AIR PASSENGER RIGHTS: TEN YEARS ON

Regulation 261/2004 on Air Passengers' Rights has been amongst the most high-profile pieces of EU secondary legislation of the past few years, generating controversial CJEU judgments, from *ex parte IATA* to *Sturgeon*. The Regulation has led to equally challenging decisions across the Member States, with domestic courts holding that a Regulation could not be relied upon by an individual claimant, or even threatening outright to refuse an application of its provisions. The economic stakes are significant for passengers and airlines alike, and despite the European Commission's recent publication of reform proposals, controversies appear far from settled.

At the same time the Regulation should, according to the Treaty, have the same direct and general application in all the Member States of the Union. How, then, can this diversity be explained? What implications does it have for the EU's regulatory strategy at large? This book brings together leading experts in the field to present a series of case studies from 15 different Member States, as well as an overview of the extra-territorial application of Regulation 261, combined with high-level analysis from the perspectives of aviation law and EU law.

Volume 3 in the series EU Law in the Member States

EU Law in the Member States

Located at the cross-section between EU law, comparative law and socio-legal studies, *EU Law in the Member States* explores the interaction of EU law and national legal systems by analysing comparative evidence of the impact landmark EU measures—from CJEU decisions and secondary legislation to soft-law—have had across different Member States. The nature and operation of EU law has traditionally been analysed in a highly 'centralised' way, through the lenses of Brussels and Luxembourg, and in terms of the Treaty and its interpretation by the Court of Justice. Beneath this orthodoxy, however, lies the complex world of the genuine life of EU law in the Member States. Judicial and administrative practices across the Union's 28 Member States considerably qualify and sometimes even challenge the long-standing assumption that doctrines such as the direct effect and supremacy of EU law ensure a uniform and effective application of its provisions.

Each volume brings together leading academics, national experts and practitioners in order to draw conclusions both for EU law generally and the specific area in question on the basis of Member State reports and broader horizontal papers, and will be of interest to generalist EU lawyers and specialists in each field across the Member States. Academic audiences will benefit from the tight integration of national case studies and doctrinal analysis, whilst practitioners and policy makers will find systematically presented comparative evidence and commentary.

Series Editors
Jeremias Prassl
Michal Bobek

Volume 1: *Viking, Laval* and Beyond
Edited by Mark Freedland and Jeremias Prassl

Volume 2: Central European Judges under the European Influence:
The Transformative Power of the EU Revisited
Edited by Michal Bobek

Volume 3: Air Passenger Rights: Ten Years On
Edited by Michal Bobek and Jeremias Prassl

Air Passenger Rights

Ten Years On

Edited by
Michal Bobek
and
Jeremias Prassl

·HART·
PUBLISHING
OXFORD AND PORTLAND, OREGON
2016

Published in the United Kingdom by Hart Publishing Ltd
16C Worcester Place, Oxford, OX1 2JW
Telephone: +44 (0)1865 517530
Fax: +44 (0)1865 510710
E-mail: mail@hartpub.co.uk
Website: http://www.hartpub.co.uk

Published in North America (US and Canada) by
Hart Publishing
c/o International Specialized Book Services
920 NE 58th Avenue, Suite 300
Portland, OR 97213-3786
USA
Tel: +1 503 287 3093 or toll-free: (1) 800 944 6190
Fax: +1 503 280 8832
E-mail: orders@isbs.com
Website: http://www.isbs.com

British Library Cataloguing in Publication Data
Data Available

Library of Congress Cataloging-in-Publication Data

Names: Bobek, Michal, 1977– editor. | Prassl, Jeremias, editor.

Title: Air passenger rights : ten years on / edited by Michal Bobek and Jeremias Prassl.

Description: Oxford ; Portland, Oregon : Hart Publishing, 2015. | Series: EU law in the
member states ; volume 3 | "The chapters are the fruits of a conference organised jointly by the
College of Europe's Law Department and the Oxford University Institute of European
and Comparative Law, which took place at the College of Europe in Bruges on
26 and 27 September 2014." | Includes bibliographical references and index.

Identifiers: LCCN 2015039420 | ISBN 9781849468244 (hardback : alk. paper)

Subjects: LCSH: European Parliament. Regulation (EC) No 261/2004 of the European
Parliament and of the Council of 11 February 2004—Congresses. |
Flight delays—Law and legislation—European Union countries—Congresses.

Classification: LCC KJE6920.A8 A38 2014 | DDC 343.2409/78—dc23 LC record available
at http://lccn.loc.gov/2015039420

ISBN: 978-1-84946-824-4

Typeset by Compuscript Ltd, Shannon
Printed and bound in Great Britain by
CPI Group (UK) Ltd, Croydon CR0 4YY

PREFACE

This book is the third volume in the *EU Law in the Member States* series, dedicated to exploring the impact of EU law—from landmark CJEU judgments and secondary legislation to a wide range of 'soft-law' measures—in legal systems across the European Union. The chapters are the fruits of a conference organised jointly by the College of Europe's Law Department and the Oxford University Institute of European and Comparative Law, which took place at the College of Europe in Bruges on 26 and 27 September 2014. In addition to those who have contributed chapters, we would like to thank Jörg Monar, Inge Govaere, Rob Lawson QC, and a significant number of colleagues and practitioners from all sides of the debate for their participation.

We are grateful to all those at the College of Europe and the Oxford Institute of European and Comparative Law who helped us in the preparation of the workshop and with the running of the conference, including Jenny Dix and Professor Stefan Vogenauer in Oxford, and Valérie Hauspie in Bruges. Professor Ulf Bernitz's continued support has been invaluable to the further development of the series, with the present volume generously supported by the Söderberg Foundation.

The contributors have attempted to capture the law (and practice) as it stood across the Member States in November 2014. In subsequent months, we received significant editorial assistance from Emily Bowly and Anna Wardell in the preparation of this volume; we are equally grateful to Sinead Moloney and her entire team at Hart Publishing and Bloomsbury Publishing for being as supportive (and patient) as ever.

We are always interested in hearing from colleagues working in all areas of EU law as regards proposals for future topics they might wish to present for inclusion in the series.

Michal Bobek
Jeremias Prassl
College of Europe, Bruges
Magdalen College, Oxford
July 2015

CONTENTS

NOTES ON CONTRIBUTORS

Mireia Artigot i Golobardes is Juan de la Cierva Researcher at the Universitat Pompeu Fabra Law School in Barcelona.

John Balfour is an English solicitor and Consultant with Clyde & Co, London.

Frank Benyon is a Senior Fellow in the Law Department of the European University Institute, Florence, after years in private practice and then as Principal Legal Adviser to the European Commission.

Michal Bobek is Professor of European Law at the College of Europe, Bruges, and research fellow at the Oxford University Institute of European and Comparative Law.

Kristián Csach is Associate Professor at Pavel Jozef Šafárik University in Košice and Of Counsel, PRK Partners, Bratislava.

Tatjana Evas is a researcher at the University of Bremen.

Silvia Ferreri is Professor of Comparative Law at Università degli Studi di Torino, Turin, and member of the International Academy of Comparative Law.

Sacha Garben is a legal officer at the European Commission, Brussels.

Irena Gogl-Hassanin is an Austrian solicitor at the Vienna law firm Fellner Wratzfeld & Partners with several years of experience in international law firms in the United Kingdom, Poland and Austria.

Brian F Havel is Distinguished Research Professor of Law at De Paul University College of Law, Chicago.

Benjamin Jones is a Senior Retained Lecturer in Law at Pembroke College, University of Oxford.

Alexander Kornezov is Legal Secretary at the Court of Justice of the EU and Associate Professor in the Law Institute of the Bulgarian Academy of Sciences.

Krystyna Kowalik-Bańczyk is a researcher at the Institute for Legal Studies, Polish Academy of Sciences, Warsaw.

Fabien Le Bot is a legal officer at the European Commission, Brussels.

Joasia Luzak is Assistant Professor at the Centre for the Study of European Contract Law of the University of Amsterdam.

David McClean is Emeritus Professor of Law at the University of Sheffield and general editor of *Shawcross and Beaumont on Air Law*.

Pablo Mendes de Leon is Professor of Air and Space Law at Leiden University.

Jiří Malenovský is Judge at the Court of Justice of the European Union.

John Q Mulligan is FedEx/United Airlines Resident Research Fellow, International Aviation Law Institute, DePaul University College of Law.

Wouter Oude Alink is Academic Coordinator and Lecturer of Air Law at Leiden University, The Netherlands.

Laura Pierallini is the founder and named partner of Studio Pierallini, a multidisciplinary law firm based in Rome and Milan.

Jeremias Prassl is an Associate Professor in the Faculty of Law, University of Oxford, a Fellow of Magdalen College, Oxford, and a research fellow at the Oxford University Institute of European and Comparative Law.

Silvia Ustav is a lawyer at the Estonian European Consumer Centre, Tallinn.

LIST OF ABBREVIATIONS

ADA	US Airline Deregulation Act
Air Law Act	Polish Act of 3 July 2002 on Air Law
APA	Estonian Administrative Procedure Act
ATA	US–EU Air Transport Agreement
BGH	Bundesgerichtshof
Black List Regulation	Regulation (EC) 2111/2005 on the establishment of a Community list of air carriers subject to an operating ban within the Community and on informing air transport passengers of the identity of the operating air carrier
BMVIT	Bundesministerium für Verkehr, Innovation und Technologie (Austria)
BVerfG	Bundesverfassungsgericht
CAA	Civil Aviation Authority (UK)
CAR	Commission for Aviation Regulation (Ireland)
CC Committee	Consumer Complaints Committee (Estonia)
CCC	Czech Civil Code
CJEU	Court of Justice of the European Union
CRD	Consumer Rights Directive (2011/83/EC)
DGAC	Direction générale de l'aviation civile (France)
DGTA	Directoraat Generaal Luchtvaart/Direction Générale Transport Aérien (Belgium)
Directive 2005/35	Directive (EC) 2005/35 on ship source pollution and on the introduction of penalties, particularly criminal penalties for infringements
ECC-Estonia	European Consumer Centre, Estonia
ECC-France	European Consumer Centre, France
ECC-Net	European Consumer Centres' Network
ECJ	European Court of Justice
ECPB	Estonian Consumer Protection Board
ELFAA	European Low Fares Airline Association
ENAC	Ente Nazionale per l'Aviazione Civile (Italian Civil Aviation Authority)
ERTA	European Road Transport Agreement
EU	European Union
European Commission Proposal	European Commission's 'Proposal for a Regulation amending Regulation (EC) 261 establishing common rules on compensation and assistance to passengers in the event of denied boarding and of cancellation or long delay of flights' (COM(2013) 130 final)

European Parliament Proposal	European Parliament's legislative resolution of 5 February 2014 on the Proposal for a Regulation amending Regulation (EC) 261 establishing common rules on compensation and assistance to passengers in the event of denied boarding and of cancellation or long delay of flights (C7-0066/2013)
ex parte IATA	Case C-344/04 *R (International Air Transport Association and European Low Fares Airline Association v Department for Transport)* [2006] ECR I-403
Germanwings I	Case C-413/11 *Germanwings GmbH v Thomas Amend* (ECJ, 18 April 2013)
Germanwings II	Case C-452/13 *Germanwings GmbH v Henning* (ECJ, 4 September 2014)
IATA	International Air Transport Association
ICAO	International Civil Aviation Organisation
ICC	Italian Civil Code
IMO	International Maritime Organisation
INC	Italian Navigation Code
KOPP	Komisja Ochrony Praw Pasażerów (Polish Commission for the Protection of Passenger Rights)
MARPOL	International Convention for the Prevention of Pollution from Ships 1973
Montreal Convention	Montreal Convention for the Unification of Certain Rules for International Carriage by Air 1999
NEB	National Enforcement Body
Nelson	Joined Cases C-581/10 and 629/10 *Nelson v Deutsche Lufthansa AG* [2012] OJ C399/3
NSA	Naczelny Sąd Administracyjny (Supreme Administrative Court, Poland)
OGH	Oberster Gerichtshof (Supreme Court, Austria)
President of ULC	Prezes Urzędu Lotnictwa Cywilnego (President of the Office of Civil Aviation, Poland)
PTD	Package Travel Directive
SCC	Slovak Civil Code
SGS	Sofiiski gradski sad (Sofia City Court, Bulgaria)
SN	Sąd Najwyższy (Supreme Court, Poland)
SOLAS	International Convention for the Safety of Life at Sea
SÖP	Schlichtungsstelle für den öffentlichen Personenverkehr (Germany)
Sturgeon	Joined Cases C-402 and 432/07 *Sturgeon v Condor Flugdienst GmbH*; *Stefan Böck and Cornelia Lepuschitz v Air France SA* [2009] ECR I-10923
TEC	Treaty establishing the European Community
TEEC	Treaty establishing the European Economic Community

TFEU	Treaty on the Functioning of the European Union
UK	United Kingdom of Great Britain and Northern Ireland
ULC	Urząd Lotnictwa Cywilnego (Office of Civil Aviation, Poland)
UN	United Nations
UNCLOS	UN Convention on the Law of the Sea
UNIDROIT	International Institute for the Unification of Private Law
US	United States of America
VCLT	Vienna Convention on the Law of Treaties
Warsaw Convention	Convention for the Unification of Certain Rules Relating to International Carriage by Air 1929
WSA	Wojewódzki Sąd Administracyjny w Warszawie (District Administrative Court in Warsaw, Poland)
ZGV Act	Zakon za grajdanskoto vazduhoplavane (Bulgarian Civil Aviation Act)

1

Welcome Aboard: Revisiting Regulation 261/2004

JEREMIAS PRASSL AND MICHAL BOBEK

As noted in the introduction to the first volume in this series,[1] the nature and operation of European Union (EU) law have traditionally been analysed in a highly 'centralised' way, through the lenses of Brussels and Luxembourg, in terms of the Treaties and their interpretation by the Court of Justice of the European Union (CJEU). In consequence, both scholarship and legal discourse have often been aimed at the European level, describing and analysing EU law primarily from a perspective akin to that of a fully-fledged and autonomous legal system. Member States and their legal systems, on the other hand, feature much less frequently in this analysis; at least beyond the supposedly obedient application and implementation of primary and secondary EU law, as a source of preliminary references and as recipients of the rulings thus issued.

I. From Landmark Cases to Landmark Legislation

This volume returns to the quest of changing our understanding of EU law by eschewing the traditional top-down, centralised and unitary perspective, and adopting a bottom-up, composite and by definition comparative approach instead. For the present study, however, neither a landmark decision, as was the case with *Viking* and *Laval*,[2] nor a large-scale socio-legal transformation of entire judicial systems in the new Member States of the Union[3] is at stake. Instead, we set out to analyse a rather discrete piece of secondary legislation: Regulation No 261/2004 establishing common rules on compensation and assistance to

---

[1] M Freedland and J Prassl, '*Viking, Laval* and Beyond: An Introduction' in M Freedland and J Prassl (eds), *EU Law in the Member States:* Viking, Laval *and Beyond* (Hart Publishing, 2014) 1.

[2] Freedland and Prassl (eds) (n 1).

[3] M Bobek (ed), *Central European Judges under the European Influence: The Transformative Power of the EU Revisited* (Hart Publishing, 2015).

passengers in the event of denied boarding and of cancellation or long delay of flights (Regulation 261).[4]

At first sight, this choice might fail to excite all but a select group of EU aviation experts. To generalist EU lawyers, Regulation 261 may appear somewhat too technical, even dry. Even specialist EU lawyers are unlikely to have studied the Regulation in their academic capacity, even though they may well have encountered its (non-) application as passengers, when their flight was delayed or, in the less lucky course of events, cancelled. Even then, however, Regulation 261 would hardly appear to be the object of much sustained academic study.

Upon further consideration, however, the EU's enactment in 2004 of a comprehensive passenger rights regime fits neatly into the identification of 'landmark' developments in Union law which our series hopes to chart.[5] First, because the form of the legislative instrument in question is a regulation. The choice of such legal instrument may appear counterintuitive: why focus on a regulation for a *comparative* study of EU law in the Member States? If 'implementation studies' are carried out, they typically examine the national transposition of directives, or other EU sources that expressly mandate national implementation. By contrast, a regulation is directly applicable across the entire Union. In the vast majority of cases, it is not to be transposed by the Member States. Thus, it ought to be the same in all Member States and comparative studies of its application may seem redundant—an assumption that stands in stark contrast with the picture conveyed by individual chapters reflecting on the national application of a nominally 'uniform EU regime'.

Secondly, Regulation 261 offers a well-arranged and compact view of a subfield of EU law. In contrast to a number of other areas of EU rules, where there are multiple sources at the EU level which make the tracking of impact and causality of individual pieces of legislation or case law on the national level difficult, air passengers' rights are a discrete area of law introduced and codified in a single, concise regulation. This allows for a reliable study of national implementation, since the area of law is clearly demarcated and can be captured even within the confines of the present volume.

Thirdly, as 10 years have passed since Regulation 261's entry into force on 17 February 2005,[6] the time is ripe for a detailed analysis of the Regulation's impact across national legal systems. Over the years, individual analyses of the Regulation have ranged from praise for providing 'a high degree of protection for passengers'[7]

---

[4] European Parliament and Council Regulation (EC) 261/2004 of 11 February 2004 establishing common rules on compensation and assistance to passengers in the event of denied boarding and of cancellation or long delay of flights, and repealing Regulation (EEC) No 295/91 (Regulation 261) [2004] OJ L46/1.

[5] Freedland and Prassl (n 1) 3.

[6] Regulation 261, Art 19.

[7] A Milner, 'Regulation EC 261/2004 and "Extraordinary Circumstances"' (2009) 34 *Air and Space Law* 215, 220.

to warnings of 'a multiple failure',[8] 'in practice lead[ing] to significant problems in the implementation of … passenger rights',[9] or even to 'serious concerns about the rule of law in the EU' itself.[10] The national reports at the core of this book allow us to revisit the controversies surrounding the EU's passenger rights regime in the broader context of individual Member States, and to observe how the Regulation has begun to be absorbed into national discourse and practice.

Fourthly, given the Regulation's explicit consumer-protective tendency,[11] it furthermore provides a good illustration, *pars pro toto*, of some of the challenges faced by the broader consumer *acquis* in its interaction with established market practices across different Member States.

Lastly, there is also the underlying conflict between Union norms and international law that clearly surfaces in this specific area, making it a good case study for a phenomenon that is of increasing importance in EU law more broadly.[12] Decisions of the Court of Justice and of domestic courts[13] in the present context may provide (and indeed already have) important clues as to different judiciaries' broader approach to the reconciliation of EU law with international norms.

II. The Multi-Layered Perspectives of a Multi-Dimensional Problem

The evidence from EU and international law, as well as from a cross-section of Member States collected in this volume, is organised as follows. Part I focuses on analysing Regulation 261/2004 at the EU level, as well as in its broader international context. Part II then turns to the Member State perspectives, surveying the (by now perhaps un-) surprisingly diverse impact of the air passenger rights Regulation in 15 EU countries, as well as its extra-territorial implications. Part III draws on these reports, as well as the EU-level perspectives in Part I, to engage in a dialogue across the various spectra, with chapters looking at the implications of

---

[8] K Arnold and P Mendes de Leon, 'Regulation (EC) 261/2004 in the Light of the Recent Decisions of the European Court of Justice: Time for a Change?!' (2010) 35 *Air and Space Law* 91, 110.

[9] L Giesberts and G Kleve, 'Compensation for Passengers in the Event of Flight Delays' (2010) 35 *Air and Space Law* 293, 303.

[10] J Balfour, 'Airline Liability for Delays: The Court Justice Rewrites EC Regulation 261/2004' (2010) 35 *Air and Space Law* 71, 75.

[11] Recital No 1, as well as the overall tone and thrust of Regulation 261, hints at the Regulation's being primarily a consumer protection measure. However, it is true that the formal legal basis for Regulation 261 was former Article 80(2) TEC, ie the title on transport policy, not consumer protection.

[12] Recently most notably Opinion 2/13 on accession to the European Convention on Human Rights (ECHR), ECLI:EU:C:2014:2454. See generally K Ziegler, 'Strengthening the Rule of Law, but Fragmenting International Law: The *Kadi* Decision of the ECJ form the Perspective of Human Rights' (2009) 9 *Human Rights Law Review* 288.

[13] J Prassl, 'EU Aviation Law before the English Courts: *Dawson, Huzar,* and Regulation 261/2004' (2014) 39 *Air and Space Law* 365.

the material thus assembled for the EU's internal market, constitutional questions and the future of the passenger rights regime.

A. EU-Level Perspectives

Part I of this book opens with a unique point of view from a key participant in the leading decisions discussed throughout this volume. Judge *Jiří Malenovský* of the Court of Justice, writing extra-judicially, boldly embraces the opportunity 'to defend the position of the Court of Justice and reply to some of the criticism expressed towards certain judgments delivered in the field of air transport'. Having set out the main lines of challenge to the Court's case law and the consistent responses provided by the Court of Justice in return, chapter two begins with a look at the relationship between EU law and international norms in order to explain the decisions' compliance with established rules of international law.

Malenovský then turns to the 'minefield' of the extraordinary circumstances provision, recounting how a series of last-minute withdrawals of preliminary reference requests hampered the Court's early efforts to provide clear guidance, before focusing on a detailed defence of the principle of delay compensation as developed in *Sturgeon v Condor*[14] and confirmed in *Nelson v Deutsche Lufthansa AG*.[15] This meticulous and hitherto unpublished explanation of the Court's reasoning replies to a long series of academic and domestic judicial criticisms, as well as points of divergence with Advocate Sharpston's Opinion, before concluding with a reflection on the broader legitimacy of the Court's work.

Frank Benyon's chapter focuses on the genesis of Regulation 261 and its broader context, in particular the EU's common transport policy: a market liberalisation long resisted by the Member States on grounds of competence, and later by the air carriers when their new-found freedoms came hand in hand with additional passenger rights. The Regulation's consumer-protective approach can, however, be defended by reference to other sectors, such as the regulation of telecoms and the maritime sector. As the Court of Justice noted in *Vodafone*,[16] market integration is not the sole decisive factor in relying on Article 114 TFEU; consumer protection may play an equally central role.

Benyon then contrasts the development of international transport policy with that in the EU, where Member States continue to participate independently in the negotiations of international agreements. This situation was complicated by the Union's ability to take measures in areas subject to international agreements, incorporating them into EU law through Regulations or Directives, even though the Union cannot conduct such negotiations directly unless it is itself a member of the relevant international organisation. This inter-institutional dimension

---

[14] Joined Cases C-402 and 432/07 *Sturgeon v Condor Flugdienst* [2009] ECR I-10923 (*Sturgeon*).
[15] Joined Cases C-581 and 629/10 *Nelson v Deutsche Lufthansa AG* [2012] OJ C399/3 (*Nelson*).
[16] Case C-58/08 *Vodafone Ltd* [2010] ECR I-4999.

of Regulation 261 is equally important within the Member States, in particular when it comes to the enforcement of its rules through non-judicial actors such as national enforcement bodies (NEBs).

The international dimension is explored further in *David McClean*'s contribution. His chapter starts with the observation that 'it has been a feature of the history of the Warsaw Convention, and will be of the Montreal Convention and Regulation 261 and its likely successor, that some courts will find ways of avoiding the clear meaning of the text'. The argument then hones in on the crucial issue when reading Regulation 261 alongside the Montreal Convention: the latter's exclusivity principle, as laid down in Article 29 of the Convention, stipulating that the Montreal Convention defines exclusively the circumstances in which a carrier may be liable in international carriage. McClean describes how the exclusivity principle has been applied in leading cases in the United States and the United Kingdom. He concludes that it is clear that the Montreal Convention was intended to regulate private rights and that some traditional categories of public international law may therefore not be applicable.

On what legal basis might a claim under Regulation 261 then be brought despite the exclusivity of the Montreal Convention? McClean's careful analysis of the distinction between types of damages suffered by delayed passengers, and the role of Article 12 of Regulation 261 in shaping compensation payments, highlights the illogicalities inherent in the leading cases when viewed from the long-established perspective of the Montreal Convention.

These contradictions are the 'fundamental fallacy' at the starting point of *John Balfour*'s contribution. Chapter five dissects the assertion in *R (International Air Transport Association and European Low Fares Airline Association) v Department for Transport*[17] (*ex parte IATA*) that there is no conflict between the provisions relating to delay in Regulation 261 and the Montreal Convention, based on the provisions in the Convention excluding and limiting the carrier's liability for delay and on the exclusivity of the Convention as regards any action for damages. The *ex parte IATA* judgment is discussed in detail, noting in particular Article 8(1)(a) of Regulation 261, which Balfour argues is not concerned with 'immediate' relief and does not operate 'at an earlier stage than the system which results from the Montreal Convention'. Instead, he suggests that it has the potential to result in compensation that is by no means standardised and the same for each passenger, and which requires case by case assessment—thus falling squarely into the regulatory domain of the Montreal Convention. This and related conflicts between EU law and the Montreal Convention are traced through the Court's jurisprudence, leading to the conclusion that the only possible way forward would seem to be an action brought by one or more non-EU parties to the Montreal Convention against some or all of the EU Member States before the International Court of Justice.

---

[17] Case C-344/04 *R (International Air Transport Association and European Low Fares Airline Association) v Department for Transport* [2006] ECR I-403.

Silvia Ferreri, on the other hand, approaches the by now well-rehearsed set of cases from the perspective of the non-transportation specialist. She highlights the complexities caused by multiple sources of law that govern the field of aviation law, from the global level to individual Member States, the 'cumulative effect' of which leads to difficult questions when different regimes come into contact with each other—in particular if one regime purports to apply exclusively. The resulting problems can be framed as a tension between the advantages of a flexible evolution of international law on the one hand, and its fragmentation on the other—a tension which the Court of Justice sought to diffuse by attempting to reconcile the interpretation of competing, yet equally binding, texts.

This approach, Ferreri suggests, must also be seen in the light of different approaches to judicial interpretation—the Court of Justice's expansive understanding may well be different from the literal reading of statutes generally adopted by the English judiciary. It is furthermore in line with the 'presumption of conformity', which exhorts judges to 'reconcile commitments stemming from different sources as long as no explicit abrogation is established in the later legislation in unambiguous terms'. It is in the light of this effort to maintain a coherent application of international sources that the cost of strained interpretation ought to be seen. This may well explain why many national judges tend to follow the Court of Justice's approach of finding an interpretation that reconciles both Regulation 261 and the Montreal Convention rather than pitting the regimes against each other.

B. Member States' Perspectives

Part II of this book turns from discussions of Regulation 261 at the European level to reports exploring Member State perspectives. Over a dozen EU states, as well as the Regulation's extra-territorial impact, are surveyed in 11 chapters, arranged in the alphabetical order of the states to which they relate, chronicling the domestic impact of the Regulation and related case law of the Court of Justice over a period of 10 years: Austria and Germany (*Irena Gogl-Hassanin*), Belgium, the Netherlands and Luxemburg (*Pablo Mendes de Leon* and *Wouter Oude Alink*), Bulgaria (*Alexander Kornezov*), the Czech Republic and Slovakia (*Kristián Csach*), Estonia (*Tatjana Evas* and *Silvia Ustav*), France (*Fabien Le Bot*), Italy (*Laura Pierallini*), Poland (*Krystyna Kowalik-Bańczyk*), Spain (*Mireia Artigot i Golobardes*), the United Kingdom and Ireland (*Benjamin Jones*) and an international contribution with a particular focus on the United States of America (*Brian Havel* and *John Mulligan*).

Each chapter is loosely structured to provide a brief introduction to the country's relevant institutional and legal framework, before setting out claims under each of the liability events, the role played by the extraordinary circumstances defence and the availability of remedies—or the lack thereof, as the case may be. Particular emphasis is placed, where possible, on the question of whether domestic judges accept the CJEU's account of Montreal Convention compatibility, as well as the role of NEBs in the (non-) application of the Regulation's norms, and the response to the Regulation and its subsequent case law in national academic commentary. From these accounts, a fascinating picture emerges. We can observe a significant degree of diversity in the legal rules that regulate passengers' rights against carriers, and especially in EU law's interaction with Member State law.

Irena Gogl-Hassanin's report on Austria and Germany finds a series of commonalities, not least in terms of a disproportionately high number of preliminary reference requests, as well as some important differences between the two countries. Whilst both jurisdictions have seen a large number of claims, in particular for Article 7 compensation and driven not least by a series of recently established claim aggregator firms, the vast majority of cases have been restricted to first instance courts. In Austria, efforts are currently underway to set up a new NEB, which will also allow claimants to participate in voluntary conciliation. The most frequent legal questions before the courts surround jurisdiction, the notions of cancellation and delay, and, in particular, the extraordinary circumstances defence, with this last usually interpreted restrictively by courts that have generally been far less critical of the CJEU rulings than their German colleagues. Indeed, the latter have played a very active role in pointing out uncertainties in the wording of Regulation 261. After *Sturgeon*, there was a significant increase in the number of cases brought before German courts. Most claims traditionally concerned the question of long delays as distinct from cancellation (no longer a problem after *Sturgeon*) and, once more, the notion of 'extraordinary circumstances'.

Pablo Mendes de Leon and *Wouter Oude Alink* set out by noting how the Netherlands, Belgium and Luxembourg each plays an important role in relation to Regulation 261, as the homes of one of the EU's busiest airports and key EU institutions respectively. Most cases in the Netherlands deal with the scope of extraordinary circumstances. Mendes de Leon and Oude Alink argue that such cases can generally be categorised in three sub-categories—weather, technical condition of the aircraft and other conditions—before analysing the Dutch courts' role in challenging the compatibility of Regulation 261 with the Montreal Convention through preliminary reference requests. In Belgium and Luxembourg, on the other hand, the number of cases dealing with Regulation 261 are comparatively low, even though some Belgian cases dealing with the distinction between cancellation and delay, extraordinary circumstances, the limitation period for actions and the powers of the NEB are addressed. Prior to *Sturgeon* and *Nelson*, the Belgian NEB had taken a narrow view of the application of Regulation 261, with its powers subsequently contested before the Council of State, which held that the former body's rulings are non-binding opinions only.

The implementation of Regulation 261 in Bulgaria has been the source of much confusion, *Alexander Kornezov* explains, due primarily to inadequate national legislation, laissez-faire administrative practices and consistently inconsistent case law. This has led to a situation where most passengers turn to alternative dispute resolution mechanisms without hardly ever taking their case to court. The Bulgarian legislator 'transposed' the Regulation into national law by simply copying its text into an executive order, and by designating an NEB which, while it has the power to issue binding instructions, merely replies to claims by simple 'letters' devoid of legal force. At the judicial enforcement level, claimants suffer from ambiguity as to whether claims should be brought before administrative or civil courts. The distinction is significant because, in civil cases, the court is a passive adjudicator, with the passenger thus bearing the burden of proving his or her claim. By contrast, at the administrative justice level, the court plays a much more interventionist role. However, the administrative courts have never had occasion to assert their jurisdiction because of the NEB's refusal to adopt a binding decision which could then be challenged. What little case law there is, appears to be equally marred by procedural and jurisdictional problems.

In the Czech Republic and Slovakia, both case law and the administrative practice of the respective NEBs are reasonably similar. *Kristián Csach* explains that both Member States have enacted detailed legislation that covers the distinction between contracts for the transport of persons and contracts for travel services, both of which are relevant when considering the liability of an air carrier. Claims under Regulation 261 are considered regular civil law claims, actionable in the same way as other private law claims. Passengers' claims, however, can be brought either as regular civil law claims or as administrative proceedings. In order to commence the latter, a complaint must first be filed with the air carrier. Only if an unsatisfactory response is given can the passenger turn to the NEB. Interestingly, the Slovak NEB tends to subsume breaches of Regulation 261 in breaches of domestic administrative law. Overall, very few claims seem to have been made in either of these Member States.

The procedural approach to the enforcement of Regulation 261 claims in Estonia similarly relies on two tracks, enabling passengers to make a complaint to the NEB or to issue proceedings in a court. *Tatjana Evas* and *Silvia Ustav* explain that as regards the former, there are two options for settling a complaint before the NEB. The first option is to submit a complaint to the Consumer Complaints Committee, which makes a binding decision. Any failure to comply with such a decision allows the passenger to file an action in a county court. Alternatively, the Consumer Complaints Committee can issue a so-called *precept*, which requires the airline to comply with a particular act. A further option is to file a complaint with the European Consumer Centre of Estonia. Evas and Ustav then analyse the enforcement of Regulation 261 in Estonian courts, noting that there have been very few court cases, and even fewer detailed decisions. Not a single case has considered the Regulation's compatibility with the Montreal Convention. This, they suggest, is primarily due to the questionable effectiveness of domestic procedural rules, as well as to the absence of public or academic discussions of the EU's passenger rights provisions.

Fabien Le Bot's contribution begins by setting out the administrative procedure to bring a claim before the NEB in France. Notably, the NEB is not allowed to take individual decisions granting compensation to passengers. Instead, it assists passengers in their relations with airlines. Sanctions can be imposed on carriers by the Minister responsible for civil aviation at the recommendation of the Administrative Commission for Civil Aviation. Individual actions for compensation must be brought before a *juge de proximité*, with no right of appeal. Even this low-value judicial procedure can be too complex and troublesome for air passengers, however, in light of the relatively low financial amount at stake. Furthermore, important case law of the CJEU, such as the decision in *Sturgeon*, does not always appear to filter through to first instance judges. A new law establishing a right to bring a class action might provide a new way for consumers to obtain individual damages from the aviation industry, which is said to have generally failed to respect its EU law obligations. Most airlines are reluctant to provide compensation when approached, especially in cases of delay, and follow a deliberate strategy of non-disclosure in an attempt to prevent passengers from knowing about their rights. It remains to be seen, however, whether the new law can be used to make a claim under Regulation 261.

In Italy, *Laura Pierallini* notes that passenger rights include not only the international and European provisions discussed thus far, but also a domestic dimension: the Italian Civil Code and the Italian Navigation Code contain provisions dealing with air passenger rights at the national level. This overlap can be illustrated in the context of Montreal Convention compatibility: Italian case law has qualified the right to compensation for a delayed flight under Regulation 261 as cumulative with the right to damages under Article 19 of the Montreal Convention. One of the most curious aspects of the Italian experience is the fact that even prior to the CJEU's decision in *Sturgeon*, the Italian courts had recognised a right to compensation where a flight is delayed. As a result, the latter case had little if any impact domestically, as a series of decisions by Judges of the Peace from across the country demonstrate. The same is true for the application of the extraordinary circumstances defence: by the time of the Luxembourg court's ruling in *Wallentin-Hermann v Alitalia*, the Italian courts had already limited the extraordinary circumstances defence to situations such as strikes affecting the industry, whereas technical failures were not generally classed as an extraordinary circumstance.

Krystyna Kowalik-Bańczyk's contribution explores the situation in Poland. Even though absolute claim numbers as a proportion of air journeys are still relatively low, the overall implementation of Regulation 261 appears to have been successful in raising the standard of passenger protection. As in many of the jurisdictions surveyed, there are different ways of enforcing the Regulation: through the NEB or before the civil courts. The interaction between these routes can sometimes lead to difficulties. In general, however, the NEB regularly exercises its power to grant compensation to passengers. The interpretation of key terms of the Regulation is ensured in line with the Court of Justice's case law, including both a narrow interpretation of the exceptional circumstances defence and generous awards of financial compensation post-*Sturgeon*. The only exception to this picture is compensation for denied boarding, where the courts have steered away from the Court of Justice's jurisprudence and regularly deny compensation.

The application of Regulation 261 in Spain is of particular interest given that nearly a quarter of all air passenger movements in the EU originate from or are destined for Spain, as *Mireia Artigot i Golobardes* notes in the introduction to her chapter. Claims usually proceed in three stages, commencing with complaints filed online directly with the relevant airline. If this does not resolve the issue, passengers can engage in mediation procedures, before progressing to file a judicial claim. Claims under the Regulation are often brought—and heard—concurrently with a claim for breach of contract under the Spanish civil code. As a small claim worth less than €2,000, passenger rights complaints can be filed without the assistance of legal counsel, making the enforcement of the Regulation straightforward on paper. In reality, however, access to the courts is slow and lengthy due to significant backlogs, which act as a major deterrent. To address this problem, claims worth less than €3,000 can no longer be appealed—which means that the vast majority of first instance decisions applying Regulation 261 cannot be challenged. In combination with lengthy judicial delays, this has resulted in 'passengers having little incentive to bring claims' and in 'airlines' systematically denying compensation, knowing that their exposure to claims before courts is remarkably small'.

Turning next to the situation in the United Kingdom and Ireland, a contribution by *Benjamin Jones* finds that the '[a]pplication of Regulation 261 in the UK has been undermined by fierce resistance from the air transport industry, a weak NEB and a lack of awareness of Regulation 261 in the lower courts'. The airlines' response to passenger claims varies dramatically between different carriers in the UK. The Civil Aviation Authority, in its role as the UK NEB, will generally not become involved in individual claims beyond forwarding them to the airline in question; indeed, even overall, 'its supervision is notably light touch'. The Irish NEB, on the other hand, appears to be more proactive in enforcing complaints in individual cases, as well as in pursuing airlines whose policies lead to repeat infringements. The number of judicial proceedings in the UK has, however, been on the rise more recently, driven in particular by the public's awareness of a right to delay compensation following media coverage of the relevant Luxembourg decisions, and the increasing availability of no-win-no-fee services provided by solicitors, sometimes in co-operation with claim aggregator firms. The dominant litigation strategy adopted by the airline industry in response to this increase in claims has been a reliance on the extraordinary circumstances defence, and in particular on a non-binding indicative list of such circumstances prepared by several NEBs—both strategies which have become more difficult following the Court of Appeal's recent interpretation of that defence in line with established CJEU case law.

The last contribution to Part II of this book explores the extra-territorial application of Regulation 261, especially as regards its enforcement before non-Member State courts. *Brian Havel* and *John Mulligan* focus in particular on the United States of America. They note the strong incentive for bringing claims before US courts given the country's long-established tradition of class action claims, where claimants can petition the court to recover not merely their own entitlement, but also that of every similarly situated individual who has suffered in similar circumstances. Such permission—which the authors emphasise has yet to be granted by a court—would significantly increase the financial exposure of air carriers. The very applicability of Regulation 261 in US law constitutes a further hurdle for claimants, who have tried to rely on a series of arguments—notably ones akin to the notion of direct effect in EU law and to contractual incorporation of Regulation 261 passenger rights. The direct effect approach has rarely been successful, as Havel and Mulligan note. In contrast, the incorporation of the Regulation's terms into an individual's contract of carriage provides a higher chance of (jurisdictional) success, with a claim's pre-emption by US or international law (in particular the Montreal Convention) as a final hurdle. The chapter concludes with a brief overview of 'copy-cat legislation' in countries ranging from Brazil to the Philippines, which draws on Regulation 261 to inspire domestic air passenger rights statutes.

C. Broader Horizontal Perspectives

On the basis of the comparative insights developed throughout Part II, the final set of chapters in Part III of the volume turns to providing broader perspectives from EU aviation law, the EU internal market, EU private law and consumer protection, as well as EU constitutional and institutional law more generally.

Sacha Garben's contribution suggests that the area of EU air passenger rights has become one of the most turbulent—and fascinating—topics in EU law and politics, turning into a veritable goldmine for scholars of various disciplines because of the many insights the debates surveyed throughout the present volume yield into the political and legal workings of the EU institutional order. Amongst these many potential topics, her analysis focuses in particular on issues of EU inter-institutional dynamics, judicial dialogue and legal culture that underlie this field, across a series of different periods that can already be distinguished in Regulation 261's relatively short life span. In setting out this timeline, Garben emphasises the institutional interaction between the European judiciary, the various legislative actors and stakeholders, the judicial dialogue (or indeed 'shouting-matches') between the Court of Justice and selected national courts, and the rising claims culture in Europe. A detailed exploration of the increasing number of preliminary references shows up important links between judicial action in several Member States, and suggests that 'the on-going preliminary referencing is due to the airlines' litigation practices rather than fundamental questions of interpretation or judicial contestation of the applicable law'. The chapter concludes with a return to three key themes identified in Garben's previous work, looking at the events of the past 10 years—and the proposed changes to come—through the lens of concerns about judicial activism, the inexorable rise of Euroscepticism and the growth of 'Euro-legalism'.

Joasia Luzak approaches the notion of passenger rights from the perspective of the EU private lawyer, with a particular view to consumer protection in the internal market: after all, there is prima facie little difference between the Union citizen in his or her capacity as a 'passenger' or as a 'consumer'. The chapter focuses on a comparison of the existing regimes granting rights to consumers when they purchase services in the EU (including rights under the Consumer Rights Directive, the Services Directive and the Package Travel Directive) with the provisions of Regulation 261, highlighting a series of protections European consumers may already be enjoying generally yet are missing when acting in their capacity as air passengers. These include consumers' information rights, a set of consumer-specific remedies in case of non-performance or improper performance of a contract, as well as a right of withdrawal in certain circumstances. Luzak goes on to question the divergences that quickly become apparent. Might there be important justifications for differences in consumer-protective measures across various service sectors, including the aim to improve the internal market or to strengthen the position of weaker parties in European private law? Luzak does not find any such account particularly convincing. A potential solution for many of the current problems might lie in the further harmonisation of European private law as regards the provision of services, restoring coherence to the rights of Union citizens as air passengers and consumers.

Given the significant controversy and practical problems identified thus far, few commentators were surprised by the Commission's announcement in the Spring of 2013 that it would seek to propose a set of reforms and extensions in an updated Regulation. *Jeremias Prassl* looks at these proposals in detail in chapter twenty, with a particular view to understanding how, if at all, the Union legislator could take account of the multiple dimensions of heterogeneity encountered by the original Regulation and its implementing case law over the past decade. In revisiting his previous conclusions on the reforms, three topics in particular are explored: a future Regulation's relationship with the Montreal Convention of 1999; on-going controversies surrounding the role of the extraordinary circumstances defence; and the role of different actors at the EU and national level in ensuring air carriers' compliance with, and the enforcement of, established and novel obligations. Close scrutiny of each of these topics suggests that despite the relatively frequent application of the Regulation, the chances of establishing a truly uniform regime across 28 different countries (and beyond) are rather slim—a conclusion that poses a non-negligible challenge to traditional assumptions about the operation of EU law in the Member States.

Michal Bobek's contribution returns to the very notion of uniformity and uniform rights in Europe. The chapter offers an overall, EU-law-generalist conclusion to this volume by placing its subject matter in the broader context of the national application and enforcement of EU law. What can the practice of Regulation 261 in the Member States tell us about the life of EU law in the Member States in general? Bobek first sets out the orthodoxy in terms of what and how a regulation is supposed to function within the legal systems of the Member States. Secondly, drawing on the individual country reports in the Part II of this volume, the operation of Regulation 261 in the Member States is examined comparatively in relation to three elements: substantive rights, institutions and procedures. Lastly, the performance of Regulation 261 is evaluated structurally in terms of its ability to unify passengers' rights in Europe, while placing the specific issues raised within the air passenger rights regime in the context of broader debates relating to EU law sources and institutions.

III. Understanding the Debate: A Primer on (EU) Aviation Law and Air Passenger Rights

Our opening section suggested that despite its highly specialised and technical nature, EU aviation law and Regulation 261 in particular offer fertile ground for a comparative study of the life of EU law in the Member States. The details of these regimes will be discussed at length in the chapters that follow; a succinct introduction to Regulation 261 and some of Court of Justice's most important decisions flowing from it may nonetheless be apposite at this juncture to help EU law generalist readers in navigating key debates and controversies.[18]

A. Regulation 261/2004

The Contract of Carriage by Air has traditionally been the subject of international law,[19] falling under a regime dating back to the Warsaw Convention of 1929.[20] Despite subsequent improvements to passenger protection,[21] its underlying regulatory design[22] was not significantly modified in the revised Montreal Convention of 1999, to which all EU Member States are signatories. The Union itself acceded to the Convention by Council Decision 2001/539,[23] with the substantive provisions of the Montreal Convention being adopted in Regulation 2027/97.[24] However, this incorporation of the Montreal Convention into the Union legal order did not spell

---

[18] For a full account, see J Prassl, 'The European Union and The Montreal Convention: A New Analytical Framework' (2013) 12 *Issues in Aviation Law and Policy* 381, on which parts of the subsequent discussion draw.

[19] D McClean, 'Carriage by Air' in H Beale (ed), *Chitty on Contract Volume II—Specific Contracts*, 32nd edn (Sweet & Maxwell 2015); D McClean (ed), *Shawcross and Beaumount's Air Law*, 4th edn (Butterworths, 1991).

[20] Convention for the Unification of Certain Rules for International Carriage by Air, signed at Warsaw in 1929.

[21] Not least because of the United States' threatened renunciation: A Lowenfeld and A Mendelsohn, 'The United States and the Warsaw Convention' (1967) 80 *Harvard Law Review* 497.

[22] Which is strongly industry-protective, not least due to historical reasons: Larsen *et al*, *Aviation Law: Cases and Related Sources* (Nijhoff 2012) 312; B Havel, *Principles and Practice of International Aviation Law* (Cambridge University Press 2014) para 4.25.

[23] Council Decision of 5 April 2001 on the conclusion by the European Community of the Convention for the Unification of Certain Rules for International Carriage by Air (the Montreal Convention) [2001] OJ L194/38.

[24] Council Regulation (EC) No 2027/97 of 9 October 1997 on air carrier liability in the event of accidents [1997] OJ L285/01, as amended by Regulation 889/2002 of the European Parliament and of the Council of 13 May 2002 [2002] OJ L140/2.

the end of the Union legislator's attempt at regulating passenger rights, which had already begun to address particular incidents such as denied boarding[25] and culminated in a broader Regulation setting out a general passenger-protective regime in 2004.

The scope of application of the Regulation's provisions is broad. Nearly all passengers departing from or to the territory of an EU Member State can invoke its protection.[26] But whilst its scope of application is therefore broader than that of the Montreal Convention (which was prima facie inapplicable in the case of purely domestic flights), it is not unlimited.[27] The Regulation's regime is mandatory and cannot be excluded, limited or waived.[28]

i. Liability Events

Four possible events are identified in the Regulation:

(1) *Denied boarding*—Article 4 provides that in case of overbookings, the airline first needs to call for volunteers, who will be entitled to a refund or re-routing pursuant to Article 8. If the denied boarding is involuntary, the full remedial suite (as laid down in Articles 7, 8 and 9) applies.

(2) *Cancellation*—In the case of flight cancellation, passengers are likewise entitled to the full range of remedies under the Regulation in accordance with Article 5, subject only to limited exceptions (such as, for example, notification of the cancellation at least two weeks before the scheduled time of departure). The Court of Justice has defined the relevant event broadly, including, for example, the return to base of a flight that had originally departed on time but had to turn around en route due to subsequent technical problems.[29]

(3) *Delay*—Article 6 of the Regulation sets out a series of distance/time pairs, delays in excess of which trigger the assistance specified in Articles 8 and 9. The judicial interpretation of this provision has become the subject of extensive controversy.

(4) *Involuntary upgrading and downgrading*—Article 10 deals with on-board responses to overbooked flights, providing that the carrier may not charge customers for involuntary upgrades, and in the case of transportation in a class lower than that for which the ticket was purchased, giving a right to reimbursement of up to 75 per cent of the original ticket price within a maximum delay of seven days.

---

[25] Council Regulation (EEC) 259/91 establishing common rules for a denied boarding compensation system in schedule air transport [1991] OJ L36/1.

[26] Regulation 261, Art 3.

[27] Case C-173/07 *Emirates v Schenkel* [2008] ECR I-5237: on a flight routing from Germany to Manila and back via Dubai, the Regulation was not applicable to the Manila–Dubai leg of the journey.

[28] Regulation 261, Art 15.

[29] Case C-83/10 *Rodriguez v Air France* [2012] ECR I-9469.

ii. The Extraordinary Circumstances Defence

The payment of compensation in case of cancellation of a flight, provided for in Article 5, is subject to a defence set out in Article 5(3) of Regulation 261. It is worded as follows:

> An operating air carrier shall not be obliged to pay compensation in accordance with Article 7, if it can prove that the cancellation is caused by extraordinary circumstances which could not have been avoided even if all reasonable measures had been taken.

As the Commission notes, '[i]n practice, experience has shown that, in most cases, airlines invoke these extraordinary circumstances when facing a cancellation. In 2005, the Commission advised all Community carriers that such a practice cannot be abused.'[30]

The CJEU's response was an unsurprisingly narrow interpretation of the provisions laid down in Article 5(3), notably in relation to technical difficulties with the designated aircraft. In its decision in *Wallentin-Hermann v Alitalia*,[31] the Court attempted to close off airline's extensive reliance on the presence of 'extraordinary circumstances'. It furthermore found that issues such as 'political instability or meteorological conditions incompatible with the operation of the flight are relevant only if they create an unexpected risk, but are not directly an exemption'.[32] In a similar vein, the Court held in *Eglitis v Air Baltic*[33] that so-called knock-on delay resulting from an earlier airspace closure was not in and of itself an extraordinary circumstance.

iii. Remedies

The original design of the Regulation as enacted draws on a three-part remedial regime to ensure the differentiated application of a range of distinct yet complementary entitlements of air passengers. They are as follows:

(1) *Right to compensation*—Article 7 provides for compensation in form of a fixed cash sum of up to €600 in the case of long-haul flights in excess of 3,500 kilometres.[34] This amount may be halved for re-routed passengers arriving within a certain window following the scheduled arrival time of the flight originally booked.

---

[30] Communication from the Commission to the European Parliament and the Council pursuant to Article 17 of Regulation (EC) No 261/2004 on the operation and the results of this Regulation establishing common rules on compensation and assistance to passengers in the event of denied boarding and of cancellation or long delay of flights, COM/2007/0168 final [5.2].

[31] Case C-549/07 *Wallentin-Hermann v Alitalia* [2008] ECR I-11061.

[32] M Rasero, 'The Capacity of the Court of Justice of the European Union to Promote Homogeneous Application of Uniform Laws: The Case for Air Carrier Liability for Flight Delays and Cancellations' *Transnational Notes* (NYU Law Blogs) of 26 October 2011, available at <http://blogs.law.nyu.edu/transnational> (accessed 1 July 2015).

[33] Case C-294/10 *Eglitis v Air Baltic* [2011] ECR I-3983.

[34] Approximately GB £430 or US$ 630 at the time of final editing in June 2015.

(2) *Right to reimbursement or re-routing*—Once Article 8 has been triggered, passengers are free to elect between reimbursement of the full ticket cost,[35] or re-routing 'under comparable transport conditions'. As regards the latter choice, the Regulation makes some further provisions (eg as regards destinations with multiple airports); the overall application of this Article in practice appears, however, to be a lot more complex than it first appears.[36]

(3) *Right to care*—Pursuant to Article 9, airlines can become responsible for the provision of meals, refreshment and hotel accommodation 'in a reasonable relation to the waiting time', as well as having to offer passengers two free telephone calls, fax messages or e-mails.

The Regulation, lastly, includes a series of automatic duties incumbent on all air carriers coming within its scope, notably an obligation to inform passengers of their rights both generally and in the case of a liability event.[37] A network of NEBs is designed to ensure compliance with passengers' rights.[38]

B. The Court of Justice's Case Law

Regulation 261 has led to a series of high-profile challenges and decisions, discussed extensively in the chapters that follow, often by some of the key actors involved. The two most important decisions of the Court of Justice revolve around the Regulation's interaction with international law and the interpretation of its remedial provisions in the case of delayed flights, respectively.

i. *Montreal Convention Exclusivity: Case C-344/04* ex parte IATA *(2006)*

The Montreal Convention of 1999 stipulates that in providing a remedy for certain kinds of damage, its provisions are to be applied exclusive of alternative remedies. Central to this is Article 29, which provides:

> In the carriage of passengers, … any action for damages, however founded, whether under this Convention or in contract or in tort or otherwise, can only be brought subject to the conditions and such limits of liability as are set out in this Convention … In any such action, punitive, exemplary or any other non-compensatory damages shall not be recoverable.

This wording is said to 'make very clear the exclusivity of the Convention rules across the whole field of air carrier liability', and judicial interpretations

---

[35] Subject to certain deductions for already-taken flights in furtherance of the journey's original purpose: Regulation 261, Art 8(1)(a), and in addition to a return flight to the point of departure where applicable.

[36] As noted by J Bech Serrat, 'Re-routing under the Air Passenger's Rights Regulation' (2011) 36 *Air and Space Law* 441, 450–51.

[37] Regulation 261, Art 14.

[38] Regulation 261, Art 16.

have generally confirmed this idea that the Convention remedies should be 'exclusive … of any resort to the rules of domestic law'.[39]

In one of the leading decisions on the interpretation of what is today Article 29,[40] *Sidhu v British Airways*,[41] for example, passengers sued in respect of their detention in Iraq following their flight's scheduled landing in Kuwait after the beginning of the Iraqi invasion there. Claims were brought at common law, as the Warsaw Convention was accepted as not applying due to a lack of physical harm to the passengers.[42] The House of Lords held that the claimants could not succeed in their alternative action, even though redress was impossible under the Montreal Convention itself.

Given the bite of Article 29, therefore, a lack of remedy *in casu* cannot be pleaded to outflank the Montreal regime's exclusivity. On the basis of this strict interpretation of exclusivity, it is not surprising that questions soon arose as to the overall compatibility of Regulation 261/2004 with the Montreal Convention, in particular as regards the relationship between the provisions regulating compensation for delay in the respective regimes. Article 19 of the Montreal Convention provides that a carrier is prima facie 'liable for damage caused by delay in the carriage by air of passengers, baggage and cargo'. These provisions rarely offer meaningful redress to delayed passengers, however, given that a carrier can avoid liability by proving that it or its agents 'took all measures that could reasonably be required to avoid the damage or that it was impossible for it or [its agents] to take such measures'. Judicial interpretations of this widely-worded exoneration mechanism have excluded technical failures as long as the aircraft was within its ordinary maintenance schedules,[43] or where a one-off delay was caused by the unreasonable actions of a third party.[44]

In what has become widely known as the *ex parte IATA* case,[45] the Grand Chamber of the CJEU responded to a preliminary reference from the High Court in London.[46] The claimants, two key industry representative bodies, had sought to challenge the validity of the EU regime, more specifically Articles 5, 6 and 7 of Regulation 261, on several grounds, including procedural irregularity in the

---

[39] D McClean, 'Carriage by Air' in H Beale (ed), *Chitty on Contracts*, 32nd edn (Sweet & Maxwell 2015) 35-013.

[40] *cf* M Clarke, *Contracts of Carriage by Air*, 2nd edn (Lloyd's List 2010) 8ff.

[41] *Sidhu v British Airways* [1997] AC 430, 436–37.

[42] This appeared to be because there was no 'accident' in either case, and some doubt as to the existence of 'bodily injury': see ibid, 441.

[43] *Martel v Air Inter* (1984 Revue française de droit administratif 298; 1981 Revue française de droit administratif 239): hydraulics failed after 179 hours, when maintenance cycle was 230 hours.

[44] *SAS v Wucherpfennig*, LG Hamburg decision of 6 April 1955, [1955] *Zeitschrift für Luft- und Weltraumrecht* 226: Hamburg customs agents refused to hand over cargo.

[45] *ex parte IATA* (n 17).

[46] Pursuant to Art 267 of the TFEU. For case commentary, see, eg, J Wegter, 'The ECJ Decision of 10 January 2006 on the Validity of Regulation 261/2004: Ignoring the Exclusivity of the Montreal Convention' (2006) 31 *Air and Space Law* 133.

legislative process and violation of the principles of legal certainty and proportionality. The primary thrust of the submissions, however, was the Regulation's
purported inconsistency with the Montreal regime—to which the EU, as well as
all of its Member States, is a signatory.

Building on the Advocate General's opinion, which had emphasised the regimes'
complementarity both in substance and legal nature,[47] the Court of Justice drew a
clear distinction between different kinds of damage,[48] suggesting that:

> Any delay in the carriage of passengers by air, and in particular a long delay, may, generally
> speaking, cause two types of damage. First, excessive delay will cause damage that is almost
> identical for every passenger, redress for which may take the form of standardised and
> immediate assistance … Second, passengers are liable to suffer individual damage, inher-
> ent in the reason for travelling, redress for which requires a case-by-case assessment …[49]

The Court of Justice then went on to hold that since Articles 19, 22 and 29 of
the Montreal Convention only dealt with the second kind of damage, it would be
wrong to suggest that the

> authors of the Convention intended to shield those carriers from any other form of inter-
> vention, in particular action which could be envisaged by the public authority to redress,
> in a standardised and immediate manner, the damage that is constituted by the inconven-
> ience that delay in the carriage of passengers by air causes, without the passengers having
> to suffer inconvenience inherent in the bringing of actions for damages before the courts.[50]

As the system prescribed in Article 6 of Regulation 261 was one of 'standardised
and immediate assistance and care measures',[51] operating at an earlier stage than
the system of compensatory damages that resulted from the Montreal Convention, and a claim brought under Regulation 261 could not inhibit a later separate
claim under the provisions of the Convention, the two regimes could therefore
co-exist,[52] and the claimants' challenge was bound to fail.

ii. *Financial Compensation for Delay: Cases C-402 &*
   432/07 Sturgeon *(2009)*

The second major controversy arose in the context of financial compensation
for passengers whose flights had been delayed but not cancelled. Regulation 261
addresses the former in its Article 6, with liability triggered depending on certain

---

[47] Opinion of AG Geelhoed of 8 September 2005 in *ex parte IATA* (n 17) paras 42, 48.

[48] Unfortunately, this distinction between different types of damage became terminologically lost
in the English translation of the decision of the Court of Justice. The ('original') French version of
the *ex parte IATA* decision establishes and maintains a conceptual distinction between 'préjudice' and
'dommage'. However, both these categories become just 'damage' in the English version, thus contributing to the confusion concerning whether or not 'damage' under the Montreal Convention is any
different from the 'damage' under the Regulation 261.

[49] *ex parte IATA* (n 17) para 43.

[50] ibid, para 45.

[51] ibid, para 47.

[52] ibid, paras 45–46. The Court has since repeated this finding on numerous occasions, including,
eg, in Case C-204/08 *Rehder v Air Baltic Corp* [2009] ECR I-6073.

time/distance pairs. Remedies are limited to Article 9 (care) initially, with Article 8 (re-route or reimbursement) applicable additionally after a period of five hours. Crucially, however, Article 7 (compensation) was not included in the original design, at least when approaching the Regulation as to its text, a distinction challenged by the CJEU's much-discussed judgment in *Sturgeon*.[53]

In July 2005, the Sturgeon family had brought a claim for cancellation compensation against Condor, an airline that had transported them from Toronto to Frankfurt with a delay of over 25 hours. In light of this length of time, the claimants alleged that their original flight had been cancelled, rather than delayed.[54] A question as to the interpretation of the term 'cancellation', and its relationship with the concept of 'delay', was eventually referred to the Court of Justice.[55] The Fourth Chamber of the Court, having rephrased the joined questions, held that cancelled flights and delayed flights were 'two quite distinct categories', and that a delayed flight could therefore not simply be re-classified as cancelled, as long as the flight was 'operated in accordance with the air carrier's original planning'. The Court then went on to hold, however, that in line with the Regulation's consumer-protective objectives, it could not 'automatically be presumed that passengers whose flights are delayed do not have a right to compensation'. Given the absence of any 'objective ground capable of justifying [the originally designed] difference in treatment of passengers suffering substantially identical problems resulting from different events', the Court of Justice extended the right to compensation in Article 7 of Regulation 261 to passengers suffering delay in reaching their final destination in excess of three hours.

This judgment triggered a veritable avalanche of academic and practitioner commentary, ranging from those praising the Court's strong role in interpreting Article 6 in line with its consumer-protective purpose to others deeply worried about the threat of 'judicial legislation'.[56] In spite of the latter observations, the Grand Chamber of the Court in 2012 confirmed the *Sturgeon* extension of delay liability in its decision in the joined cases of *Nelson* and *TUI*.[57]

IV. The Themes and their Implications

The following chapters will further explore these controversies, first from the Brussels and Luxembourg perspective and, in Part II, from the vantage point of

---

[53] *Sturgeon* (n 14).

[54] An unsurprising argument given the then prevailing airline practice of delaying flights instead of cancelling them, in an attempt to avoid triggering Regulation 261/2004. See C van Dam, 'Air Passenger Rights after *Sturgeon*' (2011) 36 *Air and Space Law* 259, 260.

[55] A similar set of questions was referred by an Austrian court concerning a long-delayed Air France flight, and joined to the original proceedings (Case C-432/07, *Böck and Lepuschitz v Air France SA*).

[56] R Lawson and T Marland, 'The Montreal Convention 1999 and the Decisions of the ECJ in the Cases of *IATA* and *Sturgeon*—in Harmony or Discord?' (2011) 36 *Air and Space Law* 99, 100.

[57] *Nelson* and *TUI* (n 15).

individual Member States. Apart from the differentiated perceptions and under-standings of the legislation and case law set out above, there are at least five further points that merit the reader's attention when diving into the chapters and the arguments that follow. What will be offered in this section, by way of an introduc-tion to discussions that follow in subsequent chapters, is a concise identification of five such themes that recur throughout the volume in one way or another.

First, what is the desired *level of uniformity* that EU legislation is supposed to achieve within the Member States? Genuine uniformity that one normally associ-ates with the notion of a common or an internal market? Or is the aim merely similarity, a sort of a legal approximation? Moreover, with regard to what precisely should we evaluate uniformity? Only with regard to the statement of substantive rights, but not their enforcement and realisation? If that is indeed the case, is such a repartition of tasks in fact ever able to deliver any reasonable degree of uniform-ity, since nobody will be able to reach the same substantive result through such variable procedures?

Secondly, how far is the same European text likely to be read and to be under-stood in the same way across the Member States? Or is there inevitably bound to be an internal, value-orientated diversity of interpretation of the same instrument? Expanding on the previous point, the reader might think about the *value prefer-ences* and value balance manifested in adjudication choices in the various systems, but nominally hidden behind the same regulation text. In particular, where pre-cisely is the balance to be put in individual cases when interpreting the Regulation? If Regulation 261 was adopted primarily as a consumer protection measure, could it therefore be argued that a certain 'consumer-friendly' interpretative tendency is in fact embedded in it, as a certain meta-rule guiding its interpretation? Is such a vision, arguably present in much of the case law of the Court of Justice, shared by the courts of the Member States?

Thirdly, in a Union with decentralised enforcement of 'federal' rules, in which Member States' authorities act as a 'servant of two masters', enforcing both national rights as well as EU law-based ones, there is always likely to be certain *institutional diversity* in realising European rules at the national level. Connected to the first point above, however, is the question of how much diversity ought to be permis-sible in fact, in order to be able to talk of a unified, or at least similar, regime in all the Member States. Is it really acceptable if, in terms of institutional structure, one Member State entrusts the enforcement of Regulation 261 to the national avia-tion authority, another to a ministry and a third to a consumer ombudsperson or trade inspectorate? How far are such institutional choices likely to rebound and decisively to shape the type and style of enforcement of the EU law measure at the national level in the longer run?

Fourthly, *national procedures* naturally connect to national institutional diver-sity. They follow the same logic of delegation to the Member States' default choice in terms of how EU law-based rights will be enforced at the national level, whilst of course remaining under residual European supervision in terms of their equiva-lence and effectiveness. However, should there not be at least some basic similarity in terms of procedural set-up, which would allow the air passenger-consumer to vindicate his or her rights within a fairly similar framework? With this assumption in mind, readers are invited to conduct a little experiment in reading the chapters in Part II of this volume. First, on the basis of Regulation 261 alone, how would one frame the expected procedure for enforcing rights in the case of a delayed flight? Secondly, the reader may compare his or her expectations with the individual procedural regimes in the Member States captured in Part II of this volume. Moreover, it is important to remember that the legislation was put in place for the benefit of the 'travelling consumer', ie a person who is often likely to originate from outside the jurisdiction in question. Thus, in realistic terms, the issues of knowledge, access and, above all, comprehensive procedures come to the fore with renewed importance.

Fifthly and lastly, Regulation 261, in the form of a case study dissected in the ensuing chapters, provides considerable food for thought with regard to many of the *grander themes* relating to EU legislation, and the debates concerning its goals, utility and nature. What is the threshold for 'legislative success' when looking back at the operation of an EU regime that might now justify adopting further EU legislation on the matter in the first place? If an EU measure is adopted in the name of establishing uniform rules, and this is apparently as good as it gets in application reality later on, was it in fact worth it? Are the transaction costs in terms of adopting EU legislation justified? Does the 'linear progression' logic used for the current version of the subsidiarity analysis in the vast majority of Commission proposals (aka 'there remains diversity on the national level thus EU action is necessary because common rules are needed and nobody else but EU can set those') make sense, if it is apparent that even further EU rules are in fact unlikely to create greater uniformity? In view of such resistance and diversity, might it not be more useful to select issues and areas within a given field and seek full unification in them, while abandoning others where the Union cannot achieve a reasonable degree of commonality? Moreover and more specifically with regard to individual sources of EU law, if a regulation, ie the strongest legal instrument the EU has at its disposal in terms of achieving uniformity, is only able to achieve such degree of legal approximation, what, then, is the state of legal uniformity achievable by directives, or previously framework decisions, or other sources of EU soft law? It is with these questions in mind that the first part of this volume now turns to an exploration of the EU-level perspective.

Part I

EU-Level Perspectives

2

Regulation 261: Three Major Issues in the Case Law of the Court of Justice of the EU

JIŘÍ MALENOVSKÝ

I. By Way of Introduction

A judge has the prerogative to decide upon the law. However, in principle he may not defend his statements—the judgments must speak for him. By contrast, scholars do not have the power to decide upon the law. On the other hand, theirs is the privilege of criticising judgments.

In light of this, I took my participation in this book also as an invitation exceptionally to put myself in an opposite role, one that would allow me to defend some judgments of the Court delivered in the field of air transport and, at the same time, to reply to some of the criticism expressed towards them. And I accepted with pleasure.

II. The Relationship Between Regulation 261 and the Montreal Convention

Regulation 261 was controversial from the outset. Pursuing the aim of guaranteeing a high level of protection for air passengers, in their roles as consumers, it came under vigorous fire from European air carriers, particularly the *low cost* ones.[1] They accused the Regulation of imposing additional obligations upon them towards their passengers,[2] and of putting them at a comparative disadvantage on the market in relation to carriers coming from outside the EU.

---

[1] K Arnold, 'Application of Regulation (EC) No 261 on Denied Boarding, Cancellation and Long Delay of Flights' (2007) 32(2) *Air and Space Law* 93.

[2] M Schladebach, 'Europäisches Luftverkehrsrecht: Entwicklungsstand und Perspektiven' [2006] *Europarecht* 789.

In order to counteract these effects, the air carriers chose to fight their legal battle on the ground of the relationship between Regulation 261 and the 1999 Montreal Convention for the Unification of Certain Rules for International Carriage by Air (Montreal Convention). This relationship became the object of a reference for a preliminary ruling in *ex parte IATA*,[3] whereby the Court was asked to decide upon the validity of several provisions of the Regulation. The referral was made to the Court in August 2004, just six months after the adoption of the Regulation and six months before its entry into force.

The air carriers maintained that the Regulation violated the Montreal Convention. Indeed, Article 29 of the Montreal Convention states that any claim for damages that could for any reason be based upon a provision of the Montreal Convention is regulated by the conditions of the same, given that, as Article 19 provides, the carrier is liable for damage occasioned by delay in the carriage by air of passengers. Yet, according to the carriers themselves, the requirement of the Regulation that the passengers receive adequate 'assistance' and are 'cared for' by the carrier does constitute a form of compensation for the damage incurred by passengers. These measures allegedly contravened the Montreal Convention's *exclusivity*. However, the European institutions considered that there was no conflict between the Regulation and the Montreal Convention, since they established two separate compensation systems pursuing different objectives.

Advocate General Geelhoed delivered his Opinion in *ex parte IATA* in September 2005.[4] In his analysis he agreed with the EU institutions, considering that the Montreal Convention and the Regulation were 'complementary and not in conflict'.[5] In his view, Article 29 of the Montreal Convention alluded to 'any action for damages', rather than 'any action in respect of delay'.[6] Therefore, the Montreal Convention is exhaustive in so far as claims for damages are concerned, but it does not preclude the adoption of measures that would not constitute 'claims for damages' as such, and in particular measures establishing minimum requirements for carriers as regards the service they must provide during the delay.[7]

The Advocate General summarised the differences between the systems created by the Montreal Convention and by the Regulation in the following way:

[T]he Montreal Convention deals with an individual passenger's right to bring an action before a court to claim damages caused to him by a delay, the situation governed by private international law, while Article 6 of the Regulation aims to establish certain obligations for the air carrier, thereby creating at the same time the right for all passengers to receive immediate care and assistance during the delay.

[3] Case C-344/04 R *(International Air Transport Association and European Low Fares Airline Association) v Department for Transport (ex parte IATA)* [2006] ECR I-403.
[4] ibid.
[5] ibid, para 42 of the Opinion.
[6] ibid, para 44 of the Opinion.
[7] ibid, para 45 of the Opinion.

In his view, it is obvious that this legal obligation is entirely different from that laid out by the Montreal Convention regarding liability for damage occasioned by delay.[8]

In the *ex parte IATA* judgment, dating from 2006,[9] the Grand Chamber broadly followed the Advocate General and took up the principal elements of his reasoning.[10] However, emphasis was placed on the notion of *inconvenience accompanying delay* in the carriage of air passengers. Given that the 'damage' constituted by the inconvenience caused by delay is almost identical for all passengers on the same flight, they can all receive the same form of standardised and immediate compensation. As a result, such 'damage' is not covered by the Montreal Convention, which only concerns claims for damages assessed and redressed on an individual basis.[11]

Later on, in the *Sturgeon v Condor* judgment,[12] the Court concretised that a *loss of time* for passengers, which is inherent in a delay, was one of the inconveniences for which redress can be sought under Regulation 261. Being irreversible, it may only be redressed by compensation.[13]

The air carriers, who were dissatisfied with the judicial construction emanating from the judgment in *ex parte IATA*, whereby the Regulation held a supplementary role to the Montreal Convention and certain 'damages' could escape its application, used the *Sturgeon* judgment in order to contest this construction. They chose the alleged 'weak link' in the Court's reasoning, namely, the relation between a 'loss of time' and the notion of damage.[14]

The Court replied to these criticisms in the Grand Chamber judgment in *Nelson v Deutsche Lufthansa*.[15] Here, the Court noted that a loss of time is not considered damage occasioned by delay under Article 19 of the Montreal Convention, but that it constitutes an inconvenience in the same vein as other inconveniences connected to denied boarding, flight cancellation and long delays. Thus, the Court disconnected the loss of time completely from the concept of damage, unlike the *ex parte IATA* and *Sturgeon* judgments[16] (it should be mentioned,

---

[8]　ibid, paras 50 and 51 of the Opinion.

[9]　*ex parte IATA* (n 3).

[10]　This is mentioned only sparsely in the scholarly reactions to *ex parte IATA*, even though it is demonstrative of a strong concordance of opinion at the Court. See, by way of exception, an analysis of the Opinion as well as the judgment, J Wegter, 'The ECJ Decision of 10 January 2006 on the Validity of Regulation 261: Ignoring the Exclusivity of the Montreal Convention' (2006) 31(2) *Air and Space Law* 133.

[11]　*ex parte IATA* (n 3), paras 43–45 of the judgment.

[12]　Joined Cases C-402 and 432/07 *Sturgeon v Condor Flugdienst* [2009] ECR I-10923 (*Sturgeon*).

[13]　ibid, para 52.

[14]　It was held that the *Sturgeon* case reversed the judgment in *ex parte IATA*, despite the latter's being handed down by a larger chamber. See, eg S Hobe, W Müller-Rostin and A Recker, 'Fragwürdiges aus Luxemburg zur Verordnung 261' (2010) 59 *Zeitschrift für Luft- und Weltraumrecht* 149, 154–55 and 166.

[15]　Joined Cases C-581 and 629/10 *Nelson v Deutsche Lufthansa AG* [2012] OJ C399/3 (*Nelson*).

[16]　As invoked by L Grard, 'Retards de vols de plus de trois heures: l'interprétation dynamique du règlement (CE) n° 261 est maintenue' (2012) 4 *Revue de droit des transports* 55.

however, that the French version, in which language both these judgments had originally been written, completely avoids the French term '*dommage*' used in Article 19 of the Montreal Convention, instead relying deliberately on the term '*préjudice*'). Furthermore, the Grand Chamber underlined the fact that there is not necessarily a causal relationship between the actual delay and the loss of time that is relevant under the Regulation. For these reasons, the Court reiterated that the loss of time inherent in a flight delay did not fall under Article 29 of the Montreal Convention.[17]

The relationship between EU law and international agreements often gives rise to various conundrums, regarding as much the compatibility of secondary law with these agreements, which have a higher ranking in the hierarchy of norms of EU law, as the distribution of competences within the EU for their conclusion. These questions are often the subject of opinions[18] or judgments[19] from the Full Court or the Grand Chamber. It is not surprising that in the field of air transport the Court has been confronted with the same conundrums. Nonetheless, this field stands out moreover in terms of the explosive debate surrounding several legal issues it raises, and in some cases also in terms of hostile scholarly reactions to the solutions offered by the Court.

This was the case, for example, as regards the method of interpretation applied in the 2010 *Walz v Clickair SA* judgment,[20] in response to a reference for a preliminary ruling by a Spanish court. The referring court enquired whether the limit of the liability set out in Article 22(2) of the Montreal Convention encompassed both material and non-material ('moral') damages. Consequently, the Court was invited to interpret a provision of an international treaty. In the absence of a definition of damage within the Montreal Convention itself, the EU judiciary referred to the ordinary meaning of 'damage' found by the Court in Article 31(2) of the Articles on the Responsibility of States for Internationally Wrongful Acts, drawn up by the United Nations International Law Commission.[21] According to this Article, the injury includes any damage, whether material or moral. In order to justify referring to this provision, the Court first indicated that Article 31(2) codifies the current state of general international law, and therefore reflects the uniform practice of the international community regarding compensable damages. It then pointed out that nothing in the Montreal Convention indicates that the contracting parties to it intended to attribute a special meaning to the term 'damage' that

---

[17] *Nelson* (n 15), paras 49–55.
[18] eg Opinion 1/13 of 14 October 2014; Opinion 2/13 of 18 December 2014.
[19] eg Case C-308/06 *Intertanko v Secretary of State for Transport* [2008] ECR I-04057; Cases C-103 and 165/12 *European Parliament and European Commission v Council* (CJEU, 26 November 2014).
[20] Case C-63/09 *Walz v Clickair SA* [2010] ECR I-04239.
[21] J Crawford, *Les articles de la C.D.I. sur la responsabilité de l'État, Introduction, texte et commentaires* (Pedone, 2003) (for the commentary on Art 31, see ibid, 241–48).

would derogate from its ordinary meaning in the context of a harmonised system of liability in private international air law.[22]

Grard disapproved of this approach with rare sarcasm:

> Here we have reasoning which will plunge the reader into a state of perplexity. The international conclusions regarding the responsibility of States are now *mutatis mutandis* transposable onto rules regarding the liability of air carriers. International law can give thanks to the CJEU, in whom it has found its ally to help spread its effects beyond the purpose for which it was conceived. Public international law concerns inter-State relations: I'm delighted to learn that it now also governs the relationships between private entities …[23]

There are two points on which the author is mistaken. First of all, the Articles on the Responsibility of States for Internationally Wrongful Acts are not 'international conclusions' but are the reflection of general international law, which translates the uniform practice of states and in this regard must, in principle, be considered obligatory for all states, including those who are parties to the Montreal Convention. Secondly, the Court did not transpose the definition of 'damage' given by the Articles *mutatis mutandis* onto the area of civil liability; rather it used this definition as an applicable international *lex generalis*. Indeed, the contracting states to the Montreal Convention could legitimately have agreed upon a particular definition of 'damage', which would have been better adapted to the objectives pursued by the Convention, but they did not do so. Consequently, in the absence of a special definition (*lex specialis*) in the Montreal Convention that would derogate from the international *lex generalis*, this 'silence' must be interpreted in the light of the rules of international treaty law. Article 31(3)(c) of the Vienna Convention on the Law of Treaties (VCLT) states that, when interpreting a treaty, the contracting states must take into account 'any relevant rules of international law applicable in the relations between the parties'. The *lex generalis* therefore had to be applied by the Court.[24]

Grard also wonders why the Court did not explore the legal traditions of the EU's Member States in order to define 'damage', given that the air route in question was an intra-European one.[25] However, the response to these musings is clear: the request for a preliminary ruling in *Walz* explicitly asked for the interpretation of the Montreal Convention. I have to admit I am not aware of a method permitting a judge to interpret a *universal* international convention taking into account

---

[22] *Walz* (n 20) para 28.

[23] L Grard, 'Droit européen des transports' (2011) 47(1) *Revue trimestrielle de droit européen* 236.

[24] Courts applying international conventions, including the International Court of Justice, regularly carry out interpretative exercises of this kind. See, eg, B Simma and D Pulkowski, *Leges Speciales and Self-Contained Regimes, The Law of International Responsibility* (Oxford University Press, 2010) 139.

[25] Grard (n 23) 236.

only the legal traditions of a certain group of states among its Contracting Parties, situated on the same continent.

III. The Notion of 'Extraordinary Circumstances'

The Court then had to navigate a minefield in order to address a reference for a preliminary ruling regarding the concept of 'extraordinary circumstances'. According to Article 5(3) of the Regulation, an operating air carrier shall not be obliged to pay compensation if it can prove the presence of 'extraordinary circumstances which could not have been avoided even if all reasonable measures had been taken'. The importance of this notion can therefore not be overstated.

The Court replied in the *Wallentin-Hermann v Alitalia* case[26] of 22 December 2008, taking the risk that its judgment would be seen rather as a poisoned chalice than a Christmas gift for the air carriers. Moreover, given the undeniable complexity of the question, one might be astonished that the chamber of five judges did not request an Opinion from the Advocate General in this case. However, the explanation for this is rather simple: the Opinion had already been delivered in another case, namely *Kramme v SAS Scandinavian Airlines Danmark A/S,*[27] in which a Danish court had requested in September 2006 a ruling from the Court regarding questions that were substantively identical to those put in the *Wallentin-Hermann* case. In particular, the Danes wanted to know whether a technical defect in an aircraft resulting in the cancellation of a flight could be considered an 'exceptional circumstance'.

Some may not know that in the *Kramme* case, the Court deliberated yet never delivered its judgment. The date of its delivery had been set for 28 February 2008 and the interested persons had been notified. However, just prior to this date, the national court informed the Court that it was withdrawing the case, since the applicant in the main proceedings, Mr Kramme, had accepted the last-minute compensation offered to him by the air carrier. Since on the fixed date of delivery there was no longer a pending case in the national court, *Kramme* was removed from the register, as is the common practice of the Court. Therefore, the position of the Court on the definition of 'extraordinary circumstances' did not become public until two years and three months after the request for a preliminary ruling in *Kramme*, and 10 months after the aborted delivery of the judgment in this case.

Following the very late withdrawal of the request for a preliminary ruling in the *Kramme* case, a discussion began between the Members of the Court and then among the Member States in order to find a way of avoiding such unfortunate events in the future. Indeed, the considerable efforts deployed by the Court are

---

[26] Case C-549/07 *Wallentin-Hermann* [2008] ECR I-11061.
[27] Case C-396/06 *Kramme v SAS Scandinavian Airlines Danmark A/S* [2008] OJ C209/37.

totally negated if a request is withdrawn *in extremis*. Moreover, it is common for the Court to be petitioned at the same time as regards more similar cases, the examination of which is put on hold while waiting for the first 'pilot' judgment. If the pilot case is later withdrawn, the Court must restart from scratch with one of the suspended cases, and this causes a considerable delay for all interested persons awaiting the outcome of an issue affecting several national courts and tribunals.

The extensive discussion of how to deal with very late withdrawals of referrals for preliminary rulings resulted in the adoption of a new procedural rule, added to Article 100 of the Rules of Procedure, which entered into force on 1 November 2012. According to this rule, the withdrawal of a request can be taken into account until notice of the date of delivery of the judgment has been issued to the interested persons, but not after this date.[28]

The Court was once again confronted with the issue of an excessively late withdrawal of a referral for a preliminary ruling in the *Germanwings v Henning*[29] case. The judgment was due on 4 September 2014, but the day before, the Court received a fax from the national court informing it that the request had been withdrawn since the parties had settled out of court (the original claim was for the modest sum of €250). Nevertheless, thanks to the new procedural rule in Article 100, the judgment could be delivered. The same situation recently arose again in *van der Lans*, the Court having received a request for withdrawal ten days before the date of delivery of the judgment.[30]

I shall not speculate as to motives and circumstances surrounding last-minute settlements, but such arrangements, which show little respect for the hard and costly work of the Court, leave a rather bad impression. They are, however, surprisingly frequent in litigation for air passenger compensation, a field in which there have been more cases withdrawn than judgments and reasoned orders from the Court. There have been at least 20 orders for removal in this field so far.[31]

On the merits, it ought to be noted that in *Kramme*, Advocate General Sharpston concluded that

> technical problems requiring an aircraft to be taken out of operation can be considered to constitute extraordinary circumstances under Article 5(3) of Regulation No 261 if they are neither of a kind typically occurring from time to time on all aircraft and/or a particular aircraft type nor of a kind known to have affected the aircraft in question before.

According to the Advocate General, it is the national judge who has the competence to determine these circumstances.[32]

---

[28] J Malenovský, 'Comment traiter le retrait tardif d'une demande de décision préjudicielle' (2013) 20(2) *Jurisprudence Research Journal* 497.

[29] Case C-452/13 *Germanwings GmbH v Henning* (CJEU, 4 September 2014) (*Germanwings II*).

[30] Case C-257/14 *van der Lans* (CJEU, 17 September 2015).

[31] eg C Naômé and L Kodrikova, 'La disparition du litige devant la juridiction de renvoi et la compétence de la Cour de justice en matière préjudicielle' (2014) 1 *Revue des affaires européennes* 216.

[32] *Kramme* (n 27) para 61.

In the *Wallentin-Hermann* judgment, the Court decided not to follow the approach of the Advocate General in its entirety. In the light of the principle of consumer protection inherent in the Regulation, it considered that the concept of 'extraordinary circumstances' should be interpreted strictly. With such an interpretation combined with recitals 12 and 14 of the Regulation, the Chamber concluded that the concept only relates to events that are not inherent in the normal exercise of the activity of the air carrier concerned, and which are beyond its actual control on account of their nature or origin. Given that air carriers are frequently confronted with various technical problems to which the operation of aircraft inevitably gives rise, resolving a technical problem caused by failure to maintain an aircraft must therefore be regarded as inherent in the normal exercise of an air carrier's activity. As a result, technical issues linked to aircraft maintenance cannot constitute, in themselves, extraordinary circumstances for the purposes of the Regulation. According to the Court, only technical problems that stem from events that are not inherent in the normal exercise of an air carrier's activity, and which are beyond its actual control, are covered by the concept of extraordinary circumstances in Regulation 261.[33]

This approach has been criticised for not having reconciled correctly the need to protect consumers with the financial cost to be borne by the carriers.[34] Nevertheless, one should bear in mind that the primary objective of the Regulation is to ensure a high level of protection for passengers, while taking into account the requirements of consumer protection in general. Therefore, this objective must take priority in clarifying the obligations that the Regulation places upon carriers as well as the rights it affords passengers. Imposing on passengers a share of the burden of the economic risk involved in a complex technical activity freely chosen by the carriers, of which passengers are but passive consumers, would be entirely contrary to this objective.

Some authors have also criticised the Court's definition of 'extraordinary circumstances' for its lack of precision, given that there is no explanation of what 'not inherent in the normal exercise of the activity' or 'beyond the actual control' of the carrier means. The hypothesis of a plane colliding with a bird, a recurring risk for carriers, has been evoked.[35] However, it would be unusual and unwise for the Court to seek to provide a detailed or even exhaustive list of all the risks that might fall into the category of 'extraordinary circumstances'. In any event, the *Wallentin-Hermann* case did not offer the right occasion for such an exercise.[36]

---

[33] *Wallentin-Hermann* (n 26), paras 19–26.

[34] L Grard, 'Voyages aériens: Les nouveaux droits des passagers' in C Bloch (ed), *Mélanges en l'honneur de Christian Scapel* (Presses universitaires d'Aix-Marseille, 2013) 235.

[35] K Arnold and P Mendes de Leon, 'Regulation (EC) 261 in the Light of the Recent Decisions of the European CJEU: Time for a Change ?!' (2010) 35(2) *Air and Space Law* 93.

[36] However, the Court pointed out quite recently that, first, an unexpected breakdown caused by the premature malfunction of certain components of an aircraft is inherent in the normal exercise of an air carrier's activity, because it remains intrinsically linked to the very complex operating system of the aircraft, which is operated by the air carrier in conditions which are often difficult or even extreme, it

The responsibility borne by air carriers is not without limits. In its *Eglītis v Latvijas Republikas Ekonomikas ministrija* judgment of May 2011,[37] the Court had the opportunity to explain that in terms of reasonable measures to be taken in order to avoid extraordinary circumstances, the carriers cannot be expected to plan a minimum reserve time that would be applicable to all carriers generally and indistinctly. The length of the required reserve time must not force the air carrier to make intolerable sacrifices in the light of the capacities of its undertaking at the relevant time.

It would seem that the EU legislator now wishes formally to confirm the definition of 'extraordinary circumstances' that has emerged from the case law of the Court. This is apparent in the recent proposal intended to amend the Regulation, where the European Commission suggests the insertion, in Article 1 of the Regulation, of the definition of 'extraordinary circumstances' given in the *Wallentin-Hermann* judgment. The Commission refers explicitly to this judgment in its accompanying comments.[38] Within the Council, the Member State delegations are also generally agreed that, as a matter of principle, air carriers should not invoke technical difficulties in order to avoid paying compensation. However, the question remains as to what precise conditions will allow carriers to derogate exceptionally from this principle.[39]

IV. Compensation in the Event of Delayed Flights and the Echo Among Scholars

Moving on to the *Sturgeon* case, this judgment opened up a right to compensation for passengers of certain delayed flights, despite there being no explicit provision for this in the Regulation.

For many scholars, the *Sturgeon* judgment seems to have been a surprise,[40] or even to have come totally out of the blue.[41] Several commentators welcomed it, as

---

being understood moreover that no component of an aircraft lasts forever; second, the prevention of such an unexpected breakdown or the repairs occasioned by it, including the replacement of a prematurely defective component, is not beyond the actual control of that carrier, since the latter is required to ensure the maintenance and proper functioning of the aircraft it operates for the purposes of its business. *Van der Lans* (n 30), paras 41–43.

[37] Case C-294/10 *Eglītis v Latvijas Republikas Ekonomikas ministrija* [2011] ECR I-03983.

[38] Commission, 'Proposal for a Regulation of the European Parliament and of the Council amending Regulation (EC) No 261/2004 establishing common rules on compensation and assistance to passengers in the event of denied boarding and of cancellation or long delay of flights and Regulation (EC) No 2027/97 on air carrier liability in respect of the carriage of passengers and their baggage by air', COM(2013) 130 final, explanatory statement, para 3.3.1.

[39] European Council, Minutes of the 3318th meeting of the Council of the European Union (Transport, Telecommunications and Energy), Doc 2013/0072 (COD) of 5 June 2014.

[40] S Prager, 'Pioneering passengers' rights: legislation and jurisprudence from the aviation sector' (2011) 12 *ERA Forum* 307.

[41] Grard (n 34) 242.

a constructive reading of the Regulation,[42] as a bold judgment for creating a civil right that is not explicitly provided for in the Regulation,[43] or even as an audacious decision that looks like an invitation by the Court to the European legislator to rewrite the Regulation in a more coherent way favouring better passenger protection.[44]

On the other hand, some authors have claimed that the Court's interpretation of the Regulation contradicts its very clear wording,[45] the explicit intention of the legislator,[46] or that it wrongly fills an intentional gap in the protection of passengers.[47] One author alleges that the Court gave a *contra legem* interpretation,[48] whereas another maintains that, contrary to the precision inherent in the Advocate General's Opinion, one could deduce from the judgment that 'judicial activism and weak legal reasoning go hand in hand here'.[49] One author has even observed that 'the text is used in order to create an ambiguity which is not obvious. Doubtless this is the most disturbing element of the judgment: the literal interpretation seems to be exclusively subordinated to the teleological one.'[50]

For some commentators the Court has taken on a law-making role for which it has been granted no power,[51] while 'the imperfections of legislation … dictate that citizens must … tolerate more or less explicable divergences in outcome, and of even greater magnitude'.[52] Lastly, one scholar holds that the *Sturgeon* judgment 'betrays a total misunderstanding of the professional environment that it affects', since 'while cancellations are rare, delays are frequent. In other words, to provide for cancellation compensation would not excessively damage the budget of an air carrier. Compensation for delays, however, involves totally different financial consequences.'[53]

By way of response to these (sometimes brutal) condemnations of the *Sturgeon* judgment, I would like first of all to recall that any judicial decision is the fruit of

---

[42] F Picod, 'La Cour de justice renforce les garanties des passagers victimes de retards' (2009) 50 *La semaine juridique* 543.

[43] J Stuyck, 'Indemnisation pour les passagers de vols retardés en Europe' (2010) 7 *La semaine juridique* 363.

[44] G Poissonnier and P Osseland, 'Le retard de plus de trois heures d'un avion donne lieu à l'indemnisation du préjudice des passagers' (2010) 23 *Recueil Dalloz* 1461.

[45] J Balfour, 'Airline Liability for Delays: The CJEU of the EU Rewrites EC Regulation 261' (2010) 35(1) *Air and Space Law* 73; Hobe, Müller-Rostin and Recker (n 14) 155.

[46] I Gogl, 'EuGH erfindet die EG-Verordnung Nr. 261 neu: Ausgleichszahlung auch für Verspätungen' (2010) 59 *Zeitschrift für Luft- und Weltraumrecht* 82.

[47] K Csach and L Širicová, 'Rozsudok Sturgeon' (2010) 2 *Výber z rozhodnutí Súdneho dvora Európskej únie* 62.

[48] A Bouveresse, 'Interprétation des notions de retard et d'annulation' (2010) 1 *Europe* 37.

[49] S Garben, 'Sky-High Controversy and High-Flying Claims? The *Sturgeon* Case Law in Light of Judicial Activism, Euroscepticism and Eurolegalism' (2013) 50 *CMLRev* 15.

[50] F Le Bot, 'La protection des passagers aériens dans l'Union européenne' (2013) 4 *Revue trimestrielle de droit européen* 773.

[51] C-I Grigorieff, 'Arrêt "Condor" et "Air France": une protection accrue des passagers aériens' (2010) 1 *Journal de droit européen* 8.

[52] K Lilleholt, 'Case: CJEU—Sturgeon and others' (2010) 6 *European Review of Contract Law* 189.

[53] Grard (n 34) 242–43.

joint efforts. Without the possibility of a dissenting opinion, all that is left in a judgment are those elements on which there was general consensus. It can therefore happen that some elements, albeit pertinent, cannot appear in full in its actual wording, yet they still remain implied.

This explains why, even though the Court followed the same reasoning in *Nelson* as in *Sturgeon*, the recurring arguments are more developed in *Nelson*. Indeed, following the criticism it received in reaction to the *Sturgeon* judgment, the Court wished to be more pedagogical in *Nelson* and to disclose its thoughts in greater detail.[54] This still does not mean that the same reasons had not already been taken into account when writing the *Sturgeon* judgment.

V. The Court's Three-Step Algorithm in *Sturgeon*

The starting point of the reasoning is obvious. The Regulation affords certain rights to air passengers in the event of cancellation, denied boarding or delay, but, as paragraph 41 of the *Sturgeon* judgment indicates, the Regulation does not explicitly provide for a specific right to compensation for the passengers of delayed flights (nor does it exclude this right explicitly). Under these conditions, the question that the Court addressed *first* was whether compensation in case of delay, which is not in the text, *is forbidden by the legislator*. It would only be if this were the case that recognising a right to compensation for passengers of delayed flights should be considered *contra legem*.

According to the scholars who have criticised the *Sturgeon* judgment, two elements in particular show that the legislator implicitly sought to deny any right to compensation to passengers of delayed flights, namely the *travaux préparatoires* and an *a contrario* reading of various Articles of the Regulation.

Concerning the *travaux préparatoires,* several authors[55] have emphasised that in point 23 of the explanatory report accompanying the initial proposal for the Regulation, it is indicated that 'the Commission considers that in present circumstances operators should not be obliged to compensate delayed passengers'.[56] However, the value of such an argument is rather modest given that, when interpreting a

---

[54] See also Le Bot (n 50) 768, fn 120. Grard maintains that the reasoning in *Nelson* is an 'improved copy' of that in *Sturgeon*, and that it is 'concentrated on arguments relating more to the text of the Regulation than its finality' and delivered 'in respect of a greater legal orthodoxy': Grard (n 16) 1–2. On the contrary, Michel holds that in *Nelson*, 'the Court has not changed its analysis at all': V Michel, 'Vols retardés: *bis repetita*' (2012) 12 *Europe* 29.

[55] eg Arnold and Mendes de Leon (n 35) 100–01; Balfour (n 45) 74; Gogl (n 46) 84; Garben (n 49) 21.

[56] Commission, 'Proposal for a Regulation of the European Parliament and of the Council establishing common rules on compensation and assistance to air passengers in the event of denied boarding and of cancellation or long delay of flights', COM(2001) 784 final.

text in EU law, only the final wording counts, rather than opinions expressed by different EU institutions during the legislative process.

Furthermore, it should be noted, by way of *analogy*, that the interpretative method relying on *travaux préparatoires* has a very limited role in international law. According to Article 32 of the VCLT, referring to preparatory work is only a supplementary means of interpretation. It can only be used:

(1) in order to confirm the interpretation arising from the general rule given in Article 31 of the VCLT, that is to say by following the ordinary meaning to be given to the terms of the treaty in their context and in the light of its object and purpose; or

(2) when recourse to the above-mentioned general rule of interpretation leaves the meaning ambiguous or obscure, or leads to a result which is manifestly absurd or unreasonable.

As a result, even if the *travaux préparatoires* may be taken into account, it must be done with great care, only in a subsidiary way and, especially, not during the initial phase of legal interpretation when the judges establish their first understanding of the text. In passing, it is interesting to note that as regards the European Commission's stance against compensating passengers of delayed flights before the adoption of the Regulation, the same institution completely changed its position after the decision in the *Sturgeon* case, and later defended the solution found in that judgment firmly before the Court. This only goes to confirm the relatively minor importance of an argument based exclusively upon preparatory work.

Next, concerning the *a contrario* argument (*qui de uno dicit, de altero negat*), the authors who criticised the *Sturgeon* judgment noted that Article 6 of the Regulation, regarding delayed flights, read in conjunction with Article 7 (right to compensation), does not envisage a right to compensation for passengers of a delayed flight, whereas Article 5 does provide for such a right in certain instances of cancellation. They deduced from this that, contrary to the situation of cancellation of a flight, the legislator implicitly ruled out any compensation in the event of delay.[57]

However, is such an argument conclusive? The response is 'no', for at least four reasons.

First, Article 6 concerns *delayed departure* only. On the other hand, however, the Regulation does not contain a definition that would limit 'delay' to departures. It is therefore not possible to deduce the legal consequences for *arrivals after the scheduled time* from Article 6 alone.

Secondly, it should be noted that even if Article 5 concerns the cancellation of a flight, it contains two provisions allowing for compensation of passengers in the case of arrival after the scheduled time of the cancelled flight. Even if these provisions expressly concern only flights re-routing passengers, it cannot therefore be

---

[57] eg Bouveresse (n 48).

asserted that the legislator excluded any possibility of compensation in the event of a *delayed arrival*.

Thirdly, the *a contrario* argument implies that the legislator intended to treat two different situations differently. Such an intent would be defeated if it could be shown that the legislator meant to provide for the similar treatment of these two situations. According to Article 5 of the Regulation concerning cancellations, the right to compensation is conditional upon the absence of extraordinary circumstances. It is true that Article 6 regarding delays says nothing about these circumstances, which seems logical since this article does not deal with the right to compensation. However, recital 15 states that air carriers can also invoke extraordinary circumstances in the event of a long delay (as highlighted in paragraph 43 of the *Sturgeon* judgment). As a result, and contrary to what the *a contrario* argument would suggest, it becomes obvious that the legislator intended, in this regard, for *similar treatments* of the different situations set out in Articles 5 and 6 of the Regulation.

Fourthly, and most importantly, it is a myth to believe that, in contrast to *delay*, *cancellation* of a flight is a constituent element that enables compensation. Of course, a glance at Article 5(1)(c) can give such an impression, since this provision lays down the principle of compensation in the event of cancellation (absence of compensation being formally envisaged as an exception to this principle). However, a more thorough look at this paragraph taken in the context of Article 5 in its entirety reveals that the compensation provided for is intended to make up not so much for the cancellation but rather for the *trouble and inconvenience* suffered by the passengers in the case of *re-routing*. In other words, the application of the provisions of Article 5, including those regarding compensation, supposes of course a cancelled flight, but it is not the cancellation in itself that is the constituent reason for compensation. Indeed, the obligation to compensate only arises when the air carrier breaches its obligation to inform the interested persons of the cancellation within the given timescale, along with an offer to re-route that does not allow the passengers to fly to their final destination within the time frame fixed by different provisions of Article 5.

It therefore seems evident that the *EU legislator does not consider the cancellation of a flight a sufficient reason for compensation*. It has decided only to compensate the inconvenience caused to passengers resulting from information of the cancellation which comes too late and from a re-routing's taking too long.

These four elements demonstrate at the very least that the Regulation is not clear enough in respect of differentiating the legal consequences of cancellation of flights, on the one hand, and those of delayed flights, on the other. On the contrary, it is rather confusing, even if the confusion is not manifest at first sight.[58] Articles 5, 6 and 7 thus do not lend themselves to a conclusive *a contrario* reading and, as a result, the Court was unable to confirm the legislator's will to deny in all circumstances the right to compensation to passengers of delayed flights.

---

[58] Le Bot seems to share this reading of the text, eg Le Bot (n 50) 773.

I come now to the *second step*: in the absence of conclusive proof that the EU legislator wished to exclude the eventuality of compensation for passengers of delayed flights, is it possible to consider the silence of the legislator as a gap in the text that can be filled with a broad interpretation by the Court? In other words, could such compensation be established *praeter legem*? In order to answer this question, we must return to the teleological method. Recourse to this approach has several consequences.

First of all, given that the first recital of the Regulation stresses that this instrument is aimed at ensuring 'a high level of protection for passengers', the rights conferred on passengers must be interpreted broadly (paragraphs 44 and 45 of the *Sturgeon* judgment). Next, if several interpretations of a provision are possible, priority should be given to a reading that safeguards its *effet utile* in light of the aim pursued by the legislator (paragraph 47). As a result, the provisions relating to compensation of passengers must also be interpreted in a way that ensures that these provisions retain their effectiveness. Lastly, it should be presumed that the legislator did not wish to violate the 'constitution', namely EU primary law, including the general principles of equal treatment and non-discrimination. This means that Regulation 261 must be interpreted, as far as possible, in such a way as not to affect its validity (paragraph 47). This is an approach regularly used by constitutional courts as well as by the Court itself, according to which the provisions relating to the compensation must be interpreted in conformity with the principle of equal treatment, in order not to discriminate between different categories of passengers.

However, a *third step* was still necessary, namely to *connect the teleological interpretation with the wording of the Regulation*, or, in other words, to identify a provision implying a gap that the Court could fill in *prater legem*. The Court identified this lacuna in *Article 5(1)(c)(iii)* (paragraph 55).

Alas, this crucial element in the Court's reasoning has been misunderstood, deformed or simply ignored by some scholars. For example, Bouveresse, who has criticised the *Sturgeon* judgment mercilessly, makes no allusion whatsoever to Article 5(1)(c)(iii) in her analysis, despite there being several explicit references in the judgment.[59]

The *Sturgeon* judgment has also been unfairly criticised for relying on a simple recital of the Regulation, despite the fact that in its *ex parte IATA* judgment the Court had considered that the sole role of the preamble to an EU act is to clarify, rather than to derogate from, the provisions of that act.[60] However, in *Sturgeon* the Court did not use this recital in order to derogate from provisions of the Regulation, but only *precisely to specify the scope of Article 5(1)(c)(iii)*.

---

[59] Bouveresse (n 48) 37.
[60] This was apparently the argument of the Amtsgericht Nürtingen, Germany, in the judgment of 5 July 2013 in which it rejected the claim of passengers who were victims of an extended delay. See, eg, (2013) 3 *Reflets de la Cour* 15.

Indeed, Article 5(1)(c)(iii) governs even the extreme situation in which *information* is given to the passengers about the cancellation of their flight as late as their actual arrival at the airport and, in such an urgent situation, the passengers concerned are completely unable to make any other arrangements in order to reach their destination at the scheduled time. However, for the legislator, even this dramatic situation does not in itself constitute a good enough reason to require the passive carrier to compensate the unfortunate passengers. The carrier can still avoid the duty to compensate if it can propose to re-route passengers within the precise time frame, fixed by the quoted provision, which takes into account the scheduled times of departure and arrival of the cancelled flight. The inconvenience for which the EU legislator wished to compensate in Article 5(1)(c)(iii) is therefore *only* the trouble linked with a re-routing that did not respect the time frame laid down in this provision; that is to say, a *loss of time, the length of which is considered intolerable by him.*

This conclusion is corroborated by recourse to the *effet utile* method. Indeed, since Article 5(1)(c)(iii) provides for compensation for the inconvenience suffered by passengers due to a number of extra hours sacrificed by them in order to reach their destination as compared to the originally planned duration, this right to compensation must be afforded whenever the same inconvenience, the same loss of time, is suffered.

The above conclusion can also be drawn from Article 5(1)(c)(iii) read in the light of the *general principles of equal treatment* and *non-discrimination.* The unforeseeable nature of a delay necessarily implies that the passengers concerned are not normally informed of it in advance, similarly to those who were informed at the very last moment of the cancellation of their flight (paragraph 31 of the *Nelson* judgment). The situation for both groups of passengers is therefore comparable. Given that they all suffer an irretrievable loss of time, there is no reason to treat them differently.

In order to avoid arriving at the conclusion that the way in which the Regulation treats passengers suffering from long delays and those re-routed is discriminatory, the Court held that, by adopting Article 5(1)(c)(iii), the legislator intended to afford air passengers of delayed flights the right to compensation whenever they suffer an inconvenience, consisting of a loss of time, the length of which is declared intolerable by that Article.

VI. The Choice of Three Hours

As far as the conclusion according to which passengers of delayed flights should receive compensation in order to fulfil the requirements of the principles of equal treatment and of non-discrimination is concerned, the judgment in *Sturgeon* does not in fact differ too much from the Opinion of Advocate General Sharpston. On the other hand, there is a clear divergence in respect of the question whether the

EU judiciary is allowed to specify, using a precise figure, the length of a delay that must be compensated.

For the Advocate General:

> The legislator has the right to pick a figure and then defend it … The actual selection of the magic figure is a legislative prerogative. To the extent that *any* figure is to some extent arbitrary, its arbitrariness is covered by that prerogative … The Court cannot [do this]. Any figure one cared to pick would involve reading into the Regulation something it plainly does not contain and would be a judicial usurpation of the legislative prerogative.[61]

The Court did not follow the Advocate General, and indicated a precise figure. However, this figure is not the Court's own invention; it *derives directly from Article 5(1)(c)(iii) of the Regulation. This figure is therefore not arbitrary.* Having interpreted Article 5(1)(c)(iii), the Court concluded that when passengers reach their final destination three hours or more after the arrival time originally scheduled, they might rely on the right to compensation, unless the delay was a result of extraordinary circumstances.

A certain number of authors display rather a hostile reaction towards this element of the case law. Some of them erroneously believe that the air carrier has an obligation to compensate passengers for a delay *in excess of* three hours, although this is already the case for a delay *equal* to three hours.[62] Others fail to take into account the provision in which this figure appears in the Regulation (Article 5(1)(c)(iii)), despite explicit clarification at paragraphs 55–58 of the *Sturgeon* judgment. Bouveresse categorically insists, in her commentary on *Sturgeon*, that the Court committed an 'arbitrary act' in fixing the threshold of three hours:[63] 'en vain, on cherche l'article du règlement où la référence à un délai de trois heures apparaît'. Seeming to believe, wrongly, that the Court derived this figure from recital 15 in conjunction with Article 6 of the Regulation, she puts the question, whether 'it is because there is a "long" delay that one more hour is necessary, and why therefore only one more hour and not two or three? There is no answer in the judgment.'[64] But there was no need for the Court to answer such a question given that the figure of three hours came from Article 5(1)(c)(iii) and not from Article 6.

Lastly, some scholars have rightly remarked that the Court's reasoning is based on Article 5(1)(c)(iii), while drawing from this Article an entirely different conclusion. In this way, Balfour states that 'in any event, the actual delay in arrival suffered by passengers whose flights are cancelled and who are offered re-routing in

---

[61] *Sturgeon* (n 12) paras 93 and 94 of the Opinion.
[62] Grard (n 16); Grard (n 34) 242; Poissonnier and Osseland (n 44) 1461.
[63] As does Grard (n 16), albeit more prudently.
[64] Bouveresse (n 48). Given that her commentary was published very soon after the delivery of the *Sturgeon* judgement and thereby served as a reference for others (eg F Le Bot or L Grard), it would have been appropriate in my view to make more of an effort to understand, in good faith, the reasoning given in the judgment, and also to choose less categorical terms being plainly incompatible with so much uncertainty which this author shows by putting to readers her unanswered strange questions.

accordance with Article 5(1)(c)(iii) is two, not three hours'.[65] However, while the *Sturgeon* judgment links the figure of three hours to a *total loss of time* suffered by the passengers (paragraph 57), Balfour contests the same figure from the point of view of a *delay in arrival*.

It should thus be explained here *how the Court read Article 5(1)(c)(iii)*. According to this provision, if the air carrier is able to re-route a passenger, departing *no more than one hour* before the scheduled time of departure of the cancelled flight, and reaching his or her final destination *less than two hours* after the scheduled time of arrival of the cancelled flight, such re-routing resulting in a *cumulated loss of time of less than three hours* as compared to the planning of the cancelled flight, there is no duty to compensate the re-routed passenger, since the inconvenience suffered would be still tolerable in the eyes of the legislator. On the contrary, any delay in excess of this 'tolerance threshold' already constitutes an unacceptable loss of time, activating the obligation to compensate. Therefore, any cumulated loss of time suffered by a passenger in consequence of re-routing *equal to or in excess of three hours* in relation to the planned duration of the cancelled flight must in any event give rise to the right to compensation.[66]

Therefore, *it is the legislator and not the Court who made the choice of three hours*. In order to avoid any discrimination and to give *effet utile* to Article 5(1)(c)(iii), the Court, also having in mind the goal of a high level of passenger protection, simply concluded that even if the threshold is literally limited to loss of time in the event of *re-routing*, it should also be so applied to passengers who, in consequence of a delay, reach their final destination three hours or more after the arrival time originally scheduled.[67] This conclusion is corroborated by reading recital 15 in conjunction with Article 6 of the Regulation.[68]

In view of the above considerations, it must be concluded that the Court did not 'usurp a legislative prerogative' by indicating the precise length of delay giving rise to the right to compensation, but simply gave *effet utile* to a choice made implicitly by the legislator himself.

There was another strong reason for the Court to specify the relevant threshold for delays entitling passengers to compensation, which appears at paragraph 68 of the *Nelson* judgment. Indeed, it was necessary to prevent national courts from qualifying 'long delay' in different ways, inasmuch as those divergences would have called into question the principle of legal certainty. Once again, the Court gave its interpretation of the Regulation taking into account the general principles of EU law.

As already mentioned, some authors maintain that the Court has gone beyond the limits of its competence, even contesting the binding force of the *Sturgeon*

---

[65] Balfour (n 45) 74.

[66] This conclusion is not contradicted by the fact that the carrier may be sometimes obliged to compensate passengers having suffered a loss of time shorter than three hours when the proposed re-routing respected only one of the time limits (either on departure or on arrival).

[67] *Sturgeon* (n 12) para 57.

[68] ibid, para 61.

judgment.[69] Their personal contestations seem to have had a real impact, since several courts and tribunals in Germany, the United Kingdom and The Netherlands were hesitant, or even refused, to recognise the passengers' right to compensation in case of delayed flights,[70] as openly suggested by the above-discussed critical authors.

In this sceptical atmosphere, the Court found itself tasked with the *Germanwings* case,[71] submitted in July 2011. Here, the national court (the Landgericht Köln) relied openly upon the idea that the EU judiciary had exceeded its prerogatives in order to question whether the interpretation of the Regulation in the *Sturgeon* judgment was 'compatible with the principle of separation of powers in the Union'.

In this context, one may wonder whether this referral might not have been inspired, other than by scholarly attacks, by the *Honeywell* decision handed down by the German Federal Constitutional Court in July 2010.[72] In this case, the Constitutional Court scrutinised the solution reached by the CJEU in *Mangold v Helm*,[73] and clarified the perimeters of its *ultra vires* competence. On that occasion, the Karlsruhe Court held that it was not legitimate to give primacy to its own interpretation of an EU act over the one given by the EU Court, provided that the latter was a result of the application of generally recognised methods of interpretation, even if recourse to some other method might have given a different solution. However, the *Honeywell* decision does not reveal whether the German Constitutional Court would be ready to accept, without reservation, the use of the *effet utile* method that extends the scope of the provisions interpreted by the CJEU beyond their literal meaning.[74]

In any case, the German Constitutional Court did not engage in a procedure to verify the eventual *ultra vires* nature of the Court's interpretation of Regulation 261. According to the criteria applied in the *Honeywell* decision, this would have involved demonstrating that in the *Sturgeon* judgment the Court had 'manifestly' exceeded its powers, causing a 'structurally significant shift to the detriment of the Member States in the structure of competences'.[75]

The Court replied to the Landgericht Köln question in April 2013, with a reasoned Order given by a chamber of three judges, stating that the interpretation

---

[69] eg Hobe, Müller-Rostin and Recker (n 14) 163–64.

[70] Garben has drawn up a list of these cases. This author has shown understanding towards the Court's approach, saying 'All the foregoing leads us to consider that the [CJEU's] judgment in *Sturgeon* was activist, but that this activism could well be considered warranted in the broader institutional framework. In light of its signature expansionist approach in the area of the four freedoms, one could deem the ECJ's forceful assertion of consumer rights in this area appropriate and justified.' Having said that, this author explains that the particularly hostile reactions to *Sturgeon* judgment could well be due to the prevailing euroscepticism in certain Member States, and also to 'eurolegalism'. Garben (n 49) 39.

[71] Case C-413/11 *Germanwings GmbH v Amend* (CJEU, 18 April 2013) (*Germanwings I*).

[72] German Federal Constitutional Court, 6 July 2010, *Honeywell*, BVerfGE 126, 286.

[73] Case C-144/04 *Mangold v Helm* [2005] ECR I-09981.

[74] eg J Malenovský, 'Sur le passé, le présent et l'avenir du contrôle *ultra vires*', *Mélanges en l'honneur de V Skouris* (Larcier, 2015) 415.

[75] *Honeywell* (n 72) paras 61 and 71.

given by the Court on passenger compensation in the event of a delayed flight did not affect the principle of the separation of powers in the EU.[76] The Court indicated that since the examination of the wording of the relevant provisions of the Regulation, along with the help of purely logical arguments, in particular the *a contrario* argument, had not led to a final conclusion in this regard, it had considered the context of these provisions as well as the objective pursued by Regulation 261, whilst also taking into account the general principle of equal treatment, to come to the solution found in the *Sturgeon* judgment.[77]

In the wake of the *Sturgeon* judgment, the Court received several referrals for preliminary rulings regarding some specific consequences to be drawn from it. In *Air France v Folkerts*,[78] the Court held that the right to compensation in the event of a long delay is not dependent on a delay in departure, and that for flights with connections, this right must be understood in terms of the delay occurring on arrival at the final destination, which means the destination of the last flight to be taken by the passenger in question. In the *Germanwings II* judgment,[79] the Court explained that the concept of 'arrival time', which is used to determine the length of the delay suffered by the passengers, refers to the time at which at least one of the doors of the aircraft is opened, provided that, at this moment, the passengers are permitted to leave the aircraft.

VII. Conclusion

The *Sturgeon* judgment gave rise to an exchange of opinions between K Lenaerts, President of the Chamber that gave this judgment, and JHH Weiler, in a wider discussion on the legitimacy of the case law of the Court. Lenaerts defended the 'reconciliatory interpretation' used in *Sturgeon*, as well as the way in which the arguments are articulated.[80] By contrast, Weiler described the judgment as a 'characteristically cryptic decision of the Court', the legitimacy of which was weak, mainly for this reason. Weiler continues more generally:

> Lenaerts has a similar facility with the case law of the European Court, as noted on display in his chapter. Contradictions? Read more carefully, think more deeply and they all fit together … To read Lenaerts, the Court is, well, perfect … You will not find a single criticism of a single decision of the Court. You will not find a shade of any other criticism of the Court … I hope I am forgiven if I suggest that it has at least the whiff of old style Marxist 'false consciousness'. If you think the Court is less than perfect, it is because we

---

[76] eg *Germanwings I* (n 71).

[77] ibid, para 20.

[78] Case C-11/11 *Folkerts v Air France* (CJEU, 23 February 2013).

[79] *Germanwings II* (n 29).

[80] K Lenaerts, 'The Court's Outer and Inner Selves: Exploring the External and Internal Legitimacy of the European Court of Justice' in M Adams *et al* (eds), *Judging Europe's Judges. The Legitimacy of the Case Law of the European Court of Justice* (Hart Publishing, 2013) 20–26.

have not explained it well enough, because you do not understand it well enough. This is a truly remarkable apologia.[81]

Without claiming that the *Sturgeon* judgment is faultless, I share Lenaerts' view. Above all, this is not a 'cryptic' judgment. In numerical terms alone, it comprises 73 paragraphs, with the reasoning concerning passengers' right to compensation in the event of delayed flights alone taking up 30 paragraphs. Of course, not everything was laid out in detail, but I believe that if one takes the time to read this judgment carefully, the Court's reasoning as a whole becomes transparent. Furthermore, a number of scholars, such as Stuyck, Picod, Poissonnier, Osseland or van Dam,[82] found neither incoherence nor inadequacy in the judgment. It is also relevant to note that the reasoning in *Sturgeon* was taken up in its entirety in the *Nelson* judgment, adopted by the Grand Chamber, in which no genuinely new arguments appear. In any case, Weiler's remark that, in defending *Sturgeon*, the current President of the Court is engaging in old-style Marxist propaganda seems to me totally unjustified.

On the other hand, I can partially agree with Weiler in his reading of the signal given by the Court in *Sturgeon*. In Weiler's view, this judgment says to the legislator, 'For legal reasons you cannot do X, but you can do Y. So we will do Y because we think that is what you intended; or because this will cure the legal defect of X instead of invalidating it.' However, as Weiler himself admits, albeit reluctantly, exceptionally this approach, which avoids invalidating the original measure, appears justified.[83] I think that the circumstances surrounding and determining *Sturgeon* were in fact exceptional: if the Court had invalidated the Regulation, this would have annihilated all passenger rights, at least temporarily, until the adoption of a new regulation. Yet guaranteeing these rights was precisely the primary objective underlying the adoption of the Regulation.[84]

I would like to recall that the European Commission has recently published a proposal for a Regulation amending Regulation 261. This proposal aims at establishing a right to compensation for air passengers in the event of a long delay, and refers explicitly in this regard to the *Sturgeon* judgment. However, for a reason unrelated to those developed in this judgment (*viz*, to prevent an increase in the number of cancellations of flights), the European Commission has proposed to increase the threshold for a compensable delay from three to five hours for all flights within the EU.[85] On its part, the European Parliament has adopted, by a

---

[81] JHH Weiler, 'Epilogue: Judging the Judges—Apology and Critique' in M Adams *et al* (eds), *Judging Europe's Judges: The Legitimacy of the Case Law of the European Court of Justice* (Hart Publishing, 2013) 235, at 237–38 and 244.

[82] C van Dam, 'Air Passenger Rights after Sturgeon' (2011) 36(4/5) *Air and Space Law* 260.

[83] Weiler (n 81) 246.

[84] See also Lenaerts (n 80) 26.

[85] Commission, 'Proposal for a Regulation of the European Parliament and of the Council amending Regulation (EC) No 261/2004 establishing common rules on compensation and assistance to passengers in the event of denied boarding and of cancellation or long delay of flights and Regulation

landslide majority, a legislative resolution that wishes to maintain the threshold of three hours.[86] These facts show, in my opinion, that the Court's case law on air passenger compensation in the event of a long delay, along with the threshold of three hours, is in line with the will of the legislator, this time already made explicit in the negotiations that should lead to a new Regulation. Of this I am glad.

(EC) No 2027/97 on air carrier liability in respect of the carriage of passengers and their baggage by air', COM(2013) 130 final, para 3.3.1.1.

[86] European Parliament, 'Legislative resolution of 5 February 2014 on the proposal for a regulation of the European Parliament and of the Council amending Regulation (EC) No 261/2004 establishing common rules on compensation and assistance to passengers in the event of denied boarding and of cancellation or long delay of flights and Regulation (EC) No 2027/97 on air carrier liability in respect of the carriage of passengers and their baggage by air' (2014) 0092.

3

Regulation 261: The Passenger Rights Framework

FRANK BENYON

I. Introduction

As the detailed content of Regulation 261 will be discussed in the contributions that follow, I propose to look at three general matters which underpin the entire measure and which can be noted in three of its recitals.

The first recital tells us that 'Action by the Community in the field of air transport should aim, among other things, at ensuring a high level of protection for passengers.' One will need to recall the general EU law dimension of the common transport policy and its development in order better to position Regulation 261.

The second important aspect is to consider the international law dimension of the EU's transport policy and the question of coherence between the two bodies of law. Mention of this can be seen in the fourteenth recital to Regulation 261.

Thirdly, and lastly, there is no point enacting rules if they are not properly enforced. Accordingly, we must look at the inter-institutional dimension of enforcement of the rules. We must look not only at relations between the CJEU and national courts, but also at the interaction between the EU institutions and the Member States, all with a view to ensuring harmonised enforcement in each Member State.

II. General Dimension

Regulation 261 is only 10 years old and, like any novel measure, has engendered much discussion amongst academics, practitioners and courts; indeed, often the highest courts. But why is it novel? And where does it sit in the general scheme of the TFEU?

Regulation 261 is novel and relatively recent in the 50 years of the EU's existence, for the simple reason that Member States, no doubt protective of their sovereignty and of their 'flag-carriers', blocked the liberalisation of the transport sector in general, relying upon articles in the TFEU that required a positive act and which gave them full discretion as to how to liberalise.[1] The European Council only acted after a CJEU judgment of 1985[2] required it to take measures to liberalise. It was not until 1992 that full freedom to provide services was introduced for all air carriers.[3] In fact, numerous restrictions maintained by various Member States at airports and otherwise[4] meant that it was in practice only later in that decade that all carriers were able to fly freely within the EU, and only well after 2000 that they could fly from the EU to third countries after the landmark *Open Skies* judgments.[5] These measures, in effect less than two decades old, did of course benefit passengers indirectly by allowing greater choice, encouraging competition and thus lowering prices. They were followed by a great number of accompanying measures of more indirect benefit to the passenger, such as on safety, on slot allocation and on better use of flight paths, but also by measures of immediate relevance to the passenger, such as the rules on security screening,[6] those establishing 'Black Lists' of airlines not allowed to fly in the Union due to safety concerns[7] and Regulation 261, the subject of this volume. These measures have thus been introduced essentially only in the last decade, and so have obviously given rise to debate and to disputes when the carriers, so soon after having been given the freedom of the skies, were required to respect certain obligations in order to continue to exercise that freedom!

What was made clear in *ex parte IATA*,[8] but had already been indicated in the very first recitals of the Black List Regulation[9] and Regulation 261, is that measures ensuring a high level of protection for passengers fall clearly within the TFEU. This is not particular to transport. The 'rise of the consumer' (of the subscriber, of the

---

[1] Now Consolidated version of the Treaty on the Functioning of the European Union [2012] OJ C326/1, Arts 56–58, 91(1) and 100(2) (TFEU).

[2] Case C-13/83 *European Parliament v Council* [1985] ECR 1513.

[3] Council Regulation (EC) 2407/1992 of 23 July 1992 on licensing of air carriers [1992] OJ L240/1, Council Regulation 2408/1992 of 23 July 1992 on access for Community air carriers into intra-Community air routes [1992] OJ L240/1 and Council Regulation (EC) 2409/1992 of 23 July 1992 on fares and rates for air services [1992] OJ L240/1, consolidated into European Parliament and Council Regulation (EC) 1008/2008 of 24 September 2008 on common rules for the operation of air services in the Community (Recast) [2008] OJ L293/3.

[4] eg Case T-260/94 *Air Inter v Commission* [1997] ECR II-997.

[5] eg Case C-467/98 *Commission v Denmark* [2002] ECR I-9519.

[6] European Parliament and Council Regulation (EC) 2320/2002 of 16 December 2002 establishing common rules in the field of civil aviation security [2002] OJ L 355/1, now Regulation 300/2008 of 11 March 2008 on common rules in the field of aviation security and repealing Regulation (EC) 2320/2002 [2008] OJ L97/72.

[7] European Parliament and Council Regulation (EC) 2111/2005 of 14 December 2005 on the establishment of a Community list of air carriers subject to an operating ban within the Community and on informing air transport passengers of the identity of the operating air carrier, and repealing Article 9 of Directive 2004/36/EC [2005] OJ L344/15 (Black List Regulation).

[8] Case C-344/04 R *(International Air Transport Association and European Low Fares Airline Association) v Department for Transport* [2006] ECR I-403 (*ex parte IATA*).

[9] Regulation (EC) 2111/2005 (n 7).

patient, of the passenger) is to be seen in Article 12 of the TFEU,[10] in Article 95 of the TEC Treaty (now Article 114(3) of the TFEU for single market measures)[11] and indeed in Article 38 of the Charter of Fundamental Rights of the European Union 2000,[12] now of legal force equal to the Treaties since the Treaty of Lisbon 2007. The user rights that so angered air carriers in 2005 are to be found in many other Treaty sectors too. If one looks at another area close to the individual—indeed close to his ear and to his typing finger—namely telecoms, the EU legislator has given the consumer universal service, the power to change supplier, number portability and, of more immediate concern to his pocket, has capped the prices charged for roaming calls, text messages and data downloads since 2007.[13] Indeed, the permitted call charge has gone down vertiginously from €0.49 to only €0.05 per minute in only seven years.[14] Telecoms operators were no more happy with this than were the air carriers with Regulation 261, but the CJEU stated clearly in *Vodafone v Secretary of State for Business, Enterprise and Regulatory Reform*[15] that consumer protection can indeed be a decisive factor in choices to be made under Article 95 of the Treaty establishing the European Community (TEC Treaty)[16] (now Article 114 of the TFEU), a very clear statement confirming that market integration does not have to be the only decisive factor in order to rely on Article 114.

This pro-consumer approach continues in all sectors. In the maritime transport sector, for example, Regulation 1177 of 2010[17] has now given rights to passengers travelling by sea, inspired by Regulation 261 but adjusted to the maritime transport sector, thus with delay compensation limited to 25 per cent of the ticket price and costs for care limited to three days at €80 per day (no doubt inspiration for the proposal to amend Regulation 261).

In the European Commission's Citizenship Report of 2010,[18] economic rights such as those in Regulation 261 are to be found amongst the more classic citizenship rights, such as voting, standing for election and consular protection by other Member States, as an essential part of EU citizenship.

---

[10] Art 12 of the TFEU provides, 'Consumer protection requirements shall be taken into account in defining and implementing other Union policies and activities.'

[11] Art 114(3) of the TFEU provides that '[t]he Commission, in its proposals envisaged in paragraph 1 concerning health, safety, environmental protection and consumer protection, will take as a base a high level of protection'.

[12] Art 38 of the Charter of Fundamental Rights of the European Union 2000 provides, 'Union Policies shall ensure a high level of consumer protection.'

[13] European Parliament and Council Regulation (EC) 717/2007 of 27 June 2007 on roaming on public mobile telephone networks within the Community [2007] OJ L171/32.

[14] eg European Parliament and Council Regulation (EU) 531/2012 of 13 June 2012 on roaming on public mobile communications networks within the Community [2012] OJ L172/10.

[15] Case C-58/08 *Vodafone v Secretary of State for Business, Enterprise and Regulatory Reform* [2010] ECR I-4999, para 36.

[16] [2002] OJ C325/33.

[17] European Parliament and Council Regulation (EU) No 1177/2010 of 24 November 2010 concerning the rights of passengers when travelling by sea and inland waterway and amending Regulation (EC) No 2004/2006 [2010] OJ L334/1.

[18] Commission, 'EU Citizenship Report 2010, Dismantling the obstacles to EU Citizens' rights', COM(2010) 603 final.

The consumer protection measures of Regulation 261 are thus here to stay and to be developed—unless international law might restrict such a policy. So, let us now consider the international dimension.

III. The International Dimension

The basic tenets of air transport law were established at the international level between sovereign states in the Chicago Convention on International Aviation in 1944, which defines various rights (to overfly, to land, to pick up passengers, etc) and, in order to follow and develop the rules, established the International Civil Aviation Organisation (ICAO), a classic, non-supranational, international organisation. States then concluded bilateral treaties to exchange flight rights and establish related agreements, and took part in discussions within the Organisation to develop rules on various aspects of civil aviation, such as safety. So what became of these obligations when the EU was established?

Article 351 of the TFEU provides that agreements concluded between Member States and third countries prior to the establishment of the EU continue in force unless incompatible with the TFEU. The Chicago Convention thus still applies.

But when further agreements are proposed in the transport sector, for example as developed within the ICAO, who is competent to conclude these? The preliminary articles of the TFEU after the Treaty of Lisbon 2007 provide that the common transport policy is a shared competence,[19] thus both the EU and the Member States have powers. However, we also see in Article 3(2) a 'special' implied exclusive EU competence, namely when the proposed international agreement 'may affect' rules already established at EU level. This in fact takes up a landmark judgment in the early 1970s, which, what is more, was in the transport sector,[20] and which established that the EU alone would have the power to conclude the European Road Transport Agreement (ERTA) because it had already adopted a Regulation on the same subject of lorry drivers' hours, etc.[21] However, there was a 'sting in the tail' of the decision, since the ECJ found that since the dispute had only been brought before it late in the day, the Member States could go ahead and conclude the agreement. Incredibly, this 'sting' still continues to hurt, because the EU is still not party to the ERTA and, what is more, the European Commission's 2002 proposals for the EU to become a member of the ICAO[22] and of the International Maritime Organisation (IMO) are still simply pending before the European Council.

---

[19] TFEU, Art 4(2)(g).

[20] Case 22/70 *Commission v Council* [1971] ECR 1971/263.

[21] It was this type of competence that allowed the ECJ, in the *Open Skies* judgments (n 5), to rule that Member States were no longer competent to conclude air transport agreements with the USA.

[22] Recommendation from the Commission to the Council in order to authorise the Commission to open and conduct negotiations with the International Civil Aviation Organization (ICAO) on the conditions and arrangements for accession by the European Community SEC [2002] 381 final. This document also contains the request in relation to the IMO.

The peculiar situation which thus arises is that, notwithstanding the EU's mixed or exclusive ERTA competence, it is the Member States that continue to work in the relevant organisations or elsewhere to develop new rules and agreements such as, in the maritime transport area, the International Convention for the Prevention of Pollution from Ships 1973 (MARPOL) or the International Convention for the Safety of Life at Seas 1974 (SOLAS). But Member States' participation in these Conventions has not prevented the EU from taking measures in the areas covered. On the contrary, it has acted to 'improve' them by making the rules apply equally to national and to international traffic, by clarifying certain vague provisions which are the result of classic international compromise and, most importantly, by making them EU law, enforceable before the CJEU, by being part of EU Regulations or Directives and not just subject to international discussion.

The relationship between MARPOL and Directive (EC) 2005/35 on ship source pollution and on the introduction of penalties, particularly criminal penalties for infringements (Directive 2005/35),[23] a maritime Directive incorporating some of MARPOL's rules into Union law, came before the CJEU in *Intertanko v Secretary of State for Transport*,[24] where, in a 2008 judgment, it was found that the mere fact that Directive 2005/35 incorporated some rules of MARPOL to which Member States were parties, did not mean that the EU, which was not a party, was bound by the MARPOL rules. In the same decision it was also held that the UN Convention on the Law of the Sea (UNCLOS), although binding on the EU as a party thereto, could not be used to assess the validity of Directive 2005/35 either, since UNCLOS does not establish rules intended to apply directly and immediately to individuals.

In the area of air passenger rights, the Member States and the EU were not content with the outdated Warsaw Convention and its various protocols with their low levels of compensation, and, after failing to persuade other states to renegotiate the Warsaw Convention, raised these limits autonomously,[25] which in turn prompted renegotiation of the Warsaw Convention into the Montreal Convention.[26] In addition, the EU, clearly competent under the ERTA, persuaded the other negotiating states to allow it to become a party alongside its Member States.[27] Regulation 889/2002 amended Regulation 2027 accordingly.[28]

In 2004 the EU adopted Regulation 261 requiring care and compensation to be provided by carriers in the event of delays, which led to the famous *ex parte IATA* case where it was alleged that the absence of the Montreal Convention's

---

[23] Council Directive (EC) 2005/35 of 7 September 2005 on ship-source pollution and on the introduction of penalties, particularly criminal penalties, for infringements [2005] OJ L255/11.

[24] Case C-308/06 *The Queen, ex parte Intertanko et al v Secretary of State for Transport* [2008] ECR I-4057 (*Intertanko*).

[25] By adopting Council Regulation (EC) 2027/97 of 9 October 1997 on air carrier liability in the event of accidents [1997] OJ L285/1.

[26] Convention for the Unification of Certain Rules for International Carriage by Air [2001] OJ L194/39 (Montreal Convention).

[27] This was not an ICAO Convention.

[28] European Parliament and Council Regulation (EC) No 889/2002 of 13 May 2002 amending Council Regulation (EC) No 2027/97 on air carrier liability in the event of accidents [2002] OJ L140/2.

'extraordinary circumstances' exemption to the carriers' obligation to provide care in the case of delays was incompatible with the EU's obligations as a party to the Montreal Convention.

As with UNCLOS in *Intertanko*, the Court's decision confirmed that the EU was indeed bound by the Montreal Convention as a party thereto, but that the subject matter of the Regulation, the provision of care, was not part of the Montreal Convention, which dealt instead with actions for damages. The Court's decision was clear and has been confirmed in later judgments.[29] Furthermore, no state party to the Montreal Convention has pursued the EU alleging a breach of the Montreal Convention.

One lesson from these cases must be that it has to be ensured that it is the entity that lays down the internal rules that must enter into the international conventions. Although the CJEU has condemned a Member State for attempting to negotiate an agreement itself, this does not mean that the EU can conduct such negotiations unless the legislator authorises it, for example by adopting the proposals for the EU to join the ICAO and the IMO. Shall we have to resort again to an action for failure to act, which was the subject of *European Parliament v Council*,[30] which unblocked the logjam for internal liberalisation?

But even when authorised to negotiate and accede to a convention, the EU must reflect carefully whether it wishes to be bound by international norms, often the lowest common denominator and not legally enforceable, and, if so, whether it nevertheless wishes to have the possibility to take measures more appropriate to its own integrationist, legal model.

IV. Harmonised Enforcement: By Whom and How?

Regulation 261's provisions on enforcement of its rules, like its substantive provisions, have given rise to a number of legal questions.

Although the rules take the form of a Regulation, and thus under Article 288 of the TFEU is directly applicable, Article 16 requires 'each Member State to designate a body responsible for the enforcement of this Regulation'. Recital 22 states that this supervision should not affect the rights of passengers to seek legal redress from national courts, but the text of Article 16 initially led to much confusion, including English decisions'[31] finding that there was no right to sue under the Regulation, as discussed in Ben Jones's chapter on the UK and Ireland (see chapter sixteen). The CJEU has ruled clearly that there is, of course, such a right.[32]

---

[29] Cases C-581 and 629/10 *Nelson v Deutsche Lufthansa AG* [2012] OJ C399/3 (*Nelson*).
[30] Case C-13/83 *European Parliament v Council* [1985] ECR 1513.
[31] *Graham v Thomas Cook Group UK Ltd* [2012] EWCA Civ 1355.
[32] Case C-12/11 *McDonagh v Ryanair* (ECJ, 31 January 2013).

But national courts cannot alone ensure uniform enforcement of the rules. They only hear the cases that are brought before them and, depending on their national procedures, only address the arguments brought before them. Although Article 267 of the TFEU requires them to refer questions to the CJEU where they have doubts regarding provisions of EU law, the CJEU's first reply to the questions posed in *ex parte IATA* shows that it is not so obvious exactly when this should take place! Nor is it guaranteed that any ruling of the CJEU will always be applied faithfully by national courts. Further, the UK report indicates a reluctance of some UK judges even to consider references with regard to the conformity of Regulation 261 with the Montreal Convention.[33]

Article 16 of Regulation 261, with its requirement for an NEB 'to take the measures necessary to ensure that the rights of passengers are respected'[34] where appropriate, has, as the European Commission explained in its 2007 and 2011 reports on the application of Regulation 261,[35] and again in the Explanatory Memorandum to its 2013 proposal to amend the Regulation,[36] been insufficient to ensure harmonised application across the EU. Again, the distinction between a 'pro-active individual redress' enforcement body, such as exists in Ireland, and the 'general, only questions of principle' approach of the Civil Aviation Authority in the UK is glaringly obvious:[37] the European Commission's Report also shows clearly the very disparate treatment of complaints by different airlines.

In the European Commission's 2013 proposed amendment to Regulation 261, we read that 'the role of the National Enforcement Bodies should be more precisely defined and clearly distinguished from the handling of individual passenger complaints'.[38] The operative texts, however, do not seem so clear: first, Article 16(2) still states that the NEBs are responsible for ensuring the respect of passengers' rights and that they may decide on enforcement actions based on individual complaints. Next, subparagraph (3) of the new Article 16a does not say how the out-of-court resolution will take place, nor set out the nature of the new body's 'final reply', which seems to be left to (differing) national laws. Would this lead to harmonised enforcement when we know that an out-of-court settlement body would not be

---

[33] In *Nelson* (n 29), both the UK and German Governments intervened to argue against a wide or pro-passenger interpretation of Regulation 261.

[34] *cf* recital 22 of Regulation 261 only requires Member States to ensure 'general compliance'.

[35] Commission, 'Communication on the operation and the results of this Regulation establishing common rules on compensation and assistance to passengers in the event of denied boarding and of cancellation or long delay of flights', COM(2007) 168 final; Commission, 'Communication on the application of Regulation 261/2004 establishing common rules on compensation and assistance to passengers in the event of denied boarding and of cancellation or long delay of flights', COM(2011) 428 final.

[36] Commission, 'Regulation of the European Parliament and of the Council' (Proposal), COM(2013) 130 final.

[37] The national reports that follow show great differences in approach: the Czech Republic and Slovakia often impose sanctions; on the other hand France and Spain rarely do so.

[38] Commission, 'Regulation of the European Parliament and of the Council' (Proposal), COM(2013) 130 final, recital 22.

able to pose a question to the CJEU?[39] Rather, this difficult task seems to be left in part to the European Commission to be resolved by a recommendation, which under Article 288 of the TFEU has no binding force! And lastly, the important question of the relationship between these procedures and the pursuit of claims before national courts is not explained at all.

The proposal does, however, endeavour to ensure harmony in the application of Regulation 261 by putting a legislative end to the debate about the time limits applicable to claims under Regulation 261:[40] Article 16a(3) clearly lays down a three-month limit for a passenger to make a claim against the carrier, and establishes time limits in which the carrier is to respond and for the new body to carry out its work. It also aims at more harmony by establishing a committee in which information can be exchanged between Member States and measures taken by way of implementing acts under the advisory procedure in the Comitology rules, and foresees the adoption of European Commission recommendations.

With all of these complexities, it is fortunate that the co-decision procedure[41] will enable the above questions to be clarified and the draft texts revised. The European Parliament will certainly be vigilant not to leave these questions to future Comitology measures, especially when a mere advisory procedure is proposed for such implementing measures; and *ex parte IATA* has showed us how much flexibility the legislative procedure can entail! However, even once the relations between the bodies are made clear, one must ask oneself whether this proposal will solve all the enforcement disparities between Member States. For example, the National Report on France states that only 2 to 4 per cent of complaints were engaged for sanctioning and that fines are very low, compared to the average maximum sanction. Could one not also consider a requirement to 'take action' on a specific number of notified complaints, although this would require serious consideration of how to establish the base figures? Might one also not consider specific amounts for sanctioning recalcitrant carriers?

The co-operation foreseen in the new Article 16b is certainly a positive measure, and such co-operation takes place in various other sectors.[42] In the telecoms sector, meetings take place between national regulators. Seminars and summer schools are conducted by the Florence School of Regulation of the European University Institute precisely in the transport sector as well as for energy and telecoms, where the exchange of experiences in the application of complex legislation has proved invaluable to both regulators and operators. Might that not fall within the new

---

[39] Case C-394/11 *Belov v CHEZ Elektro Balgaria AD & Ors* (ECJ, 31 January 2013).

[40] The CJEU had already stated that the two-month limit under the Montreal Convention did not apply to claims under Regulation 261.

[41] The first European Parliament vote took place on 5 February 2014: Commission, 'European Parliament votes on air passenger rights' (Press Release) IP/14/119 (5 February 2014).

[42] Very detailed measures were laid down in the competition sector in Council Regulation (EC) 1/2003 of 16 December 2002 on the implementation of the rules on competition laid down in Articles 81 and 82 of the Treaty [2002] OJ L1/1,when decision-making powers over infringements were transferred from the EU level to Member State level, and might provide inspiration.

Article 16b(1)? Further, without in any way prejudicing their independence, might national judges not also consider having such exchanges, perhaps in an academic framework?

The results presented in this volume will surely be invaluable to the co-legislators in their current deliberations, and to the European Commission to facilitate the establishment of the new Committee, if retained. Indeed I hope that they will clarify the two most important questions, namely the role of international law in the EU's transport policy and how best to enforce the rules in a uniform manner in every Member State.

4

EU Law and the Montreal Convention of 1999

DAVID McCLEAN

I. Thoughts on Methodology

The focus of this chapter is the exclusivity of the Montreal Convention of 1999, as expounded by the courts of a number of countries, and the treatment of that exclusivity in the case law on Regulation 261. But I begin with some reflections of a methodological nature: the dangers of reading over from one legal order to another, and the way in which interests shape interpretation.

Events such as the conference on Air Passenger Rights, 10 Years On, held in Bruges in September 2014, remind us of the different mind-sets found among those attending any international gathering of lawyers. As someone brought up in the common law tradition, on an off-shore island with no written constitution, whose comparative law work has been largely concerned with the law of other Commonwealth countries, I recognise that I approach law and legal issues in a way unlike that followed by, for example, those in the civil law tradition and accustomed to elaborate and often federal constitutions. We always have to guard against assuming that the particular categories used in our own system or our own methods of interpretation have universal effect or universal validity. I also note that it is a feature of common law systems that judges' reasoning may be expressed fully and in very trenchant and colourful language, which the CJEU can never match in its judgments (even if they can sometimes be helpfully supplemented by extra-judicial writings).

A fairly common theme in the literature about Regulation 261 and the Montreal Convention is the identification of two mind-sets, one having an internationalist perspective the other a European one. With the *Sturgeon v Condor*[1] and *Nelson v Deutsche Lufthansa*[2] decisions in mind, I think a professor may be allowed to say that we could identify a third and important mind-set, that of the CJEU.

---

[1] Cases C-402 and 432/07 *Sturgeon and Others* [2009] ECR I-10923 (*Sturgeon*).
[2] Cases C-581 and 629/10 *Nelson v Deutsche Lufthansa AG* [2012] OJ C399/3 (*Nelson*).

Another contrast goes deeper than lawyers' mind-sets. It concerns policy, and not abstract policy—if there is such a thing—but policy driven by interests: the contrast between the interests and policy aims of the aviation industry, and those of consumers and those who put consumer protection above other values. I hope the discussions here will bring those policy issues into sharper focus.

A final introductory remark: it has been a feature of the history of the Warsaw Convention, and will be of the Montreal Convention and Regulation 261 and its likely successor, that some courts will find ways of avoiding the clear meaning of the text. Judges should, of course, be loyal in their application of the law; occasionally that duty gives way to a wish to do justice in the particular case. Opinions will differ about the merits of that circumstance, but we should not be too surprised when it happens, nor when judges lament (as did the justices of the UK Supreme Court in a case I refer to later, *Stott v Thomas Cook Tour Operators Ltd*[3]) that they are driven by their loyalty to the law to reach what they expressly recognise to be an unjust decision.

II. Regulation 261 and Article 29

The main issue when we set Regulation 261 beside the Montreal Convention is, of course, the exclusivity principle of Article 29 of the Convention,[4] asserted in language if anything more emphatic than in the predecessor provision of the Warsaw Convention in its original form. The Montreal Convention, and so the exclusivity principle it contains, is part of the national legal order of every Member State and part of the EU's legal order as regards carriers established in the EU[5] (even in cases in which some version of the Warsaw Convention would be applicable under the usual rules of treaty interpretation), so that it is doubly binding in the courts of Member States.

If we want to find emphatic statements of the exclusivity principle, we can readily find them in the language of judgments in the US and the UK. Happily, we do not need to concern ourselves with the complex issues dividing the courts in the US about the precise nature of the pre-emptive effect of Article 29. But courts in the US and elsewhere have made it clear that the Montreal Convention precludes

---

[3] *Stott v Thomas Cook Tour Operators Ltd* [2014] UKSC 15, [2014] AC 1347.

[4] Art 29 of the Convention for the Unification of Certain Rules for International Carriage by Air [2001] OJ L194/39 (Montreal Convention) provides, 'In the carriage of passengers, baggage and cargo, any action for damages, however founded, whether under this Convention or in contract or in tort or otherwise, can only be brought subject to the conditions and such limits of liability as are set out in this Convention without prejudice to the question as to who are the persons who have the right to bring suit and what are their respective rights. In any such action, punitive, exemplary or any other non-compensatory damages shall not be recoverable.'

[5] Council Regulation (EC) No 2027/97 of 9 October 1997 on air carrier liability in the event of accidents, Art 3(1) as substituted by European Parliament and Council of 13 May 2002 amending Council Regulation (EC) No 2027/97 on air carrier liability in the event of accidents.

claims framed on some other basis, for example those alleging misrepresentation[6] or discrimination.[7]

The important question is whether the Montreal Convention defines exclusively the circumstances in which a carrier may be liable in international carriage. The prevailing interpretation of Article 29, and of its predecessor provision in the Warsaw Convention, is that the Convention does apply exclusively, provided of course that the claim falls within its scope. So in the leading US case on the Warsaw texts, *El Al Israel Airlines Ltd v Tseng*,[8] it was clear that a passenger whose treatment did not amount to an 'accident' within the special meaning of that term could *not* say, 'so the Convention limits do not apply'; rather it was the carrier who could say, 'so there is no liability'.

In the UK, the same view of exclusivity was adopted in two cases arising out of the same incident: one action was begun in England, the other in Scotland, and both were eventually taken to the House of Lords. A common law action in negligence was brought by passengers who had had the misfortune to land in Kuwait just as it was occupied by Iraqi forces; any claim under the Warsaw Convention was time-barred. The claim was rejected in both countries, and those decisions were upheld in the House of Lords in *Sidhu v British Airways plc*.[9] There, Lord Hope gave the reasons:

> The intention [of the relevant articles of the Convention] seems to be to provide a secure regime, within which the restriction on the carrier's freedom of contract is to operate. Benefits are given to the passenger in return, but only in clearly defined circumstances to which the limits of liability set out by the Convention are to apply. To permit exceptions, whereby a passenger could sue outwith the Convention for losses sustained in the course of international carriage by air, would distort the whole system, even in cases for which the Convention did not create any liability on the part of the carrier. Thus the purpose is to ensure that, in all questions relating to the carrier's liability, it is the provisions of the Convention which apply and that the passenger does not have access to any other remedies, whether under the common law or otherwise, which may be available within the particular country where he chooses to raise his action. The carrier does not need to make provision for the risk of being subjected to such remedies, because the whole matter is regulated by the Convention.

That passage prompts me to underline that the Montreal Convention, unlike most instruments of public international law, is intended to—its whole purpose is

---

[6] *Connaught Laboratories Ltd v British Airways* (2002) 217 DLR (4th) 717 (Ont) (affd (2005) 77 OR (3d) 34, Ont CA), followed in a Montreal Convention 1999 context in *Walton v Mytravel Canada Holdings Inc* [2006] SJ No 373 (SaskQB).

[7] *King v American Airlines Inc* 284 F 3d 352 (NY CAs, 2002), 28 Avi 16,204 (claim of discrimination under 42 USC §1981 and 49 USC §41310(a)); *Hook v British Airways Plc; Stott v Thomas Cook Tour Operators Ltd* [2014] UKSC 15, [2014] AC 1347 (claim under the Civil Aviation (Access to Air Travel for Disabled Persons and Persons with Reduced Mobility) Regulations 2007, SI 2007/1895 (now replaced by new provisions)).

[8] *El Al Israel Airlines Ltd v Tseng* 119 SCt 662 (1999), 26 Avi 16,141.

[9] *Sidhu v British Airways plc* [1997] AC 430, followed in *Morris v KLM Royal Dutch Airlines* [2001] EWCA Civ 790 and *Deep Vein Thrombosis and Air Travel Group Litigation* [2002] EWHC 2825.

to—regulate *private* rights. That means that some of the traditional categories of public international law may not be applicable.

The same understanding of exclusivity has been adopted in many other countries. They include states both within the EU (Germany[10] and Ireland[11]) and outside it (Australia,[12] Canada,[13] Hong Kong,[14] New Zealand,[15] Nigeria[16] and South Africa[17]). That wide agreement gives the Convention text a particular rank or position, even if it is implemented in many states by 'ordinary' legislation.

Of course there are limits to the reach of the Convention. For example, the case must be one concerning 'international carriage', and there has been much litigation in the US in which the physical location of the events, whether they were before embarkation began or after disembarkation was complete, was seen as determinative. The Convention applies to claims for damages and not to proceedings seeking some other remedy such as an injunction or a declaration. But I would add that it is wrong to identify actions for damages by reference to the particular procedural usages of a state or group of states: it means any means of obtaining compensation through the courts.

So the fundamental questions remain as to whether, how far and on what proper legal basis a claim under Regulation 261 can be brought despite the exclusivity of the Montreal Convention.

III. Compensation and Damages

Before I go further, it might be useful to elaborate on one more feature of English law. It may have counterparts in other countries, but I have no information. When an aviation accident causes a death, the family of the deceased passenger will suffer in various ways. The family members will, for example, no longer enjoy the income that the deceased earned. They will also suffer the distress and unhappiness of bereavement. Although that may be experienced as a very personal thing by an individual who has been bereaved, it is an experience that for all such persons is almost identical in its nature, and is suitable for relief in the form of standardised payments with no need for proof of specific damage. Under the legislation

---

[10] Bundesgerichthof, 15 March 2011, Urteil Az X ZR 99/10.

[11] Most recently in *Hennessey v Aer Lingus Ltd* [2012] IEHC 124.

[12] *South Pacific Air Motive Pty Ltd v Magnus* (1998) 157 ALR 443.

[13] *Air Canada v Thibodeau* [2012] FCA 246.

[14] *Ong v Malaysian Airline System Berhad* [2008] HKCA 88.

[15] *Emery Air Freight Corpn v Nerine Nurseries Ltd* [1997] 3 NZLR 723.

[16] *Oshevire v British Caledonian Airways Ltd* (1990) 7 NWLR (Part 163) CA 507; *Cameroon Airlines v Abdul Kareem* (2003) 11 NWLR (Part 830) CA 1; though the Nigerian courts are not unanimous, eg F Majiyagbe and A Dalley, 'The Exclusivity of the Warsaw Convention regime vis-à-vis Actions and Remedies in International Carriage by Air under Nigerian Law' (2006) 31 *Air and Space Law* 196.

[17] *Potgieter v British Airways plc* [2005] ZAWCHC 5.

in force in England,[18] a bereaved spouse is entitled to an award of £12,980 (about €16,000). That will be taken into account in applying the Montreal Convention's rules as to the limits on the carrier's liability. The point, as the reader will have realised, is that a policy decision to provide automatic and standardised compensation is entirely compatible with the Convention, but the Convention rules apply to it. It cannot be treated as an *addition* to the compensation payable, in such a case under Article 17 of the Convention. It is, rather, an exercise in the *quantification* of sums payable by carriers under the terms of the Convention.

It will not have escaped the reader's attention that what I have just said is highly relevant to the decision in *ex parte IATA*,[19] where the Grand Chamber drew a distinction between two types of damage suffered by delayed passengers. One was 'damage that is almost identical for every passenger, redress for which may take the form of standardised and immediate assistance', and the other 'individual damage, inherent in the reason for travelling, redress for which requires a case-by-case assessment of the extent of the damage caused and can consequently only be the subject of compensation granted subsequently on an individual basis'. It *could* have been the case that the automatic compensation under Regulation 261 was seen, like damages for bereavement in English law, as a *quantification* of a specific head of damage. That approach was impossible once the CJEU held that it was 'clear' that Article 19 of the Convention governed only the second type of damage.[20] The two worlds, of Regulation 261 and the Convention, operate in isolation one from another. That was re-affirmed in *Nelson*,[21] where the court elaborated a distinction between 'inconvenience', such as a loss of time and discomfort, and the damage to which the Convention relates. I need not repeat what John Balfour's contribution will say on that issue (see chapter five); like him, I cannot understand why loss of time and discomfort must be regarded as *not* being damage caused by the delay.

The *IATA* case was, of course, decided before that of *Sturgeon*.[22] There seems to be no incompatibility issue in the case of cancellation. It has always been clear that a claim based on non-performance of the promised carriage falls outside the scope of the Convention, although the precise dividing line between delay and non-performance has given the courts some difficulty. But delay is a different matter. In *Sturgeon* the court decided that delayed passengers were entitled to compensation. I add nothing to the debate about the correctness or otherwise of that decision, but it plainly makes the issue of the relationship between Regulation 261 and the Montreal Convention more pointed: both provide for payments of money to compensate passengers for the consequences of delay.

---

[18] Fatal Accidents Act 1976, s 1A.

[19] Case C-344/04 *R (International Air Transport Association and European Low Fares Airline Association) v Department for Transport* [2006] ECR I-403, para 43 (*ex parte IATA*).

[20] ibid, para 44.

[21] *Nelson* (n 2).

[22] *Sturgeon* (n 1).

The court in *ex parte IATA* also held that

> [t]he standardised and immediate assistance and care measures do not themselves prevent the passengers concerned, should the same delay also cause them damage conferring entitlement to compensation, from being able to bring in addition actions to redress that damage under the conditions laid down by the Montreal Convention.[23]

That was reiterated in *Rodriguez v Air France SA*:

> Article 12 of Regulation No 261/2004 allows the national court to award compensation, under the conditions provided for by the Montreal Convention or national law, for damage, including non-material damage, arising from breach of a contract of carriage by air.[24]

Article 12(1) goes on to provide, in terms, that the compensation granted under Regulation 261 may be deducted from such further compensation. I think there is something illogical in deciding that compensation under the Regulation for delay can be deducted from sums awarded under the Convention, when in the court's view the Convention does not cover the type of damage attracting Regulation 261.

I must refer again to the case of *Stott v Thomas Cook Tour Operators Ltd*[25] (also cited, confusingly as *Hook v British Airways*, the two cases having been joined), a decision of the Supreme Court of the UK.[26] Mr Stott, a disabled passenger, paralysed and in a wheelchair, and his wife (who had to provide personal care to him during travel) were, in the words of Baroness Hale, 'treated disgracefully by Thomas Cook', the carrier. They sought remedies, a declaration and damages under UK legislation,[27] which gave effect to the corresponding EU Regulation on the rights of disabled persons and persons with reduced mobility when travelling by air.[28] The Court of Appeal held that damages could not be awarded, for that would be incompatible with the Montreal Convention. As Lord Justice Kay, Vice-President of the Court said (and I will comment further on this passage a little later):

> Once one is within the timeline and space governed by the Convention, it is the governing instrument in international, European and domestic law. It was open to the EU and domestic legislatures to develop the law in relation to such things as the improvement of access for disabled passengers and assistance to passengers affected by delays or cancellations, provided that they did not trespass into the domain of the Convention. They have done so. In identifying that domain, it was and is not appropriate to apply a novel approach to the construction of the Convention by reference to a perceived second strand

---

[23] *ex parte IATA* (n 19), para 47.
[24] Case C-83/10 *Rodriguez v Air France SA* [2011] ECR I-9469, para 46.
[25] [2012] EWCA Civ 66.
[26] *Hook v British Airways Plc; Stott* (n 7).
[27] Civil Aviation (Access to Air Travel for Disabled Persons and Persons with Reduced Mobility) Regulations 2007, SI 2007/1895 (now replaced by the Civil Aviation (Access to Air Travel for Disabled Persons and Persons with Reduced Mobility) Regulations 2014, SI 2014/2833).
[28] European Parliament and Council Regulation (EC) No 1107/2006 of 5 July 2006 concerning the rights of disabled persons and persons with reduced mobility when travelling by air [2006] OJ L204/1.

or sea change in the European instruments. Nor would it be appropriate to depart from the comity approach [that is, on the interpretation of the Convention] which extends beyond the Member States of the European Union. The scope of the Convention cannot have been altered by these European developments.[29]

An appeal to the Supreme Court failed. In the Supreme Court, the *ex parte IATA* and *Nelson* cases were not challenged, though they were distinguished. As Lord Toulson pointed out,[30] the court in *ex parte IATA* had recognised that any claim for damages on an individual basis would be subject to the limits of the Convention: Mr Stott's claim was for damages on an individual basis.

IV. Conclusion

There are a number of points at which the approach of Regulation 261 differs markedly from that under the Montreal Convention: that reflects the difference in policy that I spoke of at the start of the chapter, for the Regulation is at almost every point of comparison more favourable to the passenger/consumer. I notice the issues as to the applicable jurisdictional rules;[31] and the rules as to limitation of actions,[32] and, perhaps most relevant to our debates, the fact that the scope for a successful defence by a carrier under Regulation 261 on the ground of 'extraordinary circumstances' is much narrower than that of taking 'all measures that could reasonably be required to avoid the damage' under Article 19 of the Convention.[33]

What about the future? I have quoted earlier Lord Justice Kay's determination in the *Stott* case in the Court of Appeal to resist an argument that European developments should influence the interpretation of the Convention. So far as the two instruments operate in different ways and cover rather different ground, that must be correct as a matter of law. In a paper published last year, Jeremias Prassl wrote that Lord Justice Kay's 'narrow approach unduly limits the potential evolution and thus the ongoing validity and legitimacy of the Convention regime'.[34] He argues that the legislation and case law of the EU 'provides a catalyst, a reaction site, in which to challenge, evaluate, and further develop the ideas embodied

---

[29] *Stott v Thomas Cook Tour Operators Ltd* [2012] EWCA Civ 66 [53].

[30] *Stott* (n 7), para 58.

[31] Case C-204/08 *Rehder v Air Baltic Corporation* [2009] ECR I-6073.

[32] Case C-139/1 *Moré v KLM* (ECJ, 22 November 2012); *Dawson v Thomson Airways Ltd* [2014] EWCA Civ 845; a 2010 decision of the Belgium Court of Zaventem discussed in International Law Office, 'Court rules on limitation period for actions under EU Denied Boarding Regulation' (1 December 2010), available at <www.internationallawoffice.com/newsletters/>, accessed 7 August 2014.

[33] eg Case C-597/07 *Wallentin-Hermann v Alitalia* [2008] ECR I-11061; *Jet2.com v Huzar* [2014] EWCA Civ 791.

[34] J Prassl, 'The European Union and The Montreal Convention: A New Analytical Framework' (2103) 12 *Issues in Aviation Law and Policy* 381, 389.

in the current liability schemes; experimenting with significantly new approaches while building on existing norms'.[35]

I would agree that new ideas, new approaches, are to be welcomed and may lead (though I suspect not very quickly) to an updating of the Montreal Convention. But some of the phrases Prassl uses, 'judicial experimentation' and 'reinterpretation of the relevant Montreal Convention provisions',[36] make me rather more cautious. I am not sure that I quite recognise what he describes as 'the ECJ's current efforts at providing an analytically coherent underpinning to the operation of Article 29 [of the Convention]', but I do agree that such an effort is much to be preferred over a hypothetical scenario, probably not to be found in practice, in which courts are tempted to ignore the exclusive application of the Montreal Convention even in cases very clearly covered by it.[37]

---

[35] ibid, 387.
[36] ibid, 383.
[37] ibid, 405.

5

Luxembourg v Montreal: Time for The Hague to Intervene

JOHN BALFOUR

On 10 January 2006 the CJEU delivered its judgment in *R (International Air Transport Association and European Low Fares Airline Association) v Department for Transport*,[1] the first of what turned out to be a long series of judgments concerned with Regulation 261. The judgment dealt with several issues, but its most significant finding was that there was no conflict between the provisions relating to delay in Regulation 261 and in the Montreal Convention 1999, contrary to the arguments of the International Air Transport Association (IATA) and the European Low Fares Airline Association (ELFAA), based on the provisions in the Convention excluding and limiting the carrier's liability for delay and on the exclusivity of the Convention as regards any action for damages.[2] The judgment has received some critical comment,[3] and has been referred to by the Court in several subsequent judgments.[4] As the fundamental fallacy on which the judgment is based does not appear to have been appreciated as widely as it should have been, it seems

---

[1] Case C-344/04 *R (International Air Transport Association and European Low Fares Airline Association) v Department for Transport* [2006] ECR I-403 (*ex parte IATA*).

[2] Art 29 of the Convention for the Unification of Certain Rules for International Carriage by Air [2001] OJ L194/39 (Montreal Convention) provides, 'In the carriage of passengers, baggage and cargo, any action for damages, however founded, whether under this Convention or in contract or tort or otherwise, can only be brought subject to the conditions and such limits of liability as are set out in this Convention without prejudice to the question as to who are the persons who have the right to bring suit and what are their respective rights. In any such action, punitive, exemplary or any other non-compensatory damages shall not be recoverable.'

[3] eg J Wegter, 'The ECJ Decision of 10 January 2006 on the Validity of Regulation 261/2004: Ignoring the Exclusivity of the Montreal Convention (2006) 36 *Air and Space Law* 133; K Arnold and P Mendes de Leon, 'Regulation (EC) 261/2004 in the Light of the Recent Decisions of the European Court of Justice: Time for a Change?' (2010) 35 *Air and Space Law* 91; P Dempsey and S Johansson, 'Montreal v Brussels: The Conflict of Laws on the Issue of Delay in International Air Carriage' (2010) 35 *Air and Space Law* 207; R Lawson and T Marland, 'The Montreal Convention 1999 and the Decisions of the ECJ in the Cases of IATA and Sturgeon—in Harmony or Discord?' (2011) 36 *Air and Space Law* 99; C Thijssen, 'The Montreal Convention, EU Regulation 261/2004, and the Sturgeon Doctrine: How to Reconcile the Three?' (2013) 12 *Issues in Aviation Law and Policy* 413.

[4] eg Case C-549/07 *Wallentin-Hermann v Alitalia* [2008] ECR I-11061; *Moré v KLM* (ECJ, 22 November 2012); Case 204/08 *Rehder v Air Baltic* [2009] ECR I-6073.

appropriate now to revisit the judgment and related subsequent jurisprudence, which has perpetuated the fallacy and exacerbated the tensions between the judgment and the Montreal Convention.

I. *Ex Parte IATA*

The reason why the Court found no conflict between the Regulation and the Convention was that it held that the scope of application of each was different:

> Any delay in the carriage of passengers by air, and in particular a long delay, may, generally speaking, cause two types of damage. First, excessive delay will cause damage that is almost identical for every passenger, redress for which may take the form of standardised and immediate assistance or care for everybody concerned, through the provision, for example, of refreshments, meals and accommodation and of the opportunity to make telephone calls. Second, passengers are liable to suffer individual damage, inherent in the reason for travelling, redress for which requires a case-by-case assessment of the extent of the damage caused and can consequently only be the subject of compensation granted subsequently on an individual basis.

> It is clear from Articles 19, 22 and 29 of the Montreal Convention that they merely govern the conditions under which, after a flight has been delayed, the passengers concerned may bring actions for damages by way of redress on an individual basis, that is to say, for compensation from the carriers liable for damage resulting from that delay.

> It does not follow from these provisions or from any other provision of the Montreal Convention that the authors of the Convention intended to shield those carriers from any other form of intervention, in particular action which could be envisaged by public authorities to redress, in a standardised and immediate manner, the damage that is constituted by the inconvenience that delay in the carriage of passengers by air causes, without the passengers having to suffer the inconvenience inherent in the bringing of actions for damages before the courts.

> The Montreal Convention could not therefore prevent the action taken by the Community legislature to lay down, in the exercise of the powers conferred on the Community in the fields of transport and consumer protection, the conditions under which damage linked to the abovementioned inconvenience should be redressed. Since the assistance and taking care of passengers envisaged by Article 6 of Regulation 261 in the event of a long delay to a flight constitute such standardised and immediate compensatory measures, they are not among those whose institution is regulated by the Convention. The system prescribed in Article 6 simply operates at an earlier stage than the system which results from the Montreal Convention.[5]

The essence of the distinction drawn by the Court was between 'standardised and immediate' compensatory measures (the subject of the Regulation, and not the Convention) and actions for damages for redress on an individual basis at a later

---

[5] *ex parte IATA* (n 1) paras 43–46.

stage (the subject of the Convention, and not the Regulation). At first sight, this appears to be a very neat solution to the question, and indeed it might well be if the Regulation was only concerned with the provision of 'refreshments, meals and accommodation and of the opportunity to make telephone calls', which are the only examples the Court gave of standardised and immediate assistance. However, the Court conveniently overlooked another important obligation imposed by the Regulation on carriers in the event of delay. Article 6 provides that in the event of delay passengers shall be offered not only the assistance specified in Article 9(1) and (2) but also, 'when the delay is at least five hours, the assistance specified in Article 8(1)(a)'. Article 8(1)(a) provides for

> reimbursement within seven days, by the means provided in Article 7(3), of the full cost of the ticket at the price at which it was bought, for the part or parts of the journey not made, and for the part or parts already made if the flight is no longer serving any purpose in relation to the passenger's original travel plan, together with, when relevant, a return flight to the first point of departure, at the earliest opportunity.

Although the Court recited the provisions of Article 8(1)(a) in its judgment, it does not otherwise mention it at all.

Article 8(1)(a) patently is not concerned with 'immediate' relief and does not operate 'at an earlier stage than the system which results from the Montreal Convention'. Moreover, it has the potential to result in compensation that is by no means standardised and the same for each passenger, and requires case-by-case assessment. In the first place, the full cost of the ticket for the part(s) of the journey not made may differ significantly as between passengers, either because they have paid different prices for the tickets (for example, because of one passenger's having bought a ticket a long time in advance and another at the last minute, at a greatly increased fare)[6] or because a passenger's ticket includes a connecting flight from the immediate intended destination. Moreover, there may be even greater individual differences in amounts due where a passenger claims reimbursement of the cost of parts of the journey already made on the basis that the flight no longer serves any purpose in relation to the passenger's original travel plan—for example, where a passenger has flown from Dubai to Barcelona with a connecting flight from Barcelona to Seville in order to attend a meeting, and the latter flight is delayed so that the passenger does not arrive in Seville until after the meeting has finished.

Two further factors that add to the doubt about the correctness of the distinction drawn by the Court were suggested by Professor David McLean in the preceding chapter. In the first place, Article 12(1) of the Regulation provides:

> This Regulation shall apply without prejudice to a passenger's rights to further compensation. The compensation granted under this Regulation may be deducted from such compensation.

---

[6] eg in December 2013 the author of this article bought a return London–Barcelona ticket on British Airways for travel in July 2014 for £130. If bought in July 2014, the same ticket would have cost £580.

This does not seem consistent with the Court's approach to two separate and distinct regimes. Secondly, in England section 1A of the Fatal Accidents Act 1976 provides, in the context of death claims, for damages for bereavement in a fixed, standardised amount. Claims brought in England in respect of deaths of passengers in the course of carriage by air under the Montreal Convention invariably include claims for such standardised bereavement damages, and the courts have no problem in allowing them.

II. *Sturgeon* and *Böck*

At the time of the *ex parte IATA* judgment, it was not contemplated by anyone that Regulation 261 conferred on passengers a right to fixed amounts of compensation in the event of delay—unsurprisingly, in view of the Regulation's clear wording in this respect—and consequently the question of fixed compensation for delay was not addressed by either the parties or the Court. However, as is now well known, in its judgment in November 2009 in *Sturgeon v Condor* and *Böck and Lepuschitz v Air France*,[7] the Court held that the principle of equal treatment required the Regulation to be interpreted so that passengers who suffer a delay so as to arrive at their final destination three hours or more after the originally scheduled arrival time are entitled to fixed compensation at the levels laid down in the Regulation for passengers whose flights are cancelled. In reaching this conclusion the Court did not discuss at all the possible relevance of the Montreal Convention, simply referring to its reasoning about standardised and immediate redress in the *ex parte IATA* judgment by stating that

> [i]n this instance, the situation of passengers whose flights are delayed should be compared with that of passengers whose flights are cancelled. In that connection, Regulation No 261/2004 seeks to redress damage in an immediate and standardised manner and to do so by various forms of intervention which are the subject of rules relating to denied boarding, cancellation and long flight delay (see, to that effect, IATA and ELFAA, paragraph 43).[8]

III. *Nelson*

The question of the relationship between the Montreal Convention and Regulation 261, interpreted so as to provide for fixed compensation in the event of delay, only received attention from the Court in October 2012 in its judgment in the

---

[7] Joined Cases C-402 and 432/07 *Sturgeon v Condor Flugdienst GmbH*; *Stefan Böck and Cornelia Lepuschitz v Air France SA* [2009] ECR I-10923 (*Sturgeon*).
[8] ibid, paras 50–51.

joined cases of *Nelson v Deutsche Lufthansa* and *IATA v CAA*.[9] The airline parties, supported by the German and UK Governments, argued that the right to fixed compensation for delay was incompatible with the Montreal Convention. However, the Court held that it was compatible, on the grounds that the loss of time suffered by passengers as a result of delay 'cannot be categorised as "damage occasioned by delay" within the meaning of Article 19 of the Montreal Convention, and, for that reason, it falls outside the scope of Article 29 of that convention' (which provides for the Convention's exclusivity). It supported this conclusion by arguing as follows:

> Article 19 of the Montreal Convention implies that the damage arises as a result of a delay, that there is a causal link between the delay and the damage and that the damage is individual to passengers depending on the various losses sustained by them.
>
> First of all, a loss of time is not damage arising as a result of a delay, but is an inconvenience, like other inconveniences inherent in cases of denied boarding, flight cancellation and long delay and encountered in them, such as lack of comfort or the fact of being temporarily denied means of communication normally available.
>
> Next, a loss of time is suffered identically by all passengers whose flights are delayed and, consequently, it is possible to redress that loss by means of a standardised measure, without having to carry out any assessment of the individual situation of each passenger concerned. Consequently, such a measure may be applied immediately.
>
> Lastly, there is not necessarily a causal link between, on the one hand, the actual delay and, on the other, the loss of time considered relevant for the purpose of giving rise to compensation under Regulation No 261/2004 or calculating the amount of that compensation.
>
> The specific obligation to pay compensation, imposed by Regulation No 261/2004, does not arise from each actual delay, but only from a delay which entails a loss of time equal to or in excess of three hours in relation to the time of arrival originally scheduled. In addition, whereas the extent of the delay is normally a factor increasing the likelihood of greater damage, the fixed compensation awarded under that regulation remains unchanged in that regard, since the duration of the actual delay in excess of three hours in not taken into account in calculating the amount of compensation payable under Article 7 of Regulation No 261/2004.[10]

To summarise, according to the Court, a loss of time caused as a result of a delayed flight does not cause the passenger 'damage' but rather 'inconvenience'; the fact that the Convention refers to 'damage occasioned by delay in the carriage by air' means that the Convention is only concerned with individual damage suffered by passengers, as opposed to loss of time suffered identically by all passengers, and with damage causally linked to the delay, and hence is not concerned with fixed compensation payable irrespective of the length of the delay.

---

[9] Joined Cases C-581/10 and 629/10 *Nelson v Deutsche Lufthansa AG* [2012] OJ C399/3 (*Nelson*).
[10] ibid, paras 50–56.

The artificiality and weakness of the distinction between 'damage' and 'inconvenience' is self-evident and highlighted by the judgment itself, when the Court cites, in paragraph 46, its reference in the *ex parte IATA* judgment to 'the damage that is constituted by the inconvenience that delay in the carriage of passengers by air causes'. Indeed, in *Sturgeon* the Court expanded on the type of damage suffered by passengers who experience delay:

> Regulation No 261/2004 has, in those measures, the objective of repairing, inter alia, damage consisting, for the passengers concerned, in a loss of time which, given that it is irreversible, can be redressed only by compensation. In that regard, it must be stated that that damage is suffered both by passengers whose flights are cancelled and by passengers whose flights are delayed if, prior to reaching their destinations, the latter's journey time is longer than the time which had originally been scheduled by the air carrier. Consequently, passengers whose flights have been cancelled and passengers affected by a flights delay suffer similar damage, consisting in a loss of time, and thus find themselves in comparable situations for the purposes of the application of the right to compensation laid down in Article 7 of Regulation No 261/2004.[11]

Furthermore, it does not follow from the Convention's use of the words 'damage occasioned by delay' that it is only concerned with individual damage and not also damage which all passengers suffer equally because of a delay, or fixed compensation paid to passengers in respect of such common damage. It is interesting to compare the Court's cavalier approach to the interpretation of damage in this context with its careful approach to the interpretation of the word in the context of damage to baggage in its judgment in *Walz v Clickair*,[12] where the Court noted:

> Since the Montreal Convention does not contain any definition of the term 'damage' it must be emphasised at the outset that, in the light of the aim of that Convention, which is to unify the rules for international carriage by air, that term must be given a uniform and autonomous meaning, notwithstanding the different meanings given to that concept in the domestic laws of the States Parties to that Convention.

> In those circumstances, the term 'damage', contained in an international agreement, must be interpreted in accordance with the rules of interpretation of general international law, which are binding on the European Union.[13]

After some discussion of the 1969 Vienna Convention on the Law of Treaties (VCLT) and the different language versions of the Montreal Convention, the Court concluded that the term 'damage' was to be interpreted in accordance with its ordinary meaning so as to include both material and non-material damage.

The Court also considered the VCLT in its original *ex parte IATA* judgment, and in particular its provision that 'a treaty such as the Montreal Convention is to be interpreted in accordance with the ordinary meaning to be given to its terms in their context and in the light of its object and purpose'. There is no reference to the VCLT, or any indication that the Court considered it, in *Nelson*.

---

[11] *Sturgeon* (n 7) paras 52–54.
[12] Case C-63/09 *Walz v Clickair* [2010] ECR I-4239.
[13] ibid, paras 21–22.

The *Walz* judgment is also notable, and very different from *Nelson*, in the regard the Court paid to the objectives of the Montreal Convention, including not only passenger protection but also the 'equitable balance of interests of air carriers and passengers' referred to in its fifth recital, which 'requires that there be clear limits on compensation relating to total damage sustained by each passenger in each of those situations, regardless of the nature of the damage caused to that passenger'.[14]

In *Nelson* the Court furthermore justified the different treatment of fixed compensation because it can be paid 'without having to carry out any assessment of the individual situation of each passenger concerned'. This is misguided. Passengers' entitlement to compensation for delay under the *Sturgeon* principle only arises where the passengers 'reach their final destination three hours or more after the arrival time originally scheduled by the air carrier'. 'Final destination' is defined by Article 2(h) of the Regulation to mean 'the destination on the ticket presented at the check-in counter or, in the case of directly connecting flights, the destination of the last flight'. Consequently, the passengers on any particular delayed flight may have a large number of different 'final destinations', and passengers may arrive at their final destination in some cases less than three hours late, and in others more than three hours late. Moreover, the amount of fixed compensation varies depending on the length of the flight (ie, either €250, €400 or €600), and this appears to mean the whole journey to the final destination, rather than the length of the delayed flight.[15] Accordingly, a careful analysis of each passenger's whole journey will be necessary in order to determine the band of compensation to which each passenger is entitled.

Moreover, by extending the scope of the carrier's obligations to include payment of fixed compensation for delay, the Court placed itself in conflict with its *ex parte IATA* judgment, where the important distinction it drew between the Convention and the Regulation was based on the fact that the former concerns after-the-event remedies, whereas the latter concerns immediate assistance or care, operating at an earlier stage.[16]

Lastly, although the parties made detailed submissions about the Montreal Convention and the case law on its interpretation, and despite its central importance to the question in issue, nowhere in its judgment did the Court discuss the scope or meaning of Article 29 of the Montreal Convention, nor any of the judgments interpreting it, including judgments from the UK and US Supreme Courts.[17] So much for comity in the interpretation of an international convention to which the EU is party!

---

[14] ibid, paras 33–35.
[15] This appears to be the logical consequence of *Sturgeon*, and to be supported by Case C-11/11 *Air France v Folkerts* [2013] OJ C 114/8, although the position is not entirely clear.
[16] eg Arnold and Mendes de Leon (n 3).
[17] *Sidhu v British Airways* [1997] AC 430 and *El Al Israel Airlines v Tseng* 525 US 155 (1999) 122 F3d 99. See, eg, Wegter (n 3) 134; Dempsey and Johansson (n 3) 209. See also, eg, D McClean (ed), *Shawcross & Beaumont: Air Law*, vol VIII (LexisNexis), paras 405–11. Most recently, on 29 October 2014 the Supreme Court of Canada, in *Thibodeau v Air Canada* [2014] SC 67, upheld the exclusivity

IV. *Rodriguez* and *McDonagh*

A very pertinent question, raised by one of the judges during the oral hearing in the *IATA* case, is whether, in the event a carrier does not comply with its obligations under the Regulation and the passenger brings an action for damages as a result, such an action is an 'action for damages' as envisaged by Article 29 of the Montreal Convention. The Court entirely avoided this important question in its judgment, but it was inevitable that the issue would resurface.

It did so in the case *Rodriguez v Air France*,[18] in which one of the questions referred to the Court was whether the further compensation provided for by Article 12 of the Regulation included, among other things, expenses incurred by passengers due to a carrier's failure to comply with its assistance and care obligations under Articles 8 and 9 of the Regulation. The Court replied that Article 12 was not concerned with reimbursement of such expenses but that 'when a carrier fails to fulfil its obligations under Article 8 and 9 of Regulation No 261/2004, air passengers are justified in claiming a right to compensation on the basis of the factors set out in those articles'.[19]

The Court confirmed this in its judgment in *McDonagh v Ryanair*[20] where, in response to arguments by the Council to the contrary, it held that an air passenger may invoke before a national court the failure of an air carrier to comply with its obligation under the Regulation to provide care, in order to obtain compensation from the carrier for those costs the carrier should have borne.

Neither of these judgments was at all surprising, given the well-established principle of the direct effect of EU regulations:[21] indeed, it was much more surprising that in 2012 the UK Court of Appeal held that breach by the carrier of its obligations under Article 8 of the Regulation to provide reimbursement or re-routing did not give rise to a civil action for damages.[22] If a passenger brings an action against a carrier in respect of the carrier's non-compliance with its obligations under the Regulation in the event of delay—for example, for the cost of hotel accommodation made necessary by a delay of a flight till the next day, or for reimbursement of the cost of a ticket, or for payment of the fixed compensation due according to *Sturgeon*—it is difficult to see how such action can be anything

---

of the Convention in the context of a claim for damages for non-compliance with Canadian requirements as to the use of the French language in the course of international carriage by air. Interestingly, the claimants argued that the Convention excludes only 'individual damages' and not 'standardised damages', on the basis of the CJEU's judgment in *ex parte IATA*. However, the Court said that even if it were to adopt this distinction, it would not assist the claimants, as the damages they sought were not standardised damages as described in *ex parte IATA*.

[18] Case C-83/10 *Rodriguez v Air France* [2011] ECR I-9469.
[19] ibid, para 44.
[20] Case C-12/11 *McDonagh v Ryanair* (ECJ, 31 January 2013).
[21] Case C-26/62 *Van Gend en Loos v Nederlandse Administratie der Belastingen* [1963] ECR 1.
[22] *Graham v Thomas Cook Group* [2012] EWCA Civ 1355.

other than an 'action for damages', of the type contemplated by Article 29 of the Montreal Convention.[23]

V. Conclusions

The distinction drawn by the Court between Regulation 261 and the Montreal Convention in its *ex parte IATA* judgment, neat though it may have seemed at first sight, was fundamentally flawed, because it overlooked key obligations imposed on the carrier by the Regulation that were not consistent with such distinction. That has not stopped the Court from repeatedly referring back to that distinction and relying on it without any further discussion, although 'even if error communis facit jus, the mere reiteration of a wrongful solution does not suffice to give it legal grounds'.[24]

The Court has made the overlap and the conflict between the Regulation and the Convention even clearer and more serious by deciding in *Sturgeon*, as confirmed in *Nelson*, that delayed passengers are entitled to fixed compensation under the Regulation.

The Court has also, by confirming that passengers have a right to take direct action against a carrier that fails to comply with its obligations under the Regulation, answered a question left unanswered in its *ex parte IATA* judgment and confirmed by implication (without of course admitting it) that the Regulation creates a right of action that falls within the scope of Article 29 of the Montreal Convention, and hence is incompatible with the Convention.

Given the Court's record to date, it seems clear that there is little to be gained by continuing to make arguments such as these to the Court. However, the issue of conflict between EU law and the Montreal Convention is not likely to go away, and indeed may well soon resurface, if the Commission's proposals on amendment of the Regulation with regard to lost, damaged or delayed baggage are adopted.[25] Continued acceptance without protest of this disregard by the EU of its obligations to the other parties to the Montreal Convention is likely only to encourage the EU in such disregard. The only possible solution would seem to be an action by one or more non-EU Montreal parties against some or all of the EU Member States before the International Court of Justice,[26] on the basis of some or all of the arguments mentioned above—and the sooner the better.

---

[23] eg Wegter (n 3) 145; V Correia, 'Air Passengers' Rights, "Extraordinary Circumstances", and General Principles of EU Law: Some Comments After the McDonagh Case' (2014) 13(2) *Issues in Aviation Law and Policy* 252.

[24] eg Correia (n 23) 276.

[25] eg J Prassl, 'Reforming Air Passenger Rights in the European Union' (2014) 39 *Air and Space Law* 39, 59. The proposals include, among other things, a provision whereby passengers with limited mobility would be allowed to make a special declaration in respect of their mobility equipment free of charge.

[26] eg Dempsey and Johansson (n 3) 220.

6

EU Regulations in the Member States: Incorporating International Norms

SILVIA FERRERI

I. International Law and European Sources of Law

In this chapter, I shall first begin with a set of specific observations on the conflicts of international norms before the European and domestic courts, before moving on to expand the discourse to include a wider number of considerations in section II.

The starting point for observations relevant in reflecting on air passengers' rights is connected with the issue, raised in front of the CJEU, of combining several international commitments at various levels: at the worldwide level, established by international treaties (such as those sponsored by the United Nations (UN)), and at the regional level, by regional agreements binding a more limited number of partners, such as those within the EU (but also in other alliances such as the Association of Southeast Asian Nations, L'Organisation pour l'Harmonisation en Afrique du Droit des Affaires, the Organisation of American States and so on).

The cumulative effect of binding documents in the field of transport law is striking, even for non-specialists, as it is a highly specialised area of competence with a large pool of literature and a wealth of periodicals. The complexity of international sources has already been highlighted in the past, examining them from a comparative point of view and with an intriguing title: *le droit uniforme desuniformisé*.[1]

---

[1] J Putzeys, 'Le droit uniforme desuniformisé' (1988) *International Uniform Law in Practice* 442 ('le *système de Varsovie* que nous appellerons irrévérencieusement le *patch-work* législatif'), in drafting a synthetic image of existing instruments in the field of transport law the author explains 'à partir de 1946, c'est le délire, sans doute provoqué, en partie, par la facilité, et le confort procuré au déplacement des négociateurs' (emphasis added) 440; K Grönfors, 'Transport Law' in UNDROIT (ed), *International Uniform Law in Practice* (Oceana/UNDROIT, 1988) 376, 390; RH Mankiewicz, 'Conflicting Interpretations of the Warsaw Air Transport Treaty' (1970) 18 *American Journal of Comparative Law* 177; RH Mankiewicz, 'The Judicial Diversification of Uniform Private Law Conventions' (1972) 21 *International Comparative Law Quarterly* 718.

Writing on the issue without being a specialist requires some daring. However, a judge's being called upon to decide on issues in this field also presupposes some self-confidence, with the difference that—contrary to academics—a judge cannot choose the area in which he or she must pronounce.

Some time ago, the great comparatist René David described the likely evolution of the process of legal unification in separate circles. Pleading in favour of flexibility, he described both laws of a wider scope and those of a more limited extension:

> A flexible approach … makes it possible to contemplate the creation of a whole network of conventions with regard to a given subject matter, those of a less demanding nature on a world-wide basis, and other more exacting conventions on a regional level or between two or more specific states. We should not limit ourselves for the sake of principle to the often illusory idea of a world law. The peaceful coexistence of states can take diverse forms from simple tolerance to highly advanced cooperation that at times may even lead to the establishment of supranational unions or communities.[2]

The disadvantage of this flexible approach has been proven to be the fragmentation of international law sources, causing a highly complex mixture of rules that must be applied, an issue that is often confronted at the UN level and in international congresses.[3] As early as 1975, Erik Jayme pointed out that some agreements among states are drawn up and ratified without giving prior consideration to the work carried out by other organisations or conferences in the same area.[4]

The Montreal Convention, promoted by the ICAO, does contain a rather limiting provision, as Article 29 seems to establish an exclusive path for obtaining damages:

> In the carriage of passengers, baggage and cargo, *any action* for damages, however founded, whether under this Convention or in contract or in tort or otherwise, can *only* be brought subject to the conditions and such limits of liability as are *set out in this Convention* without prejudice to the question as to who are the persons who have the right to bring suit and what are their respective rights. In any such action, punitive, exemplary or any other non-compensatory damages shall not be recoverable.[5]

---

[2] R David, 'The Methods of Unification' (1968) 16 *American Journal of Comparative Law* 13.

[3] Law Commission, *Fragmentation of International Law: Difficulties arising from the Diversification and Expansion of International Law* (Law Com A/CN 4/L682 2006). AC Martineau, 'The Rhetoric of Fragmentation: Fear and Faith in International Law' (2009) 22 *Leiden Journal of International Law* 1.

[4] E Jayme, 'Staatsverträge zum Internationalen Privatrecht, Berichte der Deutschen Gesellschaft für Völkerrecht' (1975) 16 *BerGes VoelkR* 7.

[5] Convention for the Unification of Certain Rules for International Carriage by Air—Montreal, 28 May 1999, Art 29 (emphasis added). Text available at <www.jus.uio.no/lm/air.carriage.unification.convention.montreal.1999/29.html>.

With Regulation 261,[6] the European legislator nonetheless introduced some additional protection for passengers, providing:

Art 5 Cancellation

1. In case of cancellation of a flight, the passengers concerned shall:
   (a) be offered assistance ...
   (c) have the right to compensation by the operating air carrier in accordance with Article 7 ...

Art 7 Right to compensation

1. Where reference is made to this Article, passengers shall receive compensation amounting to:
   (a) EUR 250 for all flights of 1500 kilometres or less ...

The Court's efforts to avoid conflict with the Montreal Convention are clearly found in the case law of the CJEU: the European judges demonstrate their attempts to reconcile various binding texts. In *ex parte IATA*,[7] the Court distinguished between actions for damages that would conflict with the Montreal Convention and any 'other form of intervention', especially an 'action ... envisaged by the public authority to redress [damage]'. The Court held that 'assistance and taking care of passengers envisaged by [Article] 6 ... constitute ... standardized and immediate compensatory measures ... they are not among those ... regulated by the Convention'. Similarly, by further extending the monetary compensation to delayed passengers in the *Nelson* judgment,[8] the Court insisted that the fixed amount granted to all passengers without proof of specific individual damages could not be defined as redress of damage.[9] A first reading of the Montreal Convention would appear to cover all sorts of additional liabilities. Yet the CJEU has drawn a subtle distinction.

---

[6] European Parliament and Council Regulation (EC) 261/2004 of 11 February 2004 establishing common rules on compensation and assistance to passengers in the event of denied boarding and of cancellation or long delay of flights, and repealing Regulation (EEC) No 295/91 (Regulation 261) [2004] OJ L46/1.

[7] Case C-344/04 R *(International Air Transport Association and European Low Fares Airline Association) v Department for Transport* [2006] ECR I-403 (*ex parte IATA*), paras 45–46.

[8] Joined Cases C-581 and 629/10 *Nelson v Deutsche Lufthansa AG* [2012] OJ C399/3 (*Nelson*).

[9] ibid, para 51: 'A loss of time is *not damage* arising as a result of a delay, but is an inconvenience, like other inconveniences inherent in cases of denied boarding, flight cancellation and long delay and encountered in them, such as lack of comfort or the fact of being temporarily denied means of communication normally available'; ibid, para 52: 'Next, a loss of time is suffered identically by all passengers whose flights are delayed and, consequently, it is possible to redress that loss by means of a *standardised measure*, without having to carry out any assessment of the individual situation' (emphasis added); see also ibid, para 57: 'It should be stated that the obligation to pay compensation which stems from Regulation No 261/2004 is *additional* to Article 29 of the Montreal Convention, inasmuch as it operates at an earlier stage than the system laid down in that Article' (emphasis added).

The interpretation of the Court's policy may be better understood by recalling the words of Advocate General Jacobs, expressed on a previous occasion speaking about the reason why it is more necessary for the ECJ to take a purposive approach considering

> the difficulty of amending the Treaty—or of amending legislation in the case of Council acts. The ECJ cannot take the approach of many English courts which determine the meaning of a provision, acknowledge that that meaning may have unfortunate consequences, but state that it is up to the legislator to alter the text if it does not like those consequences.[10]

Scholars comparing the English and US experience in interpreting statutes made a similar observation. The more restrictive attitude of English judges towards using extrinsic aids to interpretation, and their reluctant use of preparatory works, was compared to the greater readiness of the British Government to amend a piece of legislation that has proved to be defective when undergoing judicial scrutiny.[11] A literal interpretation is less damaging if the mistakes in drafting can be corrected swiftly.

The effort of the judges of the CJEU to uphold Regulation 261 and to read it in an expansive fashion is certainly different from the strictly literal reading of statutes generally conducted by English judges, and it is not surprising that the reaction in common law countries was one of shock.[12] The process of approval of the Regulation justifies uneasiness: the situation of delayed passengers was in fact considered in the preparatory works and excluded by the scope of protection at the level of the European Commission.[13]

The fact that the amount granted to claimants is standardised, independent from individual losses, as pointed out by the European judges, may nevertheless be compatible with the notion of 'liquidated damages'. It does not seem completely to preclude a definition as 'damages'. Several national reports have highlighted criticisms of the choice made by the CJEU judges.[14] Still, the prevailing approach of

---

[10] AG Jacobs, 'Lecture: How to interpret legislation which is equally authentic in twenty languages', Seminar on Quality of Legislation (Brussels, 2003). Text available at <http://ec.europa.eu/dgs/legal_service/seminars/agjacobs_summary.pdf>.

[11] PS Atiyah and RS Summers, *Form and Substance in Anglo-American Law* (Clarendon Press, 2002) 315.

[12] B Jones, 'Report on United Kingdom and Ireland', *Air Passengers Rights, Ten Years On*, Conference, Bruges, 27 September 2014, citing the critical reaction by Lord Mance in *X v Mid Sussex Citizens Advice Bureau* [2012] UKSC 59 [44] to a 'bold interpretative approach'.

[13] Cases C-402 and C-432/07 *Sturgeon v Condor Flugdienst GmbH* [2009] ECR I-10923, Opinion of AG Sharpston, at para 31, who refers to the explanatory memorandum in Commission, 'Proposal for a Regulation of the European Parliament and of the Council establishing common rules on compensation and assistance to air passengers in the event of denied boarding and of cancellation or long delay of flights', COM(2001) 784 final, Art 23.

[14] F Le Bot, 'La protection des passagers aériens dans l'Union Européenne. Réflexions sur l'interprétation du droit dérivé par la Cour de justice' (2013) 4 *Revue trimestrielle de droit européen* 753, 771. The French report refers to comments in academic literature on 'constructive reading' and '*contra legem* interpretation'; 'critical voices' on the *Sturgeon* case are mentioned in the report on the Czech and Slovak Republics (K Csach, report to the conference, para 6).

the EU judiciary is to try and reconcile both the Montreal Convention and Regulation 261, introduced to increase the level of passenger protection.

This attitude is not completely surprising, and corresponds to a widely used strategy where uniform law texts are involved, applying an interpretation based on a 'presumption of conformity'. In line with the principle of comity, later agreements are presumed not to conflict with previous obligations. They are to be interpreted in a way that reconciles commitments stemming from different sources, as long as no explicit abrogation is provided for in the later legislation in unambiguous terms.[15]

The case law dealing with treaties intended to achieve uniform legislation in certain cross-border fields (including transport) offers many examples of interpretations that are aimed at avoiding conflicts between binding texts, seeking a combination of provisions that at first sight may seem incompatible. The International Institute for the Unification of Private Law (UNIDROIT) and its *Revue de droit uniforme* offer many examples of such cases. In aviation law, an oft-quoted passage by Lord Denning may be illustrative of the effort that judges are willing to make to maintain the coherent application of international sources. In *Corocraft v Pan American Airways*, Lord Denning affirmed that '[i]t is the duty of these courts to construe our legislation so as to be *in conformity* with international law … The Convention should be given the same meaning throughout all the countries who were parties to it'.[16]

This goal may be achieved even at the cost of rather strained interpretations. When several international sources are competent to rule on one issue, the problem may not always be solved by ranking the respective legislative sources, especially where, such as in dualistic countries, the relevant legislative texts may have the same rank. If a domestic legislative act is required to transform an international obligation of the government into a binding act for all citizens, it may well be that a later legislative act may be capable of abrogating the incorporating statute. As clearly stated some time ago in England by Lord Atkin:

> Unlike some other countries, the stipulations of a *treaty* duly ratified do *not* within the Empire, by virtue of the treaty alone, have *force of law*. If the national executive, the Government of the day, decide to incur the obligations of a treaty which involve alteration of the law they have to run the risk of obtaining the assent of Parliament to the necessary statute or statutes… a treaty is *not part of English law* unless and until it has been incorporated into the law by legislation … [A]s long as Parliament has *not incorporated*, the international agreement is 'res *inter alios acta*'.[17]

---

[15] The effort to seek a reconciling interpretation is also made in relation to EU sources to avoid conflicts between domestic and European sources: eg A Wentkowska, 'A "Secret Garden" of Conforming Interpretation—European Union Law in Polish Courts Five Years after Accession' (2009) 12 *Yearbook of Polish European Studies* 127.

[16] *Corocraft v Pan American Airways* [1969] 1 QB 616, 653 (*per* Lord Denning) (emphasis added).

[17] *Attorney-General for Canada v Attorney-General for Ontario* [1937] AC 347 (Privy Council) (emphasis added).

This problem has been illustrated by the European Convention on Human Rights, signed by representatives of the UK Government early on[18] but not incorporated into domestic law until the Human Rights Act 1998. In the arguments put forward by lawyers opposing incorporation of the Convention, Lord Bingham recalls the reasoning according to which '[t]he unwritten British constitution ... has *no means of entrenching*, that is of giving a higher ... status to a law of this kind. Therefore, it is said, what one sovereign Parliament enacts another sovereign Parliament may override'.[19] This circumstance offered a strong argument, and it meant that until the 1998 Act came into force, judges could state in reference to the Convention that '[i]t is *not part* of our domestic *law* which judges can enforce'.[20]

A similar situation occurred in Italy, another dualistic country in matters of international law. Regarding aviation law, in 1985 the Constitutional Court was required to state whether the Warsaw Convention 1929 was compatible with the Constitution.[21] Indeed, the provision limiting the amount of damages that could be paid out for injuries to a person, according to Article 22, could be read as contradicting the principle established in Articles 2 and 3 of the Italian Constitution affirming the fundamental rights of the person (including *diritto all'incolumità personale*, the right not to be injured). The argument in favour of the jurisdiction of the Constitutional Court to decide on the issue was founded on the legislative force of the act incorporating the Warsaw Convention (and its amendments): an ordinary statute that was therefore subject to the Court's judicial review. The decision was favourable to the claimants and the legislation incorporating the Warsaw Convention was declared unconstitutional where it allowed a cap on the damages to be paid for the death of an Italian citizen.

II. Constitutional Amendments and New Interpretations of Previous Doctrines

In recent years several Constitutions of Member States have been amended to guarantee a higher hierarchical rank to international treaties, so that obligations arising out of such authority cannot be abrogated by ordinary statutes but may only be affected by legislative acts adopted according to special provisions

---

[18] TH Bingham, 'The European Convention on Human Rights: Time to Incorporate' (1993) 109 *LQR* 390 (the history of accession involved important political figures such as Lord Kilmuir (Lord Chancellor) and Winston Churchill, and included the signing of the Convention as early as 1951); FA Mann, 'Britain's Bill of Rights' (1978) 94 *LQR* 512.

[19] Bingham (n 18) 395.

[20] Lord Browne-Wilkinson, 'The Infiltration of a Bill of Rights' [1992] *Public Law* 398.

[21] *Coccia c. soc. Turkish Airlines*, Constitutional Court, 6 May 1985, fn 132.

(or by an official withdrawal from the treaty itself). As an example we may refer to the 2001 Italian amendment of Article 117(1) of the Constitution.[22]

Notwithstanding these amendments, introduced to increase the binding force of international sources, it is still possible to consider the situation of European sources as that of 'sovereignty in transition', according to the 'doctrine of counter-limits' affirmed by the constitutional courts, especially in Germany, Italy and Poland.[23]

The notion that EU legislation may still be subject to judicial review when it contradicts fundamental values expressed in the Member States' constitutions is somewhat strengthened by the Treaty of Lisbon, Article 5(2) of which provides:

> The Union shall *respect* the equality of Member States before the Treaties as well as their *national identities*, inherent in their *fundamental structures*, political and *constitutional*, inclusive of regional and local self-government. It shall respect their essential State functions.[24]

Judging from the national reports set out in Part II of the present volume, the issue of the respective force of the Montreal Convention and that of the Regulation 261 seems to be considered only obliquely by different Member States' courts. National judges tend to follow the CJEU's approach of finding an interpretation that reconciles both sources, rather than arguing their respective strengths. Arguments in terms of doctrines such as *lex posterior derogat legi priori* or *lex specialis derogat legi generali*, where the decision introducing the Montreal Convention into the EU legal system is followed by Regulation 261 which either introduces an exception or specifies a previous rule, are only reported in the Polish report.[25] The prevailing attitude seems to be to await further clarification with caution.

The direct effect of Regulation 261 (as well as its *primauté* or supremacy) appears generally not to have been contested before domestic courts.[26] Only in the UK has the direct effect of the Regulation been doubted, in a court decision indicating that the Civil Aviation (Denied Boarding, Compensation and Assistance) Regulations 2005 (SI 2005/975) and the Enterprise Act 2002, passed to integrate

---

[22] 'La potestà legislativa è esercitata dallo Stato e dalle Regioni *nel rispetto* della Costituzione, nonché dei vincoli derivanti dall'*ordinamento comunitario* e dagli *obblighi internazionali*' (emphasis added). A similar strategy was followed by the 1992 German amendment of Art 23 of the Constitutional Charter.

[23] N Walker, 'Late Sovereignty in the European Union' in N Walker (ed), *Sovereignty in Transition* (Hart Publishing, 2003) 3.

[24] Treaty of Lisbon amending the Treaty on European Union and the Treaty establishing the European Community, signed at Lisbon, 13 December 2007, [2007] OJ C306/1, Art 5(2) (emphasis added).

[25] K Kowalik-Banczyck, 'Poland', *Air Passengers Rights, Ten Years On*, Conference, Bruges, 26 September 2014.

[26] ibid; K Csach, 'Czech Republic and Slovakia', *Air Passengers Rights, Ten Years On*, Conference, Bruges, 26 September 2014; A Kornezov, 'Bulgaria and Romania', *Air Passengers Rights, Ten Years On*, Conference, Bruges, 26 September 2014. However, in Bulgaria the courts sometimes qualify the claim under domestic law and consider Regulation 261 to be a 'complementary tool of interpretation'.

the EU provisions, may be decisive as regards their application, causing 'confusion' on 'the position of the EU regulation within the legal order of the member states'.[27]

Apart from indications offered by the national reports, it may be worth considering the idea of a *hidden lacuna*, a metaphor put forward by some German authors, for the reintroduction of a notion used in the past in constitutional law. This explanation seems useful in situations where the EU passes legislation that is not completely unambiguous. When domestic legislators implement a Directive or integrate a Regulation through secondary legislation, they may opt for one of several possible interpretations, later contradicted by the CJEU (perhaps making use of a teleological reading of an ambiguous text). In order to justify an enforcement that contradicts, sometimes radically, the letter of the domestic law, jurists refer to a *hidden lacuna* in the original provision that must be fulfilled in harmony with the later reading provided by the CJEU. This explanation, which tries to downplay macroscopic changes in interpretation, does leave some questions open however. An issue of equality is raised between those cases where claimants brought their claims before the change in interpretation had taken place and those where the claims were brought after the change. Some uncertainty also surrounds the role of the constitutional court, which should generally deal with problems of conflict between legislative texts.

In such a complex framework, the obvious query concerns the behaviour of national judges, who find themselves in a rather difficult position. That is, finding a balance between international conventions, the domestic civil code (where one is in force) and specific codifications of transport law, consumer law and administrative law. In some civil law countries, the presence of parallel jurisdictions for civil and administrative cases has caused further uncertainty regarding the procedure to be followed by claimants, in part undermining the efficacy of consumer protection.[28]

Upon close reading, the chapters of Part II confirm that there is a problem of awareness regarding EU law and its development, especially where the claims are of limited value and they are decided by first instance judges who may be less familiar with EU law (such is the perception in France as regards the *juges de proximité*, in Italy for the *giudici di pace* and in the UK for the *small claims track* in the county courts). It seems also significant that even though Regulation 261 has been sharply criticised as unclear and the CJEU decisions are qualified as unexpected and 'creative', only a comparatively small number of references

---

[27] B Jones, 'United Kingdom and Ireland', *Air Passengers Rights, Ten Years On*, Conference, Bruges, 26 September 2014, referring to *Graham v Thomas Cook Group Ltd* [2012] EWCA Civ 1355.

[28] In Poland the Supreme Court had to rule on the possibility of bringing issues both in front of administrative and civil law courts: K Kowali-Banczyk, 'Poland', *Air Passengers Rights, Ten Years On*, Conference, Bruges, 26 September 2014. In Bulgaria 'the legislator is partly to blame for … confusion, given that he never provided explicitly for a legal remedy through which … claims should be channeled': A Kornezov, 'Bulgaria and Romania', *Air Passengers Rights, Ten Years On*, Conference, Bruges, 27 September 2014.

for preliminary rulings have been filed at the CJEU. The data collected on this issue indicate that:

— no references for preliminary rulings have been made by the Czech Republic, Slovakia, Bulgaria, France or Poland (although one reference was filed in the Chief Administrative Court in relation to the Charter of Fundamental Rights, which was rejected in 2014);
— there is no mention in Italian reports of the number of references made for preliminary rulings by the CJEU;
— two references for preliminary rulings have been made by The Netherlands;
— one reference for a preliminary ruling has been made by Ireland; and
— one reference for a preliminary ruling has been made in the UK by the Supreme Court, which led to the decision in *ex parte IATA*,[29] and there was one rejected instance of a reference in *Hook v British Airways* and *Stott v Thomas Cook Tour Operators Ltd*.[30]

Lastly, moving on to consider the position of domestic constitutional courts, we should observe that several constitutional courts still affirm their jurisdiction to verify whether international commitments are compatible with the core provisions of their fundamental charters. Such is the case in Italy, according to a decision delivered in 2007 where the reporting judge was Giuseppe Tesauro,[31] which is relevant, as he was formerly an Advocate General at the CJEU, and therefore cannot be suspected of being inimical to the application of international law.

In Germany, decisions by the Constitutional Court (Bundesverfassungsgericht, or BverfG) are also to be considered, notably the BVerfG judgment of 7 June 2000. In this decision the Constitutional Court declared itself to be incompetent as regards the verification of the protection of 'fundamental rights' by EU legislation. At the same time, however, it retained the right of domestic review for possible 'continued and repeated violations' of the most crucial human protections. According to a subsequent decision in the BVerfG (the so-called 'Lisbon' decision), the relevant standard of review is said to be whether the 'inviolable core content' of the constitutional identity of Germany's Basic Law is respected.[32]

In order to convey a more comprehensive picture, it must be added that in the UK, a distinction drawn by Laws LJ has updated the traditional doctrine according to which all legislative acts are represented as having the same strength. An important distinguishing line has been drawn, according to a decision delivered in 2002:

> *Ordinary statutes* may be impliedly repealed. *Constitutional statutes* may not. For the repeal of a constitutional Act or the abrogation of a fundamental right ... the court

---

[29] *ex parte IATA* (n 7).
[30] *Hook v British Airways* and *Stott v Thomas Cook Tour Operators Ltd* [2014] UKSC 15.
[31] Constitutional Court, 22 October 2007, fn 349 (G Tesauro).
[32] BVerG, 2 BvE 2/08 of 7 June 2000.

would apply this test: is it shown that the legislature's actual—not imputed, constructive or presumed—intention was to effect the repeal or abrogation?

…

A *constitutional* statute can *only* be repealed, or amended in a way which significantly affects its provisions touching fundamental rights … *by unambiguous* words on the face of the later statute.[33]

Observers in the UK have pointed out that certain statutes, 'while not being entrenched were not subject to implied repeal', while in more recent cases the notion has emerged that 'there may be constitutional fundamentals which even the EU law could not overcome'.[34]

III. Conclusion

The general picture we may sketch for the time being presents a situation where we see a cautious use of the courts' 'judicial review' of EU legislation: it is more likely where constitutional courts have preliminary control over legislation, less likely where an issue must be raised by the parties to a case. But it is also worth mentioning that in 2014, the first reference to a preliminary ruling by the German Constitutional Court was made 'against the Decision … of the European Central Bank [2012] concerning Outright Monetary Transactions (OMT) and the continued purchases of government bonds'.[35] This information indicates that national constitutional courts still regard their role as relevant for the development of EU law[36]—a role that may bring about interesting future litigation in the context of Regulation 261.

---

[33] *Thoburn v Sunderland City Council* [2002] EWHC 195 (Admin), [2013] QB 151, 185.

[34] A O'Neill, 'Not Waving but Drowning?: European Law in the UK Courts' 21 July 2014, available at <http://eutopialaw.com/2014/07/21/not-waving-but-drowning-european-law-in-the-uk-courts/>, referring to the position taken by Lord Mance and Lord Neuberger in *R (Buckinghamshire County Council) v Transport Secretary* [2014] UKSC 3, [2014] 1 WLR 342.

[35] Order of 14 January 2014—2 BvR 2728/13. English translation available at <www.bundesverfassungsgericht.de/SharedDocs/Entscheidungen/EN/2014/01/rs20140114_2bvr272813en.html>.

[36] G Martinico, 'National Judges and European Laws: A Comparative Constitutional Perspective' in M Cremona, P Hilpold, N Lavranos *et al* (eds), *Reflections on the Constitutionalisation of International Economic Law, Liber Amicorum for E Ulrich Petersmann* (Martinus Nijhoff, 2014) 65.

Part II

Member States' Perspectives

7

Austria and Germany: Well-Informed Passengers, Extensive Case Law and a Strong Demand for Legal Certainty

IRENA GOGL-HASSANIN

I. Introduction

Regulation 261 entered into force on 17 June 2005[1] and introduced a legal foundation for passenger claims that would occupy civil courts all over Europe as well as the CJEU, and would cause a great deal of discussion. Austria and Germany, both Member States of the EU, were no exception.

This chapter aims to outline briefly the approach and position of jurisprudence with regard to the claims available to passengers under the Regulation, as well as its development over the years. Courts in Germany and Austria have been kept quite busy, particularly with claims by passengers for compensation under Article 7 of the Regulation. However, there are hardly any Supreme Court decisions in this regard. This is due to the fact that in both countries, there is only limited access to the Supreme Courts,[2] claims under the Regulation only rarely meeting the criteria required to be fulfilled for a matter to be brought before them. Most cases are therefore dealt with by the courts of first instance[3] or appellate courts.[4] However,

---

[1] European Parliament and Council Regulation (EC) 261/2004 of 11 February 2004 establishing common rules on compensation and assistance to passengers in the event of denied boarding and of cancellation or long delay of flights, and repealing Regulation (EEC) No 295/91 OJ L 46/1, Art 19 (Regulation 261).

[2] In both countries, the Supreme Courts only deal with cases in which a legal question of significant importance in concerned. Furthermore, in Austria claims need to have a value of at least €5,000 to have a chance of being dealt with before the Supreme Court, the Oberster Gerichtshof; in Germany the Bundesgerichtshof only deals with cases in which the Appellate Court has ruled that a so-called *Revision* to the Bundesgerichtshof is permissible. Until 31 December 2014, if the Appellate Court decided that a *Revision* was not permissible, the appellant could file a so-called *Nichtzulassungsbeschwerde*, a complaint on the non-admissibility of the *Revision*, if the value of the claim was above €20,000.

[3] Regional courts, in Austria called Bezirksgericht, in Germany Amtsgericht.

[4] District courts, in Austria called Landesgericht, in Germany Landgericht.

particularly in Germany, it can be observed that the number of decisions handed down by the German Supreme Court, Bundesgerichtshof (BGH), has increased in the last few years.

It is probably accurate to say that both countries have also played a significant role in the establishment of CJEU case law and its interpretation of the Regulation. Courts in both countries initiated preliminary ruling procedures,[5] one of which concerned *Sturgeon v Condor* (Germany) and *Böck, Lepuschitz v Air France* (Austria),[6] which introduced the possibility of awarding compensation for delays, which earned criticism in the German-speaking countries[7] but which was confirmed by a German preliminary ruling request in *Nelson v Deutsche Lufthansa*.[8] *Wallentin-Hermann v Alitalia*[9] was an Austrian preliminary ruling request, which narrowed down the scope of the exception of extraordinary circumstances under Article 5(3) of the Regulation. This chapter will illustrate how these decisions affected jurisprudence in these two countries.

II. Austria

A. Enforcement of Claims under Regulation 261

As of 1 July 2006, Austria introduced the so-called Servicestelle für Fluggastrechte at the Ministry of Transport, Innovation and Technology (Bundesministerium für Verkehr, Innovation und Technologie (BMVIT)), as the designated NEB pursuant to Article 16(1) of the Regulation.[10] Any passenger whose rights under Regulation 261 are deemed to have been violated can file a complaint with the Austrian NEB. Its role is to conciliate and try to settle the dispute, or inform the parties to the dispute of their legal position. Pursuant to Article 139a of the Austrian Air Transport Act (Luftfahrtgesetz), the airlines involved are obliged to co-operate and provide any information and disclose any documentation that is considered relevant to solving the dispute. In 2013 the Austrian NEB handled a total of 1,564 cases, of which 469 concerned claims regarding cancellations, 655 dealt with delays and 79

---

[5] Austria initiated three preliminary ruling procedures (all resulting in a ruling); Germany initiated significantly more preliminary ruling procedures (but not all of them resulted in a ruling).

[6] Cases C-402 and 432/07 *Sturgeon and Others* [2009] ECR I-10923 (*Sturgeon*).

[7] eg W Müller-Rostin, 'Zu extensive Rechtsfortbildung durch den EuGH?' [2010] *Transportrecht* 93; I Gogl, 'EuGH erfindet die EG-Verordnung Nr 261 neu: Ausgleichszahlung auch für Verspätungen' (2010) 1 *Zeitschrift für Luft- und Weltraumrecht* 59; an expert opinion ordered by the Vereinigung Deutscher Fluggesellschaften provoked a judge at the LG Köln to initiate a new preliminary ruling proceedings before the ECJ. See also K Tonner, 'Die EU-Fluggasterechte-VO und das Montreal Übereinkommen' (2011) 6 *Verbraucher und Recht* 203; S Keiler, 'Vorschlag für eine Änderung der Fluggastrechte-VO—Eine Analyse aus wissenschaftlicher Sicht' (2013) 4 *Reiserecht aktuell* 163.

[8] Cases C-581 and 629/10 *Nelson v Deutsche Lufthansa AG* [2012] OJ C399/3 (*Nelson*).

[9] Case C-549/07 *Wallentin-Hermann v Alitalia* [2008] ECR I-11061 (*Wallentin-Hermann*).

[10] Luftfahrtgesetz, Art 139a.

with denied boarding.[11] The number of cases is growing steadily.[12] This, and the fact that the Austrian Government has set itself the goal of improving passenger rights by establishing a common conciliation body for all means of transport, has recently resulted in a new legislative proposal to establish an Agency for Passenger Rights (Agentur für Passagier- und Fahrgastrechte), which would be competent to handle not only air passenger claims, such as those under Regulation 261/2004, but also claims from passengers using other means of transport.[13] The new proposal provides that before the conciliation body can be called on, the airline concerned (entrepreneur) must be contacted. It also grants the conciliation body the power to refuse to handle a claim if the complaint was filed with the conciliation body more than one year after the airline became involved with the claim, or if it was filed wilfully or in a way that would compromise the conciliation body's efficient operation.[14] The draft law is meant to pave the way for the implementation of the EU Directive on consumer alternative dispute resolution.[15] It is currently undergoing the appraisal procedure, where lobbyists, other official bodies, experts and other interested parties may comment on the draft law. It remains to be seen whether, or with what amendments, the draft law will be passed.

Even though the number of cases before the Servicestelle für Fluggastrechte is increasing, this conciliation procedure is not mandatory. The passenger can also choose to file a complaint directly with the relevant civil court, as claims under the Regulation are considered civil claims under the contract for carriage, and claims for compensation, which are the most frequent claims brought before the courts, are considered a contractual penalty.[16] Since practically all claims under the Regulation have a value of less than €15,000, the relevant courts of first instance are the so-called Bezirksgerichte. Claims for money, which cover basically all claims under the Regulation that make it to court, are dealt with in a simplified order for payment procedure, the so-called Mahnverfahren.[17] The passenger can file his complaint by filling out a standard form, following which, without much reasoned explanation as to why the claim is justified, the court issues a payment order which is served on the defendant together with the complaint; the defendant then has

---

[11] According to information given by the Austrian Servicestelle für Fluggastrechte on 3 September 2014.

[12] In 2010, a total of 912 cases were reported; in 2011 the NEB handled 1,062 matters and in 2012 it handled 1,342 complaints.

[13] Ministerialentwurf betreffend Bundesgesetz, mit dem ein Bundesgesetz über die Agentur für Passagier- und Fahrgastrechte erlassen wird und mit dem das Eisenbahngesetz 1957, das Kraftfahrliniengesetz, das Luftfahrtgesetz, das Schifffahrtsgesetz und das Verbraucherbehörden-Kooperationsgesetz geändert werden (Passagier- und Fahrgastrechteagenturgesetz—PFAG), 41/ME XXV. GP.

[14] Passagier- und Fahrgastrechteagenturgesetz (draft) (n 13), Arts 5, 6.

[15] European Parliament and Council Directive 2013/11/EU of 21 May 2013 on alternative dispute resolution for consumer disputes and amending Regulation (EC) No 2006/2004 and Directive 2009/22/EC [2013] OJ L165/63.

[16] G Wilhelm, 'Of Denied Passengers, Delayed Departures and Cancelled Flights—Pausenkakao und Bußgelder' [2004] *ecolex* 81; M Aufner, 'Die neue EU-Überbuchungsverordnung' [2005] *Zeitschrift für Verkehrsrecht* 66.

[17] Zivilprozessordnung, Art 244.

four weeks to file any objections, which will initiate regular civil proceedings, or, within two weeks, to pay the amount set out in the payment order. If objections are filed within the time limit, the court will call for an oral hearing of the matter. If the requirements are fulfilled, the European order for payment procedure is also applicable.[18]

Rulings of the Bezirksgericht are open to an appeal before the relevant Landesgericht. Should the value of the claim be equal to or less than €2,700, the reasons for the appeal are limited to nullity of the procedure or that the decision was based on an incorrect legal opinion.[19]

The number of cases brought before the civil courts is, unfortunately, impossible to determine. However, it can be observed that the number increased significantly after *Sturgeon* and when claim aggregator services first began to operate in Austria. The most popular and successful such service is Fairplane, which is active in both Germany and Austria. According to its own indications, the service handled 16,408 cases in 2013, with the numbers continuing to rise. These claim aggregator services keep a significant slice of the compensation awarded as their remuneration. A cheaper option for the passenger is to reach out to consumer protection organisations, such as the Konsumentenschutzverband or the Chamber of Labour (Arbeiterkammer), which also assist in enforcing passenger claims.

Lastly, compliance with the Regulation by the airlines can also be enforced via an administrative procedure. Violations by airlines of their obligations under Regulation 261 can be subject to an administrative fine of up to €22,000.[20]

B. Case Law

The most frequent legal questions the Austrian courts have had to deal with have concerned:

(1) the relevant place of jurisdiction;[21]
(2) the notion of cancellation and delay; and
(3) the extraordinary circumstances exception.

The relevant place of jurisdiction caused some discussion before the courts, in particular when foreign airlines were involved, due to the fact that the Regulation does not provide any solution as regards the applicable forum. Passengers tend to want to establish jurisdiction in the country of their residence. While this may be possible in other consumer matters under Article 16(1) of Regulation No 44/2001,[22]

---

[18] Zivilprozessordnung, Art 252; European Parliament and Council Regulation (EC) No 1896/2006 of 12 December 2006 creating a European order for payment procedure [2006] OJ L399/1.
[19] Zivilprozessordnung, Art 501.
[20] Luftfahrtgesetz, Art 169(1).
[21] Due to the lack of a provision regarding the applicable place of jurisdiction in Regulation 261 itself.
[22] Council Regulation (EC) No 44/2001 of 22 December 2000 on jurisdiction and the recognition and enforcement of judgments in civil and commercial matters [2001] OJ L012/1.

contractual claims based on contracts of carriage are excluded from its scope.[23] Accordingly, the Austrian courts generally did not accept a reference to Article 16 of Regulation No 44/2001.[24] There was some discussion whether jurisdiction under Article 5(1) of that Regulation, pursuant to which a person domiciled in a Member State may be sued in a different Member State at the place of performance of a disputed obligation in a matter of contract, meant the place of departure or arrival; however, since *Rehder v Air Baltic*,[25] Austrian courts accept jurisdiction when the place of departure or arrival is Austria. For third country airlines (that is, non-EU airlines), Regulation No 44/2001 does not apply and jurisdiction has to be determined pursuant to international conventions or national law provisions. There is tendency to refer to Article 33 of the Montreal Convention[26] for claims under Regulation 261, even if the third-party airline does not have a separate office or representation in Austria, if the flight was booked through an agent situated in Austria.[27] In the case of a European order for payment procedure, in which the Bezirksgericht für Handelssachen Wien was nominated the court with exclusive jurisdiction to handle such proceedings,[28] jurisdiction of that court ceases when the defendant raises a timely objection to the issued payment order. In that case, the plaintiff is required to nominate the relevant court of local jurisdiction. If it does not do so within the time frame of 30 days,[29] the claim will be rejected on the grounds of lack of jurisdiction.[30]

It was also determined that claims under Regulation 261 can only be raised against the operating air carrier, even if the carriage was part of a travel package or the contract of carriage was concluded with a travel agent.[31]

Before *Sturgeon*, courts generally distinguished between cancellation and delay and its consequences. In accordance with the wording of the Regulation in Articles 5 and 6, courts only awarded compensation pursuant to Article 7(1) of the Regulation following a cancellation. The question then was whether and when a delay should in fact be considered a cancellation. The criteria pursuant to which the courts made the distinction between cancellation and delay were not so much time-driven; rather they depended on whether a new ticket was issued,

---

[23] ibid, Art 15(3).

[24] eg HG Wien, 13.03.2012, 1 R 99/11x, A Schmidt and G Saria, [2013] *Rechtsmittelentscheidungen des Handelsgerichts Wien* 13; BG Innsbruck, 26.01.2012, 26 C 1532/11p.

[25] Case C-204/08 *Rehder v Air Baltic* [2009] ECR I-6073.

[26] The Montreal Convention was made obligatory within the EU by European Parliament and Council Regulation (EC) No 2027/97 of 9 October 1997 on air carrier liability in respect of the carriage of passengers and their baggage by air (as amended by Regulation No 889/2002) [1997] OJ L285/1.

[27] HG Wien, 28.10. 2010, 34 Cg 60/10w.

[28] Zivilprozessordnung, Art 252(2).

[29] Zivilprozessordnung Art 252(3).

[30] HG Wien 13.03.2012, 1 R 99/11x, A Schmidt and G Saria, [2013] *Rechtsmittelentscheidungen des Handelsgerichts Wien* 13.

[31] HG Wien 14.9.2009, 1 R 146/09f; A Schmidt, 'Neueste Reiserechtliche Judikatur des HG Wien' [2010] *Jahrbuch Tourismusrecht* 79.

a new boarding card was handed out, whether a new check-in had to be made, whether the flight number had changed or whether other (new) passengers were carried on the same flight.[32]

When Mrs Lepuschitz and Mr Böck filed a complaint with the Bezirksgericht für Handelssachen Wien against Air France for compensation, the court rejected the claim, arguing that there had been a delay in the flight's arrival in Vienna which, even though it amounted to 22 hours, did not justify being considered a cancellation that would allow a claim for compensation under Article 7 of the Regulation. While the CJEU confirmed the view of the Austrian courts that a delay does not become a cancellation solely on the ground of time, it surprised even the Handelsgericht Wien, which initiated the preliminary ruling procedure after Mrs Lepuschitz and Mr Böck had filed an appeal, when the CJEU ruled that a delay of more than three hours justified an award of compensation.[33] After that, a delay in departure of 15 hours and in arrival in Vienna of 21 hours was considered a long delay that justified compensation pursuant to Article 7 of the Regulation.[34] Similarly, a delay of three hours on arrival on the way from Vienna to St Lucia via Madrid and London would justify an award for compensation under Article 7 of the Regulation.[35]

Another question that concerned the Austrian courts was the distinction between 'denied boarding' and 'delay' in the event of delay of a feeder flight. The Austrian Handelsgericht Wien qualified the missed continuing flight as 'denied boarding', for which the operating air carrier of the feeder flight was responsible.[36]

Extraordinary circumstances—the permitted ground for exclusion of liability under Article 5(3)—meanwhile, have been interpreted very restrictively. Most decisions in this respect concern the question whether a technical defect can be considered an extraordinary circumstance. In earlier decisions, it was held that a technical defect could be an extraordinary circumstance if the airline could prove that it complied with all mandatory and necessary maintenance measures to guarantee the security and airworthiness of the aircraft.[37] At the same time, it was also stated that it could not be reasonably expected that an airline would keep a large number of substitute aircrafts ready, in case an aircraft could not be operated due to a technical defect, or a substitute crew (on an airport outside of the airline's base) that could operate the flight if the original crew's permitted working time had ended. In another matter, an extraordinary circumstance was established when, due to an

---

[32] eg BGHS, 8 C 2016/05m; M Flitsch, 'Economical Aspects of Aviation' in S Hobe and N von Ruckteschell (eds), *Kölner Kompendium des Luftrechts* (Carl Heymans, 2010) vol 3, 364.

[33] *Sturgeon* (n 6).

[34] HG Wien 16. 3. 2010, 60 R 114/06d; Schmidt (n 31) 79.

[35] HG Wien, 26.02.2010, 50 R 76/09x; A Schmidt, 'Neueste reiserechtliche Judikatur des HG Wien' [2011] *Jahrbuch Tourismusrecht* 119.

[36] HG Wien, 29.4.2008, 1 R 206/07a = ZVR 2008, 149; Handelsgericht Wien, 16.1.2009, 60 R 44/08p = ZVR 2009/122; Schmidt (n 35) 119.

[37] BGHS, 14 C 771/08x; M Flitsch, (n 32).

electronic error, a computer broke down which usually does not need replacement, for which within 23 hours a spare part was organised and built in.[38]

In application of the principles established in *Sturgeon* and *Wallentin-Herrmann*,[39] another case that was referred to the CJEU by an Austrian court, the courts had to adapt their views. Recently a defect in the fuselage was not considered a technical defect that would justify an 'extraordinary circumstance' exception to liability. The same conclusion was reached in relation to an electronic error that caused an aircraft to experience an electrical outage.[40]

Another decision of the Handelsgericht Wien determined whether a heart attack suffered by the pilot shortly before the scheduled departure time of a flight could be considered an extraordinary circumstance. Even though the pilot's illness was unforeseeable, it was not considered an extraordinary circumstance. The crew's falling ill is a risk inherent in the airline's operation, and must therefore be taken into account.[41]

An interesting question arose before the Oberste Gerichtshof (OGH), the Austrian Supreme Court, as to whether the air carrier was responsible for the airport's delay, due to bad weather conditions, in clearing the airfield of snow and providing the airport facilities required for take-off (such as de-icing facilities). The decision concerned a claim under the Montreal Convention, but it is submitted that the findings in this matter will also be relevant to claims under Regulation 261.[42] The OGH ruled that the airport is a party that is not controlled by the airline, and therefore no influence can be exercised on how the airport performs its operation; consequently, the airport cannot be considered an agent of the airline in the sense meant under Article 19 of the Montreal Convention. A delay in the performance of the airport's tasks does not justify a claim against the airline for damage caused by delay. A year later, the OGH ruled in a case in which the airlines referred to bad weather conditions as extraordinary circumstances. The Court established that the reference to bad weather conditions per se did not suffice as justification.[43] In accordance with the principles established in *Wallentin-Herrmann*, the airline would have to prove that it took all reasonable measures to avoid the cancellation, for example use of a nearby substitute airport, waiting for improvement of the weather conditions or re-routing the passengers to a flight that did manage to take off.[44]

An extraordinary circumstance was also acknowledged when a flight had to land at another airport, around 200km from the original destination airport, due to heavy fog.[45]

---

[38] BGHS, 10 C 1537/05k; Flitsch (n 32).
[39] *Wallentin-Herrmann* (n 9).
[40] HG Wien 23.3.2010, 1 R 37/07y; A Schmidt (n 31) 79.
[41] HG Wien 18.06.2012, 1 R 153/11p.
[42] OGH 16.11.2012, 6 Ob 131/12a.
[43] See also BG Schwechat, 12.11.2001, 4 C 580/11v, in which it was established that snow in November cannot be considered an extraordinary circumstance, as it can be expected to snow at this time.
[44] OGH 3.7.2013, 7 Ob 65/13d.
[45] BG Schwechat, 28.09.2011, 4 C 612/11z LG Korneuburg, 15.03.2012, 21 R 332/11p; E Lindinger and T Labacher, *Fluggastrechte* (Manz, 2012) 49.

Before *Emirates Airlines v Schenkel*,[46] the Austrian courts argued in favour of the 'round trip theory', meaning that a flight was considered to be a round trip, which made the Regulation applicable to third-country airlines for all parts of the flight.[47] In relation to the compatibility of Regulation 261 with the Montreal Convention and the regulations that implemented the Montreal Convention into the EU *acquis*,[48] there are no noteworthy decisions available dealing specifically with this question. It seems to be undisputed that these two systems of rules co-exist and do not contradict each other.

The most recent Austrian decision of the CJEU, *Germanwings v Henning*,[49] was initiated by the Landesgericht Salzburg, which addressed to the CJEU the question of how the term 'arrival time', in the sense of Article 7, should be interpreted. The Court ruled that 'arrival' means the time when at least one of the aircraft doors has been opened and the passengers are entitled to disembark.

It must be noted that Austrian courts also like to refer to decisions of the German courts, of which there are significantly more.

III. Germany

A. Enforcement of Claims under Regulation 261

In Germany, the Federal Aviation Office (LBA—Bundes-Luftfahrtamt) was designated as the German NEB pursuant to Article 16(1) of Regulation 261.[50] Its role is to handle complaints by passengers and airlines, in that it can give an opinion (not binding) on the admissibility of the claim and enforce passenger rights under the Regulation by means of administrative law.[51] However, it is not responsible for initiating conciliation proceedings, or for filing claims on behalf of passengers with the civil courts. As in Austria, the civil courts in Germany are the competent authorities to handle and enforce claims by passengers under Regulation 261.[52]

---

[46] Case C 173/07 *Emirates Airlines v Schenkel* (ECJ, 10 July 2008).

[47] BGHS, 4.8.2006, 8 C 2016/05m = RRa 2006, 276; U Leitl, 'Die VO (EG) Nr. 261/2004, Die Rechte der Fluggäste—Ein Leitfaden für die Praxis' [2012] *Richterzeitung* 170.

[48] Leitl (n 47).

[49] Case C-452/13 *Germanwings GmbH v Henning* (ECJ, 4 September 2014).

[50] Luftverkehrs-Zulassungs-Ordnung, Art 63d), BGBl I S 370.

[51] Pursuant to Art 108(2) of the Luftverkehrs-Zulassungs-Ordnung, violations of Regulation 261 are considered to be so-called *Ordnungswidrigkeiten* (administrative failures), which can be penalised by imposing fines of up to €25,000.

[52] In Germany, the claim for compensation is considered flat-rate compensation for damages, without any requirement to prove any actual damage (see the contribution by N Ehlers and W Müller-Rostin, 'Verbraucherschutz im Übrigen' in S Hobe and N von Ruckteschell (eds), *Kölner Kompendium des Luftrechts* (Carl Heymans, 2010) vol 3, 357; E Führich, *Reiserecht* (CH Beck, 2010) 1047. However recently, partly for reasons of compatibility with the Montreal Convention, there have been considerations that the nature of the compensation claim under Art 7 of the Regulation might not be qualified as compensation for damage after all (for further discussion see Tonner (n 7)).

Since 1 November 2013,[53] there also exist two conciliation bodies in Germany, before which a conciliation procedure can be initiated in order to try to settle any claims under the Regulation out of court. One is the so-called SÖP (Schlichtungsstelle für den öffentlichen Personenverkehr eV), a privately organised conciliation body responsible for handling alternative dispute resolution proceedings against member airlines. Currently, 38 airlines are members of the SÖP. All airlines that are not members can be called before the public conciliation body established at the Schlichtungsstelle beim Bundesamt für Justiz. The intention of the German legislator was to give airlines the possibility of establishing a private body as regards which they would enjoy more freedom in determining the applicable procedural rules, in order to make airlines more amenable to conciliation and possibly make enforcement of passenger claims easier for the passengers. However, it is not mandatory to file a complaint with one of the conciliation bodies. Most claims, therefore, are addressed directly to the courts. (Due to the fact that these are new institutions, there are not yet any figures available on the performance of these two bodies.)

Similar to Austria, German civil procedure provides for simplified proceedings for monetary claims, which are handled by the courts of first instance, the so-called Amtsgerichte. Whilst in Austria there is an upper limit on the value of claims that can be brought as simplified proceedings, Germany does not have a similar threshold. The procedure itself works very similarly, though. The plaintiff makes an application to the court to issue a payment order, the so-called *Mahnbescheid*. The defendant then can either raise objections to this payment order and initiate ordinary civil proceedings, or pay the amount set out in the payment order.[54] As in Austria, the European payment order procedure is available too.

In Germany, there are also several claim aggregator services available, the largest being Flightright. According to Flightright's own information, it has successfully handled more than 400,000 claims for passengers. Another very active service is Fairplane, which originated in Austria but is also available in Germany. Around 20 to 30 per cent of all claims before the courts are brought by Fairplane. Probably around 50 per cent of the proceedings are initiated by Flightright. There are several other services, such as EUclaim, and some specialised lawyers who, however, play only a subordinated role.

Similar to Austria, Germany also has several consumer protection services, such as the regional Verbraucherzentralen. These institutions also assist passengers with issues under their contract of carriage and related matters.

B. Case Law

Due to the fact that claims under Regulation 261 are handled in the first instance by the German regional courts, the Amtsgerichte, which are spread throughout

---

[53] Bundesrat Drucksache 254/13, dated 12 April 2013 (Schlichtungsstelle für Fluggastrechte).
[54] Zivilprozessordnung, Art 688.

Germany and whose decisions are not publicly available, it is hardly possible to get a complete picture of the decisions and interpretations of the courts with regard to the articles of the Regulation. There exist several decisions of the BGH, however, but only on certain questions and without giving a complete picture on Germany's understanding of the Regulation.[55] Nevertheless, it may be observed that most decisions at first instance are rendered by the Amtsgericht Rüsselsheim, the Amtsgericht Frankfurt am Main and the Amtsgericht Erding, as the courts in which jurisdiction for claims under the Regulation is very often established. Due to the fact that there is no concerted action between the courts, and the problem that the Regulation is unclear at certain terms and leaves, particularly after the decisions in *Sturgeon*, a lot of open questions, it is not possible to give a complete overview of the legal opinions and interpretations existing in Germany. This section will, however, give an overview of some noteworthy decisions that have been reported and are regularly used as references.

German courts have been asked to decide cases across the full range of possible Regulation 261 claims. After *Sturgeon*, the number of cases brought before the courts multiplied significantly.[56] Most claims concern the question of long delays and the notion of extraordinary circumstances. Recently, the courts have also been dealing with other legal questions, which give room for different interpretations and which have not yet been resolved or addressed by the CJEU. Some of these issues will be addressed below.

Before the decision in *Sturgeon*, the courts regularly dealt with the question of whether disruption of a flight was considered a cancellation or a delay, as they awarded compensation pursuant to Article 7 of the Regulation only in the event of cancellation. Similar to Austria, the courts did not define one criterion capable of distinguishing these two events but examined the overall circumstances to determine, on a case-by-case basis, whether there was a cancellation or a delay. A cancellation was considered to comprise the calling off of the flight, but, according to the courts, this was not necessarily the case when a new flight number was allocated (although this can be an indication of a cancellation).[57] A flight that was aborted after take-off was also considered to be a cancelled flight.[58]

The decision in *Sturgeon*, which was confirmed by *Nelson* and *Air France v Folkerts*[59] (two cases also brought to the CJEU by preliminary ruling requests from German courts), still gives rise to some disbelief amongst the judges and practitioners in Germany. In 2013 the Landgericht Köln again initiated preliminary proceedings and asked the CJEU what impact *Sturgeon* has on the principle of the division of powers in the EU, in light of the fact that the CJEU held that passengers who suffer a delay of more than three hours may request compensation under

---

[55] P Wahl, 'Wer zu spät kommt … Ausgewählte Probleme der Fluggastrechte-Verordnung in der amtsgerichtlichen Praxis' [2013] *Reiserecht aktuell* 6.

[56] ibid.

[57] AG Frankfurt aM, 12.10.2006, 30 C 1726/06.

[58] LG Hamburg, 25.02.2011, 332 S 104/10.

[59] *Nelson* (n 8); Case C-11/11 *Air France v Folkerts* (ECJ, 26 February 2013).

Article 7 of the Regulation, even though Article 6, which deals with delay, does not award such a right.[60] The CJEU stated that there was no violation of international law or EU law, and that it had duly exercised its rights to interpret the Regulation.

The notion of 'extraordinary circumstances' is one extensively examined in the decisions of German courts. Even after the rulings in *Sturgeon* and *Wallentin-Herrmann*, the question of whether a technical defect can be considered an extraordinary circumstance has not been answered in the same way by all German courts. The Oberlandesgericht Köln, for example, interprets this question in the widest possible way. In this case,[61] the aircraft had been for a scheduled maintenance check two days before a flight, which subsequently was cancelled because of a defective hydro mechanical unit. This gear had been changed during the maintenance check and was working properly after that. Only four hours before the scheduled flight it stopped working and the flight had to be cancelled. In this instance, the court ruled that this technical defect was an extraordinary circumstance, which could not have been controlled by the airline and which was not part of the ordinary operating risk. Most courts, however, have evinced a more restrictive approach. The breakdown of the left-side heating system of an aircraft, which resulted in an aborted departure and the cancellation of the flight, was not considered a technical defect that would justify the 'extraordinary circumstances' exception under Article 5(3) of the Regulation.[62] Also, a burst tyre[63] and an alleged malfunction of the engines[64] were not deemed to be 'extraordinary circumstances'. Generally, the German courts do not focus on the type of technical defect. Rather, they focus on the foreseeability of the technical defect, and on whether the event was typical in the operation of commercial aviation or whether it was completely outside the control of the airline, in determining whether a technical or a safety deficit qualifies as an extraordinary circumstance; it is not relevant how often such a defect occurs.[65] In accordance with the findings of the CJEU, the BGH ruled that technical defects that occur from time to time in the normal operation of an aircraft could not be considered extraordinary circumstances, even if the airline performed all required checks and maintenance.[66]

German courts have also dealt with several other kinds of cases that concern the interpretation of 'extraordinary circumstances'. The following cases were considered to involve extraordinary circumstances:

— the allocation of a departure slot that resulted in a scheduled landing time which violated a night flight prohibition;[67]

---

[60] Case C-413/11 *Germanwings GmbH v Thomas Amends* (ECJ, 18 April 2013).
[61] OLG Köln, 27.05.2010, 7 U 199/09.
[62] AG Düsseldorf, 30.06.2011, 40 C 3590/11.
[63] AG Königs Wusterhausen, 31.05.2011, 20 C 84/11.
[64] AG Rüsselsheim, 20.07.2011, 3 C 739/11.
[65] LG Darmstadt, 20.07.2011, 7 S 46/11.
[66] BGH 12.11.2009, Xa ZR 76/07 = NJW 2010, 1070 = RRa 2010, 34.
[67] AG Erding, 18.04.2011, 2 C 1053/11.

— a medical emergency on the airfield of the aircraft concerned, in the event that this emergency situation was not foreseeable at the time of departure;[68]
— a bird strike that caused an engine defect, pursuant to which take-off was disrupted or because of which an aircraft could not be re-used after landing;[69]
— a decision by a pilot that a landing was too dangerous;[70]
— events caused by passengers;[71]
— events caused by third parties, over which the airline does not have any influence or control, for example damage to the aircraft by airport handling agents;[72] however not all courts in Germany hold this opinion;[73]
— if de-icing is not possible during a time of continued bad weather conditions, due to the fact that the airport operator has run out of de-icing fluid;[74] and
— reduction of flight movements by air traffic control due to the onset of winter.[75]

Illness, such as that of a pilot, is generally not considered an extraordinary circumstance, even if a flight needs to be aborted due to the sudden illness of the captain.[76]

A question discussed amongst the courts is whether and when industrial action is to be considered an extraordinary circumstance. In the event of a strike by ground handling personnel, an airline must at least outline how many employees are available, how many are required to dispatch an aircraft and why a delayed departure was not possible.[77] A strike can only be an 'extraordinary circumstance' if it was not foreseeable, giving the airline no chance to make other arrangements, such as hiring substitute crews or reacting in other ways to the action.[78] When the French air traffic authority went on strike, demanding reduction of air traffic by 50 per cent, and, consequently, causing a flight to be cancelled, it was considered

---

[68] AG Wedding, 28.10.2010, 2 C 115/10.
[69] BGH 24.09.2013, X ZR 160/12.
[70] AG Geldern, 3.8.2011, 4 C 242/09; it was ruled by the court that the decision of the pilot regarding safety considerations can only be reviewed in a limited way by the court.
[71] AG Rüsselsheim, 11.07.2012, 3 C 497/11 and 6.6.2013, 3 C 3405/12 (emergency slide was released by a passenger).
[72] AG Rüsselsheim, 28.03.2013, 3 C 661/12.
[73] Eg AG Frankfurt aM, 3.2.2010, 29 C 2088/09 = RRa 2010, 289.
[74] AG Königs Wusterhausen, 8.6.2011, 9 C 113/11 = NJW-RR 2012, 51; however, in 3.5.2011, 20 C 83/11 = RRa 2011, 196, another judge of the same court decided differently and argued that bad planning by the ground handler should be considered the airline's risk and therefore not an extraordinary circumstance. Similarly, in the decision of AG Frankfurt aM, 30.01.2014, 32 C 3328/13, it was considered an extraordinary circumstance that the airport had been closed due to bad weather and when it re-opened there were delays in de-icing.
[75] AG Frankfurt aM, 01.08.2014, 30 C 2922/13; here the extraordinary circumstance was the reduction of air traffic, not the weather condition (the onset of winter can be expected in December, but the decisions of air traffic control are out of the airline's hands).
[76] LG Darmstadt, 23.05.2012, 7 S 250/11; AG Frankfurt aM, 20.05.2011, 31 C 245/11, in which it was established that illness of crew members is a typical operational risk that the airline must bear.
[77] AG Düsseldorf, 9.11.2011, 40 C 8546/11.
[78] AG Frankfurt aM, 09.05.2006, 31 C 2820/05.

an extraordinary circumstance.[79] The BGH more recently decided that a strike would always have to be considered an extraordinary circumstance, regardless of whether the strikers were employees of the airline or of a third party.[80] However, a case-by-case examination must be undertaken to determine whether the airlines take all reasonable measures to avoid the cancellation (or delay) of flights. The BGH has expressed its opinion that an extraordinary circumstance is one requirement for the application of the liability exception under Article 5(3) of the Regulation, but the airline in question must take all reasonable measures to avoid the cancellation (or delay).

Another interesting decision dealt with the question of the foreseeability of a delay and the obligations of the airline to anticipate the possible consequences of a delay. An airline was found liable to pay compensation pursuant to Article 7 of the Regulation when a delay was caused by the fact that a stretcher had to be built into the aircraft to transport a passenger who was ill, which again caused the maximum working hours of the original crew to be exceeded. The court ruled that the airline should have anticipated this and provided for a substitute crew.[81]

Another question not yet completely resolved with regard to extraordinary circumstances is how long the effect of an extraordinary circumstance should continue. Usually, airlines have flights scheduled after a directly affected flight, which, as a consequence of the first flight's not being performed, cannot be performed either. Some courts hold the view that the 'extraordinary circumstances' effect should apply only to the flight directly concerned, not to subsequent flights.[82] Others argue for a wider scope and that the effect on subsequent flights should be taken into account.[83]

Several decisions have concerned the ash cloud that appeared when the Icelandic volcano, Eyjafjallajökull, erupted in 2010. It was agreed that the event was to be considered an extraordinary circumstance, but disputes arose in relation to passengers' rights to care under the Regulation.[84] German courts had ruled in favour of passengers in this regard all along,[85] and in 2013 it was clarified by the CJEU that a right to care existed even in a case like this, and that there was not an 'extra extraordinary circumstance' the scope of which would go beyond that of Article 5(3) of the Regulation.[86] A lot of passengers were forced to organise accommodation and meals themselves during that time, and then asked the airline to reimburse them. It was ruled that the airline could not defend a claim

---

[79] AG Königs Wusterhausen, 31.01.2011, 4 C 308/10.

[80] BGH, 21.8.2012, X ZR 138/11.

[81] LG Frankfurt aM, 02.09.2011, 2-24 S 47/11.

[82] LG Hannover, 18.01.2012, 14 S 52/11.

[83] Wahl (n 55).

[84] See also C Lintschinger, 'Zum rechtlichen Nachspiel in der Reisebranche aufgrund des Vulkanausbruchs in Island' [2010] *wirtschaftsrechtliche Blätter* 321.

[85] AG Rüsselsheim, 21.12.2011, 3 C 229/11; AG Nürnberg, 14.09.2011, 18 C 6053/11; AG Rüsselsheim, 11.01.2011, 3 C 1698/10.

[86] Case C-12/11 *Denise McDonagh v Ryanair* (ECJ, 31 January 2013); see also AG Nürnberg, 14.09.2011, 18 C 6053/11.

to reimburse the costs of staying at an expensive hotel solely by arguing that a cheaper one could have been booked. The airline must substantiate and prove exactly which cheaper room and which cheaper rate was available.[87] One of these decisions also concerned those passengers who had a regular booking on a flight that could take place after the ash cloud had disappeared, when flights could be performed once more. Many passengers were stranded in different airports at that time, and the airlines were confronted with the dilemma of who to transport first. The Court ruled in favour of those passengers who had a regular booking. They had priority over other passengers who were stranded.[88]

Regarding the justification of bad weather as an extraordinary circumstance, the courts considered other cases. It is generally not sufficient to refer globally to bad weather on the date of departure. The airline has to show which specific weather condition at what time caused which cancellation by air traffic control.[89]

German courts were also concerned with questions of jurisdiction. It was established, for example, that a stopover was not relevant in determining the place of departure, and therefore a possible forum, which was to be determined as the place where the first segment of a flight had started.[90] There were also different opinions represented by German courts in relation to whether a flight, in the sense of the Regulation, should be considered a round trip, or only as either the incoming or the outgoing flight.[91] *Emirates Airlines v Schenkel*[92] was initiated by the Oberlandesgericht Köln, which determined that the incoming–outgoing flight theory should be applied.

The question of whether a stopover should be considered part of a flight or as a separate destination was also examined in the guise of a different legal question, namely, whether, where the passengers had scheduled 20 hours' stay at a stopover destination before their next flight, a delayed arrival at this destination was an event that would trigger a claim for compensation under Article 7 of the Regulation. The Landgericht Hamburg ruled that a delay at a stopover would not justify compensation as long as the final destination was reached on time. If the flights were booked together, they are not to be considered separate flights.[93]

The legal questions brought before the courts are manifold and are not limited to questions of delay or cancellation, or to extraordinary circumstances. Recent questions before the courts have concerned, for example, the concept of the 'operating air carrier'. Who is responsible when an airline other than the one with which the ticket was booked, and which it was thought was going to operate the flight, in

---

[87] AG Rüsselsheim, 21.09.2011, 3 C 56/11.
[88] LG Frankfurt aM, 12.09.2011, 24 S 99/11.
[89] AG Wedding, 19.09.2006, 14 C 672/05.
[90] AG Wedding, 15.02.2010, 18 C 180/09.
[91] eg AG Berlin-Mitte, 11 C 206/05 = NJW-RR 2006, 920 = RRa 2006, 91, S Keiler, 'Reisemangel durch Vorverlegung des Rückflug—Ansprüche nach der Pauschalreise-RL und der Fluggäste-VO' (2007) 14 *Zivilrecht aktuell* 468.
[92] *Emirates Airlines v Schenkel* (n 46).
[93] LG Hamburg, 03.03.2014, 309 S 240/12; see also AG Wedding 27.06.2011, 19 C 84/11.

fact performs the flight, either as planned or on short notice? Those airlines that do not in fact perform the flight in the end, very often try to contest claims by arguing that they do not have the capacity to be a defendant. Whether this is the case or not depends on whether it was planned from the beginning that a different airline would perform the flight, or whether this was decided at short notice.[94] In another decision regarding the same notion, the question was whether an airline could be considered the 'operating air carrier' when its 100 per cent subsidiary performed the flight. It was ruled that in this case the parent company could be viewed as an 'operating air carrier', and thus as a defendant in a claim under the Regulation.[95]

Another problematic question is whether passengers who are carried free of charge or at reduced rates should have the same rights as fully paying passengers.[96] Such an exemption applies, for example, to crew members, but not to tariffs for senior citizens or children because such tariffs are always available to the public.[97]

Similar to Austria, the coexistence of the Montreal Convention and Regulation 261 is generally acknowledged,[98] in particular after the CJEU decision in *ex parte IATA*.[99] Also in academic statements, it has been established that there is no discrepancy between the Regulation and the Montreal Convention and that both rules can coexist.[100]

German case law in relation to the Regulation could go on and on; there are numerous different matters with which the courts have to deal. The cases discussed above show only a small part thereof, but it is hoped that they give an idea of the direction at which the courts are aiming.

IV. Conclusion

Ten years of Regulation 261 and still many questions remain unanswered: this is how one could summarise the overall view of judges and legal experts in Austria and Germany. The CJEU rulings have not brought much clarification with regard to the Regulation's scope, but rather have led to more cases being tried before the courts and more questions being raised by airlines, passengers and legal experts.

The German courts in particular have played a very active role in pointing out uncertainties in the wording of Regulation 261, and thus bringing these issues

---

[94] Wahl (n 55); AG Rüsselsheim, 11.04.2013, 3 C 3406/12; if an airline different from the one originally designated to perform the flight 'jumps' in at the last minute, then the flight of the original airline must be considered a cancellation for which compensation may be paid.

[95] AG Bremen, 10.10.2011, 16 C 89/11 = RRa 2012/1, 22.

[96] Regulation 261, Art 3(3).

[97] LG Stuttgart, 07.11.2012, 13 S 95/12 = RRa 2013, 130 = NJW 2013, 380 = NVZ 2013, 303.

[98] eg Tonner (n 7).

[99] Case C-344/04 *R (International Air Transport Association and European Low Fares Airline Association) v Department for Transport* [2006] ECR I-403.

[100] Tonner (n 7).

before the European Court for preliminary rulings. While the German courts have sometimes showed resistance to the results of these preliminary rulings by the CJEU,[101] in most cases the obiter dicta of the CJEU have largely been accepted and subsequently applied. Due to the rise of claim aggregator services and organised consumer protection organisations, German passengers are well aware of their rights, and do not hesitate to enforce them before the courts if the airlines do not comply. Due to the vast number of cases tried before the German courts, it seems that the current Regulation is throwing up more and more questions that require interpretation, not making the courts' workload any smaller.

Austrian passengers seem to be as well informed and litigious as German ones, but Austrian courts are less critical of the CJEU's rulings than the German courts. Austrian courts do tend to orientate themselves around German court rulings, and thus largely follow the line of jurisprudence established in Germany, but noteworthy cases, such as *Sturgeon* or *Wallentin-Hermann*, were initiated (partly) by requests for preliminary rulings from Austrian courts, showing that those courts have also independently sought clarification of certain issues in the Regulation and, thus, actively participated in forming the now applicable European jurisprudence with regard to the Regulation and the rights contained therein.

The envisaged reform of the Regulation is viewed critically by airlines and passengers alike.[102] The view has been expressed that it is very likely that the current European Commission proposal[103] will not find a majority in the European Parliament.[104] It might therefore be that the current Regulation will remain in force for a little longer. Either way, the courts will be kept busy.

---

[101] eg *Sturgeon* (n 6).

[102] eg R Schmid, 'Fluggastrechte-Reform: Eine Verbesserung nur auf den ersten Blick' (2014) 2 *Reiserecht aktuell* editorial.

[103] Commission, 'Proposal for a Regulation of the European Parliament and of the Council amending Regulation (EU) No 691/2011 on European environmental economic accounts', COM 2013 (247) final.

[104] eg S Keiler, 'Ein Vorschlag für eine Änderung der Fluggastrechte-VO—Eine Analyse aus wissenschaftlicher Sicht' (2013) 4 *Reiserecht aktuell* 163.

8

The Benelux: Small is not Less

PABLO MENDES DE LEON AND WOUTER OUDE ALINK

I. Introduction

The Benelux is formed by three founding members of the European Economic Community, namely, the Netherlands, Belgium and Luxembourg. The three countries have a close link with the subject of this book.

The Netherlands is an important aviation country, as it is the home of a principal European airline, KLM Royal Dutch Airlines, and of one of the busiest airports in the EU, namely Schiphol. Moreover, it has a distinct tradition in the field of research and teaching of air law, which influences ideas on passenger protection, in particular when checking European regulations against global regulations.

Belgium's capital, Brussels, hosts the principal European institutions, that is the European Commission, the European Council and, for most of the time, the European Parliament. Specialised law firms closely follow initiatives taken in those institutions, including those on the present subject.

Lastly, the CJEU has its offices in Luxembourg. The Court has rather demanding tasks, as it has to respond to courts in Member States regarding myriad questions on the interpretation of the terms used in Regulation 261. Aviation activities are relatively modest in Luxembourg, and so are claims for compensation on delay, cancellation and denied boarding.

This chapter will highlight the principal cases explaining the terms of Regulation 261 and comment on them. It will discuss the Benelux countries in the above order. We have found that the cases principally relate to the distinction between cancellation and delay, the notion of 'extraordinary circumstances', and the relationship between Regulation 261 and the Montreal Convention. Hence, we will focus on those subjects.

II. The Netherlands

A. Case Law

i. *The Distinction Between Delay and Cancellation*

Before the CJEU gave its decisions in the well-known case of *Sturgeon v Condor*,[1] Dutch courts had made a rather strict distinction between 'delay' and 'cancellation'. Passengers tried to argue that a flight that was delayed for more than 24 hours must be deemed to be cancelled.[2] However, the Dutch court to which the question was submitted held that Regulation 261 does not support that view. Having established this point, the same court decided that if a flight is delayed rather than cancelled, the carrier is not obliged to supply the compensation envisaged for those passengers whose flight has been cancelled.[3] Meanwhile, we know that the CJEU has other views on that distinction, as evidenced by *Sturgeon*. This view was followed by courts in Haarlem[4] and The Hague.

Between the astonishing *Sturgeon* decision and decisions in similar cases, that is *Nelson v Deutsche Lufthansa*[5] and the *Air France v Folkerts* case,[6] airlines tried to suspend payment of the standardised amounts that are available for passengers other than those whose flights have been delayed, in the hope that the CJEU would 'correct' its earlier decision, which, as we know, has not happened. However, the court in Haarlem rejected that proposal.[7] The fact that a flight is operated under the same flight number does not mean that the flight is delayed rather than cancelled. In the circumstances of the case of *Claimant v Transavia*, the flight, which was operated by the Dutch budget carrier Transavia, had another point of departure than the one scheduled, and arrived two hours late. Those combined facts implied that the original flight was cancelled, entitling passengers to the compensation provided for them under Regulation 261.[8]

---

[1] Cases C-402 and 432/07 *Sturgeon and Others* [2009] ECR I-10923 (*Sturgeon*).

[2] eg Rb Haarlem 19 September 2007, LJN BB3974; *X v Minister of Transport and Public Works*, Rb Amsterdam 21 January 2009, LJN BH5037.

[3] eg Rb Haarlem 20 December 2006, LJN AZ5276; Rb Haarlem 19 September 2007, LJN BB3974; Rb Amsterdam 21 January 2009, LJN BH 5037.

[4] eg Kantongerecht Haarlem 10 March 2010, LJN BP8512; Rb Den Haag 12 August 2010, LJN BP 8520l; Kantongerecht Den Haag 22 September 2010, LJN BP8499; Kantongerecht Den Haag 9 February 2011, LJN BP8510; these decisions state that since the *Sturgeon* decision has been handed down, no further questions should be addressed to the CJEU.

[5] Cases C-581 and 629/10 *Nelson v Deutsche Lufthansa AG* [2012] OJ C399/3; CJEU, 'The Court of Justice has confirmed its previous ruling that passengers whose flights have been delayed for a long time may be compensated', Press release 135/12, 23 October 2012.

[6] Case C-11/11 *Air France SA v Folkerts* (ECJ, 26 February 2013).

[7] Rb Haarlem 21 March 2012, ECLI:NL:RBHAA:2012:BV9537, KG ZA, 12–69; see also *Claimants v British Airways Plc*, 22 June 2012, 1263506 CV EXPL 11-21712.

[8] *Claimant v Transavia*, Rb Northern Holland 11 June 2013, 518451/CV EXPL 11-8793.

ii. The Notion of 'Extraordinary Circumstances'

a. Scope of the Notion

Most cases in the Netherlands deal with the scope of the 'extraordinary circumstances' exception. This may be explained by the rather unpredictable weather conditions in the Netherlands, which is one of the reasons why Schiphol Airport has so many runways (six), and by awareness of the narrow interpretation of this notion after yet more decisions made by the CJEU.

The Netherlands cases falling under this heading can be categorised into three subcategories: weather, technical conditions of the aircraft and safety-related conditions amounting to 'extraordinary circumstances'.

b. Weather

In a relatively early decision in 2007, a technical failure, for instance the leakage of kerosene, was regarded as a safety issue and identified as an 'extraordinary circumstance' relieving the air carrier of liability under Regulation 261.[9] In a well-reasoned decision made in 2009, the court in Haarlem held that weather conditions also justify reliance on the 'extraordinary circumstances' exclusion, as such a decision is made for reasons of safety. Safety is of principal importance in air transport; the judge should not presume to sit in the seat of the captain of the aircraft, saying that diversion of the flight was not necessary. The judge in this case referred to Recital 14 of Regulation 261.[10]

A year later, the same court also opined that weather conditions cannot be influenced and, hence, are 'extraordinary' under Regulation 261. The judge said that the defendant airline could not prevent those circumstances and rejected the claim.[11]

Heavy storms above Paris also justified the cancellation of a flight between Paris and St Maarten in the Caribbean. The defence of 'extraordinary circumstances' was, again, held justified.[12]

c. Technical Conditions of the Aircraft

In a case that was unrelated to weather conditions but was related to the technical conditions of the aircraft, and after the decision of the CJEU in *Wallentin-Hermann v Alitalia*,[13] the Court of Haarlem found that a technical failure leading

---

[9] eg *Plaintiffs v KLM Royal Dutch Airlines*, Rb District Court 9 May 2007, 791233 CV Expl 06-19812; *Nas et al v Transavia*, Rb Utrecht 27 June 2007, LJN BE9027Rb Haarlem 29 October 2009, LJN BG2720; Rb Haarlem 3 October 2007, LJN AZ5828.

[10] Kantongerecht Haarlem 15 April 2009, LJN BI6311.

[11] Kantongerecht Haarlem 29 October 2008, LJN BG2720.

[12] Rb Haarlem 23 July 2012, 547245 EJ VERZ 12–33.

[13] eg Case C-549/07 *Wallentin-Hermann v Alitalia* [2008] ECR I-11061 (*Wallentin-Hermann*); commentators argue that in practice this may lead to a strict liability regime for airlines in the event of cancellations; see also J Balfour, 'Regulation EC 261/2004 and "extraordinary circumstances"' (2009) *Zeitschrift für Luft- und Weltraumrecht* 58(2) at 224.

to the cancellation of the flight would not fall within the term 'extraordinary circumstances' unless the problem was a consequence of events that were not inherent in the normal exercise of the activities carried out by the airline.[14] Hence, the court followed the strict reasoning of the CJEU.

After that, Dutch courts continued to apply high standards for the defence pertaining to 'extraordinary circumstances' when these circumstances were caused by technical deficiencies. Thus, evidence of adequate maintenance is not good enough to successfully appeal to the defence of 'extraordinary circumstances'.[15] A defect in the weather radar system during a flight does not qualify as an 'extraordinary circumstance'; such an event should be regarded as being inherent in the normal performance of the flight operation.[16]

In 2011, well after the *Wallentin-Herman* decision, reliance on 'extraordinary circumstances' pertaining to the maintenance and technical operation of the aircraft has been at least one time successful as the defendant airline had undertaken its best efforts to identify the technical deficiency, and especially to guarantee the safety of the flight. The judge determined that the carrier had not failed to inspect the aircraft on a regular basis, and that it could not be blamed for the absence of the necessary spare parts and trained personnel in that part of the world, that is, Curaçao. Moreover, the judge stated that remedying the defect would not necessarily guarantee the safety of the operation, an opinion also voiced by the safety inspection department of the Ministry of Infrastructure and the Environment as the enforcement body.[17]

The absence of available crew because of the delayed arrival of the aircraft from another destination does not qualify as an 'extraordinary circumstance'. In the words of the court, the airline, in this case Transavia, must keep a crew on 'standby' in such cases, which procedure is part of the normal organisation of an airline.[18]

d. Safety Related Conditions

In 2014, two safety-related decisions, discussing the technical operation of the flight, dismissed arguments to consider unexpected safety problems as 'extraordinary circumstances'.[19] The judge in these cases explained that reliance on the

---

[14] Kantongerecht Haarlem 22 April 2009, LJN BI3210; see also Kantongerecht Haarlem 6 May 2009, LJN BJ2449.

[15] Court of Appeal of Amsterdam 16 February 2010, 200.017.721/01.

[16] *Passengers v Tui Nederland Airlines*, reported in 'Luchtvaartclaim TUI/Arkefly kan van kapotte weerradar geen buitengewoon omstandigheid maken' (Nederlands Juridisch Dagblad 13 June 2013) <http://juridischdagblad.nl/content/view/12591/53/> accessed 28 November 2014.

[17] *Bazin v KLM*, Rb Amsterdam 15 March 2011, CV-3399.

[18] *Claimant v Transavia*, 22 July 2013, published in 'Transavia veroordeeld tot betalen 1600 euro schadevergoeding aan passagiers', *Nederlands Juridisch Dagblad*, 22 July 2013, available at <http://juridischdagblad.nl/content/view/12689/53/>, accessed 28 November 2014.

[19] eg *Claimants v Corendon Dutch Airlines*, Kantongerecht Den Haag 7 May 2014, 2233410 RL EXPL 13-22735; *Claimant v The State of The Netherlands*, Rb Rotterdam 10 October 2013, AWB-12_04730.

'extraordinary circumstances' exception is justified when the following conditions occur:

(1) conditions that are not inherent in the normal exercise of the operation carried out by the carrier (see *Wallentin-Hermann*);
(2) conditions over which the carrier cannot exercise a decisive influence (see *Wallentin-Hermann*);
(3) the delay was caused by a safety problem that could not be prevented, in spite of the taking of all reasonable measures (Dutch jurisprudence).

The judge held that a warning signal is an unexpected safety problem that is inherent in the normal operation of the flight by the carrier.[20]

iii. Preliminary Ruling Requests

The interpretation of the provisions of Regulation 261, its compatibility with the Montreal Convention 1999, and decisions made by the CJEU on the provisions of the Regulation have also occupied, and still occupy, the minds of Dutch judges. Dutch courts have requested preliminary rulings in the following cases:

— Despite the binding force of the CJEU's decision in *Sturgeon*, courts in the EU remain entitled to pose prejudicial questions to the Court. In this case, the District Court in Breda bravely asked whether the application of Article 7 of Regulation 261 to the payment of compensation for damage caused by delay is compatible with the last sentence of Article 29 of the Montreal Convention forbidding the payment of non-compensatory damages.[21] The answer from the Court follows from its other decisions.[22]
— In April 2014, the District Court of Amsterdam addressed 10 pertinent questions to the CJEU, which are designed to define the scope of 'extraordinary circumstances'.[23] In summary, those questions pertain to the following:
  — What is the meaning of the term 'event' in Recital 14 of the Regulation?
  — Are or are not the events mentioned in consideration 22 of the *Wallentin-Hermann* decision the same as those referred to in Recital 14 of the Regulation?
  — What kinds of events are supposed to fall within 'extraordinary circumstances' in connection with flight safety and technical problems?
  — Should the words 'inherent in the normal exercise of the flight operation' be explained in such a fashion that the said conditions can only be influenced by the air carrier?

---

[20] ibid.
[21] Rb Breda 20 October 2010, LJN BO1083 (588236 cv 10-1341).
[22] *cf* Kantongerecht Den Haag 22 September 2010, LJN BP8499; Kantongerecht Den Haag 9 February 2011, LJN BP8510; Kantongerecht Haarlem 10 March 2010, LJN BP8512; these cases state that since the *Sturgeon* decision has been handed down, no further questions should be addressed to the CJEU.
[23] Case C-257/14 *C van der Lans v KLM*, decision of 17 September 2015.

— Are you able to clarify consideration 26 of the *Wallentin-Hermann* decision?[24]
— The following question is related to the reply to the earlier question regarding the meaning of technical problems in the context of 'extraordinary circumstances'. What is the scope of the term 'all reasonable measures' and its relationship with the defence regarding 'extraordinary circumstances'?
— Can air carriers, when keeping and storing spare parts in other parts of the world, take the availability of those parts in such other parts of the world, and issues pertaining to the re-booking of passengers on flights operated by other carriers, into account, even when those carriers are only incidentally subject to the scope of Regulation 261, when invoking the 'extraordinary circumstances' defence?
— Should the judge, when determining the question whether all reasonable measures have been taken to limit the damage occasioned by the delay caused by technical problems affecting the safety of flights, reckon with circumstances that can increase the flight delay, such as the fact that the aircraft must make several stops before touching down at its home base?

These questions are aimed at taking away or reducing the uncertainty and confusion the *Wallentin-Hermann* decision has produced in light of the text of Regulation 261. On 17 September 2015, the Court in Luxembourg decided that, even in the event of a flight cancellation on account of unforeseen technical problems, air carriers are required to compensate passengers thus confirming the narrow limits for the carrier's defence which were drawn in the *Wallentin-Hermann* case. The Court also pointed out that air carriers may recover damages they had to compensate from other parties such as manufactures—but that is nothing new as Article 38 of the Montreal Convention 1999, laying down a Right of Recourse against Third Parties and general civil law, has established such entitlements.

iv. Other Cases

The State, in this case the Dutch State, is obliged to enforce the provisions of Regulation 261 in cases where the airline is required to pay compensation pursuant to those provisions as there was no evidence of 'extraordinary circumstances'.[25]

---

[24] Consideration 26 of *Wallentin-Hermann* (n13) states: 'However, it cannot be ruled out that technical problems are covered by those exceptional circumstances to the extent that they stem from events which are not inherent in the normal exercise of the activity of the air carrier concerned and are beyond its actual control. That would be the case, for example, in the situation where it was revealed by the manufacturer of the aircraft comprising the fleet of the air carrier concerned, or by a competent authority, that those aircraft, although already in service, are affected by a hidden manufacturing defect which impinges on flight safety. The same would hold for damage to aircraft caused by acts of sabotage or terrorism.'

[25] *Claimant v The State of The Netherlands*, represented by *Ministerie van Infrastructuur en Milieu* [Ministry of Infrastructure and the Environment] Rb Rotterdam 10 October 2013, AWB-12_04730.

This decision was made by the administrative judge rather than by a court in civil proceedings because the defendant in the case in issue was the State.

A passenger's claim was dismissed as the claim was directed against the parent company, KLM Royal Dutch Airlines, rather than against the operating carrier, KLM City Hopper, a daughter company of KLM Royal Dutch Airlines.[26]

B. Remedies

In 2008, the air transport sector, including Dutch and foreign airlines, and the Dutch Consumer Association (Consumentenbond) signed an agreement designed to establish a special commission dedicated to the speedy, efficient and smooth resolution of questions on passenger protection arising between carriers and their clients. This commission was tasked not only with resolving claims arising under Regulation 261, but also with dealing with the protection of handicapped passengers.

Two years later, in 2010, the Dutch media reported that the air carriers and the commission were reluctant to pay compensation, or to award it, to the dissatisfied passengers. Airlines who had to pay for the procedures found them too expensive.

The commission was abolished on 1 January 2012. Passengers can now submit their claims to the inspection body of the competent Ministry, the Ministry of Infrastructure and the Environment, which has installed a special client service for this purpose. Obviously, court proceedings remain a principal option.

C. In Conclusion

In conclusion, Dutch courts, especially those established in Haarlem, which is the district where most carriers and Schiphol Airport have their (principal) places of business, but also those established in The Hague, have changed direction after the consumer-orientated decisions made by the CJEU.

The concept of 'extraordinary circumstances' keeps parties and judges busy. In 2014, 10 very important, detailed and well-articulated prejudicial questions were put to the Court in Luxembourg, which has confirmed its earlier position in its decision of 17 September 2015.

While cases in the Netherlands have focused on the distinction between delay and cancellation, and the passenger protection afforded in such instances, we have not found any decisions on the practice of denied boarding.

We also found that the special procedures providing extra protection to passengers by way of alternative proceedings had to be stopped, for the reasons set out in section B, above.

---

[26] Rb Amsterdam 27 December 2012, LJN:BY7874; Rb Amsterdam 10 May 2012, LJN:NW5486.

III. Belgium and Luxembourg

A. Introduction

The number of published court cases in Belgium is lower than in the Netherlands, which may be a result of individual State practice in publishing cases, but may also be due to the fact that, until June 2014, the Belgian NEB had the power to judge the admissibility of a claim, as explained below. The number of cases in Luxembourg is negligible and influenced by the small amount of traffic using the only airport.

On the other hand, the main reason for a potential difference in court cases between the Netherlands and Belgium may well be the differences in the amount of air passenger traffic: the total number of passengers at Belgian airports[27] in 2013 amounted to 26,665,237;[28] while the total number of passengers at Dutch airports[29] in the same year was 58,047,513.[30] In comparison, Luxembourg Airport handled only 2 million passengers in 2013.[31]

These different numbers are reflected in the amount of complaints received by the respective NEBs (in 2010):

— Belgium: 2,730
— Netherlands: 4,284
— Luxembourg: 21.[32]

The number of complaints received by the Dutch NEB is actually lower than one might expect, based on the passenger figures given above, but this could be explained by the active role played by commercial claim firms, such as EUClaim, in the Netherlands. For example, EUClaim claims a success rate of 97 per cent. According to its website, since 2007 it has dealt with more than 62,000 cases in total,[33] which therefore amounts to almost 8,000 per year on average.

In this section of the chapter, four Belgian cases are discussed dealing with the distinction between cancellation and delay, extraordinary circumstances, the

---

[27] The airports of Antwerp, Brussels, Charleroi, Kortrijk-Wevelgem, Liège and Ostend-Bruges.
[28] FOD Mobiliteit en Vervoer, 'Statistische gegevens van de luchthavens', available at <www.mobilit. belgium.be/nl/luchtvaart/luchthavens/statistieken/>, accessed 18 November 2014.
[29] The airports of Amsterdam, Rotterdam/The Hague, Eindhoven, Groningen and Maastricht.
[30] Centraal Bureau voor de Statistiek, 'Maandcijfers Nederlandse luchthavens van nationaal belang', available at <statline.cbs.nl/StatWeb/publication>, accessed 18 November 2014.
[31] Luxembourg Airport, 'Annual Report 2013', available at <http://www.lux-airport.lu/en/The-airport/News.51.html>, accessed 8 August 2014, 20.
[32] Steer Davies Gleave, 'Exploratory study on the application and possible revision of Regulation 261/2004—Final Report' (July 2012), available at <http://ec.europa.eu/transport/themes/ passengers/studies/doc/2012-07-exploratory-study-on-the-application-and-possible-revision-of-regulation-261-2004.pdf>.
[33] EUClaim, 'Onze service', available at <www.euclaim.nl/onze-service>, accessed 18 November 2014.

limitation period for actions and the powers of the NEB. A final short paragraph is dedicated to the NEB of Luxembourg.

B. Case Law

i. The Distinction Between Delay and Cancellation

In an early case involving several and, as will be shown, 'extraordinary' events dating from 9 January 2006, thus before the notorious *Sturgeon* and *Nelson* judgments by the CJEU, the Belgian NEB, the Directoraat Generaal Luchtvaart/Direction Générale Transport Aérien (DGTA), applied the provisions of Regulation 261 to the letter.[34] In this case, two Belgian citizens were waiting for their flight back to Belgium, having spent a week's holiday in Italy. One day before their flight was scheduled to depart, however, the aircraft that was supposed to operate was hit by a bird strike in Greece and was grounded for two days. As the airline had only a small number of aircraft at its disposal, its operations were disrupted. In order to be able to pick up the passengers waiting at two Italian airports, the operator planned to sublease an aircraft from another airline. Unfortunately, one of these airports then announced that it would be closed for the night for reasons of maintenance. Because of this closure, the operator of the replacement aircraft refused to carry out the flight, because it feared that its aircraft would be grounded overnight at the closed Italian airport. The passengers were brought back 13 hours late on the following day, on an aircraft operated by the Belgian airline under the original flight number. A claim was filed by two passengers with the DGTA. They claimed €400 each in compensation on the grounds that Regulation 261 provides that passengers are entitled to this compensation in respect of cancellation of flights of over 1,500 kilometres within the EU (in accordance with Articles 5(c) and 7(1)(b) of the Regulation). However, according to the airline, the event constituted a delay rather than a cancellation. It argued that Article 6(1)(c)(ii) of the Regulation includes in its definition of 'delay' circumstances in which 'the reasonably expected time of departure is at least the day after the time of departure previously announced', whereas Article 2(1) of the Regulation provides that 'cancellation' means 'the non-operation of a flight which was previously planned and on which at least one place was reserved'. From the airline's point of view, the planned flight had been provided and the passengers had only been entitled to assistance as described in Article 6(1) concerning delayed flights. According to the airline, the passengers had no further ground for complaint or further compensation, as this was not a case of denied boarding or cancellation, which are the only grounds for compensations as provided for in Article 7 of the Regulation. The passengers'

---

[34] Decision of the Directoraat Generaal Luchtvaart/Direction Générale Transport Aérien, referred to in International Law Office, 'Setback for Passengers Claiming Compensation for Delays', 8 March 2006, available at <www.internationallawoffice.com/newsletters/>, accessed 6 August 2014.

claim was rejected by the DGTA. According to the DGTA, both the bird strike and the closure of the Italian airport causing the cancellation of the sublease constituted extraordinary circumstances limiting or excluding the airline's obligations according to the Regulation.[35]

More recently the powers of the Belgian NEB have been contested successfully, as will be explained below.

ii. *'Extraordinary Circumstances'*

a. Weather

In a case that at first sight dealt with the issue of delay as opposed to cancellation, the Second District Court of Brussels ruled that there were extraordinary circumstances and dismissed the claim of the passenger.[36]

The passenger had booked a ticket for a journey with the airline, consisting of one stretch by high-speed train from Brussels to Paris, and then on by aircraft from Paris to Phnom Penh, Cambodia, via Ho Chi Minh City, Vietnam. Both stretches were scheduled to depart on 31 March 2012. When the passenger arrived that day at Brussels-South train station, he was informed by the airline that his flight from Paris to Phnom Penh would take place on the following day, 1 April. However, on 1 April the high-speed train did not have any seats available, so the passenger had to take the high-speed train to Paris on 31 March, spend the night there and fly on to Phnom Penh on 1 April. The airline held that the flight was delayed, whereas the passenger was of the opinion that the flight was cancelled, for which reason he sought €600 compensation in accordance with Article 5(1)(c) of Regulation 261—apart from reimbursement of some minor costs. The airline held that the flight was delayed by 24 hours, as a consequence of Typhoon Pakhar that was approaching Ho Chi Minh City. In its decision of 19 June 2013, the Brussels local court so ruled, so that a typhoon qualified as an 'extraordinary circumstance', relieving the air carrier of liability under Regulation 261. The claimant insisted that the flight was cancelled, and emphasised, first, that the airline should have proved that there were no alternatives available and that the airports of Hanoi and Phnohm Penh were closed because of weather conditions, and, secondly, that the phenomenon of a typhoon in South East Asia is a frequently occurring event and therefore inherent in the normal exercise of the activities of the airline.

Regarding the delay versus cancellation issue, the airline argued that it did not conduct daily flights from Paris to Phnom Penh via Ho Chi Minh City, and that the delayed flight did not coincide with an already scheduled flight on this route. The flight was therefore delayed and not cancelled. In its defence the airline further put forward that the rules laid down in *Sturgeon* and *Nelson* are contrary to the wording of the Regulation 261 itself, as well as contrary to the exclusivity of the

---

[35] ibid.
[36] Second District Court of Brussels, 19 June 2013, 12A1715.

Montreal Convention. In relation to a typhoon being an extraordinary circumstance, the airline pointed out that according to the definition used by the Royal Dutch Meteorological Institute, the season for typhoons in the south-western part of the northern Pacific Ocean normally lasts four to five months, from midsummer to the end of the autumn. The severity of Typhoon Pakhar was supported by data provided by NASA.[37]

In its ruling, the Brussels court first decided to address the argument regarding 'extraordinary circumstances' before going on to examine the question of delay versus cancellation, as resolution of the first point would make consideration of the latter superfluous. The Brussels court was of the opinion that the airline had sufficiently and convincingly proved exonerating extraordinary circumstances, consisting of the typhoon's approaching Ho Chi Ming City and Phnom Penh at the scheduled arrival time, for which reason the air carrier could not operate the flight as scheduled.[38] As a consequence, in this case the court ruled that the airline could not be held liable, and it rejected the passenger's claim.

b. Bird Strike

As an example classifying for this category, in the DGTA case discussed in section III.B.i. above, the bird strike that took place qualified as an extraordinary circumstance, leading the DGLV/DGTA court to reject the passengers' claim.[39]

iii. Other Cases

With regard to the relationship between Regulation 261 and the Montreal Convention, a judgment by the Court of Zaventem dating from 2010, on the limitation period for actions under Regulation 261, is relevant to the present discussion.[40] In this case the claimant sued TUI Airlines Belgium after having been denied boarding on a flight from Brussels to Cairo on 25 September 2008. Sixteen months later the writ of summons was served, that is on 29 January 2010. Therefore the question at issue was whether the applicable limitation period for bringing legal actions was governed by the Montreal Convention or by national Belgian law. The claimant relied on Article 35 of the Montreal Convention, stating that 'the right to damages shall be extinguished if an action is not brought within a period of two years'. The airline, however, argued that domestic Belgian law was applicable, which provided for a one-year limitation period. The court rejected the claim and

---

[37] ibid.

[38] International Law Office, 'Delayed flights: typhoon constitutes extraordinary circumstance', 24 July 2013, available at <www.internationallawoffice.com/newsletters/>, accessed 6 August 2014.

[39] International Law Office, 'Setback for Passengers Claiming Compensation for Delays', 8 March 2006, available at <www.internationallawoffice.com/newsletters/>, accessed 6 August 2014.

[40] International Law Office, 'Court rules on limitation period for actions under EU Denied Boarding Regulation', 1 December 2010, available at <www.internationallawoffice.com/newsletters/>. accessed 7 August 2014.

ruled that the Belgian law was applicable, on the basis that, as compensation was being claimed under the scheme set out in Regulation 261, the limitation period under the Montreal Convention was not applicable.[41]

C. Remedies

i. Belgium

In the event of airlines' non-compliance with the passenger rights laid down in Regulation 261, the passenger first needs to address his complaint to the airline involved. If the airline does not answer within a reasonable period of time, that is three to four weeks, or if the answer is not to the liking of the passenger, the passenger can then go to the National Enforcement Body, the DGTA, which will investigate the complaint. A digital complaint form is available on the DGTA's website.[42]

However, the Belgian Council of State (Raad van State/Conseil d'Etat) (RvS), the highest administrative court in Belgium, ruled on 3 June 2014[43] that the decisions of the Belgian NEB 'are not binding' and 'do not produce any legal effect'.[44] In this case, 'the Belgian [NEB] decided, in a formal and final notification sent to the carrier, that the carrier had to pay compensation to the passengers in question', and that otherwise criminal sanctions would be imposed. The carrier challenged this decision of the NEB before the RvS, which has the authority to judge the validity of decisions taken by the Belgian administration.[45]

The challenge of the decision by the Belgian NEB must be seen in connection with the apparent uncertainty regarding the powers of NEBs as provided for under Article 16(1) of Regulation 261. Article 16(1) provides:

> Each Member State shall designate a body responsible for the enforcement of this Regulation as regards flights from airports situated on its territory and flights from a third country to such airports. Where appropriate, this body shall take the measures necessary to ensure that the rights of passengers are respected. The Member States shall inform the Commission of the body that has been designated in accordance with this paragraph.

In its decision, however, the RvS considered that:

(1)   it is not up to an administrative authority itself to pronounce legally on the conditions under which compensation is due from a private person

---

[41]   ibid.

[42]   FOD Mobiliteit en Vervoer, available at <www.mobilit.belgium.be/nl/luchtvaart/passagiers/klachten/>, accessed 31 July 2014.

[43]   Arrêt no 227.621, 206.347/XV-2048, 3 June 2014.

[44]   Kennedy's Law LLP, 'Belgian Council of State rules that administrative decisions relating to air passengers' rights in case of delays and cancellations are without any legal effect', 20 June 2014, available at <www.kennedys-law.com/article/aipassengers>, accessed 7 August 2014.

[45]   ibid.

(the air carrier) to another private person, and that there is no such law that allows the NEB to do so;

(2)   the refusal of the carrier to comply with the decision of the NEB may not be considered *ipso facto* a violation of its obligations under the Regulation;

(3)   the Regulation does not define the nature of the powers that have to be conferred on the authority charged with its application, as long as it takes 'the measures necessary to ensure that the rights of passengers are respected'. These measures do not necessarily include the powers to decide whether passenger rights have been infringed in a specific case and to require air carriers to pay compensation;

(4)   the decision of the NEB does not have binding force but rather constitutes an opinion, which does not produce legal effects; and

(5)   judicial courts are not bound by the decisions of the NEB, which are merely of an indicative nature.[46]

Leaving aside the consequences of this ruling, with regard to court proceedings, passengers can bring a claim to the relevant court, which in Belgium is, first, the Justice of the Peace Court (Vredegerecht/Justice de Paix) and, secondly, the Court of First Instance (Rechtbank van Eerste Aanleg/Tribunal de Première Instance).

ii. Luxembourg

In Luxembourg, the NEB is the Ministry of Economic Affairs and Foreign Trade (Ministère de l'Economie et du Commerce extérieur; Direction du Marché intérieur et de la consummation).[47] According to the Luxembourg NEB, a passenger can seek recourse if the airline has not responded to the complaint within six weeks, or, as in Belgium, if the response is not to the satisfaction of the passenger.[48] According to the domestic law in Luxembourg, Article L.311-9 of the Code de la consummation,[49] its NEB can impose sanctions on airlines.[50]

D. In Conclusion

The low availability of published cases in Belgium—in comparison to the Netherlands—may be due to two things: (i) the policy of not making cases public; and (ii) the smaller amount of air traffic.

---

[46] Arrêt no 227.621, 206.347/XV-2048, 3 June 2014.

[47] Commission, 'Complaint handling and enforcement by Member States of the Air Passenger Rights Regulations' (Commission Staff Working Document) SWD (2014) 156 final, 27, 29.

[48] Le Gouvernement du Grande Duché, 'Les Droits des passagers aériens: Règlement 261/2004', available at <www.eco.public.lu/attributions/dg2/d_consommation/protection_consomateurs/>, accessed 8 August 2014.

[49] Service Central de Legislation Luxembourg, 'Code de la Consommation', available at <www.legilux. public.lu/leg/textescoordonnes/codes/Code_de_la_Consommation/Code_de_la_Consommation. pdf>, accessed 8 August 2014.

[50] Arrêt no 227.621, 206.347/XV-2048, 3 June 2014.

We have found that before the *Sturgeon* and *Nelson* rulings, Regulation 261 had been interpreted according to the letter. Furthermore, judicial decisions show a reasonable application of the 'extraordinary circumstances' exception.

With regard to the ruling on the powers of the Belgian NEB, it will be interesting to see whether this will lead to an increase in the number of court cases.

IV. Conclusions

While a substantial number of court cases on Regulation 261 have been tried in the Netherlands, the number of published cases in Belgium is much lower.

Before the *Sturgeon* and *Nelson* rulings, courts in both states relied on the distinction between delay and cancellation provided by Regulation 261, meaning that they did not consider flights that had been delayed for more than three hours to be cancelled flights. That changed after the publication of the decisions in *Sturgeon* and *Nelson*.

The concept of 'extraordinary circumstances' has been one of the core issues with which judges in both jurisdictions have had to deal. In April 2014, the District Court of Amsterdam addressed a number of well-reasoned questions to the Court in Luxembourg on the scope of the term 'extraordinary circumstances' as employed in the *Wallentin-Hermann* decision. As explained above, the Court in Luxembourg sticked with its very narrow interpretation of this defence which is available for air carriers under Regulation 261.

Since the special procedures were abolished in 2012, Dutch claimants have to resort to regular court proceedings in order to obtain compensation. While in the Netherlands court proceedings have been brought rather frequently, this seems not to have been so in Belgium. However, the ruling of the Council of State of 3 June 2014, denying the legal force of decisions made by the Belgian NEB, might lead to an increase in court cases.

9

Bulgaria: Blurred Lines

ALEXANDER KORNEZOV

I. Introduction

The implementation of Regulation 261 in Bulgaria has been the source of much confusion due to inadequate national legislation, laissez-faire administrative practice and inconsistent case law. This has led to a situation where most passengers turn to alternative dispute resolution mechanisms and rarely take their cases to court. The state has clearly taken a non-interventionist stance in the context of enforcing air passenger rights, leaving the matter mostly to extrajudicial mediation.

This status quo has resulted from the combination of several factors. First, the national legislator has failed to adequately implement Article 16 of Regulation 261. This has left behind an ambiguous legal framework, in which neither the prerogatives of the NEB nor the legal remedies available to passengers have been clearly spelled out. Secondly, the NEB has itself failed to clarify the situation: it seems to have been pursuing a laissez-faire policy by refusing to adopt binding decisions or to impose fines for non-compliance with Regulation 261. Moreover, there is hardly any publicly accessible information about its workings. None of its decisions or recommendations are published, and there are no guidelines explaining its prerogatives and the applicable procedures.[1] Thirdly, there has been a great deal of uncertainty as to the legal remedies available to passengers, fuelled both by the lack of specific rules to that effect in the domestic law and by the incoherent case law of the courts.

The discussion that follows will examine in turn the major obstacles to the effective enforcement of air passenger rights in Bulgaria. First, the role of the NEB will be extensively discussed, given the many ambiguities surrounding its prerogatives and practice. Secondly, the jurisdiction of national courts to hear claims based on the Regulation will be examined in the light of an ongoing debate about whether

---

[1] The only relevant information that is publicly available is a standardised on-line form to be filled in by the passenger and then sent to the NEB. There is, however, no indication as to the type of act by which the NEB will respond to the complaint, its legal force and the legal remedies available to the passenger.

such claims should be heard by the civil or the administrative courts. Thirdly, the available case law of the domestic courts will be analysed in an attempt to identify the potential problem areas where frictions between national and EU law may occur. Fourthly, the question of sanctions will be critically addressed in the light of the applicable legal framework. Lastly, the discussion will be concluded with an overall assessment of the combined impact of the identified obstacles to the enforcement of air passenger rights in Bulgaria.

II. First Layer of Blurred Lines: The National Enforcement Body

There is much ambiguity and uncertainty about the actual powers that have been entrusted to the Bulgarian NEB for the purpose of enforcing Regulation 261. The main reason for the present lack of clarity can be found, on the one hand, in the failure of the national legislator to implement Article 16 of the Regulation in a meaningful way and, on the other hand, in the failure of the NEB to assume a more proactive stance and to clarify the scope of its own powers.

The inability, or the unwillingness, of the national legislator to implement Article 16 of Regulation 261 in a way that clearly spells out the rules of the game, is striking. It is certainly true that Article 16 is no example of lucidity itself. Yet the national legislator could have bridged most of the gaps had it made the effort to set up an orderly national enforcement mechanism, in which every stakeholder knows its place.

The Bulgarian legislator has unfortunately made no such effort. Its intervention has been limited, in essence, to designating the national body that would be responsible for enforcing the Regulation. To that effect, in 2006 the Minister of Transport adopted Order No 261, which practically copies the Regulation verbatim, thus 'transposing' it into national law.[2] Its only added value consists of designating the General Directorate 'Civil Aviation Administration' of the Ministry of Transport as the NEB, and of vesting it, for the purpose of enforcing the Order, with the prerogatives laid down in Article 16b(1)(3) and in sections 2 to 5 of the Civil Aviation Act (Zakon za grajdanskoto vazduhoplavane) (ZGV Act).

According to these provisions, the NEB has the power to:

(1) issue 'binding instructions' for the purpose of enforcing compliance with the ZGV Act and with the relevant bylaws;[3]
(2) access all documents directly or indirectly relevant in the context of compliance with, inter alia, Regulation 261;[4]

---

[2] Oddly, Order No 261 was not formally abolished following Bulgaria's accession to the EU in 2007, but should probably be regarded as having been superseded by Regulation 261 as of 1 January 2007.
[3] ZGV Act, Art 16b(1)(3).
[4] ZGV Act, Art 16b(3)(2).

(3)   issue 'written statements of fact' that conclude the investigations carried out by the Directorate;[5] and

(4)   impose administrative sanctions.[6]

Crucially, however, the ZGV Act does not specify what kind of act the NEB is empowered to adopt following the submission of an individual claim under Regulation 261. While it is obvious that the NEB can require access to the relevant documents held by the airline in the context of such claims, it is unclear by what type of act it is supposed to conclude the enquiry, that is, whether by 'binding instructions' or by 'written statements of fact'. This is crucial, because the so-called binding instructions are obviously binding on the airline, which could then try to have them annulled by a court. By contrast, the legal nature of the so-called 'written statements of fact' is unclear. In particular, there is no guidance in the law and in the case law as to the legal nature of these statements—are they simple 'statements' deprived of legal force, do they nonetheless produce certain legal effects and are they amenable to judicial review?

The practice of the NEB adds further to the confusion. Instead of exercising the power it has been vested with for the purpose of enforcing Regulation 261 and clarifying the scope of application of each of its prerogatives, the NEB has taken a hands-off approach. It has made use neither of its power to issue 'binding instructions' nor 'written statements of fact'. Instead, it decided to reply to claims under Regulation 261 by simple 'letters' devoid of legal force.[7] Moreover, it is unclear whether such 'letters' can be relied upon by the passenger in a subsequent court proceeding, or what their evidential status is.

The above observation is confirmed by the total absence of case law of Bulgaria's administrative courts on the matter. This seems to indicate that the NEB has indeed never adopted a binding decision in the context of a claim under Regulation 261 that would then be amenable to judicial review. It thus appears that the NEB intervenes in claims under Regulation 261 as a sort of mediator, rather than as an 'enforcement' body *stricto sensu*.

The reasons behind the NEB's hands-off policy are also unclear. As mentioned above, it has been explicitly empowered with certain prerogatives for the purpose of enforcing the Regulation. The law does not therefore preclude the NEB from adopting binding decisions addressed to the airlines, for instance ordering them to pay compensation to a passenger. Rather, it seems that the NEB has made the choice to make no use of this prerogative, preferring to act simply as a mediator. Whether this choice is the result of a political decision or of simple administrative laissez-faire is also unclear.

---

[5] ZGV Act, Art 16b(4).

[6] ZGV Act, Art 16b(5).

[7] As mentioned above, there is no publicly available information with regard to the acts adopted by the NEB in the context of the Regulation. Despite our repeated requests for information, the NEB has not replied to any of them. The observations concerning the practice of the NEB in the present chapter are thus deduced from the case law of the national courts, as well as from the wording of the applicable national law.

It is equally unclear whether the NEB has ruled out the possibility of issuing binding instructions altogether, or whether it would nonetheless be prepared to do so in certain circumstances, for instance in cases of serious or systemic breaches of the Regulation. While this would be a perfectly defendable choice, there is no evidence that such a choice has ever been made. The lack of court cases, where such binding instructions have been challenged, strongly suggests that the NEB has actually never issued such instructions.

It thus appears that the passenger can either bring his or her claim directly to a court, or, alternatively, opt for one of the alternative dispute resolution bodies, such as the NEB or the European Consumer Centres' Network (ECC-Net). For example, the NEB handled 169 complaints in 2012, which was much higher than the number of complaints lodged in 2007–09.[8] There are no available data about how many of these complaints were resolved in favour of the passenger, although one source indicates that this was the case as regards about a third of all complaints in 2008–09.[9] A comparable number of complaints have also been brought to the attention of the ECC-Net.[10] In addition, the available data show that 53 per cent of the complaints brought to the NEB in 2012 concerned delay, 14 per cent cancellation, 8 per cent denied boarding and 42 per cent 'other'.[11] By contrast, the number of court cases, as explained below, has been low.

III. Second Layer of Blurred Lines: Which Court has Jurisdiction?

The confusion and uncertainties surrounding the actual powers of the NEB in the context of Regulation 261 have reflected upon the courts as well. In particular, there have been divergent views on one of the crucial questions that underpin the implementation of the Regulation at the national level, namely whether claims should be brought before the administrative or the civil courts.

The Regulation has left the matter to the Member States in accordance with the principle of national procedural autonomy. In the absence of any specific indication as to the applicable legal remedy in Bulgarian law, the answer to the query will depend on how the powers of the NEB are actually construed. If the latter is to

---

[8] Commission, 'Complaint handling and enforcement by Member States of the Air Passenger Rights Regulations' (Staff Working Document) SWD (2014) 156 final.

[9] Steer Davies Gleave, 'Evaluation of Regulation 261/2004' final (February 2010), available at <http://ec.europa.eu/transport/themes/passengers/studies/doc/2010_02_evaluation_of_regulation_2612004.pdf>.

[10] eg According to The European Consumer Centres' Network's 'ECC-Net Air Passenger Rights Report 2011', 115 complaints were lodged in 2010 (<http://ec.europa.eu/consumers/ecc/docs/ecc_net_air_passenger_report_2011.pdf>).

[11] Commission (n 8).

adopt binding decisions, then these should be amenable to judicial review by the administrative courts. Conversely, if it has no such powers, then claims should be brought before the civil courts.

Crucially, however, the crux of the problem goes far beyond the banality of determining which court has jurisdiction. Indeed, the fundamental principles of Bulgarian administrative and civil procedural law are resolutely different. In substance, in civil procedural law the court is a passive adjudicator in an adversarial process, where the applicant (the passenger) bears the burden of proving his or her claim. By contrast, in administrative procedural law the court plays a much more interventionist role, being required to act on its own motion most of the time.

The argument that administrative courts should have jurisdiction to adjudge claims under Regulation 261 has strong proponents. When interviewed, a number of judges at the Varhoven administrativen sad (Supreme Administrative Court) argued that air passenger rights have been subject to regulation by the EU. In their view, this is therefore a regulatory, not a contractual, matter. Indeed, the obligation and the amount of compensation have been imposed upon the airline by means of a legislative instrument, not by private contract. They therefore consider that an administrative body, such as the NEB, should be responsible for enforcing the regulatory measure in question, and that, consequently, its decisions should be amenable to judicial review by the administrative courts.[12]

However, the administrative courts have never had occasion to assert their jurisdiction in claims under Regulation 261: no case has ever been brought before them. This is explained by the fact that, as described above, the NEB seems never to have adopted a binding decision in reply to a claim under Regulation 261. The NEB's hands-off approach has thus deprived the administrative courts of jurisdiction.

The resulting vacuum has led Bulgaria's civil courts to fill in the gap by assuming jurisdiction in claims under Regulation 261, regardless of whether the NEB had been seized with the matter beforehand or not.[13] Nevertheless, their case law has been scarce and fragmentary, and has fuelled even more confusion, as explained further below.

It could thus be concluded that, as matters stand today, a claim under Regulation 261 should be brought before a civil court. This conclusion is, however, far from self-evident or final. It is based on time-consuming and particularly frustrating research, exacerbated by the lack of any clear guidance in the law and practice. This is in itself a major deterrent for passengers who wish to enforce their rights.

---

[12] The right to claim 'further' compensation under Art 12 of Regulation 261 is, however, not 'regulated' by the state or the EU and is therefore clearly a matter of civil law. The logical consequence of this argument would therefore be that, in practice, a passenger should first sue for the 'regulatory' compensation before administrative courts and then sue for 'further compensation' before civil courts. While from a legal point of view this is perfectly feasible, having to instigate two consecutive proceedings might be a major deterrent for passengers.

[13] In Judgment no I-25-206 from 24 October 2013 in case no 19467/2012 of Sofiiski rayonen sad, the passenger, after receiving a letter from the NEB stating that he had no right to compensation, successfully brought a claim before the civil courts.

Moreover, this conclusion might radically change, if the NEB were to assume a more assertive role by starting to adopt binding decisions in the context of Regulation 261. Indeed, this would automatically result in a shift of jurisdiction from the civil to the administrative courts.

IV. Third Layer of Blurred Lines: Legal Basis, Evidence and Limitation Periods

Even though the body of case law on claims under Regulation 261 is relatively small, a number of problems have already emerged. The main difficulty seems to be associated with determining the legal basis of a claim under Regulation 261. This is crucial, because it might potentially have far-reaching consequences in terms of evidence and the applicable prescription periods, the rules on which differ depending on the legal basis of the claim.

With regard, first, to the legal basis of a claim under Regulation 261, three approaches can be identified in the existing case law, namely:

(1)   Regulation 261 is itself the legal basis of such claims;
(2)   the legal basis is one of the provisions on contractual liability laid down in Bulgarian civil law; and
(3)   the legal basis is one of the provisions on tort liability as defined in Bulgarian civil law.

It is thus evident that civil courts have divergent views on what the legal basis of a claim under Regulation 261 should be. At first sight, it might seem odd that Bulgarian civil courts ever had any doubts as to the legal basis of such claims, since it must be fairly obvious that their legal basis ought to be Regulation 261 itself: there is hardly any doubt that the Regulation confers directly effective rights on passengers which can be enforced before the courts. But this does not necessarily resolve all the relevant issues that might arise in the context of such claims. Indeed, Regulation 261 leaves behind a number of issues that have to be addressed at the national level. For instance, it says nothing about limitation periods. Moreover, it allows room for 'further compensation' (Article 12 of the Regulation), which can be sought on the basis of national and international law. Against this background, the fact that Bulgarian civil courts have identified three potentially relevant legal bases, two of which have been derived from national law, might seem somewhat more comprehensible. The following examples illustrate this.

The case of *MV v Bulgaria Air* is an excellent example.[14] The claimant sought damages on the basis of Article 7 of Regulation 261 for a delay of eight and a

---

[14] *MV v Bulgaria Air*, Judgment no I-043 from 13 August 2012 in case no 47602/2011 of Sofiiski rayonen sad; on appeal, see judgment no 539 from 23 January 2014 in case no 6737/2013 of Sofiiski gradski sad.

half hours, plus interest. Sofiiski rayonen sad (Sofia municipal court, hereinafter 'SRS') and, on appeal, Sofiiski gradski sad (Sofia City Court) (SGS) held, first, that the legal basis of the claim was to be found in Article 7 of the Regulation, as far as the amount of compensation fixed thereby was claimed. They then added that, in accordance with the CJEU's judgment in *Sturgeon*[15]—to which they adhered uncritically and without further ado—a flight delayed by eight and a half hours should be equated to a cancelled flight. Both SRS and SGS therefore upheld the claim based on Article 7 of the Regulation. Secondly, with regard to the award of interest, both courts considered that this branch of the claim was brought not under the Regulation but under Bulgarian civil law. The interest rate was calculated as provided for under Articles 84 and 86 of the Obligations and Contracts Act (Zakon za zaduljeniata i dogovorite, hereinafter 'ZZD Act') for the period from the date of lodging the complaint with the airline until the date of delivering the judgment.

The SRS and SGS thus practically 'severed' the claim into two sub-claims, the first being based on EU law and the second on national contract law. This solution seems perfectly in line with Article 12 of the Regulation.

By contrast, in *RD v Wizz Air*, the claimant did not obtain the compensation to which she was entitled under Regulation 261.[16] In this case, the flight was cancelled due to a technical problem. Wizz Air then offered either to reimburse the price of the ticket plus 20 per cent of that price, or to re-route the passenger to her desired destination the following week. The passenger chose the first option, and then bought a ticket from another airline for a flight departing the following day. Later the passenger brought a case before the civil courts claiming the difference between the sum of money she had received from Wizz Air and the price of the ticket she had subsequently bought. That difference amounted to around €200. The SRS held that the legal basis of the claim was not the Regulation but rather Article 79 of the ZZD Act, which lays down rules on contractual liability. Although the court did not give further reasons for this conclusion, one may speculate that the reason behind it was the amount of damages claimed by the passenger. The latter could have indeed claimed the amount of compensation to which she was entitled under the Regulation—which would have been up to €400 under Article 7 of the Regulation[17]—but she chose a lower amount that offset the difference between the compensation already received by the airline and the price of the subsequently bought ticket. This seems to have led the SRS to conclude that the claim was brought under national law. In order to justify this result, the court referred to Article 12 of the Regulation, which it interpreted as meaning that compensation could be sought either under EU law or under national law. It seems, however, that the court misinterpreted this provision of the Regulation, given that

---

[15] Cases C-402 and 432/07 *Sturgeon and Others* [2009] ECR I-10923.

[16] *RD v Wizz Air*, Judgment no I-25-206 from 24 October 2013 in case no 19467/2012 of Sofiiski rayonen sad.

[17] The cancelled flight was longer than 1,500 km.

the latter allows the award of 'further' compensation, not 'smaller' compensation than provided for under the Regulation.

The judgment in *RD v Wizz Air* raises a number of further queries. In Bulgarian civil law, the courts are bound by the claim, in the sense that they cannot award something they have not been asked for.[18] In cases such as the one under discussion, where the passenger asked for less than she was entitled to under EU law—most probably because she was unaware of her EU rights—it is crucial to know whether the civil courts can go beyond the limits of the passenger's claim and award higher compensation, as provided for under the Regulation. Although this matter was not discussed in the aforementioned judgment, the SRS seemed to consider that its jurisdiction was limited to the scope of the claim brought before it. It may be argued, however, that EU law requires national courts to act on their own motion in the area of consumer protection and apply the Regulation *ex officio*. In *Rodriguez*, the CJEU emphasised that 'there is nothing in Regulation No 261/2004 that precludes the award of compensation in respect of a failure to fulfil the obligations provided for by Article 8 and Article 9 therein, if those provisions are not invoked by the air passengers'.[19] Furthermore, in *Océano Groupo*, the Court had held that national courts should in some cases apply *ex officio* the relevant EU rules on consumer protection.[20]

The third scenario that can be detected in the case law concerns the enforcement of the right to care, guaranteed by Article 9 of Regulation 261. One case worth mentioning involved a delayed flight, where the passengers were not offered any of the care to which they were entitled under Article 9. Some of the passengers then brought a claim before the SRS, which awarded them compensation of around €300 as immaterial damages for the discomfort caused, plus interest.[21] The judgment was then confirmed on appeal by the SGS.[22] There are at least two important aspects in these judgments. The first one concerns the legal basis of the claim, which, according to the SRS and SGS, was identified as the relevant national rules on tort liability.[23] The second conclusion that seems to stem from these judgments relates to the fact that both courts awarded the claimants a lump sum in order to compensate their immaterial damage. The passengers were thus not required to prove the precise amount of the financial loss they had suffered due to the breach of the right to care (in the form of receipts or similar documents), but rather were compensated for their discomfort *ex aequo et bono*. The Varhoven kasatsionen sad (the Supreme Court of Cassation) found no manifest breach of the law in the appellate judgment and refused to allow the appeal on cassation.[24]

---

[18] Grajdanskoprotsesualen kodeks, Art 6(2) (Civil Code of Procedure).

[19] Case C-83/10 *Rodríguez v Air France SA* [2011] ECR I-9469, para 45.

[20] Cases C-240, C-241, C-242, C-243 and C-244/98 *Océano Grupo Editorial SA v Quintero* [2000] ECR I-4941.

[21] *V B-S and others*, Judgment in case no 11294/2008 of Sofiiski rayonen sad.

[22] Judgment no 2682 from 10 June 2010 in case no 12460/2009 of Sofiiski gradski sad.

[23] ZZD Act, Arts 45, 49.

[24] Order no 1179 of 20 September 2011 in case no 1720/2010 of Varhoven kasatsionen sad.

Although it seems difficult to draw general conclusions from the fragmentary case law of Bulgarian civil courts, it can be assumed that, according to the latter, the legal basis of the claims for compensation due to delay or cancellation is either the Regulation itself, or the relevant national rules on contractual liability or a combination of both. In a nutshell, if the applicant claims the amount of compensation fixed by the Regulation, the legal basis of his claim will most probably be held to be that same Regulation. If he claims 'further' compensation (for example, in the guise of interest), the legal basis of that claim would be the national rules on contractual liability. That would also be the case if the passenger claims an amount of compensation lower than the one fixed in the Regulation. By contrast, Bulgarian courts seem to assume that the legal basis of the claims for compensation for breach of the right to care is the relevant national rule on tort liability. This could probably be explained by the lack of a fixed amount of compensation to that effect in the Regulation.

The co-existence of three different legal bases, all of which have been found applicable in different hypotheses related to Regulation 261, might cause a number of spill-over problems in adjacent areas of the applicable law. For example, the rules on evidence and on limitation periods vary depending on the legal basis of the claim.

For example, in Bulgarian civil law, a person will be held liable for breach of contract or in tort, only if he acted 'guiltily'.[25] In theory, therefore, if an airline manages to show that it had acted without guilt, it would be able to avoid liability. It is fairly obvious that the notion of 'guilt' is not necessarily the same as the concept of 'extraordinary circumstances' in the sense of Article 5(3) of the Regulation, as interpreted by the CJEU. This discrepancy could potentially result in a situation where an airline avoids liability in circumstances that would not qualify as 'extraordinary circumstances' under EU law but would be construed as innocent behaviour under national law.

Luckily, Bulgarian civil courts seem to have sensed this danger. They managed, through a creative interpretation of national law, to accommodate both worlds by interpreting the notion of 'guilt' in the light of the CJEU's judgment in *Wallentin-Hermann v Alitalia*.[26] In substance, they concluded that by failing to prevent or to fix in due time the technical problems affecting the aircraft, the airline had acted 'guiltily' and was, therefore, liable for the damage caused by the delay or the cancellation.[27] Thus, in practice, and regardless of the retained legal basis of the claim, Bulgarian courts have dealt with the extraordinary circumstances defence in compliance with the CJEU's case law.

---

[25] ZZD Act, Arts 45, 81.
[26] Case C-549/07 *Wallentin-Hermann v Alitalia* [2008] ECR I-11061.
[27] eg *RD v Wizz Air*, Judgment no I-25-206 of 24 October 2013 in case no 19467/2012 of Sofiiski rayonen sad.

In another case, which concerned the right to care, the airline sought to avoid responsibility by invoking the occurrence of bad weather conditions. In its view, these amounted to 'extraordinary circumstances' that exonerated it from the duty to provide care and assistance to the passengers. The courts, however, rejected the defence as irrelevant, stating that airlines could not rely upon the 'extraordinary circumstances' exception in 'right to care' cases because airlines are under an obligation to provide care for their passengers, regardless of the cause of the delay or the cancellation of the flight.[28]

The co-existence of different legal bases described above might also cause confusion with regard to the applicable limitation periods. On the one hand, the ZGV Act provides for special limitation periods, but the wording of the relevant provisions reveals that these seem to apply only to delays in delivering 'luggage or freight' or causing damage to the latter. In the case of damage, the passenger should file his complaint with the airline within seven days of receiving the luggage or 14 days of receiving the freight, whereas in the case of delays, the deadline is 21 days.[29] The airline then has two months to reply to the complaint.[30] If the passenger is not satisfied with the airline's response, he can then bring a case before a civil court, within two years in the case of international flights and within six months in the case of domestic flights.[31] There is, however, no guidance in the case law or elsewhere as to whether these time limits and limitation periods should apply by analogy to claims under Regulation 261.

If the limitation periods laid down in the ZGV Act are not applicable to claims under Regulation 261, then the ordinary limitation periods, as defined in Bulgarian civil law, should apply. This is also source of uncertainty, however, because the general limitation period is five years[32] but there is also a shorter three-year limitation period for 'claims arising from damages … from non-performed contracts'.[33] Thus, if the compensation due under the Regulation is to be considered compensation for breach of contract, the shorter three-year period should apply. Conversely, if it is to be considered as *a sui generis* right to compensation, stemming directly from Regulation 261, the longer five-year limitation period should apply. The latter should also apply to claims for compensation presented as tort liability, such as those based on a breach of the right to care, as outlined above.

Despite these difficulties, no requests for preliminary rulings have been made, nor did the courts examine such a possibility on their own motion.

---

[28] eg *V B-S and others*, Judgment in case no 11294/2008 of Sofiiski rayonen sad; Judgment no 2682 of 10 June 2010 in case no 12460/2009 of Sofiiski gradski sad; Order no 1179 of 20 September 2011 in case no 1720/2010 of Varhoven kasatsionen sad.

[29] ZGV Act, Art 127.

[30] ZGV Act, Art 133.

[31] ZGV Act, Art 135.

[32] ZZD Act, Art 110.

[33] ZZD Act, Art 111.

V. Fourth Layer of Blurred Lines: Sanctions

Although the applicable national law empowers the NEB to impose sanctions for breaches of the Regulation, it remains particularly ambiguous in this regard. While the legislator has dedicated nine particularly long, detailed and circumstantial articles to this matter, underpinned by a myriad of paragraphs and subparagraphs, which draw up with precision an impressive list of possible violations of the law and the applicable sanctions, strangely, violations of Regulation 261 have been left out of that list. The only indirect referral to the Regulation can be deduced from Article 147b of the ZGV Act,[34] which provides that a failure to grant access to the relevant documentation for the purpose of enforcing the Regulation is liable to a fine from 250 to 1,000 BGN (approximately €125 to €500) for the person responsible for the failure, and from 500 to 2,000 BGN (approximately €250 to €1,000) for the airline.

This contrasts with the way the ZGV Act deals with violations of Regulation 1107/2006, which concerns the rights of disabled persons.[35] Article 143(5) of the ZGV Act enumerates nine different breaches of that Regulation and provides for specific sanctions for each one of them, with fines ranging from 2,000 to 10,000 BGN (approximately €1,000 to €5,000). The contrast is difficult to explain. It raises a number of queries.

First, the national law is unclear as to whether a breach of Regulation 261, other than the failure to provide the relevant documentation mentioned in Article 147b of the ZGV Act, should attract a fine at all. In the absence of specific provisions to that end, it might be argued that Article 147 of the Act applies. The latter provision announces that, where no specific sanction is provided for a given breach of the ZGV Act, that breach should be subject to a fine of 100 to 500 BGN (approximately €50 to €250).

Secondly, it is unclear whether all sorts of breaches of Regulation 261 or only some of them should attract a fine, and whether the amount should vary in accordance with the type of the breach (failure to pay compensation, breach of the right to care or of the right of information, etc). In addition, it is unclear whether individual instances of non-compliance or only systemic and serious non-compliance should attract a fine.

Thirdly, and regardless of the foregoing, it is doubtful whether the above-mentioned levels of fine are dissuasive, as required by Article 16(3) of Regulation 261. A fine of €50 to €250, or of €250 to €1,000 (for failures to provide documentation to the NEB), is—objectively—insignificant for an airline. Such amounts are also considerably lower than those that can be imposed for

---

[34] This provision refers to Art 16b(3)(3) of the ZGV Act, which in its turn refers to Art 16b(2), which grants the NEB the right to access the relevant documents held by airlines in the context of Regulation 261.

[35] European Parliament and Council Regulation (EC) 1107/2006 of 5 July 2006 concerning the rights of disabled persons and persons with reduced mobility when travelling by air [2006] OJ L204/1.

other types of breaches of the ZGV Act. These range from 1,000 to 10,000 BGN (approximately €500 to €5,000),[36] and even up to 13,000 BGN (approximately €6,500) for repetitive infringements.[37] As mentioned above, the various violations of Regulation 1107/2006 are punishable by fines ranging from 2,000 to 10,000 BGN (approximately €1,000 to €5,000).

Fourthly, no evidence has been found that the NEB has actually ever imposed sanctions for breaches of Regulation 261.[38] This is hardly surprising in the light of the NEB's overall laissez-faire attitude.

VI. Conclusion: A Muddle of Blurred Lines

The combined impact of the ambiguities of national law and practice described above has led to a situation clearly detrimental to the passenger. On the one hand, the NEB refuses to adopt binding decisions in response to claims under Regulation 261, although in principle national law empowers it to do so. It has also so far abstained from imposing sanctions for breaches of Regulation 261. On the other hand, the case law of national courts has been all but coherent, in particular with regard to the legal basis of such claims.

The blame for this mass of ambiguities lies, first of all, with the national legislator. It seems that he has been misled by the fact that the EU instrument in question is a 'regulation', which does not in principle require transposition. It thus failed to put flesh onto the bones of Article 16 of the Regulation. It failed, in particular, to spell out clearly the prerogatives of the NEB in the context of the Regulation. It also failed to define the legal remedies that are available to a passenger.

Secondly, the blame also lies with the NEB, which has failed to take a more proactive stance in the context of enforcement of the Regulation. As discussed above, the ambiguities of the applicable national law certainly allow sufficient room for a more assertive NEB. It could have, for example, published guidelines explaining how it envisages enforcing the Regulation. It could also have published at least some of its decisions (or 'letters') on the matter.

But the blame also lies with the EU institutions. On the one hand, the EU legislator drafted Article 16 in a particularly lax fashion, leaving unanswered a number of crucial issues. The ball was thus thrown back to the national legislator, who was supposed to fill in the gaps. On the other hand, the European Commission never really insisted on a clear set of national rules implementing Article 16. There is

---

[36] ZGV Act, Arts 143–144.

[37] ZGV Act, Art 146.

[38] Given that the NEB does not publish any of its decisions, this conclusion is based on the fact that, to our knowledge, no action for annulment of a decision imposing a fine for breaching the Regulation has ever been brought before a court. This strongly suggests that no fines have ever been imposed, unless the airlines have actually never breached the Regulation or, conversely, have always happily paid their fines without further ado.

indeed no evidence that the European Commission has ever initiated infringement proceedings for failure to implement Article 16.

Bulgarian academia, for its part, has not addressed the problem either. First, there has not really been a long-standing scholarly tradition in the area of aviation and transport law, although more recently some general studies have appeared.[39] Regulation 261 has attracted the attention of part of academia over the past few years, with some general overviews appearing in legal journals.[40] Emphasis has been put on the extensive interpretation of the notion of 'cancellation'[41] and the distinction, stemming from Article 12 of the Regulation and the case law, between damages sought on the basis of the Regulation and those sought on the basis of national law and/or the Montreal Convention.[42] Certain aspects of EU aviation law have been also subject to criticism with regard, in particular, to the CJEU's judgment in *Air Transport Association of America v Secretary of State for Energy and Climate Change*.[43] But the implementation of Regulation 261 in Bulgaria has never been the subject of scholarly analysis.

The unfortunate result of this whole set of circumstances clearly disadvantages the passenger. In practice, he would most often turn to the NEB or to another mediator, hoping for a positive outcome. But if the airline refuses to pay, or simply does not co-operate, the best the passenger can hope for is a 'letter' stating that he is entitled to compensation. His only option in such circumstances would be going to court. But given the costs, the formalities and the delays associated with most court proceedings, as well as the relatively small amounts of compensation at stake, few passengers would actually bother to make the effort. This is confirmed by the low number of court cases in Bulgaria. In combination with the fact the NEB rarely, if ever, fines the airlines for non-compliance with the Regulation, this has created an airline-friendly environment with few incentives for timely compliance with the Regulation.

---

[39] И Владимиров, *Право на международния транспорт* [I Vladimirov, *Law of International Transport*], 2nd edn (Ромина [Romina], 2002).

[40] A Manuelyan, 'La protection des voyageurs aériens dans la récente jurisprudence de la Cour de justice: est-ce le temps des consolidations?', *Европейски правен преглед* [*Evropeiksi praven pregled*], vol VII, 186; Я Чанкова-Дочева, 'Правна регламентация в Европейския съюз на правата на пътниците във въздушния транспорт' [I Chankova-Docheva, 'Legal Regulation in the EU of Air Passenger Rights], *Правна мисъл* [*Pravna misul*] 4/2011, 69.

[41] J Grigorova, 'Compensation of Cancelled Flights—in Search of the Golden Balance between Air Passenger Rights and the Airlines' Limited Liability' (2012) 2 *Evropeiksi praven pregled* 143.

[42] ibid.

[43] Case C-366/10 *Air Transport Association of America and Others v Secretary of State for Energy and Climate Change* (ECJ, 21 December 2011). One author argued that the Court erred in defining the circumstances in which a person can rely upon an instrument of international law in order to claim the invalidity of EU secondary legislation. She also criticised the Court for having unjustifiably limited its judicial control over the compatibility of EU secondary legislation with customary international law. The author concludes that the Court's judgment was probably guided by political and general environmental considerations rather than by solid juridical arguments: see J Grigorova, 'The Compatibility of the EU Emissions Trading System with International Law—Does the Goal Justify the Means?' (2012) 3 *Evropeiksi praven pregled* 106.

The picture would have been completely different if the NEB had decided to adopt binding decisions in response to claims under Regulation 261, or to at least pursue an active policy by imposing dissuasive sanctions for non-compliance. This would have meant that if an airline were reluctant to pay compensation, it must itself take the case to an administrative court by seeking the annulment of the decision of the NEB, thus shifting the burden of initiating court proceedings from the passenger to the airline. In this scenario the airline would be the applicant, while the NEB would be the respondent, the passenger being spared the cost and effort of the judicial process. This would have certainly enhanced compliance.

It might be also worth considering whether claims under Regulation 261 could be brought and dealt with under Regulation 861/2007 establishing a European Small Claims Procedure. This alternative might not only help overcome the ambiguities with regard to the applicable national legal remedies, but might also bring down the cost of litigation, while speeding up the process of enforcing the passengers' rights guaranteed by Regulation 261.

10

A Pair of Wings: Air Passenger Rights in the Czech Republic and Slovakia

KRISTIÁN CSACH

I. Introduction

This chapter deals with the application of Regulation 261 and supplementing national provisions regulating liabilities of air carriers towards passengers in similar situations (delay or cancellations of flight, downgrading or denied boarding) in the Czech Republic and Slovakia.

The case law and the administrative practice of NEBs in both the Czech Republic and Slovakia will be analysed together. Common legal and political history, similar private law, and the tendency of the Czech Republic and Slovakia to take account of each other's case law enable a combined analysis.[1] Although the legal background, the doctrine and the method of application of law might seem almost the same, there is nevertheless a difference regarding public access to legal sources, case law and the administrative practice relevant for the report in both countries.

Slovak case law has been accessed and analysed through the web-based database led by the Ministry of Justice[2] that is supposed to include most of the final decisions of first instance (*Okresný súd*) and appellate courts (*Krajský súd*) in Slovakia. Furthermore, both the Slovak Supreme Court and the Slovak Constitutional Court publish their decisions on their web pages.[3] In addition, a private system allowing public access to Slovak case law has been consulted.[4] The administrative practice is illustrated by the accessible decisions of the Slovak Trade Inspectorate, with the Central Inspectorate being the second instance body, as the NEB.[5]

---

[1] For more details on the interaction between Czech and Slovak legal discourse in English, see M Bobek, *Comparative Reasoning in European Supreme Courts* (Oxford University Press, 2013), 152, 174, 189.

[2] <www.justice.gov.sk>

[3] Slovak Supreme Court, at <www.supcourt.gov.sk/>; Slovak Constitutional Court, at <www.concourt.sk/>.

[4] Available at <www.otvorenesudy.sk>.

[5] Available at <www.soi.sk>.

In contrast to the Slovak system of publication of judgments, including those issued by lower courts, only decisions of the Czech Supreme Court, Constitutional Court and Supreme Administrative Court are freely accessible.[6] There is no system of general publication of judgments of lower courts. The Czech NEB (Civil Aviation Authority)[7] does not publish its decisions, but a summary of complaints raised by passengers is included in its annual reports. Because of the Czech procedural law, potential claims are heard at first instance only, and do not reach the higher courts or the Czech Supreme Court. The publication of first instance case law is almost non-existent. The decisions of first instance courts might be subject to scrutiny regarding their compliance with fundamental rights and freedoms by the Czech Constitutional Court, but they are quashed only exceptionally.[8]

It is reasonable to assume that due to the same cultural and legal background in both countries, the results stated for one country will be applicable to the other, unless otherwise stated in the report. The author assumes similar consumer behaviour in the Czech Republic and Slovakia, as the demand and supply sides are somewhat interchangeable.

II. Background

Besides the unified international conventions[9] and Regulation 261, national legislation in Slovakia and in the Czech Republic also includes detailed private law regulation of contracts for the transport of persons and contracts for travel services, which is relevant when considering liabilities of air carriers. Despite the fact that the Czech Republic underwent a complex recodification of its civil law (resulting in the new Civil Code,[10] the Act on Corporations[11] and the Act on Private International Law,[12] which came into force on 1 January 2014), the general concept of claims and their judicial enforcement has remained the same; any minor differences will be brought to the reader's attention where relevant.

Both countries have also evolved administrative enforcement of the claims under Regulation 261. The NEBs (the Slovak Trade Inspectorate, the Central

---

[6] Czech Supreme Court, at <www.nsoud.cz/>; Czech Constitutional Court, at <www.usoud.cz/>; Supreme Administrative Court, at <www.nssoud.cz>.

[7] Available at <www.caa.cz/urad>.

[8] eg Czech Constitutional Court decision file Nr III ÚS 2781/14, 16.9.2014 dismissing the complaint of an air carrier against a first instance judgment; *cf* file Nr IIIÚS 2782/14, 20.11.2014, based on the very same circumstances of a delay caused by a bird strike and following necessary technical and safety maintenance procedures.

[9] Convention for the Unification of Certain Rules for International Carriage by Air [2001] OJ L194/39 (Montreal Convention).

[10] No 89/2012 Coll (NCC).

[11] No 90/2012 Coll.

[12] No 91/2012 Coll.

Inspectorate (the second instance body) and the Civil Aviation Authority)[13] are empowered to supervise the application of Regulation 261 by air carriers, and have the authority to impose sanctions upon them in the event that they fail to perform their obligations.

III. The National Application of Regulation 261

A. The Enforcement of Regulation 261: How are Claims Brought?

Claims based upon Regulation 261 are considered regular civil law claims that are actionable in the same way as any other private law claims. The proceeding is usually initiated on the basis of an application for an order for payment. However, the procedure is backed by a parallel possibility to enforce the claim in an administrative proceeding. Before an administrative proceeding can commence, though, the complaint must be filed with the air carrier. If the air carrier does not respond within six weeks, or if the passenger is not satisfied with the response, the passenger may turn to the NEB, which can initiate a public law proceeding in order to impose sanctions upon the air carrier. Interestingly, in order to enforce the regulation in a more efficient way, the Slovak NEB tends to subsume breaches of Regulation 261 under breaches of domestic administrative law defining various administrative offences and breaches of consumer law (in other words, it adjusts the national law to the Regulation).[14] In this way, the Slovak NEB uses the rules in the Regulation to interpret the rules of domestic public law.[15]

Notwithstanding the possibility of an administrative proceeding, the passenger is entitled to bring a claim before the court on the basis of Regulation 261 or other relevant legal grounds (as described in section IV below). This is done predominantly by application for an order for payment, which in fact is a conditional action, initiating a proceeding for obtaining an order for payment within a short time or automatically opening a regular civil proceeding once the defendant pleads its defence against the order for payment issued by the court. According to the case law, claims under Regulation 261 are of contractual nature. A survey has shown that a considerable number of claims brought before the court were settled after a payment order was issued.[16] In contrast to Slovak procedural law, according

---

[13] The Civil Aviation Authority has been the Czech NEB since 1 July 2006.

[14] eg Central Inspectorate, file Nr SK/0352/99/08, 11.08.2008; Slovak Trade Inspectorate Bratislava, Nr P/0064/01/2009, 28.4.2009; Slovak Trade Inspectorate Košice, Nr P/0263/08/11, 7.10.2011.

[15] This might not be the case for the Czech national authority, as §93(2)(s), (t) of Act Nr 49/1997 Coll on civil aviation, as amended, define the failure to comply with an obligation arising from directly applicable EU legislation (namely Regulation 261) explicitly as an administrative offence.

[16] eg file Nr 51C/207/2013, 11.12.2013, where the court halted the proceedings by Okresný súd Bratislava II; see also file Nr 15C/57/2012, 10.05. 2012; file Nr 50C/10/2013, 17.12.2013; file Nr 50C/226/2013, 17.12.2013.

to §202 of the Czech Code on Civil Procedure, there is no right of appeal against a first instance judgment for payment of less than 10,000 CZK (approximately €360), and therefore cases concerning compensation under the Regulation are decided at first instance only.

B. Frequency of the Application of Regulation 261: How many Cases have been Brought?

The situation in both countries is very similar with regard to the frequency of judicial enforcement of claims based upon Regulation 261. In practice, only a very limited number of cases have been brought before the courts. Besides a rather small market 'creating' only a limited number of cases, we assume that the length of the judicial proceedings, their cost and the uncertainty of the results might deter passengers from seeking judicial enforcement of their rights. In Slovakia, lengthy proceedings concerning rights arising from Regulation 261 were challenged before the Slovak Constitutional Court and held to be acceptable when resulting from procedural complications (mostly because of a foreign element),[17] but not when founded on a lack of activity on the side of the court.[18] This might also be attributed to the sometimes problematic application of EU law by Slovak courts. However, it might be argued that the main reason for the lack of case law is the passengers' choice of another enforcement model—the administrative one.

The results of the survey suggest that passengers prefer to notify the NEBs of breaches by the air carrier of obligations under Regulation 261, as suggested by the number of administrative decisions (at least those published in Slovakia), before having recourse to judicial proceedings. The risk of an administrative fine and other sanctions is a more persuasive compliance mechanism than the risk of a passenger commencing costly judicial proceedings. Based on a prima facie survey of administrative practice, air carriers are sanctioned predominantly for delays in the payment of compensation,[19] and not for their ignorance of other obligations imposed by the Regulation (not paying any compensation at all). This leads to the conclusion that the Regulation and its enforcement model are quite effective, and

---

[17] The Slovak Constitutional Court held that a complaint was clearly unfounded in Okresný súd Bratislava I, file Nr 7 C 75/2006, which had already lasted for five years due to procedural steps that had proven to be inefficient (failures in the service of documents, lengthy translations and obtaining evidence from abroad, etc). The plaintiff demanded payment of €600 because of the cancellation of the flight; see also SÚS, file Nr I. ÚS 1/2011, 27.1.2011.

[18] In File Nr IV ÚS 340/2010, 25.11.2010, the Slovak Constitutional Court held that a complaint in a similar case (where the plaintiff demanded payment of €600 because of the cancellation of the flight) was well founded, as the first instance court, Okresný súd Bratislava I, file Nr 10C 43/2006, had performed only minimal activity within the 23 months after filing of the claim, leading to a decision on the merits of the case.

[19] Slovak Trade Inspectorate Bratislava, Nr P/0584/01/2008, 7.1.2009.

that compensation is being paid, although later than expected, once the consumer initiates and files a complaint, and shows himself willing to push the case further, either with a complaint to the NEB or via recourse to the courts (generally by filing a request for a payment order).

According to the published data, the activity of the Slovak NEB peaked in 2008, when over 70 consumer complaints relating to air transport were assessed. The percentage of complaints found to be well founded was around 46 per cent, while complaints not leading to proceedings were often passed to another authority in another Member State, or dismissed in light of lack of authority to review the complaint. Within that year the NEB dealt with three cases of denied boarding, 20 cases involving cancellations, and 10 cases involving delays and complementary rights of passengers. The NEB also considered situations where passengers were not given the option of choosing between compensation and redirection.[20] As no later overall statistics were published by the Slovak NEB, it is possible to extrapolate—also based on individual published decisions—that the general distribution of the particular situations (cancellation, denied boarding, etc) remained roughly the same. The number of complaints lodged in the Czech Republic continues to rise steadily: according to published data, passengers filed 142 complaints in 2008, 143 in 2009, 192 in 2010, 190 in 2011, 196 in 2012 and 287 in 2013.[21]

C. Rights Enforced, Situations Assessed

In general, delays in the payment of compensation for denied boarding have been punished by the imposition of fines.[22] Cancellations[23] and delays[24] are the most common grounds for compensation. No Slovak cases or decisions concerning downgrading have been identified. However, the small number of claims brought before the Slovak courts does not allow for any sweeping generalisations.

Compared to Slovakia, figures in the Czech Republic do not show any significant difference between the number of complaints brought before the NEB and those brought before the court. Annual reports published by the Czech Civil Aviation Authority give a better overview of the number of complaints brought (see Table 10.1).

---

[20] Civil Aviation Authority, 'Kontrolné akcie centrálne riadené ústredným inšpektorátom za rok 2008' (2008) [5]; unfortunately, the following annual reports do not include any summary of the sector-specific complaints and the data included; the decisions used in this chapter are extracted from the published decisions of the Civil Aviation Authority, at both first and second instances.

[21] Civil Aviation Authority, 'Kontrolné akcie centrálne riadené ústredným inšpektorátom za rok 2008' (2008), Annex 1.

[22] Central Inspectorate, file Nr SK/0352/99/08, 11.08.2008.

[23] eg file Nr I ÚS 1/2011, 27.1.2011; file Nr IV ÚS 340/2010, 25.11.2010; Slovak Trade Inspectorate Bratislava, Nr P/0584/01/2008, 7.1.2009; on multiple cancellation, see Central Inspectorate, file Nr SK/0229/99/2009, 22.06.2009.

[24] Okresný súd Bratislava II, file Nr 21C/1/2011, 17.04.2013.

Table 10.1: Number of complaints brought before the Czech NEB[25]

Year	Denied boarding	Cancellation	Delays	Downgrading
2010	15	112	65	0
2011	19	91	80	0
2012	7	72	117	0
2013	11	86	189	1

D. Exceptions

According to the survey, 'extraordinary circumstances' have not generally been defined by the administrative decision-making process or within the case law. In a recent decision of the Czech Constitutional Court on a delay caused by a bird strike following a maintenance check,[26] the Court quashed the first instance decision while stating, obiter, the view that a bird strike is to be considered as a circumstance under Recital 14 of the Regulation and possibly also as an extraordinary circumstance under Article 5(3) of the Regulation.[27] The Court left the question unresolved because of its lack of competence to interpret the Regulation.

E. Remedies

According to the published information, compensation is being awarded, though the decisions on administrative sanctions show that it is not always paid within prescribed time limits. It is possible to assume that at least after an administrative proceeding is initiated, the compensation will finally be paid. A particular Slovak case has shown that an air carrier (in this case foreign) may only have limited liability to pay compensation because, in this instance, the court passed the burden of paying the rest of the compensation as prescribed by the Regulation on to the Slovakian travel agency involved.[28]

Both Czech[29] and Slovak[30] courts have reflected on the decisions of the CJEU in *Sturgeon v Condor*[31] and *Nelson v Deutsche Lufthansa*,[32] and are extending the right to compensation for delays of longer than three hours.

---

[25] Civil Aviation Authority, 'Annual Report 2010' (2010) 17; Civil Aviation Authority, 'Annual Report 2011' (2011) 13; Civil Aviation Authority, 'Annual Report 2012' (2012) 14; Civil Aviation Authority, 'Annual Report 2013' (2013) 14.

[26] Czech Constitutional Court, file Nr III ÚS 2782/14, 20.11.2014.

[27] The Constitutional Court distinguished between a circumstance under Recital 14 of Regulation 261 and an extraordinary circumstance under Art 5(3) of the Regulation.

[28] Okresný súd Bratislava II, file Nr 21C/1/2011, 17.04.2013.

[29] Obvodní soud pro Prahu 6, file Nr 19 C 292/2013-51, 22.5.2014.

[30] For a delay of 26 hours, see Okresný súd Bratislava II, file Nr 21C/1/2011, 17.04.2013.

[31] Cases C-402 and 432/07 *Sturgeon and Others* [2009] ECR I-10923.

[32] Cases C-581 and 629/10 *Nelson v Deutsche Lufthansa AG* [2012] OJ C399/3.

F. Compatibility with the Montreal Convention

The relationship between the Montreal Convention and Regulation 261 has not been clarified in the case law. This may be a result of the prevalence of administrative enforcement of claims over judicial enforcement, which means that the issue of jurisdiction and the limitation of claims has not been considered. Otherwise, the precedence of the Montreal Convention over domestic law has been accepted by courts from both countries.[33] The exclusivity of the Montreal Convention has not been expressly challenged by Czech or Slovak courts.

IV. Supplementary National Legislation

The Regulation applies without prejudice to a passenger's rights to further compensation, but any compensation granted under the Regulation may be deducted from such compensation.[34] Rights to further compensation may be derived from contract or tort (delict).[35]

The passenger might be compensated, first, within the system of contract law. Both the Slovak and the Czech legislatures distinguish between a contract for transport of persons[36] and a contract for travel services.[37] If the air carriage is part of a package of travel services,[38] the responsibilities of the parties are governed by the contract for travel services and are actionable only *inter partes*, between the consumer and the supplier of the (package) travel service. Being denied boarding, flight cancellations, delays or downgrading are all failures to perform the contract, which are generally remedied by an appropriate reduction made in the price of the travel service. The right of the passenger to reimbursement of any loss actually suffered (whether economic loss, or personal harm or injury) remains unaffected. Claims under Regulation 261 and claims based on the contract for travel services overlap, and any compensation based on the one may be deducted from compensation based on the other. However, the two claims are against different persons, and the consumer is free to decide the basis of his claim and thereby choose the defendant he wishes to pursue and the process of enforcement (claims according

---

[33] With regard to the positions of the lower courts in Slovakia with respect to the Warsaw Convention, see file Nr 3 Cdo 290/2008, 8.7.2009; file Nr 3 Cdo 213/2010, 30.6.2011. With regard to the position of the lower courts in the Czech Republic, see file Nr 23 Cdo 840/2008, 20.9.2010. With regard to the Montreal Convention, see file Nr 23 Cdo 3377/2010, 27.6.2012; file Nr 23 Cdo 1914/2013, 25.6.2014.

[34] Regulation 261, Art 12(1).

[35] Other legal grounds for a compensatory obligation (*causa obligationem*), like unjust enrichment, shall not be taken into consideration.

[36] Act No 40/1964, § 760–764 (SCC); Act No 40/1964 Coll, § 760–764 (CCC); NCC, § 2550–2554.

[37] SCC, § 741a-741k SCC; CCC, § 852a-852k; NCC § 2550-2554.

[38] For a more detailed analysis of the liability system within the contract on travel services, see R Dobrovodský, 'Ochrana práv spotrebiteľov—objednávateľov služieb cestovného ruchu—2. časť' (2010) *Justičná revue* 143.

to Regulation 261 against the air carrier, or claims arising from the failure in the performance of the travel service contract against the supplier).[39] Some authors even suggest that the direct applicability of claims under Regulation 261 against the supplier of travel services is possible.[40] It is foreseeable that, due to procedural burdens, the consumer might opt to bring the claim against the supplier of the travel service and not against the air carrier (except if the air carrier pays voluntarily), if the air carrier is a foreign entity.

If the passenger opts to bring the action on the grounds of failure to perform the contract for travel services, he does not have to substantiate the actual harm suffered because of the failure in the performance of the contract, but an appropriate deduction from the price is made by the court.[41] Interestingly, Slovak courts are willing to calculate (*mutadis mutandis*) the price deduction (as the damage arising from the breach of a contract for travel services) for the failure in performance on the basis of claims under Regulation 261. The courts also oblige the supplier of the travel service to pay the remaining portion of the claim under Regulation 261 if the air carrier does not compensate the consumer in full (if it does not pay the amount as required under the Regulation).

Besides the claims arising from the Regulation and claims based upon the failure of performance of the travel service contract (price reduction), a general right to claim any actual damages (whether economic or personal) resulting from the breach of contractual obligations remains. The proof and calculation of loss suffered might be complicated, and the courts have developed multiple criteria for a rather policy-based judgment. For example, according to the Czech Supreme Court, the passenger has the right to be reimbursed for harm suffered if he missed a connecting flight because of delay of the previous flight.[42] Absent any contractual stipulation, multiple factors for the calculation of resulting loss actually suffered by the passenger[43] are to be taken into account, including the reasons for the delay, whether the air carrier transferred the passenger to the destination later or not, whether the passenger was provided with any substitute services, the situation of the passenger after the breach of contract by the air carrier, etc.[44]

---

[39] M Hulmák, 'Cestovní smlouva' in K Eliáš *et al* (eds), *Občanský zákoník. Velký akademický komenář, 2. svazek* (Linde, 2008) 2471.

[40] R Dobrovodský, 'Ochrana práv cestujúcich v leteckej doprave' in M Jurčová *et al* (eds), *Právo cestovného ruchu, Bratislava* (CH Beck, 2014) 128.

[41] eg R Dobrovodský, 'Ochrana práv spotrebiteľov—objednávateľov služieb cestovného ruchu. 2. part' [2010] *Justičná revue* 143.

[42] A group of passengers bought return tickets from Prague to San José (Costa Rica) on 18 December 2003, with two stops. Because of the delay of the flight from Paris to Mexico City, they missed their connecting flight. While equipped for a tropical holiday, they had to spend several days in a rather cold Mexico City, where some of them fell ill. The claimant declined the air carrier's offer of another flight scheduled for 24 December 2003, even though he knew that all flights were fully booked until 26 December 2003, and bought another ticket to Cancun, where he spent the rest of his holiday (until 9 January 2004).

[43] Montreal Convention, Art 19; CCC § 760.

[44] Czech Supreme Court, file Nr 33 Cdo 1466/2007, 26.11.2008.

The distinctions between the legal grounds for the compensation (be it Regulation 261, a contract for travel services or a contract for the transport of persons) will have a significant impact on the prescribed periods for bringing a claim, which will be addressed in section V.A below.

V. National Enforcement of Claims under Regulation 261

A survey of administrative practice did not show any indication that Regulation 261 was not held to be directly applicable or effective. Both NEBs on their web pages expressly bring to the attention of consumers, as part of the first information provided, the fact that the Regulation is directly applicable. As already mentioned, the Slovak NEB sometimes redirects the claims brought according to the Regulation to national consumer law, in order to be able to impose administrative sanctions for the breach of the obligations imposed by the Regulation, but that should not be taken as evidence against the direct applicability of Regulation 261; it is merely a way of ensuring administrative application of the relevant rules.

A. Limitation Period

Although a claim for compensation according to Regulation 261 is a contractual one, it is not subject to general rules on the limitation of contractual claims (three years). Rather, special legal rules govern the time limits for claims, which differ depending on whether the claim is against the supplier of package travel services or the air carrier.

Both legal systems distinguish between two types of time limits with different consequences. One is the *premlčanie*—a general limitation period leading to the weakening of the claim (actionability) after lapse of a specified time. Any action brought before the court is to be dismissed if brought after the limitation period has passed and where the defendant has raised the limitation exemption in the proceedings. The claim is therefore time-barred only following the raising of the exemption by the defendant. On the other side, *preklúzia* leads to a termination of the right to claim *ex lege*. After the lapse of the specified time limit, the entitlement ceases to exist (even as a 'natural' right).[45]

If the transport is a part of a package of travel services, the contractual regulation of the contract for travel services, according to § 741a of the Slovak Civil Code (SCC) and § 852a of the old Czech Civil Code (CCC), applies. Any failure in the

---

[45] For more details on prescription and preclusion in both legal systems, see J Fiala *et al*, *Contract Law in Slovak Republic* (Kluwer Law International, 2010) 55.

performance of the contract by the supplier is to be notified to the supplier or its representative at the earliest opportunity, and the local representative of the supplier is to provide the consumer with written confirmation of that notification.[46] If the supplier does not fulfil its obligations following the notification, the client must file his claim with the supplier in written form without undue delay, but in any event not later than three months after his return from the journey, otherwise the claim will be time-barred *ex lege*.[47] (Under the new Czech law,[48] the notification period has been shortened to one month, but it now has a prescriptive rather than a preclusive character.)[49] If the supplier continues not to comply with its obligations, the client may resort to judicial enforcement within the three years (general prescription period) following.

According to the Czech Supreme Court, the prescription period provided in § 852i (2) of the CCC[50] applies only to claims resulting from the non-performance of, or a failure in performance of, a contract for travel services, and does not cover claims for damages for harm suffered (personal injury) resulting from the breach of such contracts.[51] The latter claims are subject to prescription periods for claims for damages under common § 106 (1) of the SCC and of the CCC, according to which the claim for compensation shall be barred two years from the date on which the injured person becomes aware of the damage and of the identity of the person responsible for it (subjective prescription period). The subjective prescription period is however limited by an objective period of three years after the event causing damage, or 10 years if damage was caused intentionally,[52] with the exception of claims for compensation for personal injuries and damage, which are not limited by any objective period (but are still limited by the subjective one). It is highly probable that this ruling would also be followed in Slovak law.

The claim against the air carrier is also a contractual claim based on the regulation of the contract for personal carriage with its own limitation periods.[53] These rules shall apply *per analogiam* even to claims brought directly against the air carrier under Regulation 261 without any direct contractual obligation existing between the passenger and the air carrier. According to common § 763 (3) of the SCC and of the CCC, the passenger must notify the claim to the air carrier without

---

[46] SCC, § 741i (1); CCC, § 852i (1).

[47] SCC § 741i (2); CCC, § 852i (2), although it does not require notice in writing.

[48] See section II, text connected with nn 10–12.

[49] NCC, § 2540.

[50] SCC, § 741i (2).

[51] Czech Supreme Court, file Nr 25 Cdo 271/2012, 19.7.2012, published also as R 134/2012 civ; file Nr 25 Cdo 51/2013, 20.3.2014. Although the subject of the cases in question was a claim for compensation for personal injury and also the generalised 'legal sentence' (a legal sentence is an abstract sentence written in a rather normative style formulated by the court for purposes of publication), which covers only claims for compensation for personal harm, the *ratio decidendi* might support a more generalised view, arching over all kinds of damage.

[52] SCC, § 106 (2); CCC, § 106 (2).

[53] SCC, § 760; CCC, § 760; NCC, § 2550.

undue delay, but in any event within six months. After six months the claim is time-barred, ie precluded. (The recodification of the Czech civil law changed the preclusion into a prescription without changing the length of the prescription periods.)[54]

Under Slovak law (and under previous Czech law), the parties are free to opt out of application of the Civil Code and into application of the Commercial Code, based on a written agreement under § 262 of the Commercial Code, following which the general part of the law on obligations as stated in commercial law applies. The Commercial Code provides a general prescription period of four years. It is therefore possible to suggest that the applicable prescription period might be extended by opting into the Commercial Code—unless such an opt-in clause were to be considered an unfair term in a consumer contract.[55]

In the Slovak legal order only, if the contracts for travel services or air carriage are consumer contracts (concluded by a consumer acting outside the scope of his commercial or professional activities),[56] special regulations on time limits apply,[57] according to which the court has to take into account the prescription of the claim against a consumer *ex officio*. Thus, in consumer contract litigation, prescription of claims against the consumer becomes preclusion.

B. National Enforcement Bodies and their Role

As has been described, the consumer protection authorities in Slovakia and in the Czech Republic play a key role in the protection of consumer rights, including those arising from Regulation 261. They not only supervise the application of Regulation 261 by the air carriers and impose sanctions, but are—at least in Slovakia—active in reviewing the standard contract terms supplied by air carriers as regards their conformity with Regulation 261.[58]

C. Claim Aggregator Services

In contrast to some high-profile examples of litigation (bank contracts), no sign of any consumer 'resistance movements', trying to bundle more consumers into a single movement or claim, has been identified so far. A special web-page offering the possibility to bring a claim based on Regulation 261 is run in the Czech

---

[54] NCC, § 2553(3). See section II, text connected with nn 10–12.
[55] The Slovak Supreme Court has held a standard term in a consumer contract, according to which the parties are able to choose application of the Commercial Code, to be unfair *per se* (file Nr 5 MCdo 20/2009, 25.1.2011, published as R 36/2013). In contrast, the Czech Supreme Court holds the opposite opinion (eg file Nr 32 Cdo 3337/2010, 24.7.2012).
[56] eg Okresný súd Nitra, file Nr 12C 135/2008, 28.2.2011.
[57] Act Nr 250/2007 Coll, § 5b.
[58] Slovak Trade Inspectorate Košice, Nr P/0263/08/11, 7.10.2011.

Republic on a rather commercial basis,[59] as in Slovakia.[60] Most of the cases decided by the courts and decisions given by consumer protection authorities have been initiated personally by affected consumers. However, consumer protection associations may play a significant role in providing support for consumers within judicial proceedings (subsidiary intervention in the proceeding, representation of the claimant, etc).

No particular consumer protection association concentrates solely on air transport or travel services, but most of the associations show willingness to provide support with claims under the Regulation too. The associations are also entitled to bring particular actions before courts on their own motion. Although not entitled to demand compensation on behalf of consumers, such an association is a 'qualified entity',[61] able to bring an action for an injunction requiring the cessation or prohibition of any infringement of consumer rights, including those arising from Regulation 261. Consumer protection associations are active in targeting contractual provisions of suppliers of travel services and air carriers.

However, according to Slovak case law, the consumer protection association is not entitled to bring an action before the court if the NEB fails to act upon their request for action (alleged breach of Regulation 261), as the consumer protection association is not a participant in the administrative proceeding and its legal position is not directly affected by a decision of the administrative body on a sanction against the defendant.[62]

The NEBs also act as a kind of a claim aggregator when deciding multiple complaints against one defendant in respect of multiple different flight delays or cancellations in a single proceeding.[63]

D. Interaction with the CJEU: Preliminary Rulings

Neither Slovak nor Czech courts have submitted any request for preliminary ruling regarding Regulation 261. It is not known whether any proceedings have been stayed because of a pending request for preliminary ruling, as decisions on staying proceedings are not published. However, the need for a reference was identified by the Czech Constitutional Court, and it is possible that a preliminary question will be referred before long.

In the 'bird strike' case,[64] the Czech Constitutional Court held, inter alia, that two questions were relevant for the decision on the merits to be in compliance

---

[59] Available at <www.kompenzomat.cz/>.
[60] Available at <http://apra.sk/>.
[61] eg European Parliament and Council Directive (EC) 98/27 of 19 May 1998 on injunctions for the protection of consumers' interests OJ [1998] L166/51, Art 3.
[62] Slovak Supreme Court, file Nr 6Sžnč/3/2010, 22.9.2010.
[63] On multiple cases of cancellations, see Central Inspectorate, file Nr SK/0229/99/2009, 22.06.2009.
[64] Czech Constitutional Court (n 26).

with fundamental rights. First, whether a bird strike was a 'circumstance' under Recital 14 of the Regulation; and, secondly, whether the obligatory airplane technical maintenance check itself was an 'extraordinary circumstance', and therefore whether the time needed to complete the check, according to the obligatory regulations on technical and safety procedures, was to be counted as part of the delay for the purposes of the Regulation. Despite presenting its position (the Constitutional Court leant towards a positive reply to the first question), the Court noted that it lacked the competence to interpret the Regulation, and concluded that these questions could be answered by the CJEU alone.[65] The Czech Constitutional Court held that the failure to refer a preliminary question on the interpretation of the Regulation constituted a violation of the fundamental right to one's lawful judge according to Article 38(1) of the Czech Charter of Fundamental Rights and Freedoms.

VI. Scholarly Analysis and Concluding Remarks

Regulation 261 and related claims are subject to analysis by scholars focusing on consumer protection and private international law, predominantly forming part of the commentaries on civil codes and the casebooks on civil law and private international law in both countries. The case law of the CJEU has been the subject of rather sparse scholarly analysis.[66] Critical voices have been raised regarding the *Sturgeon* decision and the question whether the requirement to compensate passengers whose flights are delayed is compatible with the Montreal Convention. The conclusion that the loss of time inherent in a delayed flight constitutes an inconvenience that is not governed by the Montreal Convention was not thought to be very persuasive. A more lively discussion took place on Czech and Slovak legal discussion blogs, with participants not limiting themselves to the material issues in question but also covering the resulting private international law (conflict of laws) issues.[67]

---

[65] Czech Constitutional Court, file Nr III ÚS 2782/14, 20. 11. 2014 [29].

[66] K Csach *et al*, 'Interakcia medzi medzinárodnou a európskou právnou úpravou zodpovednosti leteckého dopravcu za škodu spôsobenú cestujúcemu', *Výber z rozhodnutí Súdneho dvora Európskej únie* 2 (2010) 5; K Csach *et al*, 'Rozsudok Sturgeon—komentár', *Výber z rozhodnutí Súdneho dvora Európskej únie* 2 (2010) 61; R Dobrovodský, 'Die Rechtsprechung zum slowakischen Reiserecht', *Tourismusrecht* (Neuer wissenschaftlicher Verlag, 2014) 77; R Dobrovodský, 'Ausgewählte Probleme des slowakischen Reiserechts—theoretische Fragestellungen und praktische Erfahrungen', *Tourismusrecht* (Neuer wissenschaftlicher Verlag, 2010) 45; J Klučka, 'Rozsudok Rehder—komentár', *Výber z rozhodnutí Súdneho dvora Európskej únie* 2 (2010) 39; E Kuteničová, 'Kompenzácia poskytované pasažierom leteckými spoločnosťami' (2006) *Justičná revue* 151.

[67] M Bobek, 'Jak si Michal myslel, že se Petr (s)pletl, ale Petr autoritativním výkladem prokazoval, že se nespletl' (Jiné Právo, 9 July 2009), available at <http://jinepravo.blogspot.sk/2009/07/jak-se-petr-spletl-aneb-ja-jsem-tu.html>, accessed 30 July 2014; J Gyarfás, 'Tri hodiny na bukurešťskom letisku

Some scholars also addressed the possibility of recovering immaterial harm caused by a failure to perform a contract for travel services according to the Czech law prior to the recodification. The general concept of Slovak law (and the old Czech law) on liability[68] excludes the possibility of recovering any immaterial damage, unless the right to privacy has also been violated.[69] According to some authors, the regulation on liability within the contract for travel services[70] has to be interpreted in conformity with EU law, enabling a claim for recovery of immaterial harm to be brought too.[71]

Despite the fact that the almost non-existent case law on the subject is limiting this chapter's general conclusion, it is possible to put forward a rather paradoxical hypothesis: the lack of case law and administrative ('hard') application of Regulation 261 might be evidence as to the efficiency of Regulation 261 in daily practice. Maybe, the obedience to law and a soft application of Regulation 261 prevails over a hard one in the Czech and Slovak legal order.[72]

---

a kreatívny výklad práva' (LexForum.sk, 19 November 2009), available at <www.lexforum.sk/207>, accessed 30 July 2014.

[68] SCC, § 420; CCC, § 420.
[69] SCC, § 13; CCC, § 13.
[70] CCC, § 852i; SCC, § 741.
[71] M Selucká, 'Cestovní smlouva' in J Švestka *et al* (eds), *Občanský zákoník II*, 2nd edn (CH Beck, 2009) 2402. For Slovakia, see I Fekete, *Občiansky zákonník, Veľký komentár* (Eurokódex, 2011) 2223.
[72] The present chapter was originally prepared as part of research project, APVV-0518-11.

11

Estonia: All Well or is there Something in the Air?

TATJANA EVAS AND SILVIA USTAV

I. Introduction

This chapter examines the impact of Regulation 261 on the system of protection of air passenger rights in Estonia, and explains the reasons for the relatively modest attention to the topic by all stakeholders involved. The implementation and application of Regulation 261 in Estonia did not trigger either a substantial number of cases in the courts, or intensive public or scholarly debate. Based on the analysis of the national legislation, statistical data, court judgments and decisions of the NEB, this chapter argues that the enforcement of the Regulation in Estonia is generally in accordance with EU law and the case law of the CJEU. However, considering the very small number of claims brought before the NEB and domestic courts, this contribution questions the effectiveness of the national procedural rules.

First, we briefly outline the relevant background of the Estonian procedural system for bringing claims. Secondly, we then turn to analyse the enforcement and protection of air passenger rights guaranteed by the Regulation, through the review of the legislation and administrative and judicial practice in Estonia. Lastly, we consider scholarly publications and public debate.

II. The Estonian System of Air Passenger Rights Protection

A. General Legislative Framework Applicable to Air Passenger Rights

The main Acts regulating the system of enforcement of air passenger rights in Estonia provided for under Regulation 261, include the Aviation Act,[1] the Consumer Protection Act[2] and the Law of Obligations Act.[3]

[1] Aviation Act, RT I, 29.06.2014, 27.
[2] Consumer Protection Act, RT I, 12.07.2014, 136.
[3] Law of Obligations Act, RT I, 11.04.2014, 13.

The Aviation Act stipulates, in accordance with the requirements of Article 16 of the Regulation, that the Estonian Consumer Protection Board (ECPB) is the NEB.[4] The ECPB has competence to ensure the implementation of passenger rights, as provided for in the Regulation, on flights from airports situated in Estonia and flights from third countries landing in Estonia.[5] Moreover, the Aviation Act provides:

> Where appropriate, the Consumer Protection Board will take measures necessary to ensure that the rights of passengers are respected.[6]

The Consumer Protection Act provides a legal basis for the ECPB and the Consumer Complaints Committee.[7] The ECPB has wide powers that include, amongst others, supervision of compliance with consumer rights, the right to make a proposal for a legislative change in the area of consumer rights, and the power to settle petitions and complaints concerning violations of consumer rights.[8]

The procedures and types of sanctions available following a violation of rights deriving from the Regulation are regulated by the Aviation Act, Consumer Protection Act, Civil Code, Law on Obligations Act and Substitutive Enforcement and Penalty Payment Act.[9]

B. The Estonian Procedural Background

Those air passengers who have a claim under the Regulation have the right to take the complaint either to the ECPB or directly to a national county court.

The ECPB is a national agency under the supervision of the Ministry of Economic Affairs and Communications. The Administrative Procedure Act[10] applies to the proceedings of the ECPB, subject to exceptions specifically provided in the law. Therefore decisions of the ECPB may be challenged through administrative court proceedings. The Consumer Protection Act provides a relevant complaint procedure, which is applicable to all consumer-related complains, including by air passengers.

Affected passengers must first submit a written complaint, with relevant supporting documents, to the airline company. The airline company must confirm

---

[4] Aviation Act, RT I, 29.06.2014, 27, Art 58[4].
[5] ibid.
[6] This is verbatum transposition of Art 16 of Regulation 261.
[7] Consumer Protection Act, RT I 2004, 13, 86, Art 17.
[8] In addition to handling claims and inquiries from air passengers, the Consumer Protection Board is also, for example, responsible for implementing preventive measures to avoid violations of the passengers rights. Since one of the main functions of the Board is market surveillance and consumer education, it carries out information campaigns and other similar activities, and proactively observes compliance with the legislation in different consumer markets.
[9] Substitutive Enforcement and Penalty Payment Act, RT I, 12.07.2014, 29.
[10] Administrative Procedure Act, RT I, 23.02.2011, 8.

receipt of the passenger's complaint in writing, and must reply to the complaint within 15 days.[11] The reply must include a reasoned opinion and suggestion about how the complaint might be settled. If the company does not agree with the complaint, it must provide justifications for its refusal of the whole or part of the claim.[12] The settlement of disputes between a consumer and a trader is not deemed to be an administrative proceeding within the meaning of the Administrative Procedure Act.[13]

If agreement cannot be reached between passenger and the airline, or if the airline refuses to reply within the timeframe provided by the law, the passenger has a right to 'submit a complaint to the person or institution which settles corresponding disputes, to the consumer complaints committee through the Consumer Protection Board or to a court'.[14]

Lastly, the affected air passenger has a choice to submit a complaint to the Consumer Protection Board or the court.

C. Procedure before the National Enforcement Body

There are two options for settlement of an air passenger complaint within the ECPB. First, the passenger can submit the complaint to the Consumer Complaints Committee (CC Committee). The CC Committee is an alternative dispute resolution body within the ECPB that settles consumer disputes if the value of the dispute is at least €20.[15] The settlement of the complaint by the CC Committee is free of charge for the parties. The CC Committee may refuse to hear the complaint if the same dispute is currently pending before a court, or if there is a court judgment in force concerning the same matter. On the basis of the information provided by the parties to the dispute, the CC Committee holds a hearing and adopts a decision by a simple majority of its members. The decision is addressed to the parties. The decision of the CC Committee must be complied with within one month following the day of receipt of a copy of a decision, unless otherwise provided in the decision. The airline company must notify the Consumer Protection Board in writing when it complies with the decision of the CC Committee.[16] If a party does not consent to the decision of the CC Committee, or fails to comply with the decision, it has a right to bring proceedings in the county court for resolution of the same dispute.

If the airline fails to comply with a decision of the CC Committee, the ECPB, as well as the air passenger, has a right, subject to the consent of the passenger, to

---

[11] The airline company may extend this deadline, provided valid reasons are presented.
[12] Consumer Protection Act, RT I 2004, 13, 86, Art 19.
[13] ibid, Art 1.
[14] ibid, Art 20.
[15] ibid, Art 21.
[16] ibid, Art 37.

file an action with a county court. Additionally, the ECPB can issue a *precept* to an air operator, with a claim for compensation and assistance of passengers in the event of denied boarding, cancellation or the long delay of flights.[17] A precept is an administrative act that imposes a legal obligation on the air operator to perform a required act.[18] It must be complied with immediately, and the contesting of the precept will not suspend compliance therewith. The sanction available to the ECPB to ensure compliance with a precept is payment of a penalty. Until 30 June 2014, the maximum penalty was €640. From 1 July 2014 this has been increased to €3,500.[19] The penalty can be applied repeatedly until the air operator complies with the precept.[20]

Recently, a precept issued by the ECPB was challenged by one company.[21] The company brought a claim to the administrative court, demanding compensation from ECPB for the penalty paid. The company unsuccessfully challenged the power of the ECPB and the legal validity of the precept. The Tallinn Administrative Court dismissed the challenge and found that the ECPB has the power to issue precepts to the trader that have legally binding force. See Table 11.1 for a summary of precepts issued by the ECPB between October 2012 and March 2014.

The second option for affected air passengers is to turn to the European Consumer Centre of Estonia (ECC-Estonia). The ECC-Estonia is an independent department of the ECPB.[22] The activities of the ECC-Estonia are regulated by the Statute on the European Consumer Centre of Estonia adopted by the head of the ECPB.[23] One of the functions of the ECC-Estonia is to assist consumers with cross-border complaints and disputes, and forwarding of disputes to the alternative dispute resolution body in Estonia or in other Member States.

There are no statistical data available from commencement of implementation of the Regulation in 2005.[24] However, according to the information provided in the annual reports of the ECPB, the volume of air passenger complaints under the

---

[17] Aviation Act, RT I, 29.06.2014, 27, Art 60[3]; in case of any other infringements under Regulation 261 the Board can issue a precept under the Law Enforcement Act, RT I, 12.07.2014, 84.

[18] Substitutive Enforcement and Penalty Payment Act, RT I 2001, 50, 283, Arts 3 and 4.

[19] Aviation Act, RT I, 29.06.2014, 27, Art 60[3].

[20] Substitutive Enforcement and Penalty Payment Act, RT I 2001, 50, 283, Art 2(2).

[21] *Bakker Holland OÜ v Tarbijakaitseamet* (case ref 3-13-965). The case did not concern air passenger rights but related to unfair commercial practice.

[22] As can be read in the annual reports of ECC-Estonia, each year since 2005, air passenger rights-related inquiries and complaints have formed a considerable percentage of all appeals received. All published reports are available at <www.ecc.ee/about-the-ecc-of-estonia/>.

[23] Available (in Estonian) at <www.tarbijakaitseamet.ee/sites/default/files/ametist/el_nk_pohimaarus. pdf>.

[24] This is due to the fact that the complaints database used by the Board until 2013 did not enable differentiation of cases handled only under Regulation 261 but contained all kinds of complaints relating to air transport (including luggage, changes in timetables, ticket fares, etc).

Table 11.1: Precepts issues by the ECPB

Number	Date	Main legal issue	CJEU case law referred
EK-TRT-2014-40 SmartLynx	28.03.2014	Denied boarding Article 2, 4(3), 7 of the Regulation	Cases C-402 and 432/07 *Sturgeon and Others* [2009] ECR I-10923 Cases C-581 and 629/10 *Nelson v Deutsche Lufthansa AG* [2012] OJ C399/3 Case C-22/11 *Finnair v Lassooy* (ECJ, 4 October 2012)
EK-TRT-2014-03 Estonian Air	07.01.2014	Long delay Article 5, 7 of the Regulation	–
6-25/13-09110-001 SmartLynx	02.10.2013	Long delay Articles 3(6), 5 and 7 of the Regulation	*Sturgeon* *Nelson* Case C-294/10 *Eglītis & Ors v Latvijas Republikas Ekonomikas ministrija* (ECJ, 12 May 2011)
6-25/13-09051-001 SmartLynx	01.10.2013	Denied boarding Article 4(3), 7 and 8 of the Regulation	*Sturgeon* *Nelson* *Finnair*
6-25/13-08229-001 Pullmantur Air	05.09.2013	Long delay Article 7 of the Regulation	*Sturgeon* *Nelson*
6-25/13-08057-001 SmartLynx	30.08.2013	Long delay Article 7 of the Regulation	*Sturgeon* *Nelson* Case C-549/07 *Wallentin-Hermann v Alitalia* [2008] ECR I-11061
6-25/13-03236-001 Estonian Air	28.03.2013	Long delay Article 7 of the Regulation	*Sturgeon* *Nelson* *Wallentin-Hermann*
6-25/13-01164-001 SmartLynx	30.01.2013	Long delay	*Sturgeon* *Nelson*
6-25/12-09379-001 UTair	23.10.2013	Denied boarding Article 4 and 7 of the Regulation	–
Estonian Air	09.10.2012	Long delay	*Sturgeon*

Regulation continues to increase.[25] The ECPB handled 46 air passenger complaints in 2013[26] and 59 in 2014.[27]

D. Judicial Procedure

Two types of judicial proceedings regarding air passenger rights are possible in the Estonian courts. First, claims can be brought under the administrative law procedure. The actions of the ECPB and its subordinate departments are subject to this procedure. Thus, for example, the validity of the precept or any violation of procedural rules in the complaints procedure may be challenged through the administrative courts.

If the parties do not agree with the decision of the CC Committee, or wish to file a complaint directly with the court, the civil procedure must be followed. The Code of Civil Procedure[28] provides a simplified court adjudication process for claims worth €2,000 or below on the main claim and up to €4,000 together with collateral claims.[29] The simplified proceedings mean that the process, including the judgment itself[30] and the right of appeal, is limited.

The substantive law applicable to the air passengers is the Regulation and the Law of Obligations Act. Regulation 261 is directly applicable to all Member States,

---

[25] eg the volume of the cases in 2012 was approximately at the same level as in 2010, when the air transport sector was greatly affected by the Islandic volcanic ash crisis. In the Board's opinion, the growth in complaints might have resulted from the increased awareness of passengers of their rights, or from the overall economic crisis that raised consumer sensitivity in terms of protection of their economic interests and probably affected the quality of air transport services in general at the same time: Consumer Protection Board, *Annual Report 2012*, available (only in Estonian) at <http://issuu.com/tarbijakaitseamet/docs/tarbijakaitseameti_aastaraamat_2012>.

[26] The Board issued a precept to airlines in connection with eight (out of 46) complaints, in light of the airlines' refusal to pay compensation. In the case of four complaints, the airlines had already paid compensation after receiving a warning from the Board. A total of €13,733 was paid in 2013 by airlines to passengers who had turned to the Board for assistance (in 2012 this figure was over €4,000). In addition to complaints relating to compensation, the Board also resolved other complaints concerning rights of air passengers (such as duty to give information, return of ticket money, changes to timetables), as well as baggage complaints: Consumer Protection Board, *Annual Report 2013*, available at <http://issuu.com/tarbijakaitseamet/docs/tarbijakaitseameti_aastaraamat_2013_64c67859679694?e=0/8273691>.

[27] Those numbers concern only complaints, not information requests regarding air passenger rights under the same Regulation. A 'complaint' means the passenger's claim when, due to the specific incident (delay, cancellation, etc), he or she is asking for enforcement of his or her rights under Regulation 261. The data for 2014 cover only 11 months. According to the information provided in the Commission Staff Working Document, 'Complaint handling and enforcement by MS of the Air Passenger Rights Regulations', the Estonian NEB handled 60 complaints in 2010, 55 complaints in 2011 and 87 complaints in 2012. It is not fully clear whether the data included in the annual reports and Commission document are directly comparable. Unfortunately, the ECPB did not respond to our request to provide a statistical overview of the complaints.

[28] Code of Civil Procedure, RT I, 31.12.2014, 5.

[29] ibid, Art 405.

[30] ibid, Art 444; the adjudicating court may confine itself, in the statement of reasons for its judgment, to setting out the legal reasoning and the evidence on which the conclusions of the court are based.

including Estonia. The Law of Obligations Act[31] regulates contracts for the carriage of passengers. The provisions of the Act relating to the carriage of passengers are applicable only in so far as this area is not otherwise regulated by law or an international convention that is binding on Estonia.[32] The decisions of all courts are public, unless otherwise requested, and are publically available on the database.[33]

There is no specific regulation of the time limits for bringing actions for compensation under the Regulation. The general limitation periods provided under the General Part of the Civil Code Act apply in Estonia.[34] According to Article 146(1) of the General Part of the Civil Code Act (Tsiviilseadustiku üldosa seadus),[35] the limitation period for a claim arising from a transaction is three years. Contract for carriage of passengers by air fall within the scope of that provision, thus the general limitation period for claims under Regulation 261 is also three years.

There have been very few cases on Regulation 261 brought before the Estonian courts (see Table 11.2).[36] Considering the relatively low amounts contested in air passenger disputes and the high costs associated with the judicial proceedings, this is not surprising. The system for provision of legal aid,[37] the overall duration and complexity of the court proceedings, and claimants' inability to bring a formal class action are among those factors contributing to the low litigation rates. The low number of cases is also explained by the relatively low volume of air transport in Estonia. Tallinn Airport, the largest airport in the country, serves 37,856 flights and around two million passengers annually.[38]

---

[31] Law of Obligations Act, RT I, 11.04.2014, 13.

[32] ibid, Art. 824(3).

[33] The database of court judgments at the first and second levels is available at <www.riigiteataja.ee/kohtuteave/maa_ringkonna_kohtulahendid/main.html>; the judgments of the Supreme Court are available at <www.nc.ee>.

[34] In Case C-139/11 *Moré v KLM* (ECJ, 22 November 2012), the Court held that the time-limits for bringing actions for compensation under Arts 5 and 7 of Regulation 261 are determined in accordance with the rules of each Member State on the limitation of actions.

[35] General Part of the Civil Code Act, RT I, 13.03.2014, 103.

[36] First instance court ruling from 29 December 2011 (case ref 2-11-40908), which concerned a passenger's claim for compensation under Regulation 261 for the lengthy delay of a flight. Since the airline did not submit any objections or proofs regarding the reasons for the delay, the court held that the passenger was entitled to the compensation claimed. Similarly, the first instance court, on 24 April 2013 (case ref 2-12-51064), ruled in favour of five passengers in their claims for compensation under Regulation 261 due to cancellation of their flight. The airline accepted the claim and did not submit any objections.

[37] The survey on access to legal aid in Estonia, carried out in Winter 2014 by Factum&Ariko, confirmed that almost 50% of respondents found legal aid too costly and access to such aid limited. The results of the survey were summarised in the press release published by the insurance company for legal expenses, DAS, available at <www.das.ee/uuring-ligi-poolte-vastanute-hinnagul-on-oigusabi-teenused-liiga-kallid/>.

[38] Tallinn Airport, 'Statistics and Surveys', available at <www.tallinn-airport.ee/eng/associates/GeneralInfo/statisticsandsurveys/?articleID=1355>; Tallinn Airport, *Annual Report 2013*, available at <www.tallinn-airport.ee/upload/Editor/Aastaaruanded/Lennujaama%20aastaraamat_2013_ENG.pdf>; 12 airlines operate to and from Tallinn Airport, according to statistical data for 2014 available at <www.tallin-airprot.ee>; in 2013 the national air carrier Estonian Air carried out 10,788 flights in total, which is 44.8% less than in 2012; the total number of passengers for all flights was 551,169, which is 37.9% less than in 2012; see Estonian Air, *Annual Report 2013*, available at <http://estonian-air.ee/wp-content/uploads/2014/06/ESTONIAN-AIR-ANNUAL-REPORT-20131.pdf>.

Table 11.2: Court Cases on Regulation 261 (2005–15)

Case Number	Court	Date of Judgment	Contested Legal Issues	Facts	Outcome
2-12-51064/7	Harju County Court (1st instance)	24 April 2013	Cancellation Articles 5 and 7 of the Regulation Simplified procedure/civil law procedure	Complaint by a family	Compensation awarded to the passengers
2-12-8977/31	Tallinn Circuit Court (2nd instance)	27 February 2013	Obligation to provide care (appeal)	Dispute between tour operator and airline	Tour operator to bear the costs
2-12-8977/20	Harju County Court (1st instance)	8 October 2012	Obligation to provide care Articles 6 and 9 of the Regulation Law of Obligations Act	Dispute between tour operator and airline	Tour operator to bear the costs
2-11-40908/9	Harju County Court (1st instance)	29 December 2011	Long Delay European Small Claims Procedure Technical problem is not an exception circumstances	Complaint by a passenger delayed for 8 hours	Compensation awarded € 250
2-06-1036/5	Harju County Court (1st instance)	26 January 2007	Long delay Moral compensation under Law of Obligations Act	Delay incurred by tourists on travel package holiday	Compensation awarded in part

III. Review of the Judicial and Alternative Dispute Resolution Practice in Estonia

Since there are very few court cases in Estonia, this section will provide an overview of the available practice of the ECPB and national courts. There have been very few decisions concerning Regulation 261: four cases in the first level courts and one case in the court of appeal.[39] No cases have been brought before Supreme

---

[39] eg Table 11.2 above for an overview.

Court of Estonia, and no requests for preliminary rulings on the Regulation have been submitted to the CJEU by Estonian courts. The ECPB has issued eight precepts to airline companies, obliging them to compensate passengers in accordance with the Regulation.

A. Rights

All the available decisions adjudicated in Estonia are rather short and do not discuss the application of Regulation 261 in detail. Two cases have been decided by the courts on the basis of the simplified civil law procedure[40] or European Small Claims Procedure.[41] Two other cases concerned air passenger rights guaranteed indirectly under the Regulation: (i) awards of moral compensation in addition to the compensation provided under the Regulation;[42] and (ii) disputes between tour operators or airlines on the issue of who is responsible to cover costs relating to the obligation to provide care for delayed passengers.

The precepts of the ECPB are longer and provide more detailed discussion of the Regulation and CJEU case law. Seven cases in which a precept was issued concerned long delays, and three cases dealt with denied boarding. Five precepts have been issued against the Latvian company SmartLynx, three against the national flag airline Estonian air, and one each against the Spanish airline Pullmantur Air and the Russian UTair.

i. Scope of Application

The scope of application of the Regulation has been contested only in one proceeding in the ECPB.[43] In the precept issued against the Russian airline UTair, the airline tried to argue that the Regulation cannot be mandatory for air carriers of the Russian Federation because the Russian Federation is not a member of the EU.[44] The ECPB dismissed this argument and explained that the Regulation applies to all passengers departing from an airport located in a Member State of the EU.[45] Consequently, the Regulation also applies to a flight operated by UTair from Tallinn Airport.[46]

ii. Long Delay

The precepts relating to long delays, seven in total, form the largest group of cases addressed by the ECPB. The ECPB relies on the jurisprudence of the CJEU,

---

[40] Case ref 2-12-51064/7.
[41] Case ref 2-11-40908/9.
[42] Case ref 2-06-1036/5.
[43] Ref 6-25/12-09379-001.
[44] Ref 6-25/12-09379-001.
[45] Ref 6-25/12-09379-001.
[46] Ref 6-25/12-09379-001.

particularly *Sturgeon*, to include long delays in the scope of the protection and compensation scheme provided by the Regulation. The ECPB, directly relying on *Sturgeon*, considers cases of long delay as being comparable to cancellation, and therefore subject to compensation as provided in Article 7 of the Regulation.[47] Thus, the *Sturgeon* and *Nelson* line of jurisprudence is well understood and accepted by the ECPB. There has been only one case in the court of first instance that referred to *Sturgeon*.[48] There, the dispute was about long delay, and the court ordered payment of compensation to the passenger.

iii. Denied Boarding

Three precepts deal with the issue of denied boarding. Two cases concerned passengers who were denied boarding and who refused alternative routes offered by the airline,[49] and one case concerned 14-year-old passengers who were travelling alone and who were denied boarding.[50] In the case concerning denied boarding and re-routing, the airline attempted to argue that passengers who refused re-routing to their final destination and who did not agree to the reimbursement of the ticket price should be considered 'volunteers',[51] and thus as not entitled to compensation under Article 7 of the Regulation.[52] In all cases the ECPB provided detailed discussion of the concept and legal consequences of denied boarding as stipulated in the Regulation. The ECPB has stressed that in the case of denied boarding, the right to compensation is 'automatic and … does not depend on whether the passengers accepted the alternative route or not or claim for reimbursement'.[53]

iv. Right to Care

The only court case to have reached the appeal level concerned the interpretation of a contract between a tour operator and an airline. The question the court was asked to answer was: Who is legally obliged to provide care for passengers as provided in Article 9 (right to care) and Article 13 (right of redress) of the Regulation: an airline, or a tour operator?[54] The case was brought by the airline, which, due to a lengthy delay in the time of departure, was obliged to meet the care obligation towards those passengers suffering delay in connection with the travel package to Greece. The airline, based on the contract between the tour operator and the

---

[47] eg the first precept issued on 9 October 2012 and subsequent precepts relating to long delay.
[48] Harju County Court (Harju Maakohus), 29.12.2011 in case 2-11-40908.
[49] Ref EK-TRT-2014-40; Ref. 6-25/13-09051-001.
[50] Case ref 6-25/12-09379-001. The information published on the airline web page did not require additional documents, or adult supervision for passengers aged 12 years or older, but the two passengers, aged 14 years, holding all necessary documents, were refused boarding.
[51] 'Volunteers', as considered by the airline company in this case, should be entitled to assistance in accordance with Art 8 of Regulation 261, and benefits to be agreed between the passenger and operating air carrier.
[52] Case ref 6-25/13-09051-001.
[53] Ref EK-TRT-2014-40.
[54] Case ref 2-12-8977/20 (first instance); Case ref 2-12-8977/31 (on appeal).

airline, sought compensation for incurred costs relating to the 'right to care' provided under the Regulation.

The airline and the travel agency had entered a contract for the provision of charter flights. Article 13 of the contract referred to the liabilities of the parties to the contract. The exact meaning and interpretation of this provision was highly contested by the parties. However, the legal question was clear: Could the obligation under Articles 6 and 9 of the Regulation to provide care to the delayed passengers in certain circumstances be transferred, based on the civil law contract, to a third party (in this case, the tour operator)?

The tour operator argued that Regulation 261 must be understood as imposing the obligation to provide care on the airline company. The tour operator could only be responsible for damage caused by the action or inaction of the tour operator. The obligation of care could not be transferred by civil law contract to a third party. The airline company, however, argued that the Regulation does not preclude transfer of the obligation to provide care. The ultimate aim of the Regulation is to ensure that delayed passengers receive care. The identity of the provider of this care may be settled or negotiated by the civil law contracts. In this case, the airline company had shifted its liability and thus transferred the obligation to provide care to the tour operator, which had entered into the contract for the provision of charter flights. The first- and second-level courts agreed with the arguments of the airline company, and required the tour operator to cover the costs incurred by the airline in providing care to passengers as required by Article 6 of the Regulation. An appeal to the Supreme Court was not admitted. Thus, the decision of the second-level court became final.

v. Montreal Convention Compatibility

No cases considered by the ECPB or the courts have dealt with issues relating to the compatibility of the Montreal Convention and the Regulation.

B. Exceptions: Extraordinary Circumstances

In the precepts, where there has been a long delay, the airlines have attempted to use 'extraordinary circumstances' as a defence. However, they have not been successful. In accordance with the CJEU jurisprudence, the defence of 'extraordinary circumstance' is understood and interpreted by the ECPB narrowly.

The ECPB, with reference to *Eglītis*,[55] explained that an air carrier is obliged to implement 'all reasonable measures to avoid extraordinary circumstances'.[56] This includes an obligation, at the stage of planning the flight, to take account of 'the

---

[55] ECJ, Case C-294/10, *Andrejs Eglītis and Edvards Ratnieks v Latvijas Republikas Ekonomikas ministrija.*

[56] Ref 6-25/13-09119-001.

risk of delay connected to the possible occurrence of such circumstances'.[57] This risk may be mitigated, for example, by making provision for a certain amount of reserve time to address unexpected circumstances.[58] The ECPB, in line with the CJEU case law, also found that an airline cannot claim that 'all reasonable measures' have been taken merely by proving that minimum rules on maintenance of an aircraft have been duly complied with.[59]

In one proceeding, an airline company tried to argue that the Estonian translation of Article 5(3) of the Regulation is misleading.[60] The case concerned the delay of a flight caused by the defrosting of the plane, which could easily have been avoided by keeping the plane in the warm, covered hangar. The company argued that in the Estonian language version of the provision, the term 'reasonable measures' (in Estonian *mõistlikud meetmed*) is translated as 'necessary measures' (in Estonian *vajalikud meetmed*).[61] The company claimed that it relied on the Estonian language version of the Regulation and complied with all necessary measures to avoid extraordinary circumstances.[62] The ECPB did not accept this argument, and stated that this linguistic incoherence could not be relied on by the company to avoid its obligations following from the Regulation.[63] Although there are no legal rules regulating the storage of planes in winter-time, it is expected and predictable that, due to cold weather, a plane may be not be immediately operational (leading to delays of scheduled flights) if it is not stored in a warm hangar.[64] The airline company, in preparing the flight schedule, had to take due account of those circumstances, and could not rely on delays caused by technical problems relating to the cold weather that could be easily avoided.[65] In this context, the ECPB concluded that neither necessary nor reasonable measures had been taken by the airline.

With reference to *Sturgeon*, *Nelson* and *Wallentin-Hermann*, the ECPB has found that technical problems in an aircraft are not covered by the concept of 'extraordinary circumstances'.[66]

In establishing whether a situation can be considered an 'extraordinary circumstance', the ECPB co-operates with the Civil Aviation Administration of Estonia. The ECPB forwards documents submitted by the airline and requests the expert opinion of the Civil Aviation Administration. The Civil Aviation Administration ascertains whether the incident is of an exceptional nature (for example, as regards technical faults or weather conditions) within the meaning of the Regulation.[67]

[57] Ref 6-25/13-09119-001.
[58] Ref 6-25/13-09119-001.
[59] Ref 6-25/13-08057-001.
[60] Precept from 9.10.2012.
[61] Precept from 9.10.2012.
[62] Precept from 9.10.2012.
[63] Precept from 9.10.2012.
[64] Precept from 9.10.2012.
[65] Precept from 9.10.2012.
[66] Ref 6-25/13-08057-001; also Ref 6-25/13-05073-001; Ref 6-25/13-03236-001.
[67] eg ref 6-25/13-09119001.

C. Remedies

According to the practice of the Consumer Protection Board, in approximately 25 to 30 per cent of the cases, the airlines pay compensation under the Regulation.

In a court case where the award of compensation under the Regulation was under discussion, the court did reach a verdict in favour of the passengers, probably due to the fact that the airline did not contest the claims.

IV. Scholarly Analysis and Public Debates

There is unfortunately very little scholarly analysis or public debate in Estonia on the issue of air passenger rights in general and the application of the Regulation in Estonia in particular. The volcanic ash eruptions in 2010 and a series of CJEU casestriggered attention, and have facilitated the reform of air passenger rights in the EU. Estonian politician Siim Kallas, who was the Vice-President of the European Commission responsible for transport in 2010–14, played a central role in the current European reforms.[68] However, the debates at the European level and in various Member States have found only very modest reflections in Estonian political discussions and public debate. The Estonian Government and Parliament have supported the European Commission's proposal for reform.[69]

The ECPB carries out information campaigns, but does not really facilitate wider public discussion of the current regulatory scheme. Industry representatives have not openly expressed their positions. Regarding the framework of this chapter, information requests were sent to four major airlines operating from Tallinn Airport.[70] The airlines were asked to provide an opinion on the current regulatory scheme regulating air passenger rights and comment on their position vis-à-vis possible future reforms. Unfortunately none of the companies provided any information.

Mass media coverage of the issues relating to air travel has mostly concentrated on the continuous financial difficulties of the national flag carrier, Estonian Air, including the possible consequences for passengers in the event of insolvency of the company. Another issue that has attracted some public attention is state aid

---

[68] Kallas, as the responsible European Commissioner, was at the centre of Europe-wide public attention in the light of the volcanic ash eruptions, and equally so during the development, proposal and adoption by the European institutions of new measures to strengthen air passenger rights.
[69] Eesti lähtub Vabariigi Valitsuse 02.05.13 ja 03.10.13 istungil ning 17.05.2013 ja 04.10.2013 Riigikogu Euroopa Liidu asjade komisjoni istungil heakskiidetud seisukohtadest availalbe at <www.riigikogu.ee/?op=emsplain&page=pub_file&file_id=894a354f-b9dc-4996-be6f-3b4264fd75c2&>; see also the Parliament of Estonia, 'EL asjade komisjon toetab lennureisijate õiguste tugevdamist', 17 May 2013, available at <www.riigikogu.ee/index.php?id=176483>.
[70] Estonian Air, Lufthansa, Ryanair and Finnair.

provided to Estonian Air, currently awaiting investigation by the European Commission into whether it is contrary to EU law.[71]

Few publications have aimed at informing air passengers of their rights according to EU law. They have mostly been in the form of interviews with the representative of the ECPB.[72] There are, however, three scholarly works written in Estonian that discuss the EU system for protection of air passenger rights. One article, published shortly after Regulation 261 came into force, provides an overview of the legal obligations following from the Regulation, but does not address Estonian law or practice.[73] A more recent article reviewed developments at the EU level through analysis of the jurisprudence of the CJEU.[74] The third publication, prepared by the analytical department of the Estonian Parliament, provided a short, thematic, four-page overview of the main case law of the CJEU and legal provisions regulating the rights of air passengers.[75]

V. Conclusions

The first Vice-President of the Estonian Parliament, Laine Randjärv, stated in 2014 that

> Estonia is a small country, but we have five international airports, a military summer base in Emari, serving NATO planes, our own airline company Estonian Air, the Estonian Aviation Academy, which prepares high profile pilots, as well as an aviation museum. This underlines the success of Estonia in the sphere of aviation, but we could use the existing capacities even more effectively.[76]

This statement aptly describes the state of art in the area of air passenger rights. On the basis of the review of the administrative decisions of the ECPB and very limited court practice, it may be concluded that the Estonian administrative and

---

[71] Estonian Air is the national flagship company. The company is continually struggling for survival and is showing depressing economic results. A number of business model reorganisation projects have been carried out since 2006 to boost the economic profitability of the company. The most controversial economic restructuring plan, with a contribution of state funds of over €74 million, not only has been the subject of national political controversy, but also has resulted in an official investigation by the European Commission on the state aid.

[72] eg Äripäev, 'Lennureisija teadku oma õigusi', 29 June2013, available at <www.aripaev.ee/uudised/2013/06/29/lennureisija-teadku-oma-oigusi>; Postimees, 'Kristina Vaksmaa: lennureisija kadunud kohver ja vaevalised vaidlused', 2 July 2012, available at <http://arvamus.postimees.ee/894174/kristina-vaksmaa-lennureisija-kadunud-kohver-ja-vaevalised-vaidlused>.

[73] Mäll, A 'Lennureisija õiguste kaitse Euroopa Liidus. Viibivad lennud' (2006) 10 *Juridica* 702.

[74] Sein, K and Värv, A, 'Lennureisija õigus saada hüvitist. Euroopa Liidu lennureisijate õiguste määrus' (2013) 2 *Juridica* 107.

[75] Värv, A, 'Lennureisijate õigused Euroopa Liidus', Nr 6/25.02.2013.

[76] Parliament of Estonia, 'Randjärv tunnustas Eesti lennundust lennupäevade avamisel', 14 May 2014, available at <www.riigikogu.ee/?id=179694> (in Estonian, authors' translation).

judicial systems interpret and apply the Regulation correctly. The jurisprudence of the CJEU is central to the reasoning and decisions of the ECPB.

However, it is alarming and puzzling to note that so few complaints are submitted by air passengers, and that the case law is almost non-existent, with little attention given to the issue in public debates. The existing legal framework and institutional capacities should be used more effectively to protect air passenger rights, both through a simplification of the relevant procedural rules and through the provision of legal aid for court representation.

12

France: Air Passengers Facing Long-Haul Judicial Journeys

FABIEN LE BOT

I. Introduction

The aim of this chapter is to examine the impact of Regulation 261[1] and its accompanying case law on the protection of air passengers' rights in France. Generally, the Regulation and the case law of the CJEU have been applied and followed by French courts. However, this does not mean that the enforcement of Regulation 261 is always satisfactory. In some cases, it is perceivable that national jurisdictions hesitate to apply the Regulation directly in the way it has been interpreted: they sometimes seem uncomfortable with the case law of the CJEU, notably following the *Sturgeon* case.[2] This is true not only for the right to compensation, but also as regards the compatibility of the Regulation with the Montreal Convention.

The outline of this chapter is as follows. First, the procedural background is addressed, before briefly dealing with claims and remedies in France. Discussion then turns to details of the application of Regulation 261 by the French courts, including its scope of application, the right to compensation, extraordinary circumstances and compatibility with the Montreal Convention. The last section of this chapter is devoted to French scholarly analysis of the Regulation.

II. The French Procedural Background

Regulation 261 addresses infringements in Article 16 and establishes an administrative procedure before a National Enforcement Body (NEB). Each passenger

---

[1] European Parliament and Council Regulation (EC) 261/2004 of 11 February 2004 establishing common rules on compensation and assistance to passengers in the event of denied boarding and of cancellation or long delay of flights, and repealing Regulation (EEC) No 295/91 OJ L 46/1 (Regulation 261).

[2] Cases C-402 and C-432/07 *Sturgeon and Others* [2009] ECR I-10923 (*Sturgeon*).

may complain to such a body about any alleged infringement of the Regulation. However, the Regulation does not include any provision about the procedure before national courts. This does not mean that a judicial procedure is impossible. Indeed in *McDonagh v Ryanair*, a case concerning the right to care, the CJEU found that Article 16, establishing the administrative complaints mechanism,

> cannot be interpreted as allowing only national bodies responsible for the enforcement of Regulation No 261/2004 to sanction the failure of air carriers to comply with their obligation laid down in Articles 5(1)(b) and 9 of that Regulation to provide care.[3]

It is therefore possible for air passengers to go directly before a national court, without activating the administrative system beforehand.

In France, as well as in the other Member States, air passengers should have the possibility, after an unfruitful demand addressed to the airline company, of following the administrative procedure established by the Regulation or, alternatively, of bringing the case before a court.

A. Administrative Procedure before the National Enforcement Body

The NEB designated by the French authorities is the Direction générale de l'aviation civile (General Direction for Civil Aviation, Ministry of Transport) (DGAC), which has an office devoted to air passengers' rights. Its website[4] sets out the relevant complaint procedure for air passengers. The DGAC will handle the complaint and, if necessary, assist the passengers in their relations with airline companies. However, the NEB is not allowed to take individual decisions granting compensation to passengers.

Article 16(3) of the Regulation requires the Member States to lay down effective, proportionate and dissuasive sanctions. In France, cases of violation of Regulation 261 can be transmitted to the Commission administrative de l'aviation civile (Administrative Commission for Civil Aviation), which can recommend the Minister in charge of civil aviation to impose an administrative fine of up to €7,500.[5] Very few complaints were sent to the DGAC from 2007 to 2009. In 2010, it received more than 5,000 complaints; in 2011, about 4,500; and in 2012, 3,500.[6] Out of these, only 2 to 4 per cent of cases were recommended for sanctioning, and even fewer for effective sanctions. Fines are therefore rare, and their level in France is low compared to the average maximum sanction of €43,617 in the Member States, as calculated by the European Commission.[7]

---

[3] Case 12/11 *McDonagh v Ryanair* (ECJ, 31 January 2013), para 23.

[4] Available at <www.developpement-durable.gouv.fr/Que-faire-en-cas-de-retard-refus-d.html>.

[5] *Code de l'aviation* (Aviation Code), Arts R 330-20 and R 330-22.

[6] European Commission, 'Complaint handling and enforcement by Member States of the Air Passenger Rights Regulations' (Commission Staff Working Document) SWD (2014) 156 final.

[7] ibid, 17.

B. Judicial Procedure

As far as the judicial procedure is concerned, the CJEU, in *Cuadrench Moré*, has logically held that

> in the absence of provisions of EU law on the matter, it is for the domestic legal system of each Member State to lay down the detailed procedural rules governing actions for safeguarding rights which individuals derive from EU law, provided that those rules observe the principles of equivalence and effectiveness … [Therefore] the time-limits for bringing actions for compensation under Articles 5 and 7 of Regulation No 261/2004 are determined by the national law of each Member State.[8]

In France, such actions for compensation are subject to the ordinary time limit set by Article 2224 of the Civil Code, that is, five years. In most cases, they have to be brought before the *juge de proximité* (proximity judge),[9] who has jurisdiction for all litigation regarding amounts under €4,000. For such litigation, there is no possibility of appeal; only a *pourvoi en cassation*, limited to questions of law, is possible before the Cour de cassation (Court of Cassation). This procedural system explains why the jurisprudence on air passengers' rights is somewhat difficult to delineate in full. The decision of the proximity judge is not published. It is only if the case is brought before the Cour de cassation, or if the amount involved is more than €4,000, that it is easier to access the decision.

In *Rehder v Air Baltic Corporation*, the Court of Justice, interpreting Regulation 44/2001,[10] held that

> where there are several places at which services are provided in different Member States, it is also necessary to identify the place with the closest linking factor between the contract in question and the court having jurisdiction, in particular the place where, pursuant to that contract, the main provision of services is to be carried out … [Therefore] both the place of arrival and the place of departure of the aircraft must be considered, in the same respect, as the place of provision of the services which are the subject of an air transport contract.[11]

This case law has been followed and applied by some French courts, for instance the Cour d'appel d'Aix-en-Provence (Aix-en Provence Court of Appeal)[12] or the Cour d'appel de Grenoble (Grenoble Court of Appeal).[13]

Launching a judicial procedure is, however, often complex and troublesome for air passengers, especially in view of the relatively low financial amount at stake.

---

[8] Case C-139/11 *Cuadrench Moré* (ECJ, 22 November 2012) paras 25–26.
[9] *Code de l'organisation judiciaire* (Judicial Organisation Code), Art L 231-3; the proximity judge should nevertheless cease to act as a court on 1 January 2017 (*Lois* No 2011-1862 of 13 December 2011, No 2012-1441 of 24 December 2012 and No 2014-1654 of 29 December 2014).
[10] Council Regulation (EC) No 44/2001 of 22 December 2000 on jurisdiction and the recognition and enforcement of judgments in civil and commercial matters [2001] OJ L012/1.
[11] Case C-204/08 *Rehder v Air Baltic Corporation* [2009] ECR I-6073, paras 38, 43.
[12] CA Aix-en-Provence 9 November 2012, No 12/08544.
[13] CA Grenoble 14 May 2013, No 12/05483.

In this respect, a new feature of French law could be helpful in the near future: a class action has been created by an Act adopted in 2014.[14] The new *action de groupe* must be launched by a registered and representative consumer protection association. It is a new way for consumers in a similar or identical situation to obtain individual damages from a professional who has failed to respect his obligations. However, it remains to be seen if damages can be obtained using this procedure on the grounds set out in Regulation 261, as the new law seems to be restricted to material damages. It is not clear whether the 'standardised and automatic compensation' of Article 7 of the Regulation can fall within this category. Nevertheless, this *action de groupe* could be useful in obtaining further compensation under national law or the Montreal Convention. Also, it could be used against travel agencies, which are not bound by the Regulation as they are not operating air carriers. This new procedure could promote the role of consumer associations in the protection of air passengers. Some of them, such as the Fédération Nationale des Associations d'Usagers des Transports (FNAUT), already help passengers in their litigation with airline companies. With the *action de groupe*, they could become proper claim aggregator services.

C. Alternative Dispute Resolution Mechanisms

Apart from the administrative and judicial procedures that passengers may follow to protect their rights, alternative dispute resolution mechanisms also exist in France. In 2010, the French Government appointed a mediator for the treatment of complaints following the widespread disruptions caused by the eruption of the volcano Eyjafjallajökull in Iceland. The European Consumer Centre France (ECC-France) also has an important mediation function, and issued a report on the exercise of passengers' rights in June 2012.[15] Furthermore, a Charte de la médiation du tourisme et du voyage (Mediation Charter for Tourism and Travel) was signed in 2011. An independent mediator can propose a friendly resolution, which in most cases proves satisfactory and obviates the need for judicial proceedings.[16] This type of alternative dispute resolution mechanism is now used more frequently, and will be even more so once Directive 2013/11/EU[17] becomes effective.

---

[14] Loi No 2014-344 of 17 March 2014.

[15] European Consumer Center France, 'L'exercice des droits des passagers aériens: la mise à l'épreuve de la réglementation européenne' (June 2012).

[16] In 2013, the Mediation Tourism and Travel opened 925 files and has given 460 opinions, which were followed in 84% of cases; La Médiation Tourisme et Voyage, available at <www.mtv.travel>.

[17] European Parliament and Council Directive 2013/11/EU of 21 May 2013 on alternative dispute resolution for consumer disputes and amending Regulation (EC) No 2006/2004 and Directive 2009/22/EC (Directive on consumer ADR) [2013] OJ L165/63.

III. Claims and Remedies

A. Claims

Given the difficulties inherent in accessing most of the judicial decisions concerning the application of Regulation 261, it is impossible to know with any degree of certainty just how many claims have been brought before the courts in France. Higher courts than the proximity judge (Cours d'appel) have dealt with such claims on several occasions, but the Cour de cassation has been confronted with only a dozen cases involving the Regulation.

It is, however, easier to evaluate the number of claims before the NEB, given that the DGAC has disclosed figures on its activity. In the period 2010–12, some 13,500 complaints were brought (see section II.A above). Most of these have concerned events of cancellation and long delays (around 45 per cent each); fewer have involved events of denied boarding (around 10 per cent).

Classification of judicial decisions according to the ground for liability seems comparable, although no figures are available. Most of the published decisions deal with cancellation and long delays, and it is also noticeable that some claims were brought before the courts in order to obtain further compensation,[18] notably on the ground of the Montreal Convention. On the other hand, it does not seem that the courts have had to deal with the right to care[19] or incidental rights.

B. Remedies

It seems that most airline companies are reluctant to award compensation when approached. This is true in the case of cancellation, but even more so in the case of long delays, given the fact that compensation is not contained in the letter of the Regulation but results from its constructive interpretation by the CJEU in *Sturgeon*.[20]

Airline companies at first, in an attempt to avoid paying compensation, appear to follow a strategy of non-disclosure of information to passengers, or to provide them with incomplete information about their rights. That said, in most cases, companies comply with the right to care, in particular meals and refreshments, in the event of a delay. However, if a long delay or a cancellation occurs, it is particularly difficult to obtain compensation, as companies will often invoke exceptional circumstances, such as weather conditions, to side-step demands.

---

[18] Regulation 261, Art 12.
[19] ibid, Art 9.
[20] *Sturgeon* (n 2).

It is difficult to know whether a claim brought before the DGAC is more favourable to the passenger, given the fact that the DGAC cannot issue sanctions in individual cases. It often seems that only judicial proceedings may lead to satisfactory compensation. Indeed, most courts seem to have applied the Regulation in line with its interpretation by the CJEU. In this respect, it should be noted that no request for a preliminary ruling has been submitted to the CJEU by a French court, be it the Cour de cassation, a Cour d'appel or a proximity judge. This is at odds with the practice of many courts in other Member States, most notably in Germany.

IV. French Courts and Regulation 261

A. Scope of Application

The CJEU has ruled on several occasions on the scope of application of the Regulation. First of all, it held in *Emirates Airlines* that

> the concept of 'flight' within the meaning of Regulation No 261/2004 must be interpreted as consisting essentially in an air transport operation, being as it were a 'unit' of such transport, performed by an air carrier which fixes its itinerary ... [Therefore] Article 3(1)(a) of Regulation No 261/2004 must be interpreted as not applying to the case of an outward and return journey in which passengers who have originally departed from an airport located in the territory of a Member State to which the Treaty applies travel back to that airport on a flight from an airport located in a non-member country. The fact that the outward and return flights are the subject of a single booking has no effect on the interpretation of that provision.[21]

This is to say that the Regulation does not apply to flights departing from third countries operated by non-EU carriers. This case law was applied in France by the Cour de cassation in a decision of 21 November 2012.[22] Indeed, it refused to grant the right to compensation to passengers of a cancelled flight from Annaba to Paris operated by Air Algérie. Furthermore, the Cour de cassation logically applied the notion of 'operating air carrier' in Article 2(b) as meaning that the Regulation cannot be invoked against a travel agency.[23] But French law provides that every person or company selling or organising travel is fully liable for the execution of its contractual obligations, even if executed by other operators.[24]

---

[21] Case C-173/07 *Emirates Airlines* [2008] ECR I-5237, paras 40, 53.
[22] C Cass 21 November 2012, No 11-22552.
[23] C Cass 8 March 2012, No 11-10226.
[24] *Code du tourisme* (Tourism Code), Art L 211-16.

French courts also had to deal with the distinction between 'cancellation' and 'delay'. In *Sturgeon*, the CJEU ruled that

> where passengers are carried on a flight whose departure time is later than the departure time originally scheduled, the flight can be classified as 'cancelled' only if the air carrier arranges for the passengers to be carried on another flight whose original planning is different from that of the flight for which the booking was made.[25]

Different planning can be evidenced by a change in the flight number, as shown by a judgment of the Cour d'appel de Paris (Paris Court of Appeal).[26] On the other hand, a flight operated the following day or two days later would be delayed and not cancelled, even if the aircraft was not the same as initially planned.[27] French case law is thus in line with the distinction between 'cancellation' and 'delay' as interpreted by the CJEU.

B. Right to Compensation

The case law of the CJEU on the right to compensation has been widely commented on and criticised. In *Sturgeon*, the Court famously held that 'the damage sustained by air passengers in cases of cancellation or long delay is comparable',[28] and therefore found, on the ground of the principle of equal treatment, that

> passengers whose flights are delayed may rely on the right to compensation laid down in Article 7 of Regulation No 261 where they suffer, on account of such flights, a loss of time equal to or in excess of three hours, that is to say when they reach their final destination three hours or more after the arrival time originally scheduled by the air carrier.[29]

This extensive interpretation of the Regulation was confirmed in *Nelson v Deutsche Lufthansa*,[30] as well as in *Air France v Folkerts*.[31]

In France, before the *Sturgeon* ruling, the Cour d'appel de Paris excluded the possibility of awarding compensation in the event of a long delay, referring to Article 6 of the Regulation, which only grants a right to care in such a case.[32] Following *Sturgeon*, however, most French courts complied with the ruling of the CJEU. For instance, the Cour d'appel de Grenoble has recognised a right to compensation when a long delay occurs.[33] Lower courts sometimes seem less familiar with the case law of the CJEU, refusing the right to compensation. It has indeed

---

[25] *Sturgeon* (n 2), para 35.
[26] CA Paris, 16 June 2011, No 09/28086.
[27] CA Paris, 3 July 2008, No 06/22704.
[28] *Sturgeon* (n 2), para 60.
[29] ibid, para 61.
[30] Cases C-581 and C-629/10 *Nelson v Deutsche Lufthansa AG* [2012] OJ C399/3 (*Nelson*).
[31] Case C-11/11 *Air France v Folkerts* (ECJ, 26 February 2013).
[32] CA Paris 3 July 2008, No 06/22704.
[33] CA Grenoble 16 October 2012, No 09/02188.

been noticed that some proximity judges do not apply the *Sturgeon* ruling.[34] In its annual report, the Mediator for Tourism and Travel also noticed that the discrepancy between the text of Regulation 261 and its interpretation by the CJEU renders it difficult to apply, with airline companies generally refusing to grant compensation in the event of long delays.

C. Extraordinary Circumstances

To deny passengers the right to compensation, airline companies have widely invoked Article 5(3) of the Regulation, which provides that

> [a]n operating air carrier shall not be obliged to pay compensation in accordance with Article 7, if it can prove that the cancellation is caused by extraordinary circumstances which could not have been avoided even if all reasonable measures had been taken.

This provision has been interpreted narrowly by the CJEU, notably in *Wallentin-Hermann v Alitalia*, where the CJEU ruled:

> [A] technical problem in an aircraft which leads to the cancellation of a flight is not covered by the concept of 'extraordinary circumstances' within the meaning of that provision, unless that problem stems from events which, by their nature or origin, are not inherent in the normal exercise of the activity of the air carrier concerned and are beyond its actual control.[35]

Furthermore, the air carrier

> must establish that, even if it had deployed all its resources in terms of staff or equipment and the financial means at its disposal, it would clearly not have been able—unless it had made intolerable sacrifices in the light of the capacities of its undertaking at the relevant time—to prevent the extraordinary circumstances with which it was confronted from leading to the cancellation of the flight.[36]

The 'extraordinary circumstances' defence has also been used before courts in France. Generally, French courts have followed the restrictive approach initiated by the CJEU. For instance, the Cour de cassation has judged that a company crew strike cannot be considered, in principle, as an extraordinary circumstance.[37] By the same token, the Cour d'appel de Saint-Denis de la Réunion (Saint-Denis de la Réunion Court of Appeal) has judged that a technical problem in the aircraft is an event which is inherent in the normal exercise of the activity of an air carrier

---

[34] eg P Frühling, E Decat and S Golinvaux, 'Panorama de la jurisprudence communautaire rendue en application du règlement n° 261/2004 sur les droits de passagers' [2012] *Revue de droit des transports*, dossier 15.

[35] Case C-549/07 *Wallentin-Hermann* [2008] ECR I-11061, para 34.

[36] ibid, para 41.

[37] C Cass 24 September 2009, No 08-18177 and No 08-18178; in this respect, it should be noted that during the long strike of September 2014, Air France publicly announced that it would systematically grant compensation to the passengers of cancelled flights.

and does not find its origin in an extraordinary event.[38] The concept of 'reasonable measure' has also been interpreted narrowly in line with the case law of the CJEU, as shown, for instance, by a judgment of the Cour d'appel de Paris.[39] It is therefore only in particularly rare cases that an extraordinary circumstance will be recognised as justifying an exception to the right to compensation. This has nonetheless been the case in a judgment of the Cour d'appel de Paris, where not only technical problems but also unfavourable weather conditions had been proved by the air carrier.[40]

A recent judgment by the Cour de cassation clearly shows that French case law tends to apply the CJEU's interpretation of 'extraordinary circumstances' in a strict manner.[41] In this case, a proximity judge ruled out the right to compensation, indicating that the technical problem was an extraordinary circumstance, and that Air France was not at fault and had respected the maintenance programme of the aircraft. The Cour de cassation, using the words of *Wallentin-Hermann*, quashed this first instance judgment: the proximity judge should have verified that the technical problem stemmed from events that, by their nature or origin, were not inherent in the normal exercise of the activity of the air carrier concerned and were beyond its actual control. He should also have investigated whether this carrier had taken all necessary measures to prevent the alleged extraordinary circumstances from leading to the cancellation of the flight. In this respect, following the minimal rules of maintenance cannot be considered as the completion of all reasonable measures.

The case law of the highest court seems to respect the interpretation of Article 5(3) as laid down by the CJEU. This case law has not changed following the publication on the European Commission's website of an indicative list of extraordinary circumstances.[42]

D. Montreal Convention Compatibility

In *R (International Air Transport Association and European Low Fares Airline Association) v Department of Transport*,[43] as well as in *Nelson*,[44] the CJEU asserted the compatibility of Regulation 261 with the Montreal Convention. For the CJEU, the relevant provisions of the Montreal Convention

> merely govern the conditions under which, after a flight has been delayed, the passengers concerned may bring actions for damages by way of redress on an individual basis, that

---

[38] CA Saint-Denis de la Réunion 22 July 2011, No 10/01924.

[39] CA Paris 4 November 2011, No 10/08/581.

[40] CA Paris 16 June 2011, No 09/28086.

[41] C Cass 19 March 2014, No 12-20.917.

[42] Available at <http://ec.europa.eu/transport/themes/passengers/air/doc/neb-extraordinary-circumstances-list.pdf>.

[43] Case C-344/04 *R (International Air Transport Association) v Department for Transport* [2006] ECR I-403 (*ex parte IATA*).

[44] *Nelson* (n 30).

is to say for compensation, from the carriers liable for damage resulting from that delay … [Therefore] it does not follow from these provisions, or from any other provision of the Montreal Convention, that the authors of the Convention intended to shield those carriers from any other form of intervention, in particular action which could be envisaged by the public authorities to redress, in a standardised and immediate manner, the damage that is constituted by the inconvenience that delay in the carriage of passengers by air causes, without the passengers having to suffer the inconvenience inherent in the bringing of actions for damages before the courts.[45]

This means that both the right to care and the right to compensation provided by Regulation 261 are standardised and immediate compensatory measures that fall outside the scope of the Montreal Convention and operate at an earlier stage than the Convention's system.[46]

   This interpretation has been questioned on the ground of the principle of exclusivity of the Montreal Convention, especially as far as the right to compensation in case of delays is concerned. Nonetheless, it has been followed by the French courts, for instance by the Cour d'appel de Versailles (Versailles Court of Appeal)[47] and also by the Cour d'appel d'Aix-en-Provence.[48]

   The compatibility of the Regulation with the Montreal Convention means that air passengers can benefit from the protection granted by the Regulation but also, following its Article 12 dealing with 'further compensation', from other instruments. Indeed, as ruled by the CJEU in *Sousa Rodriguez v Air France*:

> [T]he compensation granted to air passengers on the basis of Article 12 of Regulation No 261/2004 is intended to supplement the application of measures provided for by Regulation No 261/2004, so that passengers are compensated for the entirety of the damage that they have suffered due to the failure of the air carrier to fulfil its contractual obligations. That provision thus allows the national court to order the air carrier to compensate damage arising, for passengers, from breach of the contract of carriage by air on a legal basis other than Regulation No 261/2004, that is to say, in particular, in the conditions provided for by the Montreal Convention and national law.[49]

Article 12 of the Regulation, as interpreted by the CJEU, has been applied by the French courts on several occasions. For instance, the Cour d'appel d'Angers (Angers Court of Appeal) has judged that a company can be liable under the Montreal Convention even if it has already fulfilled its obligations of care under Regulation 261.[50] The Cour d'appel de Paris has used Article 12 in order to compensate passengers for the entirety of the damage suffered by them.[51] Recently, the Cour de cassation ruled that, when the conditions to grant compensation under

---

[45] *ex parte IATA* (n 43); see also *Nelson* (n 30), para 46.
[46] *ex parte IATA* (n 43), para 46; see also *Nelson* (n 30), para 57.
[47] CA Versailles 10 July 2013, No 13/03381.
[48] CA Aix-en-Provence 9 November 2012, No 12/08544.
[49] Case C-83/10 *Sousa Rodriguez and others v Air France* [2011] ECR I-9469, para 38.
[50] CA Angers 26 January 2010, No 09/00126.
[51] CA Paris 4 November 2011 No 10/08/581.

Regulation 261 are not met (delay lasting less than three hours), the French judge must still grant compensation on the basis of the Montreal Convention.[52] The complementary nature of the relation between the two instruments is therefore favourable to the air passenger.

V. Scholarly Analysis

Regulation 261 and its accompanying case law have been commented on and often criticised by French legal scholars. The Regulation, although it grants valuable rights to passengers, is vulnerable to criticism on account of its lack of precision, which in turn has brought it under the scrutiny of the CJEU.[53] For transport law specialists, aviation transport contracts are already governed by international private law, notably the Montreal Convention, and by domestic law. An EU Regulation setting up a new regime for compensation is not a proper instrument to tackle air passengers' problems. Furthermore, legally, its compatibility with the principle of exclusivity of the Montreal Convention is questionable.[54]

However, the main target in French academic writing has not been the Regulation itself but rather the CJEU's protective and expansive interpretation of it. Especially, granting compensation to delayed passengers in *Sturgeon* and the case law that followed has been criticised as being a *contra legem* interpretation of the Regulation.[55] Several scholars have qualified the interpretation of the CJEU as purely 'consumerist'.[56] A minority of authors have considered that *Sturgeon* is a 'constructive reading' of the Regulation,[57] or that this line of case law, 'favourable to the protection of air passengers, [is] in accordance with the spirit in which Regulation 261/2004 was adopted'.[58]

Few articles have specifically assessed the enforcement of the Regulation in France, except on a case-by-case basis. The enforcement problem of EU law-based

[52] C Cass 2 April 2014, No 13-16.038.
[53] F Le Bot, 'La protection des passagers aériens dans l'Union européenne. Réflexionx sur l'interprétation du droit derive par la Cour de justice' [2013] *Revue trimestrielle de droit européen* 753; see also V Correia, 'Transport aérien—Protection des droits des passagers' [2014] *Jurisclasseur Transport*, Fasc 930.
[54] eg V Grelliere, 'Refus d'embarquement, annulation de vol, retard au départ et à l'arrivée: controverses et réécriture du règlement (CE) n° 261/2004 du 11 février 2004' [2010] *Revue de droit commercial, maritime, aérien et des transports* 4.
[55] A Bouveresse, 'Interprétation des notions de retard et d'annulation' [2010] *Europe* (case note 43).
[56] P Frühling, E Decat and S Golinvaux, 'Panorama de la jurisprudence communautaire rendue en application du règlement n° 261/2004 sur les droits de passagers' [2012] *Revue de droit des transports*, dossier 15; see also P Delebecque, 'Règlement (CE) n° 161: l'interprétation consumériste de la CJUE se poursuit' [2012] *Revue de droit des transports* (case note 8).
[57] F Picod, 'La Cour de justice renforce les garanties des passagers victimes de retards' (2009) 50 *La Semaine Juridique Edition Générale*.
[58] L Grard, 'Indemnisation des passagers aériens en cas d'annulation d'un vol: un problème technique n'a rien d'extraordinaire' [2009] *Revue de droit des transports* (case note 36).

rights has been identified in French legal literature,[59] but has not been properly addressed by academia or by the public authorities. It is also noticeable that the reform proposals made by the Commission in 2013[60] have not been widely commented on by French academia,[61] although ECC-France and consumer associations such as FNAUT took part in the public consultation on the possible revision of Regulation 261.

VI. Conclusion

Generally, Regulation 261 and its accompanying case law have been enforced by French courts and have had a positive impact on the protection of air passengers in France. Certainly, such comprehensive legislation granting the right to care and the right to compensation to passengers in the case of cancellation or long delays did not exist previously. However, the enforcement of the Regulation is not always satisfactory. First, the Regulation itself is not clear enough. Secondly, passengers are not informed properly of their rights by public authorities and air carriers. Thirdly, airline companies often refuse to grant financial compensation to passengers, citing the 'extraordinary circumstances' exception. Fourthly, the powers of the NEB are limited.

The interpretation of the Regulation by the CJEU, although favourable to passengers, can also create additional problems for them. The NEB and independent mediators often hesitate to apply these interpretations as regards air carriers, which are in any case not bound by their decisions in individual cases. Thus only the judicial procedure may ultimately be effective. To compound matters, proximity judges are not always familiar with the case law of the CJEU, and it is only when the case is referred to the highest judicial court, the Cour de cassation, that the passenger will have his rights under Regulation 261, as interpreted by the CJEU, respected in full.

---

[59] F Le Bot, 'Les juridictions nationales et la protection des passagers aériens dans l'Union européenne' [2014] *Annuaire du droit de l'Union européenne 2012* 343; see also Correia (n 54) [113]–[133].

[60] European Commission, 'Proposal for a Regulation of the European Parliament and of the Council amending Regulation (EC) No 261/2004 establishing common rules on compensation and assistance to passengers in the event of denied boarding and of cancellation or long delay of flights and Regulation (EC) No 2027/97 on air carrier liability in respect of the carriage of passengers and their baggage by air' COM(2013) 130 final.

[61] eg V Correia, 'La proposition de révision du règlement n° 261/2004: entre clarifications textuelles et perfectionnement des droits des passagers aériens' [2014] *Revue européenne de droit de la consommation* 7.

13

The Italian Experience and Trend

LAURA PIERALLINI

I. Introduction

Regulation 261 is one of the most important and discussed topics in the Italian aviation industry, as it involves the interests of both passengers and airlines—an area in which it has always been, and still is, difficult to reach a fair and effective balance.

The discussion of this topic has become even more pointed because of the long-lasting global economic recession, which has equally affected the European aviation industry and become worse due to the sharp rise in fuel prices and the increase in airport security measures imposed as a consequence of the enduring terrorist threat. It is well known that all these factors have negatively affected passenger traffic and, along with the increased competition from low-cost carriers, put more strain on airlines, leading to a significant squeeze in profits in order to remain competitive in a global market.

These short-term factors have put Italian airlines, which were already showing signs of financial weakness and economic vulnerability, at a disadvantage. The difficulties faced by national airlines have extended to Italian airports as well: some have found themselves in the undesirable position of having to deal with a reduction in traffic and a change in the type of passengers, due to the increase in services offered by low-cost carriers. In the light of the airports' inability to manage the changed circumstances of air transport with their own financial resources, they face the real risk of eventually closing down.

It therefore comes as no surprise that many European operators, along with the European Commission, agree that the applicable regulation[1] on denied boarding, cancellation and delay of flights is in need of thorough review. This has become

---

[1] European Parliament and Council Regulation (EC) 261/2004 of 11 February 2004 establishing common rules on compensation and assistance to passengers in the event of denied boarding and of cancellation or long delay of flights, and repealing Regulation (EEC) 295/91 [2004] OJ L046/1 (Regulation 261).

more urgent following *Sturgeon v Condor*,[2] *Nelson v Deutsche Lufthansa*[3] and other decisions of the CJEU, and in consideration of the inadequacy of EU legislation to safeguard passengers' rights effectively in the event of extraordinary circumstances, such as the volcanic ash cloud that occurred in April 2010, as well as airlines' insolvency.

From the foregoing perspective, the reform of Regulation 261 will necessarily have to take into consideration, on the one hand, the interests of passengers seeking recovery for poor services and, on the other hand, the interests of airlines requiring a clear definition of their potential liability.

The purpose of this chapter is to provide an overview of the Italian legislation and case law on passenger rights, highlighting the main changes and developments after the introduction of Regulation 261. Discussion will also focus on the Italian NEB's role, highlighting how its involvement is key to achieving the desired uniformity in the application and enforcement of the Regulation in Italy. In conclusion, a brief outline of the current discussions and positions of the Italian NEB as a result of the European Commission's proposed reform of Regulation 261 will be provided.

II. Italian Legal Background

Regulation 261 is not the only legislation applicable to air passengers' claims in Italy. General provisions on air carriers' liability and passenger rights are set forth in the Italian Civil Code (ICC) and the Italian Navigation Code (INC).

The ICC lays out general rules on contracts (from definition to withdrawal and termination, passing through essential elements, conditions, interpretation, effects and invalidity), as well as specific rules for certain contracts (so-called 'type contracts'). As a general principle applicable to contracts, Article 1218 of the ICC provides:

> The debtor who does not exactly render the performance due is liable for damages unless it is proven that non-performance or delay was due to impossibility of performance for a cause not imputable to the debtor.

Specifically referring to the contract of carriage, Article 1681(1) of the ICC provides:

> In addition to liability for delay and non-performance in providing transport, the carrier is liable for accidents which injure the passenger during the voyage, or for loss of or damage to the property which the passenger carries with him, unless the carrier proves that it took all appropriate measures to prevent the damage.

---

[2] Cases C-402 and 432/07 *Sturgeon and Others* [2009] ECR I-10923 (*Sturgeon*).
[3] Cases C-581 and 629/10 *Nelson v Deutsche Lufthansa AG* [2012] OJ C399/3 (*Nelson*).

Further provisions governing the contract of air carriage and the air carrier's liability are set out in Article 941 and subsequent articles of the INC (as amended by Italian Legislative Decree 96 of 9 May 2005), which also include specific rules governing the passengers' right to information,[4] as well as the right to indemnification of damage[5] and reimbursement of the ticket price[6] in cases of denied boarding, delay and cancellation.

Consistent with the provision under the aforementioned Article 1681 of the ICC, Article 949 bis of the INC provides:

> [T]he carrier is liable for the damages to a passenger or his baggage arising from the non-performance of the contract of carriage, unless it proves that it and its employees adopted, according to ordinary diligence, any necessary and possible measure to avoid the damages or that it was impossible to adopt them.

Furthermore, Article 941 of the INC expressly refers to the international and European rules governing the air transport of passengers and baggage, including the Montreal Convention[7] signed on 28 May 1999 and ratified by Italian Law 12 of 10 January 2004 and Regulation 261.[8]

III. The Montreal Convention and Regulation 261: Compatibility and Concurrent Application in the Italian Experience

The Montreal Convention (which unifies and replaces the system of liability that derived from the Warsaw Convention)[9] governs, respectively, the rights and liabilities of passengers and carriers in international air transport, fixing limits

---

[4] INC, Art 943.

[5] ibid, Art 947.

[6] ibid, Art 949.

[7] Convention for the Unification of Certain Rules for International Carriage by Air [2001] OJ L194/39 (Montreal Convention); the Montreal Convention was the product of an effort by the International Civil Aviation Organisation (ICAO) to update and 'harmonize the hodgepodge of supplementary amendments and intercarrier agreements' of which the Warsaw Convention system of liability consisted.

[8] Regulation 261 entered into force on 17 February 2005 and applies to passengers departing from a Member State airport and to passengers arriving at a Member State airport, unless they received benefits or compensation and were given assistance in a non-Member State, if the air carrier operating the flight is a EU carrier (Art 3). Art 3(1)(a) of Regulation 261 states that the Regulation shall apply to passengers departing from 'an airport located in the territory of a Member State to which the Treaty applies', referring to the Treaty of Nice signed on 26 February 2001 and entering into force on 1 February 2003, which amended the Maastricht Treaty and the Treaty of Rome.

[9] Convention for the Unification of Certain Rules relating to International Carriage by Air 1929 (Warsaw Convention). The Warsaw Convention had two primary goals: (i) to establish worldwide uniform laws for claims arising out of international carriage of passengers, baggage and cargo; and (ii) to limit the liability of air carriers for such claims.

to air carriers' liability for damage caused to passengers, baggage and cargo. The Montreal Convention provides, inter alia, for:

(1)   unlimited liability in the event of death or injury of passengers;
(2)   advance payments to meet immediate needs;
(3)   the possibility of bringing a law suit before the courts in the passenger's principal place of residence;
(4)   increased liability limits in the event of delay;[10]
(5)   the modernisation of transport documents (electronic airway bills and tickets);
(6)   the clarification of the rules on the respective liability of the contractual carrier and the actual carrier;
(7)   the obligation for air carriers to maintain adequate insurance.

Regulation 261 entered into force on 17 February 2005, establishing common rules on compensation[11] and assistance[12] to passengers in the event of denied boarding,[13] cancellation or long delay of flights, and repealing Regulation (EEC) 295/91.[14]

The compatibility of Regulation 261 with the Montreal Convention, which was questioned, has been affirmed by the CJEU.[15] The most recent Italian case law has classified passengers' right to compensation for delayed flights under Regulation 261 as cumulative with the right to indemnification of damage under Article 19 of the Montreal Convention.

---

[10] Montreal Convention, Art 22. In the case of damage caused by delay under Art 19 of the Montreal Convention in the case of carriage of persons by air, the air carrier's liability for each passenger is limited to 4,150 Special Drawing Rights. According to Art 22(5), such limit may be exceeded if it is proven that the carrier engaged in wilful misconduct under or the carrier may be found not liable if it took 'all measures that could reasonably be required to avoid the damage', or can prove that it was impossible for it to take such measures: Art 19. The Montreal Convention therefore provides a right to compensatory damages for 'damage caused by delay' in the international transport of passengers.

[11] Regulation 261, Arts 7–8. The air carrier must immediately compensate passengers affected by denied boarding or cancellation with an amount within the range €250,00 to €600,00, depending on the route of the flight, and without prejudice to passengers' right to choose between reimbursement of the full purchase price of the ticket and re-routing to the final destination at the earliest opportunity, or at a later date, at the individual passenger's convenience.

[12] Regulation 261, Art 9.

[13] Regulation 261, Art 4. The provision requires that when an air carrier cannot provide boarding for all the passengers, it must first call for volunteers, who may surrender their seats in exchange for benefits under conditions agreed *inter partes*. If the number of volunteers who come forward is not enough to allow the remaining passengers with reservations to board the flight, Art 4(2) allows the air carrier to deny boarding to passengers against their will.

[14] Council Regulation (EEC) 295/91 of 4 February 1991 establishing common rules for a denied boarding compensation system in scheduled air transport [1991] OJ L36/5.

[15] Case C-344/0 R *(International Air Transport Association and European Low Fares Airline Association) v Department for Transport* [2006] ECR I-403.

The above is reflected in, amongst others, a recent decision of the Civil Court of Rome,[16] based on the case law of the CJEU on the application of Article 12(1) of Regulation 261,[17] which stated as follows:

> The most recent case law of the European Court of Justice extended the right to compensation provided in case of cancellation or denied boarding to passengers affected by a flight delay of at least three hours in arrival, and also confirmed the possibility to claim additional damages other than the compensation, as well as the general compatibility between Regulation 261/2004 and Montreal Convention.

The air carriers' liability and the protection of passengers' rights under the Italian legal system are therefore governed by the concurrent application of:

— the internal rules set out by the ICC and the INC;
— the international rules set out by the Montreal Convention; and
— the European rules set out by Regulation 261.

The next section of the chapter will focus on the Italian case law on protection of passengers' rights and air carriers' liability, highlighting how the *Sturgeon* decision of the CJEU has had an impact on the relevant trend.

IV. Italian Case Law on the Protection of Passengers' Rights and Air Carriers' Liability

Differently from other EU jurisdictions (such as the UK and The Netherlands), passengers' right to compensation in the event of flight delay was already recognised by Italian judges even before the *Sturgeon* case,[18] based on Article 19 of the Montreal Convention and the general principles of law and equity provided by the ICC and the INC. As a consequence, whilst the aforementioned case law of the CJEU on the application of Regulation 261 (*Sturgeon*, in particular) was perceived as a 'cataclysm' in many European jurisdictions, it had no significant impact on the Italian experience.

---

[16] Tribunale Roma 10 February 2014, 3134/2014.
[17] Art 12(1) provides that '[t]his Regulation shall apply without prejudice to a passenger's rights to further compensation'.
[18] *Sturgeon* (n 2). With such a ruling, the Court determined the conditions under which a delayed flight has to be considered and classified a 'cancelled flight' within the meaning of Regulation 261. To this end, on the one hand the Court maintained that a long delay in respect of the flight's scheduled departure time is not sufficient to classify a flight as cancelled; and on the other hand, the Court extended to passengers affected by a delay in arrival of at least three hours the right to compensation provided by the Regulation for denied boarding and cancelled flights.

A. Trend Before and After *Sturgeon*

As a matter of fact, even before the *Sturgeon* case, Italian judges recognised the right to compensation of air passengers whose flights were delayed for more than three hours or cancelled (as provided by Article 7 of Regulation 261), as well as the right to be indemnified against pecuniary and/or moral damage based on the provisions of the Montreal Convention or by recalling the said general principles of law and equity provided by the ICC and the INC. For example:

— The Justice of the Peace of Sassari, in a case dated 4 November 1998, ruled that

   [t]he air carrier must indemnify the passengers for the damages suffered as a consequence of the flight delay and the long wait in the airport if the carrier does not
   provide evidence that he has taken the necessary measures to avoid the damage caused
   by delay.[19]

— The Justice of the Peace of Venice, in a case dated 13 January 1999, held:

   [T]he damage suffered by the passenger as a direct consequence of the flight cancellation and consisting of the inconvenience caused by the long wait, along with the
   trouble for not being able to join a business meeting in time, must be indemnified.[20]

— The Justice of the Peace of Milan, in a case dated 18 December 2000, ruled that

   [i]n the air transport industry the information to be provided by the air carrier
   regarding the entity of flight delay and the consequent measures to be taken is not
   only an act of courtesy, but also a specific obligation of the air carrier towards the
   passengers. As a consequence, the air carrier must indemnify the passengers in case of
   breach of the said obligation. In addition to pecuniary damages, such a breach is cause
   of non-pecuniary damages for the passengers, such as nervousness and frustration
   arising from the flight delay. Such non-pecuniary damages can be assessed by equity.[21]

— The Justice of the Peace of Naples, in a case dated 27 November 2002, ruled that:

   [t]he liability of the carrier for damages resulting from a delay to a passenger is not
   limited to the cost of the ticket but can also affect personal serenity.[22]

— The Court of Palermo, in a case dated 15 July 2003, held that

   repeated and considerable flight delays breach the air passengers' right to safety
   and quality of the services as provided by article 1, paragraph 2, letter b), of Law
   n. 281/1998 and are potentially in prejudice of further essential rights, both pecuniary
   and non-pecuniary ...[23]

---

[19] Giudice di Pace Sassari 4 November 1998, Giur It 2000, 316.
[20] Giudice di Pace Venezia Mestre 13 January 1999, Dir Trasporti 2001, 811.
[21] Giudice di Pace Milano 18 December 2000, Dir Trasporti 2002, 288.
[22] Giudice di Pace Napoli 27 November 2002, Giur Merito 2003, 693.
[23] Tribunale Palermo 15 July 2003, Argomenti di Diritto Pubblico dell'Economia 2010, 376.

— The Justice of the Peace of Maglie, in a case dated 23 April 2004, ruled that '[t]he air carrier must indemnify the passengers concerned for the non-pecuniary damages suffered as a consequence of the flight delay and the long wait in the airport'.[24]

— The Justice of the Peace of Catanzaro, in a case dated 3 July 2006, stated:

> The so called moral damage provided by article 2050 of Italian Civil Code must be indemnified and assessed by equity … In the case, the passenger suffered both physical and moral pains caused by the unlawful conduct of the air carrier … [25]

— The Justice of the Peace of Sant'Anastasia, in a case dated 14 September 2006, ruled that

> [t]he long wait in the airport as a consequence of the flight delay, in the case equal to 1 hour and a half, causes a level of stress to air passenger entitling the latter to be indemnified for the damages suffered, which can be assessed on an equity basis … The ENAC Chart on air passengers' rights (namely 'Carta dei Diritti del Passeggero') provides that air passengers must receive information within the estimated time of boarding in case of flight delay, as well as additional information every further thirty minutes.[26]

Since the *Sturgeon* ruling, most Italian judges have instead started to show a general tendency to recognise a right to compensation only pursuant to Regulation 261 in favour of the air passengers in cases of flight delay or cancellation. Such a trend is clearly reflected in the most recent Italian case law on passengers' right to compensation under Regulation 261. The Justice of Peace of Florence ruled:

> Considering that the Regulation 261 is aimed, among other things, at ensuring a high level of protection for air passengers in case of … flight delay, it is belief of this Judge that the non-pecuniary damage's indemnification—as claimed by the passenger—is already provided by the above regulation and that compensation laid down in Article 7 therein covers both pecuniary and non-pecuniary damages arising from flight delay.[27]

Further, the Justice of Peace of Leonforte held that 'air passengers have a right to compensation under to Article 7 only as consequence of flight delay, whilst any other damages claimed by them cannot be indemnified being uncertain and not proven'.[28]

B. The Extraordinary Circumstances Defence

In return for enhancing the protection of passengers, Regulation 261 provides for the so-called 'extraordinary circumstances' defence in favour of air carriers, which

---

[24] Giudice di Pace Maglie 23 April 2004, Danno e Resp 205, 309.
[25] Giudice di Pace Catanzaro 3 July 2006, Trasporto, Spedizione e Deposito Questioni Processuali 2011, 60.
[26] Giudice di Pace Sant'Anastasia 14 September 2006, 2779/2006.
[27] Giudice di Pace Firenze 31 August 2010, 8899/2010.
[28] Giudice di Pace Leonforte 1 March 2011, 33/2011.

excludes the obligation to pay passengers compensation if the carrier can prove that the cancellation or long delay is caused by extraordinary circumstances that could not have been avoided even if all reasonable measures had been taken.[29]

Italian judges had already restricted the possibility for air carriers to effectively enforce the 'extraordinary circumstances' defence, even before the restrictive approach was adopted by the CJEU in *Wallentin-Hermann v Alitalia*.[30]

An extraordinary circumstance that is generally admitted consists of industrial action, such as a strike, affecting the industry, for example air traffic control, ground handing and airport management staff strikes (but not the airline staff concerned),[31] while technical problems affecting the aircraft generally do not qualify as extraordinary circumstances.[32]

Recently, the Justice of the Peace of Massa[33] has stated:

> the airline's denial of the passenger's right to compensation affirming that the flight cancellation was caused by extraordinary circumstance ... as the aircraft was affected by an unexpected breakdown of the flight control commands is groundless. In particular, the airline did not prove that the cancellation was occurred due to extraordinary circumstances which could not have been avoided even if all reasonable measures had been taken. (Regulation 261/04, Recital 12).

Indeed, air carriers frequently struggle to satisfy the burden of proof for the 'extraordinary circumstances' defence, especially when seeking to provide evidence of *force majeure* and technical faults on aircraft. Documents provided by the air carrier, such as technical logs, may be considered difficult to understand for a non-specialist; documentation is often not adequately analysed and assessed (even though in many cases it represents the only evidence in favour of the air carriers). On the other hand, trying to satisfy the burden of proof through witnesses is not an easy task, because the result of any witness evidence always remains subject to discretionary evaluation by the judge.

C. Some Highlights of the Italian Judicial System

Having looked at the 'softer' impact of the *Sturgeon* judgment in Italy, it is worth underlining the peculiarities of the Italian legal system, in particular with respect to the proceedings, which condition the application of the Regulation 261. In terms

---

[29] Recital 14 of Regulation 261 provides a few examples of what can be considered as extraordinary circumstances, stating that 'such circumstances may, in particular, occur in cases of political instability, meteorological conditions incompatible with the operation of the flight concerned, security risks, unexpected flight safety shortcomings and strikes that affect the operation of an operating air carrier'. See also Regulation 261, Recital 15.

[30] Case C-549/07 *Wallentin-Hermann v Alitalia* [2008] ECR I-11061.

[31] eg Giudice di Pace Trieste 17 September 2012, 668/2012.

[32] eg Giudice di Pace Caserta 22 November 2007, Dir Trasporti 2008, 573.

[33] Giudice di Pace Massa 20 March 2014, 119/2014.

of procedure, around 95 per cent of passengers' claims are not dealt with by the main civil courts but fall within the jurisdiction of the Justice of the Peace (Giudici di Pace), given the fact that these claims generally involves small amounts (that is, claims under €5,000). Justices of the Peace rarely have adequate experience in aviation matters: they often apply the 'equity principle' and tend to rule in favour of passengers. The territorial jurisdiction is vested with the judge of the district where the passenger is resident, pursuant to Article 33 of the ICC.[34]

Recent case law has accepted the airlines' position, based on the CJEU decision in *Rehder v Air Baltic Corporation*,[35] that the applicant has a choice of territorial jurisdiction—the place of departure or the place of arrival of the aircraft, as those places are agreed in the air transport contract.[36]

The time limits for bringing actions in respect of Article 5 (flight cancellation) and Article 7 (compensation) of Regulation 261, as clarified by the CJEU in *Moré v KLM*,[37] are determined in accordance with the rules of each Member State on the limitation of actions. Therefore the time during which a claim for compensation may be brought varies across Member States. Articles 941 and 949-ter of the INC provide that the two-year limitation period laid down by the Montreal Convention applies to any air passengers' claims brought before Italian judges, so includes claims based on Regulation 261.

All the above, as well as taking into account the generally small size of the relevant claims, which could easily be less than the overall costs of litigation, has often led air carriers to pursue a settlement, rather than relying on judicial defences.

V. The Italian National Enforcement Body

A. Ente Nazionale per l'Aviazione Civile

Article 16 of Regulation 261 requires each Member State to designate a NEB responsible for the enforcement of the Regulation's provisions, with regard to flights from airports situated on its territory and flights from a third country to such airports. Such a body has the ability to impose measures in order to ensure respect for passengers' rights, and passengers have the right to address their complaints directly to the NEB.

The designated NEB for Italy, Ente Nazionale per l'Aviazione Civile (the Italian Civil Aviation Authority or ENAC), is the primary agency entrusted with the

---

[34] Legislative Decree 206/2005, Art 33.
[35] Case C-204/08 *Rehder v Air Baltic Corporation* [2009] ECR I-6073.
[36] eg Giudice di Pace Roma 13 April 2012, 14356/2012.
[37] Case C-139/11 *Moré v KLM* (ECJ, 22 November 2012).

responsibility of regulating aviation in Italy, as provided by Article 687 of the INC and Legislative Decree 250/97. The Ministry of Transport is the body having supervising authority over ENAC and general competence.

In general, ENAC is responsible for supervising air carriers and applying sanctions. In particular, ENAC is in charge of issuing sanctions to air carriers who are in breach of Regulation 261. The system of sanctions for breach of the Regulation was introduced by Italian Legislative Decree 69/06, which allows for the imposition of administrative fines between €2,500 and €50,000.

Table 13.1: Fines provided by Italian Legislative Decree 69/06

	Minimum (€)	Maximum (€)	Reduced (€)
Denied boarding	10,000	50,000	16,666.67
Flight cancellations	10,000	50,000	16,666.67
Delay	2,500	10,000	3,333.33
Upgrade/downgrade	1,000	5,000	1,666.67
Lack of priority and assistance to the disabled or to unaccompanied children	10,000	50,000	16,666.67
Provision of information	2,500	10,000	3,333.33

The administrative procedure for the issuing of fines by ENAC is regulated by Italian Law 689 of 14 November 1981. It entitles the defaulting carrier to seek a meeting with ENAC within 30 days, and for the carrier to file a statement of defence. Alternatively, the air carrier is entitled to ask for a discount of two-thirds of the fine, achieved by paying the discounted amount within 60 days of the service of process.

In the event that its defence is rejected by ENAC, the air carrier is allowed to challenge the fine with the competent Italian administrative court, as soon as it is served by ENAC with an order for payment.

The implementation of Regulation 261 by ENAC has sometimes proved to be affected by practical issues, for instance with regard to the slowness of the process of collecting fines.

B. Air Passengers' Charter

The Italian Civil Aviation Authority has issued the Air Passengers' Charter (Carta dei Diritti del Passeggero), detailing the rights conferred on air passengers. The Air Passengers' Charter is practically a *vade mecum* of national, European and international regulation on air passenger protection, detailing the claims and compensation procedures available to air passengers in the event of non-compliance with the above regulations. The Air Passengers' Charter was drawn up and ready to be distributed at all Italian airports in 2001.

A new version was introduced in 2005, at the same time as the entry into force of new rules governing the delay and cancellation of flights, with a view to reflecting, in particular, the increase in the amount of compensation payable by air carriers in the event of denied boarding due to overbooking, the introduction of forms of compensation and assistance in the event of flight cancellations or long delays, and the extension of such protection to passengers on charter flights.

In March 2009, ENAC approved the latest edition of the Passengers' Charter, also referring to the EU provisions on the rights of disabled passengers, as set forth by Regulation 1107/2006 concerning the rights of disabled persons and persons with reduced mobility when travelling by air.[38]

VI. A Much Needed Review of Regulation 261

A. European Commission's Proposed Reform

As outlined by the European Commission,[39] the current formulation of the Regulation 261 shows a number of shortcomings which have brought a lack of uniformity in its application and enforcement across Europe with consequent uncertainty for both operators and consumers. With the purpose of clarifying the current grey areas, simplifying the compliant handling, better coordinating the enforcement policies and ensuring a realistic financial cost for airlines, on 13 March 2013 the European Commission published its proposal for amending the 'controversial' Regulation 261.[40]

---

[38] European Parliament and Council Regulation (EC) 1107/2006 of 5 July 2006 concerning the rights of disabled persons and persons with reduced mobility when travelling by air [2006] OJ L204/1. This legislation establishes that air carriers cannot refuse carriage to persons with reduced mobility, unless for specific safety requirements or if the size of the aircraft makes the embarkation of such persons physically impossible. Instead, the person with reduced mobility and the accompanying person should be offered reimbursement or re-routing under certain conditions. Assistance without additional charge should also be offered by the managing body of the airport to persons with reduced mobility.

[39] Commission, 'The application of Regulation 261/2004 establishing common rules on compensation and assistance to passengers in the event of denied boarding and of cancellation or long delay of flights' (Communication) COM(2011) 174 final. The report was part of the European Commission's work to remove obstacles preventing citizens from effectively exercising their rights under EU law.

[40] Commission, 'Proposal for a Regulation amending the Regulation (EC) No 261/2004 establishing common rules on compensation and assistance to passengers in the event of denied boarding and of cancellation or long delay of flights and Regulation (EC) No 2027/97 on air carrier liability in respect of the carriage of passengers and their baggage by air' (Proposal) COM(2013) 130 final. While the proposal has been positively welcomed by the passengers' representatives and by the general press, airlines and the operators of the industry have already signalled their disappointment at the proposed revisions. They consider the proposal excessive as regards many aspects, and as overburdening air carriers

As expected, the European Commission codifies the position taken by the CJEU regarding passengers' right to compensation in the case of long delays, established in the *Sturgeon* judgment.[41] The European Commission's proposal has been subject to a number of changes, made by the EU Parliament on 5 February 2014.[42] A key role is also played by the NEBs, who are actively co-operating in the revision of Regulation 261, submitting comments and suggesting amendments on behalf of the respective Member States. The most up-to-date text of the European Commission proposal, as voted by the EU Parliament, was submitted to the EU Council on 22 May 2014. The Greek Presidency was unable to achieve agreement amongst the Member States before the end of the relevant semester. Thereafter, the Italian Presidency similarly chose not to continue work on the dossier, nor had the Luxembourg Presidency so far shown a different approach.

B. Italian Civil Aviation Authority's Point of View on the Proposed Reform

The Italian Civil Aviation Authority has raised some thoughts and considerations in relation to the European Commission's proposed reform of Regulation 261. In particular, having regard to the last updated text of the proposal, as submitted to the EU Council, ENAC has focused on the following main issues:

— the right to compensation should be extended to infants;
— the word 'flights' in the current text of Article 7 should not be replaced by the proposed word 'journeys'[43] for calculating the distance and determining accordingly the amount of compensation due to passengers in cases of flight delay;
— the nature of compensation should be expressly defined in order to make clear the distinction between the same and the damage indemnification provided for under the Montreal Convention;

---

operating from and within Europe, at a time when the region is seriously struggling. See, as an example, the announcement released by the Board of Airline Representatives in the UK (UK BAR) following the publication of the proposal.

[41] *Sturgeon* (n 2). One of the main innovative aspects is therefore represented by the increase of the 'time threshold' after which the right to compensation arises: five hours for intra-EU flights and other flights of 3,500 km or less; nine hours for flights between 3,500 and 6,000 km; and 12 hours for flights of 6,000 km or more.

[42] European Parliament Legislative Resolution 2013/130 of 5 February 2014. In order to codify the most recent case law of the CJEU, minimise litigation, strengthen passengers' rights and reduce the financial burden on air carriers, the European Parliament position has brought forward some relevant changes to the legislative proposal tabled by the European Commission on 13 March 2013, namely (main points): (i) the definition of 'extraordinary circumstances'; (ii) levels of compensation; (iii) the allowance regarding carry-on luggage; (iv) insolvency; and (v) denied boarding/no-show policy.

[43] The proposed new version of Art 2(p) of Regulation 261 defines 'journey' as a flight or a continued series of flights transporting the passenger from the initial airport of departure to his final destination in accordance with a single contract of carriage.

— the minimum hours of flight delay entitling passengers to compensation should be fixed at five, nine and 12 hours;
— the period during which the air carrier is obliged to provide assistance in case of flight disruption due to extraordinary circumstances other than technical fault should be limited; and
— in cases of missed connections due to delay occurring on the original flight within the same rotation, a fair threshold should be provided before passengers become entitled to compensation.

The above considerations raised by ENAC—submitted to the European institutions involved in the relevant legislative *iter*—are currently subject to further internal discussions. Moreover, a debate is currently open between ENAC and the Italian air carriers on the above issues, focused by the Italian NEB.

14

Poland: Do Not Adjust Your Seat, Passengers' Rights are Assured

KRYSTYNA KOWALIK-BAŃCZYK

I. Introduction

The aim of this chapter is to explore the impact of Regulation 261 in the Republic of Poland. It mainly presents the application of Regulation 261 by analysing the case law of Polish courts since the Regulation's entry into force in 2005. The Regulation is currently undergoing broad reform, but its scope will not be analysed in this chapter.[1]

Given the fact that the Polish airports served over 25 million passengers in 2013,[2] the number of claims against the air carriers is still not very high (3,540 claims in 2013). In that year, the District Administrative Court in Warsaw (Wojewódzki Sąd Administracyjny w Warszawie) (WSA) ruled in 29 cases concerning decisions based on the Regulation. The Regulation is regularly invoked and used by passengers in their claims against air carriers in Poland. The statistics reveal that every year the number of claims is increasing, which clearly shows that the main aims of the Regulation—to raise the awareness of passengers and to improve the standards of their treatment—have been gradually achieved. After *Sturgeon v Condor*,[3] passengers also started to claim compensation for delays in flights, which had not been common previously.[4]

In this chapter, the main references will be to the judicial control of decisions issued by the President of the Office of Civil Aviation (Prezes Urzędu Lotnictwa Cywilnego) (President of ULC), in which this body also decides upon the civil

---

[1] J Prassl, 'Reforming Air Passenger Rights in the European Union' [2014] 39 *Air and Space Law* 59.

[2] ULC 'Analiza przewozów pasażerskich w polskich portach lotniczych w 2013 roku' (ULC, 27 March 2014), available at <http://www.ulc.gov.pl/_download/statystyki/2014/analiza_2013.pdf>, accessed 1 November 2014.

[3] Cases C-402 and 432/07 *Sturgeon and Others* [2009] ECR I-10923 (*Sturgeon*).

[4] *cf* judgment of WSA of 6.10.2008 VI SA/Wa 1230/2008.

responsibility of carriers. Those decisions are subject to limited judicial review[5] before the WSA,[6] and might further be subject to cassation by the Chief Administrative Court of Poland (Naczelny Sąd Administracyjny) (NSA).[7] The WSA applies the Regulation directly and often undertakes its construction,[8] without, to date, posing any preliminary questions. No doubts have been raised on the issues of the direct effect or supremacy of the Regulation.[9]

Proceedings in front of civil courts are much less frequent, but the bankruptcy of air carrier OLT Express[10] in 2012 generated a number of civil cases brought by clients of this air carrier, most of which are still pending. Some passengers have also applied to the President of ULC against this air carrier, which confirms the possibility of using a double (or parallel) route for redress.[11] The civil courts have sole competence to judge claims based on the Montreal Convention.

In analysing the application of Regulation 261 in Poland within the last nine years, the legislative background is given first, before the rights of passengers, remedies used and the relationship with Montreal Convention are discussed. The national enforcement landscape and its scholarly analysis are presented at the end of the chapter. The analysis reveals a rather accurate picture of the adaptation of Polish practice to the requirements of the Regulation.

II. Legislative Background for the Application of the Regulation

The relevant background to the national procedural system for bringing claims is mainly set out in the Act of 3 July 2002 on Air Law (Air Law Act) with amendments.[12] According to Article 16 of the Regulation, as from 1 February 2005 the Republic of Poland was required to designate a body to which passengers might

---

[5] According to Art 1 of the Act of 25 July 2002, Law on the regime of administrative courts ([2002] *Journal of Laws* no 153, pos 1269 with amendments), an Administrative Court controls the legality of an administrative decision.

[6] There are 16 District Administrative Courts in Poland, but in this chapter only the District Administrative Court of Warsaw is relevant.

[7] In the database of the NSA, there are about 100 judgments of either the WSA or the NSA, where the decisions of the President of ULC have been reviewed; *cf* at <http://orzeczenia.nsa.gov.pl/cbo/search>, accessed 1 November 2014.

[8] In fact, in all of the judgments cited in this chapter, the Regulation serves as a legal basis for the control of legality, together with appropriate provisions of Polish law. For instance: judgment of WSA of 6.10.2008, VI SA/Wa 1230/2008; judgment of WSA of 28.04.2011, VII Sa/Wa 2208/10; judgment of WSA of 16.11.2012, VII SA/Wa 1321/12.

[9] Very clearly recently in the judgment of WSA of 30.12.2013, VII SA/Wa 1169/13.

[10] The Polish air carrier OLT Express Regional was declared bankrupt on 12 September 2012 by the Regional Court of Gdańsk.

[11] *cf* judgment of WSA of 13.08.2013, VII SA/Wa 660/13; judgment of WSA of 8.08.2013, VII SA/Wa 592/13.

[12] Act of 3 July 2002 on Air Law [2006] *Journal of Laws* No 100, pos 969 with amendments.

direct their claims regarding denied boarding, delay or cancellation of flights (the so-called NEB).[13] Under Article 205a of the Air Law Act, the NEB is the President of ULC, assisted by the Commission for Protection of Passenger Rights (Komisja Ochrony Praw Pasażerów) (KOPP).[14] The jurisdiction of this body is laid down in Article 16(2) of the Regulation and is not 'supplemented' or 'mirrored' by national provisions. In the event that a claim is brought before the wrong body, that body can pass the claim to the competent organ.[15]

In parallel, the Air Law Act provides at Article 205 that

> for contracts of air transport, including charter flights, and other civil relations linked with air transport, which are not regulated by this Act and international treaties, the provisions of civil law are applicable.

This provision was used to justify the possible jurisdiction of civil courts to rule on liability based on the Regulation. Polish law provides some guarantees to avoid cases of *déni de justice*. If a civil court refuses to adjudicate, the President of ULC cannot refuse to admit the claim.[16] On the other hand, the civil court cannot plead lack of jurisdiction in cases where an administrative body has already declared its lack of competence in the matter.[17]

At the initial stage of introduction of the Regulation, some Polish authors underlined the possible limitation of its application due to linguistic problems, as claims in the territory of Poland should in principle have been submitted in the Polish language.[18] This practice might have been perceived as discriminatory, favouring Polish passengers in comparison to passengers from other Members States. An amendment to the Air Law Act eliminated this risk, and at present Article 21a of the Act guarantees that claims brought before the President of ULC can be submitted in English; however, according to Article 21a.3 of the Act, the President of ULC may require a translation into the Polish language (requiring such a translation as a matter of course might also be perceived as discriminatory). On the other hand, those air carriers that received decisions of the President of ULC in English with reasons in Polish, questioned this linguistic solution, but the Polish NSA did not find any infringement of law in this regard.[19]

---

[13] A Konert, *Odpowiedzialność cywilna przewoźnika lotniczego* (Wolters Kluwer Polska, 2010) 237; A Kunert-Diallo, 'Ochrona konsumenta na rynku usług lotniczych w strukturze administracji publicznej' in E Jasiuk and G Maj (eds), *Wyzwania i dylematy związane z funkcjonowaniem administracji publicznej* (Wyższa Szkoła Handlowa, 2012) 309.

[14] Air Law Act, Art 205a.2.

[15] This situation was analysed by the NSA in its judgment of 23.10.2013, I OSK 1164/13, where the Court invoked, inter alia, a document, being an agreement between the competent national authorities within the EU; 'NEB-NEB Complaint Handling Procedure Under Regulation EC/261/2004', available at <http://ec.europa.eu/transport/themes/passengers/air/doc/neb/neb_complaint_handling_procedures.pdf>, accessed 1 November 2014.

[16] Code of administrative proceedings, § 4 [1960] *Journal of Laws* No 30 pos 168 with amendments, Art 66.

[17] Code of civil procedure [1964] *Journal of Laws* No 43 pos 296 with amendments, Art 1991.

[18] Konert (n 13) 237.

[19] Judgment of NSA of 6.03.2012, I OSK 328/11. The air carrier was also asking the Court to submit preliminary questions on the interpretation of Regulation 1348/2000, but the Court did not consider

The detailed rules on the possibility of claiming for breaches of the Regulation should be included in the 'Statute' or 'Rules of Transport' issued by an air carrier operating in the territory of Poland.[20] In particular, they should contain:

— priority rules for admission of passengers on board;
— the rules regarding the refund of payments for the flights that have not taken place;
— information on the limits of and ways of paying compensation; and
— information on the care of passengers who have not been allowed to board a flight.

Air carriers that transport passengers to or from the territory of Poland are obliged to provide their Statute, containing typical conditions of transport of passengers and baggage, in the Polish language, unless a particular passenger has chosen a version in another language (Article 205.2a, Air Law Act). Such an air carrier is obliged to provide the President of ULC with its Statute upon request.[21]

In the case of claims listed in Article 205a.1 of the Air Law Act,[22] the President of ULC will issue administrative decisions stating either a lack of infringement or the existence of an infringement, its scope and the sanctions provided for in Article 209b.1 of the Act.[23] The President of ULC states the obligations of air carrier and the time limit for their fulfilment,[24] including the obligation to compensate or reimburse the passenger.

The claim can be deposited in either Polish or English (Article 205b.2), not earlier than 30 days after its deposit with the air carrier.[25] The passenger is obliged to attach to the claim the following documents:

— a copy of the complaint to the air carrier;
— a copy of the response of the air carrier, or a statement that no answer was sent within the time limits set out in the transport contract or the Statute;
— a copy of the reservation for a particular flight; and
— a declaration that the copies provided are identical to the originals.[26]

The burden of proof that no rights of passengers have been infringed is on the air carrier.[27]

---

them necessary. In another case the NSA stated that the practice by which an air carrier receives documents in Polish with an informal translation in English is sufficient to keep the air carrier informed—judgment of NSA of 6.03.2012, I OSK 555/11.

[20] Air Law Act, Art 200.3.
[21] Air Law Act, Art 205.3.
[22] This provision states, 'The President of the Office controls the alignment with 1) Regulation 261/2004, 2) Regulation 2111/2005, 3) Regulation 1107/2006—and in particular it is competent to adjudicate on claims named in art. 16.2 of Regulation 261/2004 and art. 15.2 of Regulation 1107/2006.'
[23] The sanctions for various infringements of Regulation 261 are set out in detail in Attachment no 2 to the Air Law Act.
[24] Air Law Act, Art 205b.
[25] Air Law Act, Art 205b.4; unless the transport contract or the Statute provides for a shorter time limit.
[26] Air Law Act, Art 205b.
[27] Air Law Act, Art 205b.

There is a double route to claim obligations from an air carrier, either within the scope of civil proceedings rules, or according to the rules of execution in administration.[28] According to the reports of the KOPP, the practice of Polish civil courts has not been uniform as regards the granting of *exequatur* to administrative decisions of the President of ULC. Some civil courts have denied the grant of *exequatur*,[29] while others granted it.[30]

The KOPP provided detailed statistical data on its activity for the years 2006–12 (the data for 2013 are not yet complete). The number of claims rose steeply over that period, from 1,068 in 2006 to 4,021 in 2012. Table 14.1 sets out the nature of

Table 14.1: Claims for infringements of Regulation 261 in 2006–13[31]

	2006	2007	2008	2009	2010	2011	2012	2013
Proceeding in front of the President of ULC—**cancellation of flight**	467	534	816	538	611	726	1,537	
Proceeding in front of the President of ULC—**delay of flight**	240	206	142	63	324	980	1,617	
Proceeding in front of the President of ULC—**denied boarding**	78	99	78	72	65	62	92	
Proceeding in front of the President of ULC—**others**	30	28	71	43	73	47	179	
Proceeding in front of the President of ULC—**Requests for explanations**	253	341	431	319	467	380	596	
Together	1,068	1,208	1,538	1,035	1,540	2,195	4,021	3,540

[28] Law of 17 November 1964 Code of Civil Procedure [1964] *Journal of Laws* No 43, pos 296 with amendments, Art 777 § 1.3; Law of 17 June 1966 Executive proceeding in administration (Ustawa z dnia 17 czerwca 1966 roku o postępowaniu egzekucyjnym w administracji) [1966] *Journal of Laws* No 24 pos 151 with amendments.

[29] Order of Regional Court of Warsaw of 28.05.2009, II Co 735/09, given as an example of cases listed by KOPP, available at <www.ulc.gov.pl/pl/prawa-pasazera/wazne-komunikaty>, accessed 1 November 2014.

[30] Order of Regional Court of Warsaw of 9.05.2013, I Co 760/13, given as an example of cases listed by KOPP, available at <www.ulc.gov.pl/pl/prawa-pasazera/wazne-komunikaty>, accessed 1 November 2014.

[31] Lotnicza Polska, 'Skargi pasażerów—statystyki KOPP' (21 January 2013), available at <http://lotniczapolska.pl/Skargi-pasazerow-statystyki-KOPP,28248>, accessed 1 November 2014; P Szymaniak, 'Wspólnota sprzyja podróżującym, czyli jak UE chroni pasażerów' *Gazeta Prawna* (Warsaw, 30 April

claims brought before the Polish NEB and requests for information in the period 2006–13.

The most frequent claims concerned delays and cancellation of flights. There were fewer claims regarding denied boarding. There was a significant increase in the number of claims concerning delayed flights (from 240 in 2006 to 1,617 in 2012). A significant increase in 2012 can be attributed, amongst other factors, to the collapse of OLT Express in Summer 2012, after which this carrier stopped functioning and all its flights were cancelled.

Apart from the data provided in the statistics of the KOPP, there are no numbers showing the percentage of claims that are successful. Considering that in those cases where the air carrier does not respond to a claim of infringement, the President of ULC rules that there has been an infringement (due to the rules on burden of proof set out in the Air Law Act), passengers tend to be quite successful in their claims.[32]

Statistical data are not available on the number of cases brought in civil proceedings in which infringements of the Regulation were ordered to be compensated. However, it seems that passengers tend to prefer to use the cheaper administrative proceedings, which also are more efficient, at least as long as the claim is admitted. Resort to civil claims tends to occur in cases where the President of ULC refuses to adjudicate.

III. Rights of Passengers

A. Interpretation by the Polish Courts of Rights Stemming from the Regulation

The rights of passengers, as defined in Regulation 261, are as follows:

(1)   the right to compensation;[33]
(2)   the right to reimbursement of the full price of the ticket, together with a return flight if applicable;[34]
(3)   the right to re-routing under comparable transport conditions to the final destination;[35]

2014), available at <http://serwisy.gazetaprawna.pl/poradnik-konsumenta/artykuly/793924,wspolnota-sprzyja-podrozujacym-czyli-jak-ue-chroni-pasazerow.html>, accessed 1 November 2014.

[32] *cf* the reasons in the judgment of the WSA of 16.11.2012, VII SA/Wa 1321/12.

[33] European Parliament and Council Regulation (EC) 261/2004 of 11 February 2004 establishing common rules on compensation and assistance to passengers in the event of denied boarding and of cancellation or long delay of flights, and repealing Regulation (EEC) No 295/91 [2004] OJ L46/1 (Regulation 261), Art 7.

[34] ibid, Art 8(1)(a).

[35] ibid, Art 8(1)(b), (c).

(4)   the right to information on the existing following rights;[36] and

(5)   the right to care, that can be invoked in cases of three events that constitute an incorrect fulfilment of the obligations of air carrier (denied boarding, cancellation, delay).[37]

Any alleged infringement of these rights is adjudicated upon by the President of ULC and, more rarely, by the civil courts.

Following administrative decisions finding an infringement of the Regulation, the President of ULC can order compensation of the passenger whose rights have been infringed. Since early 2010, invoking the *Sturgeon* case, the President of ULC has begun to grant compensation for delayed flights, and not just for denied boarding and the cancellation of flights. The Polish Supreme Court (Sąd Najwyższy) (SN) has recently answered the question as to whether there exists a right to compensation in the case of flight delays that can be adjudicated upon by civil courts. In 2012 a three-person family was delayed by 15 hours. They brought a claim for compensation in the civil court. The air carrier claimed that the proceedings in the civil court were inadmissible because the only competent body was the President of ULC. In light of of the decision in *Sturgeon*, the court of second instance decided to stay the proceedings and ask the Supreme Court for an opinion as to whether the two ways of claiming compensation were admissible in parallel. The Court stated that compensation for delay may be claimed in the civil court, or before the President of ULC.[38]

Interestingly enough, the Polish courts referred to *Sturgeon* even when it was still pending before the CJEU,[39] without, however, staying the proceedings. In a case from 2007, the WSA in its reasoning clearly regretted that no compensation for delay was provided for in Regulation 261.[40] In another pre-*Sturgeon* case, the Court suggested that the passenger concerned should claim damages for delay under the Montreal Convention.[41]

Differently from the right to compensation, which is interpreted very broadly, in Polish practice there is a narrow interpretation of the right to reimbursement. This right is interpreted by the Polish courts as requiring that the passenger should prove that 'the flight is no longer serving any purpose in relation to the passenger's original travel plan'. Following this line of reasoning, a passenger taking a planned lengthy trip had difficulties in proving that one day's delay in the departure time meant that the trip had lost its purpose; the passenger was therefore denied any reimbursement.[42] Such a construction of this provision does not

---

[36] ibid, Art 14.

[37] ibid, Art 9.

[38] Resolution of the SN of 7.02.2014 III CZP 113/13.

[39] Judgment of WSA of 28.01.2009, VI SA/Wa 2091/08.

[40] Judgment of WSA of 18.12.2007, VI SA/Wa 2317/06.

[41] Judgment of WSA of 3.10.2007, VI SA/Wa 891/07.

[42] Judgment of WSA of 18.12.2007, VI SA/WA 2317/06; *cf* M Stec, 'Przesłanki odstąpienia od umowy przewozu w europejskim transporcie lotniczym w Rozporządzeniu Parlamentu i Rady (WE) nr 261/2004' (2010) 4 *Europejski Przegląd Sądowy* 9.

favour passengers, requiring them to prove that the journey has lost its purpose. This interpretation is not consistent with other linguistic versions of the Regulation, where this loss of purpose appears only in the context of connecting flights.[43] The right to reimbursement and to an eventual return flight cannot be limited due to the occurrence of exceptional circumstances, as Article 8 of the Regulation does not allow for this interpretation.[44]

The Polish institutions have also underlined a separate right to information that all passengers should receive in the event of any unforeseen circumstances connected to the scheduled flight. Following Article 14 of the Regulation, the administrative courts have stated that the passengers should obtain full information about their rights.[45] The KOPP undertakes regular checks to monitor whether such solutions are at place at the airports. In its judgment of 28 April 2011, the WSA stated that passengers have the right to be informed of their rights in writing and in a comprehensive way. Article 14(2) of the Regulation has been interpreted literally, so that a legible notice or oral announcement in English and Polish on its own is not enough. The passengers have to be given information in writing, and in that written information all data should be included. Therefore it is not permissible to give passengers a note setting out a few draft details (like an advertisement and not a full notice of rights).[46] Thus the Polish Court held that informing passengers that they can ask for further information does not fulfil the requirements of Article 14(2) of the Regulation.

There are some examples of cases where the right to care under Article 9 of the Regulation was infringed alongside other infringements of the Regulation,[47] but there are hardly any examples of decisions where the right to care has been considered separately, with no parallel infringement of other rights stemming from the Regulation.[48] In its judgment of 28 April 2011, the WSA stated that a passenger who consciously decides not to travel further (after being given a choice to so continue) loses his right to care (consisting of the rights to accommodation, food and communication with the outside world at the cost of the air carrier) once he opts for a reimbursement of the price of the ticket. In such circumstances the passenger cannot then claim back the costs of a taxi taken to the final destination if this was not agreed with the air carrier.[49] The fulfilment of the obligations of the air carrier

---

[43] Stec (n 42) 9ff, 9–10; invoking also Recital (17) of the Preamble to Regulation 261.

[44] ibid, 9ff, 11.

[45] Judgment of WSA of 16.11.2012, VII SA/Wa 1321/12.

[46] Reasons in the judgment of WSA of 28.04.2011, VII Sa/Wa 2208/10, 8, where the court, criticising the method of informing the passengers of their rights in a superficial manner by a very broad notice, stated, '*pol.: ulotka … zawiera treści ulotne*' (which says: 'advertisement contains only volatile content', which should be understood as not really reliable form of providing information to passengers).

[47] Judgment of WSA of 23.08.2011, VII SA/Wa 733/11; judgment of WSA of 1.12.2010, SA/Wa 1295/10.

[48] *cf* judgment of WSA of 6.05.2008, VI SA/Wa 558/07.

[49] Reasons in the judgment of WSA of 28.04.2011, VII Sa/Wa 2208/10, 10; see also judgment of the NSA of 15.01.2013, I OSK 1412/11.

set out in Article 14 of the Regulation are controlled *ex officio* by the President of ULC.[50]

B. Interpretation of the 'Extraordinary Circumstances' Defence by the Polish Courts

The Regulation allows air carriers to free themselves from liability in the event of 'extraordinary circumstances'. This expression constitutes a particular form of exemption from liability, known as *vis major*.[51]

In their interpretation of the 'extraordinary circumstances' defence, the Polish courts referred to the jurisprudence of the CJEU[52] and to Recital (14) of the Preamble to Regulation 261.[53] A certain evolution, from an interpretation supporting the air carriers to an interpretation giving broader support to passengers, can be observed.

The first case in which the 'extraordinary circumstances' defence was raised by an air carrier occurred in 2005. The passenger was not admitted to the plane after check-in due to the technical failure of the aircraft. The carrier, LOT Airlines, refused to pay damages, claiming that the technical failure could not have been remedied quickly and endangered the safety of the flight. The passenger brought a claim before the President of ULC. The claim was rejected and the WSA, in its ruling of 15 June 2006, stated that the technical failure of an aircraft constituted an extraordinary circumstance justifying the cancellation of a flight.[54] As Anna Konert underlines, the air carrier was not obliged to prove in detail the occurrence of exceptional circumstances.[55] This method of reasoning has not been maintained, and a clear evolution, influenced by the development of CJEU's jurisprudence, is visible.

In later cases, the WSA ruled that the 'extraordinary circumstances' defence can be invoked by an air carrier in cases of delay and not only in connection with cancellation of flights[56] (after stating that compensation can be granted not only for cancellations but also for delays).[57] However, a technical error in an airplane is not in itself an 'extraordinary circumstance', unless it stems from events which—'due

---

[50] Air Law Act, Art 205a.3.

[51] M Stec, 'Prawo do odszkodowania w przypadku opóźnienia lotu—glosa do wyroku TS z 19.11.2009 r. w sprawie C-402/07 Sturgeon v. Condor oraz Bock i Lepuschitz v. Air France' [2011] 2 *Europejski Przegląd Sądowy* 41.

[52] In the judgment of WSA of 16.11.2012, VII SA/Wa 1321/12.

[53] In the judgment of WSA of 16.11.2012, VII SA/Wa 1321/12.

[54] VI Sa/Wa 749/06, LEX no 502529; M Nesterowicz, *Prawo turystyczne* (Wolters Kluwer, 2009) 159; Konert (n 13) 232.

[55] Konert (n 13) 233.

[56] In the judgment of WSA of 16.11.2012, VII SA/Wa 1321/12 or the judgment of WSA of 20.11.2013, VII SA/Wa 1973/13.

[57] Following the *Sturgeon* (n 3) interpretation of Art 7 of the Regulation, confirmed in Cases C-581 and 629/10 *Nelson v Deutsche Lufthansa AG* [2012] OJ C399/3.

to their character or source—are not falling in the framework of normal activity of air carrier and are beyond his effective control'.[58] Here the Court was clearly repeating the position of the CJEU in *Wallentin-Hermann v Alitalia*[59] and *Eglītis v Air Baltic*.[60] This position, with reference to the same CJEU jurisprudence, was confirmed in further jurisprudence of the WSA. In 2012 it stated that a collision with a flock of birds might constitute an exceptional circumstance, but the delay of a flight due to the need to repair the effects of such a collision was not covered by the exemption from liability.[61] In a series of judgments of April 2014 the Court stated that a hydraulic defect in an aircraft, due to which the flight was delayed by over eight hours, did not constitute an exceptional circumstance excluding the liability of air carrier.[62] In 2013 the WSA had to consider whether an air carrier, operating a flight that departed on time but which was forced to return to the airport of departure because one of the front windows of the aircraft was broken, could use the exceptional circumstances defence. The Court did not consider that this event constituted an exceptional circumstance, and found that compensation for delay was due.[63] In another case, the WSA stated that the illness of a captain of aircraft, of which the air carrier became aware a couple of hours before departure, did not constitute an exceptional circumstance and fell within the 'employer's risk' that everyone employing others may experience.[64] In another case, the same Court stated that the circumstances, consisting of the bankruptcy of the air carrier, of which a passenger learnt from the media, did not constitute exceptional circumstances.[65]

There are few examples of cases where the Polish Court actually did find the occurrence of exceptional circumstances. The WSA admitted, however, that some natural circumstances might constitute exceptional circumstances. For instance: thick fog constitutes an exceptional meteorological circumstance;[66] deep snowfall at the airport of arrival, due to which an aircraft had to delay its landing;[67] the appearance of a herd of deer on the incoming airport runway;[68] or a collision with a flock of birds during the flight.[69] In some cases, such circumstances were found

---

[58] In the judgment of WSA of 16.11.2012, VII SA/Wa 1321/12 or the judgment of WSA of 20.11.2013, VII SA/Wa 1973/13. By this the court was clearly repeating the position of the CJEU in Case C-549/07 *Wallentin-Hermann v Alitalia* [2008] ECR I-11061 (*Wallentin-Hermann*).

[59] *Wallentin-Hermann* (n 58); *cf* A Konert, 'Glosa do orzeczenia TS z 22.12.2008 r w sprawie C-549/07, Wallentin-Hermann przeciwko Alitalia' LEX/el 2012.

[60] Case C-294/10 *Eglītis v Latvijas Republikas Ekonomikas ministrija* [2011] ECR I-03983.

[61] Judgment of WSA of 3.10.2012, VII SA/Wa 1552/12.

[62] Judgments of WSA of 23.04.2014: VII SA/Wa 2461/13, VII SA/Wa 2464/13 and VII SA/Wa 2465/13; judgments of WSA of 14.04.2014, VII SA/Wa 2463/13 and VII SA/Wa 2462/13. In all the judgments, the Court directly invoked *Wallentin-Hermann* (n 58).

[63] Judgment of WSA of 1.10.2013, VII SA/Wa 3002/12.

[64] Judgment of WSA of 5.09.2013, VII SA/Wa 2957/12.

[65] Judgment of WSA of 30.12.2013, VII SA/Wa 1169/13.

[66] Judgment of WSA of 20.07.2012, VII SA/Wa 680/12; judgment of WSA of 6.05.2008, VI SA/Wa 558/07.

[67] Judgment of WSA of 24.05.2012, VII SA/Wa 283/12.

[68] Judgment of NSA of 6.03.2012, I OSK 555/11.

[69] Judgment of WSA of 24.01.2012, VII SA/Wa 1776/11.

in cases where an air carrier, after duly controlling the aircraft, suddenly experienced technical problems resulting from a technical failure that the air carrier could have not possibly have foreseen.[70]

The publication of the European Commission industry-led indicative list of exceptional circumstances from 2012 does not seem to have influenced the jurisprudence, in this sense that it was never directly referred to by the courts. However, the definition of the exceptional circumstances defence contained therein does appear to be reflected in the Polish decisions, because both some meteorological conditions and some technical errors were considered as exceptional, exonerating the air carrier from liability for compensation.

IV. Remedies

Claims for compensation have been brought, inter alia, for denied boarding, cancellation, delay or downgrading. There is a visible increase in the number of claims for delayed flights. Whereas at the start of the Regulation's coming into force, the claims deposited with the KOPP mainly concerned cancellations, passengers have come to realise that they can also claim compensation for delays. Apart from compensation for all the infringements mentioned above, the President of ULC can impose financial sanctions upon the air carriers concerned.

As explained in section III.A above, there was a distinct reaction in the jurisprudence to the *Sturgeon* case. There has been a clear extension of the circumstances in which the compensation adjudicated by the competent body under Article 16(2) of the Regulation can be granted, to passengers delayed for more than three hours. In 2006 and 2007 the President of ULC was still refusing to regard this kind of compensation as not covered by the Regulation, and was suggesting that passengers should take the general path of civil claims for compensation. Due to the *Sturgeon* case, the WSA[71] initiated a long series of judgments in which that jurisprudence was fully applied. It referred to *Sturgeon* even when it was pending before the CJEU,[72] and has never questioned the decision's implications. It has, however, sometimes clarified the application of this jurisprudence, without, however, ever considering it necessary to submit a preliminary question to the CJEU. For instance, in 2012 the President of ULC granted compensation for a delayed flight only to the mother of an infant, holding that a child below two years of age, travelling with 'no seat', was not entitled to compensation. The WSA quashed this decision, stating that an infant is a passenger entitled to all the rights contained in Regulation, including the right to compensation for delay.[73]

---

[70] Judgment of WSA of 9.05.2013, VII SA/Wa 2894/12 (engine trouble), judgment of WSA of 9.05.2012, VII SA/Wa 2690/11 (failure of electronic system during the flight).

[71] Reasons in the judgment of WSA of 6.10.2008, VI SA/Wa 1230/2008, 2.

[72] Judgment of WSA of 28.01.2009, VI SA/Wa 2091/08.

[73] Judgment of WSA of 16.05.2012, VII SA/Wa 2793/11.

Sometimes the jurisprudence of Polish courts steers away from the CJEU jurisprudence. In 2011 the WSA had occasion to interpret the situation where compensation is due for denied boarding. It held that compensation was only due in cases of overbooking[74] and not where a passenger was denied boarding for reasons connected with incomplete documents (in the instant case, lack of a visa)[75] or for other reasons.[76] In 2012 this interpretation was confirmed by the NSA,[77] despite the fact that the CJEU had given a broader interpretation in *Finnair v Lassooy*.[78] In the judgment of May 2014,[79] the WSA did not find an infringement of the right of all four members of a family with two children, one of whom was not admitted onto the aircraft due to overbooking, in consequence of which the whole family asked to be placed on a different flight. Compensation for the one family member had been granted by the President of ULC, but the instant case concerned the other three members of the family, who were not compensated. On the other hand, there are also examples of judgments where the denial of access to the flight, without there being any overbooking, was perceived as an infringement of the Regulation,[80] and thus as wholly in line with the CJEU's jurisprudence.

The interpretation of other incidental rights, different from the right to compensation, is seldom the subject of case law. As already mentioned in section III.A above, in its judgment of 28 April 2011, the WSA held that passengers must be fully informed of their rights in writing.[81] Thus any lack of, or only partial, fulfilment of the obligations under Article 14(2) of the Regulation constitutes an infringement of the Regulation.

The NSA ruled, in a judgment of 2 December 2011,[82] that a passenger who had not been informed of the cancellation of his flights two weeks before the date of his planned departure should be granted compensation. The burden of proving that the passenger was informed of the change in the flight schedule falls on the air carrier. Copies of e-mails sent to all passengers booked on the flight are sufficient proof that the passenger concerned was correctly informed of the

---

[74] Judgment of WSA of 16.02.2011, VII SA/Wa 2314/10.

[75] This interpretation is given by R Ostrihansky in J Barcz (ed), *Prawo Unii Europejskiej. Prawo materialne i polityki* (Instytut Wydawniczy EuroPrawo, 2005) II-539.

[76] Judgment of WSA of 11.07.2007, VI SA/Wa 648/07.

[77] Judgment of the NSA of 23.10.2012, I OSK 1183/11; cf M Makowski, 'Zakres odpowiedzialności przewoźnika lotniczego z tytułu odmowy wpuszczenia na pokład na podstawie rozporządzenia Parlamentu Europejskiego i Rady z 2004 r.—glosa krytyczna do wyroku NSA z 23.10.2012 r.' [2013] 8 *Europejski Przegląd Sądowy* 39.

[78] Case C-22/11 *Finnair Oyj v Timy Lassooy* (ECJ, 4 October 2012); Case C-321/11 *Cachafeiro v Iberia* [2012] OJ C366/13; M Stec, 'Prawo do odszkodowania w przypadku odmowy przyjęcia pasażera na pokład samolotu—glosa do wyroków TS: z 4.10.2012 r. w sprawie C-321/11, Cachafeiro v Iberia oraz z 4.10.2012 r. w sprawie C-22/11, Finnair v Lassooy' (2013) 2 *Europejski Przegląd Sądowy* 45.

[79] Judgment of WSA of 22.05.2014, VII SA/Wa 276/14.

[80] Judgment of WSA of 23.08.2011, VII SA/Wa 733/11. This interpretation is confirmed by A Konert, 'Glosa do wyroku Wojewódzkiego Sądu Administracyjnego w Warszawie z dnia 11 lipca 2007 r., sygn. akt VI SA/Wa 648/07' LEX/el. 2011.

[81] Judgment of WSA of 28.04.2011, VII Sa/Wa 2208/10, 8.

[82] Judgment of the NSA of 2.12.2011, I OSK 2043/10; cf A Hauser and R Talaga, 'Review of European jurisprudence of Polish administrative courts' (2012) 5 *Europejski Przegląd Sądowy* 61.

change.[83] However, the fact that the cancellation was due to a change in the flight schedule because of the presence of a herd of wild animals at the airport, a fact known to the air carrier some time before the date of the flight, can be perceived as an exceptional circumstance within the meaning of Article 5(3) of the Regulation. The air carrier is first of all obliged to guarantee the safety of passengers, and such situations undermine their security. The concept of 'exceptional circumstances' is not limited to the 'sudden events' but can also apply to events that continue for a certain time.

V. Montreal Convention Compatibility

The Montreal Convention purports to regulate exclusively liability arising from contracts of carriage by air.[84] It was signed by the European Community on 9 December 1999 under the then Article 300(2) of the Treaty establishing the European Community[85] (now Article 218 of the TFEU), and entered into force on 28 June 2004. The Convention was ratified by Poland on 6 October 2005[86] and entered into force on 18 March 2006.[87] By definition, Regulation 261 regulates only a fragment of the issues covered by the Convention, concerning the rights of passengers perceived as consumers.[88] The Regulation is perceived by some authors even as a form of implementation of the Montreal Convention in EU law, at the same time acting as a stimulus within EU law to the development of international solutions.[89] The thesis on implementation cannot to be supported, but there is no doubt that the two legal regimes clearly blur one into the other.[90] In cases of breach of the Convention that do not also consist of breaches of the Regulation (like liability for the life and health of passengers, which is regulated in the Montreal Convention),[91] the passengers can claim damages before the civil courts.[92]

---

[83] According to Art 61 § 2 of the Civil Code, the communication of one's will in electronic form takes place at the moment of introducing the statement into the means of electronic communication.

[84] eg M Żylicz, 'Nowe prawo międzynarodowego przewozu lotniczego (system warszawsko-montrealski)' (1999) 9 *Państwo i Prawo* 22.

[85] [2001] OJ L194/38. Under Art 3 of the Air Law Act, ratified international conventions override the provisions of the Act.

[86] [2007] *Journal of Laws* No 37, pos 235.

[87] Oświadczenie rządowe z 16 października 2006 r (Government declaration of 16 October 2006), [2007] *Journal of Laws* No 37, pos 236.

[88] Stec (n 42).

[89] Konert (n 13) 59.

[90] See broader interactions between different rules on passengers' protection in A Kunert-Diallo, *Kolizje praw w międzynarodowym transporcie lotniczym* (Wolters Kluwer, 2011).

[91] Convention for the Unification of Certain Rules for International Carriage by Air [2001] OJ L194/39 (Montreal Convention), art 17.1; cf Mirosław Nesterowicz, *Prawo turystyczne* (Wolters Kluwer 2012) 175.

[92] cf judgment of WSA of 28.01.2009, VI SA/Wa 2091/08 (the passengers were wrongly informed of the delay of the flight and because of this missed the flight); judgment of Wojewódzki Sąd Administra-cyjny w Warszawie of Warsaw of 6.05.2008, VI SA/Wa 558/07 (the passenger missed a connecting flight after being granted a taxi drive instead of an annulled flight).

Because the Convention has been ratified by all the Member States of the EU and the European Union itself, some authors are of the opinion that on the basis of Article 351 of the TFEU,[93] the Montreal Convention should take precedence over the Regulation.[94] This position is not shared by the author of this chapter, as it seems that the relationship between the Convention and the Regulation should be perceived on the basis both of the principle of *lex posterior derogat legi priori* and the principle of *lex specialis derogat legi generali*. If one considers that there is no hierarchy between the Regulation and the decision introducing the Convention into the EU legal order, the Regulation should be perceived as *lex posterior*. As, in addition, the provisions of the Regulation partly touch upon the same issues as the Convention, but in a more detailed manner as far as the definition of rights, remedies and methods of redress are concerned, the Regulation should be considered to be *lex specialis*.[95] However, such a position would mean that in cases that are not covered by the Regulation, or in cases of doubt over the interpretation of terms contained in the Regulation, the Montreal Convention should be a source of reference, helping to construe their proper meaning.

In this line of reasoning, Polish doctrine is of the opinion that Article 12 of the Regulation should be interpreted consistently with Article 19 of the Montreal Convention, which means that the compensation granted should cover not only material damage but also immaterial damage (moral damage).[96] This would be in line with CJEU judgments in *Walz v Clickair*[97] and *Rodriguez v Air France*.[98]

In doctrine, the relationship between the Montreal Convention and the Regulation has been perceived as comprising a distinction between the international system (Warsaw–Montreal system) and the European system.[99] The Polish legislator opted for a solution that any damage that occurs in international transport by air (be it international or European in dimension) should first be subject to international regulation. Article 3 of the Air Law Act aims at introducing a universal liability regime for both national and international transport.[100]

In 2006 and 2007, the President of ULC relied on the Montreal Convention to find that liability for delayed flights was not the object of Regulation 261 only, but also of the Convention, so the prospective claims should have been brought before the civil courts, as the President of ULC found himself not to be competent in this matter.[101] However, this interpretation has changed due to the *Sturgeon* case, and at present the President of ULC admits such claims as being covered by the

---

[93] Treaty establishing the European Community [2001] OJ L 194/38, art 307.
[94] A Konert, 'Glosa do orzeczenia TS z 22.12.2008 r. w sprawie C-549/07, Wallentin-Hermann przeciwko Alitalia' LEX/el 2012.
[95] Stec (n 42).
[96] M Górski, 'Glosa do wyroku TS z dnia 13 października 2011 r., C-83/10' LEX/El 2012.
[97] Case C-63/09 *Walz v Clickair SA* [2010] ECR I-04239.
[98] Case C-83/10 *Rodríguez v Air France SA* [2011] ECR I-09469.
[99] Konert (n 13) 19.
[100] ibid, 20.
[101] Reasons in the judgment of WSA of 6.10.2008, VI SA/Wa 1230/2008, 2.

Regulation. But the initial refusal to adjudicate had led to a paradox. Passengers started to claim damages for delays under the Montreal Convention before the civil courts. However, after the *Sturgeon* decision the civil courts started to question their jurisdiction, claiming that it was up to the President of ULC to adjudicate on such cases. This has developed in such a way that, currently, the liability of air carriers for delays in flights can be claimed both before of the President of UCL, that is a NEB introduced in accordance with Article 16 of the Regulation, and (in parallel) also before the civil courts. This solution has recently been confirmed by the Polish Supreme Court, in answer to a question posed by a civil court considering a case on liability for delay.[102]

This development clearly shows that the initial distinction between the scope of liability defined in the Montreal Convention and that in the Regulation has been blurred. However, the scope of the Montreal Convention is narrower in respect of the protection of passengers than the scope of the Regulation. The Convention regulates cases of delay, whereas the Regulation also covers overbooking and cancellation or denied boarding.[103] One can expect that further cases 'fusing' the two regimes will occur, as both instruments belong to the *acquis communautaire*, and in Poland the distinction between them is important only for jurisdictional issues and not for substantive issues. The resolution of the Supreme Court of February 2014 shows that there is a strong will to interpret both the Regulation and the Montreal Convention in a way that allows passengers to claim their rights in as many forums as possible.

VI. National Enforcement

The Regulation is held to be directly effective both by the NEB and by civil courts. This has never been questioned by the courts, and has been confirmed by the legislator in Article 3 of the Air Law Act. The main enforcer of the Regulation is the President of ULC, the civil courts playing only a subsidiary role.

As to the limitation periods applicable to claims based on Regulation 261, there is interesting but rather controversial recent jurisprudence on this. In the Air Law Act of 2002 there is a provision stating that issues not regulated in the Act should be ruled upon on the basis of general civil law provisions.[104] In the WSA's judgment of 22 May 2014,[105] the Court clearly stated that the normal rules of civil law

---

[102] Resolution of SN of 7.02.2014, III CZP 113/13; *cf* [2014] 2 *Biuletyn Sądu Najwyższego* 8. The case concerned compensation for a delayed flight, which until *Sturgeon* (n 3) was only handled by the civil courts.

[103] Konert (n 13) 187; M Polkowska, 'Air Carrier Liability in the Passengers Transport and Protection of their rights' [2011] *Revista europea de derecho de la navegación marítima y aeronáutica* available at <http://rednma.eumed.net/air-carrier-liability-in-t … ion-of-their-rights/>.

[104] Air Law Act, Art 205.

[105] Judgment of WSA of 22.05.2014, VII SA/Wa 241/13.

are not applicable to claims based on the Regulation as far as limitation periods are concerned. The Court held that there is no basis in Article 205 of the Air Law Act to find the application of the Polish Civil Code on the issue of limitation periods. The Court directly referred to the CJEU's judgment in *Moré v KLM*,[106] in which it is stated that it is up to each Member State to fix the applicable limitation periods. However, this judgment only states that such claims can be subject to national law limitation periods; there is no obligation for the Member States to set such limits. Therefore, it can be said that claims under the Regulation are not subject to the limitations set out in the Polish Civil Code. If this judgment is retained, it would mean that passengers have gained a very strong weapon against the air carriers.

To date there have been no preliminary questions to the CJEU on the Regulation or the Montreal Convention. In a few cases brought before both the district and chief administrative courts, some parties asked the court to submit preliminary questions.[107] In 2014, one of the parties suggested that preliminary questions on the interpretation of various provisions of the Regulation and their conformity with the Charter of Fundamental Rights of the European Union,[108] as well as the definition of 'exceptional circumstances', should be assessed, but the NSA did not consider it necessary to ask those questions.[109] The Court stated that the doubts raised by the party had already been answered in the *Sturgeon* and *Wallentin-Hermann* judgments. Similarly, in 2013, the NSA did not follow suggestions to submit preliminary questions, stating that the problems raised had already been clarified by the CJEU.[110] There are no cases of hearings being stayed because of preliminary references in other countries.

In a recent case, where the Polish Supreme Court had to adjudicate on whether there was an alternative to claiming liability for the delay of a flight before a body responsible for the enforcement of the Regulation in Poland or before the civil court, no preliminary question was asked. The Supreme Court has not considered its possible obligation to raise a preliminary question with the CJEU on the interpretation of Article 16 of the Regulation. This is to be regretted, as it is not clear whether Article 16 allows for the 'double' jurisdiction of both NEBs and civil courts in cases covered by the Regulation, and this was a good opportunity to clarify this.

VII. Scholarly Analysis

The subject of civil liability of air carriers has been analysed in the Polish literature since 1960, mainly through the lens of international obligations stemming from

---

[106] Case C-139/11 *Moré v KLM* (ECJ, 22 November 2012).

[107] eg, judgment of the NSA of 2.12.2011, I OSK 2043/10; judgment of WSA of 1.12.2010, VII SA/Wa 1295/10.

[108] [2012] OJ C326/391.

[109] Reasons in the judgment of the NSA of 27.03.2014, I OSK 1971/12.

[110] Judgment of the NSA of 23.10.2013, I OSK 1164/13.

the Warsaw Convention[111] and, later, the Montreal Convention.[112] In the last few years the focus has shifted, from international law solutions to EU law solutions,[113] for two reasons: (i) Polish accession to the EU, which clearly influenced the remedies at hand for passengers, and (ii) the presumed alignment of the EU solutions with international solutions, expanding the protection of passengers rather than lessening it.

The Regulation has been criticised for its very complex and imprecise language, which leaves room for various, often inconsistent, interpretations of the same provisions. In particular, the translation of the Regulation into the Polish language on the basis of the English version of the Regulation was widely criticised as inconsistent with the Polish legal tradition of civil law, based on Continental notions.[114] It is generally perceived as not corresponding to the Polish civil law system.[115]

Discussion in recent literature has mainly concentrated on the scope of the competence of the CJEU to extend the interpretation of the rights (or even to add new rights) stemming from Regulation 261.[116] The authors underline that the teleological interpretation of the Regulation takes over its literal meaning, and that the aim of assuring the 'efficiency' of EU rules is the primary initial intention of the EU legislator.[117] Thus the CJEU seems to overstep its competence by taking policy-making steps and creating the law rather than applying it.[118]

VIII. Conclusions

Over the past nine years there has been a clear development as far as awareness of passengers of their rights is concerned. This can be seen clearly in the statistical data on the number of claims brought. Polish courts are aware of the jurisprudence

---

[111] J Rajski, *Opowiedzialność cywilna przewoźnika lotniczego w prawie międzynarodowym i krajowym* (Państwowe Wydawnictwo Naukowe, 1968); M Dragun, *Kwotowe ograniczenia odpowiedzialności przewoźnika w międzynarodowym prawie przewozowym* (Wydawnictwo Uniwersytetu Mikołaja Kopernika, 1984).

[112] M Polkowska and I Szymajda, *Konwencja montrealska Komentarz Odpowiedzialność cywilna przewoźnika lotniczego* (Liber, 2004); M Polkowska, *Umowa przewozu i odpowiedzialność przewoźnika w międzynarodowym transporcie lotniczym* (Amalker, 2003); Konert (n 13), who refers broadly to EU law.

[113] M Żylicz, *Prawo lotnicze—międzynarodowe, europejskie i krajowe* (Lexis Nexis, 2011).

[114] Stec (n 42) 12.

[115] M Stec, 'O niektórych postaciach niewykonania lub nienależytego wykonania pasażerskiej umowy przewozu lotniczego na kanwie rozporządzenia Parlamentu i Rady Unii Europejskiej z 2004 r.' in *W kierunku europeizacji prawa prywatnego. Księga pajmiątkowa dedykowana Profesorowi Jerzemu Rajskiemu* (CH Beck, 2007) 256.

[116] A Jurkowska-Gomułka, 'Glosa do orzeczenia TS z 19.11.2009 w sprawie C-402/07, Sturgeon v Condor oraz Bock i Lepuschitz v Air France' LEX/el 2010; M Stec, 'Prawo do odszkodowania w przypadku opóźnienia lotu—glosa do wyroku TS z 19.11.2009 r w sprawie C-402/07 Sturgeon v Condor oraz Bock i Lepuschitz v Air France' (2011) 2 *Europejski Przegląd Sądowy* 40.

[117] Stec (n 116) 43.

[118] A Konert, 'Zryczałtowane odszkodowanie za opóźniony lot' (2013) 2 *Glosa* 57.

of the CJEU and directly refer to it in their rulings, mainly in order to strengthen their argument for a particular interpretation of the Regulation.[119] References to the most recent CJEU jurisprudence might be perceived as a sign of good will, and even herald a certain judicial dialogue between the national counterparts and the CJEU, with only few instances of divergent lines of interpretation. However, the lack of any preliminary question in this domain shows that the dialogue remains indirect. There is particularly a need to clarify two issues: first, the problem of the double jurisdiction of the NEB (President of ULC) and the civil courts in cases of delayed flights, where the interpretation of Article 16 of the Regulation is required; and, secondly, the narrow interpretation of the right to compensation for denied boarding, often limited to cases of overbooking, which is not in line with the language of the Regulation and needs to be clarified by a preliminary question.

---

[119] Judgment of WSA of 16.11.2012, VII SA/Wa 1321/12; judgment of WSA of 22.05.2014, VII SA/Wa 241/13. In both cases the court referred to *Sturgeon* (n 3).

15

Spain: Defeating Air Passengers' Rights Through Procedural Rules

MIREIA ARTIGOT I GOLOBARDES

I. Introduction

The aim of this chapter is to present the application and impact of Regulation 261 in Spain. Air transport to and from Spain represents a remarkable amount of the air transport flying to and from the European Union (EU). Spanish air passenger transportation represents roughly 25 per cent of the total overall in the EU. This proportion has been quite steady in the last few years.[1] See Tables 15.1 and 15.2 below and Figure 15.1.

In light of the importance of the Spanish air transport market, the analysis of the impact and application of Regulation 261 in Spain is of remarkable significance. However, both of these matters have been strongly conditioned by events that have taken place in Spain since the European legislature adopted Regulation 261.

In 2006 and 2012, two Spanish airlines, Air Madrid and Spanair, had their operating licences suspended. This resulted in bankruptcy proceedings for both companies, and in a remarkable amount of litigation by affected passengers. Air Madrid was created in 2003.[2] In 2006, after failing to comply with a plan of corrective measures addressing delays and the continuous malfunctioning of the aircraft, the Ministry responsible for air navigation, the Ministerio de Fomento,[3] proceeded to suspend Air Madrid's licence to operate as an airline.[4]

---

[1] During the year 2013, 158,072,126 passengers were transported into and from Spain by air; 633,192,382 total passengers were transported by air in the 27 Member States of the EU (Croatia later became an EU Member State in July 2013).

[2] Air Madrid, available at <http://concurso.airmadrid.com/cgi-vel/concurso/www-exec.pro?web-orden=1>, accessed 30 December 2014.

[3] The Spanish Ministry of Fomento is the government department responsible for land, air and maritime transport infrastructure. Additional information can be found at <www.fomento.gob.es/mfom/lang_castellano/>, accessed 5 January 2015.

[4] Confirmed by the Spanish Supreme Court in Judgment of the Spanish Supreme Court (3rd section) RJ 2013/5659 of 1 July 2013.

Table 15.1: Total Air Passengers on Board EU (27) flights 1998–2013[5]

SCHEDULE/TIME	1998	1999	2000	2001	2002	2003	2004	2005
Total								
Scheduled								
Non-scheduled								

SCHEDULE/TIME	2006	2007	2008	2009	2010	2011	2012	2013
Total		800,498,781	803,963,457	757,541,386	786,630,027	827,068,170	832,270,854	633,192,382
Scheduled		704,301,021	710,736,018	677,183,413	704,980,144	749,174,965	756,805,538	582,837,199
Non-scheduled		96,197,760	93,227,439	80,357,973	81,649,883	77,893,205	75,465,310	50,355,183

Table 15.2: Total Air Passengers on Board Spanish flights 1998–2013[6]

SCHEDULE/TIME	1998	1999	2000	2001	2002	2003	2004	2005
Total	273	282	1,083	114,155,694	113,025,419	120,052,804	130,490,088	140,867,149
Scheduled	:	282	166	78,979,984	78,319,578	86,300,513	98,663,384	112,329,731
Non-scheduled	273	:	917	35,175,710	34,705,841	33,752,291	31,826,704	28,537,418

SCHEDULE/TIME	2006	2007	2008	2009	2010	2011	2012	2013
Total	147,962,416	162,984,822	162,236,983	148,988,842	153,915,703	165,667,780	160,385,889	158,072,126
Scheduled	121,281,599	137,825,410	138,672,645	131,211,171	136,828,499	147,755,057	143,084,925	140,975,348
Non-scheduled	26,680,817	25,159,412	23,564,338	17,777,671	17,087,204	17,912,723	17,300,964	17,096,778

5 Eurostat, 'Air passenger transport by reporting country' (Eurostat), available at <www.ec.europa.eu/eurostat>, accessed 11 April 2015.
6 Eurostat, 'Air passenger transport by reporting country' (Eurostat), available at <www.ec.europa.eu/eurostat>, accessed 11 April 2015.

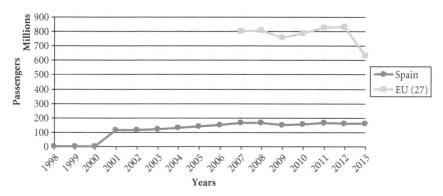

Figure 15.1: Air Passengers on Board EU (27) and Spain 1993–2013[7]

The case of Spanair was quite different, although it also ended with a bankruptcy proceeding.[8] Spanair, created in 1986, ceased its operations in 2012 after Qatar Airways decided not to pursue an investment it had been considering, because it feared potential actions by the European Commission resulting from complaints that the airline had received state aid. Qatar Airways' decision, following on the heels of the economic and financial crisis, led Spanair to cease its operations, leaving some 23,000 pasengers without flights.[9] Spanair filed for bankruptcy, and the proceeding remains pending and before the Spanish courts.

In parallel to these events, in 2011, Spanish procedural rules were amended, directly affecting the procedures through which passengers could claim compensation under Regulation 261.

The outline of this chapter is as follows. First, it provides a background to the legal context in which Regulation 261 is applied. Secondly, it discusses the interpretation, scope and burden of proof of the extraordinary circumstances exception, before presenting the analysis of Regulation 261 by Spanish scholars.

II. Legal Context of the Application of Regulation 261 in Spain

This section explores the background legal context in which Regulation 261 is applied. It will first focus on the rules of procedure through which legal claims

[7] Eurostat, 'Air passenger transport by reporting country' (Eurostat), available at <www.ec.europa.eu/eurostat>, accessed 11 April 2015.

[8] See Spanair, available at <www.spanair.com/>, accessed 30 December 2014.

[9] The compensation claims of these passengers became part of the creditors' claims in the bankruptcy proceeding. See Spanair (n 8), accessed 5 January 2015.

are brought. It will then discuss the national legislation often applied together with Regulation 261, and the impact of Regulation 261 on claims brought before Spanish courts.

A. Procedure for Claiming Compensation

Claims under Regulation 261 often have three different phases. The first phase is when passengers experience a delay or cancellation, or are denied boarding, and when airline companies are required to provide adequate information regarding passengers' rights. Airline companies generally require the filing of a complaint online, and provide compensation a few days after the event. When airline companies fail to respond to passengers' claims, passengers often engage in mediation procedures. Mediation is the second phase, and it is often carried out by public institutions and public consumer agencies.[10] If the mediation is not successful, passengers may decide to file a judicial claim—the third phase.

It is difficult to assess the performance of each of these different phases, given that the Spanish agency responsible for air traffic[11] does not provide data on flight incidents and consumer agencies do not provide information on consumer mediation procedures conducted each year. From this perspective, it is difficult to assess the percentage of incidents in which air passengers engage in mediation, how many of these mediations result in an agreement between the parties and how many end up in court.

Focusing specifically on the judicial procedure, according to the Spanish Law of Civil Procedure, passengers bring their claims against airline companies before courts using a *juicio verbal de reclamación de cantidad* (oral argument for claiming an economic amount due),[12] regulated by Articles 437 to 447 of the Law of Civil Procedure. The courts with jurisdiction to hear claims based on Regulation 261 are the commercial courts.[13]

---

[10] These public institutions are either at the national level or at the regional level. Spain is a pluri-legislative state, and some of these powers are not dependent on the national Government but on the governments of the 17 autonomous communities.

[11] The agency responsible for air traffic in Spain is Aena. Further information is available at <www. aena.es/csee/Satellite/HomeAena/en/>, accessed 30 December 2014.

[12] Spanish Law 1/2000 of 7 January on Civil Procedure, BOE no 7, of 8 January 2000, Arts 248.2.2 and 250.2; correction of errors in BOE nos 90, of 14 April 2000, and 180, of 28 July 2001 (Spanish Civil Procedure Act). The English version of the Spanish Civil Procedure Act can be found at <www. mjusticia.gob.es/cs/Satellite/1292426983864?blobheader=application%2Fpdf&blobheadername1 =Content-Disposition&blobheadervalue1=attachment%3B+filename%3DCivil_Procedure_Act_ %28Ley_de_Enjuiciamiento_Civil%29.PDF>, accessed 30 December 2014.

[13] Spanish Civil Procedure Act, Art 52.2; Law 38/1988 of Demarcación y Planta Judicial, BOE no 313 of 30 December 1988, Arts 3.1, 19 and 86.3.2(b); interim decisions issued by the Spanish Supreme Court on 10 October 2007, 3 April 2007, 5 November 2004 and 7 October 2004, when dealing with issues on courts' jurisdiction. However, it should be noted that some issues have been dealt with before administrative as well as civil courts. These administrative courts have focused more on aerial regulation, suspension of flight licences and, eventually, the bankruptcy proceedings of the flight companies whose licences had been suspended.

When the claims brought by passengers are for compensation of less than €2,000, passengers may file their claims without being assisted by legal counsel[14] and may use the templates provided by courts for filing this kind of claim. When compensation claims are above that amount, the assistance of legal counsel is mandatory.

Further, claimants, at least in theory, are not supposed to bear the litigation costs of any of the parties in the procedure, regardless of whether they prevail or not. The Spanish Law of Civil Procedure, in Article 32.5,[15] establishes that in those judicial proceedings in which the participation of a legal counsel and a *procurador* is not mandatory, as in most judicial proceedings under Regulation 261,[16] neither party will bear the litigation costs of the proceeding unless the court understands that one of the parties was reckless when initiating the proceeding before the court.

Filing judicial claims under Regulation 261 should be relatively easy in Spain, given that no legal representation is needed and, unless there has been reckless behaviour, that there might not be exposure to the litigation costs of the other party who might have legal assistance. If both conditions were to be complied with, the consumer protection goal aimed at by Regulation 261,[17] as well as by the TFEU,[18] would be fulfilled.

One of the major problems with the Spanish court system is that access to courts too often is not equivalent to access to justice. Spanish rules of procedure are old (even though they have been amended) and they are lengthy, resulting in delays and backlogs. In many cases, by the time a court issues an opinion, it is no longer relevant.[19] Further, the number of judges in Spain is low, and their selection

---

[14] Spanish Civil Procedure Act, Arts 23.2.1 and 31.2.1. It should be noted that when an individual files a claim before a Spanish court, it is generally necessary to be assisted by two different attorneys: one providing legal advice to the client, and another responsible for the interaction between the client and the courts (the *procurador*).

[15] Art 32.5 of the Spanish Civil Procedure Act provides, 'cuando la intervención de abogado y procurador no sea preceptiva, de la eventual condena en costas de la parte contraria a la que se hubiese servido de dichos profesionales se excluirán los derechos y honorarios devengados por los mismos, salvo que el Tribunal aprecie temeridad en la conducta del condenado en costas o que el domicilio de la parte representada y defendida esté en lugar distinto a aquel en que se ha tramitado el juicio, operando en este último caso las limitaciones a que se refiere el apartado 3 del artículo 394 de esta ley' ('when the assistance of legal counsel and of a *procurador* is not mandatory, the party determined to be responsible for the litigation costs of the procedure will not be responsible for the fees of these legal professionals unless the court finds reckless behaviour by this party or the party represented and assisted by counsel is domiciled outside the district in which the trial has taken place. This latter case based on domicile is governed by part 3 of article 394 of the present law').

[16] It should be noted that legal assistance and participation of a *procurador* are not required in procedures involving a claim for less than €2,000.

[17] European Parliament and Council Regulation (EC) 261/2004 of 11 February 2004 establishing common rules on compensation and assistance to passengers in the event of denied boarding and of cancellation or long delay of flights, and repealing Regulation (EEC) No 295/91 OJ L 46/1 (Regulation 261), Preamble, Recital (1).

[18] Consolidated version of the Treaty on the Functioning of the European Union [2012] OJ C326/1 (TFEU), Arts 4(f) and 169; the TFEU establishes consumer protection as one of the goals of the EU.

[19] It should be noted that Spanish judges are law graduates who can take an exam once they complete their law degree—without needing to practise law—and once they pass the exam they complete two years of judicial school before being assigned to a court. Spanish judges are public servants.

process is often questionable and questioned.[20] In order to address this situation and speed up judicial procedures, in 2011 the Spanish Government adopted Law 37/2011.[21] The relevant amendment introduced by this Law was that of Article 455.1 of the Spanish Law of Civil Procedure, which eliminated the possibility of appealing judgments in procedures involving a claim of less than €3,000.[22] The Spanish legislature adopted this law because of the exponential increase in litigation before Spanish courts during the decade prior to 2009,[23] and because of the excessive, often abusive and unnecessary, use of appeals in certain kinds of cases[24]—the Spanish Government claimed.

This amendment is of crucial importance for the application of Regulation 261 and for the enforcement of passengers' rights. As of today, there are questions as to whether the Spanish court system can ensure the proper application of European law and jurisprudence, and a coherent body of judicial opinions, that could guarantee a uniform application of Regulation 261, as well as compliance with passengers' rights as provided for the European legislature. This is of special importance when analysing the different interpretations and application of Regulation 261 in first instance courts and in Spanish appellate courts. Allowing appeals may not necessarily ensure passengers' rights. However, it could help ensure a more consistent and uniform application of Regulation 261, and protect the fundamental right of access to justice.[25]

B. Limitation Periods within which to Claim Compensation: *Moré*'s Background and Relevance

One of the major contributions to Spanish case law on the interpretation of Regulation 261 was the case of *Moré v KLM*,[26] concerning the limitation period

---

[20] Because of the past and current shortage of judges, there are a remarkable number of substitute judges who are legal practitioners, professors or other qualified legal professionals, who sit in courts or assist courts that are particularly clogged. However, these substitute judges do not take any exam and there are minor evaluation processes in these cases that often put into question the fundamental right to justice and the fundamental right to a judge pre-determined by the law, established by Art 24 of the Spanish Constitution of 1978.

[21] Law 37/2011 of October 10, on Measures for Speeding Judicial Procedures, BOE no 245 of 11 October 2011, 106726 to 106744.

[22] Since 2011, Art 455.1 of the Spanish Civil Procedure Act has read as follows: 'Las sentencias dictadas en toda clase de juicio, los autos definitivos y aquéllos otros que la ley expresamente señale, serán apelables, con excepción de las sentencias dictadas en los juicios verbales por razón de la cuantía cuando ésta no supere los 3.000 euros.' ('The judgments issued by courts in any type of trial, the final motions issued by courts and any other court procedure laws expressly determined will be subject to appeal with the exception of judgments issued in oral court proceedings claiming amounts of less than 3,000 euros.').

[23] Law 37/2011 on Measures for Speeding Judicial Procedures, Preamble II.

[24] ibid, Preamble III.

[25] eg J Garberí Llobregat, *El Recurso de Apelación en la Ley de Enjuiciamiento Civil* (Bosch, 2014) ch 3, challenging the limitation of appeals in this kind of judicial procedure and suggesting that such limitation might violate the fundamental right to justice and to a fair judicial process with all guarantees of Art 24 of the Spanish Constitution.

[26] Case C-139/11 *Moré v KLM* (ECJ, 22 November 2012).

applicable when bringing a claim under Articles 5 and 7 of Regulation 261. This case was the result of a request for a preliminary ruling of the Barcelona Court of Appeals before the CJEU,[27] on whether claims under Regulation 261 were subject to the two-year limitation period established by Article 35 of the Montreal Convention.[28] The CJEU, in its judgment of 2011,[29] established that claims brought under Articles 5 and 7 of Regulation 261 were subject to the statute of limitations of each Member State.

Since the CJEU issued this judgment there has not been much case law in Spain on this point. However, two judgments applying and discussing *Moré* might be highlighted: first, a decision of the First Instance Commercial Court of Bilbao in 2012;[30] and, secondly, a decision of the Barcelona Court of Appeals of 2013 between the same parties as in *Moré* and on the same issue, but as regards a different flight.[31]

The judgment of the First Instance Commercial Court of Bilbao in 2012[32] dealt with the interaction between the domestic laws of the Member States and European regulation, and, among other issues, dealt with the statute of limitations applicable to bringing an action under Regulation 261. The claim was filed more than two years after the flight was cancelled. However, applying the ruling of the CJEU in *Moré*,[33] the court considered that the 15-year limitation period under Article 1964 of the Spanish Civil Code[34] was applicable, and hence the claimant's action was filed in good time.

The second judgment applying the CJEU's decision in *Moré* was that of the Barcelona Court of Appeals issued in 2013.[35] This was a case between the same parties and on the same issue—whether the compensation claim under Regulation 261 was filed in time—but in connection with a different flight. In that case, the claimant's claim, based on Articles 5 and 6 of Regulation 261, was dismissed in the first instance court because it was considered that the two-year limitation period established by Article 29 of the Warsaw Convention and Article 35 of the Montreal Convention had run. On appeal, the claimant argued that the first instance court had erred in not applying the 10-year default limitation period established in Article 121.20 of the Catalan Civil Code,[36] applicable in those cases where there was no shorter and express limitation period. The claimant argued that since Regulation 261 did not include any express time limits within which to

---

[27] ibid; a reference for a Preliminary Ruling from the Barcelona Court of Appeals was lodged on 21 March 2011.

[28] Convention for the Unification of Certain Rules for International Carriage by Air [2001] OJ L194/39 (Montreal Convention).

[29] *Moré* (n 26).

[30] Judgment of the Bilbao First Instance Commercial Court AC 2013/165 of 17 December 2012.

[31] Judgment of the Barcelona Court of Appeals JUR 2013/338930 of 6 May 2013.

[32] Judgment of the Bilbao First Instance Commercial Court AC 2013/165 of 17 December 2012.

[33] *Moré* (n 26), paras 24–25.

[34] Spanish Civil Code, Royal Decree of July 24 of 1889, BOE no 206 of July 25 of 1889, 249–59 (Spanish Civil Code).

[35] Judgment of the Barcelona Court of Appeals JUR 2013/108993 of 26 February 2013.

[36] Catalan Civil Code, Law 29/2002, DOGC 3798 of 13 January 2003 and BOE no 32 of 6 February 2003.

bring claims under it, the default limitation period was the 10-year period established by Article 121.20 of the Catalan Civil Code.

The Barcelona Court of Appeals filed a request for a preliminary ruling before the CJEU that resulted in a judgment of 22 November 2012.[37] In the judgment by that Court, the CJEU established that the limitation period under Regulation 261, to bring claims under Articles 5 and 7 of Regulation 261, should be interpreted according to the domestic rules of each Member State.[38]

In light of the judgment of the CJEU, the Barcelona Court of Appeals understood that, as the claimant argued, the domestic limitation period within which to bring a claim under Articles 5 and 7 of Regulation 261 was the default 10-year period under Article 121.20 of the Catalan Civil Code, and hence the action had been filed in time.[39]

Spanish courts seem to be following and applying with no further discussion the interpretation of the limitation periods applicable for claims under Articles 5 and 7 of Regulation 261. That is, as foreseeable, Spanish courts apply domestic law when determining whether a claim based on Article 5 or Article 7 of the Regulation 261 has been brought in time or not. In this respect, it should be noted, as the two cases above show, since Spain is a pluri-legislative state, statute of limitation rules might be found in the Spanish Civil Code, as well as in other civil regulations in force in some specific territories of Spain with their own civil law.

C. National Legislation Jointly Applied with Regulation 261

As explained above, when discussing limitation periods within with to bring claims under Regulation 261, the domestic rules of the EU Member States are applicable together with the provisions of Regulation 261. However, such procedural interaction also takes place at the level of substantive law.

The compensation provided under Regulation 261 is compatible with compensation from other sources based on national legislation.[40] Spanish case law shows that a standard judicial claim under Regulation 261 is often accompanied by a breach of contract claim under the Spanish Civil Code.

The breach by the airline company of the obligations to perform the transport service is subject to compensation under Articles 1101[41] and 1107[42] of the Spanish

---

[37] *Moré* (n 26).
[38] ibid, paras 24 to 29.
[39] Judgment of the Barcelona Court of Appeals JUR 2013/108993 of 26 February 2013.
[40] Case C-12/11 *McDonagh v Ryanair* (ECJ, 31 January 2013), interpreting Art 12(1) of Regulation 261.
[41] Art 1101 of the Spanish Civil Code states that 'Quedan sujetos a la indemnización de los daños y perjuicios causados los que en el cumplimiento de sus obligaciones incurrieren en dolo, negligencia o morosidad, y los que de cualquier modo contravinieren al tenor de aquéllas' ('Whoever, when performing their duties, in any way contravenes fulfilment of their obligations through fraud negligence or default, will have to compensate for the damage caused).
[42] Art 1107 of the Spanish Civil Code states that 'Los daños y perjuicios de que responde el deudor de buena fe son los previstos o que se hayan podido prever al tiempo de constituirse la obligación y que sean consecuencia necesaria de su falta de cumplimiento. En caso de dolo responderá el deudor

Civil Code. The Spanish Civil Code and, specifically, Articles 1101 and 1107 were the legal basis of claims brought before Regulation 261 was adopted. The Spanish Aerial Navigation Law 48/1960[43] did not regulate air carriers' liability for delays. For that reason, before Regulation 261 was adopted, Spanish courts applied the general civil law rules on contractual liability resulting from a breach of contract, included in Articles 1101 and 1107 of the Spanish Civil Code. Article 1101 establishes the effects of a breach of contract in the context of intentional breach, negligent breach or delay in compliance with the terms of the obligation. Whenever there was a delay in the passengers' arrival at their final destination, Spanish courts understood that such delay constituted negligent performance and delay in performance, and that the terms of the obligation were not complied with given the irregular or different performance of the transport contract.[44] Article 1107 of the Spanish Civil Code establishes the scope of the compensation for breach of performance of the obligations to be those damages that could have been foreseeable at the time of entering into the obligation.[45]

Today, the breach of contract based on the Spanish Civil Code is often included as a subsidiary *petitum* by which, in addition to the compensation claim under Regulation 261, claimants often claim defective performance of the contract or a breach of contract. Resulting from this defective performance or from the breach, passengers often claim pain and suffering for the delay, cancellation or overbooking experienced.

Currently, case law on the issue shows that Spanish courts, in this kind of situation, typically consider two elements when determining whether there has been defective performance of contract or a breach of contract: the passenger's time of arrival compared to the initial travel plan, and the lack of extenuating circumstances that would excuse the airline company from performing under the terms of the transport contract.

---

de todos los que conocidamente se deriven de la falta de cumplimiento de la obligación' ('The damages that the good faith debtor is responsible for are those that could have been foreseen at the time of entering into the obligation and that could be a necessary result of lack of compliance with it. If the debtor intentionally did not comply with its obligation, it will answer for all damage resulting from its lack of compliance').

[43] Law 48/1960 on Air Navigation of July 21 1960, BOE no 176 of July 23 1960, 10291, as amended by Law 1/2011 establishing the security program of the State as regards civil aviation and amending Law 21/2003 of 7 July on air security of 4 March 2011, BOE no 55, 24995) (Air Navigation Law).

[44] The jurisprudence on this issue is broad. See, eg, Judgment of the Spanish Supreme Court (first section) RJ 2000/5089 of 31 May 2000 and judgments of the Madrid Court of Appeals AC 2002/1078 of 15 January 2012; Asturias Court of Appeals AC 2002/189 of 21 January 2002; València Court of Appeals AC 2002/2352 of 23 September 2002; Asturias Court of Appeals AC 2002/2310 of 22 October 2002; Barcelona Court of Appeals AC 2003/1354 of 20 March 2003.

[45] Before Regulation 261 was adopted, the element of foreseeability was an important factor when determining whether compensation was to be awarded to the air passenger and its amount, because the elements foreseeable by the air carrier and by the passenger were remarkably different due to their different information and expectations regarding the transport contract. See, eg, MG Saldaña, 'Morosidad, negligencia y contravención de compañía aérea por omission de escala en el billete y retraso en vuelo intercontinental' (2007) 4 *Indret*, available at <www.indret.com>, accessed 20 December 2014.

With respect to the passenger's time of arrival, courts have often considered that in transport contracts, punctuality is an essential element of the contract, because it is one of the main factors that passengers take into account when deciding to travel by plane instead of using alternative available methods of transport.[46] So when the airline company, responsible for performing the transport service, does not comply with the element that differentiates air transport from other alternative methods, the contract is performed defectively.[47]

The interpretation by Spanish courts of the essential nature of timing in transport contracts is in line with the Warsaw Convention,[48] with the Montreal Convention[49] and with the Spanish Aerial Navigation Law.[50]

In order to be able to claim compensation for the defective performance of contract or for breach of contract, Spanish courts require it to be shown that the air carrier has no excuse for the defective performance or for the non-performance of the contract. The different excuses that Spanish courts have considered are planes malfunctioning,[51] labour conflicts,[52] delay in the plane's arrival at an airport[53] as well as air traffic congestion.[54]

Resulting from the claim of defective performance of contract or of breach of contract, damages for pain and suffering are often requested.[55] Articles 12(1) and 15 of Regulation 261 allow claims for additional compensation and exclude the possibility of limiting such compensation contractually. It should be noted that given that these claims for defective performance of contract or for breach of contract accompany the compensation claims under Regulation 261, courts are reluctant to award damages directly resulting from the defective performance or from the breach of contract but tend to award damages for the passenger's pain and suffering.[56] In this sense, the Spanish Supreme Court has stated in different

---

[46] Judgment of the Madrid Court of Appeals AC 2004/2121 of 17 December 2004, stating that, based on Art 1256 of the Spanish Civil Code, punctuality is an essential element of an air transport contract and hence should not be left to be unilaterally decided by one of the parties to the contract.

[47] Judgment of the Barcelona Court of Appeals AC 2002/1026 of 4 March 2002, noting that passengers are not indifferent to the time they reach their final destination.

[48] Convention for the Unification of Certain Rules Relating to International Carriage by Air 1929 (Warsaw Convention), Art 19, holding the carrier liable for damage caused by the delay in the carriage of air passengers, luggage or goods.

[49] eg the Montreal Convention.

[50] Air Navigation Law, Art 94.

[51] Judgment of the Madrid Court of Appeals JUR 2007/241693 of May 17 2007; Judgment of the Seville Court of Appeals AC 2003/1686 of 31 October 2003.

[52] Judgment of the Asturias Court of Appeals AC 2001/2560 of 24 December 2001; Judgment of the Barcelona Court of Appeals AC 2002/1248 of 19 June 2002.

[53] Judgment of the Seville Court of Appeals AC 2003/1686 of 31 October 2003.

[54] Judgments of the Spanish Supreme Court (first section) RJ 1990/4089 of 28 May 1990 and RJ 1993/3718 of 20 May 1993.

[55] For a general overview of the interpretation and application of compensation for pain and suffering resulting from breach of contract in Spanish case law, see, eg, I Marín and R Milà, 'Daño moral contractual' in F Gómez Pomar and I Marín (eds), *Daño Moral* (SA Bosch, 2015).

[56] Compensation for pain and suffering is recognised in Art 128 of Royal Decree 1/2007 of 16 November 2007 adopting the General Law for the Defence of Consumers and Users and other complementary Laws, BOE no 287 of 30 November 2007, and in Arts 1.088, 1.089, 1.090, 1.091, 1.254 i

judgments that damages for pain and suffering are compatible with the compensation awarded for material damage,[57] and that delays in air transport might cause anxiety, irritation, and loss of time or even of vacation days.[58]

One of the first and most important cases regarding the requirements and scope of the concept of pain and suffering was issued by the Spanish Supreme Court in 2000.[59] In that judgment, the Spanish Supreme Court established that all nuisance or inconvenience necessarily constituted pain and suffering, and a minimum damage threshold therefore had to be met. Hence, the Supreme Court held that compensation for pain and suffering could be awarded for a delayed flight where such delay caused tension, uncertainty, inconvenience, nuisance and potential losses if the passengers affected missed a day of work.

Identifying the liable parties depends on who sold the flight that subsequently was delayed. In this regard, the Spanish Supreme Court has held the travel agency and the flight company jointly and severally liable for the pain and suffering suffered by the passengers as a result of the flight delay, when that flight was part of a holiday package purchased by the passengers.[60]

The Supreme Court, considering that all damage resulting from the defective performance of the air transport contract or from the breach of contract should be compensated, has repeatedly stated that it does not require direct evidence of pain and suffering,[61] especially with respect to its economic value, which is often

1.258 of the Spanish Civil Code. See, eg, Judgment of the Spanish Supreme Court (first section) RJ 2000/5089 of 31 May 2000, and also judgment of the Bilbao First Instance Commercial Court AC 2013/1780 of 19 September 2013. In this latter case, the court relied on the prejudicial request of another Spanish court, in case TJCE C-83/10, asking whether the compensation awarded under Regulation 261 was compatible with supplementary compensation based on another regulation. The ECJ confirmed the compatibility of Regulation 261 with other compensation sources, and the court in Bilbao awarded compensation for pain and suffering based on the Spanish Civil Code.

[57] Judgments of the Spanish Supreme Court (first section) RJ 1998/3379 of 20 May 1998; RJ 2000/5089 of 31 May 2000 and RJ 2000/7733 of 19 October 2000.

[58] eg Judgment of the Spanish Supreme Court (first section) RJ 2000/5089 of 31 May 2000; Judgment of the Madrid Court of Appeals JUR 2005/108037 of 15 March 2005; Judgment of the Madrid Court of Appeals AC 2004/212 of 17 December 2004.

[59] Judgment of the Spanish Supreme Court (first section) RJ 2000/5089 of 31 May 2000.

[60] Judgment of the Asturias Court of Appeals AC 2002/189 of 21 January 2002; Judgment of the Asturias Court of Appeals AC 2002/1099 of 28 February 2002; Judgment of the Madrid Court of Appeals JUR 2008/321002 of 17 July 2008; Judgment of the Barcelona Court of Appeals JUR 2009/242758 of 5 September 2008; Judgment of the Madrid Court of Appeals JUR 2009/238141 of 13 February 2009; Judgment of the Madrid Court of Appeals JUR 2009/472884 of 22 May 2009; Judgment of the Barcelona Court of Appeals AC 2009/2048 of 25 September 2009; Judgment of the Vizcaya Court of Appeals JUR 2010/409885 of 31 March 2010; Judgment of Las Palmas Court of Appeals JUR 2011/376218 of 1 September 2011.

[61] eg Judgment of the Spanish Supreme Court (first section) RJ 1990/6165 of 23 July 1990; Judgment of the Spanish Supreme Court (first section) RJ 1993/515 of 29 January 1993; Judgment of the Spanish Supreme Court (first section) RJ 1994/9433 of 9 December 1994. See also Judgment of the Spanish Supreme Court (first section) RJ 1994/1308 of 15 February 1994; Judgment of the Spanish Supreme Court (first section) RJ 2000/1520 of 11 March 2000, noting that compensation for pain and suffering might be awarded when such pain and suffering has quite evidently been experienced by the victims, even when not totally proved.

difficult to quantify.[62] The Court has noted the importance of awarding compensation for pain and suffering, and has made clear that lack of evidence of its existence is not sufficient to deny such compensation.[63]

D. Cases Brought before Spanish Courts and the Amount of Litigation concerning Regulation 261

The adoption of Regulation 261 has not resulted in a litigation crisis in Spain. Many factors may explain the smooth application of this instrument. Despite the lack of reliable figures provided by public authorities, since the adoption of Regulation 261 there have been around 400 opinions issued by Spanish courts. The first, and probably most important factor may be the continuing lack of awareness of passengers' rights in Spain. A second factor is the existence of mediation procedures conducted before any legal claim is filed. A third factor is that judges often focus on Spanish law and not on EU law or on the judgments of the CJEU, and this often results in a lack of consistency between judgments of the lower courts. Such inconsistency introduces uncertainty when deciding whether to file a claim before the courts. This last, important factor is enhanced by the recent amendments to the rules of procedure, which have eliminated the possibility of filing an appeal, making it even more difficult to ensure consistency and compliance with EU law in lower-court rulings.

III. Scope, Interpretation and Context of the Extraordinary Circumstances Exception

The most relevant exception claimed by airlines before Spanish courts is the 'extraordinary circumstances' exception under Article 5(3) of Regulation 261. This is the most important defence claimed by airlines, in order to avoid being held liable and hence subject to the obligation to compensate airline passengers.

The interpretation of the 'extraordinary circumstances' defence has been quite sketchy and contingent on the specific contexts in which it has been claimed. In this respect, the interpretation of this exception by Spanish courts has been strongly conditioned by airport strikes in Spain and France, and by the suspension of Air Madrid's operating licence, as well as by the jurisprudence of the CJEU in

---

[62] Judgment of the Spanish Supreme Court (first section) RJ 1993/515 of 29 January 1993; Judgment of the Spanish Supreme Court (first section) RJ 1994/9433 of 9 December 1994.

[63] Judgment of the Spanish Supreme Court (first section) RJ 1996/7235 of 21 October 1996; Judgment of the Spanish Supreme Court (first section) RJ 1994/1308 of 15 February 1994; Judgment of the Spanish Supreme Court (first section) RJ 1991/4407 of 3 June 1991, considering that awarding compensation for pain and suffering does not depend on direct evidence of its existence.

Wallentin-Hermann v Alitalia,[64] and *Eglītis v Air Baltic*.[65] The extraordinary circumstances exception has been broadly claimed by airlines in response to strikes
in Spanish airports, or in French airports, directly affecting the operation of fights
to and from Spain. Lastly, even though it is difficult to generalise, the first instance
courts and appellate courts seem to have different requirements as regards the
application and approach to this defence, and the burden of proof. It should be
noted that there has yet to be any record of Spanish administrative authorities or
courts taking into consideration the 2013 publication on the European Commission's website of the industry-led indicative list of circumstances that could be
considered extraordinary when interpreting this defence.[66]

A remarkable decision denying use of the defence of extraordinary circumstances to avoid compensating passengers can be found in a case involving the suspension of Air Madrid's operating licence: *Air Madrid Líneas Aéreas, SA*.[67] When,
in 2006, the Ministerio de Fomento suspended Air Madrid's licence to continue
operating as an airline, a claim was brought by passengers and consumer associations representing the interests of passengers affected by the suspension. The airline claimed that the suspension constituted an extraordinary circumstance, and
hence that there was no compensation obligation. The Spanish Supreme Court
held that there were no extraordinary circumstances in this case that would excuse
the airline company from having to compensate passengers for the cancellations
suffered. The Supreme Court reasoned that such a defence had been very narrowly
interpreted by the CJEU in *Eglītis* and *McDonagh v Ryanair*,[68] and that the interpretation excluded from the meaning of 'extraordinary circumstances' cancellations resulting from airlines' technical problems, even when they had complied
with all minimum measures of maintenance. The Supreme Court noted that in
this case it was the airline that had not complied with such minimum measures.
Hence, the defence was not considered available and the airline was held responsible for compensating the passengers affected. Air Madrid filed for bankruptcy in
2007 and the passengers claiming compensation became creditors in the proceeding. Claims are still pending today.[69]

In parallel with the specificity presented by the claims resulting from the Air
Madrid case, Spanish courts have followed the different judgments of the CJEU[70]
regarding the strict interpretation[71] and scope of Article 5(3) of Regulation 261,
and the elements that the EU legislature has indicated in Recital (14) of the Preamble to Regulation 261. The exceptional circumstances enumerated in the Preamble

---

[64] Case C-597/07 *Wallentin-Hermann v Alitalia* [2008] ECR I-11061.
[65] Case C-294/10 *Eglītis v Air Baltic* [2011] ECR I-03983.
[66] The list of proposed extraordinary circumstances can be found at <http://ec.europa.eu/
transport/themes/passengers/air/doc/neb-extraordinary-circumstances-list.pdf>.
[67] Judgment of the Spanish Supreme Court RJ 2013/5659 of 1 July 2013.
[68] *McDonagh* (n 40).
[69] See <http://administracionconcursal.airmadrid.com/>.
[70] *Wallentin-Hermann* (n 64).
[71] ibid, para 20.

are examples of circumstances that in certain cases may be deemed exceptional but that should be strictly interpreted. However, the list is only an indication of circumstances, and the fact that one of the circumstances on the list occurs does not necessarily imply that it is exceptional. It should be noted that the burden of proof established by the CJEU in order to prove that exceptional circumstances took place requires, first, that the circumstances were beyond the control and the ordinary activity of the airline, and, secondly, that it was not possible for the airline, even using its personal and material means, to avoid the exceptional circumstances that caused the cancellation of the flight, or that avoiding such circumstances was impossible or too burdensome for the airline.[72]

Mechanical problems resulting in flight delays and cancellations have also been the object of litigation. With respect to technical problems of the plane, following the CJEU in *Wallentin-Hermann*, Spanish courts have held that the malfunctioning of the cabin door as a consequence of a vehicle impact was not an exceptional circumstance, given that such an operation was an habitual and ordinary occurrence in the airline's activity.[73] Even when it is the technical problem of maintenance that causes the cancellation of the flight, Spanish courts have held that such an event is not an exceptional circumstance given that the activity is inherent to the normal activity of the airline.[74]

The interpretation and scope of the extraordinary circumstances exception has been broadly discussed by Spanish courts in the context of strikes in Spain affecting the normal operation of flights, as well as of strikes in France affecting flights to or from Spain. Since Regulation 261 was adopted, a significant number of airport strikes by air controllers or by other airline employees have taken place in Barcelona and Madrid, and particularly important strikes have taken place in France, in the air navigation industry, as well as general strikes that directly resulted in cancellations of and delays to Spanish flights.

Following *Wallentin-Hermann*,[75] Spanish courts have considered a strike to be an extraordinary circumstance as long as the strike and the events resulting from it are beyond the control and foreseeability of the airline. Whenever these circumstances are met, compensation is not awarded. So, when an unexpected and unannounced strike took place at Barcelona Airport, resulting in the suspension of the airport's activities, Spanish courts considered this circumstance to be within the

---

[72] ibid, para 41.

[73] Judgment of the Alicante First Instance Commercial Court AC 2010/712 of 12 February 2010. It should be noted that this court awarded compensation for pain and suffering to the claimants.

[74] eg Judgment of the Barcelona Court of Appeals AC 2014/84 of 15 January 2014; Judgment of the Vizcaya Court of Appeals JUR 2010/400506 of 28 May 2010, considering an engine failure in a flight between Frankfurt and Bangkok by itself did not constitute an extraordinary circumstance under Regulation 261. See also Judgment of the Barcelona Court of Appeals JUR 2009/409930 of 14 May 2009, finding that the cancellation of a flight due to a mechanical failure that occurred right before take off did not constitute an extraordinary circumstance.

[75] *Wallentin-Hermann* (n 64) para 23.

scope of the extraordinary circumstances exception.[76] Similarly, when the strike was called by employees of another company providing services at the airport, when the airline from which compensation was sought had no possible way of foreseeing, controlling and resolving, or minimising the effects of such strike, this event constituted extraordinary circumstances and compensation was not available, even when the strike resulted in flight cancellations and delays.[77]

Strikes in other countries, such as France, affecting air traffic in Spain have sometimes been considered extraordinary circumstances. However, the mere existence of the strike has not been sufficient to deem it an extraordinary circumstance, and it is for the airline to prove that the strike affected the normal functioning of flights departing from a specific airport and not merely claim that a strike in France constituted an extraordinary circumstance.[78]

Lastly, from a procedural and judicial perspective, it is interesting to note that the application and burden of proof required when applying this exception seem to be remarkably different depending on whether the case is before a first instance court or an appellate court. Spanish appellate courts seem to follow the spirit of the CJEU more closely when interpreting the extraordinary circumstances exception. Thus the Courts of Appeals require the two-tier burden of proof established by the CJEU: first, whether the event that triggered the flight delays or cancellations was foreseeable and within the scope of control of the airline from which compensation is sought; and, secondly, whether such circumstances were inevitable even if all reasonable measures were adopted.[79]

It is interesting to see that many of these cases that reach the Courts of Appeals, involve a reversal of the holding of the first instance courts, mostly focusing on the first instance courts' interpretation of the extraordinary circumstance exception and noting that those courts relied on generic and imprecise reasons to conclude that the exception was applicable.[80]

---

[76] eg Judgment of the Barcelona Court of Appeals JUR 2009/462901 of 8 September 2009; Judgment of the Vizcaya Court of Appeals JUR 2010/145984 of 19 February 2010, considering an illegal strike that resulted in flight cancellations as an extraordinary circumstance.

[77] eg Judgment of the Barcelona First Instance Commercial Court JUR 2012/343678 of 23 July 2008, following *Wallentin-Hermann* (n 64), where the Court held that Art 5 of Regulation 261 was not applicable because the Iberian airline did not have any influence over, control of or means of intervention in the cancellation of flights, due to the action taking place in the airport being by workers of a different company. See also Judgment of the Madrid Court of Appeals AC 2012/1413 of 13 March 2012, considering an illegal strike of airport workers as an extraordinary circumstance.

[78] eg Judgment of the Balearic Islands Court of Appeals AC 2013/52 of 21 November 2012; Judgment of the Burgos Court of Appeals AC 2011/2129 of 29 July 2011, considering that the airline did not meet its burden of proving that a general strike in France constituted an extraordinary circumstance under Regulation 261.

[79] Judgment of the Barcelona Court of Appeals JUR 2009/409474 of 21 May 2009.

[80] eg Judgment of the Barcelona Court of Appeals JUR 2009/409474 of 21 May 2009, holding that the defendant had not proved that all reasonable measures were adopted, and hence revoking the holding of the first instance court. See also Judgment of the Barcelona Court of Appeals JUR 2011/260322 of 20 April 2011, noting that the first instance court did not require the airline to prove that the event that was claimed to be an extraordinary circumstance was inevitable; Judgment of the Barcelona Court

It should be noted that Spanish Courts of Appeals have considered the concept of extraordinary circumstances under Regulation 261 to be equivalent to the concept of *force majeure* in Spanish law.[81] This equivalence has allowed differentiation between *force majeure* and *caso fortuito*. This jurisprudential distinction is based on the internal or external origin of the cause that results in the delay, cancellation or event that may result in the obligation to compensate. Whenever the circumstances at the root of the delay, cancellation or event that may result in the obligation to compensate are inherent in the activity then the case is *fortuito*, and hence there is no excuse for not meeting the obligation to compensate under Regulation 261. But if, in contrast, the circumstances are beyond the risks inherent in the activity that resulted in damage to the passengers, the circumstances will be considered *force majeure*, and hence there will be no obligation to compensate.

The nature of the *caso fortuito* does not imply that it must necessarily and specifically affect the flight delayed or cancelled. If the event causing the damage did not take place during the flight on which the passenger was supposed to be carried but on a different flight with the same airline company that caused the passenger's flight to be delayed, the nature of the event might also be considered present.[82]

The different approaches of the first instance courts and Courts of Appeals to the extraordinary circumstances exception have been of special importance since 2011, when the right of appeal for claims under €3,000 was eliminated. Claims under Regulation 261 for amounts of compensation lower than €3,000 are judged in a single instance, which makes it very difficult to ensure the unified and consistent interpretation of this exception and control of compliance with the jurisprudence of Spanish higher courts and of the CJEU and hence ensure compliance with the air passenger's protection goal of Regulation 261 in Spain. From this perspective, after this procedural amendment, it seems difficult to ensure the correct interpretation and enforcement of Regulation 261 by Spanish first instance courts, which will be the ones most usually involved in hearing claims based on the Regulation.

IV. Scholarly Analysis

The adoption of Regulation 261 has not resulted in much scholarly analysis and discussion. This could be explained as being due to the occasional domestic law

---

of Appeals JUR 2013/43728 of 25 October 2012, where the Court of Appeals reversed the first instance court judgment, holding that providing a screen-shot of meteorological conditions did not meet the standard of proof of the extraordinary circumstances exception and that the airline had to prove that flying under such conditions was impossible.

[81] Judgment of the Barcelona Court of Appeals AC 2012/630 of 25 January 2012.

[82] ibid, noting that in this case, the event resulting in the delay would constitute defective organisation of the means of transportation, and thus was not *force majeure* and hence not an extraordinary circumstance.

bias of Spanish law academic literature, but it might also be because the impact of the adoption of Regulation 261 in Spain has not resulted in a noteworthy amount of litigation and in a change as regards transportation contracts. To be sure, Regulation 261 has resulted in changes to the standard terms included in any air transport contract, but not in a remarkable change of behaviour by the contracting parties.

Some general articles presenting and discussing Regulation 261 were published when Regulation 261 was first adopted;[83] others discussed specific aspects of Regulation 261, such as the obligations of the contracting parties in the context of holiday packages[84] and in the context of flight delays generally.[85] More specifically, there has also been scholarly work discussing the remedies available to passengers in the case of flight delays resulting in passengers missing flight connections.[86]

However, to date, there has been no scholarly discussion of the practical impact and implications of the adoption of Regulation 261 for Spain, nor any articles discussing the European Commission's proposal for amending Regulation 261.[87]

V. Conclusions

The adoption of Regulation 261 has not resulted in a litigation crisis in Spain. This is an important point, and it can be explained by a variety of factors. There appears to be a lack of awareness among the Spanish public of the rights passengers have under Regulation 261. As a result, passengers do not pursue their claims before Spanish courts. At the same time, national authorities have not been as diligent

---

[83] F Gómez Pomar and M Gili, 'El coste de Volar' (2005) 3 *Indret* <www.indret.com>, accessed 20 December 2014.

[84] A Nieto Alonso, 'Viajes, vacaciones y circuitos combinados. Los remedios frente al incumplimiento—las "vacaciones frustradas"—y las facultades y derechos de los consumidores y usuarios' [2005] 13 *La Ley—Actualidad Civil* 1541, regarding the remedies available to consumers and users in case of defective performance or non-performance in contracts involving holiday packages.

[85] MJ Guerrero Lebrón, 'La regulación comunitaria de las situaciones de "gran retraso" en el transporte aéreo de pasajeros: Comentario a la Sentencia del Tribunal e Justicia de la Unión Europea de 10 de enero de 2006 (TJCE 2006/2)' (2006) 17 *Revista de Derecho Patrimonial* 543, 543–61; E Mapelli Lopez, 'Regulación del retraso en el transporte aéreo de viajeros según la legislación internacional y de la Unión Europea' (2004) 37 *Anuario jurídico y económico escurialense* 329, 329–49.

[86] M Gili Saldaña, 'Morosidad, negligencia y contravención de compañía aérea por omisión de escala en el billete y retraso en vuelo intercontinental' (2007) 4 *Indret* <www.indret.com>, accessed 20 December 2014, discussing the Judgment of the First Commercial Court of Bilbao (AC 2007/493) on whether the defendant, an airline, breached the transportation contract with the plaintiffs when the flight was delayed and such delay resulted in the plaintiffs' missing a flight connection.

[87] Commission, 'Proposal for a Regulation of the European Parliament and of the Council amending Regulation (EC) No 261/2004 establishing common rules on compensation and assistance to passengers in the event of denied boarding and of cancellation or long delay of flights and Regulation (EC) No 2027/97 on air carrier liability in respect of the carriage of passengers and their baggage by air', COM(2013) 130 final.

as might have been expected in providing information and in ensuring airlines' compliance with Regulation 261.

Lastly, the amendment of the Spanish rules of procedure in 2011 has resulted in passengers having little incentive to bring their claims before the courts, and in airlines systematically denying compensation, knowing that the risk of their exposure to claims before the courts is remarkably small.

In order to ensure the adequate enforcement of Regulation 261 and comply with the consumer protection goal the European Commission had in mind when it adopted it, there must be more widespread dissemination of information regarding passengers' rights among the Spanish public and a stronger belief in this European instrument among Spanish authorities—something that the Spanish legislature, the Spanish courts and Spanish public officials currently seem to lack.

16

United Kingdom and Ireland: Passenger Protection Turns a Corner

BENJAMIN JONES

I. Introduction

The aim of this chapter is to examine the impact of Regulation 261 and its case law in the United Kingdom of Great Britain and Northern Ireland (UK), and to consider the changes that it has helped precipitate over the last 10 years. Taking into account developments in judicial treatment, practical themes in litigation and academic commentary, this chapter outlines the obstacles that have obstructed the development of effective application of Regulation 261 in the UK, with contrasts drawn to the situation in the Republic of Ireland. Whilst written in the wake of several important judgments that give cause for optimism, trenchant resistance to the uniform application of Regulation 261 suggests that the issues of the last 10 years have not yet been wholly overcome.

The outline of this chapter is as follows. Section II provides a brief functional overview of the procedural demands placed upon claimants who seek to exercise the protections under the Regulation 261 in the UK. The discussion in section III then details the volume of applications that have been brought under Regulation 261 and the outcomes of such claims, and identifies practical issues that disincentivise or impede enjoyment of the Regulation's remedies. It also considers the judicial treatment of Regulation claims in the UK and, in some detail, the courts' responses to the main litigation strategies and arguments advanced by the aviation industry in resisting these claims. The chapter then briefly examines how far the treatment of Regulation 261 deviates from uniform application and particular domestic obstacles to effective enforcement, and considers domestic attitudes towards reform.

II. Attempts to Exercise Regulation 261 Rights

In the UK, as elsewhere, in the first instance individuals must raise a complaint under Regulation 261 directly with the airline. Such applications have proven to be of broadly varying efficacy. Whilst little information on such claims is available, a broad indication of the variety in responsiveness between airlines can be seen in the results of an August 2013 poll by a popular consumer affairs website.[1] From the sample of 3,550 respondents, the most responsive airline, as a proportion of claims submitted, was the UK's flag carrier, British Airways, who had responded to 80 per cent of applications submitted and had paid out in around two-thirds of all claims. At the other end of the range, Jet 2, a low-cost and charter carrier, had yet to respond to more than 60 per cent of claims submitted by participants in the poll, and had upheld almost no claims. Other carriers were distributed fairly evenly between these two extremes, with different airlines adopting differing strategies in relation to certain categories of application (particularly regarding the delay before application, discussed below).

Where a satisfactory resolution has not been reached, individuals have a choice between bringing proceedings directly before the civil courts or first seeking assistance from the national regulatory body. The UK's designated NEB under Article 16(1) of Regulation 261 is the Civil Aviation Authority (CAA),[2] with the Air Transport Users Council designated as another competent body under the terms of Article 16(2).[3] The CAA has various 'enforcement tools' at its disposal, which range from requesting the airline to reconsider a complaint, to bringing criminal proceedings (breaches of Regulation 261 being an offence under regulation 3 of the Civil Aviation Regulations). The CAA's regulatory powers also include authority to issue a fine of up to £5,000 for a breach of Regulation 261.[4] However, in practice, enforcement proceedings have never been employed in connection with Regulation 261.

Whilst the CAA does forward complaints to the airlines where it considers a complaint to fall within its remit and that there are grounds to take up the complaint, its supervision demonstrates a notably light touch. It used its enforcement tools in only 17 instances in 2011, 12 instances in 2012 and six instances in 2013 (these are the only years for which data are held).[5] These engagements have consisted of phone calls, meetings, letters, e-mails, undertakings under Part 8 of the Enterprise Act 2002 and compliance monitoring.[6] The CAA does not see its function as that of an ombudsman, and it denies that it has any powers for 'obtaining redress for individual consumers' or 'legal powers to impose a solution'.[7] Whilst the CAA does acknowledge an enforcement role, it will not 'generally take enforcement action based on the facts in a single complaint'. Instead it looks 'to ensure future compliance by addressing systemic non-compliance by a business'.[8]

---

[1] H Knapman, 'Flight delay compensation: It's an airline lottery for passengers', MoneySavingExpert. com, 16 August 2013, available at <http://perma.cc/66TH-CYNY>, accessed 10 July 2014.

[2] Civil Aviation (Denied Boarding, Compensation and Assistance) Regulations 2005 (SI 2005/975), reg 5(1) (Civil Aviation Regulations).

[3] ibid, reg 5(2).

[4] Enterprise Act 2002, pt 8.

[5] CAA, 'Response to Freedom of Information Act request' (31 July 2014).

[6] ibid.

[7] ibid.

[8] ibid.

As such, the CAA does not attempt to validate claims or adjudicate on disputes between individuals and airlines over the extent of a delay (the CAA maintains no database of flight information), and in more than half of the complaints brought to the CAA's attention it has agreed with the airline's adjudication that extraordinary circumstances were the cause of the delay or cancellation.[9]

Of the complaints taken up by the CAA, Table 16.1 shows the number of complaints made that have been categorised under each of the relevant heads of claim covered in Regulation 261.

Table 16.1: Complaints made to CAA within the auspices of Regulation 261[10]

	2005	2006	2007	2008	2009	2010	2011	2012	2013
Cancellations	1,583	2,383	2,062	2,183	1,471	6,740	2,497	1,349	2,357
Delays	1,719	1,079	930	795	715	2,047	1,338	2,549	20,219
Denied Boarding	170	258	281	291	277	299	274	319	424
Downgrades	0	1	–	–	–	–	–	–	91
Total	3,472	3,721	3,273	3,269	2,463	9,086	4,109	4,217	23,091

Whilst the numbers for 2013 are slightly inflated compared to previous years, due to a new system of accounting for complex claims that involve multiple alleged breaches, there is nonetheless an extremely marked growth in complaints overall, driven primarily by a huge spike in delay-based claims in the wake of *Nelson v Duetsche Lufthansa*.[11] Wide publicity around the judgment resulted in a large number of historic claims being brought forward. Data for the first two quarters of 2013 show the breakdown of the years to which complaints brought in early 2013 related (see Table 16.2).

Also notable in Table 16.1 is the increase in downgrade-based complaints. The way in which the CAA records complaints has been altered twice over the last 10 years, with downgrade complaints being so rare in 2004–06 that they were excluded from the categorisation scheme in 2007. However, there were sufficient complaints in 2013 that the CAA resumed recording them as a separate category (albeit still dwarfed by the main heads of delay and cancellation). Unfortunately no data are retained in a readily accessible format regarding duty-of-care claims under Article 9.

---

[9] CAA, 'Air passenger compensation guidelines published', CAA Press Release, 23 July 2013, available at <http://perma.cc/R9B6-F2EA>, accessed 21 March 2015.

[10] Civil Aviation Authority (n 5); Civil Aviation Authority 'UK Passenger Complaints' (*Perma.cc*, 10 December 2014), available at <http://perma.cc/R9S6-EYTK>, accessed 21 March 2015.

[11] Cases C-581 and 629/10 *Nelson v Deutsche Lufthansa AG* [2012] OJ C399/3 (*Nelson*).

Table 16.2: Years to which CAA complaints submitted in early 2013 pertained

Year	Q1 2013	Q2 2013	Total
Not specified	185	320	505
2000	0	1	1
2001	1	0	1
2004	1	1	2
2005	24	25	49
2006	54	37	91
2007	98	166	264
2008	172	293	465
2009	155	271	426
2010	417	697	1,114
2011	470	769	1,239
2012	3,042	2,217	5,259
2013	646	2,208	2,854
Total	5,265	7,005	12,270

Where an individual chooses to seek formal enforcement by the courts, he or she must issue a civil claim, which will normally be heard by a county court under the small claims track procedure (which involves payment of a court issued claim fee and limits the costs recoverable). Whilst more confident litigants in person continue on this basis, to remove exposure to costs and obtain the benefits of specialist assistance, no-win-no-fee services provided by solicitors (sometimes routed through claim aggregators) have become an important part of the UK picture. These services have largely arisen since the judgment in *Nelson*, which was well publicised by the media in the UK. These services are widely employed, with the leading provider of no-win-no-fee service[12] having handled more than 20,000 instructions since it began handling claims under Regulation 261 in February 2013.

In Ireland the designated NEB is the Commission for Aviation Regulation (CAR). The CAR adopts a more proactive approach to complaints brought by aggrieved passengers and, as well as advising members of the public in relation to their rights under Regulation 261 and directing complaints towards the airlines, seeks to 'relentlessly enforce compliance by carriers deemed to have infringed

---

[12] Bott & Co's aviation department handles the majority of claimant work under Regulation 261 in the UK (having become the UK partner for the EUClaim aggregation service shortly after the decision of *Dawson v Thompson* [2014] EWCA Civ 845, [2014] 3 CMLR 35, and gaining significant media attention for its services through subsequent media attention around Regulation 261).

Regulation 261 in individual cases or through carrier policy'.[13] To this end, unlike the UK CAA, the Irish CAR will adopt an opinion on the merits of individual claims and, where it considers airlines to be breaching passenger rights (for instance through inappropriate reliance on the extraordinary circumstances exception), will actively pursue the airlines to try to get them to provide restitution.

Table 16.3 shows the number of valid complaints received by the CAR in each of the years for which data are publicly available, and Table 16.4 shows the manner in which complaints considered to be within the scope of the CAR's remit have been handled.

Table 16.3: Valid complaints received by the Commission for Aviation Regulation[14]

	2008	2009	2010	2011	2012	2013 Jan–Jun
Cancellation	304	204	611	612	163	155
Delay	70	60	147	303	207	297
Denied Boarding	20	44	36	50	21	30
Downgrades	2	0	0	2	2	2
Total	396	308	794	967	393	484

Table 16.4: Complaint handling by the Commission for Aviation Regulation[15]

	2007	2008	2009	2010	2011	2012	2013 Jan–Jun
Compensation Paid	61	13	11	24	61	58	45
Refund of Fare Accepted	8	49	23	121	193	22	38
Extraordinary Circumstances Identified	27	26	19	48	284	59	90
Continuing Investigation	70	68	30	–	99*	73	48
Complaint Withdrawn	–	2	1	19	182	297	161
No Claim Detected	–	28	33	54			

As with the UK figures, Table 16.3 shows a peak in complaints in 2010 and 2011, with the latter seemingly being associated with the Icelandic ash cloud. The large number of complaints under continuing investigation in 2011 were specifically connected by the CAR with the ash cloud issue and the subsequent lawsuit in

[13] CAR, 'Report on Passenger Rights Complaints' (CAR, 1 July 2009), available at <http://perma.cc/R4JQ-8TWS>, accessed 29 July 2014.

[14] CAR, 'Report on Air Passenger Rights' (CAR, 2007–Q2 2013), available at <www.aviationreg.ie/air-passenger-rights/statistics-reports.317.html>, accessed 21 March 2015.

[15] ibid.

McDonagh v Ryanair.[16] This large number of complaints (marked with an asterisk (*) in Table 16.4) would turn on the outcome of the subsequent CJEU preliminary reference (discussed below). We also see in the half-year figures for January to June 2013 a significant upswing in complaints (comfortably outstripping the whole of 2012 in only six months), again mirroring the UK data.

III. Litigation Tactics and Judicial Treatment

Given the practical limitations on the CAA's enforcement capacity and the high proportion of complaints that are either rejected or receive no response, many claimants have turned to litigation to enforce their rights under Regulation 261. Amongst these actions the majority relate to delayed departures (>70 per cent), with a significant minority concerning cancellation (~15 per cent), and the remainder principally being claims for denied boarding.[17] Downgrading actions are, by their nature, rarities, and more likely to be compensated for given the nature of the passengers involved. Actions for breach of duty of care under Article 9 are also relatively rare on account of the higher level of compliance by airlines with these obligations than with the compensation provisions.[18]

In addition to the procedural argument regarding time limits, as detailed above, airlines also adopt a range of substantive arguments in countering, rejecting or discouraging claims. Focusing on the bulk of complaints covered by the delay and cancellation provisions of Regulation 261, as augmented by the CJEU in *Sturgeon v Condor* and *Nelson*,[19] the dominant litigation strategy adopted by the industry has been reliance on the extraordinary circumstances exception. Around 80 per cent of claims made direct to airlines are rejected on the basis of the extraordinary circumstances exception. To support such arguments a number of airlines have institutionalised the proactive assessment of all delayed flights so as to streamline the processing of such claims.[20] Whilst these assessments, based on the NEB's 'indicative list', are sometimes controversial (a point discussed below), this approach does mean that a minority of claims are paid without further recourse to formal legal proceedings.

Some airlines, however, most notably Jet 2, blanket reject or ignore all or most of the complaints submitted to them, and the majority of claims that have been settled have come to be so only once the claimant takes the step of filing

---

[16] Case C-12/11 *McDonagh v Ryanair Ltd* (ECJ, 31 January 2013).

[17] Figures based on sample of 2,500 actions brought by Bott & Co's aviation team between February 2013 to July 2014.

[18] One might speculate that this is due to airlines being very much more prepared to provide this assistance than they are to provide the payouts required under the other Articles of Regulation 261.

[19] Cases C-402 and 432/07 *Sturgeon and Others* [2009] ECR I-10923; *Nelson* (n 11).

[20] easyJet, for instance, holds a daily meeting at which all delayed flights are assessed by application of the NEB indicative list.

proceedings. In the very limited number of cases that go to court (probably fewer than 100 out of the many thousands of complaints initially advanced), a range of litigation strategies is adopted. Where there is any potential for an extraordinary circumstances argument to succeed, however, such arguments are routinely pleaded, often with reference to the NEB indicative list. Similarly, time bar arguments, Montreal Convention[21] exclusivity arguments (discussed below) and other substantive objections have also been raised.

Some of these arguments have yet to be tested by the higher courts and so lack binding precedent. This is in part a result of a concerted litigation strategy within the industry to avoid drawing clarification on certain arguments that might be given short shrift by the senior judiciary. There is, however, a volume of case law relating to Regulation 261, leading to a number of important domestic authorities regarding extraordinary circumstances, time limits and other issues. Most notably, notwithstanding the wary attitude of some justices of the UK Supreme Court,[22] the UK higher courts have also been the source of important EU preliminary references.[23]

Throughout the rest of this section, I examine the key case law on extraordinary circumstances, use of the NEB list, Montreal exclusivity and some emerging litigation trends. The overall picture revealed is of a slow, and often grudging, movement towards enforcing a compatible interpretation of Regulation 261 in the UK.

A. Extraordinary Circumstances

Given the industry's heavy reliance on the extraordinary circumstances arguments, the case law in this area has been of the greatest importance. Despite the clear message sent by the CJEU in *Wallentin-Hermann v Alitalia*,[24] and the even clearer messages sent in *Sturgeon, Nelson* and *McDonagh*, there has still been substantial ambiguity in domestic proceedings about the extent to which the courts are willing to take a firm line in interpreting the extraordinary circumstances exception. Part of the problem has been the publication of the NEB list, as detailed in section III.B below, which has helped propagate an approach to defining extraordinary circumstances that is incompatible with the CJEU's own interpretation.

After years of use in the lower courts, a final judicial ruling on the application of the exception in English law is now in the offing. The recent Court of Appeal judgment in *Huzar*[25] turned on the point of the proper construction of extraordinary

---

[21] Convention for the Unification of Certain Rules for International Carriage by Air [2001] OJ L194/39 (Montreal Convention).

[22] Formerly Law Lords sitting as members of the Judicial Committee of the House of Lords.

[23] eg Case C-344/04 *R (International Air Transport Association and European Low Fares Airline Association) v Department for Transport* [2006] ECR I-403 (*ex parte IATA*).

[24] Case C-549/07 *Wallentin-Hermann v Alitalia* [2008] ECR I-11061.

[25] *Huzar v Jet2* [2014] EWCA Civ 791.

circumstances. Given that the Law Lords had been critical of the direction adopted by the CJEU in interpreting Regulation 261, particularly the extension of compensation coverage to delays under *Sturgeon* and *Nelson*,[26] it was unclear whether the judgment of the Court of Appeal would surive. Hopeful of such an outcome, most, if not all, outstanding claims turning on interpretation of the extraordinary circumstances exception were successfully stayed by the airline defendants pending a final outcome. The CAA also stated that whilst it was accepting complaints based on technical problems it was prepared to stop considering such complaints if the decision is overturned.[27]

The application was however rejected and so the state of the law remains as passed under the Court of Appeal judgment in *Huzar*. The case itself involved a delay of 27 hours caused by the technical failure of a piece of wiring responsible for indicating faults in an engine fuel shut-off valve. The problem was initially misdiagnosed as involving the valve itself, and the delay was extended by the need to fly in a specialist engineer and spare wiring from the defendant's facility at Leeds Bradford airport to Malaga, where the plane was grounded. It was accepted that the wiring had failed far short of its expected lifespan and that the fault was neither discovered nor discoverable by a reasonable regime of maintenance. As such, it was an established fact, for the purposes of the appeal, that the fault was 'unforeseen and unforeseeable', and the appeal itself turned on whether the CJEU's interpretation of 'extraordinary circumstances' was sufficient to cover an unforeseen and unforeseeable fault that was, nonetheless, within the control of the airline (in the sense that it did not arise from an external factor without the influence of the airline).

Considering the CJEU's approaching in *Wallentin-Hermann*, the Court of Appeal criticised the CJEU for adopting different formulations of the test for extraordinary circumstances in paragraph 23 and following paragraph 44 of the judgment. In paragraph 44, the Court of Appeal considered the phrase 'by their nature and origin' to be used in qualifying the normal exercise of an airline's activities, whilst in paragraph 23 the Court considered the phrase to have been used to qualify the element of control exercised by the airline.[28] The Court also described it as 'curious' that the CJEU had, at paragraph 73 of the *Sturgeon* judgment, augmented the language of Article 5(3) of Regulation 261, regarding extraordinary circumstances, with the explanatory phrase 'namely circumstances beyond the actual control of the air carrier', creating another distinct test.[29] Looking at the judgment in *McDonagh*, the Court further complained that rather than using the official answer in *Wallentin-Hermann*, the CJEU had instead cited the

---

[26] eg in the case of *X v Mid Sussex Citizens Advice Bureau* [2012] UKSC 59, Lord Mance, a judge who regularly makes a sceptical response to any hint of European judicial activism, described the CJEU's approach in the two cases as constituting a 'bold interpretative approach' (at [44]).

[27] CAA, 'Response to Freedom of Information Act request' (31 July 2014).

[28] *Huzar* (n 25) [16].

[29] ibid [18].

above-distinguished construction from paragraph 23, and had thus agreed with the Advocate General's opinion that extraordinary circumstances 'relate to all cases which are beyond the control of the air carrier, whatever the nature of those circumstances or their gravity'.[30]

In the first instance in *Huzar*, His Honour Judge Platts had interpreted *Wallentin-Hermann* as saying that 'it is the consequences of the technical problem and not the problem itself which must be considered'.[31] This interpretation was challenged in the appeal, with counsel for the airline arguing that the focus on consequences rather than cause was incorrect. This submission was accepted by the Lord Justices, who agreed that

> [a] technical problem may indeed constitute an extraordinary circumstance provided it stems from an event which is not inherent in the normal exercise of the activity of the air carrier concerned and is an event which is outside the carrier's control.[32]

However, the Court of Appeal was not convinced by the submission that an unforeseen and unforeseeable technical defect was necessarily extraordinary. The Court concluded this on the basis that the CJEU in *Wallentin-Hermann* intended to lay down a two-limbed test, not a single composite test as averred by counsel for Jet 2.[33]

In the eyes of the Court of Appeal, proper understanding of the extraordinary circumstances test requires, first, consideration of 'the nature or origin of the event or events which caused the technical problem' and ensuring that they were not 'inherent in the normal exercise of the activity of the carrier', and then, secondly, ensuring that the events were beyond the 'actual control' of the airline.[34] The relationship between these limbs was accepted by the Court of Appeal to be unclear, a fault which was laid at the feet of the CJEU and its above-detailed failure to adopt a singular, consistent approach to defining and encapsulating the relevant concepts within its jurisprudence. However, notwithstanding this ambiguity, the fact that the limbs were distinct was asserted and the airline's submissions rejected on the basis that they appeared to collapse the two limbs into one (making the actual control limb an interpretative tool for assessing the first limb). Instead the Court of Appeal put emphasis on 'actual control', as an event beyond the airline's actual control could not be inherent in the normal exercise of its activity.[35] To do otherwise would have shifted the basis of the test to one of what should reasonably be discovered in advance, and thus to a question of fault, which was not the legislative intention (a conclusion reached on the basis that such a test could have been much more efficiently expressed).

---

[30] ibid [19], citing para 34 of AG Bot's Opinion in *McDonagh* (n 16).
[31] ibid [20].
[32] ibid [21].
[33] ibid [31], [23], respectively.
[34] ibid [31].
[35] ibid [36].

As such, the current binding precedent before the UK courts supports a broad construction of control when interpreting extraordinary circumstances; and in the case of mechanical failures, this sees actual control encompassing events within the potential influence of the airline, even where this heavily penalises the airline for problems that could not have been prevented by even the most exacting levels of scrutiny. With the Supreme Court having refused permission to appeal on the basis that the Court's existing case law on EU law provides a sufficient answer to the case, a great deal of uncertainty has been removed. It is to be expected that many hundreds of existing claims, as well as a growing volume of future claims, will now experience an easier, if not yet wholly clear, path to compensation.

Under the Irish jurisdiction there is little in the way of jurisprudence on Regulation 261. However, no discussion of the extraordinary circumstances exception would be complete without reference to the case against RyanAir following the April 2010 closure of European airspace due to the eruption of the Eyjafjallajökull volcano in Iceland. This case involved RyanAir's refusal to provide the care due under Article 9 of Regulation 261, and thus would not normally engage the extraordinary circumstances exception at all. However, in an attempt to prompt judicial creativity, RyanAir pleaded that a total closure of European airspace should be categorised as a form of 'super-extraordinary' circumstance that released airlines not only from their compensation obligations for delay and cancellation, but also from their other obligations under Regulation 261 (including the duty to provide care under Article 9). The Dublin Metropolitan District Court also referred questions regarding the possible caps on the amount of care provided in the case of prolonged periods during which travel could not be provided.

In the CJEU's judgment on the reference under Article 267 of the TFEU in *McDonagh*, the idea of 'super-extraordinary circumstances' was dismissed on the basis that the full range of extraordinary circumstances had been intended to fall under the definition of the term, without any limitation on the basis of gravity.[36] Similarly, any attempt to limit the amount of assistance either in absolute financial terms or in terms of a maximum period of obligation was also rejected by the Court, notwithstanding the potentially significant discrepancy between the cost of such support and the cost of many low-price tickets.

B. The National Enforcement Body List

Another matter that must not be overlooked when considering the application of the extraordinary circumstances exception, at least in the UK, is the NEB indicative list of extraordinary circumstances.[37] Whilst the impact of the NEB list going

---

[36] A decision rooted in study of the *travaux préparatoires* for Regulation 261.
[37] Commission, 'Draft list of extraordinary circumstances following the National Enforcement Bodies (NEB) meeting held on 12 April 2013: Understanding between NEB–NEB on a non-exhaustive

forward is likely to be heavily reduced by the judgment in *Huzar*, it is important to note the impact that the list has had on the interpretation of extraordinary circumstances not just by the CAA and the airlines, but also by the courts. Whilst there have been no reported judgments that refer to the NEB list, it is routinely employed by airlines both to deny claims on paper and also in their pleadings if court action is initiated.[38] Although the document is non-binding and non-exhaustive, its dissemination via the European Commission website, and application by the CAA, has granted it a practical status that has resulted in at least a dozen claims being rejected at first instance hearings.

The potential issues thrown up by judicial reliance on the list as a persuasive authority have led to the document's having been amended to include its current disclaimer,[39] following a complaint from a UK solicitor. The list is, however, still being relied upon by airlines, even in cases where the local NEBs have indicated their belief that a claim should be upheld. The ongoing application of this strategy in part reflects the courts' semi-deference to the CAA. This was most clearly seen in the case of *Graham v Thomas Cook*,[40] which was a dispute regarding the availability of damages under Regulation 261 and the interaction between Regulation 261 and the Montreal Convention. At first instance in *Graham*, Her Honour Judge Hampton concluded that Article 8 of Regulation 261 did not give rise to a civil claim for damages, as it was a matter for each state to decide how Regulation 261 would be given effect under domestic law, and in the UK this effect was achieved through the Civil Aviation Regulations 2005[41] and the Enterprise Act 2002. This finding was upheld by the Court of Appeal, which described the finding at first instance as 'plainly correct' and noted that

> the Civil Aviation Regulations make it a criminal offence to fail to comply with an obligation under the relevant articles of Regulation 261 and appoint the CAA as the designated body for the purposes of Article 16 of Regulation 261; ie for the purposes of enforcing the [R]egulation.[42]

Whilst the underlying conclusion, regarding damages in excess of those provided for under Regulation 261, is unproblematic, the notion that Regulation 261 was in some sense not directly effective is clearly not correct. That the Court of Appeal considered the UK Parliament's choices in the Civil Aviation Regulations

---

and non-binding list of extraordinary circumstances for the application of the current Regulation (EC) 261/2004', 19 April 2013, available at <http://ec.europa.eu/transport/themes/passengers/air/doc/neb-extraordinary-circumstances-list.pdf>, accessed 21 March 2015 (NEB list).

[38] Bott & Co, Interview with aviation team (10 July 2014).

[39] Stating in footnote 1 on the front page of the NEB list that 'the content of this document has not been adopted or in any way approved by the European Commission and should not be relied upon as a statement of the European Commission's position'.

[40] *Graham v Thomas Cook Group UK Ltd* [2012] EWCA Civ 1355.

[41] SI 2005/975 (n 2).

[42] *Graham* (n 40) [19].

and the Enterprise Act 2002 as, in some way, modifying or defining the force of Regulation 261, moving authority for enforcement onto the CAA rather than the courts, is confusing, as a reading both of Regulation 261's content and of the CJEU's jurisprudence, and, more fundamentally, is an incorrect approach to the fundamental position of EU regulations within the legal orders of the Member States. This confusion appears in some significant part to have been precipitated by the approach adopted to the interrelationship between Regulation 261 and the Montreal Convention, and the ongoing attempts of the airlines to advocate for a different interaction between the two instruments (despite the clear jurisprudence of the CJEU on the matter).

C. Montreal Compatibility

Whilst it pre-dates both the Montreal Convention and Regulation 261, the starting point for problems surrounding the interaction of the two is the 1997 House of Lords judgment in *Sidhu v British Airways*.[43] *Sidhu* was a high-profile case involving a claim by two passengers on a British Airways flight who sustained physical and psychological injuries after being held captive when the flight was captured by Iraqi forces, shortly after the outbreak of the first Gulf War, during a routine refuelling stop in Kuwait. In *Sidhu*, the House of Lords considered the exclusivity principle under Article 17 of the Montreal Convention's predecessor, the Warsaw Convention,[44] a provision that is replicated in Article 17 of the Montreal Convention. Their Lordships had to decide whether the passengers' common law claims in contract and tort were permissible. They concluded that the exclusion principle was effective in extinguishing tortious and contractual claims, and that the two-year time limit under Article 17 was applicable. This ruling had a significant impact through the comity principle, with the authority being cited and applied by other senior courts[45] (including, most notably, the US Supreme Court in the case of *El Al Israel Airlines Ltd v Tseng*).[46] Since Regulation 261 was passed, the Court of Appeal has applied *Sidhu* in proceedings involving the Regulation's application.

The first such instance occurred in 2008, when the Court ruled in another case against British Airways, *Barclay v British Airways*.[47] In *Barclay*, the Lord Justices

---

[43] *Sidhu v British Airways Plc* [1997] AC 430.

[44] Convention for the Unification of Certain Rules Relating to International Carriage by Air, signed at Warsaw on 12 October 1929.

[45] eg by the Singapore Court of Appeal in *Seagate Technology International v Changi International Airport Services Pte Ltd* [1997] 2 SLR(R) 57.

[46] 525 US 155 (1999); by the Canadian Federal Court of Appeal in *Thibodeau c Air Canada* 355 DLR (4th) 62; and the Malaysian Court of Appeal in *All Nippon Airways Co Ltd v Tokai Marine & Trading Co Ltd* [2012] 9 CLJ 429.

[47] *Barclay v British Airways Plc* [2008] EWCA Civ 1419.

concluded that the limiting principle under the Montreal Convention had the same effects in terms of exclusivity as that under the Warsaw Convention had.[48] *Barclay* again dealt with contractual and tortious claims rather than an argument under EU law, but in 2011 the Court of Appeal was required to deal with the interaction of the exclusivity principle under Article 29 of the Montreal Convention and EU secondary legislation, in this case Regulation 1107/2006 concerning the rights of disabled persons and persons with reduced mobility when travelling by air.[49] In this third case against British Airways, *Stott v Thomas Cook Tour Operators Ltd* (paired with another claim *Hook v British Airways*),[50] the claimant sought compensation for injured feelings resulting from a failure to take account of the claimant's disability in relation to seating. At first instance the High Court had decided that neither Regulation 1107/2006, nor regulation 9 of the domestic Regulations[51] created a private law cause of action where the Montreal Convention applied. Despite Recital 18 to Regulation 1107/2006 specifically stating that 'Member States should lay down penalties applicable to infringements of this Regulation and ensure that those penalties are applied', and stating that these penalties should be 'effective, proportionate and dissuasive', the Court considered that the requirement for penalties was discretionary and not essential to ensuring the effectiveness of the instrument. Regarding *Sidhu*, Kay LJ stated that '[i]t is abundantly clear from these authorities that, "in those cases with which it deals", the Montreal Convention has exclusivity in domestic law'.[52] This ruling was made notwithstanding the intervention of the Secretary of State for Transport in the case, arguing that Regulation 1107/2006 was complementary to the Montreal Convention and that as it concerned the prevention of disability discrimination, with which the Montreal Convention was not concerned, damages should be allowed for injuries to feelings that arose through a breach of the disability-specific rights of air passengers. Regarding Regulation 261, the Court of Appeal considered *ex parte IATA*,[53] *Rehder v Air Baltic*[54] and *Rodriguez v Air France*,[55] but did not comment upon or apply their reasoning, preferring to maintain comity through application of international jurisprudence regarding the Montreal Convention.

The recent judgment of the Supreme Court in *Stott*[56] upheld the Court of Appeal's decision. Ruling that allowing the appeal would permit claimants to undermine the Montreal Convention by 'deft pleading', the Supreme Court

---

[48] ibid [192A] (Laws LJ).

[49] European Parliament and Council Regulation (EC) 1107/2006 of 5 July 2006 concerning the rights of disabled persons and persons with reduced mobility when travelling by air [2006] OJ L204/1.

[50] *Hook v British Airways, Stott v Thomas Cook Tour Operators Ltd* [2012] EWCA Civ 66 (*Stott*).

[51] Civil Aviation (Access to Air Travel for Disabled Persons and Persons with Reduced Mobility) Regulations 2007 (SI 2007/1895).

[52] *Stott* (n 50) [36].

[53] *ex parte IATA* (n 23).

[54] Case C-204/08 *Rehder v Air Baltic* [2009] ECR I-6073.

[55] Case C-83/10 *Rodriguez v Air France* [2011] ECR I-3203.

[56] *Stott* (n 50).

stated that the Convention was comprehensive for matters occurring between embarkation and disembarkation.[57] Whilst the ruling was acknowledged to be incompatible with the developing body of EU law on equality rights, the Supreme Court concluded that while there was 'much to be said for argument that it is time for the Montreal Convention to be amended to take account of the development of equality rights ... any amendment would be a matter for the contracting parties'.[58] Handling argument based on Regulation 261 case law, the Court noted *Nelson* and the CJEU's conclusion that redress under Regulation 261 was supplemental to and distinct from the coverage of the Montreal Convention, but concluded that these cases were irrelevant as the CJEU had acknowledged that 'any claim for damages on an individual basis would be subject to the limits of the Convention' whilst Mr Stott's claim was for freestanding individual damages.[59] The Supreme Court concluded that the question was not even a question of European law, as the Montreal Convention retained exclusivity within its purview and so the only question was 'whether the claim is outside the substantive scope and/or temporal scope of the Montreal Convention'. The relevant law for the case was thus taken to be the Vienna Convention[60] (which, though not retrospective, and so not explicitly applying to the Warsaw Convention, reflected customary international legal rules that would so apply). The premise asserted by the Court was that 'there is no basis for supposing that the Montreal Convention should be given a different "European" meaning from its meaning as an international convention'.[61] A request by counsel for Mr Stott to refer the key issue in the case to the CJEU under the preliminary reference procedure was denied.

D. Time Limits

Whilst the cases discussed in the last subsection are not directly on point for a consideration of Regulation 261, they are illustrative of the UK senior courts' attitudes towards the Montreal Convention, and the apparent preference for protecting the integrity of the Convention at the expense of European law where the two come into tension. Direct consideration of the interaction between the Montreal Convention and Regulation 261 has only been seen in the case law referred to above regarding time limits, which has become an increasingly important issue, as recent decisions, particularly the well-publicised judgment in *Jet 2 v Huzar*,[62] continue to encourage large numbers of claimants to come forward with historical claims (as shown in Table 16.2). This has resulted in sustained attempts by

---

[57] ibid [61].
[58] ibid [64].
[59] ibid [58].
[60] Vienna Convention on the Law of Treaties, 23 May 1969, 1155 UNTS 331.
[61] *ex parte IATA* (n 23) [59].
[62] *Huzar* (n 25).

the industry to place a procedural obstacle in the way of claimants in the form of the Montreal Convention limitation period on claims. Under the English law, the standard period of limitation for statutory damages or contractual claims is six years.[63] However, notwithstanding the CJEU's judgments in *Nelson* and *Moré v KLM*,[64] several airlines have habitually argued that a two-year limit applies to claims under Regulation 261 (for example, Jet2 and Ryanair, who send out proforma rejections to any claim more than two years old).

The recent case of *Dawson v Thompson*[65] has now provided a domestic precedent to add weight and clarity to the CJEU's rulings that the two-year limit under Article 29 of the Montreal Convention does not apply to claims under Regulation 261. However, whilst this means that the statutory six-year limit applies as a default, and the majority of carriers have accepted this,[66] others (including Thompson and Jet2) seem intent on continuing to push for a two-year limit on the basis of express limitations in the contract for carriage. Such terms are based on the standard IATA terms, which provide for a limitation in connection with damages-based claims of two years. However, in response to CJEU clarification that Regulation 261 provides for compensation rather than damages,[67] a small number of airlines have responded by amending their contractual terms to limit both compensation and damages claims.[68] As such, whilst the majority of cases will now be accepted so long as they are submitted with six years of the journey in question, a further successful challenge to the reasonableness[69] of these terms will be required before uniform application is achieved; and if such a challenge proves unsuccessful, there is the potential, in the context of further decisions strengthening the position of passengers, for other airlines to make similar amendments to limit future exposure under Regulation 261.

IV. Conclusion

Application of Regulation 261 in the UK has been undermined by fierce resistance from the air transport industry, a weak NEB and a lack of awareness of

---

[63] Limitation Act 1980, ss 9, 5, respectively.

[64] *Nelson* (n 11); Case C-139/11 *Moré v KLM* (ECJ, 22 November 2012).

[65] *Dawson v Thompson* [2014] EWCA Civ 845.

[66] Virgin Atlantic, Flybe, easyJet, Monarch and Thomas Cook are all reported to have accepted the six-year limit when contacted by a journalist from a financial news website: This is Money, 'How to claim flight delay or cancellation compensation', 21 January 2015, available at <http://www.thisismoney.co.uk/money/holidays/article-2271213/How-claim-EU-flight-delay-compensation-EC-261-2004.html>, accessed 21 March 2015.

[67] *McDonagh* (n 16).

[68] eg Ryanair, 'General Terms and Conditions of Carriage', cl 15.2, available at <www.ryanair.com/en/terms-and-conditions>, accessed 21 March 2015; Jet2, 'Terms and Conditions', cl 31.5, available at <www.jet2.com/Terms.aspx>, accessed 21 March 2015, which attempts to extinguish all claims after two years.

[69] Under the Unfair Contract Terms Act 1977.

Regulation 261 in the lower courts. Legal arguments based on reliance on the exclusivity provisions of the Montreal Convention and blanket pleading of the 'exceptional circumstances' defence have substantially impacted upon the effective application of Regulation 261. This would not have been possible had the courts taken a firmer line and rejected these arguments. However, through avoiding precedent-generating appeals, and a couple of questionable judgments regarding the force of EU aviation regulations, consumers have not had access to an effective means of enforcing their rights.

The inactivity of the senior courts is also seen in their inconstent participation in judicial dialogue with the CJEU. Whilst the reference in *ex parte IATA* played an important early part in developing Regulation 261's jurisprudence, the UK courts have more recently avoided making references where these may solidify further development of Regulation 261. Overall the English jurisprudence demonstrates a greater care for safeguarding comity under the Montreal Convention and preserving the integrity of the Montreal Convention's system than fulfilling the spirit of Regulation 261 and its jurisprudence. The most distinctive element of academic commentary in the UK pertains to this preference[70] and the potential for a more fruitful interaction between the EU regime and the Montreal Convention, where the former provides a space for the latter to develop rather than becoming an ever greater threat to it.[71]

The judgments of the first half of 2014 may be seen by claimants as a source of hope, provisionally closing the door on a couple of the main tactics employed by the industry to avoid engaging with a large numbers of, at least potentially, well-founded claims. Now that doubt around *Huzar* has been resolved (with the Supreme Court's refusing the opportunity to liberalise the strict approach of 'actual control' adopted by the Court of Appeal), industry options for evading liability have narrowed substantially.

By comparison with the Irish system, where an active enforcement body takes a proactive approach in investigating and enforcing customer rights, the UK's resistance to European regulation is clear. In light of the changed jurisprudential picture after 2014, plans for reform will need to grapple with some fundamental questions if they are to find an effective balance between functional protection for passengers and addressing the concerns voiced (in relation to the interpretative direction taken by the CJEU) by industry, academic commentators[72] and the UK courts.

---

[70] eg J Prassl, 'Reforming Air Passenger Rights in the European Union' (2014) 39(1) *Air and Space Law* 59.

[71] J Prassl, 'The European Union and the Montreal Convention: A New Analytical Framework' (2013) 12 *Issues in Aviation Law and Policy* 381.

[72] J Balfour, 'Airline Liability for Delays: The Court Justice Rewrites EC Regulation 261' (2010) 35 *Air and Space Law* 75.

17

Extraterritorial Application: Exporting European Consumer Protection Standards

BRIAN F HAVEL AND JOHN Q MULLIGAN

I. Introduction

While the consequences of Regulation 261[1] and its accompanying case law have been predominantly experienced within the various Member States of the European Union (EU), a proper retrospective of the first decade of European passenger rights regulation would be incomplete without some consideration of Regulation 261's impact beyond the EU's territorial jurisdiction. As should be evident from the ongoing controversy surrounding the regulation of aircraft emissions, any major policy initiative involving international air transport inevitably has ramifications for states beyond the purported scope of the legislation. This chapter proposes to examine Regulation 261's legacy outside of the EU.

Though the chapter title refers to the 'extraterritorial application' of Regulation 261, the term is inapt if understood to mean the application of Regulation 261's provisions beyond the jurisdictional boundaries of the EU, which has not been an issue. Instead, the chapter focuses on the extent to which Regulation 261 is legally recognised outside the EU, and has influenced policy in non-Member States and international organisations.

Section II of this chapter examines some remarkable recent attempts to enforce the provisions of Regulation 261 in the courts of the United States of America (US). These cases have probed whether the EU might implicitly have contemplated Regulation 261 to be enforceable in non-Member State courts. Moreover, Regulation 261's possible incorporation through contract law offers a fascinating insight into the unanticipated ways in which legal rights can potentially metastasise.

---

[1] European Parliament and Council Regulation (EC) 261/2004 of 11 February 2004 establishing common rules on compensation and assistance to passengers in the event of denied boarding and of cancellation or long delay of flights, and repealing Regulation (EEC) No 295/91 (Regulation 261) [2004] OJ L 46/1.

In section III, the chapter then discusses the policy influence of Regulation 261 as demonstrated by the proliferation of copycat legislation, as well as by the elevation of passenger rights to an issue of significant concern for international organisations. Lastly, section IV offers some concluding thoughts.

II. Bringing Regulation 261 Claims in US Courts

Over the past few years, US courts have considered sporadic but noteworthy attempts to recover damages under Regulation 261 through the US judicial system.[2] The primary motivation behind bringing these claims in a US court, rather than submitting a compensation demand to the appropriate Member State enforcement body, appears to be to take advantage of the US legal system's tolerance for class action claims. In theory at least, under class actions, a plaintiff can bring a claim to recover not merely for his or her own injuries, but on behalf of every similarly situated plaintiff who suffered a related injury. This would allow a claim to be brought not merely for the €600 a passenger may be due for his or her delayed transatlantic flight, but instead for the entitled compensation of numerous aggrieved passengers whose claims have yet to be litigated. For example, in *Lozano v Continental*,[3] the complaint attempted to define the class represented as consisting of

> all people in the United States who have been on any Continental flight since November 18, 2009 that departed from an EU member state where the flight was delayed over 3 hours (or cancelled) and where the delay was not due to extraordinary circumstances.[4]

Given the low rates at which passengers collect their entitled compensation, a collective action on behalf of a class of this size represents a potentially significant increase in liability for airlines, as well as a windfall for the litigating attorneys. The US is a much more attractive system in which to attempt such a manoeuvre compared with the courts of EU Member States, which have historically been much

---

[2] *Kruger v Virgin Atl Airways Ltd*, 976 F Supp 2d 290 (EDNY 2013); *Volodarskiy v Delta Air Lines Inc*, 11 C 00782, 2012 WL 5342709 (ND Ill Oct 29, 2012); *Lozano v United Cont'l Holdings Inc*, No 11 C 8258, 2012 WL 4094648 (ND Ill Sept 17, 2012); *Polinovsky v British Airways PLC*, 11 C 779, 2012 WL 1506052 (ND Ill March 30, 2012); *Polinovsky v Deutsche Lufthansa AG*, 11 CV 780, 2012 WL 1080415 (ND Ill March 30, 2012); *Gurevich v Compagnia Aereas Italiana*, 1-11-CV-1890, 2012 WL 10759331 (ND Ill Jan 17, 2012); *Giannopoulos v Iberia Lineas Aereas de Espana SA*, 11 C 775, 2011 WL 3166159 (ND Ill July 27, 2011). Note that all but one of these cases was litigated in the federal district court for the Northern District of Illinois. As might be expected, the same law firms represented plaintiffs in all of these cases, suggesting that creative US lawyers, rather than disgruntled passengers, were behind this initial push to road-test Regulation 261 litigation outside the EU. But other lawyers have taken note, and copycat lawsuits can be expected. The most recent case was filed by an entirely different set of attorneys in a New York federal court.

[3] *Lozano v United Cont'l Holdings Inc*, No 11 C 8258, 2013 WL 5408652 (ND Ill Sept 26, 2013).

[4] ibid.

less accommodating to these collective action claims, though many EU Member States have passed legislation permitting forms of claim aggregation in recent years.[5] In researching this chapter, we spoke directly with one of the attorneys representing the passengers in the majority of these cases. He indicated that the class action mechanism is the only reasonable means by which US citizens could enforce their Regulation 261 rights in court, as retaining European counsel to proceed in the court of an EU Member State would be far too costly given the amount of compensation at stake. As oral arguments before the US Seventh Circuit Court of Appeals in *Volodarskiy v Delta Air Lines* made clear, however, US courts can be highly sensitive to the appearance of exploitation of the US class action system by plaintiffs' attorneys bringing claims that otherwise would not be litigated in US courts.[6] Perhaps for this reason, US courts have yet to certify any of the proposed classes in Regulation 261 cases for collective action.

With the prospect of significant awards available through collective action as motivation, a handful of attorneys with 'an eye for the unusual case' have demonstrated great ingenuity in devising a legal basis for why US courts should be enforcing Regulation 261. This section begins by discussing the two general legal theories passengers have advanced in support of their attempts to enforce alleged violations of their rights under Regulation 261 in US courts: (i) direct effect (or, more precisely, direct enforceability),[7] and (ii) incorporation of Regulation 261 through state contract law. The following subsections cover some of the other potential grounds for dismissing these cases prior to consideration of the merits, including the possibility of complete pre-emption by federal law or treaty as well as other procedural hurdles, concluding with an examination of the few substantive Regulation 261 questions that have been addressed by US courts.

A. Direct Effect (Direct Enforceability)

Under this theory, Regulation 261 grants passengers a private right of action without requiring that right to be enforced only through the national enforcement bodies (NEBs) established by the EU Member States. The cases litigated thus far have involved US citizens who have suffered delays or cancellations on flights operated by a US carrier and departing from an EU Member State en route to the US. These passengers contend that they should not be forced to rely on the administrative body or court of the Member State with jurisdiction over their claim, but should be able to seek enforcement of their claim via their local US court.

---

[5] TL Russell, 'Exporting Class Actions to the European Union' (2010) 28 *Boston University International Law Journal* 141, 169.

[6] Oral Argument, *Volodarskiy v Delta Air Lines*, No 13-3521 (7th Cir Apr 17, 2014).

[7] The argument resembles the concept of direct effect in European law. But instead of seeking to invoke the rights granted by Regulation 261 in a national court of one of the Member States, plaintiffs are seeking to enforce those rights in a US court.

This argument has forced US courts to confront two related questions:

— Does Regulation 261 authorise passengers to enforce their rights in foreign courts?
— Should US courts recognise legal rights created by EU regulations?

The plaintiffs in *Lozano* argued that it is a basic tenet of EU law that legislation such as Regulation 261 creates private rights of action enforceable judicially, and that Regulation 261 itself prescribes two avenues for passengers to enforce their rights: either by filing complaints with the appropriate administrative bodies, or by filing actions for compensation in civil courts.[8] Specifically, plaintiffs cited Recital (22) of the Preamble to Regulation 261, which states:

> Member States should ensure and supervise general compliance by their air carriers with this Regulation and designate an appropriate body to carry out such enforcement tasks. The supervision should not affect the rights of passengers and air carriers to seek legal redress from courts under procedures of national law.

While Recital (22) clearly authorises passengers to seek redress via the courts, it does not make explicit that the courts in question are the courts of the EU Member States. The US courts that have considered the question to date have concluded, however, that Regulation 261 implicitly limits enforcement to the courts of the Member States. The *Lozano* court, for example, concluded that the 'national law' referred to in Recital (22) of the Preamble is the national law of the Member States, because that is how 'national law' is commonly used in EU law and because Regulation 261 makes repeated reference to the Member States whenever enforcement is discussed.[9]

The court in another Illinois federal case, *Volodarskiy*,[10] building upon the *Lozano* opinion, added that US courts typically refrain from enforcing foreign legal rights except where expressly authorised to do so.[11] As there is no clear authorisation for enforcement by US courts contained in the text of Regulation 261, US judicial administration would be best served by declining to recognise claims for direct enforcement.[12]

By dispensing with the direct enforcement question on these grounds, the US courts have been able to avoid any detailed discussion of whether an EU regulation can even create a cognisable cause of action within the US courts absent some corresponding US legislation or treaty obligation.[13] In their appeal before the US

---

[8] *Lozano* (n 3) 1–2.
[9] *Lozano* (n 3) 3.
[10] *Volodarskiy v Delta Air Lines Inc*, 987 F Supp 2d 784 (ND Ill 2013).
[11] ibid, 789–91.
[12] ibid, 791.
[13] ibid, 790, fn 4, which states that '[t]he Court need not address this more fundamental question because the text of [Regulation 261] is sufficiently clear that authorisation to entertain suits under [Regulation 261] is confined to Member States. But it is not self-evident that this cause of action could be cognizable in a United States court absent any treaty obligations to the contrary'.

Seventh Circuit Court, the plaintiffs in *Volodarskiy* cited a prior case, *Kalmich v Bruno*,[14] as precedent for US courts' recognition of foreign statutes.[15] During oral argument in *Volodarskiy*, the Seventh Circuit justices distinguished the US judiciary's historical willingness to exercise jurisdiction over tortfeasors found within the US for violations committed elsewhere under different legal systems, known as the doctrine of transitory torts, from the issue of passenger rights, which has no direct analogue within the US legal system.[16] As issued, the Seventh Circuit Court opinion ultimately refused to entirely foreclose the possibility of US courts adjudicating matters of foreign law, but strongly suggested that the doctrine of forum non conveniens would cause courts to avoid it in most cases.[17]

Additionally, both the *Lozano* and *Volodarskiy* courts expressed a reluctance to undermine Regulation 261's objective of producing consistent judicial enforcement among the courts of the Member States.[18] The possibility of courts outside the EU, not subject to review by the Court of Justice of the European Union (CJEU), making determinations about what constitutes 'extraordinary circumstances', for example, could (in the US courts' view) seriously undermine the goal of consistency in enforcement.[19] The US courts' concern for international comity has been much less pronounced in the cases where Regulation 261 has been found to be incorporated into a carrier's contract of carriage, as will be discussed below, suggesting that courts may merely be using comity as an excuse to reject legal theories with which they are otherwise uncomfortable.

B. Incorporation through (State) Contract

The alternative to seeking direct enforcement of European statutory rights in US courts has been to seek to vindicate those rights under US contract law. Under this argument, plaintiffs contend that airlines have made enforceable promises within their contracts of carriage to grant passengers the compensation to which they would otherwise be entitled under Regulation 261. This line of attack has proved more fruitful for plaintiffs, because, clearly, contract-embedded violations are enforceable in US courts. Thus, courts are left to determine on a case-by-case basis whether the terms of Regulation 261 have actually been incorporated into each carrier's contract of carriage.

In *Giannapoulos v Iberia*,[20] the US district court analysed Iberia's conditions of contract, which included a notice to passengers that '[a]s established in [Regulation 261], compensation is fixed in the event of a flight cancellation unless

---

[14] *Kalmich v Bruno*, 404 F Supp 57 (ND Ill 1975).
[15] Reply Brief of Plaintiffs-Appellant, *Volodarskiy v Delta Air Lines* (No 13-3521) 2014 WL 809099.
[16] Oral Argument, *Volodarskiy* (n 6).
[17] *Volodarskiy v Delta Air Lines Inc*, 784 F 3d 349, 356 (7th Cir 2015).
[18] *Lozano* (n 3) 3.
[19] ibid.
[20] *Giannopoulos* (n 2).

the latter is due to extraordinary circumstances' and '[a]s established in [Regulation 261], in the event of a long delay in relation to the scheduled departure time of flight, passengers are entitled to immediate aid and assistance throughout the duration of the delay'.[21] The court concluded that Iberia had promised contractually to provide passengers with compensation 'as established' by Regulation 261, and that such a promise was enforceable in US courts.[22] In this case, the passengers were seeking compensation for delay, not a cancellation, leading Iberia to argue that because the text of Regulation 261 does not contemplate compensation for delay, Iberia had not contracted to provide any such relief.[23] The court concluded, however, that by contracting to provide compensation 'as established' by the EU Regulation, Iberia's contract with the plaintiffs bound it to honour the terms of Regulation 261 as interpreted by the CJEU. Accordingly, the requirement to compensate for delays of a certain duration announced in *Sturgeon v Condor*[24] was part of Iberia's contractual obligations.[25]

The US district court in *Polinovsky v Deutsche Lufthansa*[26] came to a similar conclusion with respect to Lufthansa's contract of carriage. In that document, the carrier provided that 'in the case of a flight cancellation or flight delay we offer assistance and compensation to the concerned passengers according to [Regulation 261]'.[27] But the court dismissed the plaintiff's breach of contract claims in the companion case of *Polinovsky v British Airways*[28] because British Airways' contract of carriage did not expressly incorporate the pertinent EU Regulation.[29] In contrast to the Lufthansa scenario, British Airways promised to provide passengers with 'additional assistance, such as compensation … if required to do so by any law which may apply',[30] but the terms of the contract never mentioned Regulation 261 *expressis verbis*. The court ruled that the language framed a sufficiently general commitment that British Airways was not bound to honour the terms of Regulation 261 when those terms could not otherwise be directly enforced.[31]

United States carriers have been even more circumspect about making Regulation 261 commitments in their contracts of carriage, and courts have until now uniformly rejected plaintiffs' creative arguments for incorporation. Neither Delta, in *Volodarskiy*, nor Continental, in *Lozano*, explicitly referenced Regulation 261 in their contracts of carriage. The plaintiffs were forced to take advantage of modern technology to advance more creative incorporation claims involving notices to passengers about their rights under Regulation 261 that were posted on the

[21] ibid, 3.
[22] ibid.
[23] ibid.
[24] Cases C-402 and C-432/07 *Sturgeon and Others* [2009] ECR I-10923.
[25] *Giannopoulos* (n 2) 3.
[26] *Polinovsky v Deutsche Lufthansa, AG*, 11 CV 780, 2012 WL 1080415 (ND Ill Mar 30, 2012).
[27] ibid, 3.
[28] *Polinovsky v British Airways, PLC*, 11 C 779, 2012 WL 1506052 (ND Ill Mar 30, 2012).
[29] ibid, 3.
[30] ibid.
[31] ibid.

carriers' websites as Regulation 261 requires. In both cases, the courts appraised the connection between the contracts of carriage and Regulation 261 as too tenuous to support reading Regulation 261 into the contracts of carriage.

In *Volodarskiy*, the US district court, echoing the result in *Polinovsky v British Airways*, distinguished Delta's contract of carriage from the contracts used by Lufthansa and Iberia on the ground that Regulation 261 was not expressly incorporated, or even specifically mentioned, anywhere in the contract of carriage.[32] Although the contract conceded that 'contrary law, regulation or [government] order shall prevail' over the terms of the contract, the court held that it was illogical to assume that the carrier had intended to incorporate those laws or regulations into the terms of the contract, and thereby to create a situation where a carrier in violation of those laws could then be held liable either for violating the law or for breach of contract.[33] Rather, the provision was intended to recognise that the carrier could not enter a contractual agreement absolving it of its external legal obligations.

A more interesting argument in the case posited that, regardless of the express terms used, carriers can incorporate terms into their contracts merely by posting them to their websites. The Volodarskiys argued that Regulation 261 should be considered incorporated into Delta's contract of carriage because Delta's e-tickets included hyperlinks to its website, which in turn could be searched to locate a notice informing passengers of their rights 'established by European Union regulation in the event that you have a confirmed reservation on a flight greater than 3,500 kilometers distance and your flight is delayed beyond its scheduled departure time … or your flight is cancelled'.[34] The court rejected this argument because the Volodarskiys had purchased printed boarding passes without the hyperlinks, and because the hyperlinks did not in any event connect directly to the Regulation 261 notice hosted elsewhere on Delta's website. The court conceded, however, that had Delta sold e-tickets with direct links to the page hosting its notice about Regulation 261, and not merely to Delta's home page, the outcome would have been a much closer call.[35]

Similarly, plaintiffs in *Lozano* argued that a portion of Continental's contract of carriage declaring Continental to be subject to 'any terms and conditions printed on or in any ticket, ticket jacket or e-ticket receipt, or specified on any internet site', incorporated the EU Regulation into Continental's contract by reference because information about Regulation 261 is in fact available on Continental's website.[36] The court was not persuaded, contrasting the treatment of Regulation 261 with the Montreal Convention, which had been expressly acknowledged and incorporated by Continental elsewhere in its contract of carriage.[37]

---

[32] eg *Volodarskiy v Delta Air Lines, Inc*, 11 C 00782, 2012 WL 5342709 (ND Ill Oct 29, 2012) 3.
[33] eg ibid.
[34] ibid, 4.
[35] ibid.
[36] *Lozano* (n 2) 4.
[37] ibid, 5.

C. Pre-emption

Even when plaintiffs have their rights under Regulation 261 recognised by US courts, there remains the possibility that their ability to enforce those rights will be pre-empted either by international law in the form of the Montreal Convention,[38] or by US federal law (and, in particular, by the US Airline Deregulation Act (ADA)).[39] In the US legal system, both federal law and treaties are recognised as being superior to State law, and indeed a successful plea of pre-emption may completely eliminate plaintiff's cause of action if the contradictory State law is declared unenforceable. Less clear is the extent to which foreign regulations, if legally enforceable in US courts, are also superseded by US federal or treaty law. Thus far, US courts have been sceptical of arguments that claims related to Regulation 261 are pre-empted by either the ADA or the Montreal Convention.

The ADA's pre-emption provision, intended to prevent US States from undermining the goals of federal airline deregulation, holds that

> a state, political subdivision of a state, or political authority of at least two states may not enact or enforce a law, regulation, or other provision having the force and effect of law related to a price, route, or service of an air carrier …[40]

As a consequence, any attempt to enforce such a law will be dismissed. While the ADA explicitly pre-empts State law regulating airline rates, routes or services, the US Supreme Court ruled in *American Airlines v Wolens*[41] that the ADA did not pre-empt State contract law. Therefore breach of contract claims, such as those in *Polinovksy* and *Giannopoulos*, have been allowed to proceed. The analysis does not end there, however, as *Polinovsky v Deutsche Lufthansa* revisited the question of how the approach of US State contract law to Regulation 261 would be affected by the CJEU's decision in *Sturgeon*. The US Supreme Court recently reaffirmed that State common law rules that impose policy preferences onto the terms of the contract are pre-empted by the ADA.[42] Lufthansa's question was whether the CJEU's decisions broadening Regulation 261 beyond its explicit terms, such as the decision to grant compensation for delays and not merely cancellations, should not similarly be pre-empted because the contract of carriage only incorporates the text of Regulation 261 and not the interpretive opinions of the CJEU. In a decision that appears highly questionable in the wake of the aforementioned Supreme Court ruling, the US court rejected the contention that *Sturgeon* and similar decisions

---

[38] Convention for the Unification of Certain Rules for International Carriage by Air [2001] OJ L194/39.

[39] 49 USC § 41713.

[40] 49 USC § 41713(b).

[41] *Am Airlines, Inc v Wolens*, 513 US 219 (1995).

[42] *Nw, Inc v Ginsberg*, 134 S Ct 1422, 1431–33 (2014), holding that a claim that the airline breached the implied covenant of good faith and fair dealing, a Minnesota common law doctrine applied to contracts, was pre-empted by the ADA because the implied covenant of good faith and fair dealing was a State-imposed policy that was extraneous to the terms of the contract to which the parties had agreed.

constitute an external expansion of Regulation 261, describing those judgments as merely 'guidance' on how to interpret the terms that Lufthansa had contracted to perform.[43]

Should a US court recognise a plaintiff's right to direct enforcement of the EU legislation within the US legal system, the question of ADA pre-emption may become more interesting. Because no US court has granted Regulation 261 direct enforceability within the US system, it has been unnecessary to rule on its possible pre-emption. Some federal courts have nonetheless offered comment in hopes of avoiding having to re-hear arguments on pre-emption should a federal appellate court overturn their dismissal of the direct enforceability claim. To date, most of the courts that have considered ADA pre-emption of Regulation 261 have concluded that the ADA would not apply to Regulation 261 because the ADA explicitly pre-empts only 'State' laws governing air passenger transport services: the US courts have interpreted that reference to apply solely to laws passed by one of the 50 US States and not to laws of foreign states.

The one apparent exception to this neat dichotomy between US State and foreign regulations came in 2014 in *Giannopoulos v Iberia*, where the US district court concluded that the ADA intended what is known as 'field pre-emption', meaning pre-emption of all regulation of domestic air transport services in the United States, even forms of regulation not explicitly referenced in the statute.[44] Thus, the ADA's textual definition of 'State', referring to the sub-federal bodies of the US system of governance, does not necessarily represent all of the sources of regulation that might be pre-empted. If Regulation 261, regardless of origin, defeated the ADA's objective of deregulating the entire US air passenger transport sector, it would be deemed pre-empted by implication, which is exactly what the court found in *Giannopoulos*.[45] The court determined that applying Regulation 261 only to certain airlines or certain routes, as Regulation 261 implicitly requires, would create a patchwork regulatory system with respect to those flights covered by the ADA, and would therefore undermine the ADA's purpose of uniformity.[46]

With regard to pre-emption by the Montreal Convention, US courts are split as to whether Montreal pre-empts *all* State law tort or contract claims so that they cannot even be raised in court, or whether the Montreal Convention just limits a carrier's liability for otherwise admissible tort or breach of contract claims. Most of the US courts to consider Regulation 261 claims have adopted the latter approach.

In *Volodarskiy*, the court did, if only as *dicta*, consider the possibility of pre-emption by the Montreal Convention and rejected that argument. The court only examined pre-emption by Article 29 of the Montreal Convention, which prohibits

---

[43] *Polinovsky* (n 26) 3.
[44] *Giannopoulos v Iberia Lineas Aereas de Espana, SA*, 11 C 775, 2014 WL 551603 (ND Ill Feb 12, 2014) 5–6.
[45] ibid, 5–7.
[46] ibid.

punitive, exemplary or non-compensatory damages.[47] The court held that Article 29 had no bearing on the damages covered by the EU Regulation, which it described as compensatory in nature.[48] The court did not consider the possibility that certain provisions of Regulation 261 might be pre-empted by Article 19 of the Montreal Convention governing damages for delays.

The court in *Polinovksy v Deutsche Lufthansa*, by contrast, considered and rejected the Montreal Convention Article 19 pre-emption argument, based on a Seventh Circuit Appeals Court precedent that found State contract and tort law cases not pre-empted by the Warsaw Convention.[49]

D. Other Grounds for Dismissal

The challenges passengers have to overcome to bring Regulation 261 claims in US courts do not end with pre-emption. Courts have considered a variety of potential procedural bars that would obstruct recovery in the US. In *Giannopoulos*, Iberia attempted to argue that Article 7 of the 2007 US–EU Air Transport Agreement (ATA)[50] dictates that Regulation 261 would not apply to flights departing from the US.[51] The relevant clause of the Article reads as follows:

> While entering, within, or leaving the territory of one Party, the laws and regulations applicable within that territory relating to the admission to or departure from its territory of passengers, crew or cargo on aircraft (including regulations relating to entry, clearance, immigration, passports, customs and quarantine or, in the case of mail, postal regulations) shall be complied with by, or on behalf of, such passengers, crew or cargo of the other Party's airlines.[52]

The court, however, rejected Iberia's interpretation, concluding that Article 7 was not an exclusivity clause and referred only to regulations directly concerning entry or departure, such as those governing customs and immigration, not consumer protection.[53] The court concluded that the ATA's discussion of consumer

---

[47] *Volodarskiy* (n 10) 794.

[48] ibid; *Giannopoulos v Iberia Lineas Aereas de Espana, SA*, 11 C 775, 2012 WL 5383271 (ND Ill Nov 1, 2012) 4–5, holding that Regulation 261's purpose was to compensate passengers rather than to punish airlines.

[49] *Polinovsky* (n 26) 4, citing *Sompo Japan Insurance, Inc v Nippon Cargo Airlines Co, Ltd*, 522 F3d 776 (7th Cir 2008).

[50] Air Transport Agreement between the United States of America and the European Community and its Member States, signed on 25 and 30 April 2007, as amended by Protocol to Amend the Air Transport Agreement between the United States of America and the European Community and its Member States, signed on 25 and 30 April 2007 [2010] OJ L223/3.

[51] *Giannopoulos* (n 2) 5.

[52] Air Transport Agreement between the United States of America and the European Community and its Member States, signed on 25 and 30 April 2007, as amended by Protocol to Amend the Air Transport Agreement between the United States of America and the European Community and its Member States, signed on 25 and 30 April 2007 [2010] OJ L223/3 art 7.

[53] *Giannopoulos* (n 2) 5.

protection was vague enough not to meaningfully impact the claim in this case, but that what little it did offer suggested that Regulation 261 should be enforced in the US, as both parties pledged to support consumer protection and respect the other's laws.[54]

Iberia also argued that the passengers' claims should be dismissed for failure to exhaust administrative remedies in the EU prior to bringing the claims. The court rejected this argument as well, concluding that there was nothing in either Iberia's contract or within the text of Regulation 261 that requires plaintiffs to exhaust any available administrative remedies prior to filing suit.[55] As the court ruled, '[w]hile each Member State is required to establish a responsible body for enforcing Regulation 261, passengers are not required by [Regulation 261] to complain to this body prior to filing suit'.[56]

Alternatively, Iberia argued that international law requires exhaustion of local remedies prior to turning to a foreign or an international forum to pursue a claim. Again the court was unpersuaded, holding that such an international law requirement, if it does exist, has only been recognised by US courts with regard to claims for human rights violations.[57]

Lastly, carriers have argued that US courts should decline to make determinations regarding Regulation 261 claims on international comity grounds. The rationale behind this argument is that the enforcement mechanisms established by Regulation 261 should not be upset, and also that the uniformity of adjudications should not be distorted by making substantive rulings that cannot be appealed to the CJEU.[58] Interestingly, all of the US courts to consider the issue of comity with regard to claims brought under the incorporation-by-contract theory have thus far rejected calls to decline Regulation-based cases on comity grounds. They have accordingly pronounced themselves capable of following the applicable precedents established in the courts of Member States.[59] Yet, as was discussed above, when presented with claims for direct enforcement of Regulation 261 in US courts, US federal judges have demonstrated a much greater concern for the effect their decisions may have on the EU's regulatory objectives.

E. Substantive Claims

In the exceptional instances in which claims under Regulation 261 have been allowed to proceed to the merits in US courts, all as breach of contract claims, two substantive issues have been examined: the liability of a contracting carrier as

---

[54] ibid.

[55] ibid, 6.

[56] ibid.

[57] ibid.

[58] *Giannopoulos* (n 2) 7.

[59] ibid, 'Of course, European courts are more familiar with [Regulation] 261 and its application, but the court will not be faced with an area of law so complicated that declining jurisdiction would be prudent'.

part of a codeshare, and the question of whether the delay is excused because of 'extraordinary circumstances'.

One of the passengers included in the class action against Lufthansa in *Polinovsky v Deutsche Lufthansa*, Baumeister, had a contract of carriage with Lufthansa, but claimed damages for a flight that was technically operated by regional carrier Augsburg Airways, which operates flights under a charter agreement with Lufthansa.[60] Although the EU Regulation was incorporated through Baumeister's contract of carriage with Lufthansa, from whom Baumeister's employer had purchased his ticket, according to the terms of Regulation 261 any obligations under Regulation 261 fall upon the operating carrier.[61] The US district court looked to a German case, *Xa ZR 138/8*, for guidance on how to apply Regulation 261 in such a situation. In that case, the German court found that the 'contracting air carrier' and the 'operating air carrier' can be separate and distinct entities.[62] Following the reasoning laid out in the German case for distinguishing between contracting and operating carriers under Regulation 261, the court concluded that because Augsburg Airways was designated as the operating carrier on the passenger's ticket, owned the aircraft and employed the crew used on the flight, Augsburg was the liable party under Regulation 261 and any claims against Lufthansa were dismissed.[63]

The other plaintiffs in the case, the Polinovskys, were originally scheduled to fly on British Airways and then were re-routed onto a Lufthansa flight after the British Airways flight was cancelled.[64] When the Polinovksys sought to recover compensation for delays on the Lufthansa flight, Lufthansa argued that the Polinovskys' contract was with British Airways. The court rejected this argument, concluding that British Airways had acted as an agent of Lufthansa in issuing a ticket for a Lufthansa flight and that Lufthansa's contract of carriage would govern.[65]

Lufthansa then resorted to the 'extraordinary circumstances' defence in an attempt to avoid paying damages to the Polinovskys. The US court looked to the CJEU cases *Sturgeon v Condor* and *Wallentin-Hermann v Alitalia*[66] for the appropriate standards under which to consider assertions of extraordinary circumstances.[67] The Polinovskys' flight was delayed one hour and eight minutes because of the late arrival of the inbound aircraft, which had been held up for de-icing as a result of weather conditions in Dusseldorf, and delayed an additional 24 minutes because of an 'unknown cargo issue', cumulatively causing the Polinovskys to miss their connecting flight.[68] The court denied Lufthansa's request for summary judgment on the extraordinary circumstances defence, declaring it

---

[60] *Polinovsky v Deutsche Lufthansa, AG*, 11 CV 780, 2014 WL 983255 (ND Ill Mar 13, 2014) 2.
[61] ibid.
[62] ibid.
[63] ibid.
[64] *Polinovsky v Deutsche Lufthansa, AG*, 11 CV 780, 2014 WL 1017619 (ND Ill Mar 14, 2014).
[65] ibid, 2.
[66] *Sturgeon v Condor* (n 24); Case C-549/07 *Wallentin-Hermann v Alitalia* [2008] ECR I-11061.
[67] *Polinovsky* (n 64) 3.
[68] ibid.

an open factual question whether Lufthansa took all reasonable measures to prevent the Polinovskys' delay.[69] The Polinovskys ended up settling with Lufthansa out of court.

Two passengers in the *Giannopoulos* case were delayed by the 2010 eruption of the Eyjafjallajökull volcano, but the court rejected Iberia's attempt to have the case dismissed because of extraordinary circumstances.[70] Iberia re-routed the passengers around the volcanic disruption, but only provided them with a 35-minute window to make their connecting flight, which they missed when their first flight was late. The court, quoting an CJEU case[71] that held airlines must 'take account of the risk of delay connected to the possible occurrence of extraordinary circumstances',[72] decided to allow the question of whether Iberia had taken 'all reasonable measures' to avoid the delay to proceed to a jury.[73]

The only other US case to reach the issue of extraordinary circumstances got there by skipping over some of the aforementioned procedural questions. In *Kruger v Virgin Atlantic Airways*,[74] the court held that the extraordinary circumstances defence prevented the plaintiffs from recovering damages for a delay caused by a snowstorm, and obviated any need for the court to consider the other legal questions presented.[75]

III. Copycat Legislation

Regulation 261 has not received the same attention from other non-EU courts, presumably because outside the class action-friendly US system there is little reason for passengers to seek their established compensation remedies in local courts rather than through the administrative mechanisms made available by the Member States. That does not mean that Regulation 261 has gone unnoticed elsewhere. Regulation 261's most profound global repercussions are the result of the EU's status as a 'norm entrepreneur'.[76] The term refers to an individual, organisation, state or, in this case, a regional body that attempts to promote or spread the adoption of a standard of appropriate behaviour. This is a role the EU has increasingly

---

[69] ibid, 4.

[70] *Giannopoulos v Iberia Lineas Aereas de Espana, SA, Operadora, Sociedad Unipersonal*, 11 C 775, 2012 WL 5499426 (ND Ill Nov 9, 2012) 4–5.

[71] Case C-294/10 *Eglitis v Latvijas Republikas Ekonomikas ministrija* [2011] ECR I-03983.

[72] ibid, para 27.

[73] *Giannopoulos* (n 70) 6.

[74] *Kruger* (n 2).

[75] ibid, 299–300.

[76] CR Sunstein, 'Social Norms and Social Roles' (1996) 96 *Columbia Law Review* 903, 911. The phrase 'norm entrepreneur' is often attributed to Cass Sunstein, and has come to be used in international law to describe a state or entity that attempts to elevate a particular principle or policy change from a national to a universal objective by persuading or mobilising popular or elite opinion in foreign states on the issue.

assumed on the international stage, especially with regard to the aviation sector, as is evident from its influence on the debate over international noise and emissions regulation.

In the decade since its passage, similar measures have proliferated across the globe. Obviously local political pressures, including high-profile incidents of passengers stranded at airports and struggles to maintain quality in fast-growing markets, are primarily responsible for the increased worldwide focus on passenger rights. But the EU legislation has provided a model to which besieged governments have repeatedly turned. Today more than 50 states have some form of passenger rights rules specific to aviation, at least 30 of which have been introduced in the past seven years. This section will briefly discuss a few examples and their relationship to the EU progenitor.

A. Brazil

Brazil adopted Resolution 141 in 2010, requiring airlines to reimburse passengers for overbookings, cancellations and flights delayed longer than four hours. Passengers are entitled to access to communications after a one-hour delay, food after two hours and accommodations after four.[77]

B. India

India's rules, adopted in 2010, follow the EU legislation closely. Compensation, in addition to reimbursement, is provided for denied boarding and cancellations, but not for delays. Extraordinary circumstances are recognised as a defence. Meals and accommodations are obligatory for delays, depending on the length of the delay and the duration of the flight.[78]

C. Nigeria

Nigeria's Consumer Protection Regulations, adopted in 2012, compare closely to Regulation 261.[79] For cancelled flights, passengers are entitled to reimbursement, as well as compensation of at least 25 per cent of the ticket price for domestic flights and 30 per cent for international flights.[80] Delayed passengers have a right to pastoral care, including access to communications, refreshments and accommodations, depending on the duration of the delay.[81]

---

[77] Resolução No 141/2010, *Dispõe sobre as Condições Gerais de Transporte aplicáveis aos atrasos e cancelamentos de voos e às hipóteses de preterição de passageiros e dá outras providências* (9 March 2010).

[78] Civil Aviation Requirements Section 3—Air Transport Series M Part IV Issue I (6 August 2010).

[79] Nigeria Civil Aviation Regulations, part 19, Consumer Protection Regulations.

[80] Nigeria Civil Aviation Regulations, part 19, Consumer Protection Regulations, ss 19.5–19.7.

[81] Nigeria Civil Aviation Regulations, part 19, Consumer Protection Regulations, ss 19.4, 19.8.

D. Israel

Israel's law, adopted in 2012, is largely attributed to a series of high-profile delays leaving passengers stranded at Ben-Gurion International Airport, although it also fits with a more recent agreement to eventually harmonise aviation regulation between the EU and Israel. To achieve complete harmonisation, however, more work will be required, because the Israeli passenger rights regime, while similar in spirit, differs from EU policy with respect to specific provisions. For example, Israeli law only entitles passengers to food, drink and access to a telephone for delays shorter than five hours, and allows them to cancel for a full refund of flights delayed by between five and eight hours. It is only after passengers have been delayed longer than eight hours that they become entitled to monetary compensation and overnight accommodation. 'Bumped' passengers, meaning those passengers whose seat reservations were not honoured due to overbooking, are also guaranteed compensation.

E. Turkey

Turkey's regulation on air passenger rights took effect at the beginning of 2012, and of all the copycat legislation it probably resembles the EU legislation most closely. Harmonisation with EU rules is an explicit purpose of the Turkish regulation. Article 3 refers to the fact that Turkey's regulation has been 'issued in parallel with the EU By-law 11.02.2004—261 (EC)'.[82] There is no textual provision for cancellations to become delays as under *Sturgeon*. Otherwise, however, the Turkish rules are aligned so closely with the EU legislation that the compensation levels for various cancelled flights are even set at the Turkish lira equivalent of the corresponding euro value laid down by the EU legislation for that distance of flight.

F. The Philippines

The most recent of the new passenger rights regimes was adopted as a joint administrative order between the Philippines Department of Transportation and Communications and the Department of Trade and Industry.[83] The order's preamble explicitly mentions the primary concerns that led to its adoption and the popularity of similar measures elsewhere, namely, the 'asymmetrical relationship' between carriers and passengers with regard to their contracts of carriage, and the heightened potential for 'unsound business policies and practices' in a recently 'liberalized and highly competitive aviation environment'.[84]

---

[82] Turkey, Regulation on Air Passenger Rights (1 January 2012), Art 3(b).
[83] Providing for a Bill of Rights for Air Passengers and Carrier Obligations, Joint DOTC-DTI Administrative Order No 1 (10 December 2012).
[84] ibid, Preamble, paras [7]–[8].

The Philippines regulation is one of the only models explicitly to incorporate *Sturgeon*'s holding that delays can be equivalent to cancellations. Delays longer than six hours for which the airline is responsible are treated as cancellations and the passengers are entitled to the same rights, with the addition of overnight accommodation when applicable.[85] A distinction is made between terminal delays, where passengers wait to board a flight, and tarmac delays, where they wait to depart after already boarding the aircraft.[86] For terminal delays greater than three hours, the passenger is entitled to food, drink, telephone and e-mail access, as well as a refund or rebooking should the passenger so choose. This relief is provided whether or not the airline is at fault. For tarmac delays longer than two hours, passengers are entitled to food and drink proportionate to the length of the delay.[87] Compensation is not required in cases of cancellations for force majeure, safety or security reasons.[88]

The Philippines 'Air Passenger Bill of Rights' stands out for the extent to which it surpasses Regulation 261 in the scope of the obligations placed on carriers. In addition to incorporating much of the EU legislation's conceptualisation of delays, cancellations and compensation, it also draws inspiration from recent regulatory changes in the US, imposing detailed requirements on fare advertising and treating tarmac delays as a distinct issue.[89] In some sections, the Philippines' regulation 261 goes beyond what either the EU or US legislation requires, mandating that check-in counters open a specified amount of time prior to departure, and requiring the designation of separate check-in counters for seniors and persons with disabilities.[90]

G. International Civil Aviation Organisation

The EU's leadership on passenger rights has also placed the issue on the agenda of leading international organisations. At the 2013 International Civil Aviation Organisation's (ICAO's) World Air Transport Conference there were multiple submissions concerning the desire for harmonisation of various passenger rights regimes or development of international standards regarding passenger rights.[91]

It appears unlikely that the ICAO will interfere with the work of national regulators any time soon. At most, the ICAO may decide to draft a set of core principles

---

[85] ibid, §12.2.
[86] ibid, §2.8.
[87] ibid, §12.
[88] ibid, §11.2.
[89] ibid, §§4–6.
[90] ibid, §9.
[91] International Civil Aviation Organisation, 'Consumer Protection and Definition of Passenger Rights in Different Contexts' (Worldwide Air Transport Conference, 2013); International Civil Aviation Organisation, 'Consumer Protection a Joined Up Approach Required Between Governments and Industry' (Worldwide Air Transport Conference, 2013).

to guide national passenger rights regulations, but there is no demonstrated willingness to begin work on international standards or a passenger rights convention.

The International Air Transport Association (IATA) has unsurprisingly been even less welcoming to this new area of airline regulation. The organisation has been lobbying for any international principles on passenger rights regulation to include a requirement that such regulations adhere to the terms of the Montreal Convention, a clear reference to carriers' disagreement with the CJEU's judgments allowing compensation for delays.

IV. Conclusion

When adopting Regulation 261, EU legislators likely gave little or no consideration to Regulation 261's impact on courts, legislatures and regulatory agencies outside the Member States. Anticipated or not, Regulation 261 has had consequences outside the EU. The US court system has had the opportunity to define an aspect of Regulation 261 that would likely never have surfaced in EU courts, that is, whether the rights conferred by Regulation 261 were intended to be enforceable in foreign courts. Because US courts have thus far unanimously concluded that that was not the EU's intent, the importance of that question has been largely academic. Of greater significance, and surprise, has been the discovery by air carriers that recognition of their Regulation 261 obligations within their contracts of carriage could be considered a contractual promise that extended the number of jurisdictions in which those obligations could be litigated. In the future, those cases will certainly influence airline behaviour with regard to formulation of their contracts of carriage.

In the legislative and regulatory realm, it was perhaps more predictable that the EU's adoption of a strong passenger rights regime would prove somewhat influential. After all, various Member States have played prominent roles in setting regulatory standards since the beginning of international aviation. Granted, Regulation 261 cannot be considered solely responsible for the proliferation of passenger rights provisions over the past decade: many of the same local political pressures that motivated EU lawmakers have been felt by legislatures and regulators worldwide. But textual comparisons between many foreign passenger rights laws and the EU original make clear the extent to which the EU legislation has served as a 'proof-of-concept' that has paved the way for foreign imitators.

Still to be determined is the extent to which other countries will follow the EU's lead, not merely in the adoption of passenger rights rules but in their implementation and interpretation. Of particular note is the degree to which the EU legislation, amplified through CJEU decisions, has continuously evolved over the past decade. Many non-EU states modelled their legislation after Regulation 261 as written, rather than as expanded through various CJEU rulings. Will the judiciaries in those states interpret the provisions of their indigenous laws as broadly? The US courts, for their part, have determined that to the extent that the EU legislation is incorporated into contracts of carriage with legal effect abroad, the full body of CJEU interpretation is incorporated as well. A question for future study will be to observe whether other countries update their regulations should the EU's contemplated revisions go into effect.

The image of the ICAO attempting vainly to foster some kind of international consensus on an issue on which the EU has pushed the envelope, is by now awfully familiar. This is of course reminiscent of the debates over noise and emissions. Before EU passenger rights advocates start to congratulate themselves, we should first ask whether the EU's norm entrepreneurship on this particular issue has been a good thing.

Unlike emissions, where we are confronted with a global problem requiring a solution that involves the entire international community, flight cancellations in foreign countries do not affect EU passengers.

Similarly, there is not the same level of concern with regard to quality of service standards as there is with regard to safety or security standards, namely, that looser standards in one region may jeopardise the integrity of the international aviation system.

Regulation 261 was adopted in response to specific problems experienced within the European market. Different service standards may be better suited to other regions of the world whose airline sectors are subject to far different conditions.

Rather than copying what the EU has done, states should be paying close attention to the conditions within their own domestic sectors and allowing market forces to communicate to their carriers the quality of service expected, without pricing air transport beyond the reach of their citizenry.

Additionally, Regulation 261 has been particularly irksome to airlines, who believe that legislation, especially as interpreted by the CJEU with regard to delays, revises issues the industry assumed were settled in the Montreal Convention only 15 years ago. At a time when industry co-operation is needed on the arguably more important issue of emissions, the proliferation of passenger rights rules is only antagonising a sector that has begun to view governments, formerly its biggest benefactors, as the enemy.

The questions about the compatibility of Regulation 261 with the Montreal Convention do not help in this regard, as they communicate a somewhat cavalier approach to international law, admitting that it can be twisted and stretched as needed to accommodate certain policy goals. With a more multipolar and irreconcilable international aviation community than at any time before in history, a firm, clear commitment to abide by international agreements, in letter and in spirit, is sorely needed.

Part III

Broader Horizontal Perspectives

18

The Turbulent Life of Regulation 261: Continuing Controversies Surrounding EU Air Passenger Rights

SACHA GARBEN

I. Introduction

In 2004, adding an important citizenship dimension to the liberalisation of the aviation market, the European Parliament and the European Council adopted Regulation 261 establishing common rules on compensation and assistance to passengers in the event of denied boarding and of cancellation or long delay of flights.[1] Ever since its conception, the Regulation has been characterised by controversy. While lauded by travellers and consumer organisations as one of the most tangible things the EU has ever 'done' for citizens (or in any event consumers), Regulation 261 has faced persistent resistance from the airlines—a resistance that seems to have turned into outright hatred following a number of landmark judgments of the CJEU.[2] The airlines have stubbornly refused to comply in full with their obligations, until dragged to court by equally stubborn individuals claiming their rights under Regulation 261. National courts, faced with an ever-increasing number of cases, have shown discomfort with certain concepts as laid down in Regulation 261 and, more saliently, with the judgments of the CJEU. This has resulted in some rebellious national judgments diverting from the CJEU's case law, as well

---

[1] European Parliament and Council Regulation (EC) 261/2004 of 11 February 2004 establishing common rules on compensation and assistance to passengers in the event of denied boarding and of cancellation or long delay of flights, and repealing Regulation (EEC) No 295/91 [2004] OJ L46/1 (Regulation 261). Regulation 261 is based on an earlier measure, Council Regulation (EEC) No 295/91 of 4 February 1991 establishing common rules for a denied-boarding compensation system in scheduled air transport [1991] OJ L36/5. This chapter builds on the views expressed in a previous article: S Garben, 'Sky-high controversy and high-flying claims?: the Sturgeon case law in light of judicial activism, euroscepticism and eurolegalism' (2013) 50 *CML Rev* 15. The views expressed in this article are entirely personal and do not reflect the opinion or policy of the European Commission.

[2] Case C-549/07 *Wallentin-Hermann v Alitalia* [2008] ECR I-11061; Cases C-402 and C-432/07 *Sturgeon and Others* [2009] ECR I-10923.

as a stream of preliminary references, sometimes explicitly criticising the Court's approach and reasoning. In addition, the European legislator has recently rejoined the fray, proposing a revision of Regulation 261.[3] All in all, this idiosyncratic area is turning out to be one of the most fascinating in EU law and politics.

Indeed, as shown by the present edited volume, this area has become a veritable goldmine for scholars, allowing the research of a variety of intriguing issues. Private law specialists can explore the Europeanisation in this area from their particular point of view, as can of course those specialising in consumer protection and travel law. Researchers with a taste for comparative law will delight in the opportunity to contrast judicial approaches from a variety of Member States on the same issue. International law enthusiasts are provided with an extensive case study of the interaction between international and EU legal norms, the differences between the EU legal order and the international one, and complex questions on EU law's extra-territorial application. Those interested in EU institutional dynamics will find a valuable case study in the interaction between the CJEU, the stakeholders and the European legislator. Scholars of legal culture and sociology can delve into the fascinating concepts of adversarial legalism and claim culture underlying this area. And those interested in the judicial dialogue between the CJEU and the national courts will revel in the sharply toned preliminary questions, at times explicitly criticising not only the outcome of the Court's judgments but also its legal reasoning, and even its professional ethics.

The present contribution will look in particular at the issues of EU inter-institutional dynamics, judicial dialogue and legal culture that underlie this field, across the various different periods that we can already distinguish in Regulation 261's relatively short life. Although Regulation 261 got off to a shaky start, and encountered some heavy turbulence upon ascent, it could be said that it is finally reaching cruising altitude, although the possible legislative changes on the horizon make it too early to start thinking about a safe landing. In setting out this timeline, particular attention will be devoted to the interaction between the European judiciary, the various legislative actors and the stakeholders, the judicial dialogue (or perhaps shouting-matches) between the CJEU and the national courts, and the rising claim culture in Europe. The aim is not only better to understand the specific issues and phenomena that we encounter in this corner of EU law, but also to acquire insights and draw lessons that will enrich our general understanding of EU law and politics.

---

[3] Commission, 'Proposal for a Regulation of the European Parliament and of the Council amending Regulation (EC) No 261/2004 establishing common rules on compensation and assistance to passengers in the event of denied boarding and of cancellation or long delay of flights and Regulation (EC) No 2027/97 on air carrier liability in respect of the carriage of passengers and their baggage by air' COM(2013) 130 final.

II. Period I: The Early Days or 'Off to a Shaky Start'

A. Before Regulation 261

As late as the mid-1980s, national governments retained virtually unchallenged authority to regulate air transport, something that followed quite logically from the fact that in writing the Treaty of Rome, the Member States had pointedly excluded air transport from provisions that otherwise obligated the Council of Ministers to develop common transportation policies.[4] Most of the sector operated through national airlines, state-owned enterprises with a legal status varying from being part of government to listed companies with the state as a regular shareholder. These national carriers functioned as important political instruments of the national governments, such as contribution to regional development, industrial policies and full employment by obliging airlines to serve non-profitable routes, to purchase locally manufactured planes and parts, and to maintain a large workforce.[5] Public-sector unions flourished in the industry, and successfully pressed governments to provide employment and social security.[6] In addition, this model allowed the public to influence the airlines and their behaviour directly, imposing consumer standards without having to resort to legislation. While carriers operated at a loss, governments tended to treat such losses as public policy expenditures.

At the same time, the lack of competition meant high prices and little choice, and a strong momentum for liberalisation started to build. In the words of O'Reilly and Stone Sweet:

> As cross-border exchanges (trade, passenger and freight traffic) grew, so did the costs of a rigid, inefficient and necessarily patchwork regulatory system for those (major business users, private consumers, cargo shippers and ultimately governments) who bore them. Interest groups organized at European level forged alliances with the Commission, and lobbied national governments for change. The Commission, at first timidly then ever more aggressively, pursued an increasingly comprehensive agenda for fullscale reregulation of the industry at the European level. Activated by [a preliminary reference from a national court faced with litigation involving private carriers offering intra-EC flights against the wishes of a member state government], the [CJEU] rewrote the rules governing national rule-making in the sector, placing member state governments in the shadow of the law. This shadow deepened considerably in 1986 when the Commission used the

---

[4] D O'Reilly and A Stone Sweet, 'The liberalization and reregulation of air transport' (1998) 5 *Journal of European Public Policy* 447. Art 82 of the Treaty establishing the European Economic Community (TEEC) stated that the 'provisions of Title IV shall apply to transport by rail, road, and inland waterway'; Art 84(2) of the TEEC provided the legal basis for legislating in the excluded sectors, '[t]he Council may, acting unanimously, decide whether, to what extent, and by what procedure, appropriate provisions may be laid down for sea and air transport'.

[5] O'Reilly and Stone Sweet (n 4) 448.

[6] ibid.

Court's judgment to leverage recalcitrant governments. In sum, governments, faced with declining benefits and the rising costs of maintaining national governance structures, reacted by constructing supranational governance.[7]

In the wake of the Single European Act, and in response to calls from business lobbies, parts of the industry itself and air transport consumer groups, the EU thus embarked on a 10-year process to deregulate the sector. Directive 87/601/EEC[8] on air fares was adopted as a first step, and in the following decade the EU successfully liberalised the sector by means of various reform packages, allowing all air carriers to operate EU air services under a common licence system and to freely determine their tariffs. The regime is now consolidated in Regulation 1008/2008/EC establishing common rules for the operation of air services in the EU.[9]

B. The Adoption of Regulation 261

This liberalisation was balanced with EU-level re-regulation. For instance, minimum standards of staff working conditions were laid down in Directive 2000/79/EC, implementing the Agreement on the Organisation of Working Time of Mobile Workers in Civil Aviation concluded by the Social Partners.[10] Furthermore, as regards consumer care standards, Regulation 261 was adopted.

Regulation 261 grants several categories of passengers different sets of rights. Passengers of cancelled flights are entitled to reimbursement or re-routing under Article 8, assistance in the form of meals, accommodation and two phone calls under Article 9, and compensation for up to €600 under Article 7. The same rights apply regarding passengers denied boarding. If passengers are successfully re-routed, the air carrier does not have to pay compensation if the passengers were informed of the cancellation in advance and the delay they suffer on account of the re-routing is limited, for instance when they were informed less than seven days before the scheduled time of departure and the re-routing allowed them to depart no more than one hour before the scheduled time of departure and to reach their final destination less than two hours after the scheduled time of arrival (Article 5(1)(c)(iii)). In all other instances of re-routing, the carrier may limit the compensation to be paid to 50 per cent of the amounts listed in Article 8, if the delay in reaching the final destination is no more than two hours in respect of flights of less than 1,500 kilometres, three hours in respect of all intra-EU flights of more than 1,500 kilometres, and for all other flights between

---

[7] ibid, 3.

[8] Council Directive 87/601/EEC of 14 December 1987 on fares for scheduled air services between Member States [2008] OJ L374/12.

[9] European Parliament and Council Regulation (EC) 1008/2008 of 24 September 2008 establishing common rules for the operation of air services in the Community (Recast) [2008] OJ L293/3.

[10] Council Directive (EC) 2000/79 of 27 November 2000 concerning the European Agreement on the Organisation of Working Time of Mobile Workers in Civil Aviation concluded by the Association of European Airlines (AEA), the European Transport Workers' Federation (ETF), the European Cockpit Association (ECA), the European Regions Airline Association (ERA) and the International Air Carrier Association (IACA) [2000] OJ L302/57.

1,500 and 3,500 kilometres, or four hours in respect of all other flights. Compensation does not have to be paid at all if the carrier 'can prove that the cancellation is caused by extraordinary circumstances which could not have been avoided even if all reasonable measures had been taken'. Passengers of flights delayed for more than two hours for distances under 1,500 kilometres, three hours for distances between 1,500 and 3,500, or four hours for distances over 3,500, can claim assistance in the forms of meals, accommodation and phone calls under Article 9. If the delay is over five hours, passengers have the same rights to reimbursement or re-routing under Article 8 as passengers of cancelled flights and those denied boarding. However, for these passengers no reference is made to Article 7, and so compensation is not explicitly provided for in the case of delays.

Regulation 261 contains a number of additional provisions, relating, inter alia, to upgrading and downgrading, to persons with reduced mobility or special needs, and obligations to inform passengers of their rights. In particular, Article 14(1) provides:

> The operating air carrier shall ensure that at check-in a clearly legible notice containing the following text is displayed in a manner clearly visible to passengers: 'If you are denied boarding or if your flight is cancelled or delayed for at least two hours, ask at the check-in counter or boarding gate for the text stating your rights, particularly with regard to compensation and assistance'.

Lastly, Article 16 requires each Member State to designate an enforcement body. It states that '[w]here appropriate, this body shall take the measures necessary to ensure that the rights of passengers are respected'.

C. Early Case Law: *Ex Parte IATA* and *Wallentin-Hermann*

Almost immediately after its adoption, the International Air Transport Association (IATA) and the European Low Fares Airline Association (ELFAA) sought to annul Regulation 261.[11] The claimants argued that it was inconsistent with the Montreal Convention,[12] and breached the legal certainty principle and the general principle of equal treatment. The Court, however, was not convinced, and upheld Regulation 261.

Disgruntled travellers quickly started to make use of the opportunities offered by Regulation 261, and airlines were faced with ever-increasing numbers of claims for assistance, care and compensation. The airlines engaged in a consistent practice of completely ignoring claims, or invoking extraordinary circumstances as a ground to refuse to make payments, unless taken to court.[13] It was therefore

---

[11] Case C-344/04 *R (International Air Transport Association and European Low Fares Airline Association v Department for Transport)* [2006] ECR I-403 (*ex parte IATA*).

[12] Convention for the Unification of Certain Rules for International Carriage by Air [2001] OJ L194/39 (Montreal Convention).

[13] M Brignall, 'Thomas Cook won't refund the cost of a taxi fare home', *Guardian* (18 December 2010); R Colbey, 'European Court rules on airline compensation', *Guardian* (21 March 2009). Consumer surveys confirm this lack of compliance by practically all airlines. See, eg, Verbraucherzentrale,

not surprising that in 2008, the Court was called on to interpret the concept of 'extraordinary circumstances'.[14] The cancellation in question resulted from a complex engine defect in the turbine, which had been discovered the previous day during a check. The carrier had been informed of the defect during the night preceding that flight, at 1.00am. The repair of the aircraft necessitated the dispatch of spare parts and engineers, and could not be completed in time before the flight, which was therefore cancelled. One of the affected passengers, Mrs Wallentin-Hermann, claimed compensation in accordance with Article 7 of Regulation 261, but the carrier argued that this technical defect constituted an extraordinary circumstance, which exonerated it from paying compensation under Article 5(3).

In reply to the preliminary question, the Court considered that as a derogation from a main rule, the concept has to be interpreted strictly. The indicative list of possible instances in which such extraordinary circumstances might occur, provided in Recital 14, mentions 'unexpected flight safety shortcomings'. The Court held that although a technical problem may be amongst such shortcomings, the circumstances surrounding such an event can be characterised as 'extraordinary' only if they relate to an event 'which is not inherent in the normal exercise of the activity of the air carrier concerned and is beyond the actual control of that carrier on account of its nature or origin'. The Court added that in the light of the specific conditions in which carriage by air takes place, and the degree of technological sophistication of aircraft, air carriers are confronted as a matter of course in the exercise of their activity with various technical problems to which the operation of those aircraft inevitably gives rise. It is in order to avoid such problems and to take precautions against incidents compromising flight safety that those aircraft are subject to regular checks, which are particularly strict and which are part and parcel of the standard operating conditions of air transport undertakings. The resolution of a technical problem caused by failure to maintain an aircraft therefore had to be regarded as inherent in the normal exercise of an air carrier's activity, and technical problems that come to light during maintenance of aircraft or on account of failure to carry out such maintenance cannot constitute, in themselves, 'extraordinary circumstances'. This would be different only if the technical problems would stem from events not inherent in the normal exercise of the activity of the air carrier and beyond its actual control, for example in the situation where it was revealed by the manufacturer of the aircraft comprising the fleet of the air carrier concerned, or by a competent authority, that those aircraft, although already in service, are affected by a hidden manufacturing defect that impinges on flight safety, or damage to aircraft caused by acts of sabotage or terrorism.

'Fluggastrechte—Anspruch und Wirklichkeit. Ergebnisse einer Online-Umfrage der Verbraucherzentralen' (Potsdam, 2010); Centre Européen des Consommateurs France, 'Synthèse du rapport sur l'exercice des droits des passagers aériens en Europe: la mise à l'épreuve de la règlementation européenne' (7 September 2010), available at <www.europe-consommateurs.eu/>, accessed 21 March 2015. See also C van Dam, 'Air Passenger Rights after Sturgeon' (2011) 36 *Air and Space Law* 260.

[14] Case C-549/07 *Wallentin-Hermann v Alitalia* [2008] ECR I-11061.

D. The *Sturgeon* Judgment

If the outcome in *ex parte IATA*[15] and *Wallentin-Hermann v Alitalia*[16] were not to the airlines' liking, this was nothing compared to what was about to follow in the 'spectacular'[17] *Sturgeon v Condor* judgment, in which the Court established that not only passengers of cancelled flights and those who were denied boarding, but also those who suffered long delays could qualify for compensation of up to €600.[18] In the judgment, the Court held that although it did not 'expressly follow from the wording' of Regulation 261, these passengers are to be treated, for the purposes of the application of the right to compensation, as passengers whose flights are cancelled, and they may thus rely on the right to compensation laid down in Article 7 'when they reach their final destination three hours or more after the arrival time originally scheduled by the air carrier'.[19]

The Court based this outcome on numerous considerations, some more persuasive than others. First, it considered that although the possibility of relying on extraordinary circumstances was provided for only in Article 5(3) concerning cancellation, Recital 15 in the Preamble to Regulation 261 stated that that ground could also be relied on 'where an air traffic management decision in relation to a particular aircraft on a particular day gives rise to a long delay'. The Court deduced that 'as the notion of long delay is mentioned in the context of extraordinary circumstances, it must be held that the legislature also linked that notion to the right to compensation'. This argument attaches a lot of weight to the Preamble to justify a conclusion contrary to the actual provisions. In *ex parte IATA*, the Court had specifically stated that while a preamble may explain the latter's content, it cannot be relied upon to derogate from the actual provisions of the measure; and in that same case it held that although there were some inconsistencies between the Preamble and the Regulation's provisions, this did not affect its legality, as Articles 5 and 6 were 'themselves entirely unambiguous'. Now it came to a completely different reading of these supposedly unambiguous articles on the basis of the Preamble.[20]

The Court's second line of reasoning based on the general principle of equal treatment is more convincing. Comparing the situation of passengers whose flights are delayed with that of passengers whose flights are cancelled, the Court considered that the damage redressed by compensation is that of a loss of time, which is suffered equally by both types of passengers. Indeed, passengers of cancelled

---

[15] *ex parte IATA* (n 11).

[16] *Wallentin-Hermann* (n 14).

[17] C van Dam, 'Luchtvaartmaatschappijen zijn niet gek op passagiersrechten' (2010) 85 *Nederlands Juristenblad* 672.

[18] Cases C-402 and 432/07 *Sturgeon and Others* [2009] ECR I-10923.

[19] ibid, para 61.

[20] P Mendes de Leon and De vulkaan, 'IJsland en de *Sturgeon*-zaak uit Luxemburg leiden tot uitbarstingen' (2010) 85 *Nederlands Juristenblad* 1221.

flights who are re-routed are afforded the right to compensation only where the carrier fails to re-route them on a flight that departs no more than one hour before the scheduled time of departure and reaches their final destination less than two hours after the scheduled time of arrival. The Court concluded:

> [T]hose passengers thus acquire a right to compensation when they suffer a loss of time equal to or in excess of three hours in relation to the duration originally planned by the air carrier. If, by contrast, passengers whose flights are delayed did not acquire any right to compensation, they would be treated less favourably even though, depending on the circumstances, they suffer a similar loss of time, of three hours or more, in the course of their journey.

Hence, it would amount to an unjustifiable difference in treatment to deny compensation to passengers of delayed flights, especially since the aim sought by Regulation 261 is to increase protection for all air passengers. However, instead of annulling Regulation 261 for a violation of this principle, as suggested by the Advocate General, the Court interpreted Regulation 261 expansively.[21] Advocate General Sharpston had concluded that the underlying problem could not 'be "fixed" by interpretation, however constructive',[22] opining that it was impossible for the Court to provide a particular time limit after which passengers of delayed flights qualified for compensation, since this was the legislator's prerogative. The Court disagreed and, 'to counter the separation of powers objection',[23] it deployed the argument that the concept of 'long delays' had already been linked to compensation indirectly via the provision that re-routed passengers of cancelled flights would be entitled to compensation only after a delay of three hours or more.

III. Period II: The *Sturgeon* Fallout, or 'Hitting Heavy Turbulence'

A. A Critical Reception

Beyond the predictably strong reactions from those directly affected, ie consumer groups applauding the ruling and air carriers fiercely critical, the *Sturgeon* judgment triggered a considerable amount of controversy. Indeed, as *Sturgeon* is 'one of the most interesting recent judgments exploring the boundaries of the CJEU's function vis-à-vis the political process',[24] it has a significant importance

---

[21] *Sturgeon* (n 18), Opinion of AG Sharpston.

[22] ibid, para 97.

[23] K Lenaerts and J Gutiérrez-Fons, 'The Constitutional Allocation of Powers and General Principles of EU Law' (2010) 47 *CML Rev* 1637.

[24] N Baeten, 'Judging the European Court of Justice: The Jurisprudence of Aharon Barak through a European Lens' (2011) 18 *Columbia Journal of European Law* 148.

beyond the realms of travel and consumer protection law. Recent years have seen a clear rise of concerns among national authorities and judiciaries, and within European civil society, about the Court's judicial activism.[25] At the same time, EU legal academics have become increasingly critical of the Court's approach. Although the debate is effectively an old one,[26] it has been gaining momentum. A large part of the criticism is directed at instances when the market freedoms are (are perceived as) being applied to the detriment of social values, as for example in *Viking Lines v ITF*[27] and *Laval v Byggnadsarbetareforbundet*.[28] But also the application of general principles of EU law (perhaps even furthering social rights), reaching outcomes that seem to be circumventing the will of the European legislature, has given rise to widespread criticism, such as in the much-discussed *Mangold v Helm* case.[29] The criticism of activist judgments often stems either from a general (horizontal) separation of powers objection that entails that the unelected judiciary should respect the prerogatives of the democratically accountable legislature, or from a federal (vertical) division of powers objection that when the CJEU issues activist judgments, this tends to advance the reach of EU law to the detriment of national powers. A third often-raised objection is directed at the quality of legal reasoning. Fourthly, critical reactions are especially strong when the Court's activism leads to the imposition of obligations on private parties that were not, on a strict reading of the law, foreseeable, and therefore potentially at odds with the

[25] M Dawson, 'Judicial activism at the Court of Justice (Judicial Activism at the CJEU Conference, Maastricht University, 10–11 October 2011). See, eg, R Herzog and L Gerken, *Stoppt den Europäischen Gerichtshof* (Frankfurter Allgemeine Zeitung, 2008) 8; H de Waele, *Rechterlijk Activisme en het Europees Hof van Justitie* (Boom Juridische Uitgevers, 2009). For the purposes of this chapter, activism will be defined as the Court's engaging in broad and teleological interpretation beyond the text (and/or likely intention) of the law.

[26] H Rasmussen, *On Law and Policy in the European CJEU. A Comparative Study in Judicial Policy-Making* (Martinus Nijhoff, 1986). See also de Waele (n 25) 21; T Tridimas, 'The Court of Justice and Judicial Activism' [1996] *European Law Review* 199. For a defence of the CJEU's approach, see eg A Arnull, 'The European Court and Judicial Objectivity: A Reply to Professor Hartley' [1996] *LQR* 411; A Albors-Llorenc, 'The European CJEU, More Than a Teleological Court' [1999] *The Cambridge Yearbook of European Legal Studies* 373.

[27] Case C 438/05 *Viking Line v ITF* [2007] ECR I-10779. For a full account, see vol 1 in the present series.

[28] Case C 341/05 *Laval v Byggnadsarbetareforbundet* [2007] ECR I-11767; C Joerges, 'A new Alliance of De-Legalisation and Legal Formalism? Reflections on Responses to the Social Deficit of the European Integration Project' (2008) 19 *Law and Critique* 246; N Londstrom, 'Service Liberalization in the Enlarged EU: A Race to the Bottom or the Emergence of Transnational Political Conflict' (2010) 48 *Journal of Common Market Studies* 1307; U Belavusau, 'The Case of Laval in the Context of the Post-Enlargement EC Law Development' (2008) 9 *German Law Journal* 2279; N Reich, 'Free Movement v Social Rights in an Enlarged Union—the Laval and Viking Cases before the CJEU' (2008) 9 *German Law Journal* 159; C Kilpatrick, 'Laval's Regulatory Conundrum: Collective Standard-Setting and the Court's New Approach to Posted Workers' (2009) 34 *European Law Review* 844.

[29] Case C 144/04 *Mangold v Helm* [2005] ECR I-09981; for interesting discussions of the judgment, see M Beyer-Katzenberger, 'Judicial activism and judicial restraint at the Bundesverfassungsgericht: Was the *Mangold* judgment of the European CJEU an *ultra vires* act?' (2011) 11 *ERA Forum* 517; M Dougan, 'In Defence of Mangold?' in A Arnull *et al* (eds), *A Constitutional Order of States? Essays in EU Law in Honour of Alan Dashwood* (Hart Publishing, 2011) 219.

principle of legal certainty. Especially the first, third and fourth objections played an important role in the *Sturgeon* controversy.[30]

B. Reactions from National Courts

National courts, faced with a flood of cases arising out of compensation claims denied by the airlines, started to show discomfort with the *Sturgeon* judgment by referring a stream of preliminary questions. While many of these questions formally asked for clarification of the judgment, it is evident that this was national court's way of entering into dialogue with the Court of Justice, in reality expressing their concerns and asking it to revisit its case law.

The first national court to refer a preliminary question regarding the *Sturgeon* judgment was the German Amtsgericht Köln, in *Nelson v Deutsche Lufthansa*.[31] The three preliminary questions focused on the relationship between *Sturgeon*, the Montreal Convention and the *ex parte IATA* case. Most strikingly, the third question asked straightforwardly how 'the interpretative criterion' underlying *Sturgeon* could be 'reconciled' with the interpretative criterion that the Court applied to that Regulation in *ex parte IATA*. The judgment can be seen as a strong criticism of *Sturgeon* and the quality of its legal reasoning, as it does not ask for a clarification so much as a justification or revision of that judgment.[32] This first reference foreshadowed a flood of cases from other German courts. In January 2011, the Bundesgerichtshof referred two preliminary questions in *Folkert v Air France*,[33] inquiring whether passengers have a right to compensation in the case where departure is delayed for a period below the limits specified in Article 6(1) of Regulation 261, but arrival at the final destination is at least three hours later than

---

[30] K Riesenhuber, 'Interpretation and Judicial Development of EU Private Law. The Example of the Sturgeon-Case' (2010) 6(4) *European Review of Contract Law* 384; Lenaerts and Gutiérrez-Fons (n 23) 1637; C van Dam, 'Air Passenger Rights after Sturgeon' (2011) 36 *Air and Space Law* 260, 265; J Struyk, 'Indemnisation pour les passagers de vols retardés en Europe' (2010) 7 *La Semaine Juridique, Edition Générale* 201; K Arnold and P Mendes de Leon, 'Regulation (EC) 261 in the Light of the Recent Decisions of the European CJEU: Time for a Change?!' (2010) 35(2) *Air and Space Law* 100; K Haak, 'De rol van het Europees Hof van Justitie in het passagiersvervoer door de lucht' [2010] *Tijdschrift voor Privaatrecht* 493; M Mok, 'Het arrest *Sturgeon*' (2010) 85 *Nederlands Juristenblad* 1234; A Staudinger, 'Das Urtel des BGH in den Rechtssachen Sturgeon und Böck' (2010) 1 *Reise Recht Aktuell* 12; M Van Dam, 'De bus komt zo, toch? Een onderzoek naar de rechten van passagiers bij vertraging en annulering in het Nederlandse stads- en streekvervoer in verhouding tot de Europese verordeningen voor passagiersrechten' (Master Thesis, Erasmus University, 2011) 11.

[31] Reference for a preliminary ruling from the Amtsgericht Köln (Germany), lodged on 13 December 2010—*Emeka Nelson, Bill Chinazo Nelson, Brian Cheimezie Nelson v Deutsche Lufthansa AG* (Case C-581/10). The reference was joined with a reference from the UK, and the Court handed down its ruling in Cases C-581 and 629/10 *Nelson v Deutsche Lufthansa AG* [2012] OJ C399/3 on 23 October 2012.

[32] In May 2011, the Amtsgericht Geldern referred similar questions on the relationship between the Montreal Convention and *Sturgeon*. See, eg, Reference for a preliminary ruling from the Amtsgericht Geldern (Germany) lodged on 24 May 2011—*Nadine Büsch and Björn Siever v Ryanair Ltd* (Case C-255/11), radiated by Order of 30 November 2012 following the request from the CJEU to the national court whether the reference was still necessary after the *Nelson* judgment.

[33] Case C-11/11 *Folkerts v Air France* (ECJ, 26 February 2013).

the scheduled arrival time. *Sturgeon* is crystal clear on the point that passengers of delayed flights qualify for compensation where they suffer a loss of time equal to or in excess of three hours, 'that is to say when they reach their final destination three hours or more after the arrival time originally scheduled by the air carrier', and this reference can therefore also be seen as a challenge to the Court.[34]

One other German preliminary reference that should be mentioned in particular is from the Landgericht Köln of 5 August 2011 in *Germanwings*.[35] Not mincing its words, the Landgericht asks: Is it compatible with the principle of the separation of powers in the European Union if, in order to remedy what would otherwise be unequal treatment, Regulation No 261 is interpreted as meaning that a passenger who is affected by a mere delay of more than three hours is entitled to compensation under Article 7 of Regulation 261, although Regulation 261 provides for this only in the case of denied boarding or cancellation of the booked flight but, in the event of delay, restricts the passenger's claims to assistance under Article 9 of Regulation 261 and, if the delay is for more than five hours, also assistance under Article 8(1)(a) of Regulation 261?

Not very often do we get to see such open contestation by a national court of the CJEU and its methods, and if we do, it is usually played out at the highest level between national constitutional or supreme courts and the CJEU. Here we witness a rebellion of lower courts, who are traditionally well disposed and more receptive to the CJEU, its claims of supreme authority and its teleological reasoning than the higher courts.

As Prager states, 'also within the English jurisdiction *Sturgeon* gave rise to astonishment on the part of lawyers and howls of anguish on the part of airlines'.[36] On 24 December 2010, the High Court of Justice of England and Wales, Queen's Bench Division made a preliminary reference to the CJEU in a case brought by TUI Travel, British Airways, easyJet and IATA against the Civil Aviation Authority (UK NEB), asking in essence whether *Sturgeon* is indeed the applicable law.[37] The fact that the High Court decided to stay the proceedings and refer these questions to which there was already an answer, was grist to the airlines' mill. It allowed them to stall the process further, and to refrain from paying out compensation, while

---

[34] Reference for a preliminary ruling from the Bundesgerichtshof (Germany) lodged on 11 January 2011—*Société Air France SA v Heinz-Gerke Folkerts and Luz-Tereza Folkerts* (Case C-11/11). In August 2011 the Bundesgerichtshof referred another two cases to the CJEU, with questions identical to the *Folkerts* reference. Reference for a preliminary ruling from the Bundesgerichtshof (Germany) lodged on 26 August 2011—*Ekkerhard Schauß v Transportes Aéreos Portugueses SA* (Case C-437/11); Reference for a preliminary ruling from the Bundesgerichtshof (Germany) lodged on 26 August 2011—*Sandra Schüsslbauer, Martin Schüsslbauer, Maximilian Schüsslbauer v Iberia Lineas Aéreas de España SA* (Case C-436/11). C-436/11 Order of the Court of 22 May 2013 *Schüsslbauer v Iberia*.

[35] Reference for a preliminary ruling from the Landgericht Köln (Germany) lodged on 5 August 2011—*Germanwings GmbH v Amend* (Case C-413/11).

[36] S Prager, 'Pioneering passengers' rights: legislation and jurisprudence' (2011) 12 *ERA Forum* 308 (issue 2).

[37] Reference for a preliminary ruling from High Court of Justice (England & Wales), Queen's Bench Division (Administrative Court), lodged on 24 December 2010—*TUI Travel plc, British Airways plc, easyJet Airline Co Ltd, International Air Transport Association, The Queen v Civil Aviation Authority* (Case C-629/10).

it also strengthened their cases before other courts, giving extra weight to their argument that the legal situation was unclear.

Indeed, this could be seen with some Dutch courts that had initially faithfully followed *Sturgeon*.[38] In October 2010, the district court of Breda referred a question to the CJEU on the compatibility of Regulation 261 with Article 29 of the Montreal Convention.[39] This reference added to the confusion and strengthened the case of the airlines in their fight against *Sturgeon* and Regulation 261 more generally, as could be seen from a subsequent judgment of the Haarlem district court,[40] which had applied *Sturgeon* without any difficulties only a few months earlier. In this new judgment, the Haarlem court took into account the preliminary reference of the High Court of England and Wales, as well as the judgment of the Breda district court. While it still insisted that the Court had already implicitly ruled on Article 29 of the Montreal Convention, it also referred to the legal uncertainty that had come about by these divergent approaches. As such, and since the district court admitted that it did in fact see some merit in the argument that Regulation 261 was incompatible with Article 29, it felt that it was desirable for the Hoge Raad der Nederlanden (Supreme Court of the Netherlands) to rule on the issue. The district court hence signalled that it would request the Procurator General of the Supreme Court to take on the case in cassation in the interest of the uniform application of the law.

Further adding to the controversy, on 19 January 2012, the district court of Den Bosch issued a remarkable judgment.[41] The applicant had suffered a delay of more than three hours on a flight with Ryanair from Eindhoven to Pisa, and claimed compensation under Regulation 261. The district court rejected the claim, however, considering that it concerned a delay and not a cancellation, for which Regulation 261 did not provide a right to compensation. The court stated that the *Sturgeon* judgment did not change anything in that respect, 'considering the fact that the CJEU does not constitute the European legislature and it is therefore not competent to legislate by means of its case law'.[42] Even though several other Dutch courts remained unconvinced and continued to apply *Sturgeon*,[43] the Hoge Raad

---

[38] Gerechtshof Amsterdam, 16 February 2010, *X v Surinaamse Luchtvaart Maatschappij NV*, 200.017.721/01, LJN BM5267; Rechtbank Haarlem, Sector Kanton, 15 July 2010, *EUclaim BV v China Southern Airlines Company Limited* 395168 / CV EXPL 08-10281, LJN BN2126.

[39] Case 314/85 *Foto-Frost v Hauptzollamt Lübeck-Ost* [1987] ECR 4199.

[40] Rechtbank Haarlem Sector kanton, 10 March 2011, *X v Martinair Holland NV*, 407708/CV EXPL 08-15073, LJN BP8512.

[41] Rechtbank 's-Hertogenbosch Sector kanton, 19 January 2012, X v. Ryanair Limited, 774709, LJN BV1931.

[42] Paragraph 4.3. Author's translation.

[43] Rechtbank Amsterdam, 11 August 2011, *X v Koninklijke Luchtvaart Maatschappij NV*, 1152144 CV EXPL 10-16769, LJN BR6267. Similarly, in December 2011, the Amsterdam Court of Appeal confirmed the *EUclaim v China Southern Airlines* judgment of the Haarlem district court on appeal in Gerechtshof Amsterdam, 6 December 2011, *China Southern Airline Company v Euclaim BV*, 200.077.860/01, LJN BU6840. See also Rechtbank Zwolle Sector kanton, 18 January 2012, *X v Martinair Holland NV*, 522140 CV 10-14685, LJN BV1731; Rechtbank Zwolle Sector kanton, 22 June 2011, *X v.*

decided to stay the proceedings in eight *Sturgeon*-related cases before it, until the judgment in *Nelson*, *TUI* and *Germanwings*.[44]

On 23 October 2012, the CJEU handed down its judgment in the joined *Nelson* cases, confirming its interpretation of EU law in the *Sturgeon* judgment.[45] The Court reiterated that the principle of equal treatment requires that passengers whose flights are delayed and those whose flights are cancelled at the very last moment must be regarded as being in comparable situations as regards the application of their right to compensation, because those passengers suffer similar inconvenience, namely a loss of time. Since passengers whose flights are cancelled are entitled to compensation where their loss of time is equal to or in excess of three hours, the Court therefore found that passengers whose flights are delayed may also rely on that right where they suffer the same loss of time, bar extraordinary circumstances in which airlines are discharged of their compensation duties altogether. The CJEU also confirmed its view that the loss of time inherent in a flight delay constitutes an inconvenience that is not governed by the Montreal Convention. It firmly rejected the arguments that the obligation to award compensation to passengers of delayed flights would be contrary to the principles of legal certainty and proportionality. The judgment is clear and consistent, and deals with the preliminary questions in a serious manner, but it does not address the burning issue: that so many national courts have expressed their doubts about the legitimacy of *Sturgeon*. The CJEU had clearly chosen to respond to the flow of questions in a factual manner, simply restating its previously established principles, and disposing of repetitive questions by means of orders and suggestions to national courts to withdraw their questions, instead of seeking an open confrontation.

On 18 April 2013, by means of an order published only in German and French, the CJEU delivered its judgment in *Germanwings*, where the national court had asked about the compatibility of the Court's judgment in *Sturgeon* with the principle of separation of powers.[46] The Court decided the case by means of motivated order and not by regular judgment, because, in its opinion, 'la réponse à la question posée ne laisse place à aucun doute raisonnable' (the answer to the question leaves no reasonable doubt). As to the merit of the question (or perhaps rather allegation) of the national court, the CJEU first noted that the principle of separation of powers regulates the relations between the different EU institutions and characterises the Union as operating on the basis of the rule of law. The Court referred to Article 13(2) of the Treaty on the European Union (TEU), in accordance with which each institution shall act within the limits of the powers conferred on it in the treaties, and in conformity with the procedures, conditions and objectives set out in them, and Article 19(1) of the TEU, following which the Court

[44] Hoge Raad, 15 June 2012, Koninklijke Luchtvaart Maatschappij N.V. v. X, 12/00187, LJN BW5515.
[45] Joined Cases C-581/10 and C-629/10, *Nelson v Deutsche Lufthansa AG and TUI Travel plc v Civil Aviation Authority*, ECLI:EU:C:2012:657.
[46] Order of the Court (Ninth Chamber) of 18 April 2013, *Germanwings GmbH v Thomas Amend*, General Report—Section 'Information on unpublished decisions', ECLI:EU:C:2013:246.

'shall ensure that in the interpretation and application of the Treaties the law is observed', notably through ruling at the request of national courts on the interpretation and/or validity of EU law. It was in exercising that task that the Court interpreted Regulation 261 in *Sturgeon*. As to its reasoning, the Court held:

> L'examen du libellé des dispositions pertinentes du règlement n° 261, ainsi que l'utilisation d'arguments de valeur purement logique, tels que, notamment, l'argument a contrario, n'ayant pas permis de parvenir à une conclusion définitive à cet égard, c'est en se fondant sur l'analyse du contexte dans lequel s'inscrivent les dispositions interprétées, ainsi que sur l'objectif poursuivi par la réglementation en cause, tout en prenant en considération le principe général du droit de l'Union de l'égalité de traitement, que la Cour est parvenue à la solution mentionnée au point précédent.[47]

Unsurprisingly, the Court concluded that this interpretation of Regulation 261 does not conflict with the principle of the separation of powers.

IV. Period III: The Post-*Nelson* Phase or 'Finally reaching Cruising Altitude?'

A. Continuing Controversies

If anyone thought that the Court's judgment in *Nelson* would end the turbulent times of EU air passenger rights, they were mistaken. Airlines continue to refuse compensation to passengers, passengers continue to take their claims to national courts, and national courts continue to refer cases to the CJEU on ever-more specific and detailed questions of interpretation of Regulation 261. In 2013 and 2014 in the Netherlands, over 100 cases were judged by various courts across the country on issues relating to Regulation 261. The German Bundesgerichtshof dealt with 13 cases involving Regulation 261 in that same period, which can be expected to show only the tip of the iceberg considering that it is the court of last instance in these cases. In France and the UK matters seem somewhat calmer, but still several judgments from higher courts have been rendered recently applying Regulation 261.[48]

---

[47] Paragraph 20 of the Order. 'As the examination of the wording of the relevant provisions of Regulation 261/2004 and the logical arguments used, such as the a contrario argument, did not allow a definite conclusion as to [the question whether passengers of delayed flights could be equated to those of cancelled flights as regards the right to compensation], it was on the basis of the analysis of the context of the relevant provisions, as well as the objective pursued by the regulation at issue, taking into account the general principle of EU law of equal treatment, that the Court arrived at the abovementioned solution [ie granting the right to compensation for a delay over 3 hours]'. Author's translation.

[48] Cour administrative d'appel de Paris N° 12PA03835, N° 12PA02993, Cour de Cassation 19 mars 2014, 12-20.917l; *Murial Vergara v Ryanair Ltd* [2014] SCAYR 35 ScotSC 80; *Dawson v Thomson Airways Ltd* [2014] EWCA Civ 845; *Jet2.com Ltd v Huzar* [2014] EWCA Civ 791; *Stott v Thomas Cook Tour Operators Ltd* [2014] UKSC 15.

More than 20 applications for a preliminary ruling were made in 2013[49] and 2014.[50]

But although the flood of references is continuing, the references no longer continue to challenge the very existence of a right to compensation in cases of delays as held by the Court in *Sturgeon*. Furthermore, the references do not seem to criticise the Court or its previous interpretations of Regulation 261 anymore— at least not overtly. Instead, they seem to concern genuine questions about the concept of 'extraordinary circumstances' and, to a more limited extent, other concepts of Regulation 261, in ever-more specific circumstances. The fact that these references are made is in part a reflection of the reality that there are still a number of unresolved issues surrounding Regulation 261; but, moreover, it also is a simple consequence of the airlines' strategies to let passengers' claims play out in court and to pressure national courts to refer references to the CJEU with inventive arguments that exploit any detectable inconsistency or uncertainty in Regulation 261 or the Court's interpretation thereof.[51] More and more, it seems that the on-going preliminary referencing is due to the airlines' litigation practices, rather than fundamental questions of interpretation or judicial contestation of the applicable law. Therefore, one could argue that, regardless of some continuing turbulence, we have at least reached cruising altitude.

B. Extraordinary Circumstances

In *Spitzner*, the Landgericht Hannover had asked whether an 'extraordinary circumstance causing a delay to a flight also constitutes an extraordinary circumstance, within the meaning of that provision, for another, subsequent flight, in the case where the effect of the extraordinary circumstance causing a delay affects the later flight solely by reason of the operational organisation of the air carrier',[52]

---

[49] Case C-575/13 *Thomas Etzold and Others v Condor Flugdienst GmbH* [2014] OJ C15/10; Cases C-475 and C-476/13 *Jubin v easyJet Airline Co Ltd* [2014] OJ C184/24; Case C-471/13 *Link v Condor Flugdienst GmbH* [2014] OJ C184/24; Case C-452/13 *Germanwings v Henning* (ECJ, 4 September 2014); Case C-431/13 *Vietnam Airlines v Voss* [2014] OJ C315/46; Case C-353/13 *Hein v Condor Flugdienst GmbH* [2014] OJ C184/24; Case C-347/13 *Pickert v Condor Flugdienst GmbH* [2014] OJ C184/24; Case C-262/13 *Hein v Condor Flugdienst GmbH* [2013] OJ C215/7; Case C-259/13 *Recinto-Pfingsten v Swiss Internaitonal Air Lines AG* (ECJ, 14 April 2014); Case C-68/13 *Weiss v Condor Flugdienst GmbH* [2013] OJ C114/25.

[50] Case C-365/14 *Liebler v Condor Flugdienst GmbH* [2014] OJ C329/10; Case C-337/14 *Mandl v Condor Flugdienst GmbH* [2014] OJ C431/17; Case C-119/14 *Niessen v Condor Flugdienst GmbH* [2014] OJ C159/13; Case C-118/14 *Kieck v Condor Flugdienst GmbH* [2014] OJ C184/11; Case C-79/14 *TUIfly GmbH v Walter* [2014] OJ C315/47; Case C-46/14 *Kaiser v Condor Flugdienst GmbH* [2014] OJ C261/21; Case C-680/13 *Condor Flugdienst GmbH v Plakolm* [2014] OJ C85/14; Case C-658/13 *Spitzner v TUIfly GmbH* [2014] OJ C85/14.

[51] Another part of the strategy appears to be to prevent inconvenient precedents by ensuring that the preliminary reference is withdrawn by the national court if it looks like the case will be decided in the claimant's favour, by quickly settling before the judgment can be rendered by the CJEU. It is doubtful that these opportunistic practices will put the CJEU judges in a pro-airline mood, and one might therefore wonder about the long-term effectiveness of these litigation strategies.

[52] Case C-658/13 *Spitzner v TUIfly GmbH* [2014] OJ C85/12.

but this reference was withdrawn.[53] The Högsta domstolen in Sweden had asked the Court for guidance on the question whether a technical problem with the airport, which alone or together with weather conditions makes landing impossible, constitutes an 'extraordinary circumstance',[54] but similarly withdrew its request.[55]

Currently pending is a set of different references from the Amtsgericht Rüsselsheim, asking whether the 'extraordinary circumstances' concept includes 'adverse actions by third parties acting on their own responsibility and to whom certain tasks that constitute part of the operation of an air carrier have been entrusted',[56] whether these circumstances must 'relate directly to the booked flight' or 'how many earlier flights involving the aircraft to be used for the scheduled flight are relevant to the existence of an extraordinary circumstance',[57] and whether the airline should 'prove that it took all reasonable measures to avoid the foreseeable consequences of an extraordinary circumstance in the form of cancellation or considerable delay or that no such reasonable measures were available to it'.[58] Furthermore, on 29 April 2014, the Amsterdam district court referred 10 highly detailed further questions to the Court on the responsibilities of airlines in the context of extraordinary circumstances.[59]

C. Delay

On 26 February 2013, the CJEU confirmed in *Air France v Folkerts*[60] that only the time of arrival has to be taken into account for the purpose of establishing a delay, and that if this arrival is delayed for three hours or more, compensation is due, regardless of the departure time. Many other references were withdrawn following this ruling.[61] Still, it is clear that *Nelson* had not resolved all the possible questions on compensation in cases of delay, as is illustrated by an intriguing reference by the Landgericht Hannover about the consequences of the bringing forward of a flight. The national court mused that the aim of Regulation 261, namely, to

[53] Case C-658/13 Order of the President of the Court of 13 May 2014, *Spitzner v TUIfly GmbH* [2014] OJ C261/20.
[54] Case C-150/12 *Brännström v Ryanair Holdings plc* [2012] OJ C157/6.
[55] Case C-150/12 Order of the President of the Court of 22 October 2012, *Brännström v Ryanair Holdings plc* [2013] OJ C9/34.
[56] Case C-365/14, *Liebler v Condor Flugdienst GmbH* [2014] OJ C329/10; Case C-353/13 *Hein v Condor Flugdienst GmbH* [2013] OJ C215/7.
[57] Case C-364/14 *Lorch v Condor Flugdienst GmbH* [2014] OJ C339/14; Case C-575/13 *Etzold v Condor Flugdienst GmbH* [2014] OJ C15/10; Case C-347/13 *Pickert v Condor Flugdienst GmbH* [2014] OJ C184/24; Case C-68/13 *Weiss v Condor Flugdienst GmbH* [2013] OJ C114/25.
[58] Case C-337/14 *Mandl v Condor Flugdienst GmbH* [2014] OJ C431/17; Case C-46/14 *Kaiser v Condor Flugdienst GmbH* [2014] OJ C261/21.
[59] Case C-257/14 *van der Lans v Koninklijke Luchtvaart Maatschappij NV* [2014] OJ C303/12.
[60] Case C-11/11 *Air France v Folkerts* (ECJ, 26 February 2013).
[61] Similar questions had also been referred by the Portugese Tribunal de Pequena Instância Cível de Lisboa on 8 July 2011 in Case C-365/11 *Coelho dos Santos v TAP Portugal* [2011] OJ C282/10, which was withdrawn by the national court on 16 February 2012.

compensate for the damage arising from a loss of time, might also be affected if the passenger were to arrive earlier and therefore time arrangements before the flight would be concerned.[62] This reference has been withdrawn.[63]

Furthermore, questions have arisen as to what time is relevant for the term 'time of arrival':

(1) the time that the aircraft lands on the runway ('touchdown');
(2) the time that the aircraft reaches its parking position and the parking brakes are engaged or the chocks have been applied ('in-block time');
(3) the time that the aircraft door is opened; or
(4) a time defined by the parties in the context of party autonomy?

The CJEU rendered its judgment in this case on 4 September 2014.[64] The Court held that the situation of passengers on a flight does not change substantially when their aircraft touches down on the runway at the destination airport, when that aircraft reaches its parking position and the parking brakes are engaged, or when the chocks are applied, as the passengers continue to be subject, in the enclosed space in which they are sitting, to various constraints. It is only when the passengers are permitted to leave the aircraft, and the order is given to that effect to open the doors of the aircraft, that they may in principle resume their normal activities without being subject to those constraints. Therefore, 'arrival time' corresponds to the time at which at least one of the doors of the aircraft is opened, the assumption being that, at that moment, the passengers are permitted to leave the aircraft.

D. Other Questions

Other questions are focusing on cancellation, rather than delay.[65] For instance, the Bundesgerichtshof has asked the Court to clarify whether a right to compensation granted under national law, which is intended to reimburse additional travel costs incurred as a result of the cancellation of a booked flight, should be deducted from the compensation granted under Article 7 of Regulation 261 if the air carrier has fulfilled its obligations under Articles 8(1) and 9(1) of Regulation 261.[66]

---

[62] Case C-79/14 *TUIfly GmbH v Walter* [2014] OJ C142/23.
[63] Case C-79/14 Order of the President of the Court of 19 June 2014 (request for a preliminary ruling from the Landgericht Hannover, Germany); *TUIfly GmbH v Walter* [2014] OJ C315/47.
[64] Case C-452/13 *Germanwings GmbH v Henning* (ECJ, 4 September 2014).
[65] In Case C-680/13 *Condor Flugdienst GmbH v Andreas Plakolm* [2014] OJ C85/14, the Landgericht Frankfurt am Main asks whether the expression 'cancellation', which is defined in Art 2(l) of Regulation 261(1), is to be interpreted as meaning that, in a situation such as that in the present case, it also applies where, although the flight departed under the original flight number, it was not a non-stop flight as originally planned but involved a stopover scheduled before departure, and another aircraft and airline company were used in a sub-charter arrangement.
[66] Case C-476/13 *Retzlaff v easyJet Airline Co Ltd* [2014] OJ C261/19.

In addition, there are questions about 'double compensation' when the passenger has already been reimbursed by a third party.[67]

V. Period IV: The Proposed Revision or 'Safe Landing or Go-around?'

A. The Road to the Legislative Proposal

The revision process was launched by a European Commission Communication of 11 April 2011,[68] which assessed the current Regulation against the background of a number of factors. The Communication framed the issues in a consumer-orientated way, placing them in the context of EU Citizenship Report 2010, 'Dismantling the obstacles to EU citizens' rights'.[69] In particular, the Communication noted that the growth of the sector has negatively affected the perceived quality of air transport, due to avoidable delays caused by airspace congestion, crowded airports and insufficient contingency planning in the event of severe bad weather, stricter security measures, bigger airports with longer distances, which imply risks in retrieving luggage and missing flights, and commercial practices of air carriers that may negatively impact upon passengers (such as the so-called 'no-show policy' or practices linked to the mishandling of luggage that show loopholes and deficiencies in the application of current legislation). Furthermore, the Communication reflected on the difficulty for passengers to enforce their individual rights and the lack of uniform enforcement through the EU. As such, the Communication concluded that 'there are three areas where measures are still necessary to improve the application of Regulation 261: effectively harmonised enforcement of EU rights, facilitation of their enjoyment in practice, and raising awareness about these rights'. The Communication furthermore affirmed the Court's judgment in *Sturgeon*, simply stating that 'since the CJEU rulings are directly applicable and legally binding from the date that the relevant Regulation came into force, all the carriers are legally obliged to respect them'.

---

[67] In Case C-431/13 *Vietnam Airlines Co Ltd v Voss* [2015] OJ C315/46, the Landgericht Frankfurt am Main asks: Is a passenger entitled to receive in full the compensation provided for in Article 7 of Regulation 261(1) for long delay of flights, even when a third party, other than a passenger, has already made a payment to the passenger as compensation for the delay suffered, or should such payment be deducted?

[68] Commission, 'Communication from the Commission to the European Parliament and the Council on the application of Regulation 261 establishing common rules on compensation and assistance to passengers in the event of denied boarding and of cancellation or long delay of flights' (Communication) COM(2011) 174 final.

[69] Commission, 'EU Citizenship Report 2010, Dismantling the obstacles to EU citizens' rights' (Report) COM(2010) 603 final.

However, the final conclusion in the Communication, which specifically announced the revision process, strikes a somewhat different tone, as it resolves to

> [l]aunch in 2011 an Impact Assessment to assess the proportionality of the current measures in the light of experience and the costs of Regulation 261 for stakeholders, with a view to propose further measures on Air Passenger Rights and in coordination with the ongoing revision of the Package Travel Directive (90/314/EEC), including of a legislative nature, in 2012.

While the Communication did discuss the specific situation of the 2010 Icelandic volcano eruption, and the fact that Member States and the European Commission needed to reflect 'on how to ensure that, in the future, this vital support which in the volcano crisis was provided solely by part of the industry is correctly shared and financed', the proposal to revise the entire Regulation in light of 'the costs of Regulation 261 for stakeholders' somehow came falling out of the sky without advance warning.

Between 19 December 2011 and 11 March 2012, a public consultation was carried out, comprising an open online public consultation, as well as a bilateral consultation involving interviews and direct submissions from a sample of key stakeholders. In the context of the online consultation, respondents were asked for their view on a number of questions relating to Regulation 261's current scope and possible changes thereto.[70] Four hundred and ten submissions were received,

---

[70] The many questions included the following (re-structured for readability): (1) Do you agree on the need to take action to address the above-mentioned problems? (2) Do you agree that there is a need to revise Regulation 261 to address at least part of these problems? (3) Is further clarification needed of (i) extraordinary circumstances involving technical reasons, (ii) for other reasons (eg strikes), (iii) of the requirements for the triple choice reimbursement/re-routing/rebooking? (iv) on the definition of re-routing at the earliest opportunity? (4) Should automatic compensation be introduced where airlines fail to offer the option of re-routing when Regulation 261 requires it? (5) Is the current 3 hour delay after which compensation is payable in cases of delays appropriate? (6) Should Regulation 261 be amended to (i) introduce consistent time periods, after which there would be a right to assistance (such as refreshments and telephone calls), regardless of whether the disruption was caused by delay or cancellation and regardless of the length of the flight, (ii) specify under what circumstances passengers whose flights are rescheduled in advance have a right to a refund, (iii) specify rules regarding the 'no show' policy of some airlines? (7) Should Regulation 261 be amended to require that airlines allow passengers to correct booking errors without charge? (8) Should airlines and travel agents be required to provide a standard format 'Key facts' document to passengers (either in paper or in electronic format) before they confirm a reservation of tickets? (9) Should the scope of Regulation 261 be extended to include flights to the EU from non-EU airports operated by non-EU airlines? (10) Should airlines be required to transport delayed baggage to passengers' final destination (not only to the airport, but also to their residence (home/hotel))? (11) Should airlines be required to refund any baggage fees where the baggage is lost, on top of the possible compensation due? (12) Should airlines be required to provide automatic compensation per day, in cases of delayed baggage? (13) Should airlines' liability to pay compensation be further limited, and if so, how? (14) Should airlines explicitly be given the right to claim costs of compliance from third parties, where these are responsible, even if this is not permitted by their contract? (15) Should airlines' liability be limited for providing accommodation in exceptional circumstances? (15) Should certain routes, which are particularly vulnerable to disruptions, be fully or partially exempted from Regulation 261? (16) Should Member States' sanctioning policies be better harmonised? (17) Should the airlines' operating manuals and procedures with regard to flight disruptions regularly be checked by the competent authority (NEB or licensing authority)? (18) Should compliance with consumer protection legislation become a condition for issuing or maintaining an

of which 181 were from individuals and the remainder from organisations. The industry (airlines associations, airports, travel agents) submitted 155 replies, and the submission *in verbatim* by some 'individuals' of responses also submitted by airlines, travel agents or travel retailers suggests that a proportion of the substantial number of individual respondents may have had some connection with the industry.[71] Consumer and passenger associations accounted for 30 responses.

As expected, the representatives of the operators of air services (airlines, associations, travel agents and tour operators) were not supportive of any amendments that were likely to incur additional costs for the industry, but did express support for amendments to limit their liability to pay compensation and clarify extraordinary circumstances; and they were almost unanimous in expressing disapproval of the CJEU's *Sturgeon* judgment and the resulting right to compensation for delays longer than three hours. In contrast, consumer associations and, to a lesser extent, public authorities agreed in most cases that change was desirable, and expressed support for many of the options proposed in the consultation, where they provided for additional passenger redress or entailed more stringent enforcement activities by the NEBs. Where a range of options was set out (as in the case of the length of a cooling-off period, for example), the more generous option from the passengers' point would in general be preferred by these stakeholders, whereas the airlines would invariably opt for the least generous and potentially lower-cost option. Although in the majority of cases airlines and passenger representatives expressed opposing views, there were some areas of agreement—for example, the need for clarification of extraordinary circumstances (although not about how), or requiring airlines to provide sufficient information to passengers regarding flight disruption.

On 29 March 2012, the European Parliament replied to the Communication in a Resolution.[72] The European Parliament expressed its belief that proper application of the existing rules by Member States and air carriers, enforcement of sufficient and simple means of redress, and providing passengers with accurate information concerning their rights should be the cornerstones of regaining passengers' trust. The Parliament regretted that the NEBs do not always ensure effective protection of passenger rights. Specifically with regard to Regulation 261, the Parliament asked the European Commission to propose a clarification of passengers' rights,

---

air carrier's operating licence? (19) Should airlines be required to produce contingency plans to manage major disruption, and provide these to the relevant authority (eg NEB, licensing authority) which could sanction non-compliance? (20) Should airlines be required to clearly indicate their complaint handling procedures and to allow easy and non-costly submission of complaints in accessible formats (eg phone numbers at no special fee, e-mail addresses and complaints forms on their websites and in various languages)? (21) Should airlines be required to provide a substantive response to passenger complaints within a specified time period?

[71] European Commission, 'Passenger rights, public consultations', available at <http://ec.europa.eu/transport/themes/passengers/consultations/2012-03-11-apr_en.htm>, accessed 21 March 2015.

[72] European Parliament Resolution of 29 March 2012 on the functioning and application of established rights of people travelling by air (2011/2150(INI)).

in particular the notion of extraordinary circumstances. The European Parliament was unequivocal in its support of the Court's case law on Regulation 261, calling on the European Commission to take note, in any upcoming revision of Regulation 261, 'of the level of passenger protection provided by the CJEU rulings as well as the Court's interpretation of "extraordinary circumstances"', and noting that

> recent rulings of the European Court of Justice concerning passenger entitlement to compensation in the event of delays confirm the need for measures aimed at equitable treatment, ensuring appropriate compensation in the event of long delays, regardless of the cause of such delays, in order to take full account of the damage a passenger has suffered; [the European Parliament] urges the Commission, therefore, to propose measures to that effect, without cancelling the right to be transferred to the next available flight … [and] [s]tresses that giving equal treatment to long delays and flight cancellations provides an incentive for airlines to cancel a delayed flight which could perhaps still have taken off.

B. The European Commission's Proposal

On 13 March 2013, the European Commission published its proposal to amend Regulation 261. The proposal acknowledges more explicitly than the initial Communication that at least part of the reason for the revision is to accommodate the airlines in their protests against Regulation 261 and the case law of the Court, particularly in *Sturgeon*, but it is still presented mainly as being concerned about consumer protection and passenger rights. The proposal explains that 'airlines often fail to offer passengers the rights to which they are entitled in instances of denied boarding, long delays, cancellations or mishandled baggage', refers to the EU Citizenship Report of October 2010 on dismantling obstacles to EU citizens' rights and reiterates the problem that 'it is difficult for passengers to enforce their individual rights'. It then continues to say that case law has had a decisive impact on the interpretation of Regulation 261, referring to *ex parte IATA, Wallentin-Hermann* and *Sturgeon*, concluding that the proposal

> aims to promote the interest of air passengers by ensuring that air carriers comply with a high level of air passenger protection during travel disruptions, while taking into account the financial implications for the air transport sector and ensuring that air carriers operate under harmonised conditions in a liberalised market.

The proposal tables a host of changes, the most important of which are the following.

i. Limitation of Compensation for Delayed Flights

The proposed revision will increase the minimum delay for flight compensation from three hours, in all cases except extraordinary circumstances (as held by the Court in *Sturgeon*), to five hours for intra-European flights, nine hours for flights of less than 6,000 kilometres and 12 hours for all other flights.

ii. Limitation of Airlines' Obligations to Provide Care in Exceptional Circumstances

Under the proposal, the provision of accommodation for delayed and cancelled flights will be limited to three nights in exceptional circumstances. The obligation to provide accommodation is abolished altogether for passengers of flights of less than 250 kilometres and with aircraft with less than 80 seats. This limitation does not apply to passengers with reduced mobility, persons accompanying them, unaccompanied children, pregnant women and persons with specific medical needs. This amends the current situation, where Regulation 261 does not limit the obligation to provide care in exceptional circumstances such as the Icelandic volcano eruption.[73]

iii. Strengthened Right to Care and Assistance for Long Flights

The proposal lowers the trigger for passengers' rights to care and assistance for delayed flights above 1,500 kilometres. Currently the required delay is three hours for distances between 1,500 and 3,500, or four hours for distances over 3,500; under the proposal it will be generally set at two hours, as is now already the case for flights under 1,500 kilometres.

iv. Partial Prohibition of No-show Policies

The proposal establishes a new right that a passenger may not be denied boarding on the return flight of his ticket on the ground that he did not use the outbound part of the return ticket. The ban does not affect the right of airlines to impose particular rules with regard to the sequential use of flights within a same journey.

v. Right to Correct Spelling Mistakes in Bookings

Under the proposal, the passenger may request—free of charge—the correction of spelling mistakes in his name up to 48 hours before departure.

vi. Clarification of 'Extraordinary Circumstances'

In line with *Wallentin-Hermann*, the proposal defines 'extraordinary circumstances' as circumstances which are not inherent in the normal exercise of the activity of the air carrier concerned and are beyond its actual control. It provides examples of circumstances which are considered extraordinary: natural disasters or strikes by air traffic controllers should be seen as extraordinary, but technical problems identified during routine aircraft maintenance should not.

---

[73] Case C-12/11 *McDonagh v Ryanair Ltd* (ECJ, 31 January 2013).

vii. *Clarification of Re-routing*

Where the air carrier cannot ensure the re-routing within 12 hours on its own services, it must offer re-routing with other air carriers or on other transport modes where available.

viii. *Clarification of Delay of Connecting Flights*

Where a passenger misses a connecting flight as a result of a delay to a preceding connecting flight, the passenger shall have a right to compensation. For these purposes, the delay shall be calculated by reference to the scheduled time of arrival at the final destination.

ix. *Complaint Handling*

Airlines will have to provide clear complaint-handling procedures (web form, e-mail address). They will also have to reply to passengers within given deadlines (one week for the acknowledgement of receipt, and a formal reply within a deadline of two months). Where disputes arise, passengers will be able to turn to out-of-court complaint handling bodies that will seek to resolve the dispute.

C. European Parliament's Position

On 5 February 2014, the plenary session of the European Parliament adopted its position on the revision of Regulation 261.[74] Five hundred and eighty Members supported the amendments that had been voted on in December 2013 by the Transport and Tourism Committee, whereas 41 Members voted against and 48 abstained. The European Parliament position has changed the legislative proposal in a number of significant ways.

i. *Trigger Points for Delay and Compensation Levels*

For delays at departure, the trigger point for care is after two hours, irrespective of the flight distance; the trigger point for assistance (re-routing, reimbursement, accommodation) has been changed to three hours (instead of five hours).

---

[74] European Parliament legislative resolution of 5 February 2014 on the proposal for a regulation of the European Parliament and of the Council amending Regulation (EC) No 261 establishing common rules on compensation and assistance to passengers in the event of denied boarding and of cancellation or long delay of flights and Regulation (EC) No 2027/97 on air carrier liability in respect of the carriage of passengers and their baggage by air P7_TA-PROV (2014)0092.

For delays at arrival, three trigger points for compensation in case of long delays have been maintained, but the parameters have been amended to:

— delays of three hours for all journeys of 3,500 kilometres or less;
— delays of five hours for all journeys between 3,500 and 6,000 kilometres; and
— delays of seven hours for journeys of more than 6,000 kilometres.

ii. Care in Case of Extraordinary Circumstances

The obligation to accommodate passengers is limited to five nights (instead of three). If the passenger arranges his or her own accommodation, the reimbursement can be limited to €125 per night/per person. The European Parliament deleted any reference to the European Commission proposal to exempt flights of less than 250 kilometres from the obligation to accommodate passengers in cases of disruptions.

iii. The Definition of Extraordinary Circumstances

The European Parliament amended the definition by removing the word 'inherent'. The nature of the annex listing the circumstances is now exhaustive. The annex can be amended by delegated acts by the European Commission (with a possibility for the European Parliament and the European Council to object). Technical problems can still be considered as extraordinary circumstances, but this is limited to problems caused by natural disasters, acts of sabotage, terrorism or hidden manufacturing defects. Any other technical defect detected before or after the release to service is not considered as extraordinary. Other cases of extraordinary circumstances that have been added to the annex are: damage in-flight or after service release caused by meteorological conditions; bird strikes; war and political unrest; unforeseen air traffic control restrictions and runway closures; and unforeseen labour disputes (both internal and external to the air carrier).

iv. Re-routing

Passengers will have the right to be re-routed on other air carriers or on another mode of transport (if reasonable and comparable alternatives exist), if the initial carrier cannot transport the passenger on its own services to arrive at the destination within eight hours of the scheduled time of arrival (instead of 12 hours). The carrier has the obligation to inform passengers within 30 minutes after the scheduled departure time whether it will re-route them on its own services.

v. Right of Assistance and Compensation in Case of Missing a Connecting Flight

Only where a passenger misses a connecting flight as a result of a change of schedule or a delay to a preceding connecting flight of 90 minutes or more, calculated by reference to the time of arrival at the transfer point, shall the passenger have a right to compensation.

vi. Claim Procedure

A time limit within which to submit claims/complaints to the airlines is fixed at three months; however, the passenger is free to take legal steps through the judicial system or out-of-court settlement also if the complaint is submitted after these three months. The air carrier must provide a full answer to the claim/complaint within two months, otherwise the claim is deemed accepted by the carrier. Both 'extraordinary circumstances' and 'all reasonable measures' have to be documented by the carrier in its answer to the passenger, which should also include the contact details of the NEBs responsible for the out-of-court resolution of disputes between air carriers and passengers. It is made compulsory that airlines are affiliated to these out-of-court dispute resolution bodies.

D. Outlook

It has been reported[75] that despite intense work undertaken in Council Working Group negotiations, it was clear that further work and time would be needed to find compromises on a number of significant outstanding issues, specifically the trigger points for when delay compensation is due and connecting flights. As a result, the Greek Presidency decided not to seek any form of agreement at the Transport Council on 5 June 2014, and instead submitted a progress report. The dossier was not treated as a priority by the Italian Presidency,[76] nor by the Latvian Presidency. In addition, the British-Spanish territorial dispute over Gibraltar has stalled the implementation of all EU aviation legislation since 2012, which would have to be resolved before the passenger rights proposal can move forward.[77] It is therefore difficult to predict whether any decision will be reached in 2015 or even 2016.

VI. Assessment

In a previous article on this topic, I tried to offer some explanations for the depth and vigour of the controversy surrounding Regulation 261, especially in national

---

[75] UK House of Commons European Scrutiny Committee, 'Sixth Report of Session 2014–15' (House of Commons, 9 July 2014) 9.

[76] UK House of Commons European Scrutiny Committee, 'Sixth Report of Session 2014–15' (House of Commons, 9 July 2014) 9.

[77] Euractiv, 'Brussels considers withdrawing draft EU law on air travellers' Rights,' 30 April 2015.

judiciaries. It was argued that a trigger for the controversy was the 'activism' of the CJEU's *Sturgeon* judgment. It was also argued that an increase in Euro-scepticism might have served as a facilitating factor. Most importantly, however, it was argued that in essence, the situation should be viewed and explained as a prime example of what Daniel Kelemen has dubbed 'Euro-legalism'.[78] The EU-level liberalisation of the air travel sector in the 1980s and 1990s led to a need to re-regulate at European level, which was done in the form of actionable individual rights. This approach relocates the regulatory battle field from 'informal and cooperative mechanisms' to courts (both national and European). I argued that this (together with the financial interest of the airlines) explains the volume of cases in the national courts, as well as their unease with dealing with it. Looking at the situation now, as it has evolved over the past couple of years, and in particular taking into account the proposed revised Regulation, we should revisit these issues.

A. Judicial Activism

The first and most obvious reason for the critical reactions to *Sturgeon* is the idea that the CJEU engaged in excessive judicial activism. The most outspoken national courts, in the *Germanwings* reference and the Den Bosch *Ryanair* ruling, explicitly opine that *Sturgeon* amounts to illegitimate judicial law-making. The *Germanwings* reference is especially interesting in this regard, because by asking whether the CJEU deemed it compatible with the principle of the separation of powers to interpret Regulation 261 the way it did, it placed the issue of the boundaries of the judicial function and the hot potato of judicial activism at the core of the preliminary question, and thereby under the Court's nose. Of course it is true that *Sturgeon* is a striking example of jurisdictional self-empowerment, seeing that the Court allowed itself to essentially write a detailed legal rule into a Regulation, something the Advocate General had explicitly warned against. Even if the argument could be made that Regulation 261 did not explicitly exclude the compensation in cases of delay, but instead did not provide for it, and even if passengers of cancelled flights who were re-routed were effectively granted compensation for delays of three hours and above, meaning that the Court did not completely conjure up the magical 'three hour' benchmark out of thin air, few would deny that *Sturgeon* takes teleological reasoning to its extremes. But although the Court acted not as the *bouche de la loi* but instead very much like a legislator, it is not immediately clear that it did so at the cost of the legislature beyond what is normal in a system that allows for judicial review. In the EU legal order, the legislative prerogative does not encompass infringing constitutional principles, and the CJEU has been specifically empowered to decide on that issue. Finding a

---

[78] RD Kelemen, *Eurolegalism. The Transformation of Law and Regulation in the European Union* (Harvard University Press, 2011).

piece of legislation in breach of a higher norm requires either annulment of the law, or conform interpretation. Either choice sees the CJEU thwarting the will of the legislature, asserting itself and its power to control the legislature, as is inherent in the concept of judicial review. Opting for conform interpretation rather than annulment can even be seen as choosing the lesser evil. Most national constitutional courts aim to avoid annulment and use conform interpretation—'adding in' or 'reading down' legislative provisions—as a common technique to avoid a stand-off with the legislature.[79]

An argument could therefore be made that an interpretation of Regulation 261 in conformity with the principle of equal treatment was more deferential and respectful of the legislative process than an annulment of Regulation 261, or parts of it, would have been. Of course, it would be naive to paint *Sturgeon* as a picture of judicial restraint. Using 'very teleological'[80] conform interpretation, as de Visser points out, 'courts can engage in judicial law-making by re-drafting legislation in a way that can contradict the legislature's intentions',[81] as *Sturgeon* illustrates perfectly. But one could argue that in choosing between the two evils of either annulling Regulation 261 or interpreting it in conformity with the equal treatment principle by extending the right to compensation to the unduly excluded group, the CJEU actually chose the option that was closest to the legislator's intention. For the piece of legislation was adopted in the interest of consumer protection, and it can hence be assumed that it would be closer to the legislator's intention— itself of course a difficult fiction—to extend that notion of protection to an extra group than to do away with that protection altogether by annulment of the relevant provisions.

And indeed, although like in most cases of judicial activism there certainly is a self-serving element in the judgment, one could also choose a less cynical perspective and suggest that the Court acted out of a genuine concern for consumer protection. In any case, regardless of the Court's motive, the judgment is a victory for consumer protection. What would have been the consequence had the CJEU invalidated the relevant provisions of Regulation 261, as proposed by the Advocate General? The airline companies would have had a field day. They would, for the time being, not have been required to pay compensation to anyone, neither the passengers of delayed flights nor those of cancelled flights. The European legislature would most likely have sought to address the issue, but this would have left a significant time-gap in which the travelling European citizen would have had to pay the price. It is true that on the basis of Article 264(2) of the TFEU, the CJEU could have decided to maintain the effects of Regulation 261 for a brief

---

[79] M de Visser, 'A Cautionary Tale. Some Insights Regarding Judicial Activism from the National Experience', *Judicial activism at the Court of Justice*, Conference, Maastricht University, 10–11 October 2011.

[80] Case C-363/12 *Z v A Government Department and the Board of Management of a Community School* (ECJ, 26 September 2013), Opinion of AG Wahl, qualifying the judgment in *Sturgeon*.

[81] ibid.

period, to be fixed in such a way as to allow the Council to remedy the infringements. That way, passengers of cancelled flights would have retained their right to compensation during that period. Nevertheless, the outcome of new negotiations would have been unsure. Airlines would most certainly have seized this opportunity to try to turn the legislation in their favour by major lobby-investments, and it is not at all certain that a new compensation regime would have been put in place. The achieved result could just as well have been to remedy the unequal treatment by levelling-down, doing away with compensation for all passengers. It could be argued that as long as there is a certain degree of capture of the European legislative process by pro-business lobbyists,[82] accompanied by a neo-liberal bias in that same process,[83] the Court is right to counterbalance some of these defects.[84]

One might point out that this very thing is happening now: a revision of Regulation 261, at least partially as a reaction to *Sturgeon*, and the significant lobbying efforts on behalf of the airlines. But the starting point of the revision process is fundamentally different now that the Court did not annul Regulation 261 but interpreted it protectively and expansively. Even if it seems clear that the European legislature is planning to revise the Court's case law at least to some degree, with the European Commission's proposal changing the trigger point for compensation from a delay of three hours in all cases to a delay of to five hours for intra-European flights, nine hours for flights of less than 6,000 kilometres and 12 hours for all other flights, this has been significantly nuanced by the European Parliament (three hours for journeys of 3,500 kilometres or less, five hours for journeys between 3,500 and 6,000 kilometres, and seven hours for journeys of more than 6,000 kilometres) and, most importantly, the essence of the Court's judgment will be respected. Entering into the political negotiating process with the right to compensation after three hours as a point of departure instead of a general consideration that 'there should be equal treatment as regards compensation for passengers of delayed and cancelled flights', makes a pro-consumer outcome far more likely.

---

[82] This is what Follesdal and Hix have called a variant of the fifth main claim of the standard version of the democratic deficit. They formulate this critique as follows: '[S]ince a classic representative chamber, such as the European Parliament, is not the dominant institution in EU governance, private interest groups do not have to compete with democratic party politics in the EU policy-making process. Concentrated interests such as business interests and multinational firms have a greater incentive to organize at the European level than diffuse interests, such as consumer groups or trade unions, and the EU policy process is pluralist rather than corporatist. These features skew EU policy outcomes more towards the interests of the owners of capital than is the case for policy compromises at the domestic level in Europe' (A Follesdal and S Hix, 'Why There is a Democratic Deficit in the EU: A Response to Majone and Moravcsik' (2006) 44(3) *Journal of Common Market Studies* 537). On this point Follesdal and Hix refer to W Streeck and P Schmitter, 'From National Corporatism to Transnational Pluralism: Organized Interests in the Single European Market' (1991) 19(2) *Politics and Society* 133.

[83] eg F Scharpf, *Crisis and Choice in European Social Democracy* (Cornell University Press, 1999). For a critical response, see A Moravcsik, 'In Defence of the "Democratic Deficit": Reassessing Legitimacy in the Eruopean Union' (2002) 44(4) *Journal of Common Market Studies* 603.

[84] eg C Kaupa, 'What if the CJEU is NOT an activist court, but still has a neoliberal bias?' *Judicial activism at the Court of Justice*, Conference, Maastricht University, 10–11 October 2011.

It is of course still the legislature's prerogative, as it should be in a democratic legal system, to change the rules and to set different concrete criteria and limits to the rights laid down in the legislation, or to do away with them altogether, within the constitutional parameters set by the Court. And of course this may lead to a less consumer-protective outcome than the Court's interpretation. And while there are elements in the current proposal as amended that level down some of the protection, particularly as regards delay and as regards care and assistance in extraordinary circumstances, it should be observed that the main thrust of Regulation 261 as interpreted by the Court is respected, incorporated and thereby democratically validated. The revision attempts to balance an elevated level of passenger protection with a limitation of the financial responsibilities of airlines, and not everybody will agree that the balance has been appropriately struck by either the European Commission or the European Parliament, nor in any final outcome. But that is inherent in democracy, and what we are seeing is—I would argue—a healthy process of law-making, where the Court was called on to interpret and remedy problematic provisions in a piece of legislation, where it sought an outcome that served the goals of the legislation in question, and where these judge-made solutions were passed back to the legislature, which is now able to revise and/or to validate these solutions. While it would be naive to say that the Court's 'activism' has not made any difference to the final outcome, it cannot be denied that any final arrangement on compensation for passengers of delayed flights will now be the explicit choice of the legislator.

B. Legal Certainty

Such revised legislation will also resolve what is perhaps the most powerful argument against the *Sturgeon* case law, namely, that of legal certainty. This principle is of particular importance, especially when it concerns obligations on private parties, such as in the case of airlines. Indeed, the legal certainty of private parties is the central argument why the CJEU has denied the direct effect of EU directives. Regulations, of course, are of direct application, and therefore can impose obligations on individual parties. But judicial activism in the interpretation of such regulations can lead to unforeseeable obligations on those private parties. Indeed, some of the most contentious cases in recent EU law history share this common thread: they impose obligations on private parties that could not be foreseen.[85]

However, while this argument might be valid as a reason to limit the temporal effects (that is, retroactive application) of the judgment,[86] it no longer applies from

---

[85] Case C-144/04 *Mangold v Helm* [2005] ECR I-09981, concerning an employer; Case C-341/05 *Laval un Partneri Ltd v Byggnadsarbetareförbundet* [2007] ECR I-11767, concerning a trade union.

[86] Which is rarely done by the Court, but for this very reason in the landmark Case 43/75 *Defrenne v Société anonyme belge de navigation aérienne Sabena* [1976] ECR 00455, para 70.

the moment the contentious ruling is handed down. From that point onwards, the law is known, and private actors can adjust their behaviour accordingly. In terms of legal 'clarity', the situation is perhaps not entirely the same as in the case of enacted legislation, which is arguably more accessible to private parties than court case law, and where in addition the private parties often would have a more generous adjustment phase. But, especially in the case of powerful companies such as airlines, who have proven to dispose of a sophisticated legal support system that allows them to analyse the case law in minute detail, it is hard to take seriously any concerns about legal certainty from that point onwards.

Indeed, it should also be pointed out that while in the heated debates about Regulation 261 and its interpretation by the CJEU airlines have consistently referred to legal certainty as one of their main complaints, they have at the same time deployed deliberate tactics to avoid establishing legal certainty, if that certainty would not be in their favour. In particular, as was noted above, it has been reported that in many cases, airlines convinced national courts to pose preliminary questions arguing that the situation was unclear, subsequently using those preliminary references in other courts to convince them of the legal uncertainty and to stall the procedure or to refer further questions, dragging out the procedure just up until the moment that a judgment from the Court was expected, and then—when projecting an unfavourable outcome—quickly settling the claim and thereby forcing the national court to withdraw the reference. Now that the Court has amended its rules of procedure, a reference cannot be withdrawn after a hearing has taken place, which will put a stop to this inelegant (and potentially counter-productive) strategy. But it does make one turn a deaf ear to the howls and cries from the industry in the name of the sacred principle of legal certainty.

C. Eurolegalism

In attempting to offer some explanations for the depth and vigour of the controversy surrounding Regulation 261, I argued that the root cause behind the controversy was that it is a manifestation of the increasing 'claim culture' or 'compensation culture' in Europe. Many will have noted that the distinctly American approach to governance, which has been dubbed 'adversarial legalism', is on the rise in the EU, leading to what Kelemen has called the spread of 'Eurolegalism'.[87] Adversarial legalism is characterised by detailed, prescriptive rules; legalistic and adversarial approaches to regulatory enforcement and dispute resolution; costly legal contestation and mega-lawyering techniques; active judicial review of administrative decisions and practices, and frequent judicial intervention; and frequent private litigation concerning regulatory policies.[88] Overall, it empowers private actors to assert their legal rights through the emphasis on the enforcement of legal norms through transparent legal rules.

---

[87] Kelemen (n 78).
[88] R Kagan, *Adversarial Legalism: The American Way of Law* (Harvard University Press, 2001).

Such 'regulation through litigation' was for a long time alien to Europe, where more informal, co-operative, and opaque approaches to regulation dominated, relying much less on lawyers, courts and private actions.[89] In fact, as Kelemen points out, Europeans take distinctive pride in the absence of adversarial legalism.[90] Some will remember taking scornful pleasure in the urban legend according to which US courts awarded a seven-figure amount in compensation to the unfortunate cat-owner who put her even more unfortunate cat in the microwave in an attempt to dry it after it had become wet in the rain, on the ground that the instructions had unhelpfully not warned that microwaves were not suitable for cat-drying.[91] Indeed, many Europeans view the American legal and regulatory style, featuring ambulance-chasing lawyers, class action lawsuits and massive punitive damages awards, 'with a mixture of amusement and horror—and perhaps a touch of Schadenfreude'.[92] However, as Kelemen points out, Europe is slowly but surely succumbing to the same disease.

This shift is caused by the process of deregulation and EU re-regulation linked to the creation of the internal market, where economic liberalisation has undermined the traditional, co-operative national regulatory approaches. The EU-level reregulation differs from the national regulation it replaces, because the increased volume of—and diversity in—the market, pressures EU policy-makers to rely on a more formal and transparent approach to regulation, backed by vigorous enforcement, often by private parties. Another contributing factor is the fragmented institutional structure of the EU, meaning that the re-regulation takes place in the context of a fragmented regulatory state with a powerful judicial system but a weak administrative apparatus:

> In the absence of a Eurocracy powerful enough to enforce EU law from Brussels, the EU is encouraging the spread of adversarial legalism as a mode of governance that can harness private litigants and national courts for the decentralized enforcement of European law. Eurolegalism is emerging as a quite unexpected—and in many circles unwanted—stepchild of European integration.[93]

Indeed, the saga relating to Regulation 261 is an example *par excellence* of the rise of Eurolegalism.[94] The entire chain of events has shown an EU-level deregulation of the air transport sector, the adoption of consumer protection legislation providing clearly identifiable rights, the EU launching campaigns calling on consumers to enforce these rights, airlines forming pan-European interest groups to bring legal challenges against EU rights, the European Commission taking coercive action against Member States that do not enforce consumer rights, and passengers bringing floods of claims before national courts, either individually or through newly erected firms such as Aviaclaim, EUclaim and Ticketclaim that are

---

[89] Kelemen (n 78) 7, referring to K Viscusi (ed), *Regulation through Litigation* (Brookings Institution Press, 2002).

[90] Keleman (n 78) 7.

[91] P Ryan, 'Revisiting the United States Application of Punitive Damages: Separating Myth from Reality' (2003) 10(1) *Journal of International and Comparative Law* 69.

[92] Kelemen (n 78).

[93] ibid, 8–9.

[94] ibid.

widely advertising their services on the Internet, soliciting clients to bring compensation claims against airlines. Master of manipulating public opinion through media-genic controversial statements, Ryanair has already tried to play into Europeans' dislike of American-style claim culture, by publicising that it had received a claim in relation to the flight disruption caused by the eruption of the Iceland volcano in 2010 from an Irish passenger who had paid €34 to travel to the Canary Islands and was demanding €2,900 to cover food and accommodation. True colours shone through when Ryanair said that it would respond to the 'claims coming from bastards who paid €30 and are seeking €3,000 back' by taking on '10 or 20 of the most ludicrous claims as test cases'.[95]

It is not unlikely that the strong reactions by the national courts, as well as from commentators, are at some level related to the rise of Eurolegalism and Europeans' disapproval thereof. In any event, the passenger rights saga can indeed be seen as a powerful illustration of Kelemen's theory. But although it might be legitimate to object to the Americanisation of our legal systems, it would be wrong therefore to side with the airlines on this issue and to resist an approach in support of consumers. For it should be remembered that the re-regulation, in the form of transparent and enforceable rights and the ensuing claims and legal proceedings, is the consequence of, and perhaps even defence mechanism against, the deregulation and liberalisation connected to the internal market. To resist re-regulation would be to create an undesirable 'market without rules',[96] in which important public interests are left unprotected. The CJEU's aforementioned activism is therefore not only a necessary part of Eurolegalism, it is also desirable, as a counterweight to the deregulatory effects of market liberalisation.

As was noted above, before the liberalisation of air transport, most of the sector operated through national airlines, state-owned enterprises with a legal status varying from being part of government to stock companies with the state as a regular stockholder, which allowed the public to influence the airlines and their behaviour directly. Quality standards could be imposed and adapted without having to resort to the (arduous) enactment of static legislation, to be enforced in courts. Not only has privatisation meant that private parties have been able to generate profit from what used to be a public service, banking on the guaranteed demand of transport as a necessity of modern life, it has also become more difficult for the public to make sure that common interests and values are served. Of course, privatisation can also be projected to bring about advantages to the consumer (wider variety of choice in terms of price and quality) and the public at large (no public risk, no public costs). But it should be recognised that bolstering the rights of the consumer is necessary to counterbalance the loss of control by the citizen. This indeed means that we are increasingly turned into market citizens, who relate to each other and to society at large in a rational, individualistic and

---

[95] D Milmo, 'Ryanair to reject "ludicrous" Iceland volcano claims', *Guardian* (1 June 2010).

[96] Case C-442/02 *Caixabank France v Ministère de l'Économie, des Finances et de l'Industrie* (ECJ, 5 October 2004), Opinion of AG Tizzano, para 63.

self-interested mind-set. But if this sounds unappealing, or un-European, then the idea of market integration through deregulation and liberalisation should be challenged, not the idea of consumer protection or EU-level re-regulation.

The proposed revision of Regulation 261 can be seen as 'simply one of the pieces in the "tricky balance" between market liberalisation and consumer protection, which the CJEU will continue to fine-tune'.[97] It does not break with the Eurolegalistic nature of its predecessor, as it attempts to resolve the issues by making the rules even more detailed and prescriptive. But by providing important clarifications (such as on the issue of extraordinary circumstances) it attempts to reduce the pressure on courts to fill in the things left uncertain, and while it boosts the enforcement and dispute resolution mechanisms of Regulation 261, it does seek to get most disputes resolved out of court (in particular by making it compulsory that airlines are affiliated to out-of-court dispute resolution bodies). While it can be expected that airlines will still try to avoid paying compensation and providing care by contesting provisions in Regulation 261 and by seeking out unresolved or even new legal grey areas, it can also be expected that such practices would have less traction with national courts, in the sense that they would be less likely to put into doubt the legitimacy of the rules and refer questions to the CJEU. Any concerns that they would have with the initial judicial activism of the Court would have been resolved by the adoption of a new Regulation, and they would have more legislative guidance on the crucial concept of 'extraordinary circumstances', the definition of which has become the hottest topic in national courts since *Sturgeon* was settled by *Nelson*. So it can reasonably be expected that the revised Regulation will, in the long run, make the application and the enforcement of Regulation 261 easier, and thereby will make the entire state of affairs less adversarial.

While it cannot be excluded that the Court will pull another *Sturgeon* out of the hat, this is unlikely considering the breadth of questions now already covered by rulings and possibly circumscribed by new rules in the future. And, as the Court sometimes tends to do in a two-steps-forward-one-step-back approach,[98] it may now turn the page on its strongly pro-passenger approach and adopt a slightly more restrictive stance in cases to come, as suggested in its recent judgment on a national law prohibiting airlines from charging for checked-in luggage that was struck down by the Court.[99]

---

[97] J Prassl, 'Reforming Air Passenger Rights in the European Union' (2014) 39 *Air and Space Law* 78.

[98] eg in relation to education, Case C-39/86 *Lair v Universitat Hannover* [1988] ECR 3161, Case C-197/86 *Brown v Secretary of State for Scotland* [1988] ECR 3205, Case C209/03 *Bidar v London Borough of Ealing and Secretary of State for Education and Skills* [2005] ECR I-02119, Case C-158/07 *Forster* [2008] ECR I-08507, Case C-65/03 *Commission v Belgium* [2004] ECR I-6427, Case C-147/03 *Commission v Austria* [2005] ECR I-05969, Case C-73/08 *Bressol v Gouvernement de la Communauté française* [2010] ECR I-02735; in the area of citizenship see, eg, Case C-34/09 *Zambrano v Office national de l'emploi* [2011] ECR I-01177, Case C-434/09 *McCarthy v Secretary of State for the Home Department* [2011] ECR I-03375, Case C-256/11 *Dereci v Bundesministerium für Inneres* [2011] ECR I-11315.

[99] Case C-487/12 *Vueling Airlines SA v Instituto Galego de Consumo de la Xunta de Galicia* (ECJ, 18 September 2014).

D. Judicial Dialogue

Lastly, we should briefly reflect on the implications of all the foregoing on the judicial dialogue between the CJEU and national courts. It is clear that the area of air passenger rights has seen prolific preliminary referencing over the past few years, and the tone of the dialogue is at times surprisingly sharp. As discussed above, this can be explained by several factors, such as a resistance against the Court's judicial activism, especially in private law settings, an aversion to an increasingly adversarial legal culture stemming from EU integration, and—rather bluntly—by the sheer pressure exerted by the airlines on the national courts. Big business has for a long time known how to use EU law litigation in national courts to its advantage, and while it may be displeased by the increasing counterbalancing of EU market liberalisation with EU public interest re-regulation, it still knows how to play the legal system to its advantage. Even if it may also be noted that, as described by a number of contributions in this book, many national courts in Member States other than Germany, The Netherlands and the UK have apparently found no particular problem with the application of Regulation 261 or the case law of the Court, the *Sturgeon* fallout remains a noteworthy episode in the relationship between national courts and the CJEU. But is it a problematic episode? Should we regard this as an unfortunate set of events that should somehow be prevented in the future?

We can look at this question from different angles. On the one hand, we may take it as a sign of maturity of the relationship between the CJEU and the national courts that the latter dare to speak up and express their concerns. Indeed, it is still a well-known reality that many national courts refrain from asking preliminary references, resolving the cases before them on the basis of national law or by their own interpretation of the relevant EU law, even though strictly speaking they should have addressed a question to the CJEU. From the viewpoint of the uniform application of EU law, such practices are much more problematic than asking critical and/or repetitive preliminary questions. Perhaps that is why the CJEU has shown a measure of patience with all these questions concerning Regulation 261, and has generally not bluntly disposed of them as *acte clair* or as contrary to the doctrine in *Wünsche v Germany*.[100] Even if it may not always like the tone of these questions, the Court might be happy that these national courts are engaging in the conversation at all.

---

[100] Case 69/85 *Wünsche v Germany* [1986] ECR 947. Since the *Wünsche* judgment, it has been settled case law that 'the authority of a preliminary ruling does not preclude the national court to which it is addressed from properly taking the view that it is necessary to make a further reference to the CJEU', for instance 'when the national court encounters difficulties in understanding or applying the judgment, when it refers a fresh question of law to the Court, or again when it submits new considerations which might lead the Court to give a different answer'. However, in *Wünsche* the Court also expressly held that 'it is not permissible to use the right to refer further questions to the Court as a means of contesting the validity of the judgment delivered previously, as this would call in question the allocation of jurisdiction as between national courts and the CJEU'.

On the other hand, the entire saga shows the limits of the doctrine of the uniformity of EU law, as well as the limits of the EU judicial order conceived as a hierarchical, centralised one with the CJEU as the sole and central authority to interpret EU law, supported by the preliminary reference procedure as this system's main mechanism.[101] Most pieces of EU legislation are not as hotly contested as Regulation 261, perhaps because the economic stakes are lower and the interests are less polarised, but in theory it would be possible to raise an equal number of interpretation and validity questions on other pieces of EU law as have been raised in the context of Regulation 261. I do not think that this Regulation is a particularly poorly drafted piece of legislation, and I also do not think that overall the case law of the Court concerning this Regulation has been much more far-reaching than case law in other areas. The problem is that once an area sees opposing parties prepared to spend a lot of time and money contesting the legislation in national courts, exploiting every existing inconsistency and uncertainty in the text and the case law, it is no longer tenable to hold onto the principle of uniform application of EU law and the ultimate authority of the CJEU, as doing so results in hundreds of slightly different questions on slightly different factual situations and how they relate to the applicable EU law, further blocking the already clogged arteries of the EU judicial system. Therefore, in circumstances such as these, we may have to give up the pursuit of uniformity as the Holy Grail, and instead trust national courts to find appropriate solutions in individual cases, while accepting that there may be a degree of difference between them. Such slightly differing outcomes seem inherent in law, and especially EU law, anyway. It is an everyday reality that it is not equally easy to enforce EU rights across the EU territory. Under the principle of national procedural autonomy, Member States are free to decide on fundamental procedural elements such as remedies and prescription periods, only under the supervision of the principles of equivalence and effectiveness, meaning that it can make a big difference whether a citizen lodges his claim in the UK or in Germany. While as a matter of principle the most crucial central concepts of EU law should have a uniform interpretation, the application thereof lies with the national court, and in this application the national courts can also, to a certain extent, shape the interpretation of the rules. This is not to be feared but to be fostered. And practically speaking, in areas as adversarial as the one under discussion, it seems the only viable way forward.

This decentralisation of the EU judicial system should ideally be supported by horizontal dialogue between national courts. The national case law on EU air passenger rights already shows signs of this promising, alternative way of conceiving the EU judicial order, with courts from different Member States referencing each other's case law. We saw that many Dutch, UK and German courts explicitly

---

[101] For a powerful argument against this current organisation of the EU judicial system and for placing more trust in national courts, see J Komarek, '"In the Court(s) We Trust?" On the Need for Hierarchy and Differentiation in the Preliminary Ruling Procedure' (2007) 32 *European Law Review* 467.

engaged in a discussion of case law across their borders in their judgments involving Regulation 261. In a grown-up European legal order, it would seem that only the most important questions of law should be sent to the overburdened CJEU, and that for all other issues the national courts should be considered competent to find their own solutions, in co-operation with each other. If anything, this would instill a more 'European' dimension in the work of the national judges than under the current system, where the European dimension of national law is 'outsourced' to the CJEU in Luxembourg. For this system to function optimally, the accessibility of national judgments in different languages, as well as the existence of formal and informal co-operation networks of national courts, should be encouraged.[102]

VII. Conclusion

While, no matter what happens, the developments of the past years in this area will continue to provide food for thought for years to come, perhaps the most obvious remaining question is whether and how we can expect the on-going controversies to halt. Will the CJEU be able to come up with an all-answering judgment, providing a final word on what Regulation 261 requires and what it does not? This seems impossible. Will the airlines give up their law-avoiding practices? Probably not. Will passengers give up claiming their rights? Highly unlikely. Will national courts stop referring preliminary references to the CJEU? Perhaps, and if they would, that could be a viable way out of all this turbulence, as set out above. But in the meantime, all eyes are now on the European legislator. Will the new Regulation put all controversies to rest? Of course, it is to be hoped that new Regulation, if adopted, will bring about quieter times through more clarity and better enforcement mechanisms. But the opposing forces are so strong that it is difficult to see how any revision of the rules can please and appease all concerned. The airlines are hoping that their financial obligations will be limited, while passengers are hoping that their rights to assistance and compensation, and the enforcement thereof, will be strengthened. It will be interesting to see where the EU institutions will strike the balance, if anywhere. As much as Regulation 261 has tested the workings of the EU judicial process, it will now test the workings of the political, legislative process. So it is much too soon to think about safe landings. Alas, but there is also something to be said for the excitement of the loopings and nosedives that we have seen up until now—especially when one is not on the plane but looking at it from the ground.

---

[102] eg M de Visser and M Claes, 'Courts United? On European Judicial Networks' in A Vauchez and B de Witte (eds), *Lawyering Europe, European Law as a Transnational Social Field* (Hart Publishing, 2013) 75.

19

European Private Law: Up in the Air?

JOASIA LUZAK

I. Introduction

In the past decade the European institutions have placed the harmonisation of European private law and more specifically of European contract law at the top of their list of priorities.[1] Due to the growing importance of the tourism market in the EU, we could expect that at least some of the harmonisation effort in European private law would be directed at improving the regulation of passenger transport services.[2] However, the main harmonisation projects of the last few years have not, or only barely, addressed this issue. This holds true even for the most recent European private law harmonisation project, the proposal of the Common European Sales Law. The European Commission chose not to develop an optional instrument applicable to services, but merely an instrument for sales contracts.[3] The other important measure introduced recently in European private law, the Consumer Rights Directive (CRD),[4] applies to consumer contracts for both the

---

[1] V Reding, 'The optional Common European Sales Law—Seizing the opportunity!' (Conference on European Contract Law, Warsaw, 10 November 2011); V Reding, 'Opening trade and opportunities: From the Hanseatic League to European Contract Law' (Informal meeting of the Council of Justice Ministers, Sopot, Poland, 19 July 2011); V Reding, 'The Next Steps Towards a European Contract Law for Businesses and Consumers' in R Schulze and J Stuyck (eds), *Towards a European Contract Law* (Sellier, 2011) 9; European Parliament, 'Full harmonisation no longer an option' (Press Release, 17 March 2010).

[2] Commission, 'Europe, the world's No 1 tourist destination—a new political framework for tourism in Europe' COM(2010) 352 final; J Karsten and G Petri, 'Towards a Handbook on European Contract Law and Beyond: The Commission's 2004 Communication "European Contract Law and the Revision of the *Acquis*: The Way Forward"' (2005) 28 *Journal of Consumer Policy* 31, 43.

[3] Commission, 'Proposal for a Regulation on a Common European Sales Law' COM(2011) 635 final (Common European Sales Law). Except that if agreed by the parties it may regulate services related to the sale of goods or digital content supplied on the basis of the Common European Sales Law, eg Common European Sales Law, Recital (19), Arts 2(m) and 3; Commission, 'European Commission proposes an optional Common European Sales Law to boost trade and expand consumer choice' (Press Release) IP/11/1175.

[4] European Parliament and Council Directive 2011/83/EU of 25 October 2011 on consumer rights, amending Council Directive 93/13/EEC and Directive 1999/44/EC of the European Parliament and of the Council and repealing Council Directive 85/577/EEC and Directive 97/7/EC of the European Parliament and of the Council [2011] OJ L304/64 (Consumer Rights Directive).

sale of goods and the provision of services. However, Article 3(3)(k) of the CRD excludes the application of most of this Directive's provisions to passenger transport services, and therefore the CRD barely grants any rights to air passengers. While the European institutions have heavily debated the improvement methods of the currently binding framework of the Package Travel Directive[5] (PTD) and of Regulation 261,[6] over the past few years this has not yet led to the improvement of the European regulation of transport services.[7] There seems to be a consensus that the existing rules need a thorough makeover; however, the form and the content thereof remain controversial.[8] Therefore, amongst other problems, the final version of the new European legislation with regard to air passengers' rights is still not in sight.

This chapter compares the existing rights granted to consumers when they purchase services in the EU, whether in a shop or within a distance selling scheme, with the provisions of Regulation 261.[9] While work on the new European rules on air passengers' rights is still ongoing, it is important to examine what protection measures air passengers are currently missing that European consumers may already be enjoying while concluding contracts other than for air transport services. I also discuss whether certain air passengers' rights in Europe, and the methods of providing these rights, could serve as a model for the further development of European consumer protection measures. The assumption underlying this comparison is that air transport services are just one of many services that European consumers purchase. Conceivably, consumers should enjoy similar, if not the same, protection regardless of the type of service they are interested in. Special justifications, for example, of an economic nature, could, however, justify the introduction of divergent rules with respect to air transport services. Therefore, where my research indicates such differences in the protection levels of

---

[5] Council Directive 90/314/EEC of 13 June 1990 on package travel, package holidays and package tours [1990] OJ L158/59 (Package Travel Directive).

[6] European Parliament and Council Regulation (EC) 261/2004 of 11 February 2004 establishing common rules on compensation and assistance to passengers in the event of denied boarding and of cancellation or long delay of flights, and repealing Regulation (EEC) No 295/91 OJ L 46/1 (Regulation 261).

[7] Commission, 'Bringing The EU Package Travel Rules into the Digital Age' COM(2013) 513 final, available at <http://ec.europa.eu/justice/consumer-marketing/files/com_2013_513_en.pdf>, accessed 28 January 2015; Commission, 'Commission acts to improve consumer rights for 120 million holiday makers' (Press Release) IP/13/663; European Parliament Resolution of 19 March 2012 on the functioning and application of established rights of people travelling by air [2011] INI 2150.

[8] Commission, 'European Parliament votes on air passenger rights' (Press Release) IP/14/119; Bureau Européen des Unions de Consumateurs Aisbl, 'Air Passenger's Rights. Revision of Regulation 261/04 on the rights of air passengers in the event of denied boarding, cancellation and long delays' (Bureau Européen Des Unions de Consumateurs Aisbl, 16 July 2013) 56, available at <www.beuc.org/publications/2013-00505-01-e.pdf>, accessed 28 January 2015; J Prassl, 'Reforming Air Passenger Rights in the European Union' (2014) 39 *Air and Space Law* 59, 60.

[9] Linking the air passengers' rights to European private law has already been argued for in the literature, eg J Karsten, 'Passengers, consumers, and travelers: The rise of passenger rights in EC transport law and its repercussions for Community consumer law and policy' (2007) 30 *Journal of Consumer Policy* 117, 120.

air passengers and consumers concluding contracts other than for air transport services, I consider whether these differences could be justified due to the need to protect the interests of one of the contractual parties, or due to the internal market's objectives.

To set the parameters for the intended comparison I analyse, first, justifications for introducing special protection measures in European consumer law and in the field of air transport services. It is important to examine how the European institutions have set up the legal framework within European private law for the adoption of these measures, and what similarities and differences there are. Within this section I also compare the notions of a 'passenger' and of a 'consumer', considering the possibility of either notion applying to natural persons purchasing goods or services at least partially for professional purposes. The following sections focus on specific rights that consumers have in European law when concluding contracts other than for air transport services. I begin with the illustration of consumers' information rights, followed by the description of various consumer remedies in case of non-performance or improper performance of a contract, finally discussing their right of withdrawal. In these three sections I present the European consumers' rights as established by the CRD, the Services Directive[10] and the PTD. The relevant provisions in these European consumer protection measures are compared to the rights granted to air passengers in Regulation 261, as well as in the European Commission's proposal for the new regulation on air passengers' rights (European Commission's Proposal)[11] and as amended by the European Parliament (European Parliament's Proposal).[12] This comparison will show that there are important differences in the framework of consumer and air passenger protection, not necessarily justified through differences in the services that consumers and air passengers respectively purchase. I also consider other justifications for the adoption of divergent protection measures, such as the aim to improve the internal market or to strengthen the position of weaker parties in European private law. None of the above-mentioned justifications seems overly convincing upon closer inspection. Therefore, I argue in the conclusions for further harmonisation

---

[10] European Parliament and Council Directive 2006/123/EC of 12 December 2006 on services in the internal market [2006] OJ L376/36 (Services Directive).

[11] Commission, 'Proposal for a Regulation amending Regulation (EC) 261 establishing common rules on compensation and assistance to passengers in the event of denied boarding and of cancellation or long delay of flights' (Proposal) COM(2013) 130 final (European Commission's Proposal).

[12] European Parliament, 'Legislative resolution of 5 February 2014 on the Proposal for a Regulation amending Regulation (EC) 261 establishing common rules on compensation and assistance to passengers in the event of denied boarding and of cancellation or long delay of flights COM(2013) 130 final' P7_TA-PROV (2014) 0092 (European Parliament's Proposal). I would like to remark here that while the air transport service providers have certain duties towards air passengers, they may not necessarily have a contractual relationship with them: the majority of European consumer law applies only to contractual relationships between consumers and service providers. However, for example, the Package Travel Directive also places certain obligations on travel organisers, even if the contract was concluded between a consumer and a travel retailer. Considering the current trend of purchasing air travel online directly from air transport service providers, it is also likely that the number of concluded contracts is growing. Therefore, this difference will not be discussed further in this chapter.

of European private law in the area of provision of services, so that positions of air passengers and consumers would be more similar. I consider both the extension of air passengers' rights in the proposal for the new air passengers' rights regulation, and the reduction of the scope of protection granted to European consumers concluding contracts for provision of other than air transport services. Lastly, I shall draw conclusions as to what European consumer law could learn from the current and from the forthcoming regulation of air passengers' rights in Europe.

II. Air Passengers' Rights v Consumers' Rights—Legal Framework and Notions

The introduction of specific air passengers' rights as well as of specific consumers' rights to the European private law system has been justified twofold. On the one hand, some academics see the explanation for the introduction of an additional protection in European contract law in the lack of bargaining power of one of the contractual parties.[13] Both consumers and air passengers have been considered as such weaker contractual parties, whose lives could be improved through an intervention of the European legislator on their behalf.[14] On the other hand, further development of certain sectors of the internal market, such as distance selling as well as air transport services, required the introduction of additional regulations, with the aim to set fair rules for cross-border competitors.[15] In order to strengthen the internal market and to prevent its failure, this additional protection also aims at counteracting existing information asymmetries between the parties.[16]

Interestingly, despite the fact that the European legislator justified the introduction of special protection measures in the areas of both consumer law and air transport services in the same way, the legislative bases used for the adoption of these measures differ. Regulation 261 has been adopted on the basis of Article 100(2) of the TFEU,[17] which gives the Member States the authority to adopt provisions on air transport, and not on the basis of Article 114 of the TFEU, which allows for the adoption of consumer protection measures to strengthen the internal market. It could be argued that the use of a different legal basis for the adoption of rules on air passengers' rights allowed the European institutions to interpret the notion of 'passengers' more broadly than what the traditional notion of a 'consumer' entails. In this way, the scope of application of air passengers' rights could

---

[13] JM Bech Serrat, 'Why is there a Separation between Distance Selling in EU Law and the Tourism Industry?' (2010) 33 *Journal of Consumer Policy* 75, 76.

[14] Regulation 261, Recitals (1) and (4); see also: Karsten (n 9) 121–22.

[15] Consumer Rights Directive, Recital (5); Regulation 261, Recital (4).

[16] eg KJ Cseres, 'What Has Competition Done for Consumers in Liberalised Markets?' (2008) 4 *Competition Law Review* 77; KG Grunert, 'The Consumer Information Deficit: Assessment and Policy Implications' (1984) 7 *Journal of Consumer Policy* 359.

[17] Treaty on the Functioning of the European Union [2007] OJ C326/1.

be broader than the scope of application of consumers' rights. Moreover, it could lead to the creation of a stand-alone system of air passengers' rights, not centred on the need to benefit the internal market. It seems plausible, however, that the European legislator could have introduced similar protection measures based on the general competence of consumer protection, especially since Article 12 of the TFEU requires the European institutions to consider demands of consumer protection when developing policies and actions in all areas.[18] And so, Recital (1) of Regulation 261 clearly states that the aim thereof is not only to ensure a high level of air passengers' protection, but also to take full account of general consumer protection measures. The choice to set Regulation 261 within the framework of European legal measures related to transport must have, therefore, been a political one. Aside from Regulation 261, the European legislator also based other measures that address passengers' rights in other transport services, for example in rail or road transport, on Article 100(2) of the TFEU.[19]

As mentioned above, the European legislator may have made the decision to adopt Regulation 261 on a basis different from that used for other European consumer protection measures, to broaden the scope of the notion of a 'passenger' in respect of that of a 'consumer'. Interestingly, though, Article 2 of Regulation 261 does not contain the notion of a 'passenger' in its definitions' list. It may only be certain that, just like the notion of a 'consumer', a 'passenger' refers to natural persons due to the character of the services offered.[20] However, no further limitations are imposed on the notion of a 'passenger' in Regulation 261. Neither the European Commission's Proposal nor the European Parliament's Proposal defines the 'passenger', and for this reason I shall briefly address the benefits and disadvantages of introducing such a definition into European consumer law, harmonised with the existing definitions of a 'consumer' either in the CRD or in the PTD.

European consumer law generally defines consumers narrowly, for example in Article 2(1) of the CRD, as 'any natural person who … is acting for purposes which are outside his trade, business, craft or profession'. The scope of this definition excludes from consumer protection not only persons acting for professional

---

[18] N Reich, 'A European Contract Law, or an EU Contract Law Regulation for Consumers?' (2005) 28 *Journal of Consumer Policy* 383, 399.

[19] European Parliament and Council Regulation (EC) 1371/2007 of 23 October 2007 on rail passengers' rights and obligations [2007] OJ L315/14; European Parliament and Council Regulation (EU) 181/2011 of 16 February 2011 concerning the rights of passengers in bus and coach transport [2011] OJ L55/1. The rights granted to passengers in these other European measures have not been harmonised and, generally, the scope of protection of air passengers is the broadest. Currently, the European institutions are also considering harmonisation of the whole area of passenger law, regardless of the transportation method used, eg European Parliament, 'Transport Committee calls for a fair deal for all passengers' (Press Release, 28 February 2012), available at <www.europarl.europa.eu/news/en/pressroom/content/20120227IPR39347/html/Air-travel-Transport-Committee-calls-for-a-fair-deal-for-all-passengers>, accessed 28 January 2015; European Parliament resolution of 23 October 2012 on passenger rights in all transport modes [2012] INI 2067.

[20] J Luzak, 'The quest for transparency of flight prices to enable passengers' informed choice' (2013) 3 *Zeitschrift für Europäisches Unternehmens- und Verbraucherrecht* 170, 174; Karsten (n 9) 131.

purposes, but also those acting for mixed purposes.[21] If the European legislator had introduced this definition into Regulation 261 then air passengers travelling not only for business but also combining travel for business and pleasure would have been left out of its scope of application, even if the latter purpose of travel was predominant.[22] After all, the CJEU decided in its judgment in *Gruber v Bay Wa AG* that unless the professional purpose of a person's action had a merely negligible character, this person could not qualify as a consumer.[23] It is hard to imagine that a court would attach such a qualification of negligibility to mixed purpose travel, since in many cases the business opportunity determines the travel's destination and timing. Therefore, if a lucky traveller managed to add some free time to her business trip, the main characteristics thereof would still have been determined by the traveller's professional needs. This definition would thus hardly be practical to introduce in the area of air transport services.

The 'consumer' notion is not homogeneous in European consumer law and, for example, the PTD, another travel-related European measure, in Article 2(4) defines a consumer as 'a person who takes or agrees to take the package'. This provision clearly does not refer to the requirement that the consumer's travel has to be conducted only for personal purposes. Therefore, travellers could also enjoy the protection of the PTD if they purchased travel packages for professional purposes.[24] If the European legislator defined the 'passenger' in Regulation 261 accordingly, then any person who purchased air transport services, regardless of their purpose, would be encompassed by the scope of protection of Regulation 261. Preferably, the European Commission's Proposal would introduce the notion of a 'traveller' instead of a 'passenger', to harmonise it with the currently drafted proposal for the new rules on package travel.[25] While the introduction of the notion of a 'traveller' to both the European Commission's Proposal and the Proposal for the PTD would distinguish it further from the notion of a 'consumer', it would help to achieve more clarity and consistency as to the scope of these notions. In this respect, the travel sector would be a step ahead of European consumer law, where the definition of a 'consumer', instead of being related to the type of contract being concluded, depends on the purpose of the transaction as

---

[21] *cf* Consumer Rights Directive, Recital (17).

[22] On the effects of the introduction of such an artificial distinction, see also Karsten (n 9) 128.

[23] Case C-464/01 *Johann Gruber v Bay Wa AG* [2005] ECR I-439. Of course, whether this decision, made by the CJEU to interpret rules of European private international law, would apply in European substantive consumer law could be contested. *Cf* opinion of AG Cruz Villalón, case C-110/14 *Costea* [2015] ECLI:EU:C:2015:538, para 41–47. Unfortunately, in its judgment of 3 September 2015 in this case, the CJEU did not deliberate on this issue.

[24] Karsten (n 9) 129.

[25] Commission, 'Proposal for a Directive on package travel and assisted travel arrangements' (Proposal) COM(2013) 512 final (Proposal for Package Travel Directive), Art 3(6). This provision introduces a new notion of a 'traveller', but it still allows both travellers for business- or non-business-related purposes to enjoy the consumer protection measures of this Directive. It excludes from its scope only persons travelling on the basis of a framework contract concluded with a trader specialising in the arrangement of business travel. See also Karsten (n 9) 126, arguing for a harmonised definition of a 'passenger'.

well.[26] The European institutions have already made an attempt to broaden the scope of protection of European consumer law to mixed purposes transactions in the preparatory works on the CRD. In the end, however, the final version of the CRD still narrowly defines consumers in its Article 2(1). Only Recital (17) of the CRD mentions a possibility to apply its provisions to dual purpose contracts, where the professional purpose of the transaction is not predominant.[27]

Considering that the European legislator has set the same legal objectives for Regulation 261 and for the European consumer protection measures, in the following sections I compare their provisions. I indicate to what extent European consumer law measures could provide additional protection to air passengers by granting them information rights, additional remedies and the right of withdrawal, if not for the fact that the European legislator explicitly excluded their application to passenger transport services. The European legislator supported some of these exclusions with the argument that air passengers are already protected by other European measures.[28] In order to verify this statement, I compare the rights of, respectively, consumers and air passengers, to establish whether air passengers indeed enjoy similar rights when they are not included in the scope of application of European consumer protection measures.

More specifically, I examine whether air passengers have the same rights as other consumers concluding distance selling contracts for the provision of other than air transport services. Since nowadays air passengers often book their flights online, they conclude, therefore, more distance selling contracts. The applicability of provisions on consumer distance selling as currently regulated by the CRD to such contracts, could provide air passengers with an additional layer of protection.[29] However, the European legislator has excluded passenger transport services from the scope of application of the CRD's provisions in its Article 3(3)(k), following the reasoning that they are already subject to other European legislation.[30] Only a few provisions of the CRD may still grant more protection to such air passengers who are travelling just for pleasure and could be considered consumers. For example, the prohibition on service providers' charging fees resulting from a consumer's choice of payment at a cost exceeding their actual expenses.[31]

Additionally, I look into the PTD's provisions, since they could apply to air passengers, but only when they purchased air transport services as part of the 'package travel' as defined in Article 2(a) of the PTD. If a travel agency would book the air passenger's transportation alongside her accommodation or other tourist services, and the travel would last longer than 24 hours and the whole tourist package

---

[26] Especially if the notion of the 'traveller' were to be introduced to other passenger regulations.
[27] It remains to be seen to what extent national courts and the CJEU will apply the Consumer Rights Directive's rules to mixed purpose contracts in practice. *Cf* opinion of AG Cruz Villalón (n 23) para 41–47.
[28] eg Consumer Rights Directive, Recital (27).
[29] Bech Serrat (n 13) 76, 88.
[30] Consumer Rights Directive, Recital (27); against Bech Serrat (n 13) 77–79.
[31] eg Consumer Rights Directive, Art 19 together with Art 3(3)(k).

was prearranged, this would fall under the notion of the 'package travel'. The CJEU determined, in its judgment in *Club-Tour v Garrido*, that if a consumer arranged the package together with a trip organiser prior to the contract's conclusion, the national court should still perceive such services as a prearranged package.[32] Regardless of a certain flexibility thus added to the interpretation of the notion of 'package travel' in practice, and even with the European institutions currently working on a more flexible notion of 'package travel' for the new proposal for the PTD,[33] some air passengers would still fall outside this definition. Therefore, they could not enjoy the PTD's protection, for example with regard to the possibility to claim non-material damages due to the non-performance of air transport service providers.[34] Since the modern travel sector is very dynamic, it could be beneficial and more up-to-date to discard the notion of 'package travel' altogether. Instead, the European legislator could jointly regulate any travel-related contracts, whether they would concern transportation arrangements, accommodation, tourist services or any combination of the above-mentioned services, regardless of whether they were offered or arranged through one or more service providers.[35] Therefore, the following comparison of the PTD's provision to the provisions of Regulation 261 could also clarify existing differences in the protection granted to various travellers in Europe.

Lastly, I consider what impact the Services Directive could have had on air passengers' protection if it had applied to passenger transport services. The Services Directive aims to benefit European consumers concluding contracts for the provision of services. At the moment, however, the Services Directive excludes, in its Article 2(2)(d), its application to services in the field of transport, without justifying this choice.[36] I briefly examine what kind of rights air passengers could enjoy if the Services Directive applied to them too.

III. Information Rights

A. Scope

Regulation 261 requires air service providers to inform air passengers in full about their rights in the event of cancellation, long delay or denied boarding.[37] Amongst other things, air passengers should receive full disclosure of their rights to assistance and compensation. This disclosure should mention when air passengers

---

[32] Case C-400/00 *Club-Tour v Garrido* [2002] ECLI:EU:C:2002:272.

[33] Proposal for Package Travel Directive, Art 3(2).

[34] Case C-168/00 *Leitner v Tui Deutschland GmbH & Co* [2002] ECLI:EU:C:2002:163 interpreting Package Travel Directive, Art 5.

[35] eg Commission, 'Bringing The EU Package Travel Rules into the Digital Age' (n 7).

[36] Services Directive, Recitals (17) and (21).

[37] Regulation 261, Recital (20).

obtain their rights, their scope and how to claim them. This disclosure's scope signifies that Regulation 261 aims to grant air passengers information rights with regard either to the non-performance of the air transport service provider's main contractual obligations, in the case of the flight's cancellation or denied boarding, or to their improper performance, in the case of the flight's long delay. Consequently, Regulation 261 does not address the issue of other disclosures that could be relevant for air passengers, for example with relation to the air transport service's characteristics, or to contractual rights and obligations of the parties in situations other than non-performance or improper performance by the air transport service provider. This is the main difference between the scope of information rights as provided in Regulation 261, and those provided in the other European consumer law measures analysed here. All three European consumer law measures discussed below, which could potentially apply to air transport services, provide a longer, more detailed list of information that the service provider or a trader has to give to consumers.

The CRD specifies in Article 6 what information traders need to provide to consumers concluding either distance or off-premises contracts, or, in Article 5, any other contracts. Contrary to the information provisions in Regulation 261, these two provisions not only aim to inform consumers about their rights in the case of non-performance of the contract, but are more general in nature. That is to say, they refer to all contractual rights and obligations of the parties, requiring definition of the main characteristics of the purchased services, etc. Keeping this in mind, it is surprising that the European legislator decided to exclude contracts for the provision of air transport services from the CRD's scope of application. After all, air passengers may need extensive pre-contractual and contractual information, just like customers in any other service transaction.[38] For example, if an air passenger books a flight online, she concludes a distance contract and could benefit from the mandatory information on the main characteristics of the provided air service, information on the trader's identity and geographical address, etc. Just like any other customer of an online service provider, such an air passenger will not be directly in touch with the air transport service provider. She may thus not have much knowledge about the provider and, consequently, may not be aware how to contact the provider when it improperly performs the service and when its representatives are not present at the airport.[39] Aside from the better-known, bigger air transport service providers, which even a first-time traveller can easily identify, there are many small, local air transport service providers operating in Europe. Therefore, a first-time air passenger in particular could have difficulties trying to establish the service provider's reputation and contact details, particularly since many flights are nowadays performed jointly by various airlines.

As has already been mentioned, the Services Directive also excludes air transport services contracts from its scope of application. Without this exclusion, air

---

[38] Bech Serrat (n 13) 77.
[39] ibid, 76.

passengers could have been entitled to the special protection granted to service users in the Services Directive. For example, Article 7 of the Services Directive ensures that service providers inform their consumers about the means of redress against such service providers, as well as of contact details of competent authorities responsible for the enforcement of these rules. Article 22 of the Services Directive prescribes what information service providers should reveal to consumers with respect to their respective contractual rights and obligations, for example the main features and price of the service, insurance details, the existence of after-sale guarantees, the name and contact details of the service provider. These information requirements are, therefore, again more general than the information requirements under Regulation 261, since they cover the whole contractual relationship between the parties and do not only refer to the consequences of non-performance or improper performance by the service provider. These information duties bind service providers alongside the information duties specified in the CRD, pursuant to Article 6(8) of the CRD.

An organiser or a retailer of a package travel needs to provide similar information to consumers concluding package travel contracts, pursuant to Articles 3 and 4 of the PTD. These provisions are, however, again unlikely to apply to air passengers unless they have purchased a whole package travel, apart from their air transport services. The scope of the information rights granted to consumers in the PTD is more travel-orientated. Therefore, if these provisions applied to air passengers, this could benefit them more than if only the provisions of the CRD applied to them. For example, while the CRD requires in general the identification of the main characteristics of services that consumers plan to purchase, the PTD specifies that an organiser or a retailer of package travel needs to inform consumers about the travel's itinerary, meal plan, general passport and visa requirements, health formalities, insurance policies, etc. This specificity could grant more certainty to both parties to an air transport services contract, regarding what information air passengers need to receive. Additionally, both directives require that the consumer is informed about the contact details of the service provider (CRD) or of the travel organiser (PTD), so that she can easily refer to this information if the contract is improperly performed. Travelling consumers who may benefit from travel-specific information rights in the PTD could still, however, require the more general consumer protection granted to them by the CRD. After all, the European legislator specifically tailored certain provisions of the CRD to the conclusion of distance contracts and to the uniqueness of providing information to consumers at a distance. For instance, Article 6(1)(f) of the CRD obliges service providers to inform consumers about the cost of using the means of distance communication for the contract's conclusion, whenever that cost differs from the basic rate that a consumer could have expected.[40] If this provision applied to air transport services, then if an air passenger decided to book his flight on the phone, and the use of the

---

[40] The same exclusion applies to package travel contracts, which are also often concluded at a distance and where consumers could benefit from this additional level of protection as well.

telephone line of the air transport service provider would incur a special, higher than usual charge, the provider would need to inform the air passenger of that fact, clearly and in advance.

In general, the scope of the information rights in the European consumer law measures analysed above is much broader than in Regulation 261. Surprisingly, while the European legislator has repeatedly considered provision of certain information necessary for the proper conclusion of a consumer contract, it does not establish it as mandatory information for contracts for the provision of air transport services. The European Commission's Proposal aims to 'proactively inform passengers about their rights', but it still defines air passengers' right to information as the 'right to information about the flight disruption'.[41] This right consists of information about air passengers' rights in the case of flight disruption, as well as their right to be informed about the disruption's cause. However, it does not extend the air transport service provider's information duties so as to require the provision of information on the parties' contractual rights and obligations, or on the characteristics of the service.[42] Air passengers will thus only receive information about the complaint handling procedures of a given air transport service provider, and about the claims they have at their disposal, including necessary contact details to file a complaint, as well as information about competent complaint handling bodies.[43] Air passengers are also supposed to receive this information when they booked their tickets through an intermediary established in a Member State.[44]

The European Parliament does not consider that this draft sufficiently clarifies the question of who has responsibility for informing stranded air passengers about their rights, and who is then responsible for providing them with care, assistance and reimbursement. Therefore, the European Parliament calls for the introduction of further information duties that would be more specific.[45] It would also like to oblige air transport service providers to inform air passengers about the 'simplest and most rapid' procedures for making claims and complaints.[46] Furthermore, the European Parliament suggests that air transport service providers should procure accurate and objective information about the environmental impact and energy efficiency of air passengers' travel, and share it with the latter.[47] This addition is interesting, since for the first time it exceeds the original scope of the information duties, that is only informing air passengers about their rights when the air transport service is not performed properly. This suggests that the European Parliament could supplement its Proposal with even further-reaching information duties. For instance, it could follow the example set out in the above-discussed

---

[41] European Commission's Proposal, Explanatory Memorandum ss 1.1 and 3.3.1.1.
[42] European Commission's Proposal, Recital (20).
[43] European Commission's Proposal, Recital (22) and Art 16a(1).
[44] European Commission's Proposal, Recital (20).
[45] European Parliament's Proposal, amendment 13.
[46] European Parliament's Proposal, amendment 25.
[47] European Parliament's Proposal, amendment 116.

European consumer law measures, and attempt to introduce more generic and important information duties to the European Commission's Proposal.

B. Formal Requirements

A novelty, in comparison with other European consumer laws, is the formal requirement, introduced in Article 14(1) of Regulation 261, regarding how to notify air passengers of their rights. This provision requires a notification to be displayed at the check-in desks, stating:

> If you are denied boarding or if your flight is cancelled or delayed for at least two hours, ask at the check-in counter or boarding gate for the text stating your rights, particularly with regard to compensation and assistance.

This statement, with this exact wording, has to constitute a part of a clearly legible notice displayed to consumers. As described below, other European consumer law measures limit themselves to demanding the legibility and clarity of disclosures, without dictating to service providers at the outset how to inform consumers that they have certain rights to obtain disclosures. The air transport service providers need to provide the information on air passengers' rights in writing, and must list all air passengers' rights, as well as contact details of the national designated body responsible for the enforcement of Regulation 261, pursuant to Article 14(2). Air passengers should therefore know the information to which they are entitled, and to whom they should complain if they do not receive it or do not receive it in a timely fashion. Currently, air service transport providers are incentivised by Regulation 261 to inform air passengers of the cancellation of flights or long delays before the scheduled departure time, as well as of re-routing possibilities in such circumstances.[48]

The CRD entails a few provisions listing the formal requirements applicable to the provision of information.[49] How the information is to reach consumers depends on the contract's type, in general, however, all information needs to be drafted in 'plain and intelligible language' and, for example, in the case of distance contracts it has to be provided to consumers 'in a way appropriate to the means of distance communication used'. The European legislator has not specified in the CRD how the consumer's attention should be drawn to the fact that she has certain information rights. There is no provision similar to Article 14(1) of Regulation 261 in the CRD that would determine that traders and service providers need to clearly and in a standardised manner inform consumers about their information rights. Moreover, contrary to Regulation 261, the provisions of the CRD do not set a specific timeframe for traders and service providers to give consumers the information about changes in the service, and do not attach specific

---

[48] Regulation 261, Recital (12). The incentive is further discussed in section III.D below on sanctions.
[49] Consumer Rights Directive, Arts 7 and 8.

consequences if this information is conveyed late. The only exception to this rule is the consequence determined in the CRD for delay in providing consumers with information about their right of withdrawal.[50]

The organiser of a package travel has to notify consumers 'as quickly as possible' that it intends to change the essential contractual terms, pursuant to Article 4(5) of the PTD. Other information needs to be provided to consumers 'in good time before the start of the journey', in writing or in any other appropriate form. Again, therefore, just like with the CRD, there is no specific timeframe given to service providers regarding provision of this information, nor is there an incentive to act within this timeframe. Neither does the PTD determine how the consumer is to receive notification about all the information rights to which she is entitled. Furthermore, the PTD does not even require the information to be provided in a legible and clear form.

Pursuant to Article 22(2) of the Services Directive, service providers need to reveal the required information to consumers of their own initiative. They should also make sure that their customers can easily access this information in the place where the service is provided or the contract is concluded. This resembles the provision under Regulation 261 in drawing the consumer's attention to the fact that she has certain information rights, but, unlike in Regulation 261, the language of the notification is not standardised in the Services Directive. The required information has to be provided 'in a clear and unambiguous manner, and in good time before conclusion of the contract or, where there is no written contract, before the service is provided', pursuant to Article 22(4) of the Services Directive. Again, this provision simply gives air transport service providers a general timeframe for conveying all the information to consumers, without granting them any incentives to do so; and it does not introduce certainty between the parties as to how and when this information should be provided.

The formal requirements adopted in Regulation 261 are, therefore, quite unique among the European consumer law measures, and seem to grant more legal certainty as between the contracting parties. Behavioural researchers had previously showed that a trader could more easily capture the consumer's attention through the use of a standardised message, as well as that disclosures could be more effective if they informed consumers separately that they have certain information rights.[51] It would be interesting to conduct a study into whether such standardised disclosures to air passengers do indeed reach them more easily, and whether they perhaps also leave them better informed than non-harmonised European

---

[50] Further discussed in section III.D below on sanctions.

[51] On drawing attention through repetitive, standardised message display, see, eg, C Castro *et al*, 'Worded and Symbolic Traffic Sign Stimuli Analysis Using Repetition Priming and Semantic Priming Effects' (2007) 53 *Advances in Psychology Research* 17; JR Bettman, MF Luce and JW Payne, 'Constructive Consumer Choice Processes' (1998) 25 *Journal of Consumer Research* 187; C Pechmann and DW Stewart, 'Advertising Repetition: A Critical Review of Wearin and Wearout' (1990) 11 *Current Issues and Research in Advertising* 285.

consumer law disclosures. It should also be mentioned here that the introduction of an economic incentive for the air transport service providers to provide their customers with the mandatory information in a timely fashion is a novelty in European contract law. Although the Services Directive clearly states that provision of information to consumers should occur on the service provider's initiative,[52] it still does not sanction non-performance of this obligation. With respect to its formal requirements regarding information rights, Regulation 261 might, therefore, be a step ahead of other European consumer law measures in ensuring the information's effectiveness.[53] Of course, whether these additional incentives and notifications actually work in practice, and whether the European legislator should consider their adoption with respect to other disclosures to European consumers, should first be empirically tested.

The new Article 14 of the European Commission's Proposal still provides for a standardised notice about air passengers' information rights. The novelty is that air transport service providers will now need to place this notice not only on check-in desks, but also on self-service check-in machines. Considering the development of the airports' structure, including the possibility of air passengers checking-in for their flight online and never having to approach the check-in desk at the airport, this development follows at least partially these new trends. Some air passengers may still not check in their luggage, and therefore will use neither the check-in desk nor the self-service check-in machine. For them, it could be handy to display general notices throughout the airport, or to provide them on the air transport service provider's website during the air passenger's online check-in. Interestingly, the European Parliament suggested introducing an amendment that would oblige air transport service providers to set up contact points at airports, where air passengers could obtain the necessary information.[54] These contact points should be open not only during the air transport service provider's operating hours, but also until the last air passenger disembarks from the last plane.[55] The information duties rest no longer only on air transport service providers, but also on the airport's managing body, which needs to ensure that information on air passengers' rights is clearly displayed in the air passengers' area of the airport.[56] Furthermore, in order to ensure that passengers' complaints and claims are handled more effectively in the future, the European Commission's Proposal establishes a duty for

---

[52] For the Consumer Rights Directive this has been clarified in the CJEU's judgment in Case C-49/11 *Content Services Ltd v Bundesarbeitskammer* (ECJ, 6 March 2012).

[53] Of course, this will only hold true if these information obligations are performed properly and in a timely fashion by the air transport service providers, and when enforcement of compliance with the Regulation's provisions is efficient.

[54] European Parliament's Proposal, amendments 14, 68 and 106.

[55] European Parliament's Proposal, amendment 106. This amendment could be improved further by obliging the contact point's employees to wait for the moment when the last passenger collects her checked-in baggage and leaves the airport, since only then might the air transport service provider be reasonably sure that no more assistance would be necessary.

[56] European Commission's Proposal, Art 14(4).

air transport service providers to disclose certain information to passengers at the time of making the reservation.[57]

Another amendment introduced by the European Parliament addresses the issue of air passengers' not always obtaining relevant information about their flight in good time. Therefore, the amendment proposes that air transport service providers inform air passengers about their flight's cancellation or delay at the latest 30 minutes after the scheduled departure time, and as soon as possible about the new estimated departure time.[58] If the ticket was issued by a European intermediary and not directly by the air transport service provider, then the air passenger needs to consent explicitly in writing to the transfer of her contact details to the air transport service provider. The European Commission outlined that this consent might only be given on an 'opt-in' basis.[59] The air transport service provider may use such acquired contact details to inform air passengers about any changes to a flight, but is required to delete the acquired air passenger data within 72 hours of the completion of the contract of carriage.

Under the European Commission's Proposal, air transport service providers would need to provide air passengers with electronic means to submit a complaint. They are also obliged to confirm receipt of the air passenger's complaint within eight days thereof, and to respond to the air passenger's claim or complaint within two months.[60] The European Parliament also argues for the introduction of a formal requirement that air transport service providers issue, on the electronic tickets and on all versions of boarding cards, clearly legible and transparent information about the air passengers' rights and about the contact details that are necessary to ask for help and assistance.[61] Another suggestion put forward by the Parliament is to oblige air transport service providers to procure accessible and effective telephone assistance for all air passengers who have booked their flight. Using this telephone line should not cost air passengers more than if they were making a local call.[62] Furthermore, any electronic communication made to the air passenger to notify her about the flight's cancellation, long delay or change of schedule, shall, in a prominent manner, state that the air passenger is entitled to compensation and assistance under Regulation 261.[63]

---

[57] European Commission's Proposal, Explanatory Memorandum s 3.3.1.3. This information would explain, amongst other things, the air carriers' claim and complaint-handling procedures, provide electronic means to submit complaints and give information about competent handling bodies.

[58] European Commission's Proposal, Art 14(5).

[59] European Commission's Proposal, Art 14(6).

[60] European Commission's Proposal, Explanatory Memorandum point 3.3.1.3. and Art 16a(2). Interestingly, Recital (22) only mentions the obligation to respond to passengers' complaints within a reasonable time period, while the Parliament's amendment changes it to 'the shortest period possible', without further specifying this deadline either (amendment 28).

[61] European Parliament's Proposal, amendment 107.

[62] European Parliament's Proposal, amendment 113. This amendment is consistent with the general trend of obliging service providers not to overcharge their customers for using telephone helpdesks provided by these service providers: see, eg, Consumer Rights Directive, Art 21.

[63] European Parliament's Proposal, amendment 117.

C. Burden of Proof

Article 5(4) of Regulation 261 specifies that the air transport service provider has the burden of proving that it informed the air passenger of the cancellation. The CRD also places the burden of proof, that the trader provided the information to the consumer, on the trader.[64] Equally, the Services Directive declares that the burden of proof that the information was provided to consumers rests on service providers.[65] Only the PTD does not expressly address the issue of the burden of proof, but it is hard to imagine why a different division of the burden of proof should apply with respect to the fulfilment of these information duties. The new proposal does not change this default.[66] This is one area where the discussed measures are similar.

D. Sanctions for the Breach of Information Duties

Regulation 261 tries to incentivise air transport service providers to notify their customers about the flight's cancellation in good time. Air transport service providers may avoid the need to compensate air passengers just by notifying them about the cancelled flight well in advance of the scheduled departure time.[67] The necessity to compensate air passengers if they are not informed about the flight's cancellation in a timely manner is a very clear sanction for the breach of the air transport service providers' information duties. It could serve as an example for other European consumer law measures, since they often do not prescribe either a specific timeframe within which a trader or a service provider has to give the information to consumers, or a specific sanction for non-performance of such information duties. Additionally, Regulation 261 clearly prevents potential attempts by air transport service providers at undermining it with regard to their obligation to pay compensation to air passengers. When an air passenger receives incorrect information about the compensation due to her as a result of a cancelled or a delayed flight, and accepts an amount of compensation lower than the one to which she is entitled, Article 15(2) of Regulation 261 determines that this does not discharge her right to claim additional compensation that would normally be awarded to her. The CJEU has also decided, in its judgment in *Rodríguez v Air France*, that when the air transport service provider does not inform a consumer about the assistance to which she is entitled in the case of a flight's cancellation or a long delay, that consumer does not have an obligation to inquire about that assistance with the air transport service provider. Instead, she may claim the reimbursement

---

[64] Consumer Rights Directive, Art 6(9).
[65] Services Directive, Art 27(4).
[66] European Parliament's Proposal, amendment 127.
[67] If they follow the timeframe set in Art 5(1)(c) of Regulation 261.

of costs she has incurred to provide herself with necessary assistance, for example in the form of meals and refreshment.[68]

The CRD does not contain any sanction for breach of the duty to inform consumers, with two exceptions. If a service provider does not fully and properly inform a consumer about all additional charges or costs relating to her purchase of a given service, or when she receives no information about the cost of returning this service when she chooses to exercise her right of withdrawal, then the consumer may not be charged these additional costs.[69] Secondly, if the service provider does not give consumer the information about her right of withdrawal, then the cooling-off period is prolonged by 12 months.[70] If the service provider then provides this information to the consumer within this 12-month timeframe, the cooling-off period starts running from the day on which the consumer receives this information. These sanctions may bring about significant economic consequences for service providers, unless they comply with the relevant information duties. However, the CRD contains a long list of information duties, and the European legislator introduced sanctions with respect to breach of only a few of them. A general conclusion as to the service providers' motivation to comply with these information duties thus has to be that it may vary, depending on what sanctions the Member States introduce at the national level for breach of those duties.[71]

Unfortunately, neither the PTD nor the Services Directive specifies any sanctions for breach of any of the information duties set out in those directives. The Services Directive clearly leaves any such sanctions to be determined by national laws of the Member States.[72]

Legal scholars have argued for the introduction of harmonised sanctions for the breach of information duties at a European level.[73] The lack of effective enforcement of consumer rights often results either from the lack of specificity and certainty with regard to the scope of the rights that have been granted to consumers, or, indeed, from the gap in defining the consequences for non-performance of the professional parties' obligations towards consumers.[74] In this respect, while the European legislator has traditionally left it to the Member States to introduce sanctions for the breach of contractual information duties towards consumers, so that they can adjust them to better fit their national legal systems, this flexibility should only accompany, and not act as a substitute for, more general European sanctions.

---

[68] Case C-83/10 *Rodríguez v Air France* [2011] ECR I-09469, para 45.

[69] Consumer Rights Directive, Art 6(6).

[70] Consumer Rights Directive, Art 10.

[71] Art 24 of the Consumer Rights Directive obliges the Member States to introduce effective, proportionate and deterrent sanctions, but their scope and effectiveness may differ.

[72] Services Directive, Art 27(4).

[73] eg C Twigg-Flesner and D Metcalfe, 'The Proposed Consumer Rights Directive—Less Haste, More Thought?' (2009) 5 *European Review of Contract Law* 368, 380–81; W van Boom and M Loos, 'Effective Enforcement of Consumer Law in Europe' (2008), available at <http://ssrn.com/abstract=1082913>, accessed 28 January 2015, 6–7; Cseres (n 16) 87.

[74] eg A Ogus, M Faure and N Philipsen, 'Best Practices for Consumer Policy: Report on the Effectiveness of Enforcement Regimes' (2006) OECD DSTI/CP(2006)21/FINAL.

The European Commission's Proposal leaves in place the above-described sanctions that are already binding under the current Regulation 261. The European Parliament's amendments to the proposal introduce a new sanction for the air transport service provider when it fails to respond in a timely manner and thoroughly to the air passenger's complaint. In such a situation, the air transport service provider will be deemed to have accepted the air passenger's claims.[75] This measure could increase the efficiency of enforcement of air passengers' claims, since the air passenger could then use a presumption of her claim's acceptance in a case against the air transport service provider. Moreover, the European Parliament argues that the air transport service provider should be obliged to issue to the air passenger a written notice about the reason for the existence of any extraordinary circumstances that have caused the flight's cancellation or delay. If it does not provide such a written notice to air passengers, passengers would be entitled to claim compensation.[76] The adoption of this provision could also improve air passengers' protection by minimising the air transport service provider's ability to change the reason for the flight's cancellation or delay after the air passenger has already raised her claim, by suddenly bringing up extraordinary circumstances as an excuse.[77]

IV. Remedies

Since the main focus of Regulation 261 is to grant rights to air passengers in the case of non-performance or improper performance of the air transport service provider's obligations, it is not surprising that at its core lies the regulation of air passengers' remedies. When air passengers are denied boarding, when their flight is cancelled or when it is delayed for a long time, they enjoy four general rights: reimbursement, re-routing, assistance and care, as well as compensation.[78] Pursuant to Article 8 of Regulation 261, the right to reimbursement obliges air transport service providers to return to air passengers the full cost of the ticket at the price at which it was bought for the part of the journey not yet made. Since the air transport service provider does not fulfil its part of the contract, it should not benefit from the fact that the air passenger performed her contractual obligation to pay the full price of the air transport service. This rule prevents unjust enrichment of air transport service providers and leads to the partial termination of a contractual relationship, since the parties need to return those benefits that they have received during the contract's duration for which no counter-performance has

---

[75] European Parliament's Proposal, amendment 128.
[76] European Parliament's Proposal, amendment 65.
[77] For references to such practices see, eg, Prassl (n 8) 62; S Garben, 'Sky-high Controversy and High-flying Claims? The *Sturgeon* Case Law in Light of Judicial Activism, Euroscepticism and Eurolegalism' (2013) 50 *CML Rev* 15, 17.
[78] Regulation 261, Arts 7–9.

been provided. Re-routing, defined in the same Article of Regulation 261, obliges air transport service providers to continue with the performance of their contractual obligations to help the air passenger reach her originally chosen destination. When the air transport service provider does not perform, or improperly performs, its original contractual obligation, the air passenger has a choice between claiming reimbursement, and thus terminating the contract, or re-routing, which gives the air transport service provider an additional chance to perform its obligations. Additionally, in certain cases of non-performance or improper performance by the air transport service provider, the air passenger may acquire a right to compensation.[79] This right aims to abstractly compensate air passengers at least for some inconvenience they have experienced due to the non-performance or improper performance of the air transport service provider's obligations. At the same time, this right does not prevent air passengers from raising other claims they may have against the air transport service provider if they suffered any damage as a result of the breach of its contractual obligations.[80] Lastly, due to the fact that, on the one hand, it is not always immediately obvious whether the air transport service provider will have a chance to perform its contractual obligations and, on the other hand, that the air passenger, as a result of a flight's cancellation or a long delay, may be unexpectedly stranded in a foreign place, the air passenger receives certain additional rights to assistance and care.[81]

While Regulation 261 grants a very specific set of remedies to air passengers, other European travellers may be less certain of their rights. For example, when we look at Article 5 of the PTD, we may notice that the Directive leaves it to the Member States to determine what remedies should be granted to consumers who have purchased package travel, when this contract is then subsequently improperly performed, or not performed at all. However, the few rights that the European legislator has specified in the PTD correspond with the rights that air passengers have under Regulation 261. Accordingly, if the organiser cancels the package before the agreed date of departure, the consumer has the right either to a substitute package of equivalent or higher quality, or to reimbursement pursuant to Article 4(6) of the PTD. These two rights correspond to the air passengers' rights of re-routing or reimbursement. The choice between these rights is similarly left to the consumer. A consumer is also supposed to be promptly assisted when she finds herself in difficulties due to the improper performance, or lack of performance, of the package travel contract. However, the European legislator has not determined the scope of this right to assistance further, contrary to what we find in the provisions of Regulation 261. Lastly, Article 5 of the PTD specifies that the organiser and/or

---

[79] For details as to the amounts of compensation see, eg, Regulation 261, Art 7. Due to the CJEU's judgment in Case C-402/07 *Sturgeon v Others* [2009] ECR I-10923, this compensation is due to air passengers not only in the event of the flight's cancellation, but also on its delay.

[80] Regulation 261, Art 12. See also *Rodriguez* (n 68).

[81] For description of these rights see, eg Regulation 261, Art 9. See also Case C-12/11 *McDonagh v Ryanair* (ECJ, 31 January 2013).

retailer of package travel is liable for any damage the consumer has suffered as the result of the improper performance, or lack of performance, of the package travel contract. From the CJEU's judgment in *Leitner v Tui Deutschland GmbH & Co*,[82] we know that this encompasses both material and non-material damage the consumer might have suffered. This provision does not, however, provide for compensation *in abstracto*, unrelated to the consumer's damage. In this respect, the scope of protection granted in Regulation 261 is broader than in the PTD.

The CRD and the Services Directive do not provide any remedies to consumers, leaving it to the Member States to regulate issues relating to the non-performance or improper performance of a given contract. Traditionally, consumer law remedies in case of non-performance or improper performance of a contract have been divided into two groups, depending on whether they give traders another chance to perform their original contractual obligations,[83] or whether they allow consumers to terminate the contractual relationship and to claim damages or repayment of (a part of) the price.[84] If a consumer has more than one remedy at her disposal, she usually has the ability to choose between them.[85] Of the remedies mentioned above, it is clear that only re-routing enables air transport service providers to perform their contractual obligations anew, and that, on the other hand, reimbursement signifies the end of the contractual relationship. The air passenger's free choice between these two remedies complies with the general default used in European consumer law. At first glance, the air passenger's right to compensation could be compared to the consumer's right to claim damages resulting from non-performance or improper performance of other contracts. However, this right is not related to any actual damage that an air passenger has suffered; on the contrary, the air passenger retains the right to claim compensation in the amount prescribed by Regulation 261 just as a result of the non-performance of the air transport service provider's contractual obligation. This right to compensation resembles, then, more a penalty imposed on the air transport service provider for improper or lack of performance of its contractual obligations, and is intended to provide it with an incentive to prevent such situations from happening. It could also be compared to a price reduction, since the air passenger receives not an agreed service but a service of a lesser quality, for example due to

---

[82] *Leitner* (n 34).

[83] eg in case of non-conforming goods, this would be the right to repair or replacement, pursuant to the Consumer Sales Directive; see, eg, European Parliament and Council Directive 1999/44/EC of 25 May 1999 on certain aspects of the sale of consumer goods and associated guarantees [1999] OJ L171/12 (Consumer Sales Directive).

[84] Consumer Sales Directive, Art 3(2) prescribes here a possibility to terminate the contract or to demand a price reduction (partial termination).

[85] eg Consumer Sales Directive, Art 3. However, the Consumer Sales Directive prescribes a certain hierarchy of remedies, since traditionally, in civil law systems, preference is given to the right to cure of contractual parties and to the remedy of specific performance, rather than to the right to terminate the contract and to claim damages.

the prolongation of the travelling time.[86] The CJEU has further confirmed the distinction between the compensation in Regulation 261 and the air passengers' right to claim damages in its judgment in *Rodriguez*.[87] There, the CJEU interpreted Article 12 of Regulation 261 and clarified that the air passengers' right to claim damages is not in any way influenced by their right to compensation as set in Article 7 of Regulation 261. Lastly, the right to assistance and care also falls outside one of the above-described categories. If we compared this last right to consumer law remedies, the closest to it would be the right of a consumer to a replacement good whilst the product purchased by her is being repaired. Providing consumers with a replacement product, for example a substitute computer when the non-conforming computer is being repaired, intends to compensate any inconvenience that consumers may experience related to the remedying of the originally improperly performed or unperformed contractual obligation. However, whether this right to a replacement good exists in European consumer law could be debated. In many situations traders could grant it to consumers on their own initiative. It could also be argued that when the trader knew, or could expect, that the consumer would need to take measures to cover the time between handing over the good for repair and receiving back the repaired good, and the repair would take more than just a few days, the duty to provide a replacement good could be inferred from Article 3(3) *in fine* of the Consumer Sales Directive. That is to say, the obligation to repair the good without any significant inconvenience to the consumer.[88] The purpose of the right to care is the same as the right to a replacement good, that is, to make consumers more comfortable and to diminish their inconvenience resulting from the improper performance or lack of performance of the service provider's contractual obligations. However, the right to care does not provide air passengers with a 'replacement' for the air transport service they were supposed to receive.

This comparison clarifies that the remedies provided to air passengers in Regulation 261 follow the patterns used by the European legislator in introducing remedies for non-performance or improper performance of other consumer contracts. Additionally, the adoption of a very detailed right to assistance and care places air passengers in a privileged position, for example in comparison with other travellers who may be less certain what the scope of this right would be under the provisions of the PTD.[89] The fact that the European legislator does not grant this right to consumers in case of breach of other consumer contracts could be justified due to the specific character of a transport services contract, and to the fact that, in

---

[86] Unless, however, we follow the CJEU's reasoning that the compensation should be granted to air passengers in the event of a flight's delay or cancellation, due to the loss of their freedom to manage their own time, rather than due to the non-performance or improper performance of the service. See *Sturgeon* (n 79) paras 52–54.

[87] *Rodríguez* (n 68) paras 37–38.

[88] eg M Loos, *Consumentenkoop* (Kluwer, 2014) 83–84.

[89] It should be considered here that some consumers who have purchased package travel could also be air passengers, and their rights may overlap here and confuse them due to the varied scope of these rights.

the event of its non-performance or improper performance, the traveller may find herself stranded in a foreign place. However, this justification would then call for the European legislator to extend the scope of application of this right to passengers other than air passengers as well. The air passengers' right to compensation unrelated to any actual damage is even more unusual in European consumer law, since it has certain qualities of a penalty that generally is left to the contracting parties to determine. Considering the often grave consequences that may follow from the non-performance or improper performance of the air transport services contract, the introduction of an economic incentive for air transport service providers to properly and timely fulfil their contractual obligations may be justified.

The European Commission's Proposal introduces even more specific provisions on air passengers' right to assistance and care, mentioning, amongst other things, in its revised Article 6(5), their rights during any delay on the tarmac, for example to free-of-charge access to drinking water and toilet facilities, as well as the right to disembark if the delay lasts longer than five hours.[90] Additionally, the new Article 6a grants air passengers the right to assistance and care when they have missed their connecting flights and are awaiting the new connection. Due to the heavy economic burden placed on the air transport service provider when it needs to provide its customers with hotel accommodation during any delay, even if it was caused by a long-lasting extraordinary circumstances,[91] the European Commission has introduced a limit to this assistance obligation in the new Article 9(4). The air transport service provider would only need to provide accommodation for up to three nights, and may limit its cost to €100 per night. Moreover, if the flight was supposed to be no longer than 250 kilometres, or was to occur on an aircraft with fewer than 80 seats, this right to accommodation would be excluded altogether.[92] Additionally, when the air passenger decides to choose reimbursement while being at the departure airport of her journey, or re-routing at a later date over continuation of her travel plans at the earliest opportunity, then she waives her right to assistance and care, pursuant to Article 9(6). The European legislator thus adjusted the right to compensation to lessen the financial burden on air transport service providers. As a result, this right is likely to apply in the future to fewer cancelled or delayed flights.[93] However, the Regulation also clearly determines that air passengers who have suffered a long delay to their flight have a right to claim compensation, which will thus extinguish the controversies related to the CJEU's judgment in the *Sturgeon* case.[94] Furthermore, the European Commission's

---

[90] The European Parliament suggests changing this timeframe to two hours in the European Parliament's Proposal, amendment 76.

[91] eg *McDonagh* (n 81).

[92] The European Parliament intends to raise these limits to five nights and €125 respectively, and to cancel the introduced exceptions for short flights or small aircraft in the European Parliament's Proposal, amendments 96 and 97.

[93] There is, however, a dispute between the European Commission and the European Parliament as to the precise circumstances in which air passengers should be granted these rights; for example, whether compensation should apply only to flight delays lasting three or five hours.

[94] European Commission's Proposal, Art 6(2); see also Garben (n 77) 15; see also *Sturgeon* (n 79).

Proposal allows air transport service providers to conclude voluntary agreements with their passengers to replace the statutory compensation, but only when the agreement lists the air passengers' right to compensation under Regulation 261.[95]

The European Parliament's Proposal also suggests the addition of a specific provision addressing the issue of the air transport service provider's insolvency.[96] It states that the air passenger retains all her rights in such circumstances, apart from the right to compensation. The air transport service provider needs to take out an insurance policy, or create a sufficient guarantee fund for this purpose. Furthermore, if the air transport service provider fails to offer its passengers the choice of re-routing, they may arrange such re-routing themselves and claim the corresponding costs thereof.[97]

As we can see, the new provisions limit the air passengers' rights to compensation in certain circumstances that proved in practice to be quite burdensome to air transport service providers. At the same time, the European institutions are broadening the scope of the right to assistance and care, and specify it in even more detail. It remains to be seen what measures the final version of the proposal will introduce. However, from the above analysis, it follows that the current rights of air passengers should overall be strengthened by the amendments, even though air passengers' remedies will still not be equal to consumer remedies.

V. Right of Withdrawal

While Regulation 261 grants air passengers certain information rights and remedies when the air transport service they purchased is disrupted, it does not empower them with the right of withdrawal. That is to say, the right to terminate the contract within days of its conclusion, without having to justify this termination and without having to pay any penalty. Granted, the right of withdrawal is a special consumer protection measure that European consumers enjoy only while concluding certain transactions, the character of which is deemed to justify the introduction of the right of withdrawal.[98] After all, the general contractual

---

[95] European Commission's Proposal, Art 7(5). The European Parliament adds, at amendment 83 of the European Parliament's Proposal, that this agreed compensation should contain benefits of at least equivalent value to the monetary compensation, but could be issued in a non-monetary form, eg through issuing air travel vouchers without an expiration date.

[96] European Parliament's Proposal, amendment 69.

[97] European Parliament's Proposal, amendment 90.

[98] eg J Luzak, 'To Withdraw or Not to Withdraw? Evaluation of the Mandatory Right of Withdrawal in Consumer Distance Selling Contracts Taking into Account its Behavioural Effects on Consumers' (2014) 37 *Journal of Consumer Policy* 91; H Eidenmüller, 'Why Withdrawal Rights?' (2011) 1 *European Review of Contract Law* 1; C Twigg-Flesner and R Schulze, 'Protecting rational choice: information and the right of withdrawal' in G Howells *et al* (eds), *Handbook of Research on International Consumer Law* (Edward Elgar, 2010) 145; P Rott and E Terryn, 'The Right of Withdrawal and Standard Terms' in H-W Micklitz, J Stuyck and E Terryn (eds), *Consumer Law* (Hart Publishing, 2010) 239; M Loos, 'Rights of Withdrawal' in G Howells and R Schulze (eds), *Modernising and Harmonising Consumer Contract Law* (Sellier, 2009) 241.

rule of *pacta sunt servanda* obliges contractual parties to consider carefully, before the contract's conclusion, whether they want to be bound by the given transaction's terms and conditions. If they decide to conclude a contract, they are held to the decision they have made. Still, the European legislator has already introduced exceptions to this rule, for example in the CRD, and it is important to consider whether he should also give air passengers the same or a similar measure of protection.

Since the sector of air transport services is an industry similar to package travel, it helps to look at measures the European legislator has adopted in the PTD. Article 5 of the PTD allows consumers to 'withdraw' from the contract if, prior to the trip, the travel organiser significantly alters essential terms of the contract, such as price. Clearly, this is not a typical right of withdrawal. First, it is not limited in time from the moment of the contract's conclusion. Secondly, it sets a condition for its use, in the form of the travel organiser's having significantly changed an essential contractual term. This right should, then, rather be characterised as the consumer's right to terminate the contract without having to pay a penalty.[99] The new proposal for the revised Package Travel Directive renames this right as the 'right to terminate the contract before the start of the package against payment of a reasonable cancellation fee'.[100] Consumers concluding package travel contracts are therefore also not capable of changing their minds free of any consequences as to the contract's conclusion a few days thereafter. However, at least in the case of package travel contracts, the European legislator aimed to balance the contractual parties' interests by allowing consumers who have made early reservations to terminate the contract before their trip starts, if they need to do so. Such consumers still need to consider the organiser's interests and agree to compensate the organiser reasonably for the cancellation of their contracts. Consumers concluding a package travel contract also have the right to transfer their package to another person who satisfies all the conditions applicable to the package, on the basis of Article 4(3) of the PTD. Again, if a consumer is unable to make use of the package travel she has booked in advance, she would have the option not to lose her money by finding a replacement traveller for the package travel's organiser. The European legislator has not given this option to air passengers in Regulation 261.

Article 9 of the CRD provides for the right of withdrawal for distance and off-premises contracts. The European legislator justified the adoption of the right of withdrawal in distance contracts due to the lack of physical contact between consumers and traders prior to the contract's conclusion. Legal scholars perceive this method of concluding contracts as often hindering consumers in their ability fully and properly to assess the value of the services they are purchasing, which disadvantage may leave them distrustful both of the trader and as regards the

---

[99] Even if in practice travel organisers often introduce provisions requiring a certain cancellation fee to be paid, contrary to the PTD's provisions. See, eg, Bech Serrat (n 13) 85.

[100] Proposal for Package Travel Directive, Art 10.

transaction.[101] Scholars have also argued that without the right of withdrawal's introduction to distance contracts, consumers would be less willing to participate in cross-border transactions, which often occur at a distance.[102] After all, since consumers would not be able to familiarise themselves with the quality of the services they were purchasing at a distance, they would not be willing to pay higher prices for better quality services. This could lead to the creation of the 'market for lemons' phenomenon, where the quality of goods and services offered to consumers would gradually drop due to consumers' unwillingness to pay higher prices when they could not easily verify the quality of goods or services.[103] With regard to off-premises contracts, the right of withdrawal is seen as an effective instrument to protect consumers from often surprising and aggressive sales techniques that are found in this method of concluding contracts.[104] If a door-to-door salesman ambushes a consumer in her own house, and she then signs a contract just to get rid of him, she will have the ability to reverse the legal situation in which she has found herself due to undue pressure having been exercised.

Pursuant to the derogation introduced in Article 3(3)(k) of the CRD, the provisions of the CRD on the right of withdrawal do not apply to air transport services.[105] This derogation has been introduced even though air transport service providers may, and often do, sell their services through various distance communication schemes, as well as off-premises. For example, a travel agent may visit an air passenger's home; air transport service providers may sell air travel at a travel fair, or at the airport itself.[106] An air transport service provider may also induce a passenger into concluding a contract too hastily, without her considering all the consequences of her decision and without her having been granted all the necessary information to compare the offer made to her off-premises with other available offers. Emotional, hasty purchasing may even occur at a distance, for example when a consumer purchases air transport services online, led by the discount price offered on one website, without having the time or skills necessary to compare the price offered with those on other websites, or even without examining her finances to check whether she would be able to afford a trip at all.[107] Why, then, would the European legislator not grant air passengers the same protection as enjoyed by customers of other services when concluding distance or off-premises contracts? After all, the same biases and detriments of distance and

---

[101] eg Luzak (n 98) 96; O Ben-Shahar and EA Posner, 'The right to withdraw in contract law' (2011) 40 *The Journal of Legal Studies* 115, 121.

[102] eg Bech Serrat (n 13) 82–83; Loos (n 96) 246–47.

[103] eg Luzak (n 98) 96; Eidenmüller (n 98) 7–9; Cseres (n 16) 80–81; P Rekaiti and R van den Bergh, 'Cooling-Off Periods in the Consumer Laws of the EC Member States. A Comparative Law and Economics Approach' (2000) 23 *Journal of Consumer Policy* 371, 380.

[104] eg Bech Serrat (n 13) 82; Loos (n 98) 244–45.

[105] Moreover, even despite this exemption, there is an additional provision in Art 16 of the CRD that disallows application of the right of withdrawal to transport services that would fall under the scope of application of the CRD.

[106] Bech Serrat (n 13) 82.

[107] ibid, 83.

off-premises selling should apply in these cases too. The reasons given for such a derogation are twofold.

First, air transport services occupy a flexible, rapidly changing market, where the price of air tickets fluctuates from day to day, only partly remaining within the air transport service provider's control.[108] The CRD excludes in any case the application of the right of withdrawal to such markets in its Article 16(b). It may be imagined that if an air passenger were to book air transport services for a certain trip in advance, and a few days later the price of those services dropped, given the opportunity she would choose to withdraw from the contract, only to subsequently purchase the air transport services for the same date at a lower price. This could, of course, be detrimental to the marketing strategies of an air transport service provider, which may want to boost the sale of the last few available seats by lowering their price at the last minute. However, when the difference in price is dependent on the air transport service provider's marketing strategy, and the special promotion introduced by it could motivate air passengers to use their withdrawal rights, this should be at the air transport service provider's risk. It should be able to calculate in its strategy the number of potential withdrawals from the contract, which would be limited to those contracts most recently concluded, and their impact on its business. If the drop in air transport services prices were not to depend on the air transport service provider, if, for example, fuel prices were significantly to decrease, then the air passenger's withdrawal should not harm the trader, since its costs would be lower as well. Of course, if the price of the services were to change after the contract's conclusion, this would not normally be a ground for a contract's termination. Therefore only in cases when this price fluctuation occurred within the cooling-off period, could it lead the air passenger to withdraw from a contract. This occurs due to the air passenger's possibility to use her right of withdrawal for any reason. Again, this right should not overly burden the trader, since its use would be predictable and, additionally, the cooling-off period could be limited in time to appropriately fit the situation of air transport service providers. It seems, therefore, that we could question this justification to exclude the application of the right of withdrawal from air transport services.

The exclusion of the right of withdrawal from travel-related contracts has also been motivated by the potential inability of the service provider to fill in the capacity that it has set aside for the air passenger purchasing an air transport service, if this air passenger later decides to withdraw from the contract.[109] The CJEU decided in *easyCar v Office of Fair Trading*[110] that, for example, car hire companies should fall within the scope of the derogation introduced for the transport

---

[108]   eg E Gornall, 'Low-cost air fares: How ticket prices fall and rise' (*BBC*, 21 June 2013), available at <www.bbc.co.uk/news/business-22882559>, accessed 28 January 2015; S McCartney, 'Whatever You Do, Don't Buy an Airline Ticket On ...' (*Wall Street Journal*, 27 January 2011), available at <http://online.wsj.com/articles/SB10001424052748704062604576105953506930800>, accessed 28 January 2015.

[109]   Bech Serrat (n 13) 84.

[110]   Case C-336/03 *easyCar v Office of Fair Trading* [2005] ECR I-01947.

sector in the Distance Selling Directive.[111] The CJEU recalled that the purpose of this derogation was to protect these industries where late cancellations could have disproportionate effects, such as the passenger transport industry.[112] Clearly, this reasoning could apply to air transport service providers too. Advocate General Stix-Hackl argued, in her Opinion in that case, that with regard to car hire services, unused capacity comes often with increased costs and liability when compared to other consumer services. Therefore, the CJEU should not allow passengers of car hire companies to cancel reservations at short notice, which would be likely to economically weaken traders in this sector.[113] The travel industry used this reasoning when it lobbied in the European institutions for the right of withdrawal not to apply to air transport services on the basis of the 'empty chair' syndrome.[114] They argued that if an air passenger's cancellation were to come at a short notice, the air transport service provider would be unable to find another customer without a cost to the air passenger, and consequently this practice should not be allowed. It seems, however, that the European legislator could avoid this 'empty chair' syndrome and introduce the right of withdrawal to protect air passengers with, for example, an additional time limit as to when it could be performed. Air passengers often purchase air transport services months prior to their intended travel date. If the introduced cooling-off period were to be no longer than 14 days, it should not weaken the air transport service provider's capacity to find another customer to take the seat of an air passenger who decides to withdraw from the contract she concluded, for example, six months in advance of the flight. To protect air transport service provider's interests, the European legislator could exclude the use of the right of withdrawal for air passengers purchasing their tickets, for example, within just one month of their intended travel date. After all, the short timeframe between the conclusion of the contract and the intended travel date could leave air transport service providers with insufficient time to find a substitute for the air passenger withdrawing from a contract. Another variation that the European legislator could introduce to the right of withdrawal, in order to make it more attractive to air transport service providers, would be through the introduction of cancellation fees dependent on the time left between the time of the contract's cancellation and the intended travel date. Such cancellation fees could compensate for the air transport service provider's risk of not being able to find a substitute air passenger. This practice would, of course, weaken the right of withdrawal's significance, since it is supposed to facilitate air passengers' cancellation of contracts without their having to bear any financial burdens related thereto. The introduction of cancellation fees would, however, be preferable to the existing status quo, where once the air transport services are purchased, air passengers are often unable

---

[111] European Parliament and Council Directive 97/7/EC of 20 May 1997 on the protection of consumers in respect of distance contracts [1997] OJ L144/19 (Distance Selling Directive), Art 3(2).

[112] *easyCar* (n 110) para 28 and 29 related to the interpretation of the exclusion of the application of the right of withdrawal to contracts concluded among other for transport services pursuant to art 3 para 2 Distance Selling Directive.

[113] *easyCar* (n 110), Opinion of AG Stix-Hackl, para 61.

[114] Bech Serrat (n 13) 84.

to cancel the contract without having to pay the whole ticket price. Additionally, it could be argued that air transport services are not the only ones that depend on reservations and could be harmed by cancellations at short notice. Medical or legal services are an example of such other services that could be harmed by the 'empty chair' syndrome.[115] If service providers in these markets are capable of operating successfully with the right of withdrawal protecting their customers, why would this not be a possibility for the air transport services industry? It may also be noticed here that nowadays many air transport service providers enable their passengers to effect such cancellations of their own initiative, while including cancellation fees in their prices.[116]

Unfortunately, neither the European Commission's nor the European Parliament's Proposals mention the possibility of providing air passengers with either the right to withdraw or the right to terminate the contract before the air transport service is performed upon paying a reasonable cancellation fee.

VI. Conclusions

While the European legislator continues to harmonise European private law and gives it more attention overall, the regulation of air passengers' rights seems to be 'up in the air' rather than securely established, as the title of this chapter suggests. Air passengers' rights are not yet safely grounded, and not only as the result of the unfinished legislative process on the new rules that would govern this area of European private law. A careful analysis of Regulation 261 in comparison to other measures adopted in European consumer law that apply to contracts similar to air transport services contracts, shows us that many divergences exist between these measures. This, while the justifications for these differences are often quite ambiguous.

One thing that astonishes when we take a look at the European Commission's Proposal is the continuation of the infamous tradition of not defining the notion of the 'passenger'. It does not seem necessary to differentiate this notion from the broadly interpreted notion of a 'consumer' as applied, for example, in the PTD. Of course, the European legislator could insist on limiting the application of the notion of a 'consumer' to situations in which it applies in its narrow meaning, that is to a natural person who does not act even partly for professional purposes when concluding a contract. However, then the European legislator should at least consider the introduction of common terminology in Regulation 261 and in the PTD. Therefore, the European legislator should consider incorporation of the newly prepared notion of a 'traveller', from the proposal for the new PTD, in the European Commission's Proposal as well. The adoption of the common nomenclature

---

[115] Bech Serrat (n 13) 87.
[116] eg S McCartney, 'Your Bad Luck is a Windfall For Airlines' (*Wall Street Journal*, 30 July 2009), available at <http://online.wsj.com/articles/SB10001424052970204563304574318212311819146>, accessed 28 January 2015.

could reduce air passengers' uncertainty as to what other European consumer law measures could apply to them.

Generally, the European institutions have granted consumers concluding contracts other than for air transport services a higher standard of protection, as we can observe especially as regards the example of information duties and the right of withdrawal. The justifications for exempting air passengers from the scope of these European consumer law measures are unconvincing. Especially since it seems that air passengers may be quite vulnerable when concluding air transport services online, which method of contracting is nowadays used on a regular basis.[117] Those air passengers who purchase air transport services online may also have difficulty locating the online service provider when they want to raise certain claims, and could use more detailed information about the characteristics of the service provided to them etc. The expansion of the information duties for air transport service providers does not necessarily demand the addition of a whole new list of information duties to Regulation 261. It could suffice, for example, to extend the scope of application of the CRD so that it equally covered air transport service contracts. Aside from the inferior information rights that air passengers have in comparison to other European consumers, the above-analysed reasons for excluding the right of withdrawal from applying to air transport services contracts also seem far-fetched. The problems listed as standing in the way of efficient use of the right of withdrawal in this market could be reduced or prevented if the right of withdrawal were to be modified so as to fit the air transport services industry. For example, it could be limited in time, or it could be phrased more like a passenger's right to terminate the contract upon paying a reasonable cancellation fee, dependent on the time between the contract's cancellation and the intended travel date, proportional to the risk of the air transport service provider in finding a substitute air passenger. All in all, it seems warranted to call for a more careful review of the European Commission's Proposal in light of existing consumer protection measures, with the aim of raising the level of air passengers' protection to the same standard that other European consumers enjoy.

Nevertheless, it should be observed here that certain air passenger protection measures introduced by Regulation 261 go beyond the scope of protection that European consumers enjoy. This applies specifically in the case of the duty to issue a standardised notification to air passengers that they have certain information rights, the establishment of clear sanctions for breach of information duties by air transport service providers, which may further incentivise them to inform their customers properly, and providing air passengers with the detailed remedy of the right to assistance and care. These measures are either completely missing from European consumer law, or the European legislator drafted them in an inferior way in comparison with the provisions laid down in Regulation 261. Any future drafters of European consumer law measures should therefore take a closer look at these provisions, since they may find some useful inspiration in them.

---

[117] Bech Serrat (n 13) 88.

20

Tackling Diversity Through Uniformity? Revisiting the Reform of Regulation 261/2004

JEREMIAS PRASSL

The present collection of essays is the third volume in the *EU Law in the Member States* series. One of the core goals of that series is to explore the operation of EU law across the Member States, with a particular view to understanding the reality behind the interaction of Union-level norms, as laid down by the Union legislator, interpreted by the Court and enforced, where appropriate, by the Commission, with different layers of regulation—be that on a domestic level in the form of Member State law and practice, or on an international level, in the form of treaties and related obligations to which the Member States, the EU or indeed both may be signatories.

As the preceding parts of this volume have demonstrated, Regulation 261/2004 on compensation and assistance to passengers in the event of denied boarding and of cancellation or long delay of flights has become one of the most high-profile areas of EU law[1]—whether in the perception of the travelling public, industry, academe, or policy makers at domestic and European level. The Regulation has, on the one hand, been one of the most successful areas of EU action in the field of consumer protection, contributing to the creation of an internal market in aviation services: following early action to ensure market liberalisation, the Union is now working to ensure that service recipients' rights are protected when travelling across the Continent.[2] On the other, the Regulation has come in for heavy criticism from the aviation industry: the obligations as laid down in its provisions, and later expanded upon by the CJEU, are said to impose financial burdens on air operators, and pose challenging questions as regards the relationship between EU

---

[1] Regulation (EC) No 261/2004 of the European Parliament and of the Council of 11 February 2004 establishing common rules on compensation and assistance to passengers in the event of denied boarding and of cancellation or long delay of flights, and repealing Regulation (EEC) No 295/91 [2004] OJ L46/1.

[2] See, eg, J Prassl, 'Liberalisation, Information, and Transparency: Three Tales of Consumer Protection in EU Aviation Law' (2015) 11 *European Review of Contract Law* 281.

law and international norms, notably in the form of the Montreal Convention,[3] which purports to regulate exclusively all liability arising from the contract of carriage by air.

I. Introduction: EU Law in the Member States and the Case for Legislative Reform

In one sense, therefore, EU aviation law might be said to be a rather unique and specialist discipline, with many of the problems encountered in previous parts explicable by the EU's comparatively late involvement in, and re-opening of, long-settled international bargains. In another sense, however, the resulting turbulent controversy in the field of EU aviation law is in many ways reminiscent of the aftermath of the two landmark decisions in *Viking* and *Laval*,[4] which were the subject of scrutiny in the first volume.[5] There, the Court's decisions in the area of the internal market brought into sharp conflict provisions governing free movement at Union level and the domestic (and international) regulation of the right to take industrial action. For present purposes, the potential conflicts share a surprising number of similar aspects, with Regulation 261 taking the place of the Court's interpretation of the economic freedoms enshrined in Articles 49 and 56 of the TFEU, and the Montreal Convention of 1999 that of key provisions of the European Convention on Human Rights[6] and the International Labour Organisation[7] in shaping domestic practice in many Member States before the Union's regulatory involvement.

Furthermore, the framework developed in analysing the multi-faceted impact of the landmark cases in that volume, can similarly be applied to Regulation 261: there are at least three dimensions of heterogeneity as regards the reception and operation of the Regulation's passenger rights regime across the countries surveyed. Michal Bobek's concluding chapter explores these differences and divergences in detail; suffice it to say for the moment that an extensive list of examples may be found in the *systemic* dimension (such as notably pre-existing attitudes to Montreal Convention exclusivity), the *conceptual* dimension (in particular as regards different avenues for enforcing passenger rights, ranging from tort law

---

[3] Convention for the Unification of Certain Rules for International Carriage by Air, signed at Montreal in 1999.

[4] Case C-438/05 *International Transport Workers' Federation and Finnish Seamen's Union v Viking Line APB* [2007] ECR I-10779; Case C-341/05 *Laval un Partneri Ltd v Svenska Byggnadsarbetareförbundet* [2007] ECR I-11767.

[5] M Freedland and J Prassl (eds), *EU Law in the Member States:* Viking, Laval *and Beyond* (Hart Publishing 2014).

[6] V Velyvyte, The Right to Strike in the EU after Accession to the ECHR: A Practical Assessment' in Freedland and Prassl (eds) (n 5) 75.

[7] A Bogg, 'Viking and Laval: The International Labour Law Perspective' in Freedland and Prassl (eds) (n 5) 41.

and contract law to administrative law), and the *procedural or remedial* dimension (with enforcement responsibilities diverging or even overlapping between national enforcement bodies (NEBs) and traditional court systems).

Perhaps the most important difference between the two volumes, on the other hand, relates to the lessons that may be learnt from a comparative analysis of the national impact chapters—in particular as regards considerations for future law reform. In the case of *Viking* and *Laval*, any such insights came too late—the ill-fated proposal for a *Monti II* Regulation, designed to rebalance the competing claims of workers and cross-border employers at stake, had already become 'the first "casualty" of the so-called yellow card procedure triggered by 12 reasoned opinions issued by national Parliaments on the basis of the subsidiarity Protocol introduced by the Lisbon Treaty'.[8] In the case of Regulation 261, on the other hand, regulatory reform is still very much on the cards: the only issue all parties involved in the long-running litigation surrounding the validity and interpretation of the Regulation seemingly agree upon is an urgent need for reform—whilst of course disagreeing entirely as to what shape such measures should take. Industry representatives have expressed hopes that a reformed measure would reduce the scope of obligations imposed on carriers, whilst passenger representatives appear primarily interested in affirming the Court's development and interpretation of existing provisions, as well as in improving the Regulation's patchy enforcement record.

After extensive deliberations and preparation spanning a period of two years, the European Commission put forward a set of proposals for a new Regulation to amend, and potentially extend, the existing regime of passenger rights protection on 13 March 2013.[9] The European Parliament's Transport Committee in turn replied with an extensive set of amendments, confirmed with an overwhelming majority by the Parliament on 5 February 2014.[10] At the time of finalising this contribution in the Spring of 2015, negotiations appeared to be on-going,[11] with many a compromise yet to be reached—or possible new avenues found to respond

---

[8] The Adoptive Parents, 'The Life of a Death Foretold: The Proposal for a Monti II Regulation' in Freedland and Prassl (eds) (n 5) 95–96.

[9] Commission Proposal for a Regulation amending Regulation 261/2004, COM(2013) 130 (European Commission Proposal).

[10] European Parliament legislative resolution of 5 February 2014 on the proposal for a regulation of the European Parliament and of the Council amending Regulation (EC) No 261/2004 establishing common rules on compensation and assistance to passengers in the event of denied boarding and of cancellation or long delay of flights and Regulation (EC) No 2027/97 on air carrier liability in respect of the carriage of passengers and their baggage by air (COM(2013)0130—C7-0066/2013—2013/0072(COD)) (European Parliament Proposal).

[11] See, eg, the Commission's Answer to Gabriel Mato MEP, suggesting that it 'has been actively assisting the Latvian Presidency in its efforts to make progress on this file since discussions were resumed at the beginning of January 2015. The Commission hopes that the Council will soon define its own position on this important proposal so that the interinstitutional negotiations can start this year. / The priority for the Commission in this field is for a clear, easily enforceable and ambitious amending Regulation to be adopted by the co-legislators as quickly as possible.' (Parliamentary Questions, 11 March 2015, E-000074/2015)

to some of the challenges which have become evident over the course of the preceding parts. The key question that the present chapter hopes to address is firmly located in that context: to what extent can the Union legislator's current reform project overcome the difficulties resulting from the heterogeneous impact Regulation 261 has had on domestic legal systems?

In order to answer that question, discussion in this chapter returns to a previous article by the present author,[12] which had analysed the Commission's original reform proposals, arguing that while the reforms purported to address a wide range of important concerns, only some were fully resolved, with other longstanding questions left unanswered and several new queries raised. Subsequent sections set out to re-evaluate the reform proposals, as well as the European Parliament's subsequent amendments and additions, albeit from a different perspective: the previous part's description of the diverse implementation and application of Regulation 261/2004 across the Member States sits uneasily with long-established assumptions surrounding the uniform application of Union norms. Given the fact that the original choice of legal instrument—a Regulation—would suggest that the opposite should in fact be the case, it is surprising that one of the most pressing problems with Regulation 261, *viz* its inconsistent and unpredictable application in different countries, has received comparatively little attention in discussions surrounding the pending reforms.

In turning to that very issue, the present chapter scrutinises three particularly salient aspects of the reform proposals in the light of the Member States' experiences. It is structured as follows. Section II. is dedicated to the perennial problem of the Montreal Convention's purported exclusivity in regulating passenger claims; a problem which the reform proposals ignore nearly entirely, though not necessarily unjustifiably. Discussion in section III. then turns to an analysis of the proposals' attempts to clarify key terms, such as notably which 'exceptional circumstances' can be invoked by air carriers to avoid financial liability. Planned changes to the role of NEBs, finally, are analysed in section IV., suggesting that the current reform plans would do little to address the problems identified; indeed, they may well make matters even more difficult and unpredictable.

II. EU Law and the Montreal Convention

As discussed extensively in Part I of the present volume, the relationship between the Montreal Convention and EU law was one of the earliest points of contention raised by carriers opposing passenger claims, leading to repeated references questioning the very possibility of EU regulatory action in a field already covered

---

[12] J Prassl, 'Reforming Air Passenger Rights in Europe' (2014) 39 *Air and Space Law* 59.

by international law,[13] given the exclusive coverage provided for in Article 29 of the latter.

As explained by Judge Malenovský in chapter two,[14] the Court of Justice had rejected this challenge by drawing a clear distinction between different kinds of damage:

> Any delay in the carriage of passengers by air, and in particular a long delay, may, generally speaking, cause two types of damage. First, excessive delay will cause damage that is almost identical for every passenger, redress for which may take the form of standardised and immediate assistance ... Second, passengers are liable to suffer individual damage, inherent in the reason for travelling, redress for which requires a case-by-case assessment ...[15]

Upon a detailed reading of Articles 19, 22 and 29 of the Montreal Convention, it was apparent that they only dealt with the latter kind of damage, which made it unlikely that the

> authors of the Convention intended to shield those carriers from any other form of intervention, in particular action which could be envisaged by the public authority to redress, in a standardised and immediate manner, the damage that is constituted by the inconvenience that delay in the carriage of passengers by air causes, without the passengers having to suffer inconvenience inherent in the bringing of actions for damages before the courts.[16]

The system of 'standardised and immediate assistance and care measures'[17] found in Regulation 261 could therefore not be seen as an interference with the Montreal regime.[18] This analysis drew a significant amount of ire from a range of commentators,[19] but was firmly approved of by the Grand Chamber's decision in *Nelson v Deutsche Lufthansa*.[20]

The reform debate, on the other hand, sidesteps the question of Montreal Convention exclusivity almost completely. The explanatory memorandum released together with the draft proposal for an amended passenger rights regulation simply asserts that '[c]ase law has had a decisive impact on the interpretation of the Regulation. In case C-344/04 (*ex parte IATA*), the ECJ confirmed its full compatibility with the Montreal Convention and the complementarities between the

---

[13] Case C-344/04 *The Queen on the application of International Air Transport Association and European Low Fares Airline Association v Department for Transport* [2006] ECR I-403 (*ex parte IATA*).

[14] J Malenovský, 'Regulation 261: Three Major Issues in the Case Law of the Court of Justice of the EU', ch 2 of the present volume.

[15] *ex parte IATA* (n 13) para 43.

[16] ibid, para 45.

[17] ibid, para 47.

[18] ibid, paras 45–46. The Court has since repeated this finding on numerous occasions, including, eg, in Case C-204/08 *Rehder v Air Baltic Corp* [2009] ECR I-6073.

[19] See, eg, P Dempsey and S Johansson, '*Montreal v. Brussels:* The Conflict of Laws on the Issue of Delay in International Air Carriage' (2010) 35 *Air and Space Law* 207; as well as chs 4 and 5 of the present volume.

[20] Cases C-581 and 629/10 *Nelson v Deutsche Lufthansa AG* [2012] OJ C399/3.

two legal instruments.'[21] During the proposal's passage through the European Parliament, there was even less scrutiny on point—indeed, neither in the reports and committee papers,[22] nor in the plenary discussion of 5 February 2014,[23] is there any evidence of the issue's being raised, despite the fact that the Convention's substantive provisions form part of EU law.[24]

In light of the Member State experience, this lack of engagement with a key challenge from the perspective of international aviation law is potentially problematic: given the wide range of ways in which claims for compensation under Regulation 261 are conceptualised in different legal systems, the stark complementarity between 'damage that is almost identical for every passenger, redress for which may take the form of standardised and immediate assistance' and 'individual damage, inherent in the reason for travelling, redress for which requires a case-by-case assessment' will only rarely be borne out in domestic legal systems. In several countries, an initial hurdle often faced by claimants is that as to the very classification of their claims under Regulation 261: is it a straightforward private law claim, given the underlying contractual nature of the parties' relationship, or a matter of public law, given the standardised redress specified in the Regulation? Furthermore, are any potential disputes to be adjudicated by a regular civil law court, or before specialised administrative jurisdictions?

As regards the classification of claims for cancellation or delay compensation under the EU regime, first, the distinction between 'almost identical' and 'individual' damage is not in any way consistently mirrored in the legal systems surveyed. In Bulgaria, for example, the case law has endorsed three distinct approaches to passengers' claims, seeing them as potentially founded in the Regulation itself, the relevant domestic provisions on contractual liability, or even the relevant domestic provisions on tortious liability.[25] In the Czech Republic and Slovakia, the claim is firmly based in contract law, even though the passenger's action might take on an additional public law dimension through the NEB's involvement;[26] whereas in the UK, claims for compensation under Regulation 261 would usually be approached as a 'Eurotort' claim for breach of statutory duty.[27]

As the national reports suggest, secondly, even the very attempt of drawing the clear-cut distinctions at the heart of the Court's complementarity analysis does

---

[21] European Commission Proposal (n 9) 3.
[22] Report on the proposal for a regulation of the European Parliament and of the Council amending Regulation (EC) No 261/2004 establishing common rules on compensation and assistance to passengers in the event of denied boarding and of cancellation or long delay of flights and Regulation (EC) No 2027/97 on air carrier liability in respect of the carriage of passengers and their baggage by air (COM(2013)0130—C7-0066/2013—2013/0072(COD)), A7-0020/2014 (22 January 2014).
[23] European Parliament Debate, Strasburg, 5 February 2014, CRE 05/02/2014—5.
[24] Council Decision 2001/539 [2001] OJ L194/38, paving the way for the adoption of Regulation 2027/97 [1997] OJ L285/01; as amended by Regulation 889/2002 [2002] OJ L140/2.
[25] A Kornezov, 'Bulgaria: Blurred Lines', ch 9 of the present volume.
[26] K Csach, 'A Pair of Wings: Air Passenger Rights in the Czech Republic and Slovakia', ch 10 of the present volume.
[27] European Communities Act 1972, section 2(1); *Garden Cottage Foods Ltd v Milk Marketing Board* [1984] 1 AC 130 (HL).

not easily correspond to the ways in which claims will be framed by litigants in different countries. In Spain, for instance, claims under the Regulation may be brought—and are regularly heard—concurrently with a claim for breach of the transportation contract pursuant to Articles 1101 and 1007 of the Spanish Civil Code.[28] This conflation of different claims is taken even further by Italian case law, which has continued to treat under Regulation 261 as cumulative with passengers' entitlements pursuant to Article 19 of the Montreal Convention[29]—the very opposite approach to that originally proposed by Advocate General Geelhoed in *ex parte IATA*.

It is in the light of these stark differences between various Member States' characterisations of claims under the Regulation that the relative silence of the reform proposals must be evaluated: are there any measures that could be adopted at the legislative level to remedy the implications different domestic solutions will have for the relationship between a recast passenger rights regulation and the Montreal Convention's exclusivity provisions? One potential avenue might lie in improving linguistic clarity, in particular by developing a much more careful use of specific terms. Any such attempt, however, might soon run into problems of translation: whereas in *ex parte IATA* a significant amount of the Court's reasoning hinges on a conceptual distinction between the French notions of 'préjudice' and 'dommage', both are merely translated as 'damage' in English. It is furthermore unlikely that even a more prescriptive design of terms would be able to overcome the deep-rooted systemic heterogeneity of national legal systems—not least because, at least as regards the question of Montreal Convention compatibility, the long-standing tension between effective judicial protection of EU law rights and national procedural autonomy does not appear to be an immediate problem in practice.[30]

Indeed, it might even be possible to argue that the experience in the vast majority of Member States suggests that the relationship between the two regimes of passenger protection might in fact be less of a practical challenge than the litigants' arguments in cases such as *ex parte IATA* and *Sturgeon*[31] suggest, and that the diversity observed in this regard does not require further attention on the Union legislator's part. With few exceptions, such as a Dutch district court's preliminary reference questioning the compatibility of Article 7 of the Regulation with the Montreal Convention's limitation on the payment of non-compensatory damages,[32] the Court of Justice's case law as regards Montreal Convention compatibility seems—eventually, in some jurisdictions—to have been accepted by national judiciaries. By not forcing the point at this stage, the simple adoption of the Court's

---

[28] M Artigot i Golobardes, 'Spain: Defeating Air Passengers' Rights Through Procedural Rules', ch 15 of the present volume.

[29] L Pierallini, 'The Italian Experience and Trend', ch 13 of the present volume.

[30] Though *cf* A Arnull, 'The Principle of Effective Judicial Protection in EU law: an Unruly Horse?' (2011) 36 *European Law Review* 51.

[31] Joined Cases C-402 and 432/07 *Sturgeon v Condor Flugdienst* [2009] ECR I-10923 (*Sturgeon*).

[32] Rb Breda 20 October 2010, LJN BO1083 (588236 cv 10-1341).

complementarity analysis might thus foster the sort of 'atmosphere of cooperation' between legal systems often envisaged in the constitutional literature.[33]

A second aspect of the reform plans in which the direct applicability of the *ex parte IATA* reasoning is questionable concerns passengers' rights as regards their checked baggage.[34] Beyond the general question of enforcement, discussed further in section IV., below, however, there is little that is specific to the Member State experience in this regard, and it can accordingly be dealt with most briefly. The Montreal Convention regulates compensation for damaged baggage in its Article 17(2)–(4), setting out clear liability limits in its Article 22: damages arising from lost or delayed luggage are capped at 1131 Special Drawing Rights, unless a higher value has been declared by the passenger. Article 2 of the proposed Regulation stipulates that passengers with limited mobility or a disability must be allowed to make such high-value declarations in regard of their mobility equipment under Article 22(2) free of charge, and that the carrier and its agents shall make passengers aware of their rights in that regard.[35] It furthermore introduces several procedural changes in terms of providing information about luggage allowances, and facilitating the submission of claims pursuant to the Montreal Convention.

Article 2 of the proposed Regulation thus amends Regulation 2027/97 to deal with various aspects of baggage handling,[36] including, for example, an obligation on carriers to accept baggage irregularity reports as an appropriate complaint form under Article 31(2) of the Montreal Convention.[37] It is not immediately clear how this is compatible with Article 29 of the Convention (*Basis of Claims*), as set out above. Under its terms, claims 'can only be brought *subject to the conditions* and such limits of liability as are set out in this Convention'[38]—the complementarity analysis as put forward by the ECJ in *ex parte IATA* is therefore somewhat more questionable. Whether this would lead domestic courts to re-open the issue of Montreal Convention complementarity, however, is rather doubtful; not least given the wide range of accepted approaches to overlaps and complementarities between the regimes as discussed in earlier paragraphs.

III. Clarifying Extraordinary Circumstances

Heeding a 2012 resolution passed by the European Parliament,[39] a key part of the Commission's reform strategy was to ensure the clarification and extension

---

[33] N Barber, 'Legal Pluralism and the European Union' (2006) 12 *European Law Journal* 306, 329.

[34] Prassl (n 12) 73.

[35] European Parliament Proposal (n 10), amendment 146.

[36] European Commission Proposal (n 9) 9.

[37] European Parliament Proposal (n 10), amendment 144.

[38] Emphasis added.

[39] European Parliament resolution of 29 March 2012 on the functioning and application of established rights of people travelling by air, 2011/2150(INI).

of key terms defined in the Regulation in line with the Court of Justice's case law[40]—in particular as regards the so-called 'extraordinary circumstances defence'. Article 5(3) of the Regulation exempts airlines from paying compensation if the relevant event was due to 'extraordinary circumstances'. This provision has been the source of significant litigation, in spite of an early and clear indication by the CJEU in *Wallentin-Hermann v Alitalia* that the defence was to be interpreted restrictively:[41] issues such as 'political instability or meteorological conditions incompatible with the operation of the flight are relevant only if they create an unexpected risk, but are not directly an exemption'.[42] This approach was confirmed by the Court's decision in *Eglitis v Air Baltic*,[43] which held that delays resulting from airspace closure that had affected previous flights could not in and of themselves constitute an extraordinary circumstance. It was up to the operator to design its schedules in such ways as to build in sufficient '"reserve time" which will allow [it] to operate the flight in its entirety once the extraordinary circumstances have come to an end'.[44]

Despite these repeated judicial clarifications, however, the extraordinary circumstances defence has caused a significant amount of difficulty and confusion in litigation across the Member States. To some extent, of course, this is unsurprising, given the diversity of circumstances that might interrupt flight operations (and make for some of the most colourful reading in Part II!): to what extent can it be extraordinary if Austrian airports struggle with snow and Polish ones with deer incursions on the apron;[45] fog, wind and generally unpredictable weather make life difficult at Schiphol despite its large number of runways; French industrial action leads to airspace closures affecting the Iberian peninsular; and a significant domestic carrier (Air Madrid) suffers bankruptcy in Spain? Seen from the perspective of traditional accounts of EU law, however, such differences should have little impact on the effective and uniform application of Regulation 261: the Court's repeated explanation of the terms contained within the Regulation should permit Member State courts to apply its provisions consistently to the full range of diverse and complex fact patterns before them. In reality, on the other hand, that picture varies dramatically, with at least three broad approaches discernible from the national reports.

---

[40] Explanatory Memorandum (n 4) 3.

[41] Case C-549/07 *Wallentin-Hermann v Alitalia* [2008] ECR I-11061.

[42] M Rasero, 'The Capacity of the Court of Justice of the European Union to Promote Homogeneous Application of Uniform Laws: The Case For Air Carrier Liability For Flight Delays And Cancellations' Transnational Notes (NYU Law Blogs), 26 October 2011. See also U Steppler and K Meigel, Advocate General Affirms Controversial *Sturgeon* Decision' Client Update, Arnecke Siebold June 20, 2012 (last accessed 1 September 2013).

[43] Case C-294/10 *Eglitis v Air Baltic* [2011] ECR I-0000.

[44] Holman Fenwick Willan, 'Aerospace Bulletin December 2011—EC Regulation 261/2004' <www.hfw.com/publications/bulletins/aerospace-bulletin-december-2011/aerospace-bulletin-december-2011-ec-regulation-2612004-update> accessed 1 May 2015.

[45] Judgment of Naczelny Sąd Administracyjny of 6.03.2012, I OSK 555/11.

A first group of countries seems to have followed the Luxembourg jurisprudence without much ado: indeed, in Italy many courts had already begun to read the extraordinary circumstances defence very narrowly by the time of the *Wallentin-Hermann* judgment, limiting it to instances of industry-wide strikes and excluding technical failures. In Austria, an initially broader interpretation, which included mechanical problems in the range of available defences, was soon abandoned to bring domestic jurisprudence into line with the CJEU. Following *Wallentin-Hermann* (itself a reference from the Handelsgericht Wien), the courts appear to have come to interpret the defence very narrowly indeed, even holding that a pilot's heart attack shortly before departure could fall within risks inherent in the airline's operations.[46]

A second approach can be discerned in countries such as France, where interpretative differences were rife at first instance, until superior jurisdictions intervened to quash the occasional first-instance decision that had given too broad a meaning to the extraordinary circumstances defence.[47] Similarly, first instance courts in Spain tend to be more generous as regards the scope of the defence; a fact swiftly corrected where cases go to appeal before senior courts applying the much narrower understanding developed at the Union level.[48] Indeed, in one much-discussed ruling, the Spanish Supreme Court went as far as to hold that even the suspension of an operating licence could not fall within the scope of the exception.[49]

In a third set of countries the defence seems to have created significantly more problems. The Netherlands stand out in this regard, with most passenger rights claims turning on the definition of what might constitute an extraordinary circumstance. Even after *Wallentin-Hermann*, the courts have continued to diverge in their interpretations of the defence, leading to yet another preliminary reference in April 2014.[50] When looking at the referring court's 10 detailed questions there, the range of competing approaches amongst Dutch first instance courts quickly becomes apparent. Some of the questions, on the other hand, appear, with respect, to be so abstract that any answer from Luxembourg could only bring about further confusion, and could therefore be seen as a political challenge as much as the more traditional request for clarification and interpretation.[51] In the UK, the extraordinary circumstances defence similarly continued to be interpreted widely in the face of the CJEU's definition, not least as a result of the industry's focus on basing defence claims on the contents of a non-binding indicative list of such circumstances prepared by several NEBs, discussed further in subsequent paragraphs. The tide turned, however, with the Court of Appeal's 2014 judgment in *Huzar*,

---

HG Wien 18.06.2012, 1 R 153/11p.

C Cass 19 March 2014, No 12-20.917.

Judgment of the Barcelona Court of Appeals JUR 2009/409474 of 21 May 2009.

Judgment of the Spanish Supreme Court RJ 2013/5659 of 1 July 2013.

C-257/14 *C van der Lans v KLM*. The Court's judgment (in line with previous decisions) was handed down on 17 September 2015, too late however for detailed discussion.

ibid, eg question 9 (determining stock levels of spare part in other places around the world) and question 10 (multiple stops required by defective plane returning to home base).

which brought the interpretation of the defence back into line with established Court of Justice's case law.[52] In refusing the carrier's further appeal, the Supreme Court of the UK ruled that it was 'not necessary to request the [European] Court of Justice to give any ruling, because the Court's existing jurisprudence already provides a sufficient answer'.[53]

As this brief survey of Member State experiences shows, the interpretation of key terms contained within the Regulation, notably the extraordinary circumstances defence, continues to present a significant challenge to the uniform protection of passengers' rights, at least in a number of countries. Against this backdrop, the reform proposals aim to provide clarity and consistency through three related mechanisms: an explicit definition of extraordinary circumstances, modelled on paragraph 23 of the Court's decision in *Wallentin-Hermann*, to be included in the Regulation itself; a power for the Commission to examine diverging cases and issue clarifications where necessary; and a list of relevant circumstances to be included as a new Annex 1 to the Regulation.

As regards the first of these changes, Article 2(m) of the Commission's proposal for a recast regulation provides that

> 'extraordinary circumstances' means circumstances which by their nature or origin, are not inherent in the normal exercise of the activity of the air carrier concerned, and are beyond its actual control. For the purposes of this Regulation, extraordinary circumstances shall include the circumstances set out in the Annex.[54]

The defence itself is reworded so as to limit carriers' ability to invoke the defence, 'only … in so far [the extraordinary circumstances] affect the flight concerned or the previous flight operated by the same aircraft'; the European Parliament, furthermore, amended the relevant provisions to ensure that the onus of proving the existence of an extraordinary circumstance was clearly on the carrier.[55]

A new Article 16b(4), second, is to give the Commission the power to become active in case of diverging interpretations:

> At the request of a Member State, or on its own initiative, the Commission shall examine cases where differences in the application and enforcement of any of the provisions of this Regulation arise and particularly concerning the interpretation of extraordinary circumstances; and shall clarify the provisions of the Regulation, with a view to promoting a common approach.

---

[52] *Huzar v Jet2.com* [2014] EWCA Civ 791.

[53] J Prassl, 'EU Aviation Law before the English Courts: *Dawson, Huzar*, and Regulation 261/2004' (2014) 38 *Air & Space Law* 365, 384. A series of cases that had been stayed in lower courts pending the Court of Appeal's clarification are underway at the time of writing; it is likely that they will be decided in line with the Court's narrow approach to extraordinary circumstances.

[54] Compare to this the Parliament's amended definition: '(*m*) "extraordinary circumstances" means circumstances *beyond the control of the air carrier concerned* in the normal exercise of *its* activity *and outside the obligations imposed by the relevant safety and security rules to be observed.* For the purposes of this Regulation, extraordinary circumstances *are limited to the circumstances set out in Annex 1.*' (European Parliament Proposal (n 10), amendment 45, with changes highlighted *in italics.*)

[55] European Parliament Proposal (n 10), amendments 65 and 75. See also amendments 128 and 160.

A list of examples set out in Annex 1, lastly, includes natural disasters, security risks, air traffic control restrictions and labour disputes.[56] According to the Commission's original proposal, this list was to be non-exhaustive; a Parliamentary amendment has now stipulated the opposite,[57] whilst at the same time leaving room for the Commission to adopt delegated acts, which may add items to the resulting exhaustive list of circumstances considered to be exceptional.[58]

The motivation behind all three changes is to ensure 'further legal certainty'.[59] As Recital (3) to the proposed regulation suggests, in 'order to increase legal certainty for air carriers and passengers, a more precise definition of the concept of "extraordinary circumstances" is needed'.[60] Given the experience of Regulation 261 in the Member States, however, it is not entirely clear that the new approach will bring about a significant change in domestic practices. Including an explicit definition of extraordinary circumstances should, from an orthodox point of view, not have been necessary, given the binding force of the Court's case law which is no different from that of Regulations;[61] it is, furthermore, unlikely to settle interpretative questions in circumstances where challenges are politically motivated. That said, an inclusion of the definition in the very text of the directly applicable regulation will in any event make the Court's approach more readily accessible to passengers, as well as ensuring that first instance courts unaware of the latest twists and turns in the Luxembourg case law adjudicate the defence question with greater consistency.

Perhaps the starkest innovation in the proposals' clarification efforts is the annexed list of extraordinary circumstances. This Annex builds on a draft list of extraordinary circumstances, first published by a number of NEBs in April 2013. However, as previously argued,[62] it had long been doubtful whether that so-called 'NEB List' should play a central (or indeed any) role in determining the outcome of passengers' claims. The original document at the heart of these arguments merely set out an 'Understanding NEB-NEB on a non-exhaustive and non-binding list of extraordinary circumstances'.[63] At face value, its role was no more than that of an internal draft document agreed by several NEBs, and in consequence it was usually ignored by domestic courts. The NEB list had little persuasive value, for several reasons: its content, first, was simply agreed internally by several NEBs

---

[56] For a series of significant changes made by the European Parliament, see European Parliament Proposal (n 10), amendments 160–68.

[57] European Parliament Proposal (n 10), amendment 2.

[58] European Parliament Proposal (n 10), amendment 141.

[59] European Commission Proposal (n 9) 6.

[60] See also European Parliament Proposal (n 10), amendment 31, inserting a new Recital (26a).

[61] Case C-34/73 *Variola v Amministrazione delle Finanze* [1973] ECR 981; S Weatherill, *Cases & Materials on EU Law* (11th edn, Oxford University Press, 2014) 75ff.

[62] Prassl (n 53) 380–82.

[63] Commission, 'Draft List of Extraordinary Circumstances Following the National Enforcement Bodies (NEB) Meeting Held on 12 April 2013' (Commission, 19 April 2013), available at <http://ec.europa.eu/transport/themes/passengers/air/doc/neb-extraordinary-circumstances-list.pdf>, accessed 1 May 2015 (Draft NEB List).

in 'engagement with technical experts and discussion with the airline industry',[64] none of whom have a norm-setting role in secondary EU legislation. Furthermore, as the document itself notes, its content 'does not necessarily reflect the position of all NEBs ... [and] has not been adopted or in any way approved by the European Commission'.[65]

As regards the substantive contents of the original NEB list, furthermore, several of its provisions clearly contradicted the Court's decision in *Wallentin-Herman*, both in its general definitional principles and in specific examples. Note 1 to the list, for example, suggests that extraordinary circumstances are 'defined by the following general principle: the event has to meet the three criteria, unpredictable, unavoidable and external'. The illustrations (30 of which are said to be extraordinary, and only five of them not so) then include, for example, 'Any other technical defects which become apparent immediately prior to departure or inflight (where the system or part had been maintained in accordance with the required maintenance programme) and which require investigation and/or repair before the aircraft is airworthy for the intended flight.'[66] The list's general approach, and its inclusion of a broad category of 'unexpected flight safety shortcomings' in particular, was therefore out of line with both the Regulation and subsequent case law—not least because of its implicit adoption of a fault standard.

The proposed Annex clearly overcomes the first of these problems, as its substantive provisions have been be shaped by a wide range of actors and interest groups over the course of the ordinary legislative procedure, and will continue to be developed through the Article 16b(4) procedure. As regards the technical content proposed, secondly, both the definition in Article 2(m) and the examples in the Annex have been designed to come much more closely in line with the Court of Justice's approach, thus ensuring continuity with the current case law, which seems to have found increasing acceptance by domestic courts.

While any attempt at legislative clarification should therefore of course be welcomed, it remains questionable whether this development will lead to any significant changes in terms of uncertainty, and thus litigation. A first concern surrounds the question whether the detailed definition of key terms is really one for the legislator to lay down as a general rule *ex ante*, or whether the question might best be left for judicial determination.[67] Secondly, and perhaps more controversially, the differing experiences in various Member States raise the question whether it is really the lack of clarity in the Court's decision in *Wallentin-Hermann* that causes problems for the uniform application of passenger rights. Sacha Garben observes

---

[64] Civil Aviation Authority, 'Air Passenger Compensation Guidelines Published' (Civil Aviation Authority, 23 July 2013), available at <www.caa.co.uk/application.aspx?catid=14&pagetype=65&app id=7&newstype=n&mode=detail&nid=2263>, accessed 1 May 2015.

[65] Draft NEB List (n 63) fn 1.

[66] ibid, Circumstance [26]; see more generally the category of 'unexpected flight safety shortcomings'.

[67] A prime example in this regard are general definitional issues of tort law, which in common law jurisdictions are generally left to the courts. See, eg, S Deakin, A Johnston and B Markesinis, *Markesinis and Deakin's Tort Law* (7th edn, Oxford University Press, 2012) 81ff.

that recent years have seen a continuing stream of preliminary reference requests, with over 20 requests filed in 2013–14 alone. As she notes, whilst general challenges questioning the regime's validity seem to have abated, the focus is now both on 'genuine questions about the concept of "extraordinary circumstances"' and airline litigation tactics.[68]

Even before embarking on the reform process, the European Commission had long pointed out a series of problems with the Regulation, from airlines' resisting compliance outright to NEBs providing industry and passengers alike with unclear and inconsistent guidance.[69] This is echoed in Judge Malenovský's observation that the extraordinary circumstances provision has become a definitional 'minefield', not least because of a series of last-minute withdrawals of preliminary reference requests, which continue to hamper the Court's efforts to provide clear guidance.[70] To the extent that divergence across the Member States is driven by such tactics, rather than by a genuine difference in judicial approaches, the exhaustive list and explicit definitions contained with the Regulation itself may well be important steps towards the uniform protection of air passengers' rights. At the same time, however, it is unlikely that the judicial dialogue between domestic courts and Luxembourg will come to an end any time soon, not least given the fact that such 'dialogue conducted within the context of the exercise of [the Court's] judicial powers has helped refine the rules applicable in particular areas', a dialogue which, as this section has demonstrated, 'may also occur when [the political institutions of the Union] take the case law of the ECJ into account in exercising their own decision-making powers'.[71]

IV. Domestic Enforcement

As the Union's passenger rights regime is cast in a Regulation, the question of enforcement should in principle need little attention: the TFEU itself provides unequivocally that 'A regulation shall have general application. It shall be binding in its entirety and directly applicable in all Member States.'[72] The fact that Regulation 261 also provides for the establishment or designation of so-called NEBs does not detract from the fact that individual claims for compensation can therefore

---

[68] S Garben, 'The Turbulent Life of Regulation 261: Continuing Controversies Surrounding EU Air Passenger Rights', ch 18 of the present volume, 273, 288.

[69] See, eg, European Commission, Communication from the Commission to the European Parliament and the Council on the application of Regulation 261/2004 establishing common rules on compensation and assistance to passengers in the event of denied boarding and of cancellation or long delay of flights COM(2011) 174 final, and the documents cited therein.

[70] Malenovský (n 14) 30.

[71] A Arnull, 'Judicial Dialogue in the European Union' in J Dickson and P Eleftheriadis (eds), *Philosophical Foundations of European Union Law* (Oxford University Press, 2012) 114–15.

[72] TFEU, Art 288.

be brought in the appropriate domestic judicial forum.[73] Indeed, in *McDonagh v Ryanair* the Court explicitly rejected a submission disputing the admissibility of the passenger's claim on the basis that individual passengers lacked *standing* to challenge carriers' compliance with Articles 5 and 9 of the Regulation before domestic courts as a result of the provision for NEBs in Article 16 of the Regulation.[74]

Despite this affirmation of the independent nature of NEBs' enforcement powers, the national reports present an extremely complicated picture as regards the dual-track nature of judicial and administrative enforcement. Michal Bobek's overview of the institutional and procedural dimensions of Regulation 261 in chapter twenty-one explores these divergences in detail;[75] suffice it to say that the roles played by designated NEBs vary drastically. These differences across legal systems (including sometimes even uncertainties and contradictions *within* a single Member State) have led to significant complications in the effective protection of passengers' rights.

It is therefore unsurprising that the Commission's reform proposals strive to '[e]nsure effective and consistent sanctioning' and to clarify

> the role of [NEBs] by clearly allocating the role of general enforcement to the NEBs while out-of-court handling of individual complaints will be a role for complaint handling bodies which may become Alternative Dispute Resolution (ADR) Bodies under the new ADR Directive. Both types of bodies will closely cooperate.[76]

These lofty goals are translated into Articles 16 and 16a of the amended Regulation. Article 16(2), as amended by the European Parliament, for example, provides that

> The National Enforcement Body shall closely monitor compliance with the requirements of this Regulation and take the measures necessary to ensure that the rights of passengers are respected … It shall take enforcement actions based on individual complaints transmitted by the body designated under Article 16a. Member States shall ensure that their respective National Enforcement Bodies are given sufficient power to penalise effectively with infringements.

This broad-ranging power is supplemented by Article 16a, which provides for a further (and, as currently drafted, rather bewildering) set of alternatives:

> (2) If a passenger wants to make a complaint to the air carrier with regard to his rights under this Regulation, he shall submit it within 3 months from the date on which the flight was performed or was scheduled to be performed. The submission of a complaint within three months and after the expiry of that three-month period shall be without prejudice to his right to enforce his claims under this Regulation within the framework of the judicial system and an out-of-court resolution …

---

[73] Toulson LJ's suggestion, in *Graham v Thomas Cook* [2012] EWCA Civ 1355 [19], that the judge at first instance was 'right to hold that breach of [Regulation 261/2004 obligations] does not give rise to a civil action for damages' is, therefore, with respect, inaccurate as a matter of EU and English law.

[74] Case C-12/11 *Denise McDonagh v Ryanair* (ECJ, 31 January 2013).

[75] M Bobek, 'Uniform Rights? The Nature of Regulations Revisited', ch 21 of the present volume, sections IV and V, respectively.

[76] European Commission Proposal (n 9) 7–8.

(3)   Member States shall ensure that air passengers are able to submit disputes with air
      carriers concerning rights and obligations established by this Regulation to inde-
      pendent, efficacious and efficient out-of-court resolution mechanisms. ...

At first sight, these additional powers and procedures are clearly intended to
assist passengers (and national regulators) in challenging airlines' deliberate
non-compliance with Regulation 261: there seems to be a wide-spread culture of
carriers 'boycot[ting] European legislation or at least not tak[ing] it seriously',[77]
and the same is said of the future, where 'it is likely that some airlines will try to
avoid compensating their passengers'.[78] As Arnold notes, airlines 'generally do not
compensate their passengers, unless a claim is submitted. It is unlikely that this
practice will change.'[79] In the face of such practices, changes such as the provision
of clear claim channels and tight time limits under a new Article 16a might have
the potential to make a significant difference to passengers.

Will the proposals help to address the problems arising as regards the disparate
enforcement, however? There are at least three potential problems with the NEB
reform proposals' failure to react to the heterogeneous Member State experience.
The first of these concerns is that a strengthening of the role of NEBs, such as the
Civil Aviation Authority (CAA) in the UK, will not necessarily guarantee more
effective protection. Whilst some NEBs, such as those in the Czech Republic and
Slovakia, have taken a very proactive role in the enforcement of individual claims
brought to their attention, the CAA's understanding of its role suggests that it will
not 'generally take enforcement action based on the facts in a single complaint',
looking instead 'to ensure future compliance by addressing systemic non-
compliance by a business'.[80] The creation of alternative mechanisms will similarly
not guarantee automatic success: as the Dutch experience shows,[81] a commission
established by agreement between consumer and airline representatives and
tasked to operate very much along the lines of the provisions of Article 16a(3) was
abolished after a comparatively short life span, given wide-spread dissatisfaction
with its operation across the Netherlands.

Indeed, the very fact that two distinct bodies might now be tasked with enforcing passengers' rights in addition to the courts might lead to significant confusion.
As Benyon has highlighted:

[F]irst, Article 16(2) still states that the NEBs are responsible for ensuring the respect of
passengers' rights and that they may decide on enforcement actions based on individual

---

[77] C van Dam, 'Air Passenger Rights after Sturgeon' (2011) 36 *Air & Space Law* 259, 260.
[78] K Arnold and P Mendes de Leon, 'Regulation (EC) 261/2004 in the Light of the Recent Decisions
of the European Court of Justice: Time for a Change?!' (2010) 35 *Air & Space Law* 91, 110.
[79] K Arnold, 'EU Air Passenger Rights: assessment of the proposal of the European Commission for
the amendment of Regulation (EC) 261/2004 and of Regulation (EC) 2027/97' (2013) 38 *Air & Space
Law* 403, 422.
[80] Civil Aviation Authority, 'Response to Freedom of Information Act request' (31 July 2014), as
reported in B Jones, 'United Kingdom and Ireland: Passenger Protection Turns a Corner', ch 16 of the
present volume, 230.
[81] P Mendes de Leon and W Oude Alink, 'The Benelux: Small is not Less', ch 8 of the present volume.

complaints. Next, sub-paragraph (3) of the new Article 16a does not say how the out-of-court resolution will take place, nor set out the nature of the new body's 'final reply', which seems to be left to (differing) national laws. Would this lead to harmonised enforcement when we know that an out-of-court settlement body would not be able to pose a question to the CJEU?[82] Rather, this difficult task seems to be left in part to the European Commission to be resolved by a recommendation, which under Article 288 of the TFEU has no binding force![83]

The proposed regime thus contains ample scope for further confusion. This will only be potentiated by the stark differences in NEBs' roles—whether as actors in civil proceedings, at public law, or even without any meaningful legal power whatsoever.[84]

Building on Benyon's criticism, the final potential problem with strengthened NEBs for the uniform application of the passenger rights regime is the fact that the Court has generally chosen to adopt a rather laissez-faire attitude to their operation. When asked to rule on the powers of an NEB established in the context of a Regulation governing Rail Passengers' Rights and Obligation[85] in *ÖBB Personenverkehr*,[86] the Court placed significant emphasis on national procedural autonomy in determining the scope of an NEB's enforcement powers.[87] It is unclear how this deferential approach will sit with the modified Article 16 powers and procedures once (the inevitable?) differences in domestic implementation and practice become evident.

When seen through the lens of the Member State experiences, then, it appears that several aspects of the proposed reforms to the role of NEBs have the potential to create at least as many problems as they hope to resolve. This is in no small part due to the fact that they present a half-way solution between leaving matters entirely to national procedural autonomy, and designing a detailed mechanism for enforcement. Given the stark differences in national legal systems, this approach is likely to lead to significant complications, which may well have the very opposite effect on passengers and carriers from that intended by the reform's framers.

V. Conclusion: Uniformity as a Herculean Task?

In the original evaluation of the reform proposals, it was suggested that whilst 'the reforms purport to address a wide range of important concerns, only some

---

[82] Case C-394/11 *Belov v CHEZ Elektro Balgaria AD & Ors* (ECJ, 31 January 2013).

[83] F Benyon, 'Regulation 261: The Passenger Rights Framework', ch 3 of the present volume, 53–54.

[84] Such as the Belgian NEB: see Arrêt no 227.621, 206.347/XV-2048, 3 June 2014.

[85] Regulation (EC) No 1371/2007 on Rail Passengers' Rights and Obligations [2007] OJ L315/14, Art 30(1).

[86] Case C-509/11 *ÖBB Personenverkehr AG* (ECJ, 26 September 2013) (*ÖBB*). See further J Prassl, 'Compensation for Delayed Rail Journeys: EU Passenger Rights on Track. Case C-509/11 *ÖBB Personenverkehr AG*' (2014) 4 *Transportrecht* 158.

[87] *ÖBB* (n 86) para 64.

are fully resolved. Several long-standing questions, however, are left unanswered, and even some new ones thrown up'.[88] The present contribution has added to this conclusion a further set of complications, which will play a crucial role in determining whether a recast passenger rights regulation can succeed in providing consumers with uniform redress, or at least rights to redress, across the EU.

As a result of a survey of three core problems that had been the source of extensive litigation in the first decade since Regulation 261 came into force over 10 years ago—its compatibility with the Montreal Convention, the definition of important terms such as the extraordinary circumstances defence, and the role of NEBs—it has become evident that even following various amendments in the course of the proposal's passage through the European Parliament, several problems arising from the current heterogeneous implementation of the EU's passenger rights regime remain to be resolved.

At the same time, however, it is crucial not to lose sight of an important, if somewhat delicate, underlying question: according to the fundamental design of the Union legal order, Regulations are the strongest form of unification, yet the evidence presented in this volume points towards a series of significant systemic obstacles to the development of a uniform and effective system. Which actor, then, is best suited to overcome these obstacles? The legislator, in defining terms as precisely as possible; the Court of Justice, in (continuing) to be consistent in its interpretation of those provisions; litigants, in stopping abusive practices such as late reference withdrawals or repeated challenges based on near-identical points; or NEBs, in clarifying their role and acting according to common standards?

In reality, the answer to this conundrum lies in the realisation that it is unlikely that all problems could be resolved successfully by any one of these parties as long as the focus of the reform proposals continues to fail to take full account of the *de facto* situation in the 28 Member States. It is only by acknowledging and attempting to grapple with the heterogeneity of underlying Member State experiences that an implementation of the EU's passenger rights regime much closer to what its framing as a Regulation envisaged will become a possibility.

---

[88] Prassl (n 12) 61.

21

Uniform Rights? The Nature of Regulations Revisited

MICHAL BOBEK

I. Introduction (30 Minutes to Touchdown)

Ladies and Gentlemen, welcome to the end of this volume! If you have arrived here, the local time is bound to be late, since you had to travel through 20 connecting chapters. The temperature is high, since the debates surrounding Regulation 261 are heated, as clearly visible in a number of the previous chapters. Without offering too many additional forced air travel metaphors, this chapter revisits the subject matter of this volume within the broader context of national application and enforcement of EU law—the very subject of this series of books. What can the operation of Regulation 261 in the Member States tell us about the life of EU law in the Member States in general?

The chapter proceeds as follows: first, the orthodoxy, in terms of what and how a regulation is supposed to function within the legal systems of the Member States, is set out. Secondly, the operation of the Regulation 261 in the Member States, as captured by the individual country reports in the second part of this volume, is examined comparatively in relation to three elements in turn: substantive rights, institutions and procedures. Thirdly and lastly, the performance of Regulation 261 in terms of genuinely unifying passenger's rights in Europe is evaluated. How much internal institutional and procedural diversity can there be if we want to talk of uniform rights and a unified regime?

II. An EU Regulation: The Orthodoxy

In a standard EU law textbook,[1] a regulation is likely to be introduced as one of the typical sources of EU law, with reference made to the wording of Article 288 TFEU:

---

[1] eg P Craig and G de Búrca, *EU Law: Text, Cases, and Materials* (5th edn, Oxford University Press, 2011) 105–06; D Chalmers, G Davies, and G Monti, *European Union Law* (2nd edn, Cambridge University Press, 2010) 98–99; C Barnard and S Peers (eds), *European Union Law* (Oxford University Press,

A regulation shall have general application. It shall be binding in its entirety and directly applicable in all Member States.

To facilitate students' understanding, a regulation is likely to be equated with a European 'statute' or 'law'. It enters the legal orders of all the Member States directly, without any need for its further domestic implementation.

A textbook definition of a regulation could be thus said to centre on three elements: first, the regulation is, as Article 288 TFEU itself states, directly applicable. Today, for all practical purposes, this essentially means directly effective. The text of the regulation itself is the source of rights and obligations. It is relied upon by national judges or administrative authorities, who work directly with the text as published in the *Official Journal*. Secondly, a regulation, in contrast to a directive, requires, unless it provides to the contrary, no further implementing or transposing measures on the part of the Member States. Thirdly, a regulation is the EU's primary tool for legal unification. In contrast to a directive or other sources of EU law allowing flexibility in national transposition, the very purpose of a regulation is to create uniform rights that apply equally across the Union.

The operation of Regulation 261 as set out in Part II. of the present volume, however, challenges this account, in particular as regards the second and third definitional elements of what a regulation is, and how it ought to be applied domestically. The national reports show a striking diversity in application in the Member States, in spite of the object of this study being a regulation, that is, the strongest tool the EU legal order has at its disposal in terms of generating uniformity across its Member States. These challenges will now be assessed comparatively with regard to three elements: first, substantive rights of air passengers provided for in the Regulation 261; secondly, the institutions in the Member States that have been put in place for safeguarding these rights, in particular the nebulous position of the national enforcement bodies (NEB); and, thirdly, the ensuing diversity in procedures, both administrative and judicial, for enforcing passenger rights.

III. Substantive Rights

Regulation 261 is concerned primarily with rights, or rather entitlements, guaranteed to air passengers in cases of delay, cancellation and denied boarding.[2] On the level of substantive entitlements of the passengers and duties of the air carriers, Regulation 261 can be said to provide a uniform set of substantive rules applicable across the Union. Certainly, Regulation 261 could be said to be replete with

---

2014) 99–100; K Lenaerts *et al*, *European Union Law* (3rd edn, Sweet and Maxwell, 2011) 893–96; T Oppermann, *Europarecht* (3rd edn, CH Beck, 2005) 164–65; JP Jacqué, *Droit institutionnel de l´Union européenne* (7th edn, Dalloz, 2012) 546–47.

[2] For a thorough description, see above, ch 1.III.

indeterminate legal notions in need of interpretation: What is an 'extraordinary circumstance'? What is a 'delay'? What is a 'cancellation'? What is, as a matter of fact, a 'flight'?

However, the fact that even such basic notions tend to be understood differently in different Member States, or even differently by different courts within one and the same Member State, is perhaps not as tragic as some ardent opponents of Regulation 261 would like one to believe. It is rather legal and judicial 'business as usual'. Any new piece of legislation, be it on the national or even more so on supranational or European levels, is in its initial phase in need of interpretation, of judicial fleshing out of common notions.[3] Naturally, these will, for some time at least, diverge. The process is the same as on the national level. There too, before the supreme national judicial authority steps in and starts unifying the case law, there is likely to be divergence in opinions within the judicial system, with, for example, the various courts of appeal having different ideas from one another.

From this point of view, labelling Regulation 261 as a 'deficient' piece of legislation just because it did not provide, from the moment of its entry into force, an exhaustive and ironclad definition of a 'delay' or a list of 'extraordinary circumstances', is either evidence of an acute variety of legislative optimism that believes that the legislator can or should provide for everything,[4] or may be advanced in order to dissimulate the genuine, rather economic reasons for dissatisfaction with the Regulation 261.

What is nonetheless remarkable from the systemic point of view is the specific way in which judicial definitions of the indeterminate legal notions of Regulation 261 are being fleshed out. Claims for compensation brought under the Regulation are small claims. They tend to be excluded from the possibility to be heard before the national supreme jurisdiction, or sometimes even from appellate review.[5] Within such settings, it is the CJEU that is called to unify the case law and its interpretation, in an exclusive exchange with the lower national courts, typically bypassing the higher national courts. Thus, a peculiar judicial structure is brought

---

[3] In both legal traditions, civilian as well as the common law one. There is of course a clear difference in drafting style. In civilian legislative drafting, indeterminate legal notions and broader notions left to judicial interpretation are a common feature. In contrast, an English statute would typically contain a long list of initial definitions that seek to provide terminological clarity. To what degree such an approach may be successful in terms of removing definitional problems may be open to discussion; a glance at the normal interpretative business carried out in English or common law courts generally might indicate that even such an approach to legislative drafting does not eliminate the natural need for later judicial interpretation. It rather pushes the ensuing interpretative endeavours to a different level of abstraction. For an overall comparative evaluation, see, eg, N MacCormick and RS Summers (eds), *Interpreting Statutes: A Comparative Study* (Dartmouth, 1991).

[4] Such a modernist idea, as alluring at it might be, has never worked and, unless we replace humans with robots, is unlikely to work in the future. For an early effort in this regard, see, eg, the *Allgemeines Landrecht für die Preußischen Staaten* of 5 February 1794. Whilst it contained over 17,000 paragraphs, it could hardly be said that it enhanced legal certainty and removed interpretative uncertainties.

[5] In, eg, Austria and Germany (ch 7.I); the Czech Republic and Slovakia (ch 10.III.A); France (ch 12.II.B); Italy (ch 13.IV.C); Spain (ch 15.II.A).

about, encompassing primarily lower national courts and the CJEU. This means, amongst other things, that the Regulation 261 regime provides an example against the sometimes discussed possibility of limiting the power to request a preliminary ruling to the highest national jurisdictions.[6] If such an option were to be contemplated in the future, it would exclude an entire area of law from the possibility of ever reaching the CJEU.

The fact that a number of different actors coming from different backgrounds are asked to read and to interpret the same substantive provisions provides fertile grounds for socio-legal comparisons. The contested distinction between a 'delay' and 'cancellation', as culminating in *Sturgeon*,[7] offers an intriguing case study in this regard. Diving into the national reports, one notices a considerable difference in approach, reflecting perhaps to some degree differences in approach to statutory interpretation: from the Dutch textual reading of Regulation 261, sustaining a clear distinction between a delay and a cancellation; through some German anticipation and doubts; to the rather surprising example of Italy, where the Italian courts took the same approach as the CJEU in *Sturgeon* even before the latter decision was issued.

Furthermore, after *Sturgeon*, the approaches of various national courts differed again: from embracing the expansion of the scope of passengers' rights protection carried out in *Sturgeon* in a number of states like Poland, Bulgaria or, understandably, Italy; through occasional grumbling but generally applying the position of the CJEU as in the Netherlands or in France; through a 'disbelief amongst the judges and practitioners',[8] coupled with a rather singular request for a preliminary ruling enquiring whether the CJEU is familiar with the principle of separation of powers, as applicable in Germany;[9] to the national courts falling conspicuously silent in terms of even requesting preliminary rulings on the interpretation of Regulation 261, as in England, since where there are no questions, there will be no answers.[10]

Could such a difference in approach be viewed as driven by deeper-seated convictions relating to 'proper' way of statutory interpretation[11] in each of the systems studied, and the margin of creativity allowed to a judge within such a system? Or are the correct explanations perhaps much more down to earth, combining a set of economic and geographical factors (such as a country's size, or amount of air traffic) with a correlating degree of air industry interest present within the

---

[6] See especially J Komárek, 'In the Court We Trust? On the need for hierarchy and differentiation in the preliminary ruling procedure' (2007) 32 *EL Rev* 467.

[7] Joined Cases C-402/07 and 432/07 *Sturgeon v Condor Flugdienst* [2009] ECR I-10923.

[8] Above ch 7.III.B.

[9] Case C-431/11 *Germanwings GmbH v Thomas Amend* ECLI:EU:C:2013:246.

[10] Above, ch 16.IV, tracing the origins of this position already back to the *ex parte IATA* decision of the CJEU.

[11] For an in-depth discussion, see, eg, S Vogenauer, *Die Auslegung von Gesetzen in England und auf dem Kontinent: Eine vergleichende Untersuchung der Rechtssprechung und ihrer historischen Grundlagen* (Mohr Siebeck, 2001).

jurisdiction in question, which are able to prod the perception, discussion and, accordingly, judicial approach in certain directions?

Be it as it may, in terms of substantive rights provided to the passengers in the European Air Space, Regulation 261 goes furthest in delivering what a regulation arguably ought to deliver, taken at its textbook definition provided above. Certainly, there are interpretative uncertainties across the Member States of the Union. These are, however, not 'extraordinary circumstances' but a normal state of affairs in the case of any new piece of legislation, both in quantity as well as in quality.

IV. Institutions

If, at the level of substantive rights, Regulation 261 provides for a fairly comprehensive list of entitlements for the air passengers, the picture becomes much fuzzier and problematic at the level of the enforcement of such claims.

In the EU constitutional system, when establishing common European rules, regulations included, enforcement is left to the Member States.[12] Thus, even if the title of a legislative act may induce a different impression, EU law always provides for only partial unification, most frequently just in relation to substantive rules. The designation of the institutions for enforcing these rules, as well as procedures for doing so, is left to the Member States. This principle is referred to as the principle of 'national procedural autonomy'.[13] This expression is not entirely correct, because also within their seemingly autonomous space of choice, the Member States remain under EU supervision as far as the equivalence and effectiveness of their choices are concerned.[14] However, it may be properly said that provided that EU law itself contains no explicit provisions in this regard, the 'default choice' with regard to institutions and procedures rests with the Member States.

Regulation 261 is no exception in this regard. Its provisions on enforcement procedures are frugal indeed, consisting of just one Article. It reads as follows:

Article 16   Infringements

1. Each Member State shall designate a body responsible for the enforcement of this Regulation as regards flights from airports situated on its territory and flights from a

---

[12] Which may therefore be labelled as 'cooperative federalism'—see further R Schütze, *From Dual to Cooperative Federalism: the Changing Structure of European* Law (Oxford University Press, 2009).

[13] In the more recent case law of the CJEU discussed rather under the heading of the requirement of 'effective judicial protection'. See, eg, Case C-268/06 *Impact* [2008] ECR I-2483, paras 43–48; Case C-279/09 *DEB* [2010] ECR I-13880, paras 29–33; Case C-177/10 *Rosado Santana* [2011] ECR I-7907, paras 87–89; Case C-320/08 *Alassini* [2010] ECR I-2213, paras 46–49; Case C-93/12 *ET Agrokonsulting-04-Velko Stoyanov* ECLI:EU:C:2013:432, para 59.

[14] See, eg, M Bobek, 'Why There is no Principle of "Procedural Autonomy" of the Member States', in H-W Micklitz and B de Witte (eds), *The European Court of Justice and the Autonomy of the Member States* (Intersentia, 2012) 305.

third country to such airports. Where appropriate, this body shall take the measures necessary to ensure that the rights of passengers are respected. The Member States shall inform the Commission of the body that has been designated in accordance with this paragraph.

2. Without prejudice to Article 12, each passenger may complain to any body designated under paragraph 1, or to any other competent body designated by a Member State, about an alleged infringement of this Regulation at any airport situated on the territory of a Member State or concerning any flight from a third country to an airport situated on that territory.

3. The sanctions laid down by Member States for infringements of this Regulation shall be effective, proportionate and dissuasive.

There is certainly a difference across the Member States in terms of defining the exact contours of and the borders between private and public law.[15] There might be also difference in terms of classifying the exact type of claims that Regulation 261 generates for air passengers. There is, however, little doubt that claims arising under Regulation 261 are, in terms of jurisdiction, private or civil law claims, although stemming from a regulation (ie a 'statute'). An individual (the passenger) is suing another individual (the air carrier) for standardised damage. Thus, as all the national reports confirm, the proper place for such claims are civil courts of first instance in the Member States.

Article 16, however, adds two further enforcement layers to this primarily civil law claim. Both are administrative. First, Article 16(1) provides for a *general supervisory* activity of competent administrative bodies. Read in conjunction with Recital (22), first sentence, this supervisory activity ought to relate to the overall compliance of air carriers with the provisions of Regulation 261, in the same way as they monitor and enforce any other rules applicable to the aviation industry. Certainly, individual cases of Regulation 261 violations may be relevant for such supervision, but only as indicators of overall compliance.

Secondly, and on the top of that, Article 16(2) introduces a right of *individual complaint*: 'each passenger may complain'.[16] This provision is clearly aimed at individual complaints that may be lodged with the designated national enforcement authority, which the authority must process and decide, in one way or another, on its basis.

However, these two types of administrative enforcement of Regulation 261 follow quite a different logic. In the first case, the national authority acts as a regulator of a given sector. Administrative procedures, if launched, will be instituted against

---

[15] On a theoretical level, see, eg, EJ Weinrib, *The Idea of Private Law* (Harvard University Press, 1995); O Dawn, *Common Values and the Public-Private Divide* (Butterworths, 1999). For a comparative study, see, eg, M Freedland and J-B Auby (eds), *The public law/private law divide: une entente assez cordiale?* (Hart Publishing, 2006).

[16] 'Tout passager peut saisir tout organisme désigné en application du paragraphe 1, ou tout autre organisme compétent désigné par un État membre, d'une plainte concernant une violation du présent règlement' in French, or 'jeder Fluggast [kann] bei einer gemäß Absatz 1 benannten Stelle oder einer sonstigen von einem Mitgliedstaat benannten zuständigen Stelle Beschwerde wegen eines behaupteten Verstoßes gegen diese Verordnung erheben' in German.

economic operators, the air carriers, and will concern overall non-compliance. In the second case, the logic is one of an ombudsperson or an office for the protection of consumers, which is obliged to deal with every individual case lodged and, explicitly or not, to provide protection for the individual air passengers in their capacity as consumers.

As is evident from the individual country reports in the previous part of this volume, as well as from the comprehensive list of the designated national enforcement bodies (NEBs) compiled by the European Commission,[17] what follows is a considerable diversity in the selection of the NEB at the national level. Three approaches can be distinguished. First, a majority of the Member States entrusted both types of administrative enforcement to one single authority: either to the national civil aviation authority (eg the Czech Republic, Denmark; Germany; Greece; Poland;[18] Ireland; Italy; Lithuania; Portugal; or Spain), or to a specialised department of the national ministry of transport (eg Austria; France; Belgium; Bulgaria; the Netherlands;[19] or Slovenia). Secondly, several Member States also designated one single authority for both types of administrative enforcement, but quite a different one in its nature: the national consumer protection body (eg Estonia; Latvia; or Romania). Thirdly, there is also a handful of Member States that, perhaps after pondering on the quite different nature of the functions the administrative body is supposed to fulfil under Article 16(1) as contrasted with Article 16(2) of Regulation 261, decided to split the enforcement regime and to designate two or even three NEBs: the national civil aviation authority for overall enforcement, and the national consumer protection body or the trade inspectorate for the handling of individual complaints (eg Finland; Hungary; Slovakia; Sweden; or the UK).

As is evidenced in the national reports, such institutional choices are not merely cosmetic. They tend to have a considerable impact on the enforcement of Regulation 261, in particular on individual case handling by the administrative authorities. It may not be that surprising that if the designated NEB is a national consumer protection body, its enforcement stance in individual cases is likely to be more proactive and assertive. Conversely, some national civil aviation authorities might consider themselves to be an expert body, the sector regulator, whose task it is emphatically not to provide individual redress for consumers.[20]

In sum, the national institutional diversity or uncertainty reflects in a way the double nature of Regulation 261 itself: is it primarily a consumer protection

---

[17] See especially Commission Staff Working Paper accompanying the Communication from the Commission to the European Parliament and the Council on the operation and the results of Regulation (EC) 261/2004, document COM(2011) 174 final of 11 April 2011, point 3.

[18] It ought to be added that although in Poland, the formally designated body is the President of the Office of Civil Aviation, when handling individual complaints, the President is assisted by a dedicated Commission for Protection of Passengers Rights within the Office. Thus, the system might be seen as a mixed one. See further ch 14.I.

[19] As from 1 January 2012. Further ch 8.II.B.

[20] *cf* above ch 16.I. and the example of the UK Civil Aviation Authority, explicitly confirmed by the statements made by the Authority (text to nn 7 and 8 in ch 16).

measure, or a market harmonisation and regulation measure?[21] In terms of functions, logic and operation of public administration, a phenomenon known in other areas[22] becomes equally apparent in the context of the national enforcement of Regulation 261: the *hybridisation* of national administrative bodies. The EU level requires a certain type of activity to be carried out at the national level. Since no national governments wish to establish new administrative bodies on every such occasion, they tend to, when implementing EU law, rather just add such new competences to already existing national bodies. Sometimes, the new competences may be a logical extension of the latter's extant powers. Ever so often, however, they are just added because there is some tenuous, area-related link. If that happens, a national administrative body is likely to find itself left with an incongruous collection of competences assembled over the years, or even a true competence goulash.[23]

V. Procedures

The previous section outlined that the substantive provisions of the Regulation 261 can be enforced in three different ways:

(1) *Administrative-general*—overall regulatory oversight by the designated national enforcement body (Article 16(1));

(2) *Administrative-individual*—handling of individual complaints brought by passengers to the designated NEB (Article 16(2));

(3) *Civil*—individual actions filed against the air carriers before national civil courts.

---

[21] Although Recital (4) mentions both aims in one sentence, Recital (1) as well as the overall tone and thrust of Regulation 261 clearly point at a consumer protection measure. The formal legal basis for Regulation 261 was, however, former Art 80(2) TEC, ie the title on transport policy, not consumer protection.

[22] See generally the various contributions in J-B Auby *et al* (eds), *L'influence du droit européen sur le catégories du droit public* (Dalloz, 2010).

[23] To give just one other example of the same phenomenon: Art 13 of the Council Directive 2000/43/EC of 29 June 2000 implementing the principle of equal treatment between persons irrespective of racial or ethnic origin [2000] OJ L180/22, requires the Member States to designate a body or bodies for the promotion of equal treatment of all persons without discrimination on the grounds of racial or ethnic origin. Such a body shall, amongst other things, conduct independent surveys concerning discrimination and publish independent reports and make recommendations on any issue relating to such discrimination. In the Czech Republic, no such body existed before the implementation of the Directive. The designated body then became the Ombudsperson, since the subject matter had 'something [to do] with discrimination', which was already before investigated by the Ombudsperson, but only in the context of individual complaints. The Ombudsperson objected to this new competence, stating that its task was to provide informal, flexible redress in individual cases, not to design and executive overall governmental policies, write reports, etc. Eventually, a new department within the Ombudsperson Office had to be created, the task of which become to carry out these activities that are conceptually rather remote from the overall competence of the Ombudsperson.

Leaving aside the institutional uncertainty concerning the question of which administrative authority shall be designated as the NEB (civil aviation authority, or the consumer protection body or both), discussed above, there is also a bifurcation at the level of enforcement of individual claims. Is an individual claim for compensation provided for by Regulation 261 to be brought before civil courts (3), before the designated administrative authority (2) or even both at the same time?

Regulation 261 as interpreted by the CJEU allows for both. Recital (22) states that the administrative supervision carried out by the NEBs 'should not affect the rights of passengers and air carriers to seek legal redress from courts under procedures of national law'. Furthermore, in *Denise McDonagh v Ryanair Ltd*,[24] responding to the Council's argument concerning admissibility of a request for a preliminary ruling, the CJEU replied:

> The fact, noted in this connection by the Council, that each Member State designates a body responsible for the enforcement of Regulation No 261/2004 which, where appropriate, takes the measures necessary to ensure that the rights of passengers are respected and which each passenger may complain to about an alleged infringement of that regulation, in accordance with Article 16 of the regulation, is not such as to affect the right of a passenger to such reimbursement.

> Article 16 cannot be interpreted as allowing only national bodies responsible for the enforcement of Regulation No 261/2004 to sanction the failure of air carriers to comply with their obligation laid down in Articles 5(1)(b) and 9 of that regulation to provide care.[25]

The underlying idea behind such an approach might perhaps have been that by opening multiple avenues for the enforcement of Regulation 261 and the rights individuals derive from it, the overall national enforcement of Regulation 261 was bound to become more effective. The national enforcement practices, however, as evidenced in a number of national reports in the preceding part of this volume, rather confirm the idiom about too many cooks in the kitchen spoiling the broth. The national enforcement hesitations relating to this bifurcated enforcement regime can be conceptualised on two levels: systemic and practical.

On a *systemic* level, the Member States' legal systems operate various types of division between public and private law.[26] In a number of Member States, the divide is defined by the nature of the parties and/or the type of legal relationship between them.[27] Therefore, rights and entitlements between private parties are a matter for private law, and hence to be adjudicated upon by civil courts. Thus, disputes between an individual (consumer, air passenger) and another individual (undertaking, air carrier) fall within the competence of civil courts. The fact that

---

[24] Case C-12/11, *Denise McDonagh v Ryanair Ltd*, ECLI:EU:C:2013:43.
[25] ibid, paras 22–23.
[26] Above (n 15).
[27] For the EU law perspective, see, eg, Case C-49/12 *Sunico ApS* ECLI:EU:C:2013:545, para 34, or Case C-645/11 *Sapir* ECLI:EU:C:2013:228, para 33.

there is a fair number of rules applicable because they were imposed by the public will and public interest does not change the original private nature of the legal relationship. For example, the entire area of consumer protection is in fact a (public law) regulation intervening into the law of contract, which, however, does not alter the competence of the courts.

From the inherent competence of civil courts for disputes between two private individuals also follows the fact that a public authority, such as an administrative body, cannot step into the legal relationship between two private parties and start altering their mutual rights and obligations. This is within the exclusive competence of civil courts, following an action brought by one individual against another. The underlying idea there is one of separation of powers.

Against this background, Article 16(2) of Regulation 261 asks the NEB, ie an administrative authority, to step into a private relationship in order to pass authoritative decisions about the compensation to be paid by one private party to another private party due to, essentially, non-performance of a contract (of carriage). On the level of principle, such competence is problematic for a number of Member States' legal systems.

Such systemic hesitations are visible already when deciding on the procedure in which an administrative authority would be authorised to intervene and what form its decisions should take. When handling individual cases under Article 16(2) of Regulation 261, is the administrative authority entitled to issue merely non-binding 'letters' to the air carrier, making suggestions as to when compensation is due? If this is indeed true, it may be hardly surprising that a number of specialised, expert civil aviation agencies might not be attracted by the idea of serving as a type of polite consultation place for consumers and sending around humble letters to the air carriers. Or is the NEB entitled to launch a (full?) administrative procedure, resulting in a binding administrative decision, which then, however, may be subject to review before administrative courts?

Two of the case studies presented in the previous part of this volume stand out in this regard. First, the problem of definitional 'blurred lines' introduced by the Regulation 261 is picked up and extensively discussed in the Bulgarian report. It dissects the uncertainties faced by the Bulgarian Directorate-General for Civil Aviation of the Ministry of Transport in deciding how to decide, eventually settling for simple 'letters' devoid of legal force.[28]

Secondly, faced with the same legal question but within the Belgian legal context, the Belgian Council of State (Conseil d'Etat/Raad van State) stated in its decision of 3 June 2014[29] that decisions formally taken by the Belgian NEB (the Mobility and Transport Service of the Federal Public Service, ie a department of the federal Government) are devoid of any binding, legal force.[30] In the case in question, the Belgian NEB, following a complaint filed with it by two passengers

---

[28] Above ch 9.II.
[29] Arrêt no 227.621 du 3 juin 2014, 206.347/XV-2048 (*Etihad Airways*).
[30] Above ch 8.III.C.i.

whose flights with Etihad Airways were considerably delayed, addressed a letter to the air carrier, recognising in substance the claims made by the passengers and urging the carrier to pay out compensation to the passengers. In examining the nature of the challenged act, the Council of State noted that under Belgian constitutional rules, administrative authorities are not competent to pass judgements on damages or compensation due between private parties. Therefore, irrespective of the wording of the letter addressed to the air carrier, which, if viewed on its substance, looked a lot like an administrative decision, the act had no binding force. The air carrier can therefore disregard the opinion of the NEB without any sanctions being imposed on it, certainly in the individual case. Moreover, the non-binding opinion of the NEB is equally not binding on civil courts in potential subsequent civil proceedings.[31]

Furthermore, within those systems that allow for (fully-fledged and binding) administrative decisions to be issued by the NEBs, while allowing also for a claim to be brought before the civil courts directly against the air carrier, a number of practical, jurisdictional issues arise. Is it possible to have the same claim for compensation being treated in parallel before an administrative authority and before a civil court? In the event that the passengers fails to obtain a favourable decision by the administrative authority, may they start an action for administrative review before administrative courts while simultaneously pursuing their claim before civil courts?

From the limited evidence there is on this account, perhaps also due to the fact that such hard jurisdictional issues are bound to come only later, with some delay, parallel claims within both systems of jurisdiction, civil and administrative, appear possible in some systems, for example in Poland.[32] However, the vision that might fill an ardent complainer with joy may be less reassuring for some national practitioners and judges: what about *lis pendens*? *Res iudicata*? What if a national administrative court, while reviewing a negative decision of the NEB, annuls the decision, thus de facto recognising the substance of the compensation claim, while a civil court seized in parallel by the identical claim rejects it, stating that the conditions of Regulation 261 were not met?

True, as is visible in some of the national reports, the potential competence conflict between civil and administrative courts is in most cases likely to be settled by the degree of 'customer satisfaction'. In cases where the NEB in question appears to be able and ready to seize its role as an assertive consumer rights enforcement body, most of the enforcement regime on the national level is likely to be channelled into administrative action and administrative judicial review. In realist terms, filing in a complaint with an administrative body and leaving the state to 'deal with' the air carrier will always be a more attractive option for passengers than having to go to a civil court, in particular for such a comparably low sum of money.

---

[31] Arrêt no 227.621 (n 29) [XV-2048-9/11—XV-2048-10/11].
[32] Above ch 14.I, n 11.

Revisiting, against this specific background of Regulation 261, the more general question: how is EU law to be enforced at the national level? The somewhat blurry and unsettling jurisdictional picture painted in this section, in which the enforcement of passenger rights derived from Regulation 261 oscillates between public and private enforcement, presents an excellent case study for a number of key questions in the debate on enforcement of EU law. The debate on the suitable balance between public and private enforcement of EU law at the national level is certainly nothing new. It has been argued and re-argued a number of times, be it in the context of individual EU law policies, notably EU competition rules, but also, for example, equality law and the prohibition of discrimination, or at the meta-level, in relation to the entire structure of EU law and its judicial architecture.[33]

The enforcement of competition rules as well as, for example, equality rules originally had its roots in essentially public law regimes. The rules certainly always had some private law implications,[34] but their primary enforcers at the level of the Member States were national administrative bodies. Over the years, there has been a push towards encouraging more of their private law enforcement, supplementing and enhancing extant administrative enforcement and oversight. The *leitmotif* of the day thus appears to be more private initiative and more private enforcement.[35]

The Regulation 261 regime appears to be going in the opposite direction. In its previous incarnation,[36] the Regulation was entirely silent on enforcement. Thus, its enforcement was likely to ensue before civil courts, with the imposed public law rules being de facto added to contractual obligations. Since 2005, however, and the entry into force of the new Regulation 261, the enforcement regime has started sliding more and more towards administrative enforcement, with private initiative and potential cases before civil courts being pushed into the background.

Leaving aside the grand debate whether or not EU law is in general better enforced publicly or privately, the enforcement of Regulation 261 rights is peculiar for another reason too: it opens up both ways in parallel, from the very beginning. The two ways are not construed as complementary and as one enhancing the other. They are fully-fledged alternatives. An identical claim may be brought within two systems of jurisdiction.

---

[33] By introducing the doctrine of direct effect, the CJEU has been said to have structurally provided for a diffused, decentralised way of EU law enforcement. By making EU law directly applicable in individual disputes in the Member States' courts, it supplemented the structural enforcement mechanisms of the infringement action with a powerful private oversight. On this account, see the various contributions in Court of Justice of the European Union, *50th Anniversary of the Judgment in Van Gend en Loos 1963–2013: Conference Proceedings* (Office for Official Publications, 2013).

[34] Such as, eg, the sanction of automatic nullity for contracts violating Art 101(1) TFEU, provided for in Art 101(2) TFEU, but also in all its previous numerical embodiments since the Rome Treaty.

[35] Certainly, in how far it has been actually successful is a different question. With tongue-in-cheek, a critical observer might suggest that, in competition law, there might be more articles dealing with its private enforcement that there is actual private enforcement, certainly on the European Continent (ie outside the UK).

[36] Council Regulation (EEC) No 295/91 of 4 February 1991 establishing common rules for a denied-boarding compensation system in scheduled air transport [1991] OJ L36/5.

Whatever ideological conviction one may harbour about the proper enforcement of the law and the role of the individual within it, such a way of enforcing one and the same instrument is simply problematic in *practical*, functional terms, as evidenced in a number of national reports in Part II of this volume. On their basis, it becomes evident that increasing the number of avenues for legal challenge is not necessarily conducive to increased access and greater justice. It may also lead to chaos, in which shared responsibility degenerates into shared irresponsibility: the individual blames the administrative body for being inactive, and the administrative body in turn blames the legislator for its lack of competence. Eventually, everybody turns against the EU legislator, wondering whether any serious thought was given to how such a parallel system would operate in practice, or whether certain provisions are simply mechanically copied from one regulation into another without giving a second thought to their implications within the specific regime in question.

Thus, as a matter of general policy in terms of effectively enforcing EU law-based rights at the national level, what the post-Regulation 261 approach to passengers' rights teaches us might be very simple. It is perhaps wiser to channel the enforcement of one EU law instrument into one and the same stream at the level of a Member State. It might be civil, it might be administrative, but it ought to be one only. Within that chosen enforcement stream, appropriate measures for facilitating and easing access should be taken. Put metaphorically: it is always better to have, for sea as well as air navigation in fact, one deeper and well-regulated channel than to have several parallel, but shallow and chaotic, ones.

Lastly, beyond the fundamental question of who is entitled to enforce passengers' rights stemming from Regulation 261, and according to which procedures, the individual country reports also evidence an enhanced degree of further procedural diversity within the Member States. Three of them will be mentioned by the way of a conclusion to this section.

First, the question marks that arise in the context of jurisdictional competence in terms of enforcement are then naturally mirrored within other procedural elements: the search for the specific nature of the claim[37] on which an action for compensation may be brought before the national courts spills over into issues of limitation periods for the same action. The national responses range from equating limitation periods for Regulation 261 claims with the next comparable type of claim[38] to, somewhat surprisingly perhaps, stating that since Regulation 261 is an EU law-specific regime, claims brought under Regulation 261 are subject to no temporal limitations at all, since the Regulation does not provide for them itself.[39]

---

[37] ie as a 'public law' or 'private law' one, and/or stemming directly from the Regulation 261 as a free-standing claim or as an additional rule being grafted onto the general contract of carriage—see, eg, Bulgaria (ch 9.IV); the Czech Republic (ch 10.V.G) or Spain (ch 15.II.C).

[38] Above ch 10.V.G (Czech Republic and Slovakia); ch 11.II.D (Estonia); or ch 16.III.D (UK).

[39] Apparently the position adopted for the moment by the Polish administrative courts—above ch 14.VI.

Secondly, some Member States' legal systems facilitate access to the civil courts in matters of Regulation 261 compensation. This is carried out either by channelling the enforcement of such claims into the generally available, simplified way of enforcing small claims, or specifically with regard to Regulation 261 claims. Examples of the latter type of arrangements include various private aggregator services.[40]

Thirdly and lastly, there is the question of language. It would appear that, without there being specific provisions to this effect in Regulation 261, most of the NEBs are ready to receive and process a complaint form in English in addition to the official language of the Member State concerned.[41] Such a model offers an intriguing, bottom-up elaborated alternative to the official top-down language regime of EU law.[42]

VI. Conclusions: Of Uniformity and Salami

Considerable diversity. That is, in a nutshell, the conclusion of the comparative enforcement study of Regulation 261 carried out in this volume. Translated into a metaphor, the different institutional and enforcement mechanisms in the Member States resemble a car that, by virtue of crossing the borders into another Member State, changes its shape and properties. Thus, in terms of enforcement in one Member State, there is the comfort of a BMW; by crossing the borders, the car becomes a Škoda, ie a design which perhaps, in the past, did not excite that much but certainly delivered good service for a reasonable price; crossing yet another border, the car becomes a veteran Trabant, and in the next it is just a coach, moving occasionally when pulled by horses, since apparently the engine has yet to be installed. In all these cases, there is some common proto-idea of a vehicle serving for personal transportation, but with striking differences as to its shape, function and efficiency.

There are two ways in which such findings can be interpreted. First, there is the optimistic one. Regulation 261 does precisely what a good EU regulation, in the spirit of the principles of subsidiarity and national procedural autonomy, ought to do: it provides a partial unification of the substantive rules, while leaving an appropriate space for the Member States to realise their preferences and to channel the enforcement of the common rules into the extant national structures.

---

[40] eg in Austria and Germany (ch 7.II.B) or in the Czech Republic or Slovakia (ch 10.V.I).

[41] Without, however, going for the moment as far as the Polish Supreme Administrative Court in authorising intriguing linguistic hybrids in terms of the form of a national administrative decision with the air carriers receiving decisions of the President of the Polish NEB in English with reasons stated in Polish—above ch 14.II.

[42] See also M Bobek, 'The Multilingualism of European Union Law in the National Courts: Beyond the Textbooks' in AL Kjær and S Adamo (eds), *Linguistic Diversity and European Democracy* (Ashgate, 2011).

In the vision of some actors and some Member States, this is precisely what 'Brussels' should do, with the keywords being flexibility and legislative minimalism.

Secondly, the less charitable reading of the same results is likely to stress that the current national enforcement regimes of Regulation 261 provide for a bit too much diversity. Or, put in less diplomatic terms, it is rather a dysfunctional muddle. This starts with the conceptually questionable Article 16 of Regulation 261, unable to make up its mind about the enforcement channel and disrespecting the public/private law divide present in arguably a majority of the Member States. This problem then becomes echoed and multiplied at the level of the Member States. It could be counter-claimed that there still remain the same substantive rules relating to passengers' claims and compensation, which apply in all the Member States. A social-legal realist reply to such a claim might question what good are the same substantive rules in books if, in reality, they cannot be enforced effectively? What good are EU uniform rights that are available only in some Member States, thus becoming non-uniform by definition?

The Regulation 261 case study offered in this volume therefore brings to the fore with striking sharpness the classic conundrums relating to the need for and utility of EU legislation. If an EU regulation is adopted in the name of establishing uniform rules and uniform rights, and this is apparently as good as it gets in application reality later on, was it in fact worth it? Are the transaction costs in terms of adopting EU legislation justified? Or should the EU legislator, as a matter of policy, focus on adopting fewer legislative instruments but, within those, go into the appropriate regulatory depth?

In terms of our understanding of sources of EU law and their effects, regulations tend to be described as tools of legal unification within the Union: directly applicable and without the national transposition legislation interposing, they are the 'European laws', providing for the same set of rights in all the Member States.[43] In practical terms, however, as the Regulation 261 case study again demonstrates, there is a considerable diversity at the level of Member States even in cases of a regulation. Now if this is true generally, and not just the consequence of a somewhat questionable procedural design of Regulation 261, then what would it imply about the degree of 'uniformity' achievable by other sources of EU law, notably directives or former framework decisions, not to speak of EU soft law?

Perhaps the picture may not be as gloomy as it seems when approaching and understanding sources of EU law at a textbook level. The reason for this lies in the fact that over the years, the Treaty categories in Article 288 TFEU and the corresponding doctrinal distinction between a regulation and a directive have became more and more blurred in reality. There happen to be, perhaps more and more than before, regulations that mandate their own transposition. Conversely, directives tend to be longer and much more detailed, in fact not leaving that much room for transposition manoeuvres. More and more, therefore, resigned Member States just mechanically copy the text of the directives into their national legal

---

[43] Section II of this chapter.

orders. They simply remove the initial parts of the sentences stating that 'Member States shall' and decide on whether the new rules will be passed as a new piece of legislation, or adopted as an amendment to an already extant law or a codification.

Such blurring of lines between types of legislative acts may not be welcome in constitutional terms. In terms of the uniformity or diversity debate, however, it means that the degree of diversity in transposing EU law at the level of Member States may not be great, depending on whether a given area of EU law is governed by directives as opposed to regulations.

What of unity or uniformity in EU law application and interpretation then? The heretical question creeping into one's mind might be that if this is as good as it gets, should uniform application of EU law keep being considered as the 'sacrosanct idol' of EU law adjudication, overriding any other interests, in particular those of the Member States in keeping a differentiated regime? For example, why cannot Spain keep its specific regime within the European Arrest Warrant Framework Decision,[44] refusing to execute an EAW if the warrant was based on a conviction issued *in absentia* in the requesting state,[45] since there already is so much differentiation within the EAW regime anyway?[46] What difference does one further difference make?

The traditional answer from the CJEU to this question would be on the institutional side: somebody has to do it. Somebody has to look after the values of unity and uniform application of EU law. Since the Member States, and apparently the EU legislative process trapped in political haggling and trade-offs, will not do it, the CJEU should. However, even with such a normative proposition, it is fair to admit that there is and that there has always been a certain leeway in terms of judicially accepting internal diversity within the body of EU law.[47]

Lastly, the on-going process of the Regulation 261 revision reflects a number of well-known themes from the world of EU law and legislation. Since the fate, and above all the precise shape, of the eventual Regulation 261 recast remains uncertain, with the European Parliament suggesting over a hundred amendments[48]

---

[44] Council Framework Decision No 2002/584/JHA of 13 June 2002 on the European arrest warrant and the surrender procedures between Member States [2002] OJ L190/1.

[45] Case C-399/11, *Melloni* ECLI:EU:C:2013:107.

[46] For a comparative overview, see, eg, N Keijzer and E van Sliedregt (eds), *The European Arrest Warrant in Practice* (TMC Asser, 2009).

[47] Which of course changes in time. The CJEU, like any other institution, certainly engages and reacts, at least to some extent, to the external world. Thus, in spite of the *Melloni* example (n 45), the CJEU of the past years has been more inclined towards accepting some degree of differentiation and diversity. See, eg, Case C-110/05 *Commission v Italy (motorcycles trailers)* ECLI:EU:C:2009:66, para 65, where the CJEU was ready to introduce the notion of 'margin of appreciation', awarded to the Member States, into the area of free movement of goods, a development arguably difficult to imagine in the past.

[48] Report on the proposal for a regulation of the European Parliament and of the Council amending Regulation (EC) No 261/2004 establishing common rules on compensation and assistance to passengers in the event of denied boarding and of cancellation or long delay of flights and Regulation (EC) No 2027/97 on air carrier liability in respect of the carriage of passengers and their baggage by air of 22 January 2014 (COM(2013)0130—C7 0066/2013—2013/0072(COD)).

to the original Commission proposal,[49] only two more general themes will be outlined here in conclusion.

First, the gradual evolution of EU law in the area covered by Regulation 261 is a great example of the 'salami development' of EU law. The first regulation on the matter of compensation for delayed and cancelled flights from 1991 had no provisions on its enforcement.[50] Regulation 261 of 2004 opened up the question of enforcement by inserting a new Article 16. As is apparent from this chapter, as well as those in the second part of this volume, the design of Article 16 is far from ideal, perhaps generating more problems than offering solutions. However, it opened the regulatory space in terms of enforcement at the national levels for EU law action. On its basis, the Commission recast proposal of 2013, acknowledging the enforcement deficiencies, rewrites and extends Article 16, whilst also adding Articles 16a, 16b and 16c. The new system envisaged would make the individual complaint-handling role of the NEB optional only.[51] At the same time, however, it would require the Member States to channel Regulation 261 claims into alternative dispute resolution.[52] It would also build up a complete Regulation 261 network, facilitating communication between the NEBs horizontally, as well as vertically with the Commission, and considerably expand on the reporting duties of the NEBs.

In sum, a much more robust enforcement and institutional system is now being envisaged. In terms of the subsidiarity of such a proposal, the Commission states that

> most of the problems with air passenger rights refer to divergences of application/ enforcement of Regulations (EC) No 261/2004 and (EC) No 2027/97 across Member States weakening passengers' rights and affecting the level-playing field between air carriers. Only coordinated EU intervention can address these problems.[53]

This is certainly true. A more incisive fault-finder might add that most of these enforcement problems were actually caused by the ill-conceived Article 16 in the first place. However, once the space has been opened up for EU legislation, the gradual salami logic starts to apply, inevitably increasing the number of EU rules

---

[49] Proposal for a Regulation of the European Parliament and of the Council amending Regulation (EC) No 261/2004 establishing common rules on compensation and assistance to passengers in the event of denied boarding and of cancellation or long delay of flights and Regulation (EC) No 2027/97 on air carrier liability in respect of the carriage of passengers and their baggage by air of 13 March 2013, COM(2013) 130 final (the Commission Proposal).

[50] Council Regulation No 295/91 (n 36).

[51] Art 16(2), last sentence, of the Commission Proposal (n 49).

[52] Which is already being introduced by the new Directive 2013/11/EU of the European Parliament and of the Council of 21 May 2013 on alternative dispute resolution for consumer disputes and amending Regulation (EC) No 2006/2004 and Directive 2009/22/EC, OJ L 165/63 of 18 June 2013. The directive is to be transposed by the Member States by 9 July 2015.

[53] Commission Proposal (n 49), point 3.2.

in the given area,[54] and gradually building up a fully-fledged enforcement regime as well.

Secondly, the *EU Law in the Member States* series explores the interaction of EU law and national legal systems by analysing comparative evidence of the impact landmark EU measures have had across different Member States. Similar studies inevitably engage with national specialised epistemic communities[55] that do not, perhaps, to a great extent engage with EU law as a matter of routine. Within such communities, with the vantage point being the area-dependent specialised perspective, the appreciation of some pieces of EU legislation or decisions of the CJEU might not always be a positive one, since the latter are likely to follow a different logic and pursue different aims.

However, when approaching and discussing the area of EU aviation law and the CJEU's case law in this area as a EU law generalist, one is struck by the absence of what might be called a middle-ground, compromise-seeking academic debate. There is certainly some quite heated debate relating to Regulation 261 and the case law of the CJEU interpreting it. The debate appears to be, however, at least to a non-specialist in the field, strikingly one-sided: either an author defends the interests of the air industry, or she defends the interests of consumers. This might be understandable in terms of the area of law being a niche topic within which there are some very strong and organised industry interests. It is, however, regrettable in terms of the availability of a critical, genuinely independent approach to the subject-matter studied that could help to improve the law in the given field. In this regard, it is hoped that the present volume may contribute to remedying the situation at least a little.

---

[54] In terms of Commission technique also gradually taking over and codifying the case law of the CJEU. In the context of Regulation 261, this would not be the case with regard to the institutions or procedures, but is likely to happen to a considerable degree with regard to the substantive rules—see especially the Commission Proposal (n 49), points 2.2 or point 3.3.1.1.

[55] eg, national labour, tax, contract or other lawyers. See also M Bobek, 'EU Law in National Courts: Viking, Laval and Beyond' in M Freedland and J Prassl (eds), Viking, Laval, *and Beyond* (Hart Publishing, 2014) 335–37.

SELECTED BIBLIOGRAPHY

Albors-Llorenc A, 'The European CJEU, More Than a Teleological Court' [1999] *Cambridge Yearbook of European Legal Studies* 373

Arnold K and Mendes de Leon P, 'Regulation (EC) 261/2004 in the Light of the Recent Decisions of the European Court of Justice: Time for a Change?' (2010) 35 *Air and Space Law* 91

Arnold K, 'Application of Regulation (EC) No 261 on Denied Boarding, Cancellation and Long Delay of Flights' (2007) 32 *Air and Space Law* 93

—— 'EU Air Passenger Rights: assessment of the proposal of the European Commission for the amendment of Regulation (EC) 261/2004 and of Regulation (EC) 2027/97' (2013) 38 *Air and Space Law* 403

Arnull A, 'The European Court and Judicial Objectivity: A Reply to Professor Hartley' [1996] *Law Quarterly Review* 411

—— 'The Principle of Effective Judicial Protection in EU law: an Unruly Horse?' (2011) 36 *EL Rev* 51

—— 'Judicial Dialogue in the European Union' in J Dickson and P Eleftheriadis (eds), *Philosophical Foundations of European Union Law* (Oxford University Press, 2012)

Atiyah P and Summers R, *Form and Substance in Anglo-American Law* (Clarendon Press, 2002)

Auby J-B et al (eds), *L'influence du droit européen sur les catégories du droit public* (Dalloz, 2010)

Aufner M, 'Die neue EU-Überbuchungsverordnung' [2005] *Zeitschrift für Verkehrsrecht* 66

Baeten N, 'Judging the European Court of Justice: The Jurisprudence of Aharon Barak through a European Lens' (2011) 18 *Columbia Journal of European Law* 148

Balfour J, 'Regulation EC 261/2004 and "extraordinary circumstances"' [2009] *Zeitschrift für Luft- und Weltraumrecht* 58

—— 'Airline Liability for Delays: The Court of Justice Rewrites EC Regulation 261' (2010) 35 *Air and Space Law* 75

Barnard C and Peers S (eds), *European Union Law* (Oxford University Press, 2014)

Bech Serrat J, 'Why is there a Separation between Distance Selling in EU Law and the Tourism Industry?' (2010) 33 *Journal of Consumer Policy* 75

Belavusau U, 'The Case of Laval in the Context of the Post-Enlargement EC Law Development' (2008) 9 *German Law Journal* 2279

Ben-Shahar O and Posner E, 'The right to withdraw in contract law' (2011) 40 *Journal of Legal Studies* 115

Bettman J, Luce M and Payne J, 'Constructive Consumer Choice Processes' (1998) 25 *Journal of Consumer Research* 187

Beyer-Katzenberger M, 'Judicial activism and judicial restraint at the Bundesverfassungsgericht: Was the Mangold judgment of the European CJEU an ultra vires act?' (2011) 11 *ERA Forum* 517

Bingham T, 'The European Convention on Human Rights: Time to Incorporate' (1993) 109 *LQR* 390

Bobek M, 'The Multilingualism of European Union Law in the National Courts: Beyond the Textbooks' in AL Kjær and S Adamo (eds), *Linguistic Diversity and European Democracy* (Ashgate, 2011)

—— 'Why There is no Principle of "Procedural Autonomy" of the Member States' in H-W Micklitz and Bruno de Witte (eds), *The European Court of Justice and the Autonomy of the Member States* (Intersentia, 2012)

—— *Comparative Reasoning in European Supreme Courts* (Oxford University Press, 2013)

—— 'Of Feasibility and Silent Elephants: The Legitimacy of the Court of Justice through the Eyes of National Courts' in M Adams et al (eds), *Judging Europe's Judges: The Legitimacy of the Case Law of the European Court of Justice* (Hart Publishing, 2013)

—— 'EU Law in National Courts: Viking, Laval and Beyond' in M Freedland and J Prassl (eds), Viking, Laval, *and Beyond* (Hart Publishing, 2014)

Bogg A, 'Viking and Laval: The International Labour Law Perspective' in M Freedland and J Prassl (eds), *EU Law in the Member States:* Viking, Laval *and Beyond* (Hart Publishing, 2014)

Bouveresse A, 'Interprétation des notions de retard et d'annulation' (2010) 1 *Europe* 37

Brignall M, 'Thomas Cook won't refund the cost of a taxi fare home', *Guardian* (18 December 2010)

Browne-Wilkinson, 'The Infiltration of a Bill of Rights' [1992] *Public Law* 398

Castro C et al, 'Worded and Symbolic Traffic Sign Stimuli Analysis Using Repetition Priming and Semantic Priming Effects' (2007) 53 *Advances in Psychology Research* 17

Chankova-Docheva I, 'Legal Regulation in the EU of Air Passenger Rights' (2011) 4 *Pravna* 69

Commission, 'Proposal for a Regulation of the European Parliament and of the Council establishing common rules on compensation and assistance to air passengers in the event of denied boarding and of cancellation or long delay of flights' COM(2001) 784 final

—— 'Communication on the operation and the results of this Regulation establishing common rules on compensation and assistance to passengers in the event of denied boarding and of cancellation or long delay of flights' COM(2007) 168 final

—— 'EU Citizenship Report 2010, Dismantling the obstacles to EU Citizens' rights' COM(2010) 603 final

—— 'Communication from the Commission to the European Parliament and the Council on the application of Regulation 261 establishing common rules on compensation and assistance to passengers in the event of denied boarding and of cancellation or long delay of flights' (Communication) COM(2011) 174 final

—— 'Proposal for a Regulation on a Common European Sales Law' COM(2011) 635 final

—— 'Communication on the application of Regulation 261/2004 establishing common rules on compensation and assistance to passengers in the event of denied boarding and of cancellation or long delay of flights' COM(2011) 428 final

—— 'Draft list of extraordinary circumstances following the National Enforcement Bodies meeting held on 12 April 2013—Understanding between national enforcement body on a non-exhaustive and non-binding list of extraordinary circumstances for the application of the current Regulation (EC) 261' (European Commission, 19 April 2013)

—— 'Complaint handling and enforcement by Member States of the Air Passenger Rights Regulations' (Staff Working Document) SWD (2014) 156 final

—— 'Europe, the world's No 1 tourist destination—a new political framework for tourism in Europe' COM(2010) 352 final

—— 'European Commission proposes an optional Common European Sales Law to boost trade and expand consumer choice' (Press Release) IP/11/1175

—— 'European Parliament votes on air passenger rights' (Press Release) IP/14/119

—— 'Proposal for a Directive on package travel and assisted travel arrangements' (Proposal) COM(2013) 512 final

—— 'Proposal for a Regulation of the European Parliament and of the Council amending Regulation (EC) No 261/2004 establishing common rules on compensation and assistance to passengers in the event of denied boarding and of cancellation or long delay of flights and Regulation (EC) No 2027/97 on air carrier liability in respect of the carriage of passengers and their baggage by air' COM(2013) 130 final

—— 'Proposal for a Regulation of the European Parliament and of the Council amending Regulation (EU) No 691/2011 on European environmental economic accounts' COM(2013) 247 final

—— 'Commission acts to improve consumer rights for 120 million holiday makers' (Press Release) IP/13/663

Correia V, 'La proposition de révision du règlement n°261/2004: entre clarifications textuelles et perfectionnement des droits des passagers aériens' [2014] *Revue européenne de droit de la consommation* 7

—— 'Transport aérien—Protection des droits des passagers' [2014] *Jurisclasseur Transport* 930

—— 'Air Passengers' Rights, "Extraordinary Circumstances", and General Principles of EU Law: Some Comments After the McDonagh Case' (2014) 13(2) *Issues in Aviation Law and Policy* 252

Court of Justice of the European Union, *50th Anniversary of the Judgment in Van Gend en Loos 1963–2013: Conference Proceedings* (Office for Official Publications, 2013)

Court of Justice of the European Union, 'The Court of Justice has confirmed its previous ruling that passengers whose flights have been delayed for a long time may be compensated' (Press Release 135/12, 23 October 2012)

Craig P and de Búrca G, *EU Law: Text, Cases and Materials* (Oxford University Press, 2011)

Crawford J, *Les articles de la CDI sur la responsabilité de l'État, Introduction, texte et commentaires* (Pedone, 2003)

Csach et al, 'Interakcia medzi medzinárodnou a európskou právnou úpravou zodpovednosti leteckého dopravcu za škodu spôsobenú cestujúcemu' (2010) 2 *Výber z rozhodnutí Súdneho dvora Európskej únie* 5

—— et al, 'Rozsudok Sturgeon—komentár' (2010) 2 *Výber z rozhodnutí Súdneho dvora Európskej únie* 61

—— and Širicová L, Rozsudok, 'Sturgeon' (2010) 2 *Výber z rozhodnutí Súdneho dvora Európskej únie* 62

Cseres K, 'What Has Competition Done for Consumers in Liberalised Markets?' (2008) 4 *Competition Law Review* 77

D Milmo, 'Ryanair to reject "ludicrous" Iceland volcano claims', *Guardian* (1 June 2010)

Daniel Kelemen R, *Eurolegalism. The Transformation of Law and Regulation in the European Union* (Harvard University Press 2011)

David R, 'The Methods of Unification' (1968) 16 *American Journal of Comparative Law* 13

Dawson M, 'Judicial activism at the Court of Justice', *Judicial activism at the Court of Justice*, Conference, Maastricht University, 10–11 October 2011

de Visser M and Claes M, 'Courts United? On European Judicial Networks' in A Vauchez and B de Witte (eds), *Lawyering Europe, European Law as a Transnational Social Field* (Hart Publishing, 2013)

de Visser M, 'A Cautionary Tale. Some Insights Regarding Judicial Activism from the National Experience', Judicial activism at the Court of Justice, Conference, Maastricht University, 10–11 October 2011 de Waele H, *Rechterlijk Activisme en het Europees Hof van Justitie* (Boom Juridische Uitgevers, 2009)

Dawn O, *Common Values and the Public-Private Divide* (Butterworths, 1999)

Deakin S, Johnston A and Markesinis B, *Markesinis and Deakin's Tort Law* (7th edn, Oxford University Press, 2012)

Delebecque P, 'Règlement (CE) n° 161: l'interprétation consumériste de la CJUE se poursuit' (2012) 1 *Revue de droit des transports* 8

Dempsey P and Johansson S, 'Montreal v Brussels: The Conflict of Laws on the Issue of Delay in International Air Carriage' (2010) 35 *Air and Space Law* 207

Dobrovodský R, 'Ochrana práv cestujúcich v leteckej doprave' in M Jurčová et al (eds), *Právo cestovného ruchu* (CH Beck, 2014)

—— 'Die Rechtsprechung zum slowakischen Reiserecht' *Tourismusrecht* (Neuer Wissenschaftlicher Verlag, 2014)

—— 'Ochrana práv spotrebiteľov—objednávateľov služieb cestovného ruchu—2. časť' [2010] *Justičná revue* 143

—— 'Práva leteckých pasažierov v Európskej únii' [2010] *Výber z rozhodnutí Súdneho dvora Európskej únie* 14

—— 'Ausgewählte Probleme des slowakischen Reiserechts—theoretische Fragestellungen und praktische Erfahrungen' *Tourismusrecht* (Neuer Wissenschaftlicher Verlag, 2010)

Dougan M, 'In Defence of Mangold?' in A Arnull et al (eds), *A Constitutional Order of States? Essays in EU Law in Honour of Alan Dashwood* (Hart Publishing, 2011)

Dragun M, *Kwotowe ograniczenia odpowiedzialności przewoźnika w międzynarodowym prawie przewozowym* (Wydawnictwo Uniwersytetu Mikołaja Kopernika, 1984)

Ehlers N and Müller-Rostin W, 'Kölner Kompendium Luftrecht' in S Hobe and N von Ruckteschell (eds), *Kölner Kompendium des Luftrechts* (Carl Heymans, 2010)

Eidenmüller H, 'Why Withdrawal Rights?' (2011) 1 *European Review of Contract Law* 1

European Parliament, 'Full harmonisation no longer an option' (Press Release, 17 March 2010)

—— 'Resolution of 19 March 2012 on the functioning and application of established rights of people travelling by air' [2011] INI 2150

—— 'Legislative resolution of 5 February 2014 on the proposal for a regulation of the European Parliament and of the Council amending Regulation (EC) No 261/2004 establishing common rules on compensation and assistance to passengers in the event of denied boarding and of cancellation or long delay of flights and Regulation (EC) No 2027/97 on air carrier liability in respect of the carriage of passengers and their baggage by air' [2014] P7TA 92

Fiala J et al, *Contract Law in Slovak Republic* (Kluwer Law International, 2010)

Follesdal A and Hix S, 'Why There is a Democratic Deficit in the EU: A Response to Majone and Moravcsik' (2006) 44(3) *Journal of Common Market Studies* 537

Freedland M, and Auby J-B (eds), *The public law/private law divide: une entente assez cordiale?* (Hart Publishing, 2006)

Freedland M and Prassl J (eds), *EU Law in the Member States: Viking, Laval and Beyond* (Hart Publishing, 2014)

Frühling P, Decat E and Golinvaux S, 'Panorama de la jurisprudence communautaire rendue en application du règlement n° 261/2004 sur les droits de passagers' [2012] *Revue de droit des transports* 15

Garben S, 'Sky-high Controversy and High-flying Claims? The Sturgeon Case Law in Light of Judicial Activism, Europscepticism and Eurolegalism' (2013) 50 *CML Rev* 15

Garberí Llobregat J, *El Recurso de Apelación en la Ley de Enjuiciamiento Civil* (Bosch, 2014)

Gili Saldaña M, 'Morosidad, neglicencia y contravención de compañía aérea por omission de escala en el billete y retraso en vuelo intercontinental' *Indret* (online working paper) 4/2007

Gogl I, 'EuGH erfindet die EG-Verordnung Nr 261 neu: Ausgleichszahlung auch für Verspätungen' (2010) 1 *Zeitschrift für Luft- und Weltraumrecht* 59

Gómez F and Gili M, 'El coste de Volar' *Indret* (online working paper) 3/2005

Grard L, 'Indemnisation des passagers aériens en cas d'annulation d'un vol: un problème technique n'a rien d'extraordinaire' 36 (2009) *Revue de droit des transports* 27

—— 'Droit européen des transports' (2011) 47(1) *Revue Trimestrielle de Droit Europeen* 236

—— 'Retards de vols de plus de trois heures: l'interprétation dynamique du règlement (CE) n° 261 est maintenue' (2012) 4 *Revue de droit des transports* 55

—— 'Voyages aériens: Les nouveaux droits des passagers' in C Bloch (ed), *Mélanges en l'honneur de Christian Scapel* (Presses universitaires d'Aix-Marseille, 2013)

Grelliere V, 'Refus d'embarquement, annulation de vol, retard au départ et à l'arrivée: controverses et réécriture du règlement (CE) n° 261/2004 du 11 février 2004' (2010) 4 *Revue de droit commercial, maritime, aérien et des transport* 4

Grigorieff C, 'Arrêt "Condor" et "Air France": une protection accrue des passagers aériens' [2010] *Journal de droit européen* 8

Grigorova J, 'Compensation of Cancelled Flights—in Search of the Golden Balance between Air Passenger Rights and the Airlines' Limited Liability' (2012) 2 *Evropeiksi praven pregled* 143

—— 'The Compatibility of the EU Emissions Trading System with International Law— Does the Goal Justify the Means?' (2012) 3 *Evropeiksi praven pregled* 106

Grunert K, 'The Consumer Information Deficit: Assessment and Policy Implications' (1984) 7 *Journal of Consumer Policy* 359

Guerrero Lebrón M, 'La regulación comunitaria de las situaciones de "gran retraso" en el transporte aéreo de pasajeros: Comentario a la Sentencia del Tribunald e Justicia de la Unión Europea de 10 de enero de 2006 (TJCE 2006/2)' (2006) 17 *Revista de Derecho Patrimonial* 543

Haak K, 'De rol van het Europees Hof van Justitie in het passagiersvervoer door de lucht' [2010] *Tijdschrift voor Privaatrecht* 493

Herzog R and Gerken L, *Stoppt den Europäischen Gerichtshof, Frankfurter Allgemeine Zeitung* (Frankfurter Allgemeine Zeitung, 2008)

Hobe S, Müller-Rostin W and Recker A, 'Fragwürdiges aus Luxemburg zur Verordnung 261/2004' (2010) 2 *Zeitschrift für Luft- und Weltraumrecht* 59

Hobe S and von Ruckteschell N (eds), *Kölner Kompendium Luftrecht* (Carl Heymanns Verlag, 2008)

Hulmák M, 'Cestovní smlouva' in K Eliáš et al (eds), *Občanský zákoník. Velký akademický komenář 2 svazek* (Linde, 2008)

International Civil Aviation Organisation, 'Consumer Protection a Joined Up Approach Required Between Governments and Industry' (Worldwide Air Transport Conference, 2013)

—— 'Consumer Protection and Definition of Passenger Rights in Different Contexts' (Worldwide Air Transport Conference, 2013)

Jacqué JP, *Droit institutionnel de l´Union européenne* (7th edn, Dalloz, 2012)

Jayme E, *Staatsverträge zum Internationalen Privatrecht, Berichte der Deutschen Gesellschaft für Völkerrecht* (CF Müller, 1975)

Joerges C, 'A new Alliance of De-Legalisation and Legal Formalism? Reflections on Responses to the Social Deficit of the European Integration Project' (2008) 19 *Law and Critique* 246

Kagan R, *Adversarial Legalism: The American Way of Law* (Harvard University Press, 2001)

Karsten J, 'Passengers, consumers, and travelers: The rise of passenger rights in EC transport law and its repercussions for Community consumer law and policy' (2007) 30 *Journal of Consumer Policy* 117

Karsten J and Petri G, 'Towards a Handbook on European Contract Law and Beyond: The Commission's 2004 Communication "European Contract Law and the Revision of the Acquis: The Way Forward"' (2005) 28 *Journal of Consumer Policy* 31

Kaupa C, 'What if the CJEU is NOT an activist court, but still has a neoliberal bias?', *Judicial activism at the CJEU*, Conference, Maastricht University, 10–11 October 2011

Keiler S, 'Ein Vorschlag für eine Änderung der Fluggastrechte-VO—Eine Analyse aus wissenschaftlicher Sicht' (2013) 4 *Reiserecht aktuell* 163

Kilpatrick C, 'Laval's Regulatory Conundrum: Collective Standard-Setting and the Court's New Approach to Posted Workers' (2009) 34 *EL Rev* 844

Klučka J, 'Rozsudok Rehder—komentár' (2010) 2 *Výber z rozhodnutí Súdneho dvora Európskej únie* 39

Komárek J, '"In the Court(s) We Trust?" On the Need for Hierarchy and Differentiation in the Preliminary Ruling Procedure' (2007) 32 *EL Rev* 467

Konert A, *Odpowiedzialność cywilna przewoźnika lotniczego* (Wolters Kluwer Polska, 2010)

—— 'Zryczałtowane odszkodowanie za opóźniony lot' (2013) 2 *Glosa* 57

Kunert-Diallo A, *Kolizje praw w międzynarodowym transporcie lotniczym* (Wolters Kluwer, 2011)

—— 'Ochrona konsumenta na rynku usług lotniczych w strukturze administracji publicznej' in E Jasiuk and G Maj (eds), *Wyzwania i dylematy związane z funkcjonowaniem administracji publicznej* (Wyższa Szkoła Handlowa, 2012)

Kuteničová E, 'Kompenzácia poskytované pasažierom leteckými spoločnosťami' [2006] *Justičná revue* 151

Law Commission, Fragmentation of International Law: Difficulties arising from the Diversification and Expansion of International Law (Law Com A/CN 4/L682 2006)

Lawson R and Marland T, 'The Montreal Convention 1999 and the Decisions of the Court of Justice in the Cases of IATA and Sturgeon—in Harmony or Discord?' (2011) 36 *Air and Space Law* 99

Le Bot F, 'La protection des passagers aériens dans l'Union européenne' (2013) 4 *Revue Trimestrielle de Droit Européen* 773

Le Bot F, 'Les juridictions nationales et la protection des passagers aériens dans l'Union européenne' [2014] *Annuaire du droit de l'Union européenne* 2012

Lenaerts K et al, *European Union Law* (3rd edn, Sweet & Maxwell, 2011)

Lenaerts K and Gutiérrez-Fons J, 'The Constitutional Allocation of Powers and General Principles of EU Law' (2010) 47 *CML Rev* 1637

—— 'The Court's Outer and Inner Selves: Exploring the External and Internal Legitimacy of the European Court of Justice' in M Adams, H de Waele, J Meeusen and G Straetmans (eds), *Judging Europe's Judges. The Legitimacy of the Case-Law of the European Court of Justice* (Hart Publishing, 2013)

—— 'Case: CJEU—Sturgeon and others' (2010) 2 *European Review of Contract Law* 189

Lintschinger C, 'Zum rechtlichen Nachspiel in der Reisebranche aufgrund des Vulkanausbruchs in Island' [2010] *Wirtschaftsrechtliche Blätter* 321

Londstrom N, 'Service Liberalization in the Enlarged EU: A Race to the Bottom or the Emergence of Transnational Political Conflict' (2010) 48 *Journal of Common Market Studies* 1307

Loos M, 'Rights of Withdrawal' in G Howells and R Schulze (eds), *Modernising and Harmonising Consumer Contract Law* (Sellier, 2009)

—— *Consumentenkoop* (Kluwer, 2014)

Luzak J, 'The quest for transparency of flight prices to enable passengers' informed choice' (2013) 3 *Zeitschrift für Europäisches Unternehmens- und Verbraucherrecht* 170

—— 'To Withdraw Or Not To Withdraw? Evaluation of the Mandatory Right of Withdrawal in Consumer Distance Selling Contracts Taking into Account Its Behavioural Effects on Consumers' (2014) 37 *Journal of Consumer Policy* 91

MacCormick N and Summers RS (eds), *Interpreting Statutes: A Comparative Study* (Dartmouth, 1991)

Majiyagbe F and Dalley A, 'The Exclusivity of the Warsaw Convention regime vis-à-vis Actions and Remedies in International Carriage by Air under Nigerian Law' (2006) 31 *Air and Space Law* 196

Makowski M, 'Zakres odpowiedzialności przewoźnika lotniczego z tytułu odmowy wpuszczenia na pokład na podstawie rozporządzenia Parlamentu Europejskiego i Rady z 2004 r—glosa krytyczna do wyroku NSA z 23.10.2012 r' [2013] 8 *Europejski Przegląd Sądowy* 39

Malenovský, 'Comment traiter le retrait tardif d'une demande de décision préjudicielle' (2013) 20(2) *Jurisprudence Research Journal* 497

—— 'Sur le passé, le présent et l'avenir du contrôle' *ultra vires*, in Collectif (eds), *Liber Amicorum V Skouris* (Bruylant, 2015)

Mäll A, 'Lennureisijate õiguste kaitse Euroopa Liidus. Viibivad lennud' (2006) 10 *Juridica* 702

Mankiewicz R, 'Conflicting Interpretations of the Warsaw Air Transport Treaty' (1970) 18 *American Journal of Comparative Law* 177

—— 'The Judicial Diversification of Uniform Private Law Conventions' (1972) 21 *International and Comparative Law Quarterly* 718

Mann F, 'Britain's Bill of Rights' (1978) 94 *Law Quarterly Review* 512

Manuelyan A, 'La protection des voyagers aériens dans la récente jurisprudence de la Cour de justice: est-ce le temps des consolidations?' (2013) 7 *Evropeiksi praven pregled* 186

Mapelli Lopez E, 'Regulación del retraso en el transporte aéreo de viajeros según la legislación internacional y de la Unión Europea' (2004) 37 *Anuario jurídico y económico escurialense* 329

Marín I and Milà R, 'Daño moral contractual' in G Pomar and I Marín (eds), *Daño Moral* (SA Bosch, 2015)

Martineau A, 'The Rhetoric of Fragmentation: Fear and Faith in International Law' (2009) 22 *Leiden Journal of International Law* 1

Martinico G, 'National Judges and European Laws: A Comparative Constitutional Perspective' in M Cremona, P Hilpold, N Lavranos et al (eds), *Reflections on the Constitutionalisation of International Economic Law, Liber Amicorum for E Ulrich Petersmann* (Martinus Nijhoff, 2014) 65

McClean D, 'Carriage by Air' in H Beale (ed), *Chitty on Contract Volume II—Specific Contracts*, 32nd edn (Sweet & Maxwell 2015)

—— (ed), *Shawcross and Beaumount's Air Law* 4th edn (Butterworths, 1991)

Mendes de Leon P, 'De vulkaan in IJsland en de *Sturgeon-zaak uit Luxemburg leiden tot uitbarstingen*' (2010) 85 *Nederlands Juristenblad* 1221

Michel V, 'Vols retardés' [2012] *Europe* 29

Mok MR, 'Het arrest Sturgeon' (2010) 85 *Nederlands Juristenblad* 1234

Moravcsik A, 'In Defence of the "Demoratic Deficit": Reassessing Legitimacy in the European Union' (2002) 44(4) *Journal of Common Market Studies* 603

Naômé C and Kodrikova L, 'La disparition du litige devant la juridiction de renvoi et la compétence de la Cour de justice en matière préjudicielle' (2014) 1 *Revue des affaires européennes* 216

Nesterowicz M, *Prawo turystyczne* (Wolters Kluwer, 2009)

Nieto Alonso A, 'Viajes, vacaciones y circuitos combinados. Los remedios frente al incumplimiento—las "vacaciones frustradas"—y las facultades y derechos de los consumidores y usuarios' (2005) 13 *La Ley—Actualidad Civil* 1541

Oppermann T, *Europarecht* (CH Beck, 2005)

O'Reilly D and Stone Sweet A, 'The liberalization and reregulation of air transport' (1998) 5 *Journal of European Public Policy* 447

Ogus A, Faure M and Philipsen N, 'Best Practices for Consumer Policy: Report on the Effectiveness of Enforcement Regimes' (2006) *OECD DSTI* 21

Pechmann C and Stewart D, 'Advertising Repetition: A Critical Review of Wearing and Wearout' (1990) 11 *Current Issues and Research in Advertising* 285

Picod F, 'La Cour de justice renforce les garanties des passagers victimes de retards' (2009) 50 *La Semaine Juridique: Juris Classeur Periodique* 543

Poissonnier G and Osseland P, 'Le retard de plus de trois heures d'un avion donne lieu à l'indemnisation du préjudice des passagers' (2010) 23 *Recueil Dalloz* 1466

Polkowska M, *Umowa przewozu i odpowiedzialność przewoźnika w międzynarodowym transporcie lotniczym* (Amalker, 2003)

—— 'Air Carrier Liability in the Passengers Transport and Protection of their rights' (2011) 28 *Revista europea de derecho de la navegación marítima y aeronáutica*

—— and Szymajda I, *Konwencja montrealska. Komentarz. Odpowiedzialność cywilna przewoźnika lotniczego* (Liber, 2004)

Prager S, 'Pioneering passengers' rights: legislation and jurisprudence from the aviation sector' (2011) 12 *ERA Forum* 307

Prassl J, 'The European Union and the Montreal Convention: A New Analytical Framework' (2013) 12 *Issues in Aviation Law and Policy* 381

—— 'EU Aviation Law before the English Courts: *Dawson, Huzar,* and Regulation 261/2004' (2014) 38 *Air and Space Law* 365

—— 'Compensation for Delayed Rail Journeys: EU Passenger Rights on Track. Case C-509/11 ÖBB Personenverkehr AG' (2014) 4 *Transportrecht* 158.

—— 'Reforming Air Passenger Rights in the European Union' (2014) 39 *Air and Space Law* 39

—— 'Liberalisation, Information, and Transparency: Three Tales of Consumer Protection in EU Aviation Law' (2015) 11 *European Review of Contract Law* 281

Putzeys J, *Le droit uniforme desuniformisé* (International Uniform Law in Practice, 1988)

Rajski J, *Opowiedzialność cywilna przewoźnika lotniczego w prawie międzynarodowym i krajowym* (Państwowe Wydawnictwo Naukowe, 1968)

Rasmussen H, *On Law and Policy in the European CJEU. A Comparative Study in Judicial Policy-Making* (Martinus Nijhoff, 1986)

Reding V, 'The Next Steps Towards a European Contract Law for Businesses and Consumers' in R Schulze and J Stuyck (eds), *Towards a European Contract Law* (Sellier, 2011)

—— 'The optional Common European Sales Law—Seizing the opportunity!', Conference on European Contract Law, Warsaw, 10 November 2011

Reich N, 'A European Contract Law, or an EU Contract Law Regulation for Consumers?' (2005) 28 *Journal of Consumer Policy* 383

—— 'Free Movement v Social Rights in an Enlarged Union—the Laval and Viking Cases before the CJEU' (2008) 9 *German Law Journal* 159

Riesenhuber K, 'Interpretation and Judicial Development of EU Private Law. The Example of the Sturgeon-Case' (2010) 6(4) *European Review of Contract Law* 384

Rott P and Terryn E, 'The Right of Withdrawal and Standard Terms' in H-W Micklitz, J Stuyck and E Terryn, *Consumer Law* (Hart Publishing, 2010)

Russell T, 'Exporting Class Actions to the European Union' (2010) 28 *Boston University International Law Journal* 141

Ryan P, 'Revisiting the United States Application of Punitive Damages: Separating Myth from Reality' (2003) 10(1) *Journal of International and Comparative Law* 69

Scharpf F, *Crisis and Choice in European Social Democracy* (Cornell University Press, 1999)

Schladebach M, 'Europäisches Luftverkehrsrecht: Entwicklungsstand und Perspektiven' [2006] *Europe* 789

Schmid R, 'Fluggastrechte-Reform: Eine Verbesserung nur auf den ersten Blick' [2014] *Reise Recht Aktuell* 2

Schmidt A, 'Neueste Reiserechtliche Judikatur des HG Wien' [2010] *Jahrbuch Tourismusrecht* 79

—— 'Neueste reiserechtliche Judikatur des HG Wien' [2011] *Jahrbuch Tourismusrecht* 119

Schütze R, *From Dual to Cooperative Federalism: the Changing Structure of European Law* (Oxford University Press, 2009)

Sein K and Värv A, 'Lennureisija õigus saada hüvitist. Euroopa Liidu lennureisijate õiguste määrus' (2013) 2 *Juridica* 107

Selucká M, 'Cestovní smlouva' in J Švestka et al (eds), *Občanský zákoník II* (2nd edn, CH Beck, 2009)

Simma B and Pulkowski D, *Leges Speciales and Self-Contained Regimes, The Law of International Responsibility* (Oxford University Press, 2010)

Staudinger A, 'Das Urtel des BGH in den Rechtssachen Sturgeon und Böck' (2010) 1 *Reise Recht Aktuell* 12

Stec M, 'O niektórych postaciach niewykonania lub nienależytego wykonania pasażerskiej umowy przewozu lotniczego na kanwie rozporządzenia Parlamentu i Rady Unii Europejskiej z 2004 r.' in *W kierunku europeizacji prawa prywatnego. Księga pamiątkowa dedykowana Profesorowi Jerzemu Rajskiemu* (CH Beck, 2007)

—— 'Przesłanki odstąpienia od umowy przewozu w europejskim transporcie lotniczym w Rozporządzeniu Parlamentu i Rady (WE) nr 261/2004' (2010) 4 *Europejski Przegląd Sądowy* 12

—— 'Prawo do odszkodowania w przypadku opóźnienia lotu—glosa do wyroku TS z 19.11.2009 r w sprawie C-402/07 Sturgeon v Condor oraz Bock i Lepuschitz v Air France' (2011) 2 *Europejski Przegląd Sądowy* 40

—— 'Prawo do odszkodowania w przypadku odmowy przyjęcia pasażera na pokład samolotu—glosa do wyroków TS: z 4.10.2012 r w sprawie C-321/11, Cachafeiro v Iberia oraz z 4.10.2012 r w sprawie C-22/11, Finnair v Lassooy' (2013) 2 *Europejski Przegląd Sądowy* 45

Streeck W and Schmitter P, 'From National Corporatism to Transnational Pluralism: Organized Interests in the Single European Market' (1991) 19(2) *Politics and Society* 133

Struyk J, 'Indemnisation pour les passagers de vols retardés en Europe' (2010) 7 *La Semaine Juridique* 201

Sunstein C, 'Social Norms and Social Roles' (1996) 96 *Columbia Law Review* 903

The Adoptive Parents, 'The Life of a Death Foretold: The Proposal for a Monti II Regulation' in M Freedland and J Prassl (eds), *EU Law in the Member States:* Viking, Laval *and Beyond* (Hart Publishing, 2014)

Thijssen C, 'The Montreal Convention, EU Regulation 261/2004, and the Sturgeon Doctrine: How to Reconcile the Three?' (2013) 12 *Issues in Aviation Law and Policy* 413

Tonner K, 'Die EU-Fluggastrechte-VO und das Montrealer Übereinkommen' 2011 (6) *Verbraucher und Recht* 203

Tridimas T, 'The Court of Justice and Judicial Activism' (1996) 21 *EL Rev* 199

Twigg-Flesner C and Metcalfe D, 'The Proposed Consumer Rights Directive—Less Haste, More Thought?' (2009) 5 *European Review of Contract Law* 368

Twigg-Flesner C and Schulze R, 'Protecting rational choice: information and the right of withdrawal' in G Howells et al (eds), *Handbook of Research on International Consumer Law* (Edward Elgar, 2010)

UK House of Commons European Scrutiny Committee, 'Sixth Report of Session 2014–15' (House of Commons, 9 July 2014)

van Boom W and Loos M, 'Effective Enforcement of Consumer Law in Europe' (2008), available at <http://ssrn.com/abstract=1082913>, accessed 28 January 2015

van Dam C, 'Luchtvaartmaatschappijen zijn niet gek op passagiersrechten' (2010) 85 *Nederlands Juristenblad* 672

—— 'Air Passenger Rights after Sturgeon' (2011) 36 *Air and Space Law* 259

Velyvyte V, 'The Right to Strike in the EU after Accession to the ECHR: A Practical Assessment' in M Freedland and J Prassl (eds), *EU Law in the Member States:* Viking, Laval *and Beyond* (Hart Publishing, 2014)

Viscusi K (ed), *Regulation through Litigation* (Brookings Institution Press, 2002)

Vladimirov I, *Law of International Transport* (Romina, 2002)

Vogenauer S, *Die Auslegung von Gesetzen in England und auf dem Kontinent: Eine vergleichende Untersuchung der Rechtssprechung und ihrer historischen Grundlagen* (Mohr Siebeck, 2001)

Wahl P, 'Wer zu spät kommt…-Ausgewählte Probleme der Fluggastrechte-Verordnung in der amtsgerichtlichen Praxis' [2013] *ReiseRecht aktuell* 6

Walker N, 'Late Sovereignty in the European Union' in N Walker (ed), *Sovereignty in Transition* (Hart Publishing, 2003)

Weinrib EJ, *The Idea of Private Law* (Harvard University Press, 1995)

Wegter J, 'The ECJ Decision of 10 January 2006 on the Validity of Regulation 261: Ignoring the Exclusivity of the Montreal Convention' (2006) 31 *Air and Space Law* 133

Weiler J, 'Epilogue: Judging the Judges—Apology and Critique' in M Adams, H de Waele, J Meeusen and G Straetmans (eds), *Judging Europe's Judges—the Legitimacy of the Case-Law of the European Court of Justice* (Hart Publishing, 2013)

Wentkowska A, 'A "Secret Garden" of Conforming Interpretation—European Union Law in Polish Courts Five Years after Accession' (2009) 12 *Year Book of Polish European Studies* 127

Wilhelm G, 'Of Denied Passengers, Delayed Departures and Cancelled Flights—Pausenkakao und Bußgelder' [2004] *Ecolex* 81

Żylicz M, 'Nowe prawo międzynarodowego przewozu lotniczego (system warszawsko-montrealski)' (1999) 9 *Państwo i Prawo* 22

—— *Prawo lotnicze—międzynarodowe, europejskie i krajowe* (Lexis Nexis, 2011)

INDEX